Spanish Fever

STORIES BY THE NEW
SPANISH CARTOONISTS

FANTAGRAPHICS BOOKS

Contents

"Here
you
are."

INTRODUCTION
EDDIE CAMPBELL

WHEN I FIRST MET HIM IN BARCELONA, SPAIN, IN 2010, Santiago Garcia—the editor of this anthology of contemporary Spanish comickers— had just had another book published. It was titled *La Novela Gráfica*, and was about the graphic novel, or the *roman graphique*. (University Press of Mississippi has since published it in English as *On the Graphic Novel*.) In our conversation, we noticed that—almost as an afterthought—a key aspect of the new comics, as compared to the old, is that they are called the same thing everywhere and are part of an international picture. They have stood apart from the old national differentiations and separate traditions (bande dessinée, tebeo, fumetti, manga, and comics are the old names in their various countries) and share the same concept and a new set of priorities. They share the idea, for example, of the importance of the authorial voice. In this new situation, characters are a function of this voice rather than a property that the artist must service like a gardener on an estate. The reader expects to hear the voice as clearly as possible (allowing for translation of course), but no longer accepts the adaptation and reformatting that used to be required whenever the once improbable leap was made from one domain to another.

The first Spanish comicker that I was conscious of was the great Javier Mariscal, when Art Spiegelman introduced him in the cosmopolitan *Raw* anthology many years ago. Mariscal's attraction was that he was quintessentially Spanish. His Los Garriris were a couple of hedonistic figures that spent all their time going to the beach, fishing, and introducing themselves to girls. It didn't really need to be translated, as the entire meaning was evident in the appearance of it. It meant as much as a fresh oyster, whose attraction must always be that it makes us feel over and again the precious moment when we are hit in the face by the surf. However, the new lot is working nearer to the concerns of the rest of us. Paco Roca made a graphic novel about a man suffering from Alzheimer's. It has won awards and been adapted into an animated film. Alfonso Zapico drew a wonderful biography of the Irish novelist James Joyce. He drew a lighter—but just as compelling—travel book about following the route of Joyce's travels to research the first book, taking us to Dublin, Trieste, Paris, and Zurich. One day we could hope to get all their books in translation as easily as we can nowadays get an espresso doble.

Until then, we have this anthology, which is like meeting them all at a party. While mingling I see David Sanchez and hear that he is still living at that address in Weirdsville where Daniel Clowes used to reside, and he has planted his own stuff in the garden. And I am introduced to Clara-Tanit Arqué, whose piece about a woman and her baby is so sprightly and fresh. And there are some wild characters over there by the booze that I am too timorous to approach. And here you are. How are you doing? Have you met...?

"We used
to visit
international
festivals to
buy rights to
foreign books...

TEBEOS:
THE COMICS THAT
WOULDN'T DIE
SANTIAGO GARCÍA

Now we go
to sell."

IN 1997, I COULDN'T HAVE IMAGINED THAT ALMOST twenty years later I would be in the privileged position of singing the praises of contemporary Spanish comics for an American reading audience. If you had asked me then, I would have told you that Spanish comics were dead and would never come back. I remember reading the words of Daniel Clowes in his "Modern Cartoonist" manifesto: "I suspect that even in the face of utter indifference there are those of us who will continue to create comics, if only because of the vast unexplored prairie between what has been done and the thrilling possibilities that lie around us in all directions."

A bittersweet declaration of defiance from a twilight art form, sure, but one that I could read only with longing. Yes, maybe you in America would be exploring those "thrilling possibilities," I thought, but back here in old Spain the only possible future seemed to be to keep on reading unending translations of American, French, and Japanese comics. And for those of us who dreamed of making our own "art comics," the only hope might have been to become one of those few that Clowes mentioned—and maybe dive into the wasteland of the fanzines, minicomics, and other forms of marginal and generally ignored small-press production.

Fifteen years later here we are, enjoying a burgeoning market and a growing readership, even though the nation at large is barely holding together under one of the most gruesome crises we have ever faced. It is in these times that our comics boast plush production values and are sold in general bookstores alongside the latest literary releases; it is now when our pages are exhibited in museums; national media gives us a lot of attention (it has been a long time since a journalist felt the need to explain that "comics aren't for kids anymore"); it is today that we win prestigious awards and we license our works all over the world, from France to Japan and even the United States. Not bad for a medium that was all but buried in 2000. How did this miracle come to pass?

The history of comics in Spain is very similar to the history of other Western traditions of this art form. We had our own satirical cartoons in the nineteenth century, and our kids' magazines and comic books (we call them "tebeos") during the mid-twentieth century. Our historical peculiarity, not only in comics, but in every aspect of society, was that for almost forty years we lived under an isolationist fascist dictatorship.

Dictator Franco died in 1975 and La Transición, the political process that changed the government structures from authoritarianism to democracy and which finished with the victory of the Socialist Party in the 1982 election, ushered in an earthquake in every facet of life in Spain. In terms of culture, it was a revolution.

Democracy brought freedom of press and speech and introduced us to the modern customs of our Western capitalist neighbors, and suddenly everything that was in any way related to the gray years of Franco was considered outdated. That included tebeos. In the mid-'80s, Editorial Bruguera, the giant company that had finally come to embody comics during the last four decades, fell apart. At the same time, new kinds of comics (or comix) were starting to get in touch with the new youth, eager to absorb every international current we were being exposed to. This was called the "adult comix boom." On one hand, it was caused by the release of the backlog of international comics previously banned (Richard Corben and Milo Manara, and lots of stuff from Humanoïdes Associés), and on the other by the new blood of Spanish cartoonists: the underground school of the magazine *El Víbora* (Max, Nazario, Mariscal, Martí, Gallardo, and others), and a bunch of talents that were ready for the prime time on the international market (Miguelanxo Prado, Daniel Torres, Abulí and Bernet's *Torpedo 1936*).

But it didn't take.

One by one, magazines for adults were cancelled. The "Boom" became a bust, revealed as a cruel mirage. At the end of the '90s, the comics industry had withdrawn to the minimum. The only viable offerings were translations of DC Comics and (especially) Marvel Comics (very popular in Spain since 1969), and the manga trend that had exploded in 1992 with *Dragon Ball*. Art comics were reduced to cheap, black-and-white stapled comic books, where you could find the crop of Fantagraphics titles and other rising stars of American alternative comics. *City of Glass* by Paul Karasik and David Mazzucchelli was dismantled in three paltry comic books, because no publisher in its right mind would publish a book of comics like that. The first part of *Maus* by Art Spiegelman appeared in 1989, and was so poorly received that the second one was never printed. We had to wait until the one-volume edition to have a complete translation, and it was already 2001 when that happened.

Young and promising Spanish cartoonists seemed doomed. The fate of anyone born after 1970 who wanted to make a living drawing comics seemed to be lending their talents to the French or American industries. Spanish artists had worked overseas since at least the times of Pepe González (*Vampirella*) and Esteban Maroto (*Creepy*), but now it seemed they had no other choice. Following the steps of pioneering Carlos Pacheco, many Spanish artists arrived at Marvel and DC. At the same time, a growing host of hopeful Spaniards visited the Angoulême festival with their portfolios under their arms. Today, there are a bunch of well-renowned names working both sides of the Atlantic: talents like David Aja, Marcos Martín, and Emma Ríos in the U.S., and Juan Díaz Canales and Juanjo Guarnido, creators of the best-selling *Blacksad*, over in France. It is no surprise that the big revival of *Corto Maltés* was trusted to that same Díaz Canales, teaming up with another Spanish artist, Rubén Pellejero.

At the same time that migration was established as the professional way for many Spanish cartoonists during the first decade of the twenty-first century, something happened to the ones that stayed. Since the traditional comics industry all but died during the '90s, in the Oughts a new kind of industry slowly started to rise. New companies appeared that modeled themselves not in the image of traditional comics publishers, but on literary publishers. Comics began to move from the newsstands to the bookstores, and not only specialty stores, but general bookstores as well. If you paid attention, you could feel that some engines had been set in motion. And the most powerful of those engines was "la novela gráfica."

The graphic novel was an international movement which rose on the shoulders of a bunch of influential works published in the wake of *Maus* between 2000 and 2005, most prominently *Persepolis* by Marjane Satrapi, *Palestine* by Joe Sacco, *Fun Home* by Alison Bechdel, and *Epileptic* by David B. In Spain, it rose with unexpected strength, maybe because of the void left by the traditional industry. Graphic novels simply had no rival. 2004 was a decisive year. Astiberri, one of the new companies (publisher of the original version of this anthology) released Craig Thompson's *Blankets*. Nobody had ever successfully published a comic of more than 600 pages, so the initial impulse of Astiberri was to divide it in three installments. Covers were ready to go to print when at the last minute they changed their minds and pulled the trigger. The massive and expensive one-shot volume of *Blankets* was a success, and publishers began to understand that there was a new dynamic and hopefully a new readership waiting for a different kind of comic.

We still needed to prove that this new "novela gráfica" venue was feasible for the new Spanish artists, and that happened in 2007, when Astiberri (again) published *María y yo* [*Maria and I*] by Gallardo and *Wrinkles* by Paco Roca. Both had strong sales (*Wrinkles*, with more than 70,000 copies sold, is the biggest hit of recent Spanish comics), both were made into feature films (the first as a documentary and the second one as animation) and both proved that there were new subject matters and narrative styles to be discovered. It wasn't only a new kind of package for the same old comics. It was really a new strain of tebeos. *María y yo* told the moving and bittersweet story of the relationship between cartoonist Gallardo and his autistic daughter. *Wrinkles*, on the other hand, was pure fiction, but firmly rooted in a somber reality. Nobody had thought before of making a bunch of old people suffering from Alzheimer's disease the heroes of an adventure, and nobody could expect that it would end up being such a runaway success. These were stories that caught the eye of an audience that was ready for them, even if they didn't know it yet.

After 2007, nobody doubted anymore that the graphic novel was it. That was also the first year that the government conceded the prestigious National Prize to comics, acknowledging officially that it was an art form on the same level of literature, music, fine art, or cinema. The first winner was, symbolically, *Bardín the Superrealist* by Max, a survivor from underground comix from the 1980s who had kept drawing comics and would serve as a father-like figure for the new generation of graphic novelists. The second one went to *Wrinkles*.

If I insist on the importance of this award, it is because in a historically prestige-deprived art form such as comics, institutional recognition allowed access to a new audience. Each and every one of these graphic novels became general media. In some ways, it was the signal that comics were transitioning from the margins of culture to the mainstream.

In 2009, *El arte de volar* [*The Art of Flying*] (another National Prize) by Antonio Altarriba and Kim appeared, signaling the first real masterwork of the new Spanish graphic novel. It wouldn't be the last. The story of the suicidal father of the writer, *El arte de volar* was in part a personal retelling of the combative history of twentieth-century Spain. 2013 saw the superb *Los surcos del azar* [*The Wrinkles of Fate*], by Paco Roca, another masterpiece of historical memory. It's about the first (and mostly forgotten) allied company that entered Paris during the war, made up of leftist Spaniards—exiled from their country after they lost the civil war, and suddenly thrown into a new world conflict. Spain's graphic novel output has been steadily growing in quantity and quality during these last few years, so it seems reasonable to expect that the best is yet to come. These books sell scores of thousands of copies in Spain, and sometimes even more abroad (*El arte de volar* is a hit in South Korea). New, younger artists added to the movement: Alfonso Zapico, Álvaro Ortiz, David Rubín, Cristina Durán y Miguel Ángel Giner, and many more, all of them with their own distinct voices. Like a Spanish publisher likes to say: "Before, we used to visit international festivals to buy rights to foreign books; now we go to sell."

I edited *Panorama* (retitled *Spanish Fever* for the American audience) in 2013. My goal was to take a snapshot of this time in Spanish comics. We decided not to include creators who were working (mainly) for foreign markets, because we wanted to show what was happening in the local scene. Also, we left out the satirical and political cartoons that still exist in newsstands, newspapers, and on the Internet. We have excellent satirical cartoonists in Spain, but we wanted to focus on narrative comics. We were left with the diverse, rich, and exultant sample of current comics that we are proud to offer here.

It's been three years since *Spanish Fever* was released in Spain, and what a three years these have been for all who make comics in our country. We have seen the emergence of newer and sometimes even younger talents like Nadar, Antonio Hitos, José Jajaja, Ana Oncina, Moderna de Pueblo, and Martín López Lam. The fanzines and minicomics scene has exploded with names like Klari Moreno, Ana Galvañ, Conxita Herrero, Gabriel Corbera, Irkus M. Zeberio, and Alexis Nolla. The trend with the latest generation is toward artier comics, heavy on graphic experimentation. There are stunning pages uploaded every day to sites like tiktokcomics.com, and now we have an independent art comics festival similar to SPX that takes place twice a year in Madrid and Barcelona: Grafcomic.

Many Spanish cartoonists have started to make inroads even in the U.S., a market that has never been easy for translated work to enter into. After publishing Max and Joan Cornellà, Fantagraphics has published *Wrinkles* by Paco Roca and has slated, for 2017, *Las Meninas* [*Maids of Honor*], by Javier Olivares and me, which won the latest National Prize in 2015. David Rubín has worked with Paul Pope on *Aurora West* and has been translated by Dark Horse (*The Hero*). José Domingo is known through Nobrow (*Adventures of a Japanese Businessman*). Arcade has brought over another National Prize with *James Joyce* by Alfonso Zapico. And the list keeps growing every year.

This is a difficult time for Spain, because the economic crisis is still ravaging the country and the unemployment rate is well over 20 percent. Most of the print runs are small for a country of almost 50 million, but it is no longer impossible to imagine that we can reach a bigger audience with our tebeos. And most importantly, we feel that we can do it with the utmost freedom, without being pressured by a big industry, pacing ourselves and maturing as creators alongside our readership. Times have never been better and the prevalent feeling is that we are living in a creatively golden age for comics. We can speak again what Juanjo Sáez, at the beginning of *Spanish Fever*, calls "our mother tongue," because "most of us who are in this book grew up reading comics." And we want to express ourselves through comics, tell our stories and our world through this fascinating mix of words and drawings that we love so much. That is why today we can also have hope that we too will have the right to get lost in our own stroll through "the vast unexplored prairie between what has been done and the thrilling possibilities that lie around us in all directions."

Sure, we don't know where we are going—but we know we are going to be there.

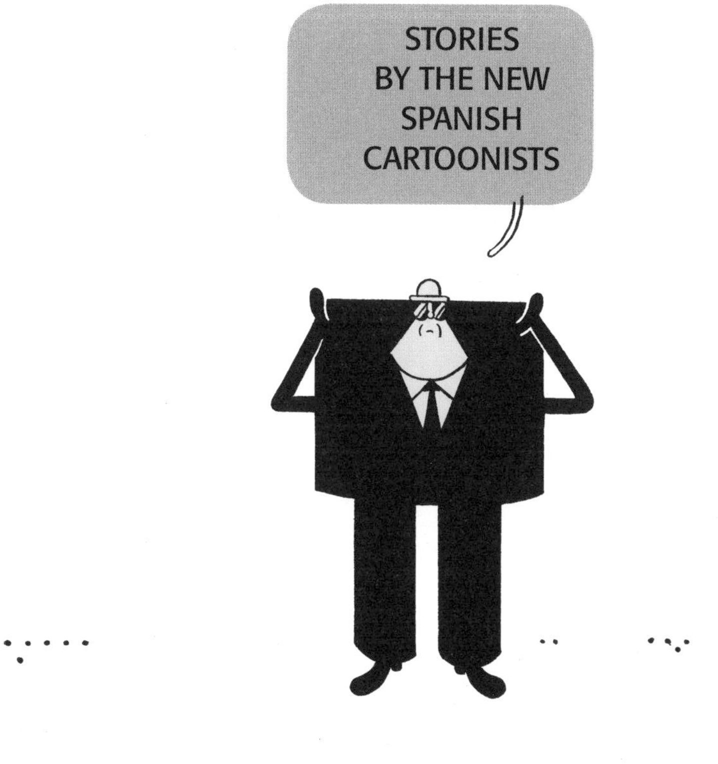
STORIES
BY THE NEW
SPANISH
CARTOONISTS

JUANJO SÁEZ

ADULT COMICS
THE GRAPHIC NOVEL

Born in Barcelona in 1972, Juanjo Sáez studied at the Escola Massana and got his start in the Barcelona fanzines of the '90s, among which *Circulo Primigenio* [*Primitive Circle*] stands out. He's contributed to the music publications *Rockdelux*, *aB*, and *Punto H*, and worked on publicity campaigns for companies like Diesel, Nike, and San Miguel. His first graphic novel with a major publisher was the 2004 best-seller *Viviendo del cuento* [*Living the Story*], which was followed by *El arte, conversaciones imaginaries con mi madre* [*Art: Imaginary Conversations with my Mother*] (2006), *Yo, otro libro egocéntrico* [*Me: Another Narcissistic Book*] (2010), *Crisis (de ansiedad)* [*Crisis (of Anxiety)*] (2013), and *Hit Emocional* [*Emotional Hit*] (2015). He is the creator of the animated television series *Arròs covat* (2009), which gave rise to the graphic novel *Arroz pasado* [*Overcooked Rice*] (2009), based on its scripts.

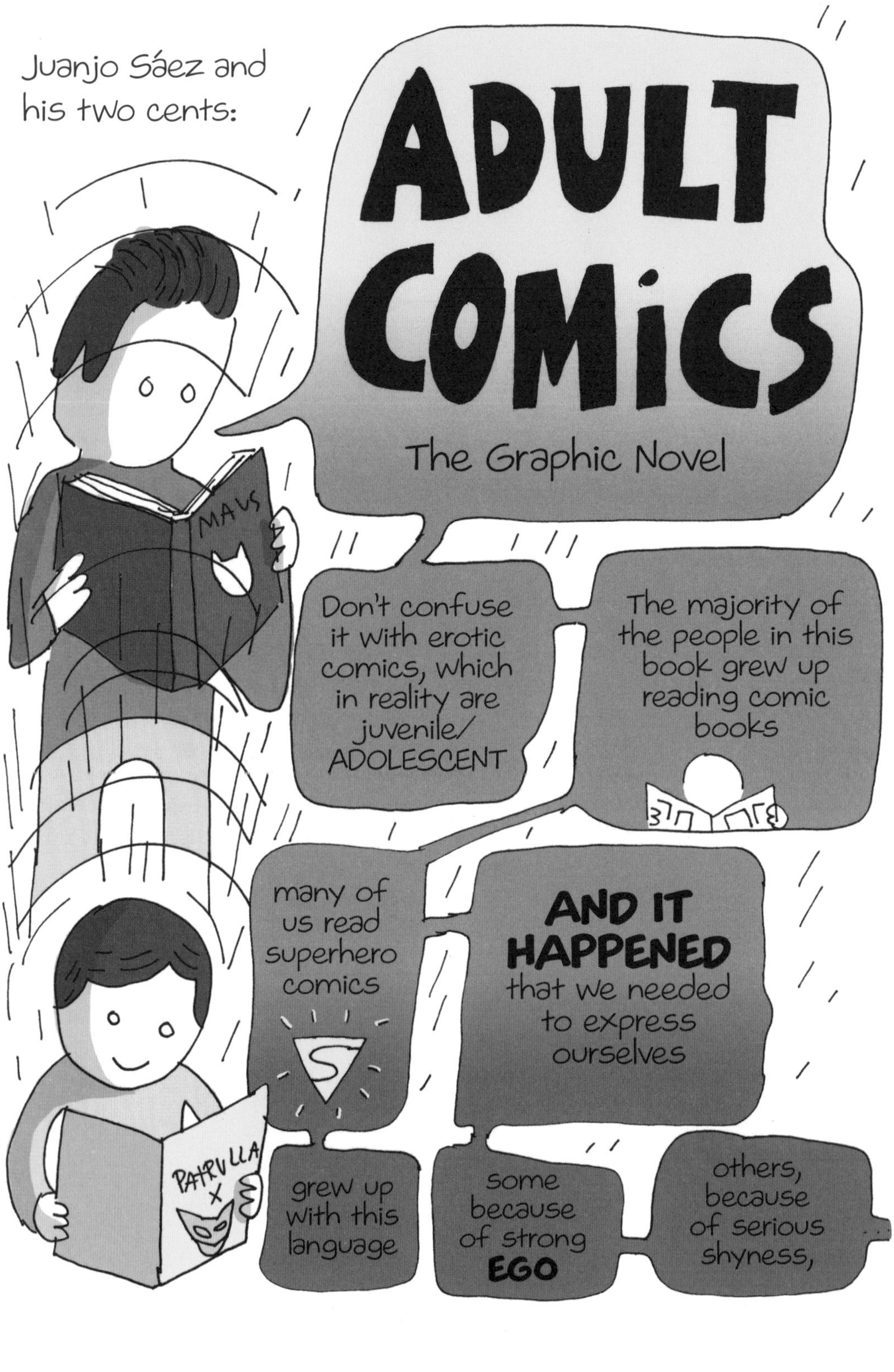
Juanjo Sáez and his two cents:
ADULT COMICS
The Graphic Novel
MAUS
Don't confuse it with erotic comics, which in reality are juvenile/ ADOLESCENT
The majority of the people in this book grew up reading comic books
many of us read superhero comics
AND IT HAPPENED that we needed to express ourselves
PATRULLA X
grew up with this language
some because of strong EGO
others, because of serious shyness,

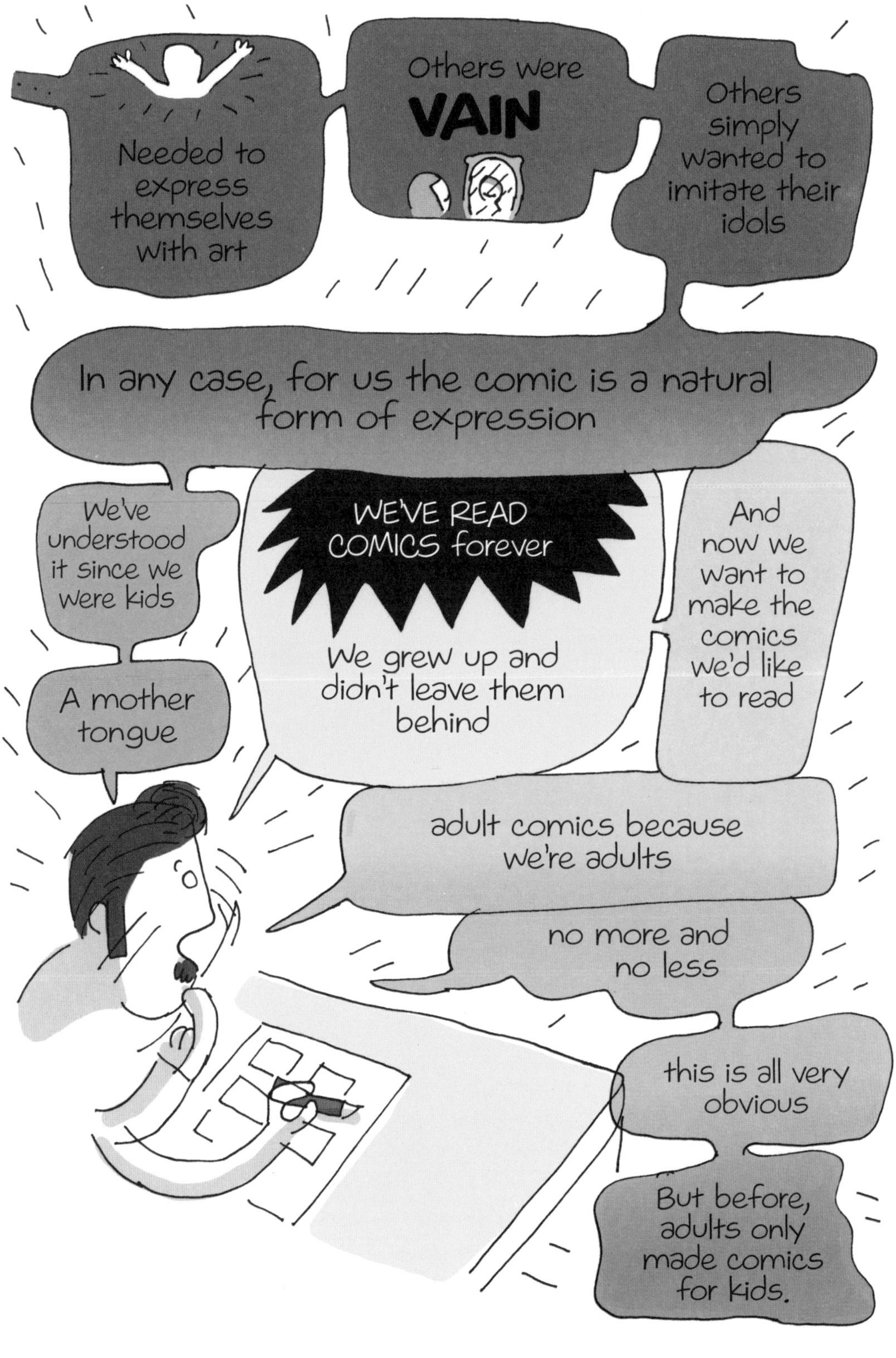
Needed to express themselves with art
Others were VAIN
Others simply wanted to imitate their idols
In any case, for us the comic is a natural form of expression
We've understood it since we were kids
A mother tongue
WE'VE READ COMICS forever
We grew up and didn't leave them behind
And now we want to make the comics we'd like to read
adult comics because we're adults
no more and no less
this is all very obvious
But before, adults only made comics for kids.

ANTONIO ALTARRIBA
KIM
THE HOUSE OF THE RISING SUN

Antonio Altarriba was born in Zaragoza in 1952. A French literature professor at the Universidad del País Vasco, Antonio Altarriba has developed an extensive body of work in the fields of visual narrative and erotic literature, both in theory and in practice. He authored *La España del tebeo* [*Spain in Comics*] (2001), *Tintín y el loto rosa* [*Tintin and the Pink Lotus*] (2007), *Maravilla en el país de la Alicias* [*Wonder in the Country of Alices*] (2010), and comics like *Amores locos* [*Crazy Loves*] (2005), *El brillo del gato negro* [*The Brightness of the Black Cat*] (2008), both with Laura (Laura Pérez Vernetti-Blina), *El arte de volar* [*The Art of Flying*] (2009), with Kim (Joaquim Aubert Puigarnau), which won the Premio Nacional del Cómic, and *El paso del tiempo* [*The Passing of Time*] (2011) with Luis Royo. His latest graphic novel, *Yo, asesino* [*I, Murderer*] (2014), illustrated by Keko, won the Grand Prize of the ACBD of Critics in France.

Kim (Joaquim Aubert Puigarnau) was born in Barcelona in 1941. He is one of the founding members of the satirical magazine *El Jueves*, to which he has contributed every week from 1977 to the present; as such, his series *Martínez el Facha* [*Martinez the Dreadful*], is more than 1,800 pages long. *Las pelis de tu vida* [*The Movies of Your Life*] (2011) collects many of his film parodies published in the same journal. In 1995, he won the Grand Prize at the Barcelona Salón del Cómic. The graphic novel *El arte de volar* [*The Art of Flying*] (2009), on which he collaborated with the writer Antonio Altarriba, won the Premio Nacional del Cómic. This *Spanish Fever* entry is the first time they've worked together since the publication of that book.

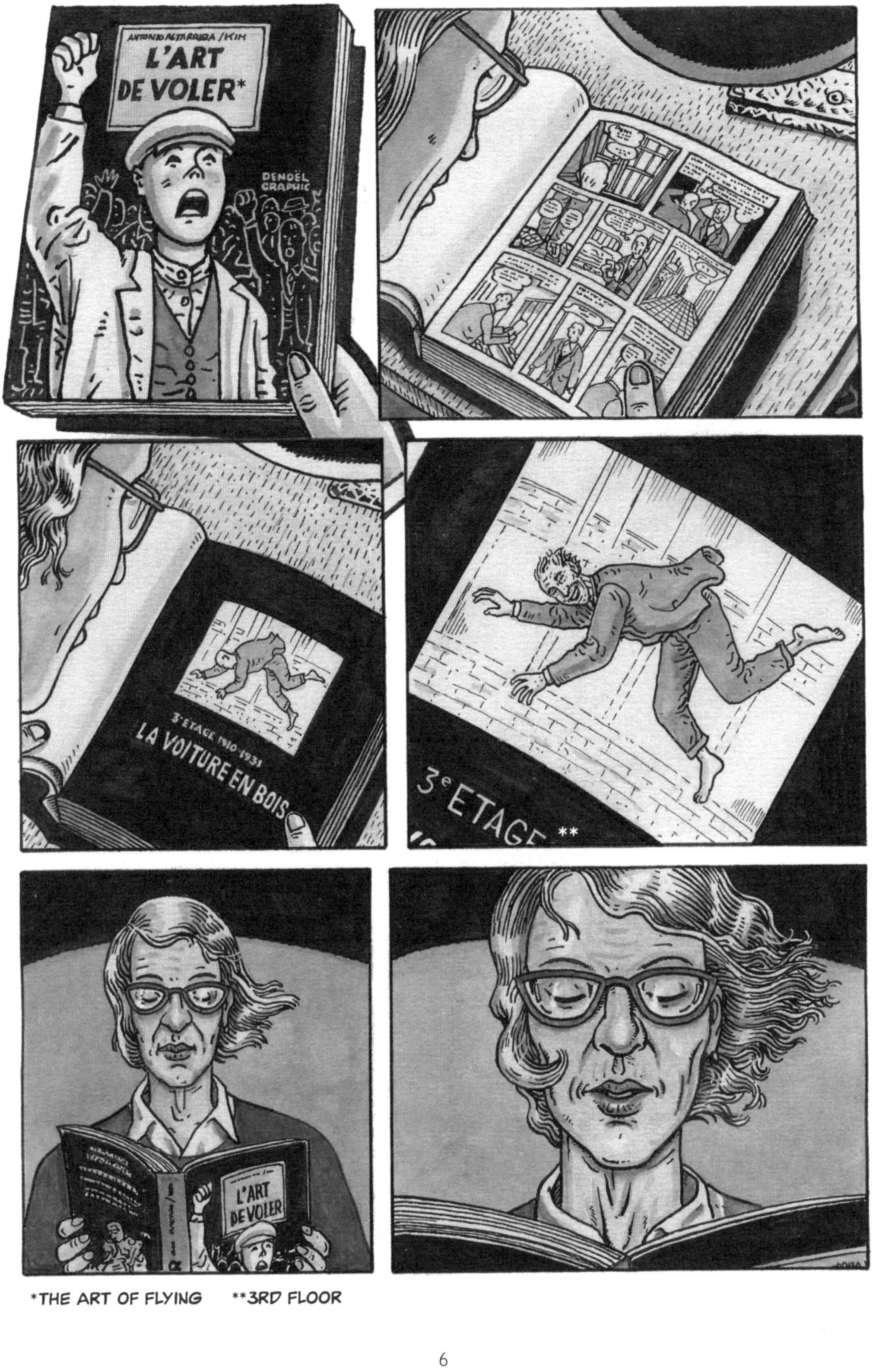
ANTONIO ALTARRIBA / KIM
L'ART DE VOLER*
DENOËL GRAPHIC
3e ETAGE 1910-1931
LA VOITURE EN BOIS
3e ETAGE **
L'ART DE VOLER

*THE ART OF FLYING **3RD FLOOR

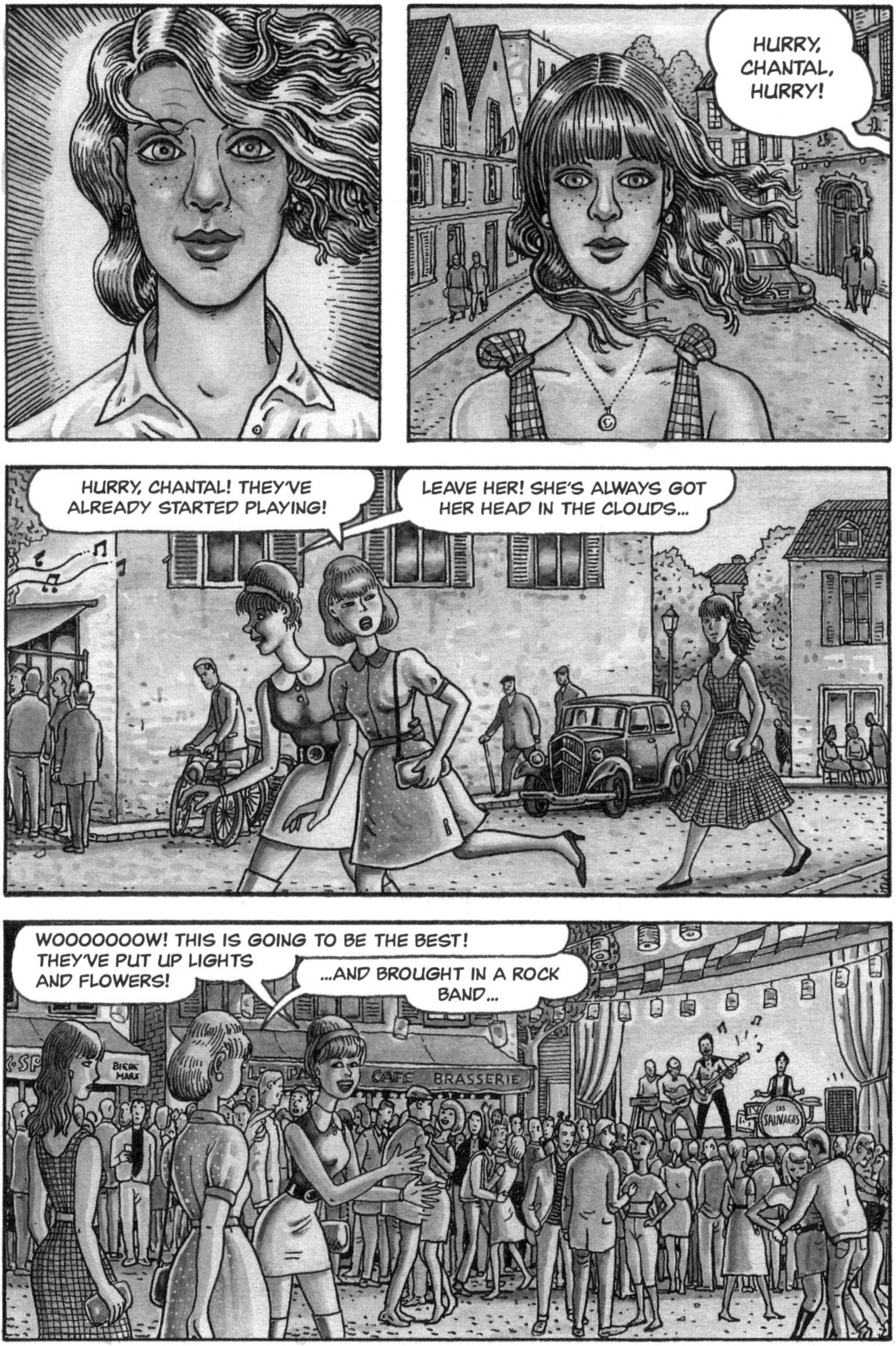
HURRY, CHANTAL, HURRY!
HURRY, CHANTAL! THEY'VE ALREADY STARTED PLAYING!
LEAVE HER! SHE'S ALWAYS GOT HER HEAD IN THE CLOUDS...
WOOOOOOOW! THIS IS GOING TO BE THE BEST! THEY'VE PUT UP LIGHTS AND FLOWERS!
...AND BROUGHT IN A ROCK BAND...
CAFE
BRASSERIE
SAUVAGES

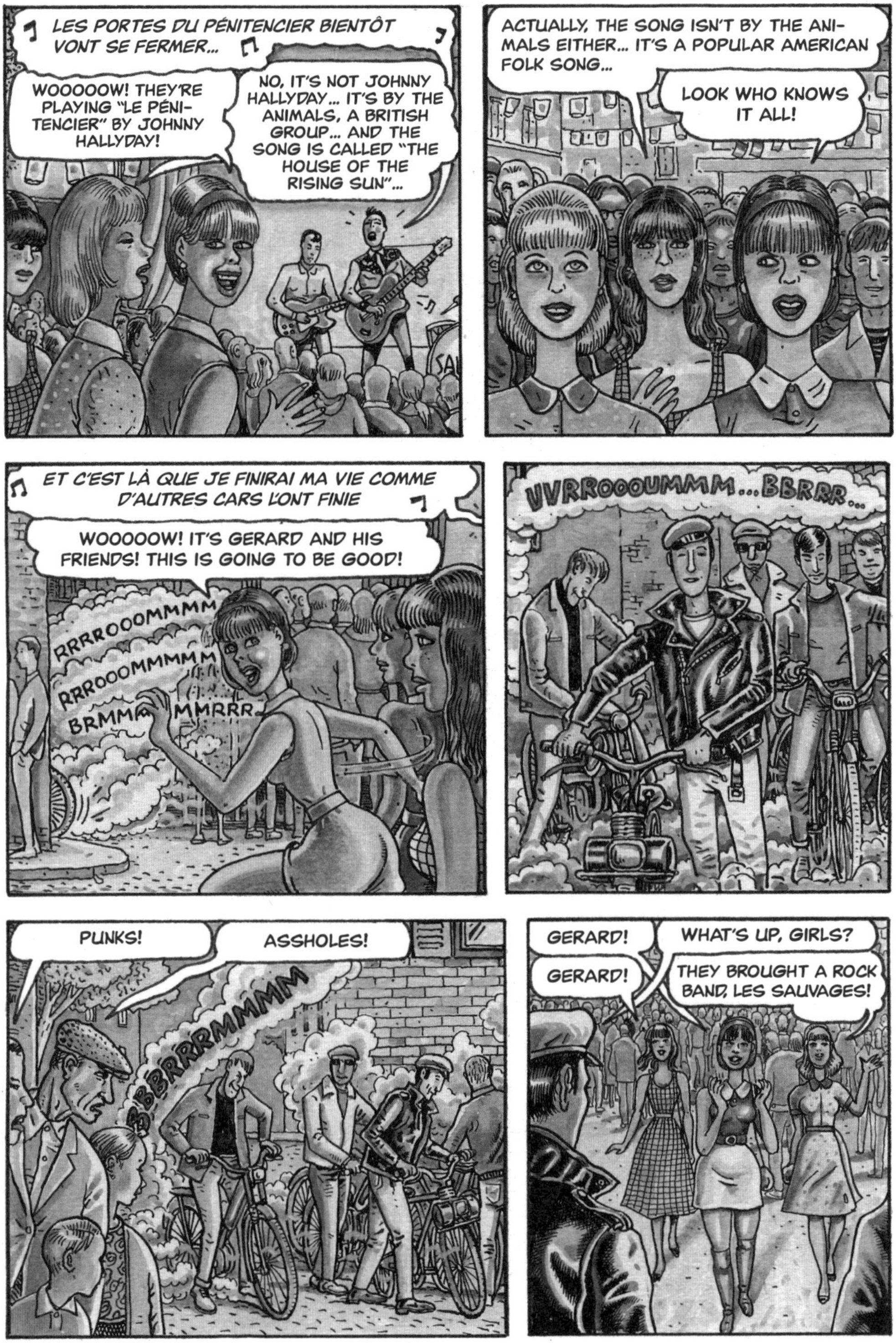
LES PORTES DU PÉNITENCIER BIENTÔT VONT SE FERMER...
WOOOOOW! THEY'RE PLAYING "LE PÉNITENCIER" BY JOHNNY HALLYDAY!
NO, IT'S NOT JOHNNY HALLYDAY... IT'S BY THE ANIMALS, A BRITISH GROUP... AND THE SONG IS CALLED "THE HOUSE OF THE RISING SUN"...
ACTUALLY, THE SONG ISN'T BY THE ANIMALS EITHER... IT'S A POPULAR AMERICAN FOLK SONG...
LOOK WHO KNOWS IT ALL!
ET C'EST LÀ QUE JE FINIRAI MA VIE COMME D'AUTRES CARS L'ONT FINIE
WOOOOOW! IT'S GERARD AND HIS FRIENDS! THIS IS GOING TO BE GOOD!
RRRROOOMMMM
RRROOOMMMMM
BRMMMMMMRRR
VVRROOOUMMM...BBRRR...
PUNKS!
ASSHOLES!
BBBRRRMMMM
GERARD!
GERARD!
WHAT'S UP, GIRLS?
THEY BROUGHT A ROCK BAND, LES SAUVAGES!

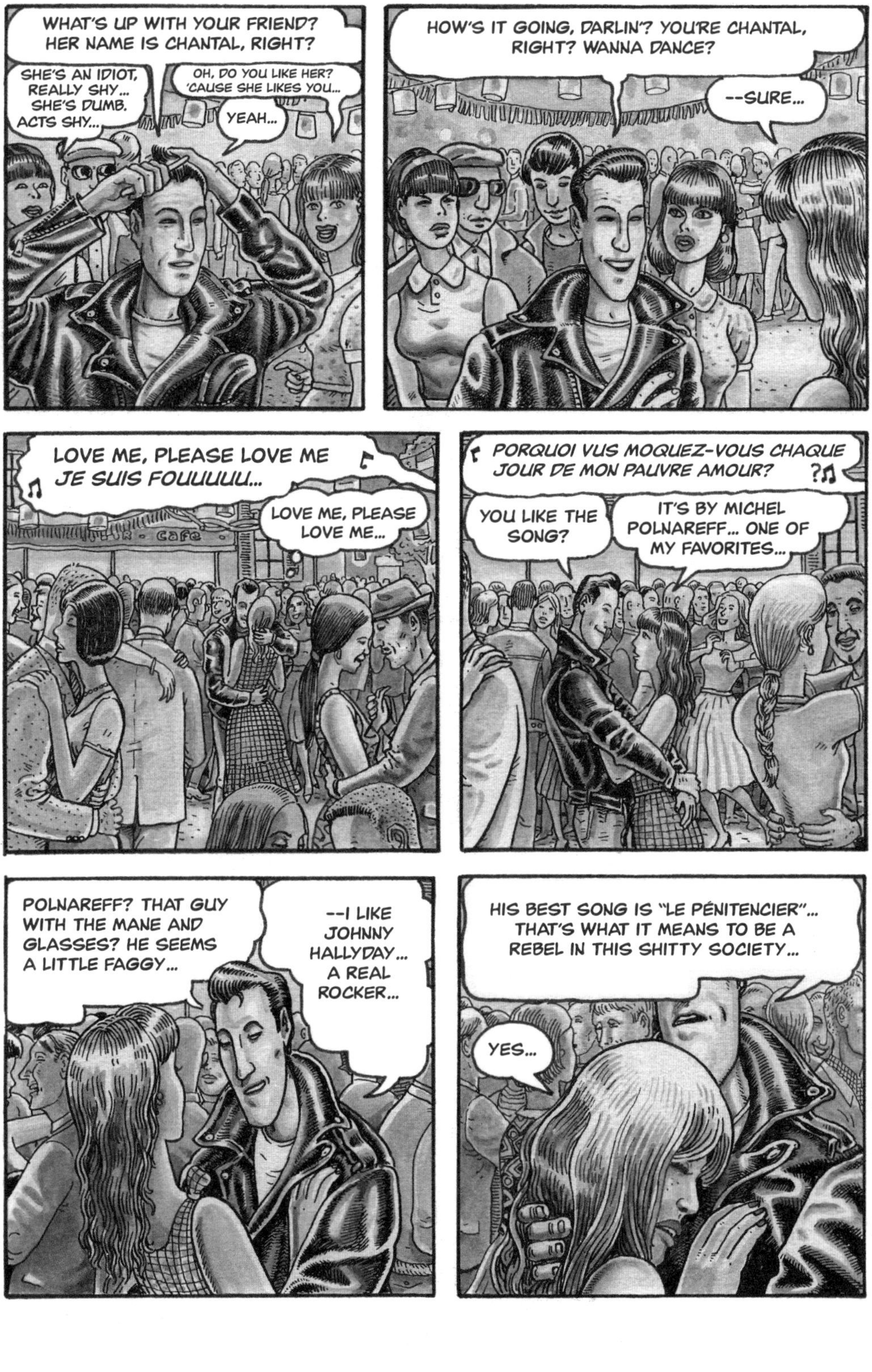
WHAT'S UP WITH YOUR FRIEND? HER NAME IS CHANTAL, RIGHT?
SHE'S AN IDIOT, REALLY SHY... SHE'S DUMB. ACTS SHY...
OH, DO YOU LIKE HER? 'CAUSE SHE LIKES YOU...
YEAH...
HOW'S IT GOING, DARLIN'? YOU'RE CHANTAL, RIGHT? WANNA DANCE?
--SURE...
LOVE ME, PLEASE LOVE ME JE SUIS FOUUUUU...
LOVE ME, PLEASE LOVE ME...
CAFE
PORQUOI VUS MOQUEZ-VOUS CHAQUE JOUR DE MON PAUVRE AMOUR?
YOU LIKE THE SONG?
IT'S BY MICHEL POLNAREFF... ONE OF MY FAVORITES...
POLNAREFF? THAT GUY WITH THE MANE AND GLASSES? HE SEEMS A LITTLE FAGGY...
--I LIKE JOHNNY HALLYDAY... A REAL ROCKER...
HIS BEST SONG IS "LE PÉNITENCIER"... THAT'S WHAT IT MEANS TO BE A REBEL IN THIS SHITTY SOCIETY...
YES...

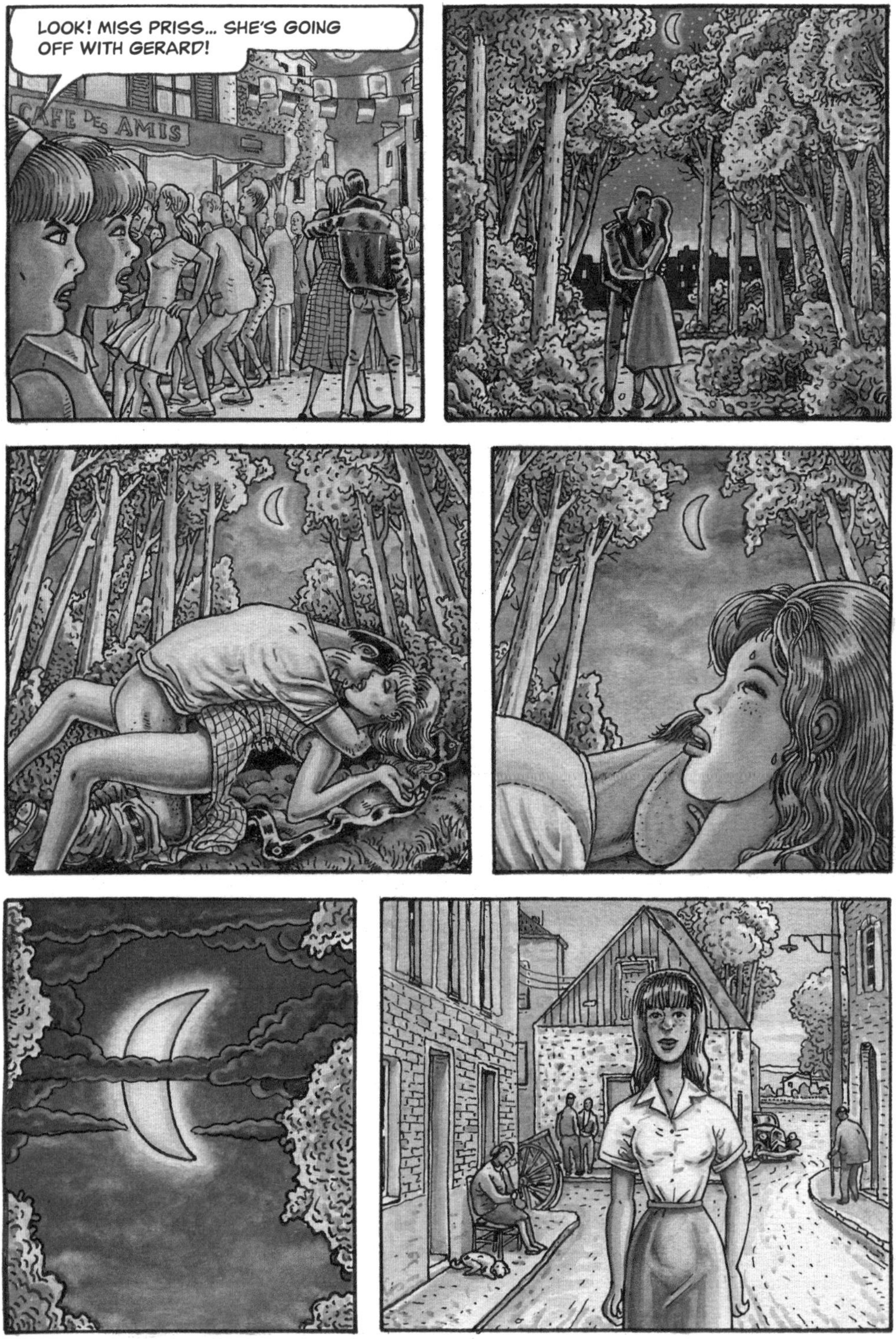
LOOK! MISS PRISS... SHE'S GOING OFF WITH GERARD!
CAFE DES AMIS

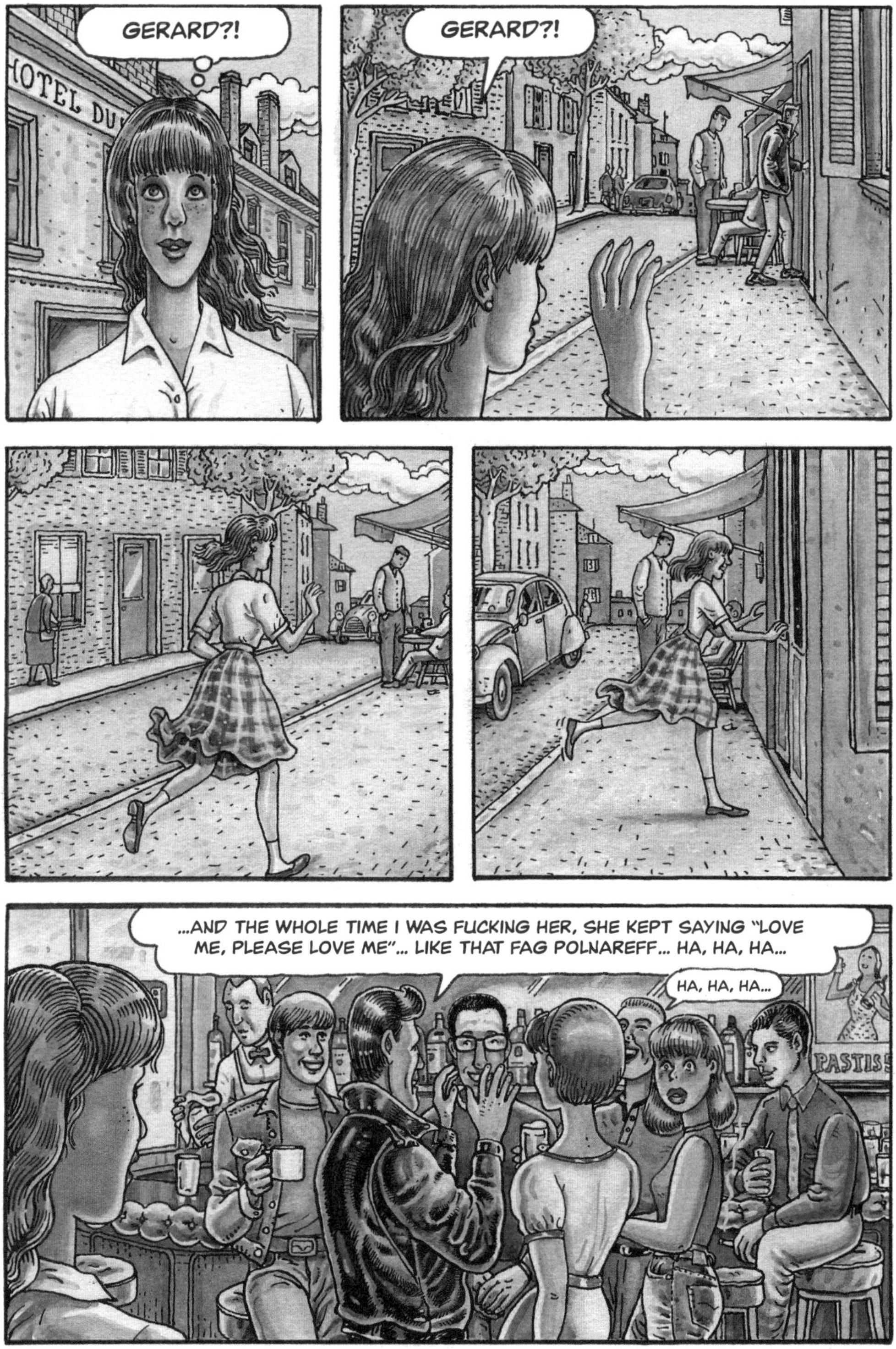
GERARD?!
HOTEL DU
GERARD?!
...AND THE WHOLE TIME I WAS FUCKING HER, SHE KEPT SAYING "LOVE ME, PLEASE LOVE ME"... LIKE THAT FAG POLNAREFF... HA, HA, HA...
HA, HA, HA...
PASTIS

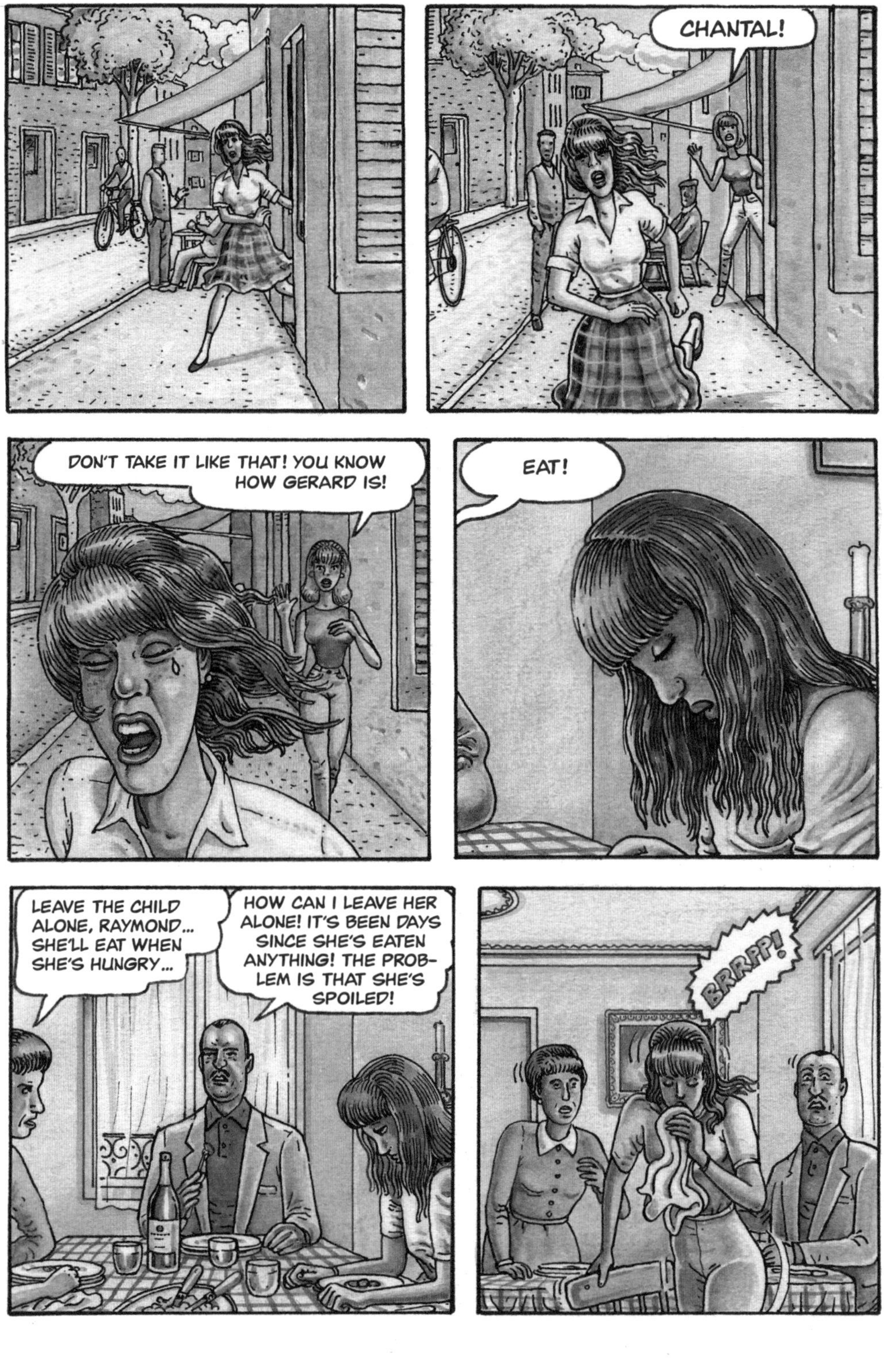
CHANTAL!
DON'T TAKE IT LIKE THAT! YOU KNOW HOW GERARD IS!
EAT!
LEAVE THE CHILD ALONE, RAYMOND... SHE'LL EAT WHEN SHE'S HUNGRY...
HOW CAN I LEAVE HER ALONE! IT'S BEEN DAYS SINCE SHE'S EATEN ANYTHING! THE PROB-LEM IS THAT SHE'S SPOILED!
BRRPP!

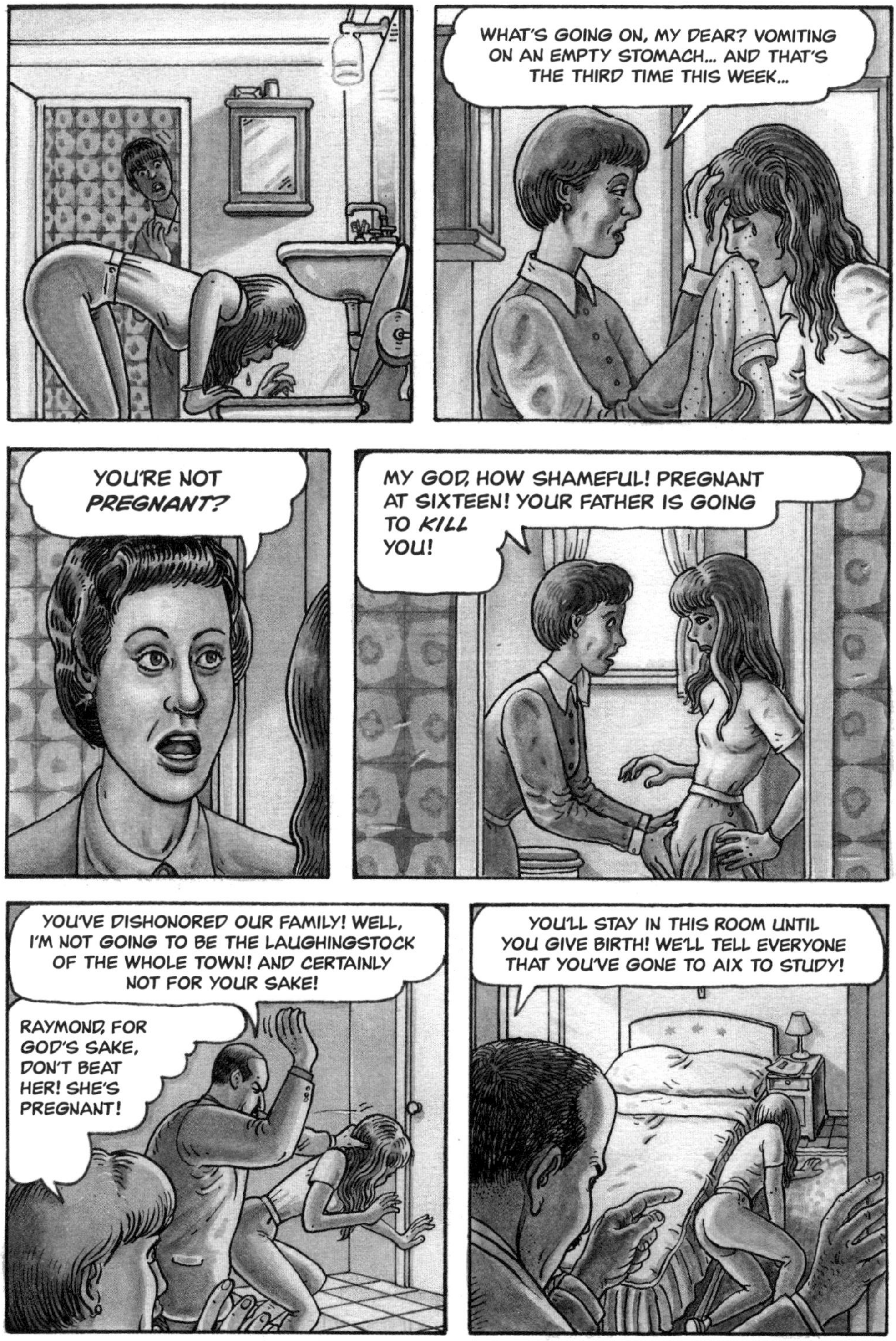
WHAT'S GOING ON, MY DEAR? VOMITING ON AN EMPTY STOMACH... AND THAT'S THE THIRD TIME THIS WEEK...
YOU'RE NOT *PREGNANT?*
MY *GOD,* HOW SHAMEFUL! PREGNANT AT SIXTEEN! YOUR FATHER IS GOING TO *KILL* YOU!
YOU'VE DISHONORED OUR FAMILY! WELL, I'M NOT GOING TO BE THE LAUGHINGSTOCK OF THE WHOLE TOWN! AND CERTAINLY NOT FOR YOUR SAKE!
RAYMOND, FOR GOD'S SAKE, DON'T BEAT HER! SHE'S PREGNANT!
YOU'LL STAY IN THIS ROOM UNTIL YOU GIVE BIRTH! WE'LL TELL EVERYONE THAT YOU'VE GONE TO AIX TO STUDY!

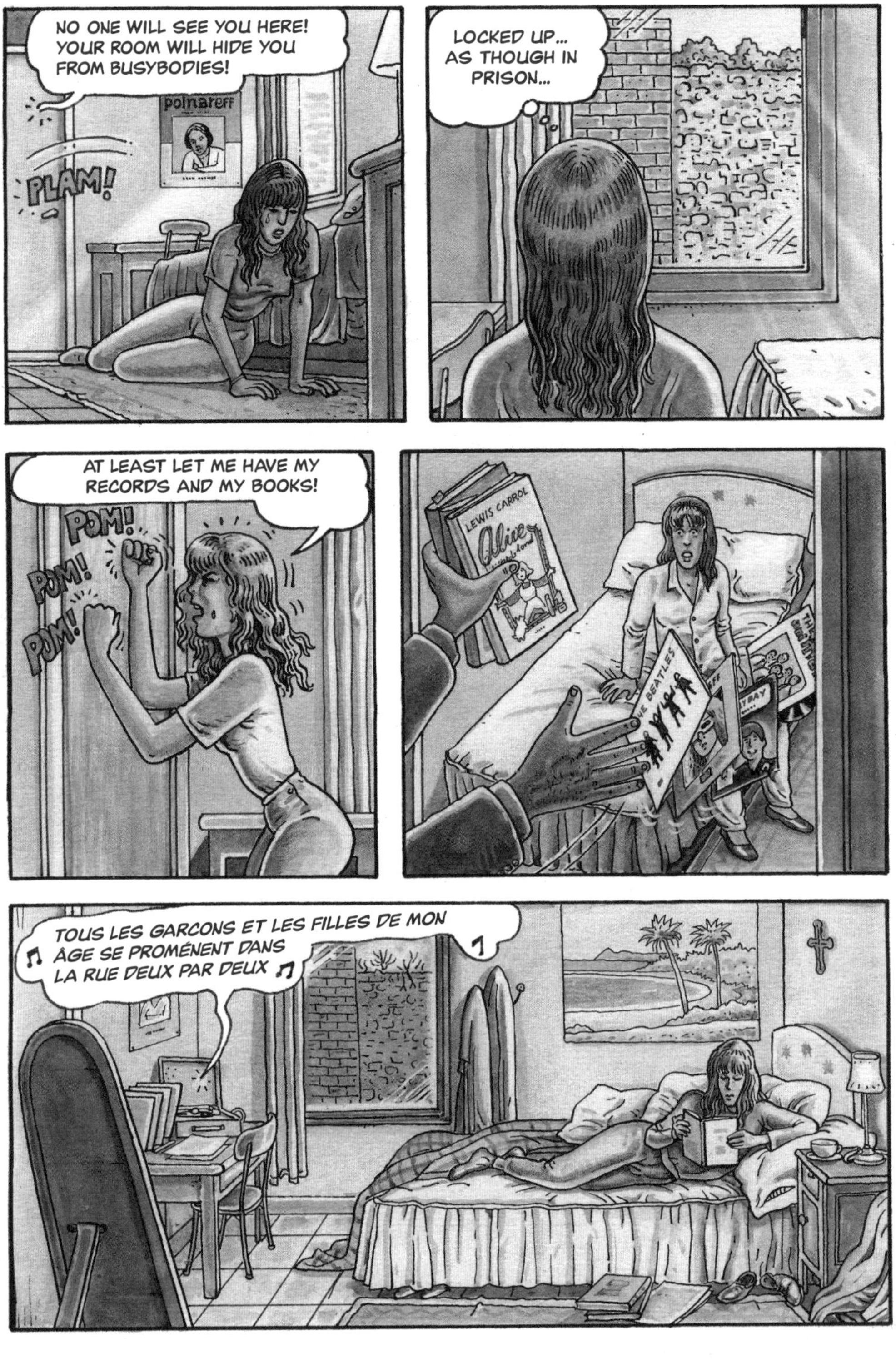
NO ONE WILL SEE YOU HERE! YOUR ROOM WILL HIDE YOU FROM BUSYBODIES!
PLAM!
polnareff
LOCKED UP... AS THOUGH IN PRISON...
AT LEAST LET ME HAVE MY RECORDS AND MY BOOKS!
POM!
POM!
POM!
LEWIS CARROL
Alice
THE BEATLES
TOUS LES GARCONS ET LES FILLES DE MON ÂGE SE PROMÉNENT DANS LA RUE DEUX PAR DEUX

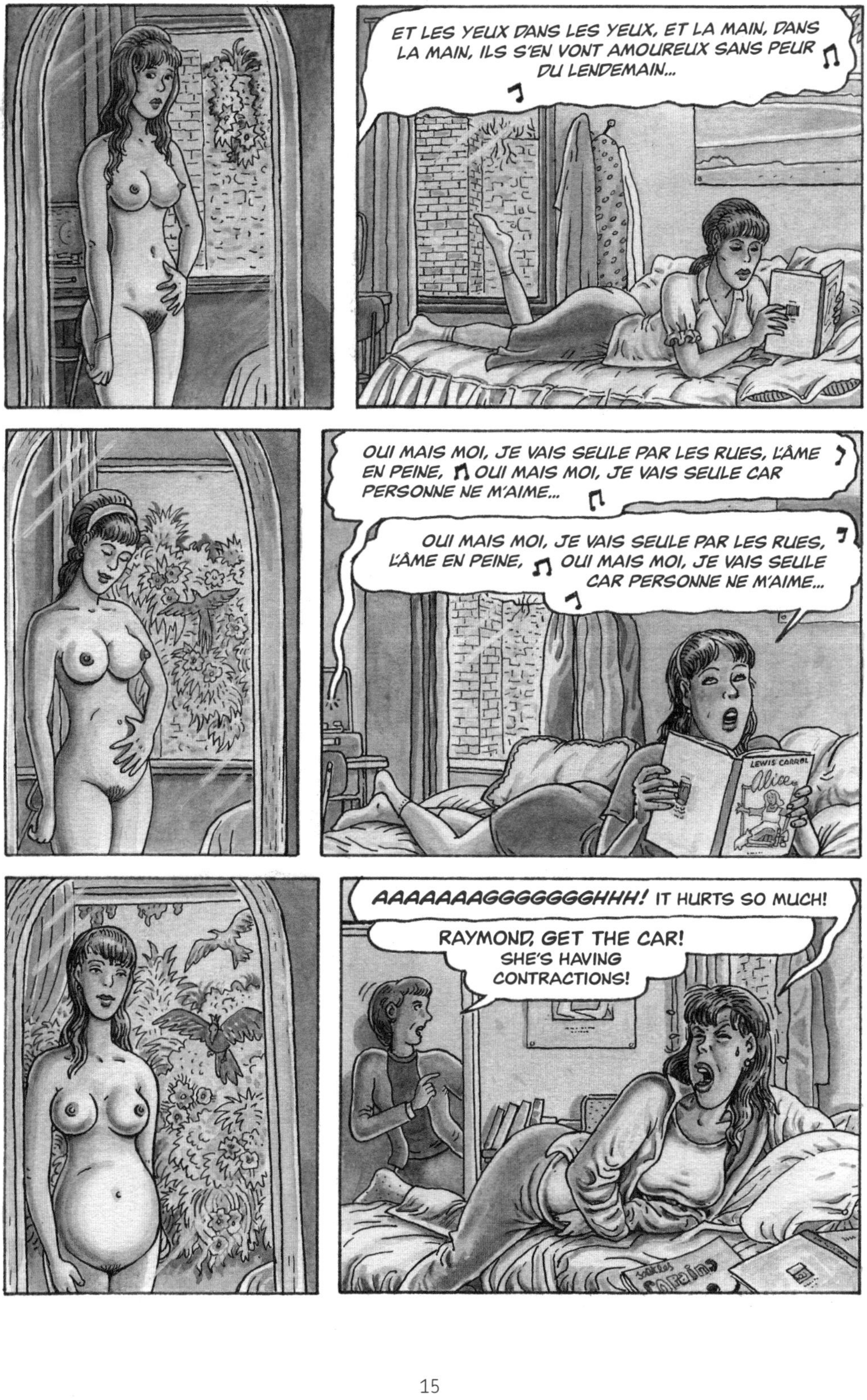
ET LES YEUX DANS LES YEUX, ET LA MAIN, DANS LA MAIN, ILS S'EN VONT AMOUREUX SANS PEUR DU LENDEMAIN...
OUI MAIS MOI, JE VAIS SEULE PAR LES RUES, L'ÂME EN PEINE, OUI MAIS MOI, JE VAIS SEULE CAR PERSONNE NE M'AIME...
OUI MAIS MOI, JE VAIS SEULE PAR LES RUES, L'ÂME EN PEINE, OUI MAIS MOI, JE VAIS SEULE CAR PERSONNE NE M'AIME...
LEWIS CARROL
Alice
AAAAAAAGGGGGGGHHH! IT HURTS SO MUCH!
RAYMOND, GET THE CAR! SHE'S HAVING CONTRACTIONS!

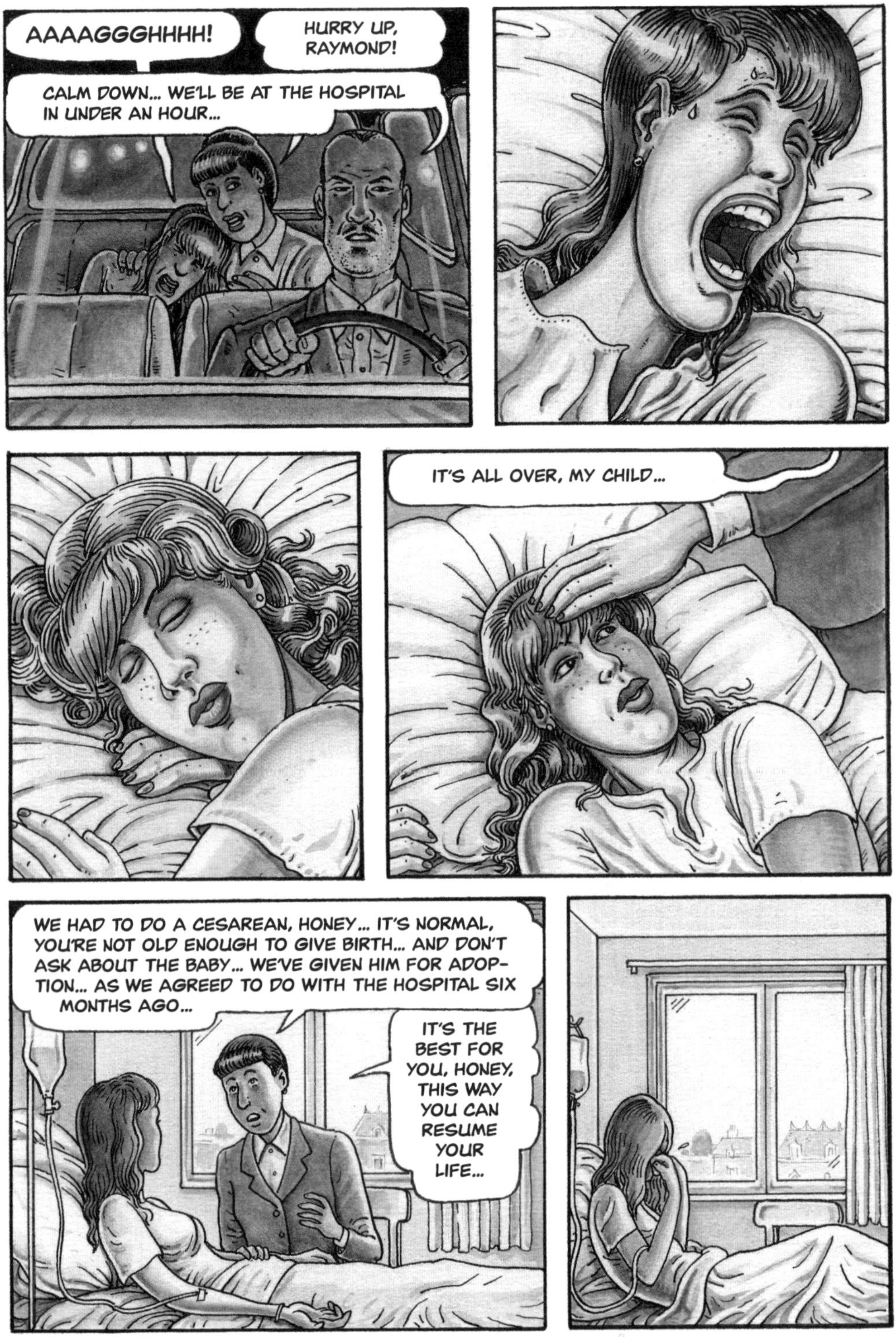
AAAAGGGHHHH!
HURRY UP, RAYMOND!
CALM DOWN... WE'LL BE AT THE HOSPITAL IN UNDER AN HOUR...
IT'S ALL OVER, MY CHILD...
WE HAD TO DO A CESAREAN, HONEY... IT'S NORMAL, YOU'RE NOT OLD ENOUGH TO GIVE BIRTH... AND DON'T ASK ABOUT THE BABY... WE'VE GIVEN HIM FOR ADOPTION... AS WE AGREED TO DO WITH THE HOSPITAL SIX MONTHS AGO...
IT'S THE BEST FOR YOU, HONEY, THIS WAY YOU CAN RESUME YOUR LIFE...

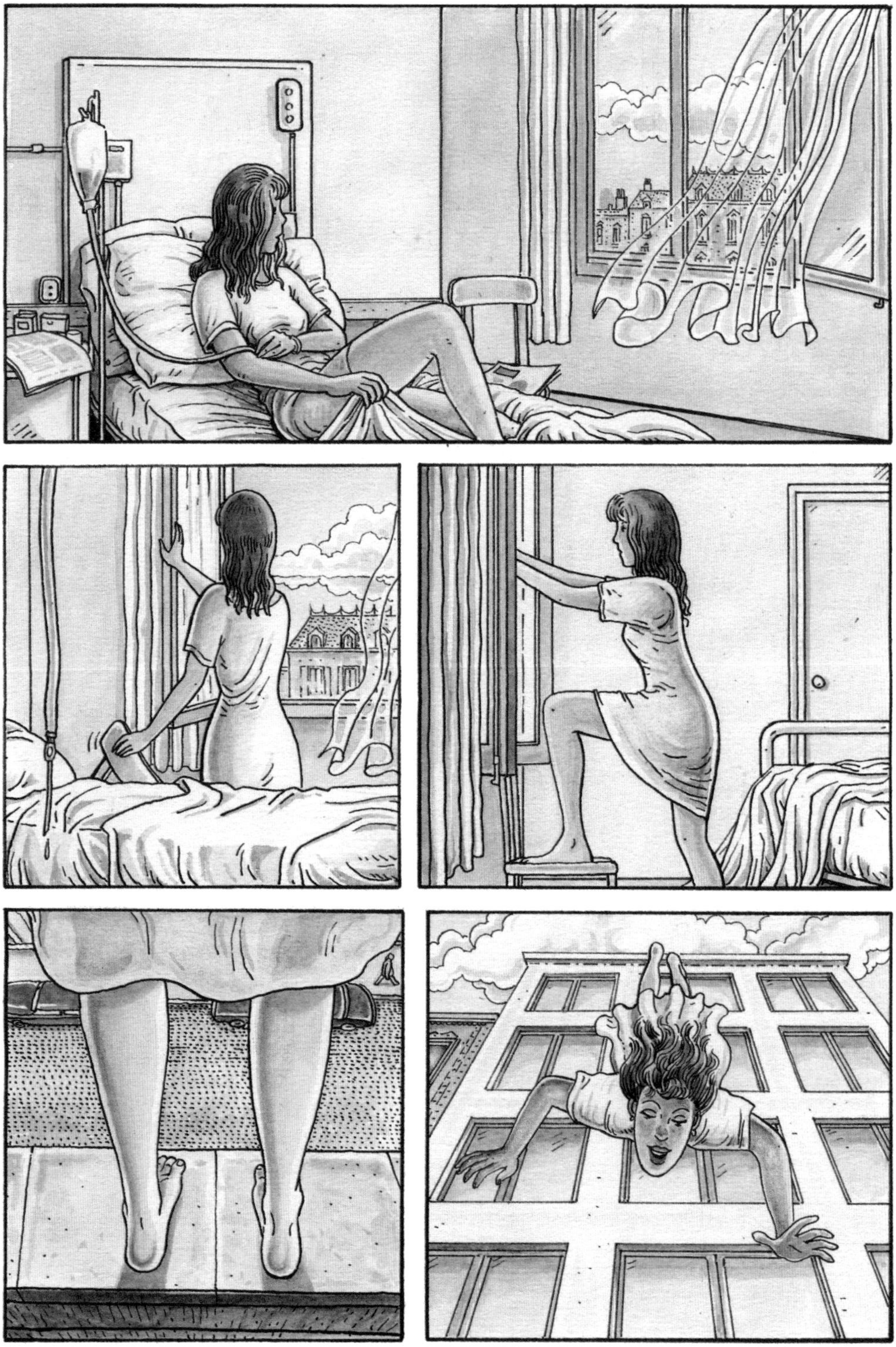

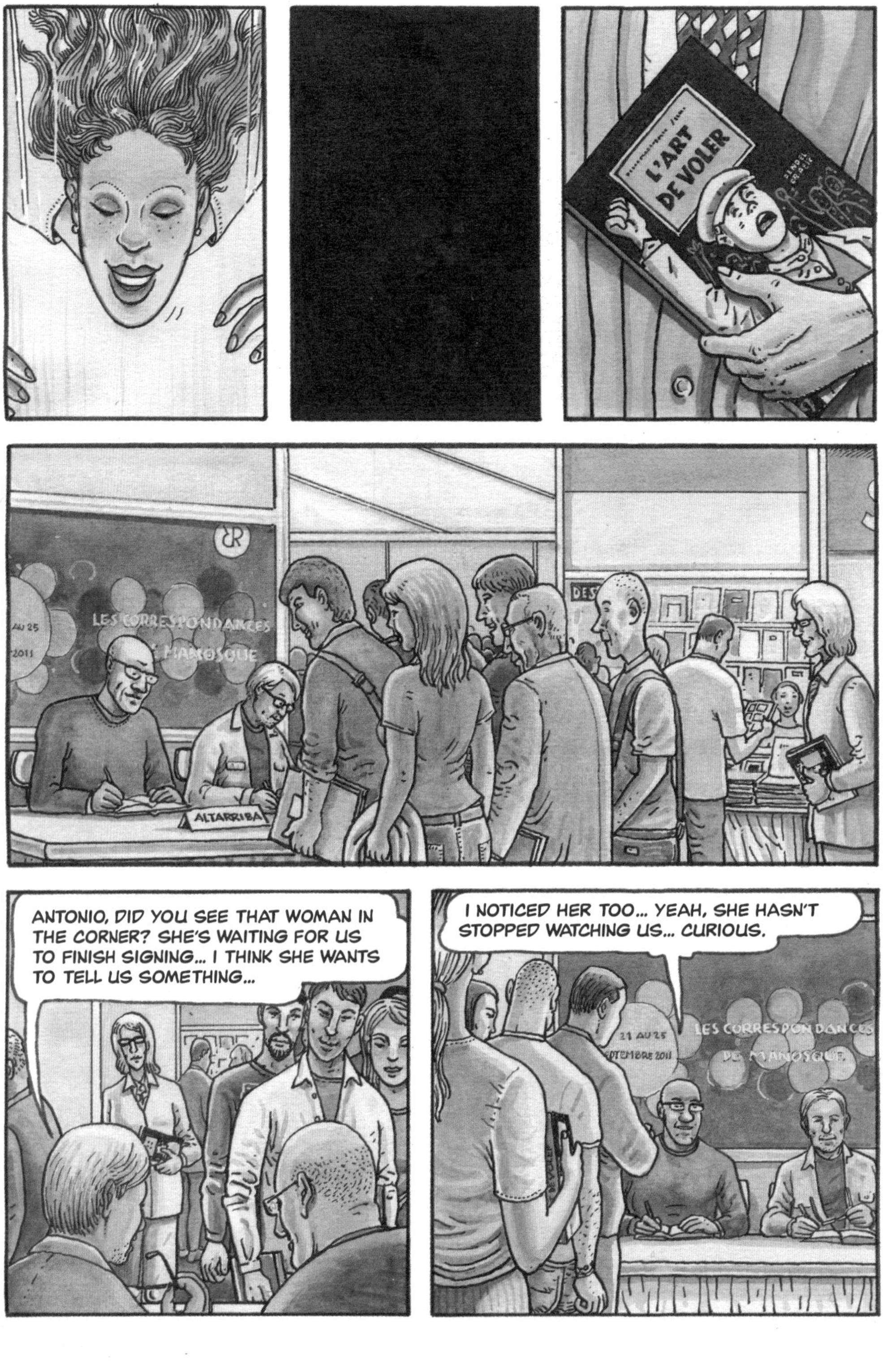
L'ART DE VOLER
ALTARRIBA
ANTONIO, DID YOU SEE THAT WOMAN IN THE CORNER? SHE'S WAITING FOR US TO FINISH SIGNING... I THINK SHE WANTS TO TELL US SOMETHING...
I NOTICED HER TOO... YEAH, SHE HASN'T STOPPED WATCHING US... CURIOUS.
LES CORRESPONDANCES DE MANOSQUE

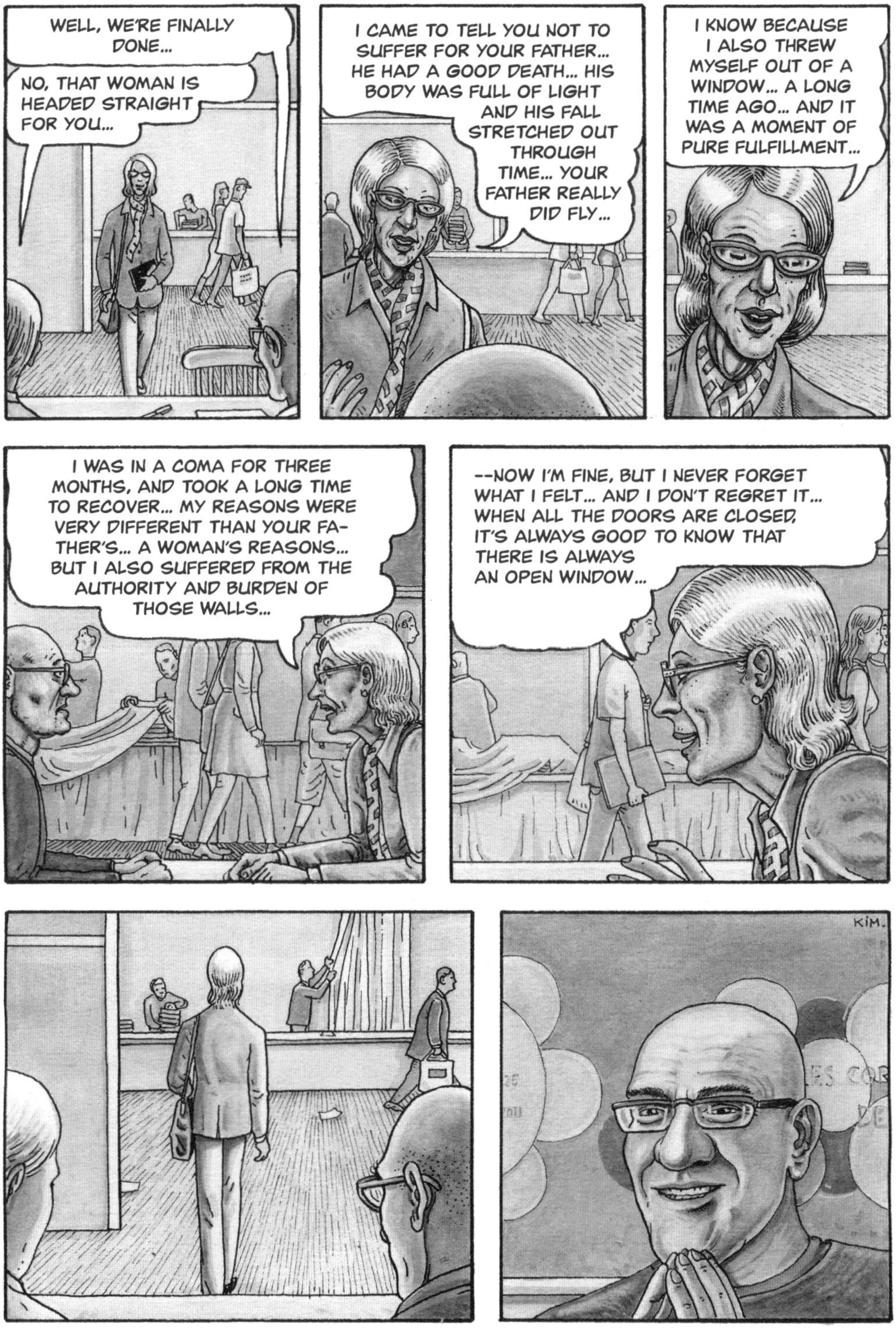
WELL, WE'RE FINALLY DONE...
NO, THAT WOMAN IS HEADED STRAIGHT FOR YOU...
I CAME TO TELL YOU NOT TO SUFFER FOR YOUR FATHER... HE HAD A GOOD DEATH... HIS BODY WAS FULL OF LIGHT AND HIS FALL STRETCHED OUT THROUGH TIME... YOUR FATHER REALLY DID FLY...
I KNOW BECAUSE I ALSO THREW MYSELF OUT OF A WINDOW... A LONG TIME AGO... AND IT WAS A MOMENT OF PURE FULFILLMENT...
I WAS IN A COMA FOR THREE MONTHS, AND TOOK A LONG TIME TO RECOVER... MY REASONS WERE VERY DIFFERENT THAN YOUR FA-THER'S... A WOMAN'S REASONS... BUT I ALSO SUFFERED FROM THE AUTHORITY AND BURDEN OF THOSE WALLS...
--NOW I'M FINE, BUT I NEVER FORGET WHAT I FELT... AND I DON'T REGRET IT... WHEN ALL THE DOORS ARE CLOSED, IT'S ALWAYS GOOD TO KNOW THAT THERE IS ALWAYS AN OPEN WINDOW...
KIM.

ÁLVARO ORTIZ

MELTED

Álvaro Ortiz was born in Zaragoza in 1983. He studied at Escola Massana in Barcelona, and he won the 2003 Injuve Prize. Álvaro Ortiz has published *Julia y el verano muerto* [*Julia and the Dead Summer*] (2005) and *Julia y la voz de la ballena* [*Julia and the Voice of the Whale*] (2009), as well as the self-published *Fjorden* (2010). After winning the Alhóndigakomik grant he finished his graphic novel *Cenizas* [*Ashes*] (2012). Following that he published *Murderabilia* (2014). Both titles have been translated into French. His most recent graphic novel is entitled *Rituales* [*Rituals*] (2015).

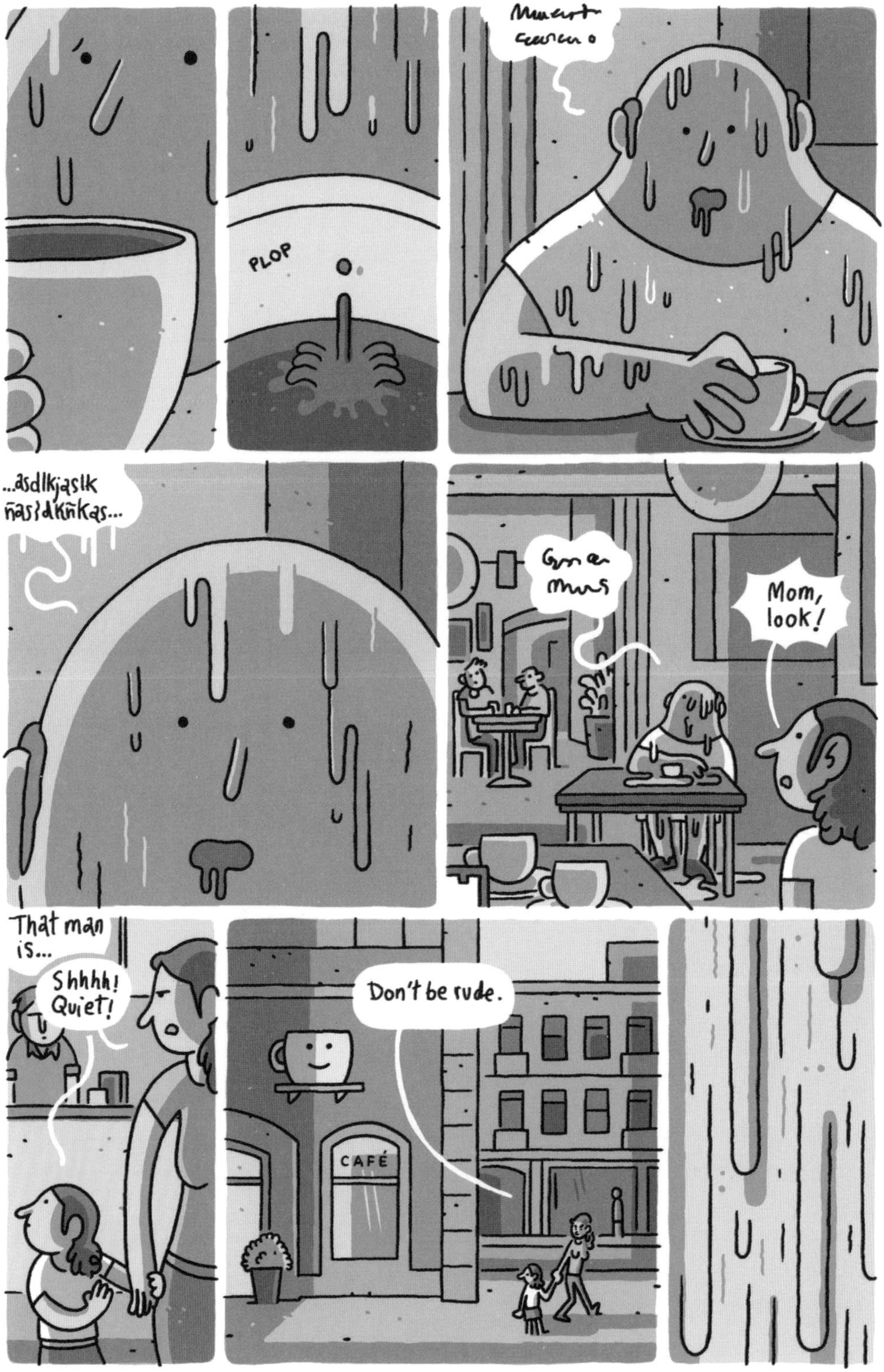
PLOP
...asdlkjaslk ñas!dkñkas...
Mom, look!
That man is...
Shhhh! Quiet!
Don't be rude.
CAFÉ

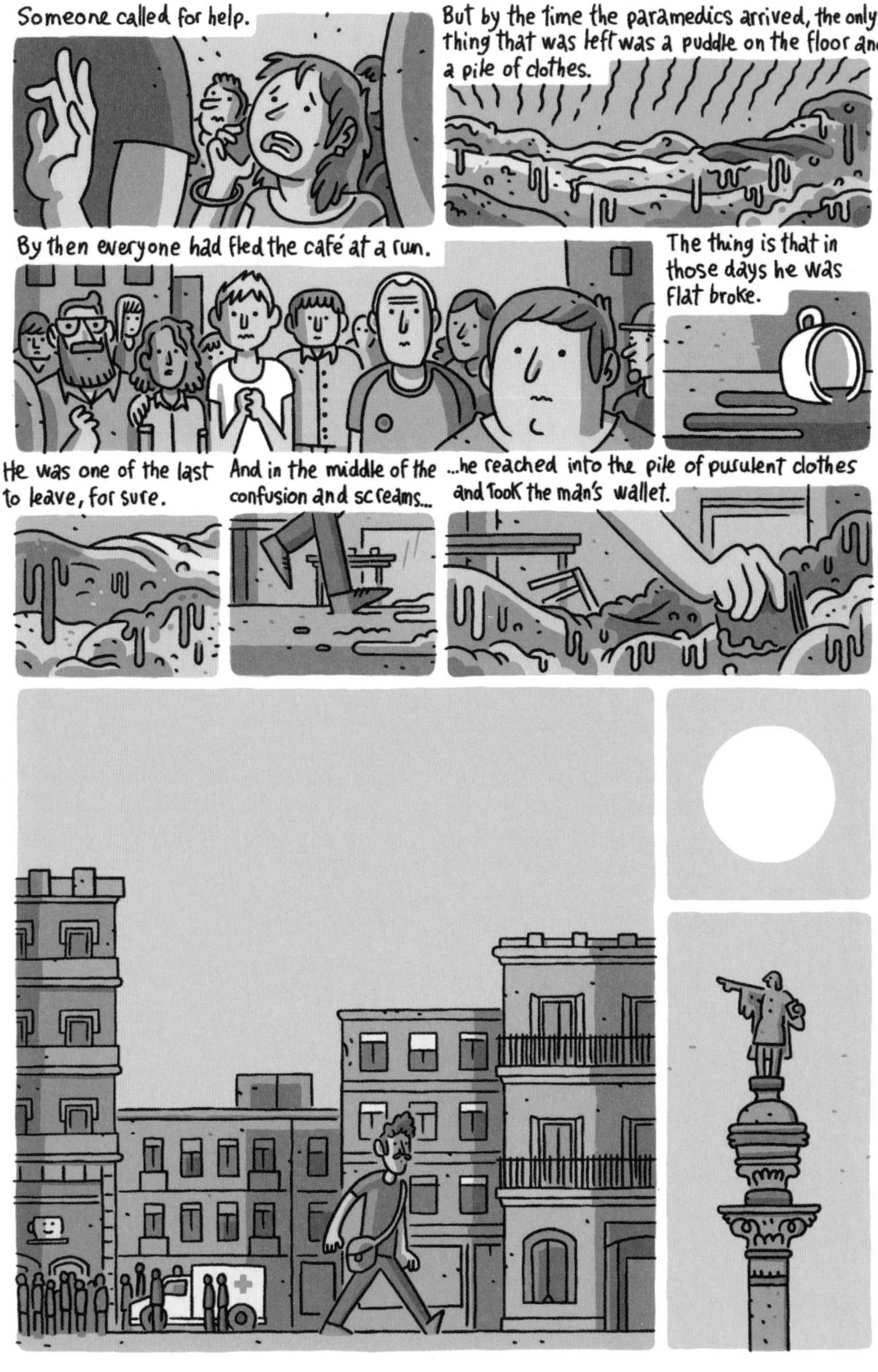
Someone called for help.
But by the time the paramedics arrived, the only thing that was left was a puddle on the floor and a pile of clothes.
By then everyone had fled the café at a run.
The thing is that in those days he was flat broke.
He was one of the last to leave, for sure.
And in the middle of the confusion and screams...
...he reached into the pile of pusulent clothes and took the man's wallet.

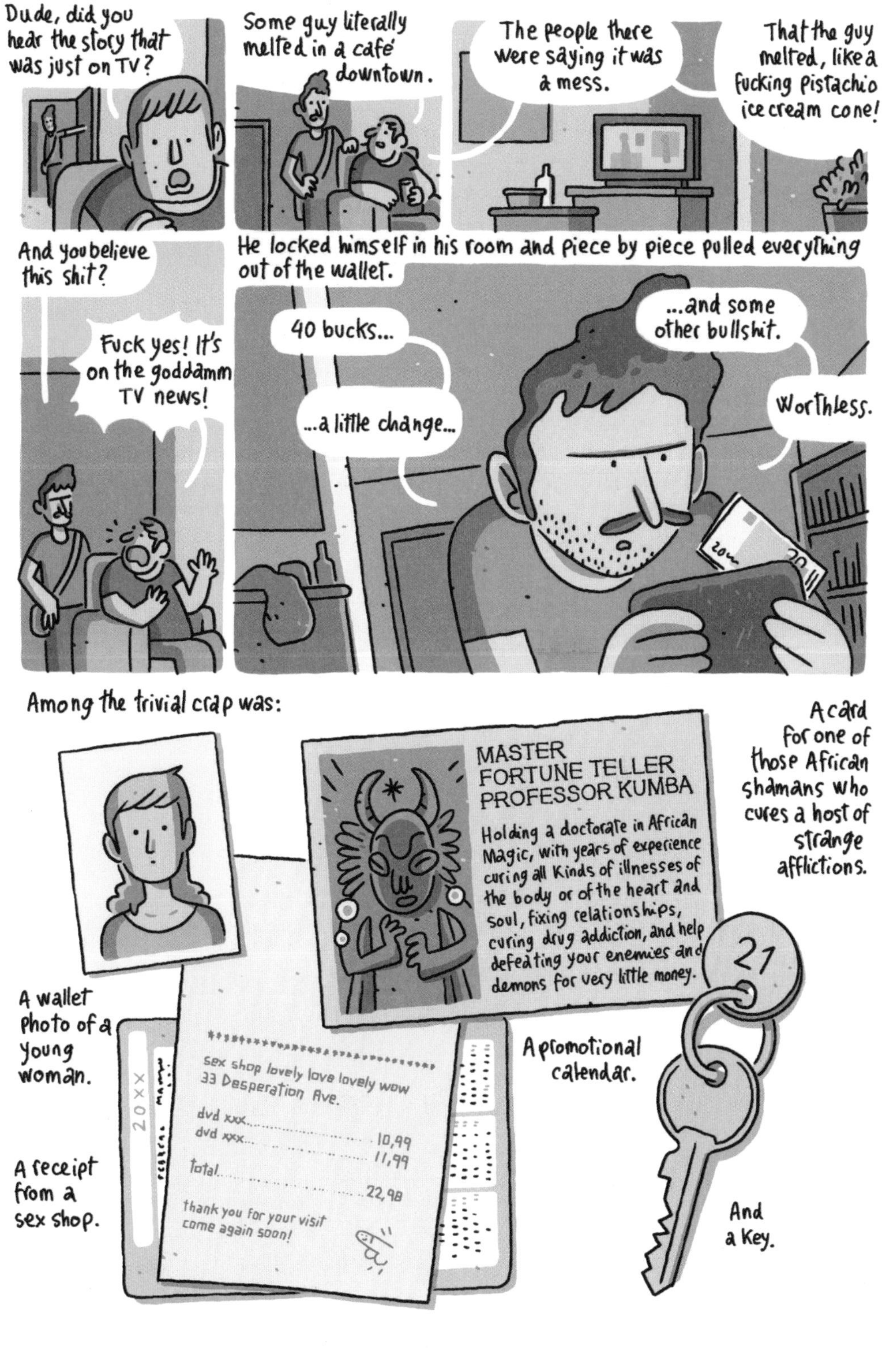
Dude, did you hear the story that was just on TV?
Some guy literally melted in a café downtown.
The people there were saying it was a mess.
That the guy melted, like a fucking pistachio ice cream cone!
And you believe this shit?
Fuck yes! It's on the goddamn TV news!
He locked himself in his room and piece by piece pulled everything out of the wallet.
40 bucks...
...a little change...
...and some other bullshit.
Worthless.
Among the trivial crap was:
MASTER FORTUNE TELLER PROFESSOR KUMBA
Holding a doctorate in African Magic, with years of experience curing all kinds of illnesses of the body or of the heart and soul, fixing relationships, curing drug addiction, and help defeating your enemies and demons for very little money.
A card for one of those African shamans who cures a host of strange afflictions.
21
A wallet photo of a young woman.
20XX
sex shop lovely love lovely wow
33 Desperation Ave.
dvd xxx.......... 10,99
dvd xxx.......... 11,99
total.......... 22,98
thank you for your visit
come again soon!
A promotional calendar.
A receipt from a sex shop.
And a key.

The really strange thing was that there was no ID, no driver's license, no identification, nothing to indicate who the guy in the café was.
Not having anything else to do, he ate some leftover pizza that he found in the fridge and decided to take advantage of the nice night and go for a walk.
He had recognized the logo on the key as belonging to a locker at the bus station, because he'd had to use one a few months before.
19
20
21
22
27
28
29
30
35
36
37
38
Since the first day he saw them, they captured his fancy. Every day that passes, it gets more expensive to retrieve the contents.
So every time he passes by he looks at the price and wonders what it is that people are storing there.
And if the price on the locker is very high, whether people are going to come back for their belongings, or if they are going to leave them there forever.
PAGO SUPLEMENTARIO
IMPORTE A PAGAR
125.00
Luckily, locker number 21 had not been closed very long.
15.50
Hey! Pepe!

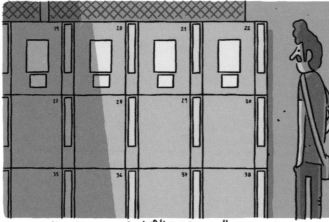

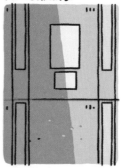

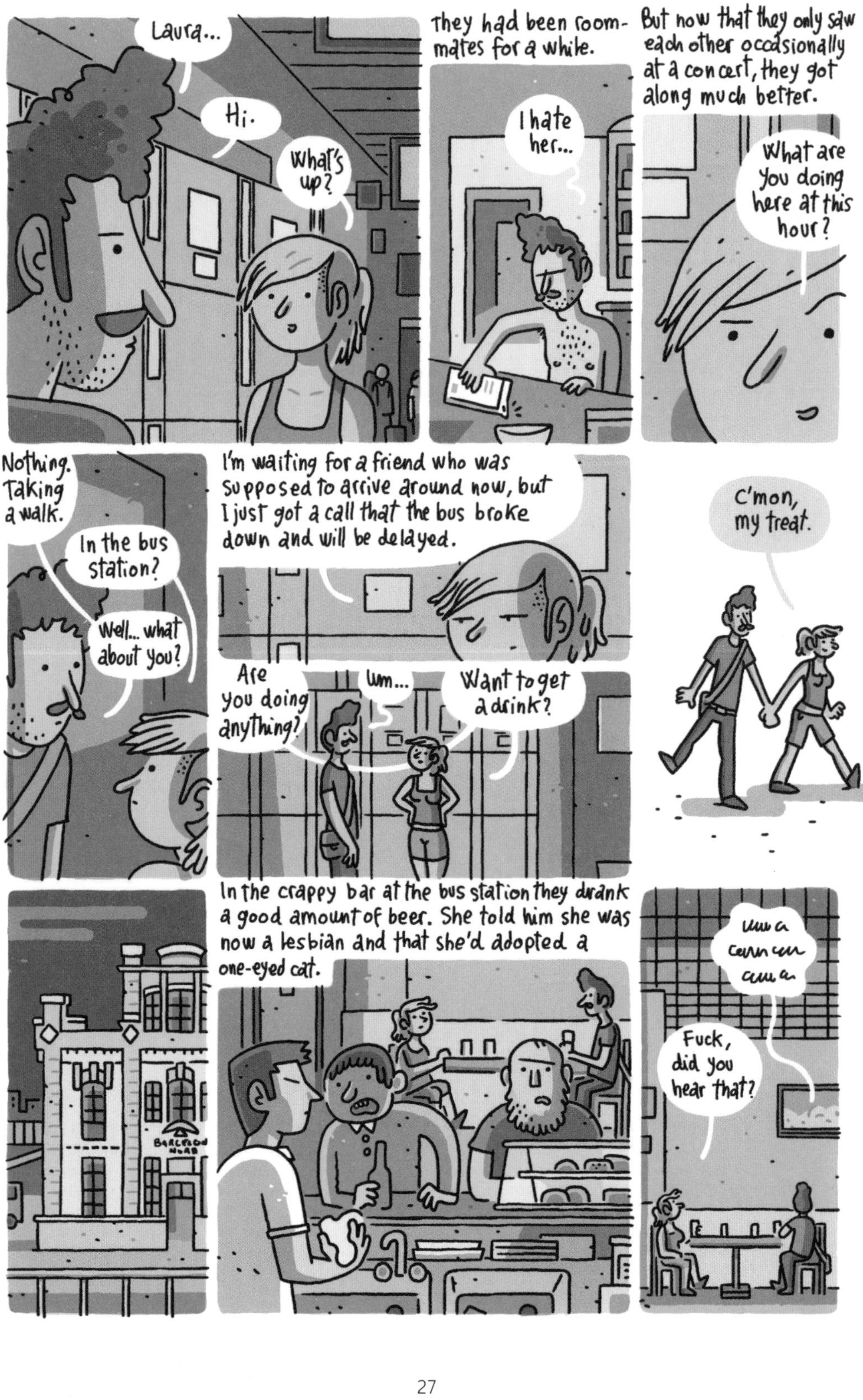
Laura...
Hi.
What's up?
They had been roommates for a while.
I hate her...
But now that they only saw each other occasionally at a concert, they got along much better.
What are you doing here at this hour?
Nothing. Taking a walk.
In the bus station?
Well... what about you?
I'm waiting for a friend who was supposed to arrive around now, but I just got a call that the bus broke down and will be delayed.
Are you doing anything?
um...
Want to get a drink?
C'mon, my treat.
In the crappy bar at the bus station they drank a good amount of beer. She told him she was now a lesbian and that she'd adopted a one-eyed cat.
Fuck, did you hear that?

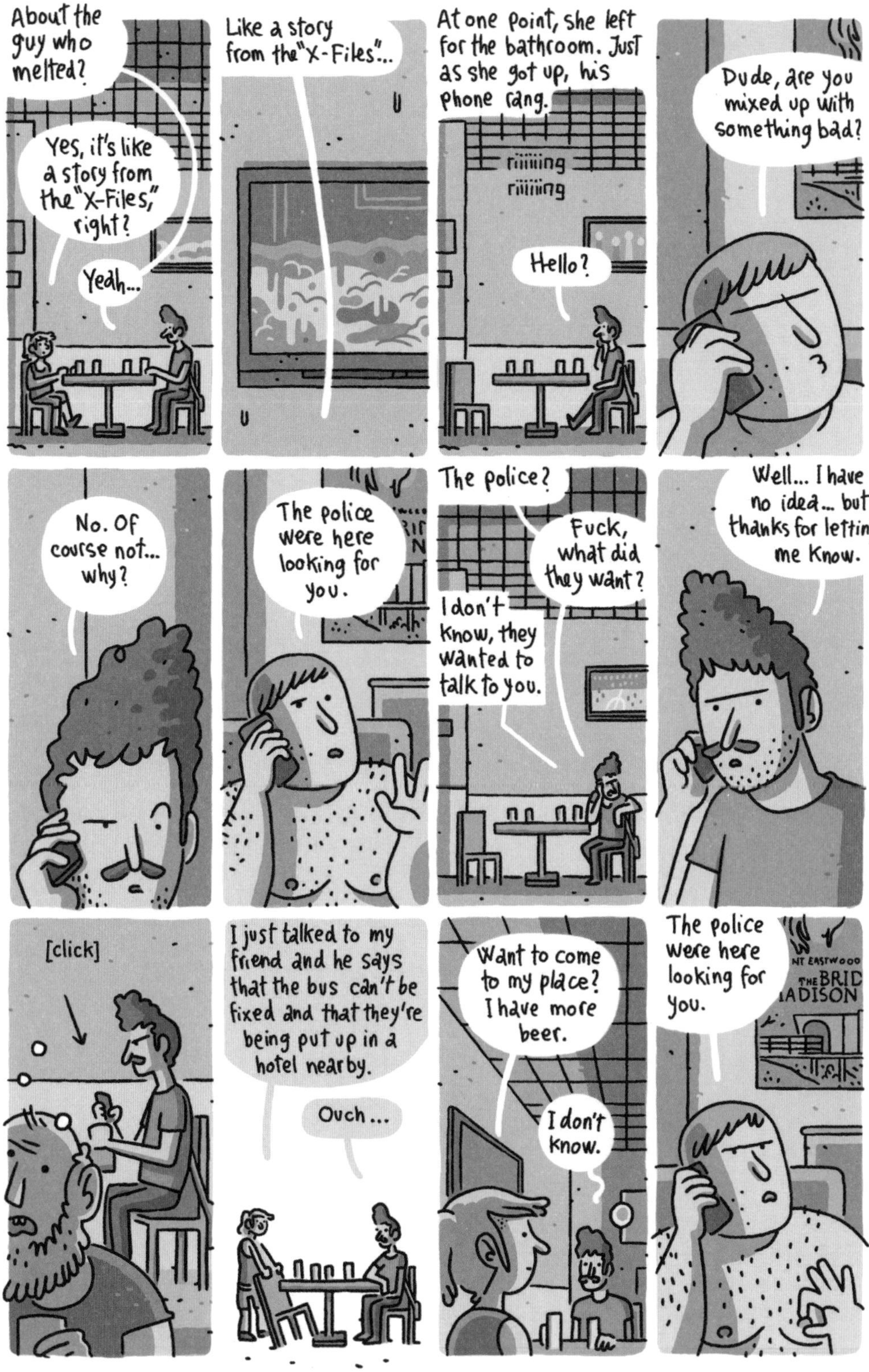
About the guy who melted?
Yes, it's like a story from the "X-Files," right?
Yeah...
Like a story from the "X-Files"...
At one point, she left for the bathroom. Just as she got up, his phone rang.
riiiiing
riiiiing
Hello?
Dude, are you mixed up with something bad?
No. Of course not... why?
The police were here looking for you.
The police?
Fuck, what did they want?
I don't know, they wanted to talk to you.
Well... I have no idea... but thanks for letting me know.
[click]
I just talked to my friend and he says that the bus can't be fixed and that they're being put up in a hotel nearby.
Ouch...
Want to come to my place? I have more beer.
I don't know.
The police were here looking for you.
NT EASTWOOD
THE BRID
ADISON

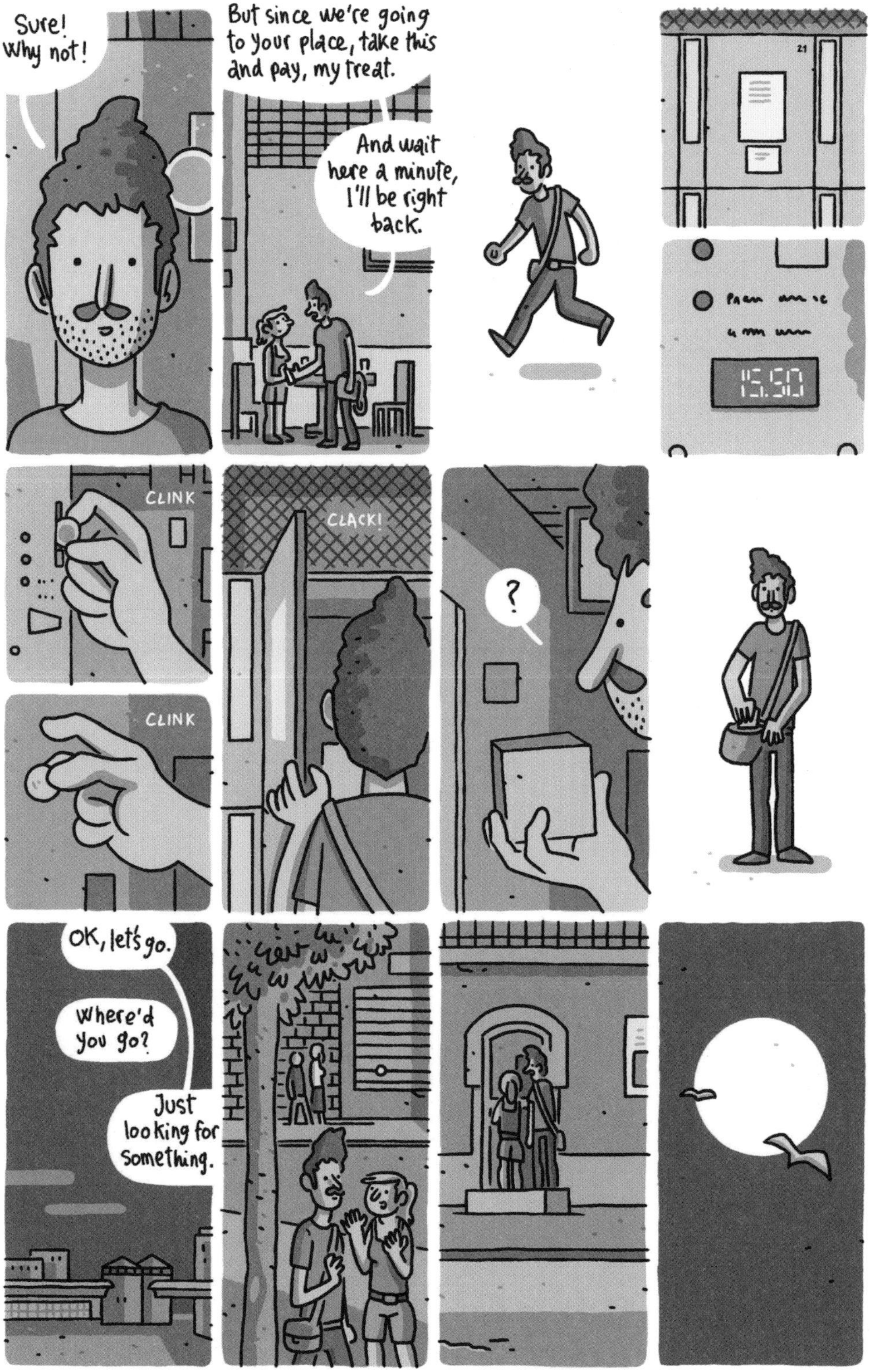
Sure! Why not!
But since we're going to your place, take this and pay, my treat.
And wait here a minute, I'll be right back.
15:50
CLINK
CLINK
CLACK!
?
OK, let's go.
Where'd you go?
Just looking for something.

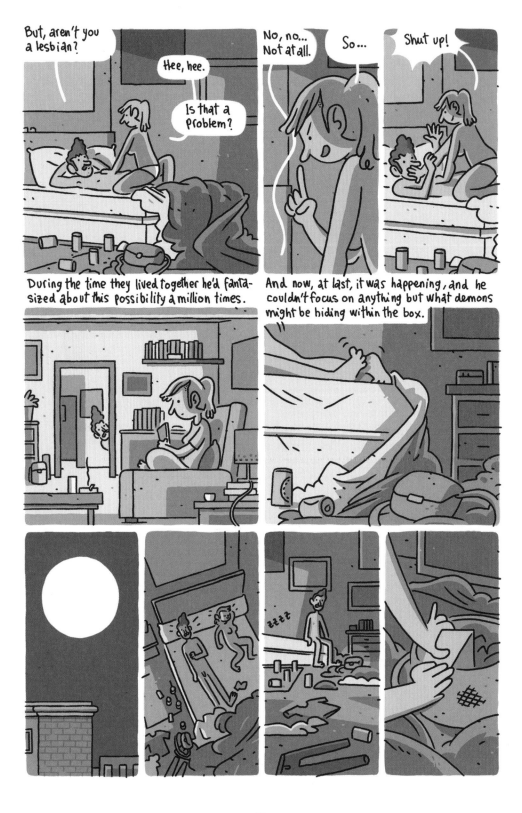

But, aren't you a lesbian?

Hee, hee.

Is that a problem?

No, no... Not at all.

So...

Shut up!

During the time they lived together he'd fantasized about this possibility a million times.

And now, at last, it was happening, and he couldn't focus on anything but what demons might be hiding within the box.

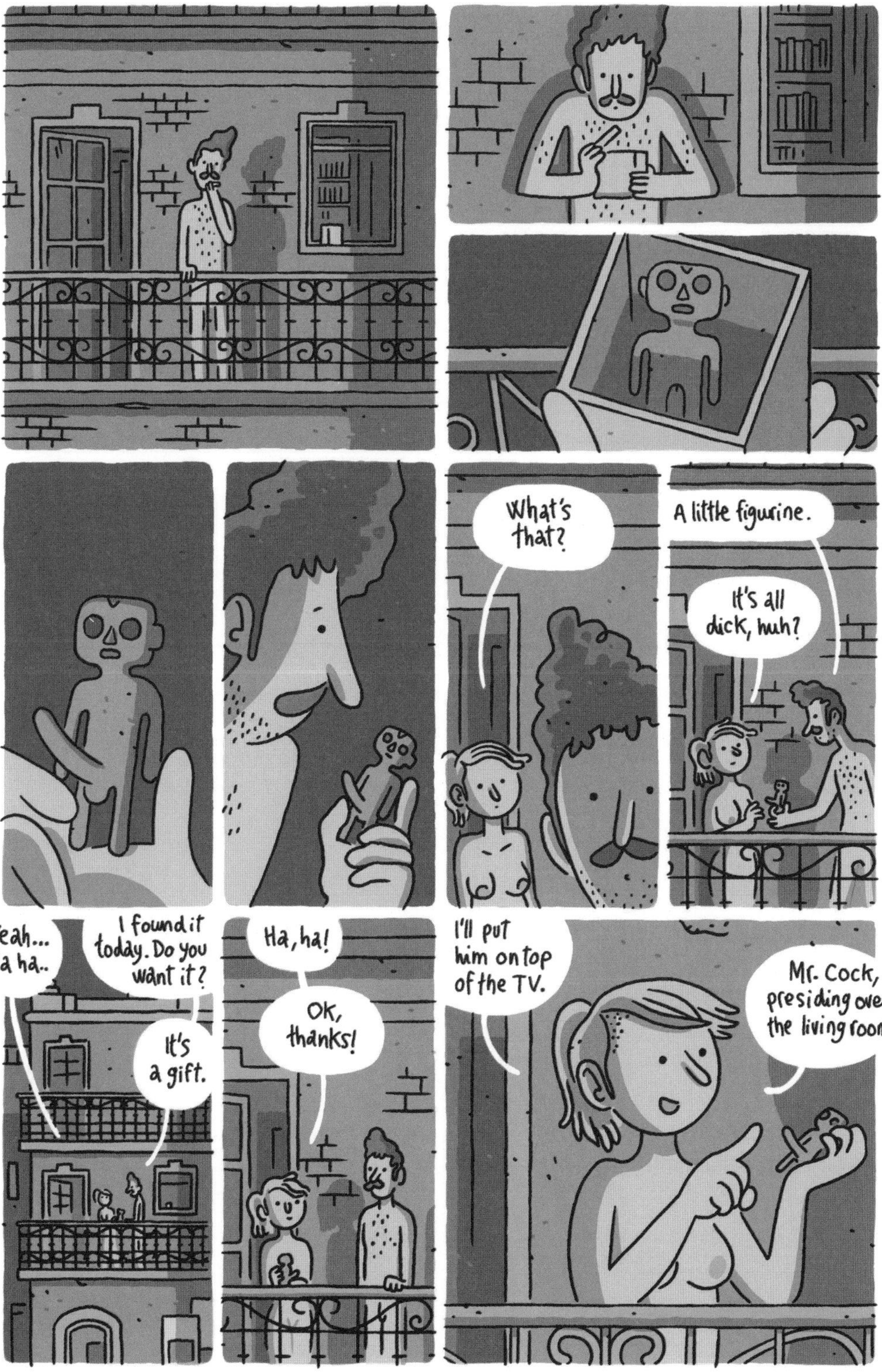
What's that?
A little figurine.
It's all dick, huh?
Yeah... Ha ha..
I found it today. Do you want it?
It's a gift.
Ha, ha!
Ok, thanks!
I'll put him on top of the TV.
Mr. Cock, presiding over the living room.

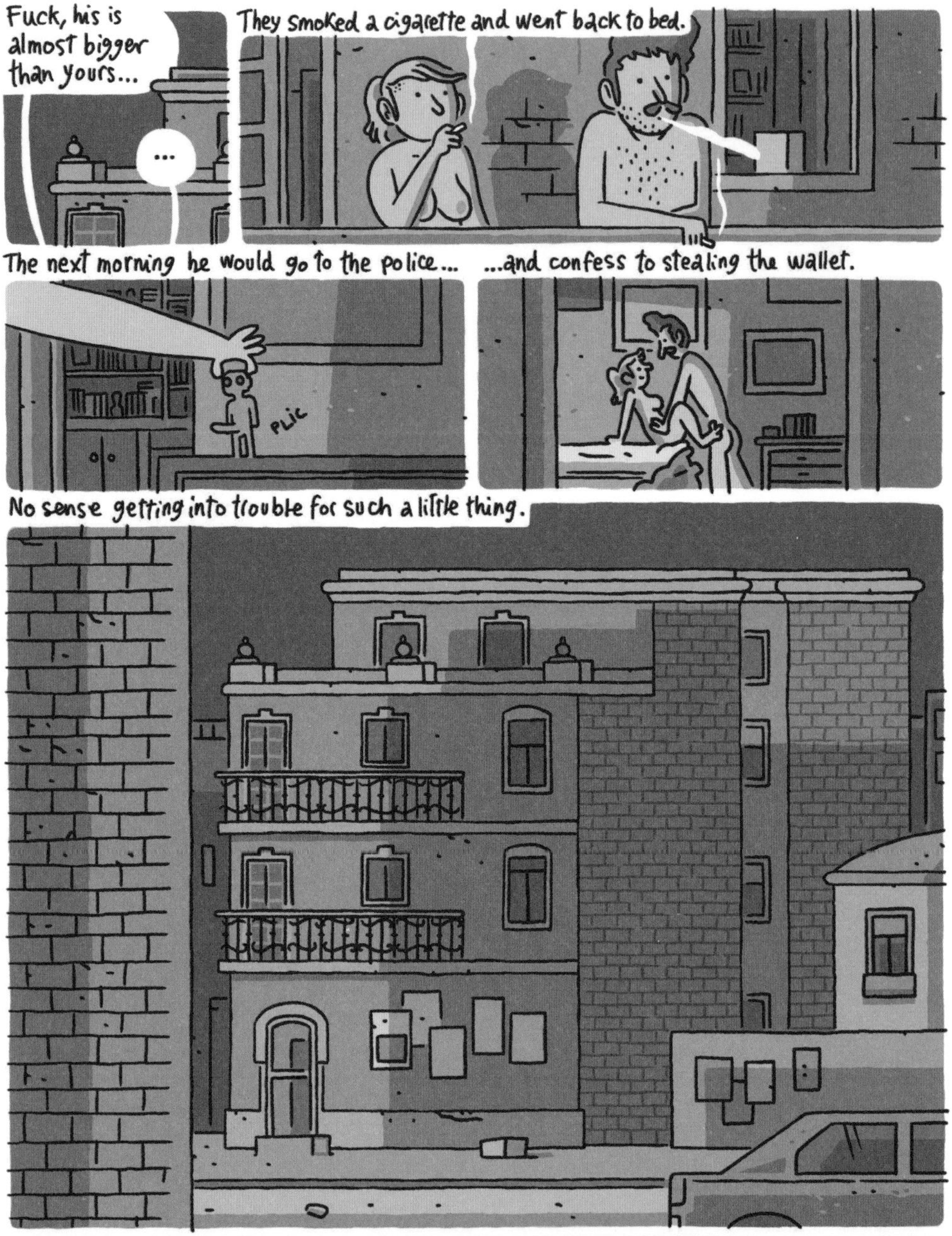

Fuck, his is almost bigger than yours...
...
They smoked a cigarette and went back to bed.
The next morning he would go to the police...
PLIC
...and confess to stealing the wallet.
No sense getting into trouble for such a little thing.
álvaro ortiz / 2015

PACO ROCA

CHRONICLE OF A CRISIS FORETOLD

Paco Roca was born in Valencia in 1969. He helped instigate the Spanish graphic novel boom, thanks to the success of *Arrugas* [*Wrinkles*] (2007), which earned him the Premio Nacional del Cómic and was made into a feature-length animated film. It's currently out from Fantagraphics in English translation. Over the last few years, he's balanced his work as an illustrator and his frequent trips and lectures with the publication of comics like *Las calles de arena* [*Streets of Sand*] (2009), *El invierno del dibujante* [*The Winter of the Cartoonist*] (2010), *Memorias de un hombre en pajama* [*Memoirs of a Man in Pajamas*] (2011), and *Andazas de un hombre en pajama* [*The Travels of a Man in Pajamas*] (2014). The last two books collected the series—published biweekly in *El País Semanal*, the Sunday supplement to the newspaper with the largest circulation in Spain—*El hombre en pajama* [*The Man in Pajamas*] in its entirety. In 2012, the MuVIM (Museo Valenciano de la Ilustración y la Modernidad) [Valencia Museum of Illustration and Modernity] held a retrospective of his work; another large exhibition at the Fundación Telefónica de Madrid followed in 2014–2015. *Los surcos del azar* [*The Wrinkles of Fate*] (2013) his most recent graphic novel, is about the exiled Spanish Republicans who fought with the Allies for the liberation of Paris, and has been met with resounding acclaim in both Spain and France. His new comic, *La casa* [*The House*], came out in 2015.

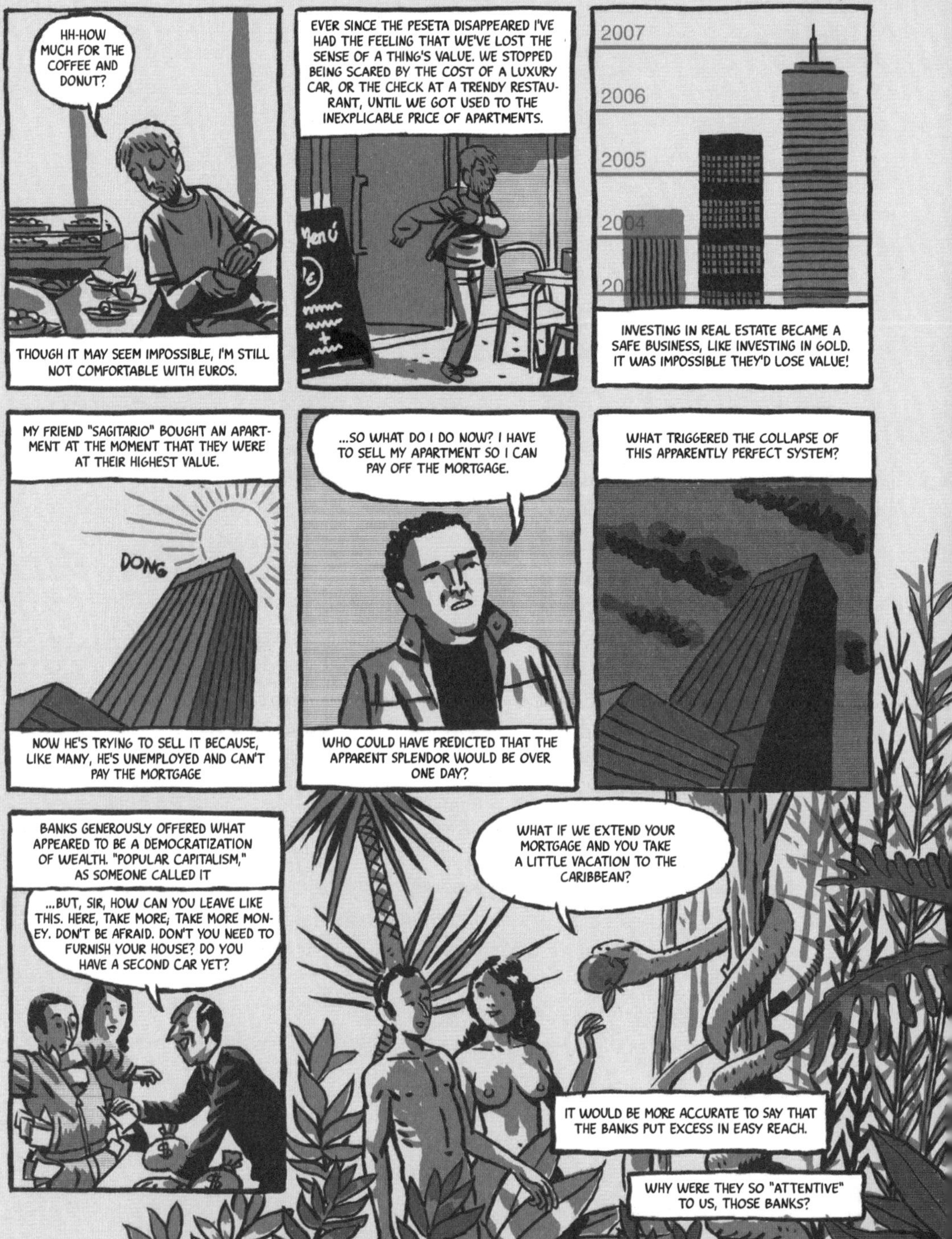
HH-HOW MUCH FOR THE COFFEE AND DONUT?
THOUGH IT MAY SEEM IMPOSSIBLE, I'M STILL NOT COMFORTABLE WITH EUROS.
EVER SINCE THE PESETA DISAPPEARED I'VE HAD THE FEELING THAT WE'VE LOST THE SENSE OF A THING'S VALUE. WE STOPPED BEING SCARED BY THE COST OF A LUXURY CAR, OR THE CHECK AT A TRENDY RESTAURANT, UNTIL WE GOT USED TO THE INEXPLICABLE PRICE OF APARTMENTS.
2007
2006
2005
2004
INVESTING IN REAL ESTATE BECAME A SAFE BUSINESS, LIKE INVESTING IN GOLD. IT WAS IMPOSSIBLE THEY'D LOSE VALUE!
MY FRIEND "SAGITARIO" BOUGHT AN APARTMENT AT THE MOMENT THAT THEY WERE AT THEIR HIGHEST VALUE.
DONG
NOW HE'S TRYING TO SELL IT BECAUSE, LIKE MANY, HE'S UNEMPLOYED AND CAN'T PAY THE MORTGAGE
...SO WHAT DO I DO NOW? I HAVE TO SELL MY APARTMENT SO I CAN PAY OFF THE MORTGAGE.
WHO COULD HAVE PREDICTED THAT THE APPARENT SPLENDOR WOULD BE OVER ONE DAY?
WHAT TRIGGERED THE COLLAPSE OF THIS APPARENTLY PERFECT SYSTEM?
BANKS GENEROUSLY OFFERED WHAT APPEARED TO BE A DEMOCRATIZATION OF WEALTH. "POPULAR CAPITALISM," AS SOMEONE CALLED IT
...BUT, SIR, HOW CAN YOU LEAVE LIKE THIS. HERE, TAKE MORE; TAKE MORE MONEY. DON'T BE AFRAID. DON'T YOU NEED TO FURNISH YOUR HOUSE? DO YOU HAVE A SECOND CAR YET?
WHAT IF WE EXTEND YOUR MORTGAGE AND YOU TAKE A LITTLE VACATION TO THE CARIBBEAN?
IT WOULD BE MORE ACCURATE TO SAY THAT THE BANKS PUT EXCESS IN EASY REACH.
WHY WERE THEY SO "ATTENTIVE" TO US, THOSE BANKS?

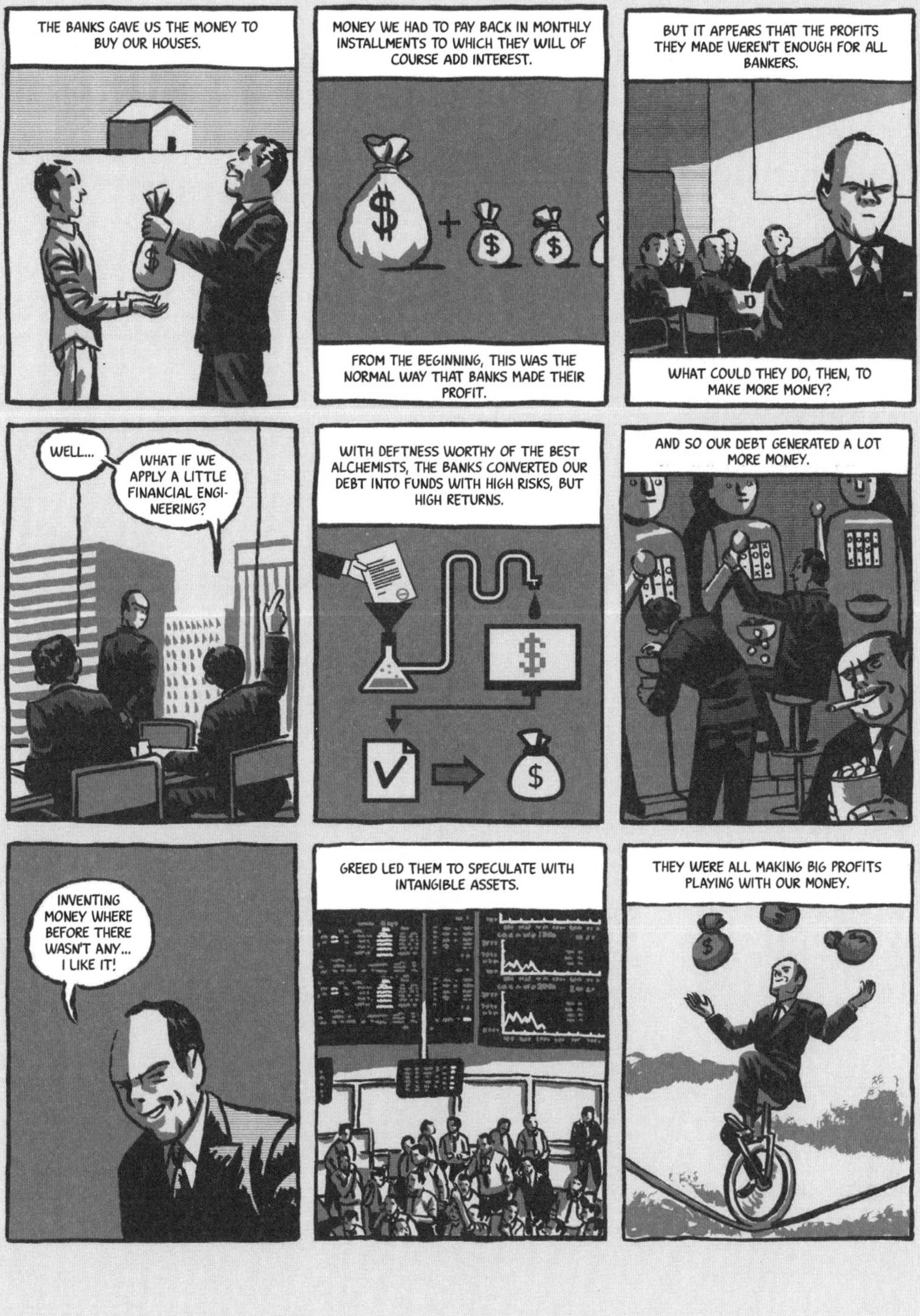
THE BANKS GAVE US THE MONEY TO BUY OUR HOUSES.
MONEY WE HAD TO PAY BACK IN MONTHLY INSTALLMENTS TO WHICH THEY WILL OF COURSE ADD INTEREST.
FROM THE BEGINNING, THIS WAS THE NORMAL WAY THAT BANKS MADE THEIR PROFIT.
BUT IT APPEARS THAT THE PROFITS THEY MADE WEREN'T ENOUGH FOR ALL BANKERS.
WHAT COULD THEY DO, THEN, TO MAKE MORE MONEY?
WELL...
WHAT IF WE APPLY A LITTLE FINANCIAL ENGI-NEERING?
WITH DEFTNESS WORTHY OF THE BEST ALCHEMISTS, THE BANKS CONVERTED OUR DEBT INTO FUNDS WITH HIGH RISKS, BUT HIGH RETURNS.
AND SO OUR DEBT GENERATED A LOT MORE MONEY.
INVENTING MONEY WHERE BEFORE THERE WASN'T ANY... I LIKE IT!
GREED LED THEM TO SPECULATE WITH INTANGIBLE ASSETS.
THEY WERE ALL MAKING BIG PROFITS PLAYING WITH OUR MONEY.

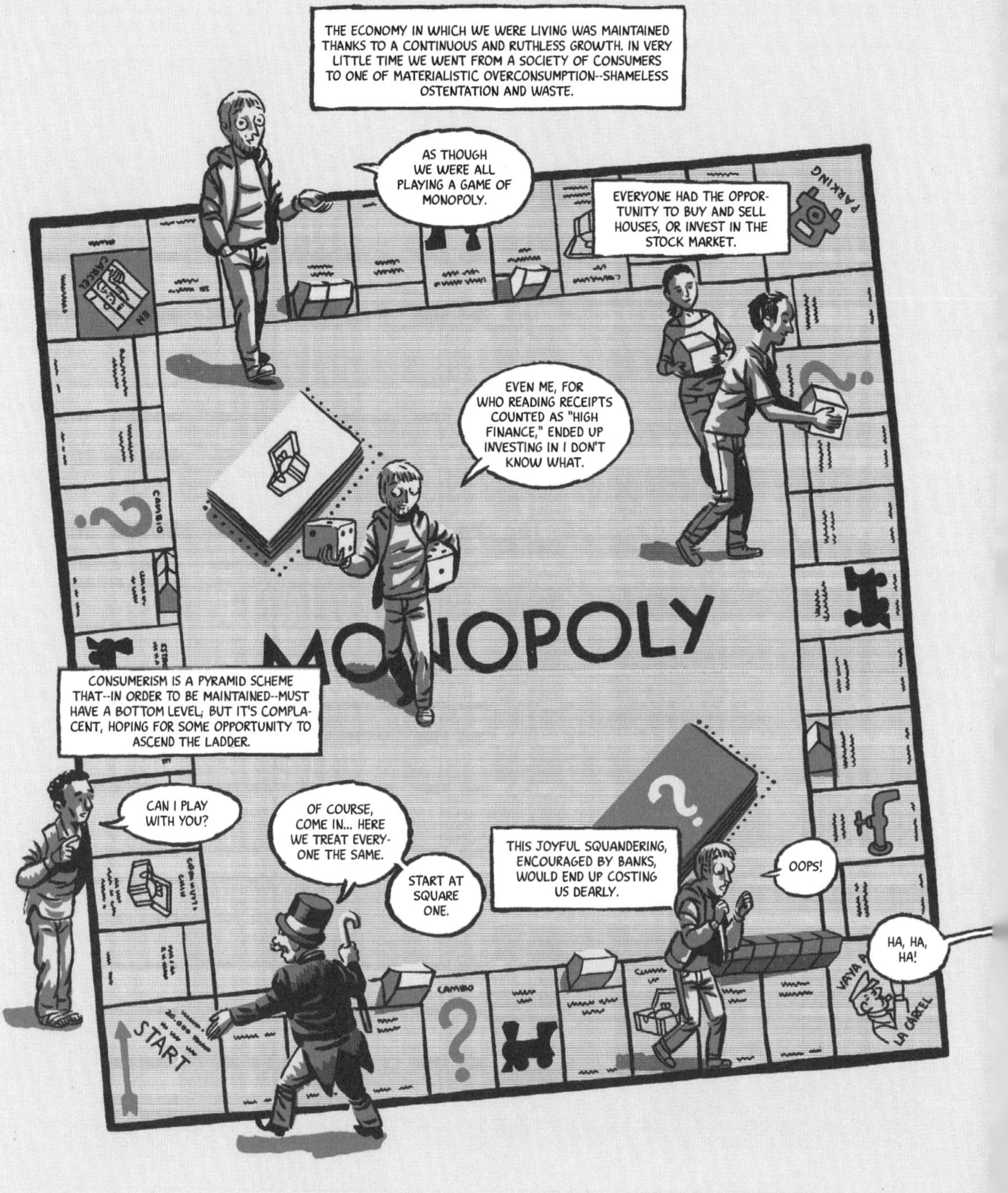
THE ECONOMY IN WHICH WE WERE LIVING WAS MAINTAINED THANKS TO A CONTINUOUS AND RUTHLESS GROWTH. IN VERY LITTLE TIME WE WENT FROM A SOCIETY OF CONSUMERS TO ONE OF MATERIALISTIC OVERCONSUMPTION--SHAMELESS OSTENTATION AND WASTE.
AS THOUGH WE WERE ALL PLAYING A GAME OF MONOPOLY.
EVERYONE HAD THE OPPORTUNITY TO BUY AND SELL HOUSES, OR INVEST IN THE STOCK MARKET.
PARKING
CARCEL
EVEN ME, FOR WHO READING RECEIPTS COUNTED AS "HIGH FINANCE," ENDED UP INVESTING IN I DON'T KNOW WHAT.
CAMBIO
MONOPOLY
CONSUMERISM IS A PYRAMID SCHEME THAT--IN ORDER TO BE MAINTAINED--MUST HAVE A BOTTOM LEVEL; BUT IT'S COMPLACENT, HOPING FOR SOME OPPORTUNITY TO ASCEND THE LADDER.
CAN I PLAY WITH YOU?
OF COURSE, COME IN... HERE WE TREAT EVERYONE THE SAME.
START AT SQUARE ONE.
THIS JOYFUL SQUANDERING, ENCOURAGED BY BANKS, WOULD END UP COSTING US DEARLY.
OOPS!
HA, HA, HA!
START
CAMBIO
VAYA A LA CARCEL

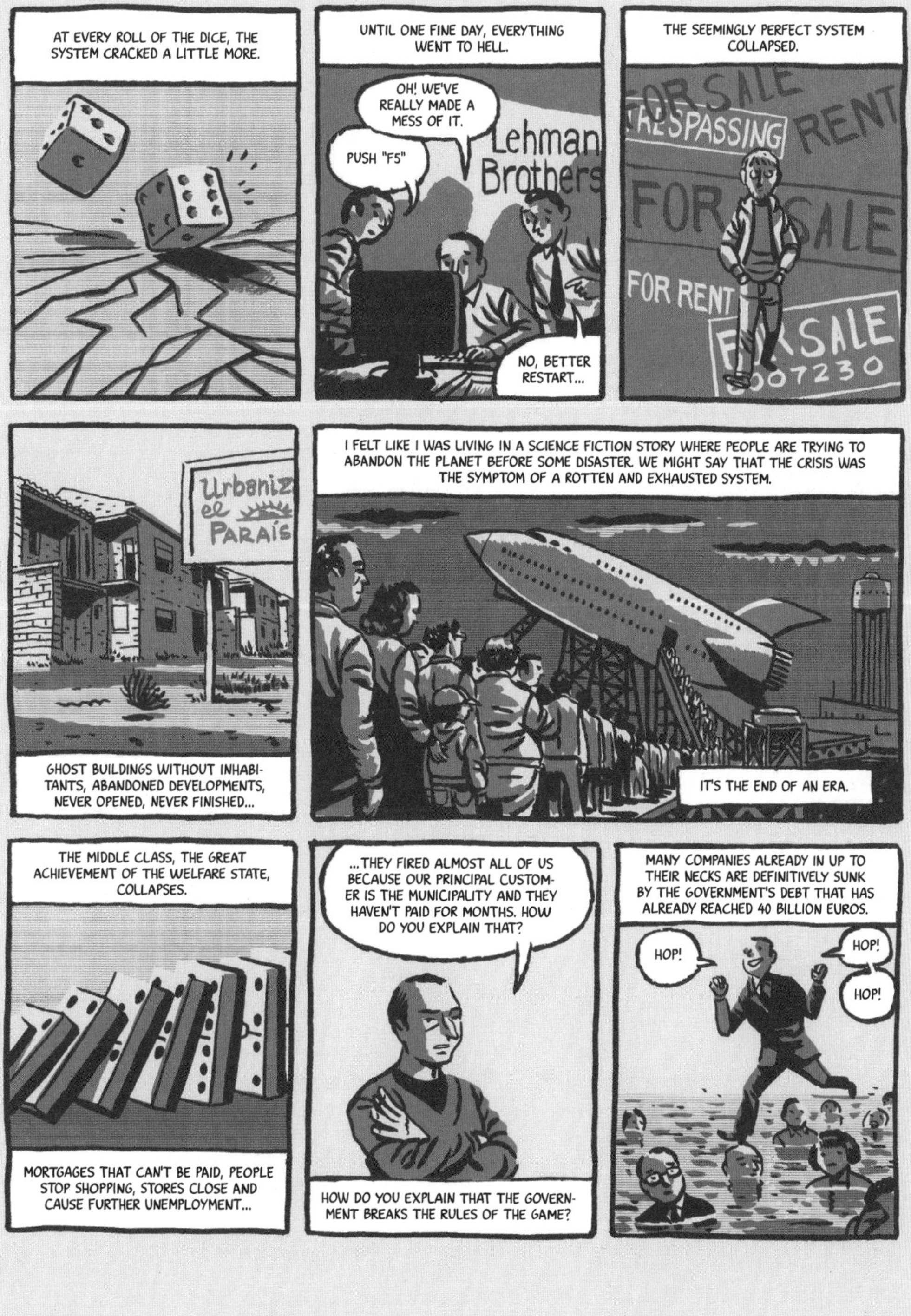
AT EVERY ROLL OF THE DICE, THE SYSTEM CRACKED A LITTLE MORE.
UNTIL ONE FINE DAY, EVERYTHING WENT TO HELL.
OH! WE'VE REALLY MADE A MESS OF IT.
Lehman Brothers
PUSH "F5"
NO, BETTER RESTART...
THE SEEMINGLY PERFECT SYSTEM COLLAPSED.
FOR SALE
TRESPASSING
RENT
FOR SALE
FOR RENT
SALE
Urbaniz el Paraís
GHOST BUILDINGS WITHOUT INHABITANTS, ABANDONED DEVELOPMENTS, NEVER OPENED, NEVER FINISHED...
I FELT LIKE I WAS LIVING IN A SCIENCE FICTION STORY WHERE PEOPLE ARE TRYING TO ABANDON THE PLANET BEFORE SOME DISASTER. WE MIGHT SAY THAT THE CRISIS WAS THE SYMPTOM OF A ROTTEN AND EXHAUSTED SYSTEM.
IT'S THE END OF AN ERA.
THE MIDDLE CLASS, THE GREAT ACHIEVEMENT OF THE WELFARE STATE, COLLAPSES.
MORTGAGES THAT CAN'T BE PAID, PEOPLE STOP SHOPPING, STORES CLOSE AND CAUSE FURTHER UNEMPLOYMENT...
...THEY FIRED ALMOST ALL OF US BECAUSE OUR PRINCIPAL CUSTOMER IS THE MUNICIPALITY AND THEY HAVEN'T PAID FOR MONTHS. HOW DO YOU EXPLAIN THAT?
HOW DO YOU EXPLAIN THAT THE GOVERNMENT BREAKS THE RULES OF THE GAME?
MANY COMPANIES ALREADY IN UP TO THEIR NECKS ARE DEFINITIVELY SUNK BY THE GOVERNMENT'S DEBT THAT HAS ALREADY REACHED 40 BILLION EUROS.
HOP!
HOP!
HOP!

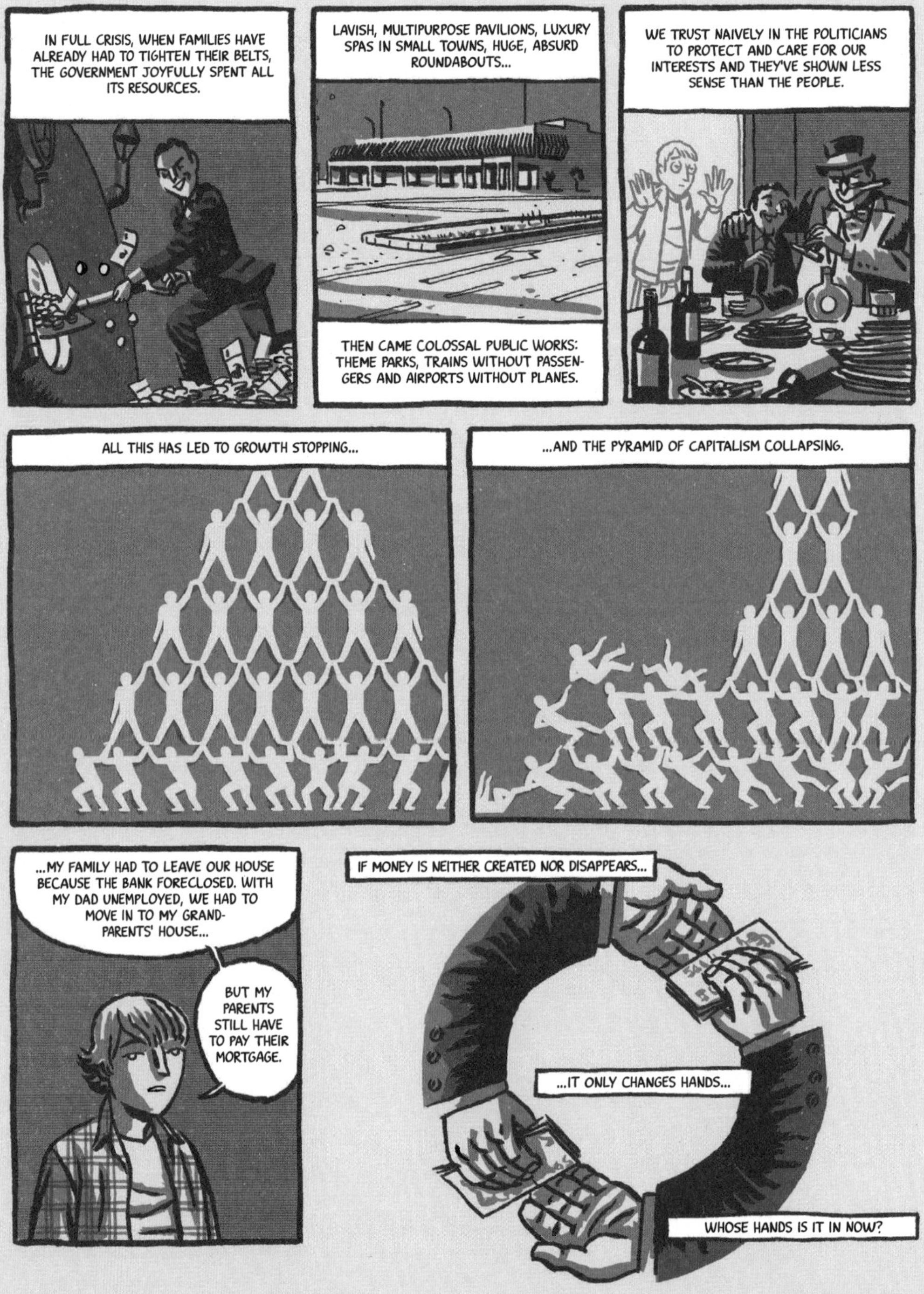
IN FULL CRISIS, WHEN FAMILIES HAVE ALREADY HAD TO TIGHTEN THEIR BELTS, THE GOVERNMENT JOYFULLY SPENT ALL ITS RESOURCES.
LAVISH, MULTIPURPOSE PAVILIONS, LUXURY SPAS IN SMALL TOWNS, HUGE, ABSURD ROUNDABOUTS...
THEN CAME COLOSSAL PUBLIC WORKS: THEME PARKS, TRAINS WITHOUT PASSENGERS AND AIRPORTS WITHOUT PLANES.
WE TRUST NAIVELY IN THE POLITICIANS TO PROTECT AND CARE FOR OUR INTERESTS AND THEY'VE SHOWN LESS SENSE THAN THE PEOPLE.
ALL THIS HAS LED TO GROWTH STOPPING...
...AND THE PYRAMID OF CAPITALISM COLLAPSING.
...MY FAMILY HAD TO LEAVE OUR HOUSE BECAUSE THE BANK FORECLOSED. WITH MY DAD UNEMPLOYED, WE HAD TO MOVE IN TO MY GRANDPARENTS' HOUSE...
BUT MY PARENTS STILL HAVE TO PAY THEIR MORTGAGE.
IF MONEY IS NEITHER CREATED NOR DISAPPEARS...
...IT ONLY CHANGES HANDS...
WHOSE HANDS IS IT IN NOW?

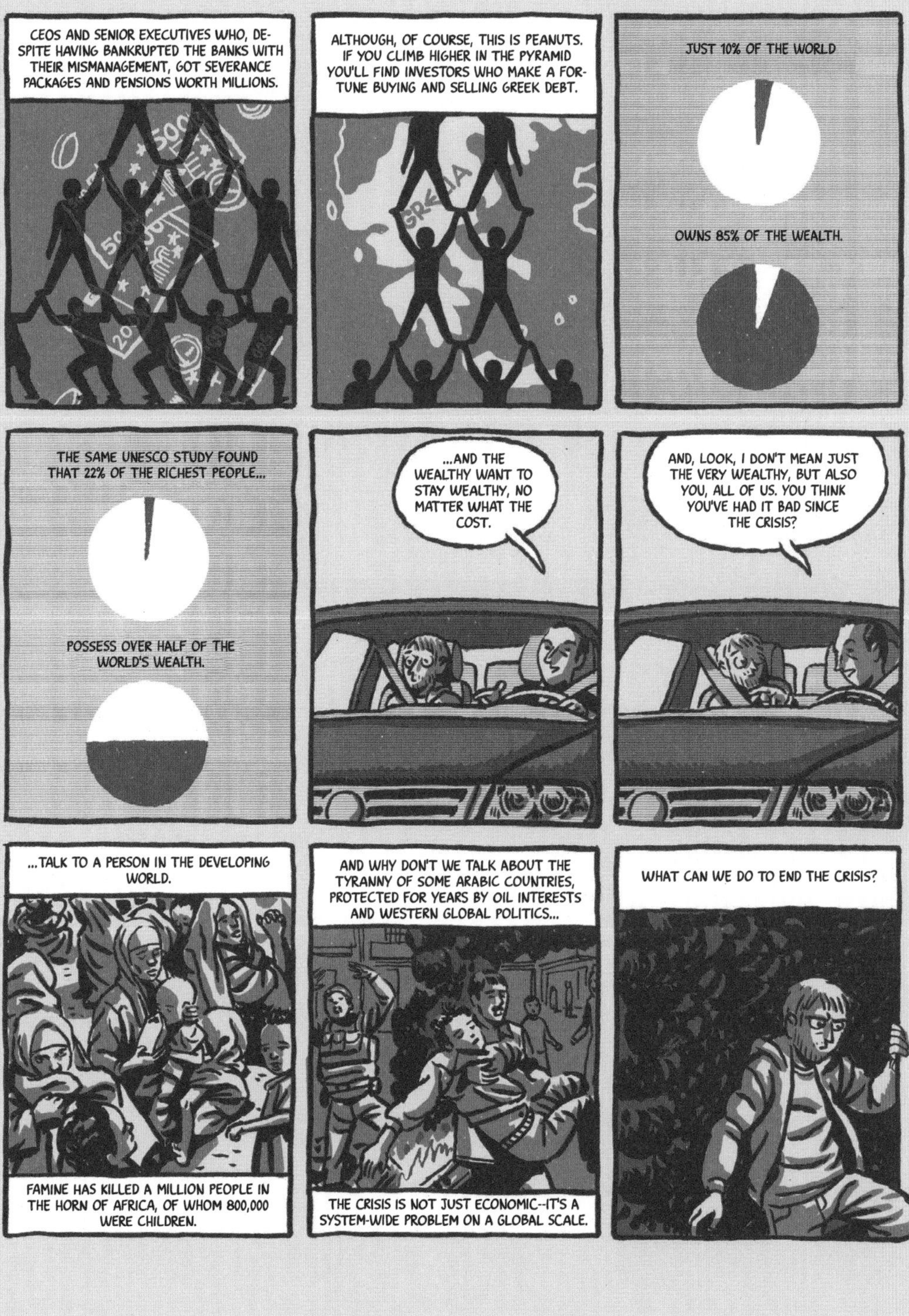
CEOS AND SENIOR EXECUTIVES WHO, DESPITE HAVING BANKRUPTED THE BANKS WITH THEIR MISMANAGEMENT, GOT SEVERANCE PACKAGES AND PENSIONS WORTH MILLIONS.
ALTHOUGH, OF COURSE, THIS IS PEANUTS. IF YOU CLIMB HIGHER IN THE PYRAMID YOU'LL FIND INVESTORS WHO MAKE A FORTUNE BUYING AND SELLING GREEK DEBT.
JUST 10% OF THE WORLD
OWNS 85% OF THE WEALTH.
THE SAME UNESCO STUDY FOUND THAT 22% OF THE RICHEST PEOPLE...
POSSESS OVER HALF OF THE WORLD'S WEALTH.
...AND THE WEALTHY WANT TO STAY WEALTHY, NO MATTER WHAT THE COST.
AND, LOOK, I DON'T MEAN JUST THE VERY WEALTHY, BUT ALSO YOU, ALL OF US. YOU THINK YOU'VE HAD IT BAD SINCE THE CRISIS?
...TALK TO A PERSON IN THE DEVELOPING WORLD.
FAMINE HAS KILLED A MILLION PEOPLE IN THE HORN OF AFRICA, OF WHOM 800,000 WERE CHILDREN.
AND WHY DON'T WE TALK ABOUT THE TYRANNY OF SOME ARABIC COUNTRIES, PROTECTED FOR YEARS BY OIL INTERESTS AND WESTERN GLOBAL POLITICS...
THE CRISIS IS NOT JUST ECONOMIC--IT'S A SYSTEM-WIDE PROBLEM ON A GLOBAL SCALE.
WHAT CAN WE DO TO END THE CRISIS?

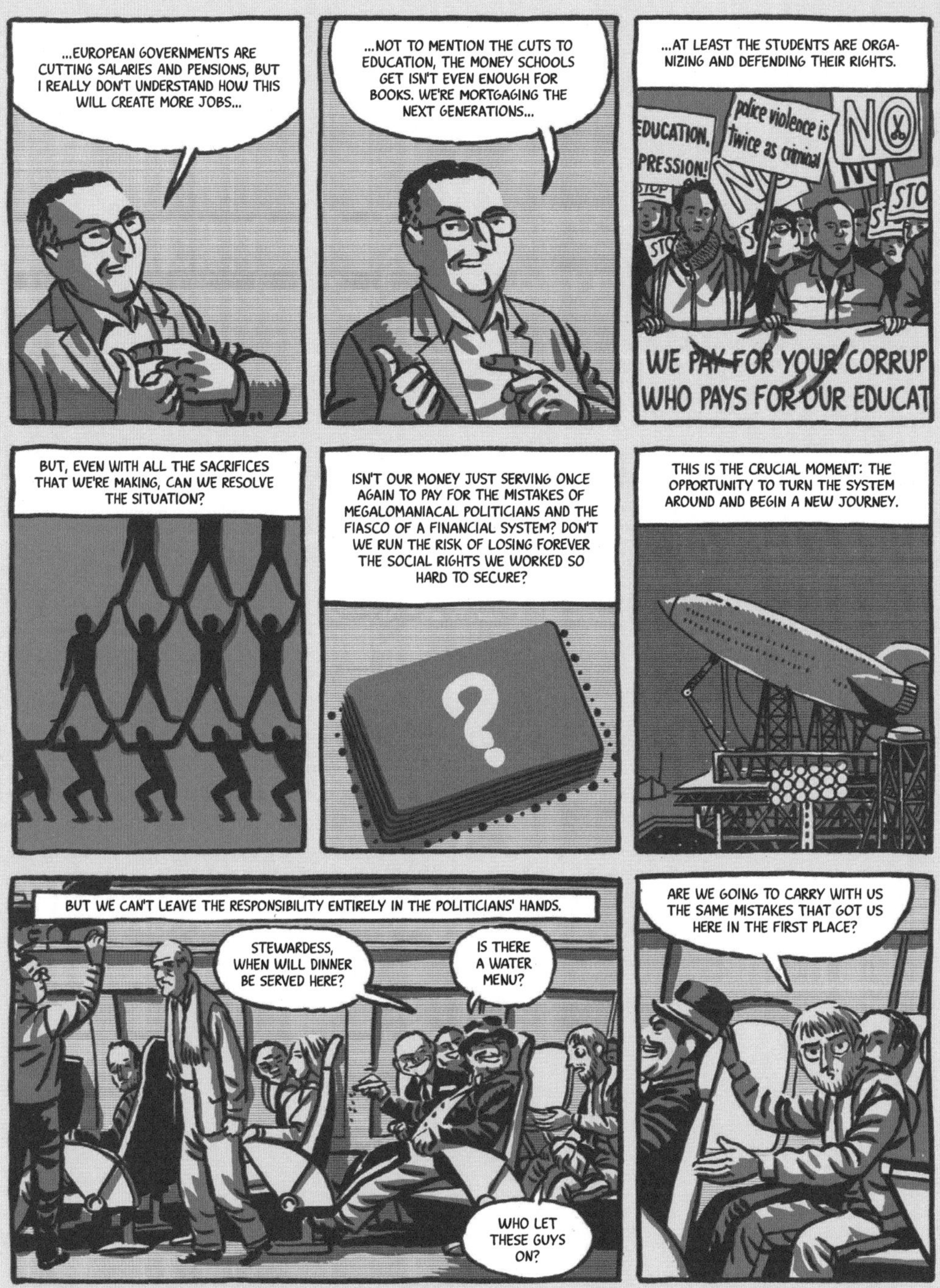
...EUROPEAN GOVERNMENTS ARE CUTTING SALARIES AND PENSIONS, BUT I REALLY DON'T UNDERSTAND HOW THIS WILL CREATE MORE JOBS...
...NOT TO MENTION THE CUTS TO EDUCATION, THE MONEY SCHOOLS GET ISN'T EVEN ENOUGH FOR BOOKS. WE'RE MORTGAGING THE NEXT GENERATIONS...
...AT LEAST THE STUDENTS ARE ORGANIZING AND DEFENDING THEIR RIGHTS.
EDUCATION,
PRESSION!
police violence is twice as criminal
NO
WE PAY FOR YOUR CORRUP
WHO PAYS FOR OUR EDUCAT
BUT, EVEN WITH ALL THE SACRIFICES THAT WE'RE MAKING, CAN WE RESOLVE THE SITUATION?
ISN'T OUR MONEY JUST SERVING ONCE AGAIN TO PAY FOR THE MISTAKES OF MEGALOMANIACAL POLITICIANS AND THE FIASCO OF A FINANCIAL SYSTEM? DON'T WE RUN THE RISK OF LOSING FOREVER THE SOCIAL RIGHTS WE WORKED SO HARD TO SECURE?
?
THIS IS THE CRUCIAL MOMENT: THE OPPORTUNITY TO TURN THE SYSTEM AROUND AND BEGIN A NEW JOURNEY.
BUT WE CAN'T LEAVE THE RESPONSIBILITY ENTIRELY IN THE POLITICIANS' HANDS.
STEWARDESS, WHEN WILL DINNER BE SERVED HERE?
IS THERE A WATER MENU?
WHO LET THESE GUYS ON?
ARE WE GOING TO CARRY WITH US THE SAME MISTAKES THAT GOT US HERE IN THE FIRST PLACE?

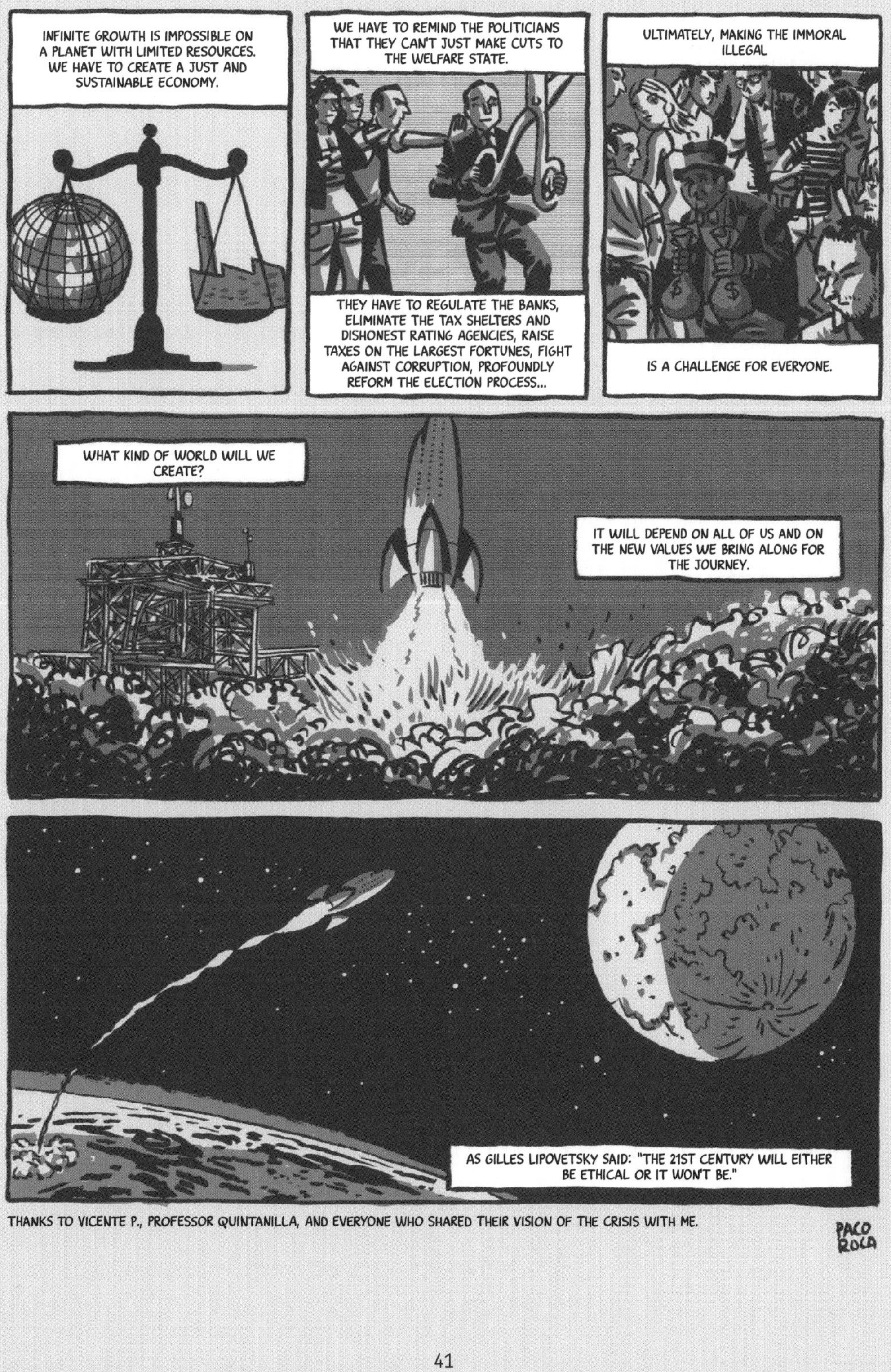
INFINITE GROWTH IS IMPOSSIBLE ON A PLANET WITH LIMITED RESOURCES. WE HAVE TO CREATE A JUST AND SUSTAINABLE ECONOMY.
WE HAVE TO REMIND THE POLITICIANS THAT THEY CAN'T JUST MAKE CUTS TO THE WELFARE STATE.
THEY HAVE TO REGULATE THE BANKS, ELIMINATE THE TAX SHELTERS AND DISHONEST RATING AGENCIES, RAISE TAXES ON THE LARGEST FORTUNES, FIGHT AGAINST CORRUPTION, PROFOUNDLY REFORM THE ELECTION PROCESS...
ULTIMATELY, MAKING THE IMMORAL ILLEGAL
IS A CHALLENGE FOR EVERYONE.
WHAT KIND OF WORLD WILL WE CREATE?
IT WILL DEPEND ON ALL OF US AND ON THE NEW VALUES WE BRING ALONG FOR THE JOURNEY.
AS GILLES LIPOVETSKY SAID: "THE 21ST CENTURY WILL EITHER BE ETHICAL OR IT WON'T BE."

THANKS TO VICENTE P., PROFESSOR QUINTANILLA, AND EVERYONE WHO SHARED THEIR VISION OF THE CRISIS WITH ME.

PACO ROCA

RAYCO PULIDO
GREAT-GRANDPARENTS

Rayco Pulido was born in Telde (Gran Canaria) in 1978. He has published short comics and several graphic novels: *Final feliz* [*Happy Ending*] (2004), with a script by Hernán Migoya; *Sordo* [*Deaf*] (2008), in collaboration with David Muñoz; and two works of his own—*Sin título 2008–2011* [*Untitled 2008–2011*] (2011) and *Nela* (2013), adapted from the classic fourteenth century Spanish novel *Marianela* by Benito Pérez Galdós. He is currently working on his new comic, *Lamia*. The story collected here was originally published in the magazine *Terry*, and with it begins a series dedicated to the saga of the imaginary Fundador family.

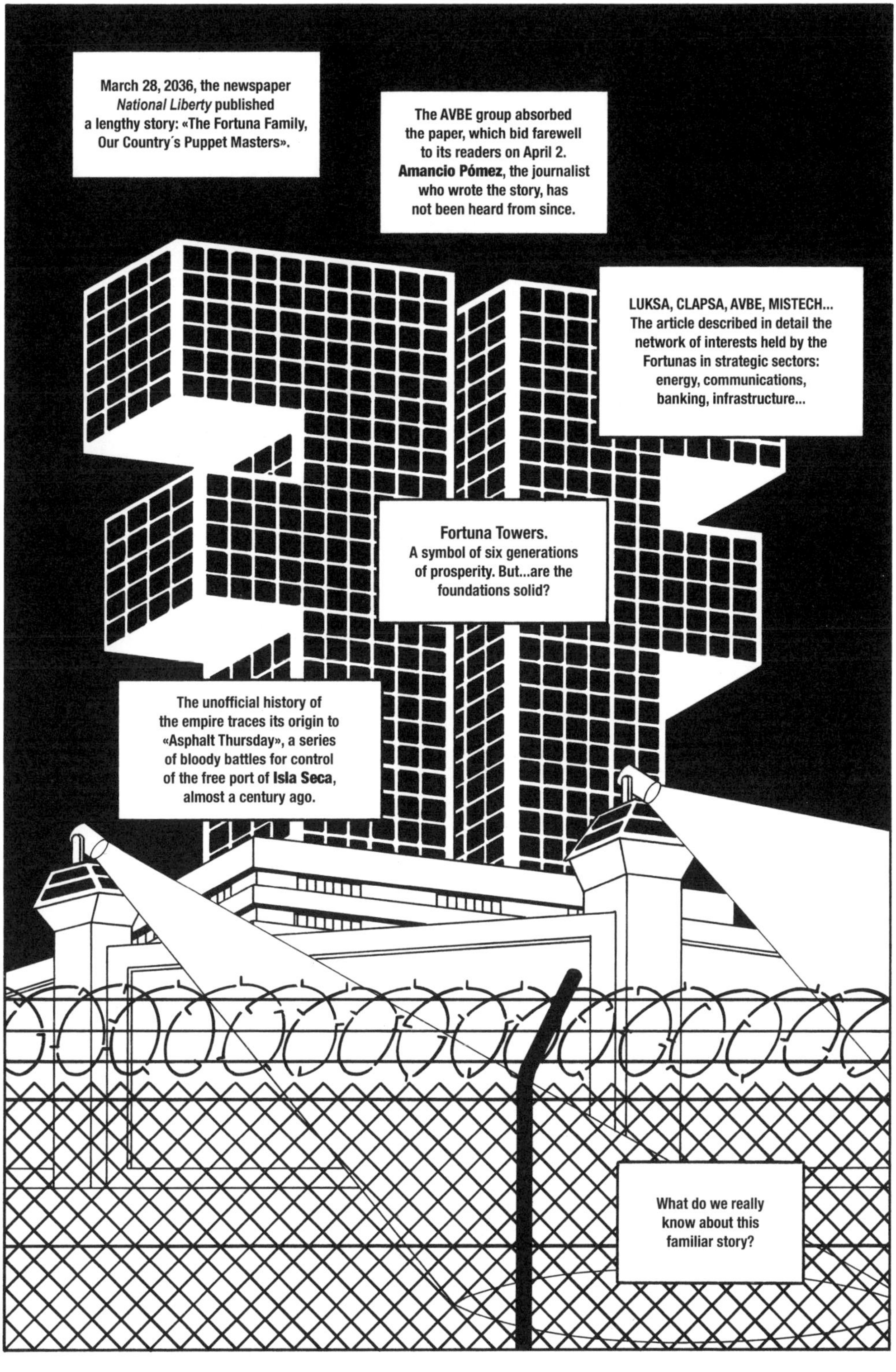
March 28, 2036, the newspaper *National Liberty* published a lengthy story: «The Fortuna Family, Our Country´s Puppet Masters».
The AVBE group absorbed the paper, which bid farewell to its readers on April 2. **Amancio Pómez**, the journalist who wrote the story, has not been heard from since.
LUKSA, CLAPSA, AVBE, MISTECH... The article described in detail the network of interests held by the Fortunas in strategic sectors: energy, communications, banking, infrastructure...
Fortuna Towers. A symbol of six generations of prosperity. But...are the foundations solid?
The unofficial history of the empire traces its origin to «Asphalt Thursday», a series of bloody battles for control of the free port of **Isla Seca**, almost a century ago.
What do we really know about this familiar story?

1 BISABUELOS

(1.GREAT-GRANDPARENTS)

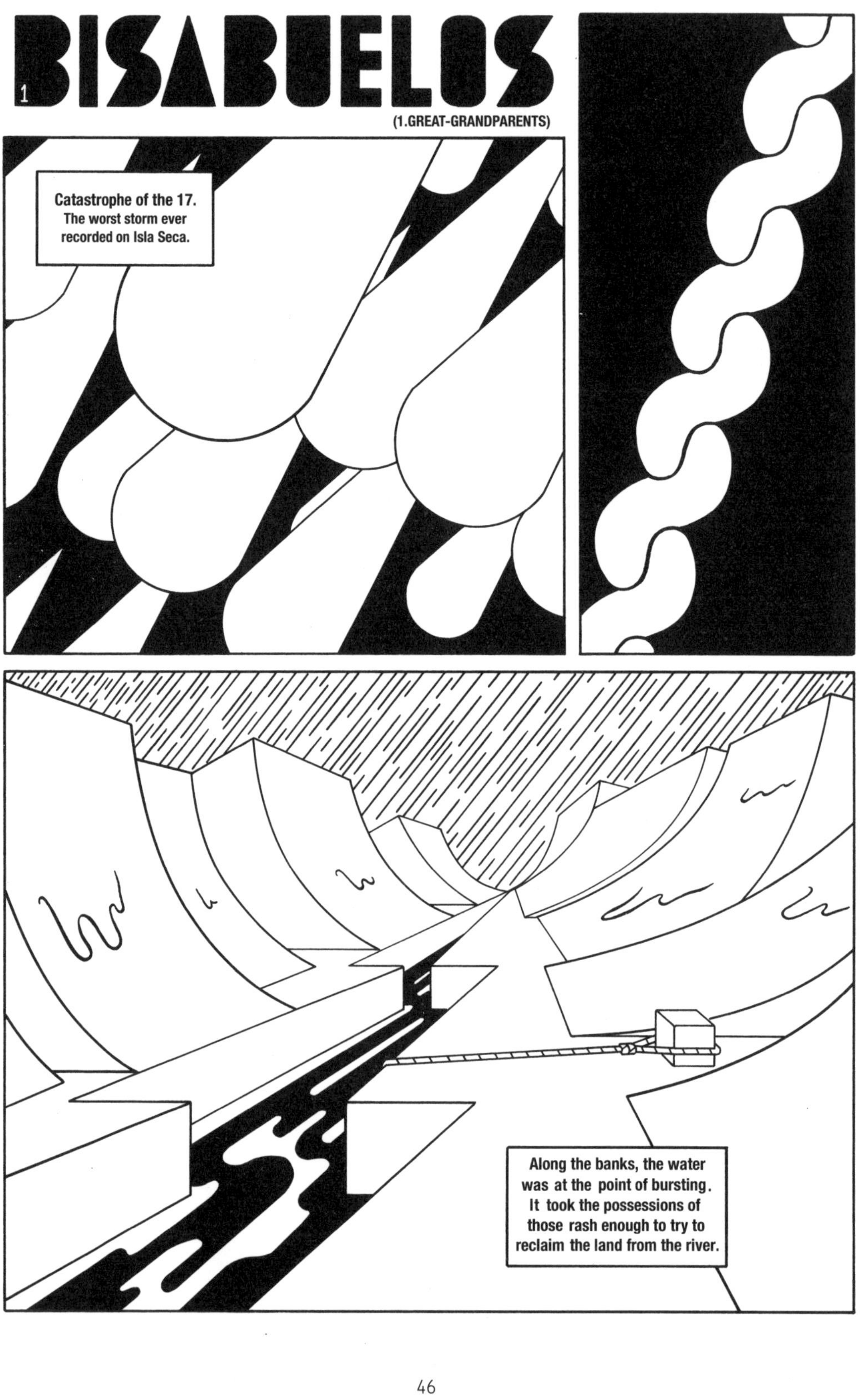
Catastrophe of the 17.
The worst storm ever recorded on Isla Seca.
Along the banks, the water was at the point of bursting. It took the possessions of those rash enough to try to reclaim the land from the river.

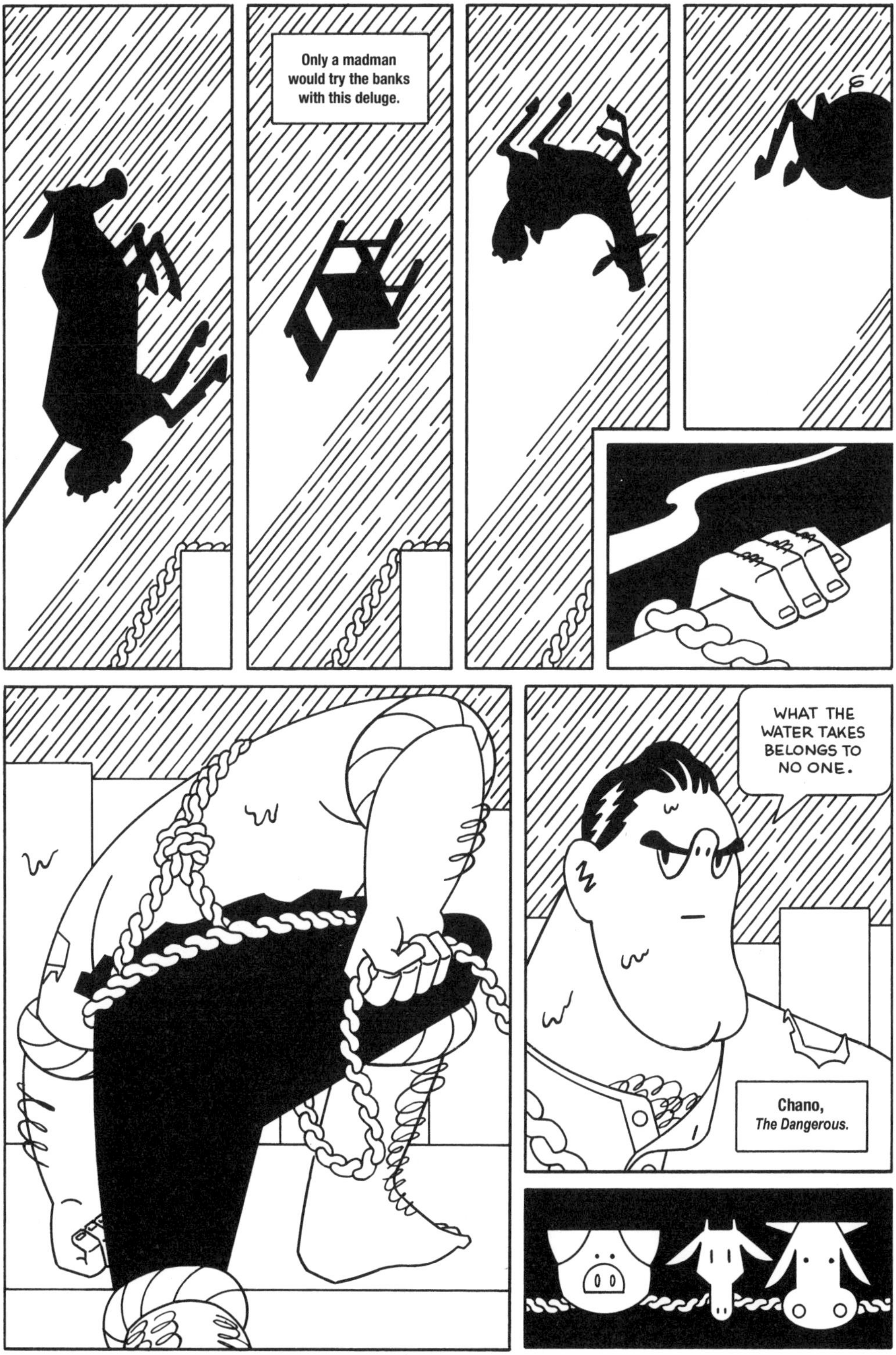
Only a madman would try the banks with this deluge.
WHAT THE WATER TAKES BELONGS TO NO ONE.
Chano, The Dangerous.

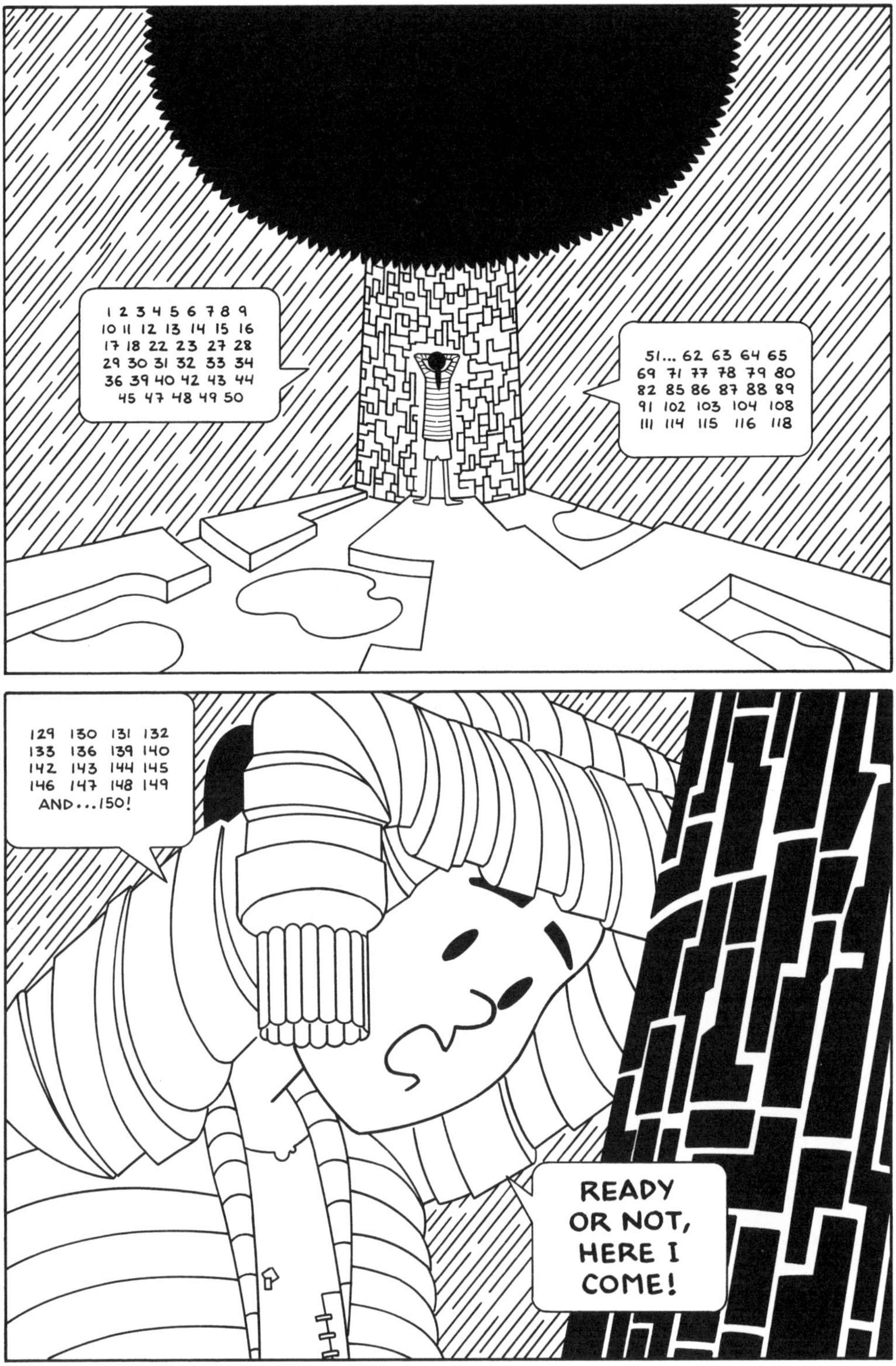
1 2 3 4 5 6 7 8 9 10 11 12 13 14 15 16 17 18 22 23 27 28 29 30 31 32 33 34 36 39 40 42 43 44 45 47 48 49 50
51... 62 63 64 65 69 71 77 78 79 80 82 85 86 87 88 89 91 102 103 104 108 111 114 115 116 118
129 130 131 132 133 136 139 140 142 143 144 145 146 147 148 149 AND...150!
READY OR NOT, HERE I COME!

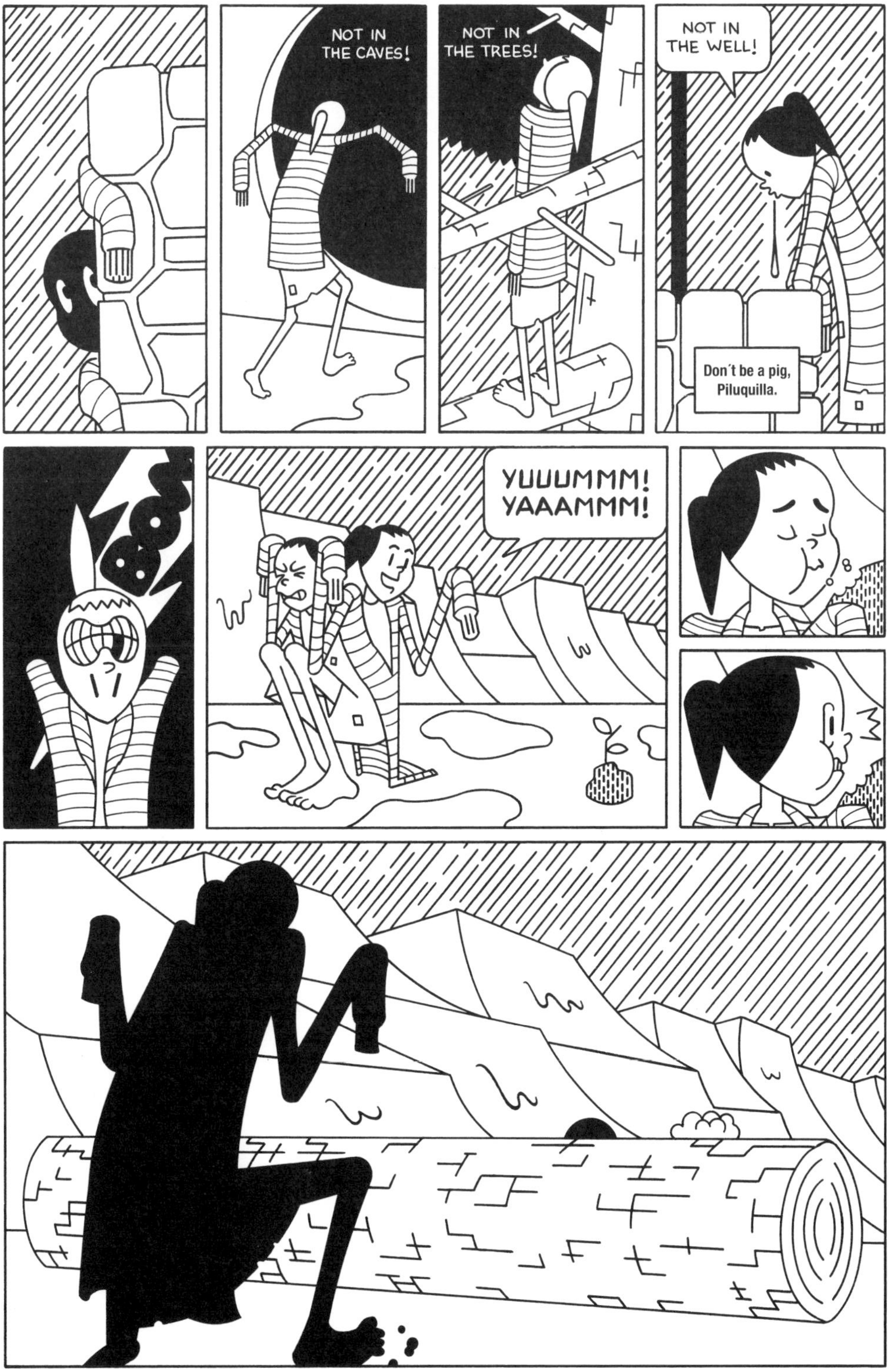
NOT IN THE CAVES!
NOT IN THE TREES!
NOT IN THE WELL!
Don´t be a pig, Piluquilla.
YUUUMMM! YAAAMMM!

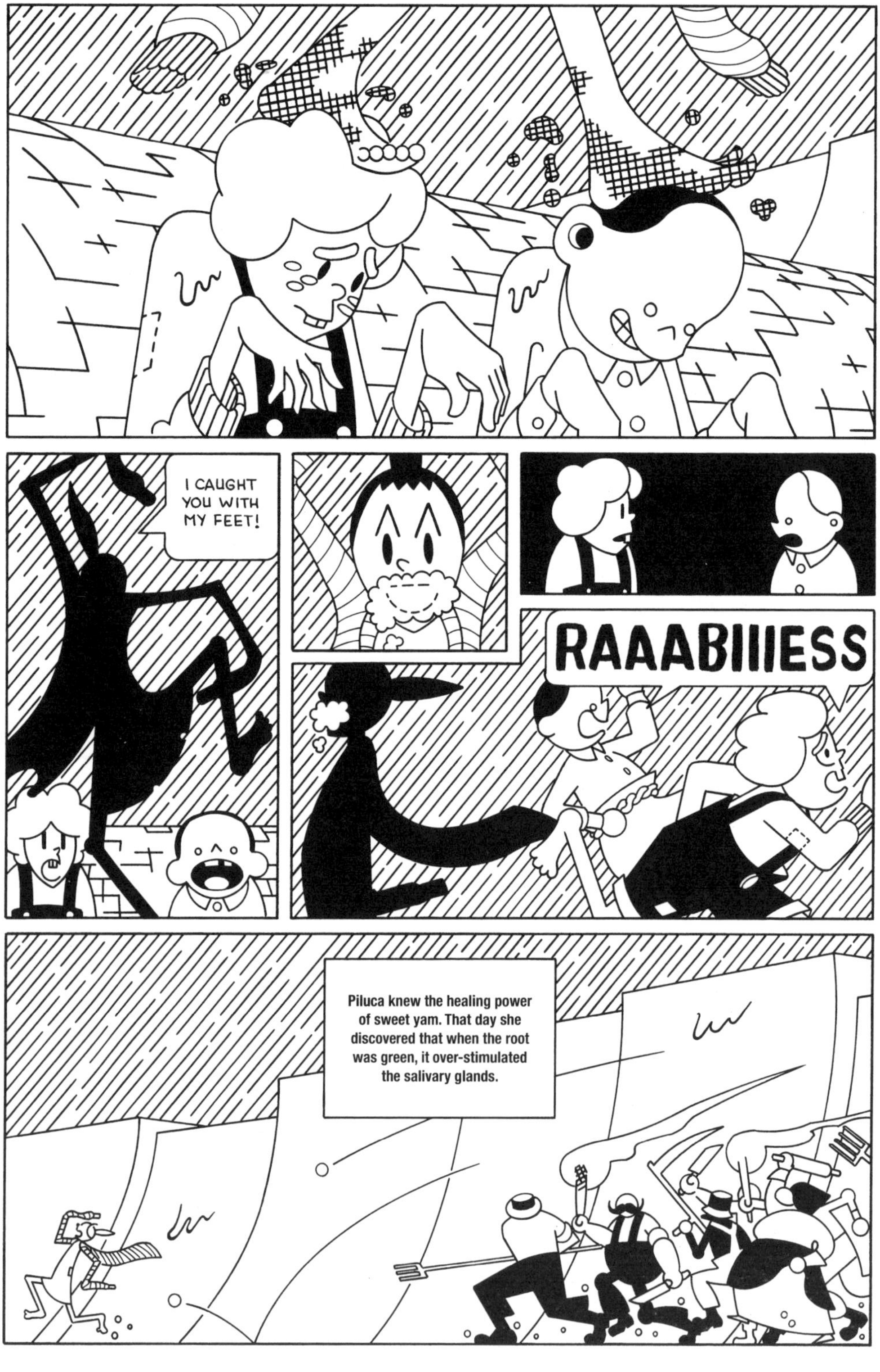
I CAUGHT YOU WITH MY FEET!
RAAABIIIESS
Piluca knew the healing power of sweet yam. That day she discovered that when the root was green, it over-stimulated the salivary glands.

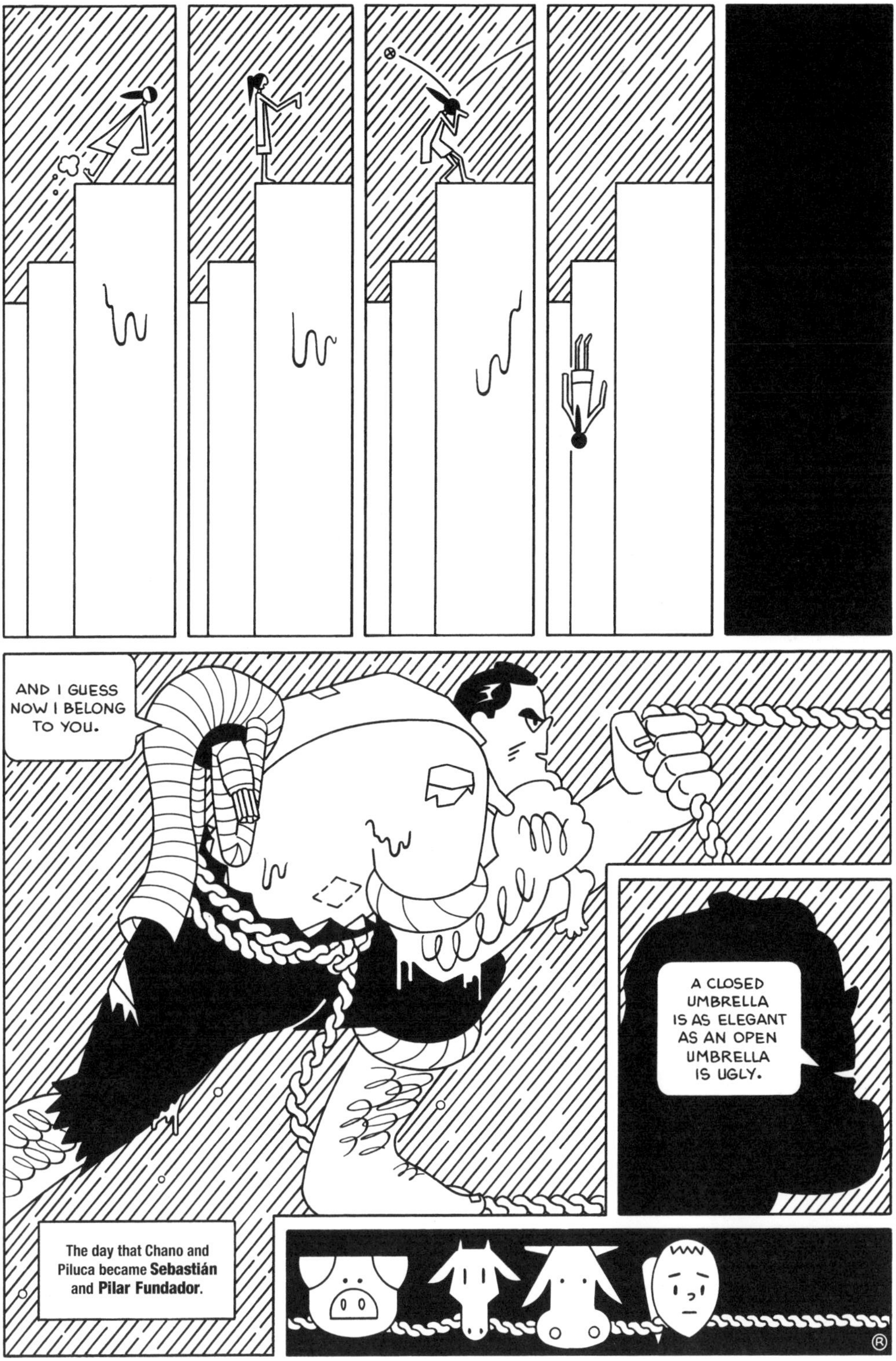
AND I GUESS NOW I BELONG TO YOU.
A CLOSED UMBRELLA IS AS ELEGANT AS AN OPEN UMBRELLA IS UGLY.
The day that Chano and Piluca became **Sebastián** and **Pilar Fundador**.
®

FERMÍN SOLÍS
LITTLE MARTÍN

Fermín Solís was born in Cáceres in 1972. Cofounder of the magazine *Usted está aquí* [*You are Here*], his work has been translated in the United States, France, and Canada. A newspaper illustrator, book author, and writer of children's comics, his best known works of adult-audience graphic literature are *Los días más largos* [*The Longest Days*] (2003), *Buñuel en el laberinto de las tortugas* [*Buñel in the Labyrinth of Turtles*] (2008), and *Mi organismo en obras* [*My Body in the Works*] (2011). For this collection he revived Martín Mostaza, his alter ego /the protagonist of his autobiographical stories.

THE JAR

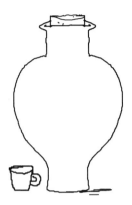

IN MY GRANDMOTHER'S HOUSE IN THE VILLAGE, WATER WAS KEPT IN A JAR.

EVERYONE DRANK FROM IT WITH THE SAME CHIPPED, DENTED CUP...

I'VE NEVER DRUNK SUCH GOOD WATER AS I DID THERE.

THE WATER IS GOOD, ISN'T IT?

YES, I'M GOING TO PLAY!

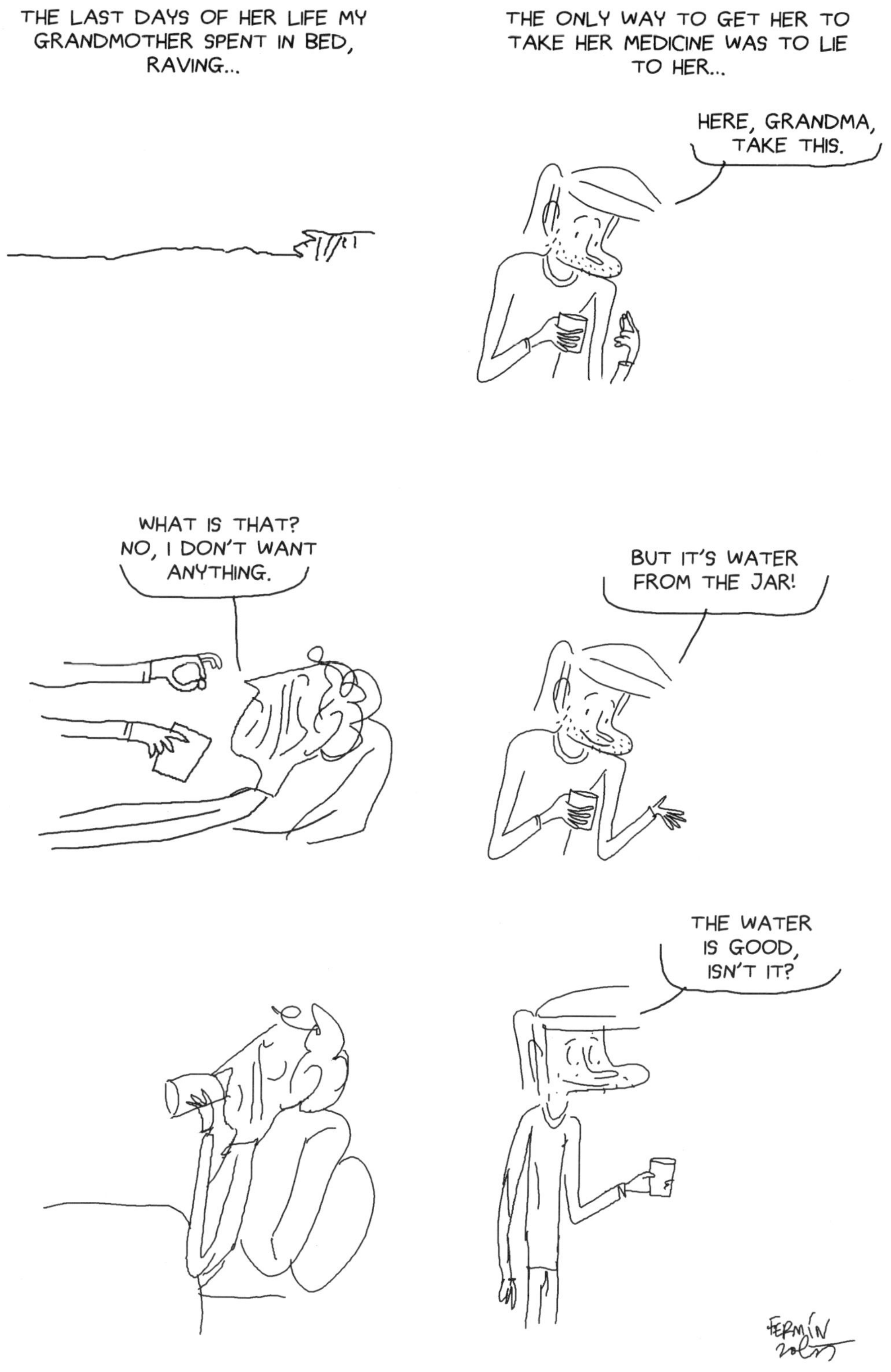
THE LAST DAYS OF HER LIFE MY GRANDMOTHER SPENT IN BED, RAVING...
THE ONLY WAY TO GET HER TO TAKE HER MEDICINE WAS TO LIE TO HER...
HERE, GRANDMA, TAKE THIS.
WHAT IS THAT? NO, I DON'T WANT ANYTHING.
BUT IT'S WATER FROM THE JAR!
THE WATER IS GOOD, ISN'T IT?

La china

PARDON ME; IT'S THE WHISKY!

PRRFFF

A GIRL WE'D NEVER SEEN BEFORE CAME TO SPEND THE SUMMER ONE YEAR.

WE CALLED HER "LA CHINA" BECAUSE SHE HAD SLANTED EYES, BUT SHE WAS REALLY JUST CROSS-EYED.

SHE CLIMBED TREES BETTER THAN ANY OF US.

IDIOTS!

AND NO ONE DARED GET INTO IT WITH HER BECAUSE SHE HAD A KILLER PUNCH.

THEY SAY THAT GIRLS DEVELOP FASTER THAN BOYS, BUT SHE WAS LEADING BY A MILE.

I WIN AGAIN!

YOU CAN SEE HER PANTIES

HER MOUTH COULD HAVE BEEN THE GATEWAY TO HELL ITSELF FOR ALL THE PROFANITY THAT CAME OUT OF IT...

MY FRIEND JUANITO, ALSO KNOWN AS "PUBES," TRIED TO ASK HER OUT A FEW TIMES...

WITHOUT SUCCESS.

LA CHINA WASN'T INTERESTED AT ALL IN BOYS.

AT THE END OF THE SUMMER, LA CHINA LEFT AND WE NEVER SAW HER AGAIN.

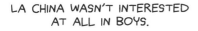

Joselito

MY FRIEND JOSELITO'S MOTHER LOOKED EXACTLY LIKE LOU REED.

JOOOOSE... YOUR PIGS IN A BLANKET ARE GETTING COLD!

I REALIZED THAT YEARS LATER, OF COURSE, BECAUSE AT EIGHT I HAD NO IDEA WHO LOU REED WAS.

WE'LL KEEP PLAYING AFTER LUNCH!

HIS FATHER HAD A SMALL SHOE REPAIR SHOP...

AND HE ALWAYS HAD THE LATEST TECHNOLOGY. HE WAS THE FIRST PERSON IN THE VILLAGE TO HAVE A CAMCORDER.

YOU'RE NOT FILMING ME...

NO.

YOU HAD TO CARRY THE VCR

THEIR HOUSE WAS RIGHT UP AGAINST MY GRANDMOTHER'S, WALL TO WALL, AND THEIR BEDROOM WINDOW FACED OUR PATIO.

C'MERE, BABYDOLL!

OH, MY SWEETHEART...

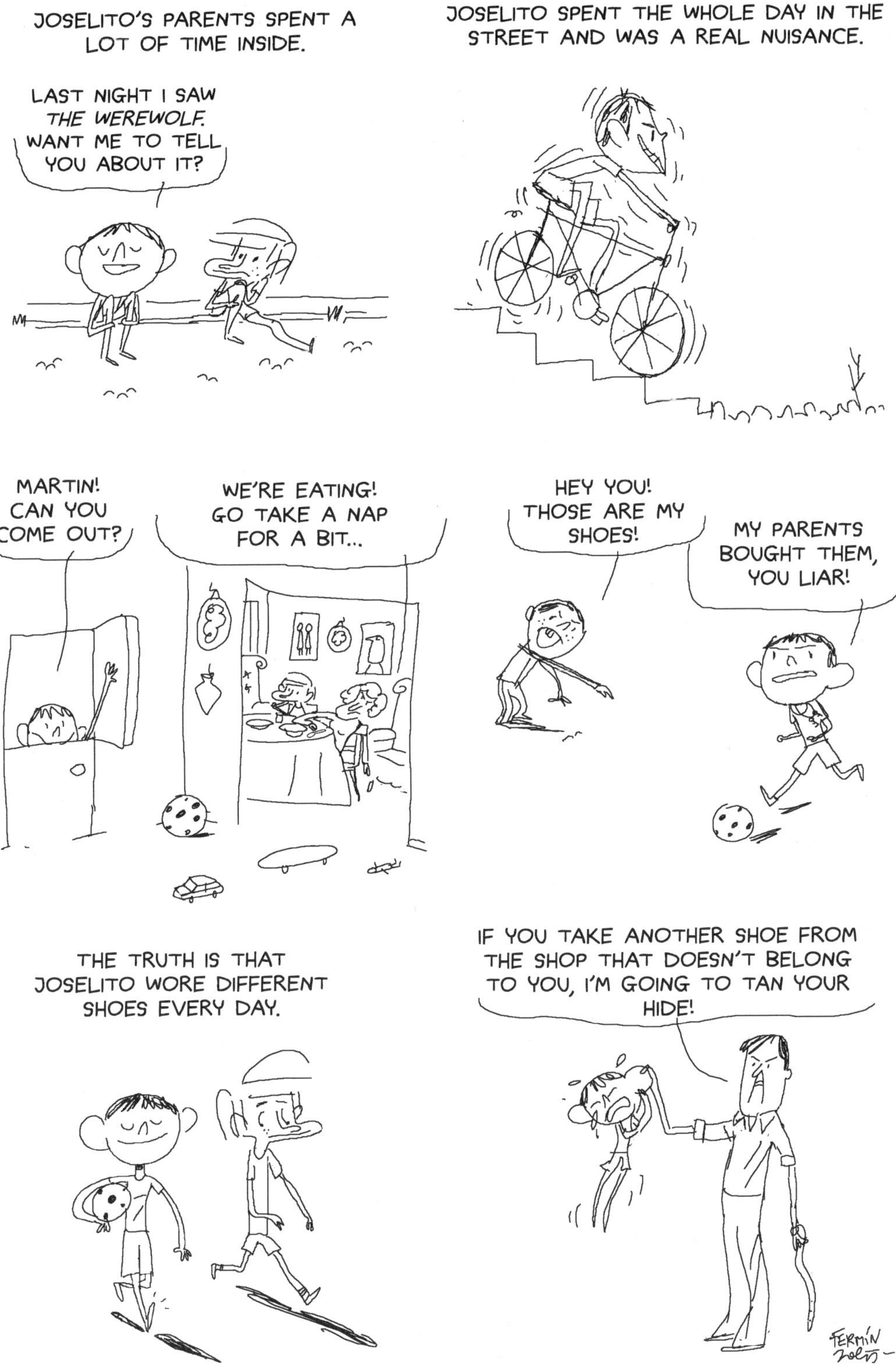
JOSELITO'S PARENTS SPENT A LOT OF TIME INSIDE.
LAST NIGHT I SAW *THE WEREWOLF*. WANT ME TO TELL YOU ABOUT IT?
JOSELITO SPENT THE WHOLE DAY IN THE STREET AND WAS A REAL NUISANCE.
MARTIN! CAN YOU COME OUT?
WE'RE EATING! GO TAKE A NAP FOR A BIT...
HEY YOU! THOSE ARE MY SHOES!
MY PARENTS BOUGHT THEM, YOU LIAR!
THE TRUTH IS THAT JOSELITO WORE DIFFERENT SHOES EVERY DAY.
IF YOU TAKE ANOTHER SHOE FROM THE SHOP THAT DOESN'T BELONG TO YOU, I'M GOING TO TAN YOUR HIDE!

THE END OF THE WORLD

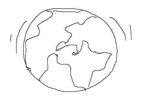

FOR ME THE END OF THE WORLD ARRIVED EVERY FRIDAY WHEN I GOT MY REPORT CARD AND I HAD AN F...

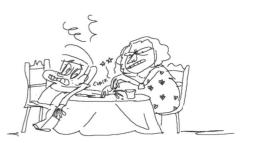

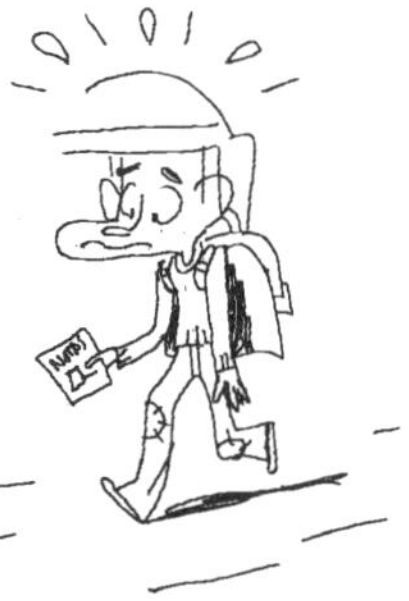

OR WHEN I WAS PLAYING IN THE STREET AND DISLOCATED A FINGER...

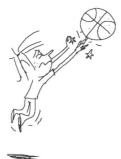

MY MOTHER BROUGHT ME TO A HEALER IN THE NEIGHBORHOOD WHO PUT IT BACK IN PLACE.

CLACK

AND IT WAS THE END OF THE WORLD WHEN MR. JOSE ORELLANA CALLED ON ME TO COME UP TO THE BOARD AND I DIDN'T KNOW HOW TO SOLVE THE EQUATION.

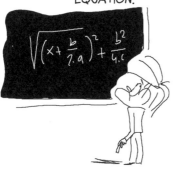

OR WHEN I NEEDED TEN PESETAS MORE TO BUY A "SPIDER-MAN" COMIC BOOK AND I DIDN'T KNOW WHERE TO GET IT.

THE PRICE HAS GONE UP
SPIDER-MAN

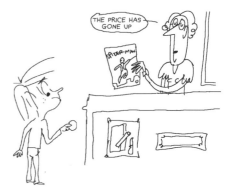

FOR ME THE END OF THE WORLD WAS WHEN MY MOM MADE ME LET AN OLD LADY WITH LIPSTICK KISS MY CHEEK.

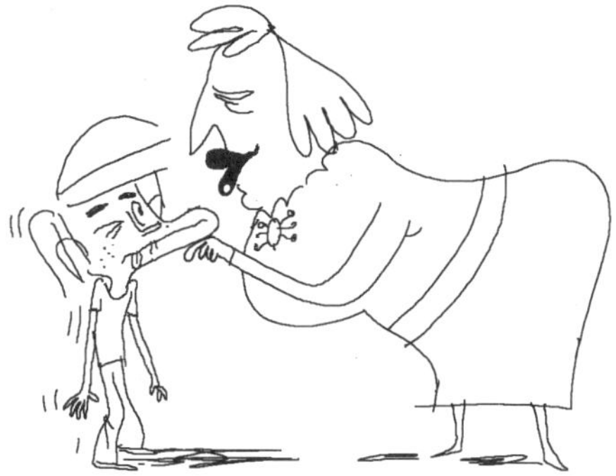

OR WHEN WE LOST THE SIGNAL AT THE END OF A MOVIE.

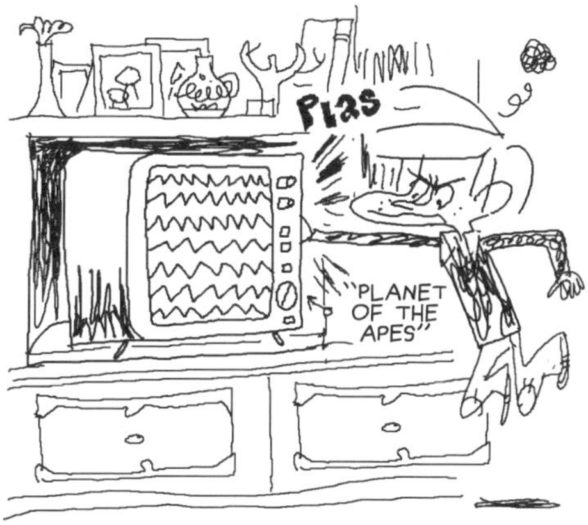
PLAS
"PLANET OF THE APES"

WHEN MY ICE CREAM FELL OFF THE CONE.

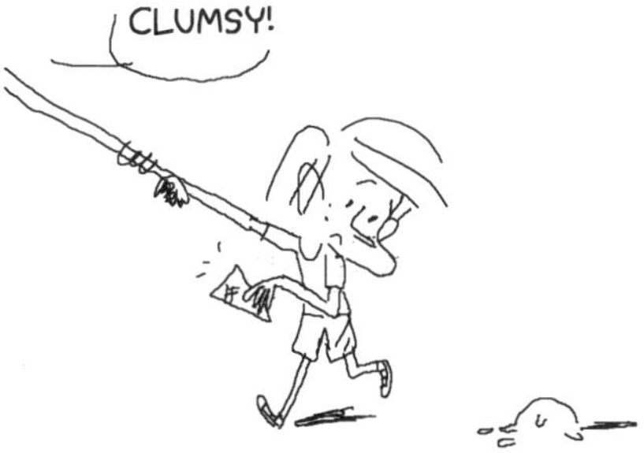
CLUMSY!

FOR ME THE END OF THE WORLD WAS WHEN MY FATHER WROTE A PHONE NUMBER OR THE LOTTERY NUMBERS DOWN ON THE COMIC I'D JUST BOUGHT.

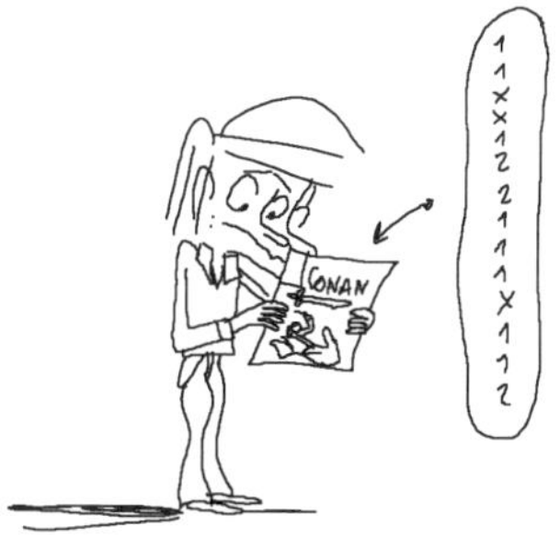
CONAN

OR WHEN I GOT OUT OF THE POOL AND MY TRUNKS FELL OFF.

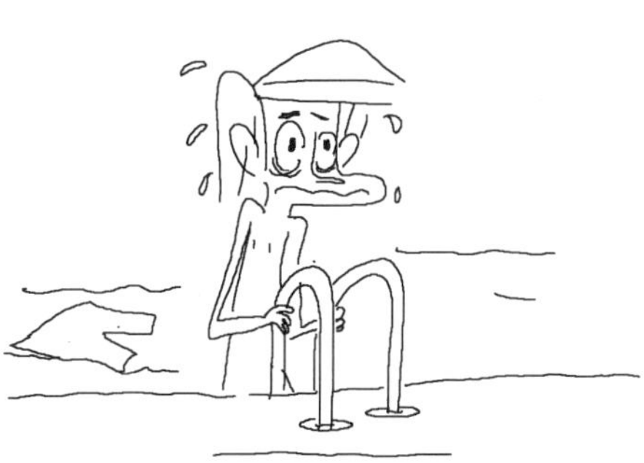

OR WHEN I LOST MY PARENTS IN THE CROWD FOR A MINUTE THAT FELT LIKE AN ETERNITY.

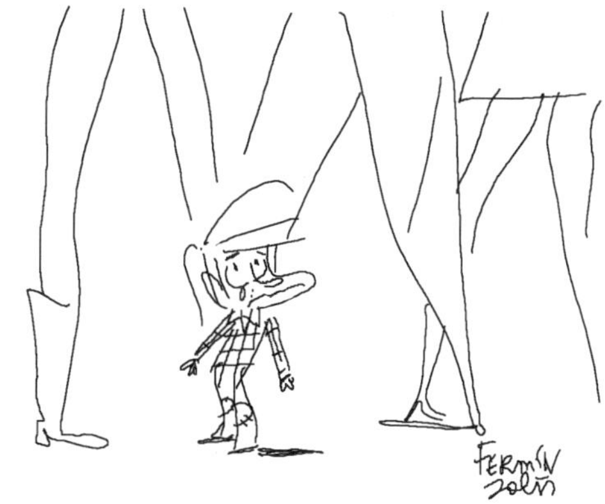

ALFONSO ZAPICO

CHOP CHOP

Alfonso Zapico was born in Blimea (Asturias) in 1981. He has worked as an illustrator for a number of advertising agencies, publishers, and institutions. He has drawn for regional Asturian newspapers *La Nueva España* and *La Cuenca del Nalón*. *La Guerra del professor Bertenev* [*Professor Bertenev's War*] (2006) was published in France. His first graphic novel is *Café Budapest* [*Budapest Café*] (2008), which in a way is echoed in his contribution to this anthology. With the publication of *Dublinés* [*Dubliners*] (2011), a biography of James Joyce, he won the Premio Nacional del Cómic. Since then he's published *El otro mar* [*The Other Ocean*] (2013) and *La balada del norte* [*The Ballad of the North*] (2015).

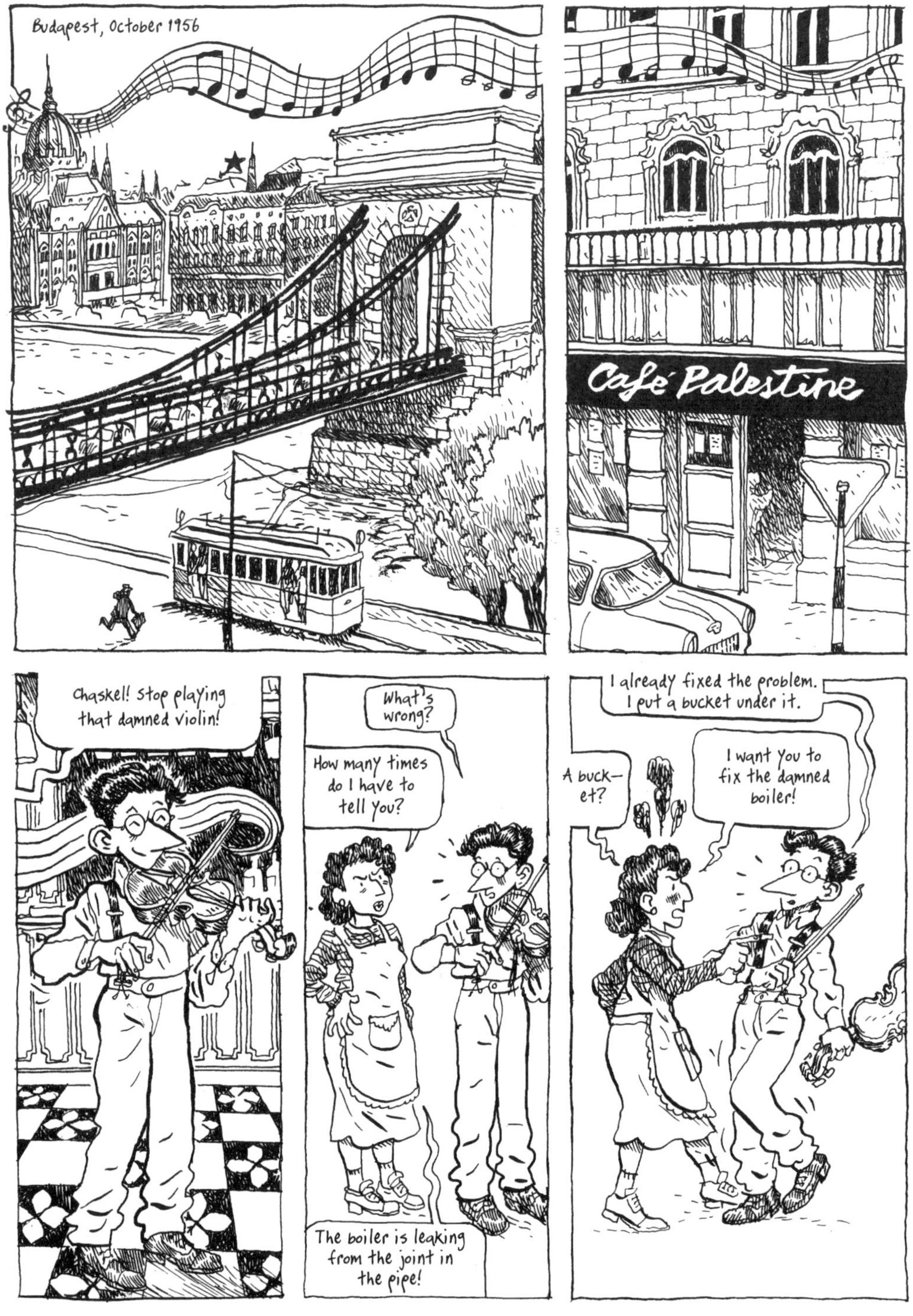
Budapest, October 1956
Café Palestine
Chaskel! Stop playing that damned violin!
How many times do I have to tell you?
What's wrong?
The boiler is leaking from the joint in the pipe!
I already fixed the problem. I put a bucket under it.
A buck-et?
I want you to fix the damned boiler!

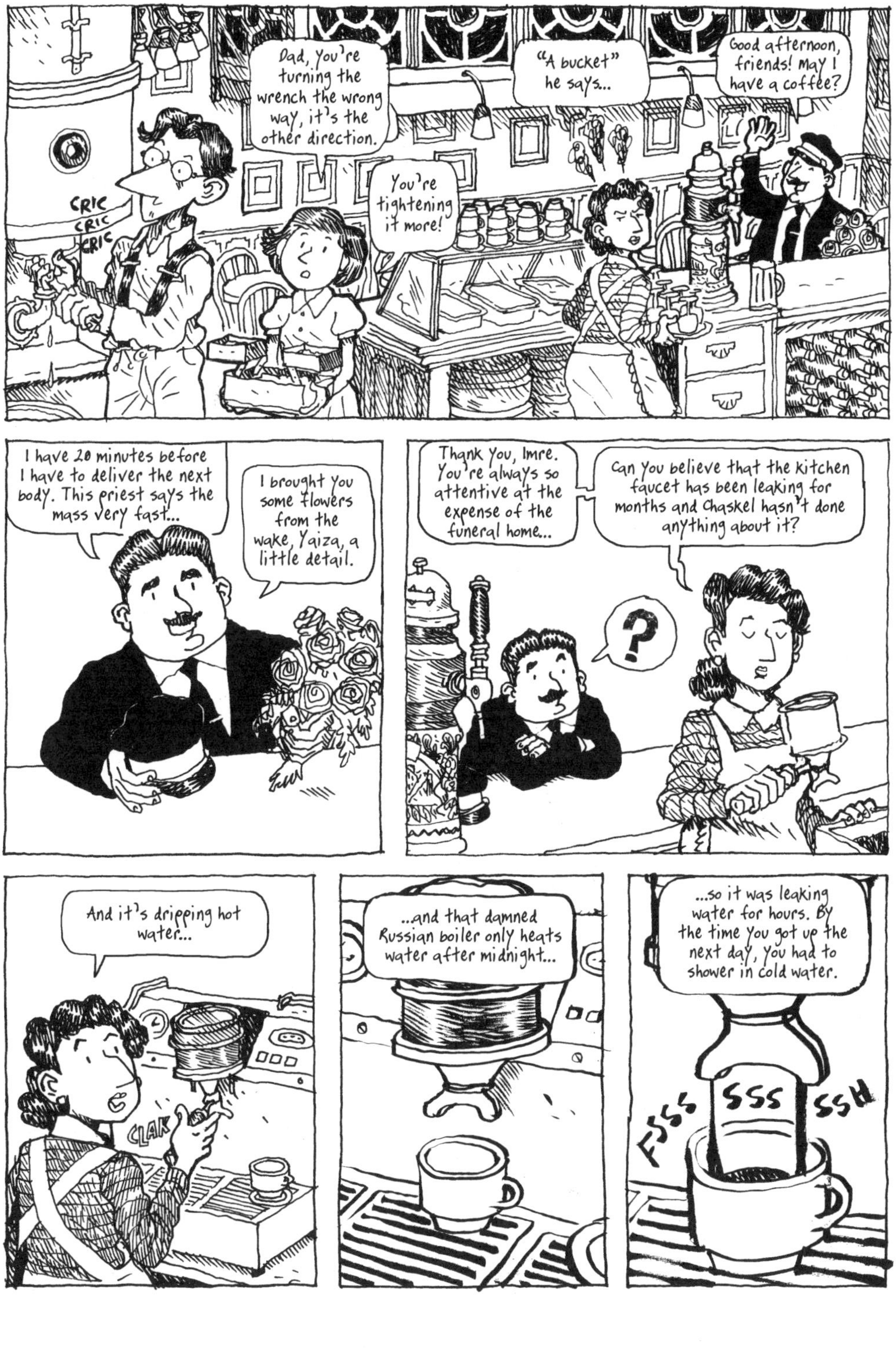
Dad, you're turning the wrench the wrong way, it's the other direction.
CRIC CRIC CRIC
You're tightening it more!
"A bucket" he says...
Good afternoon, friends! May I have a coffee?
I have 20 minutes before I have to deliver the next body. This priest says the mass very fast...
I brought you some flowers from the wake, Yaiza, a little detail.
Thank you, Imre. You're always so attentive at the expense of the funeral home...
Can you believe that the kitchen faucet has been leaking for months and Chaskel hasn't done anything about it?
?
And it's dripping hot water...
CLAK
...and that damned Russian boiler only heats water after midnight...
...so it was leaking water for hours. By the time you got up the next day, you had to shower in cold water.
FSSS SSS SSH

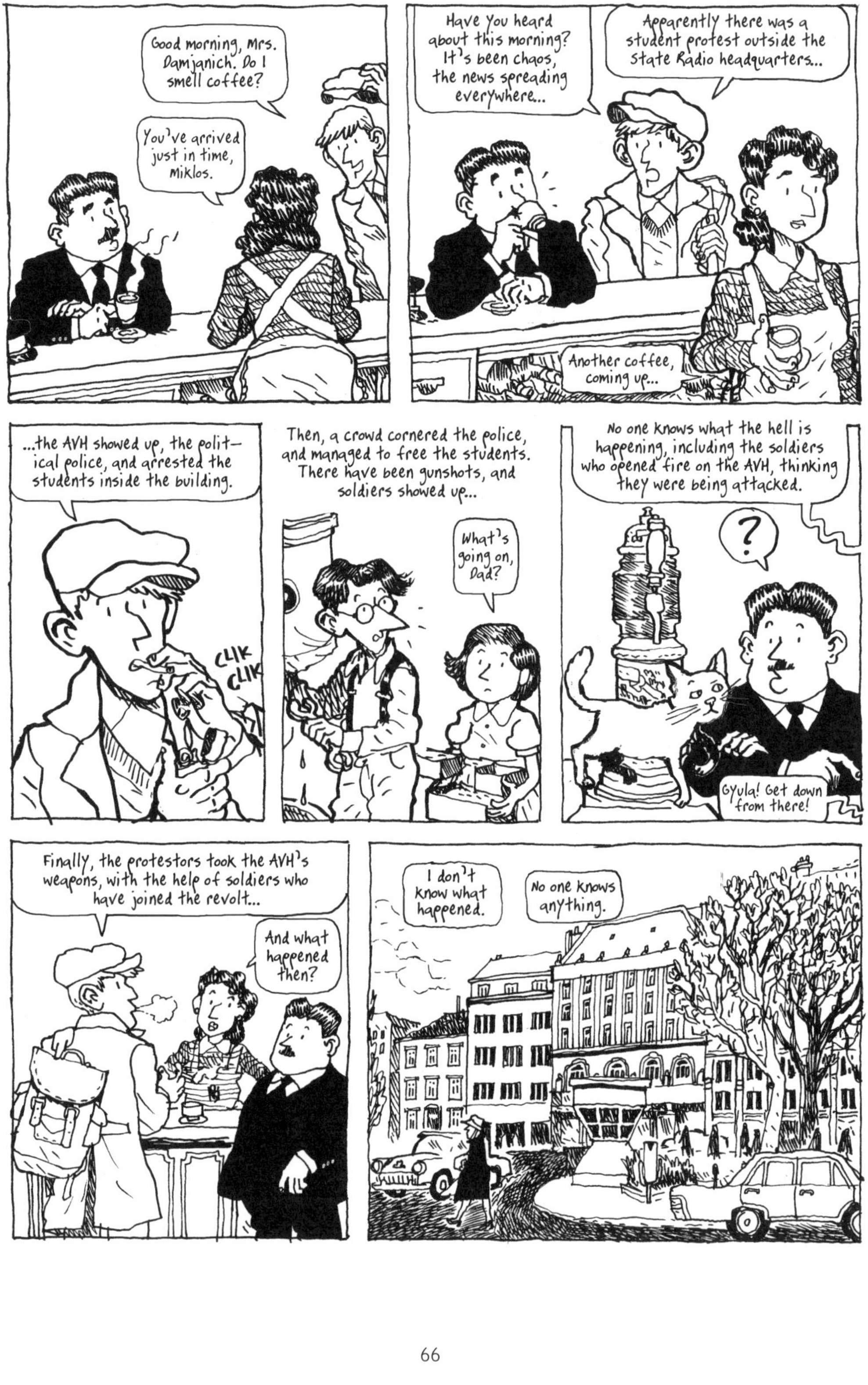
Good morning, Mrs. Damjanich. Do I smell coffee?
You've arrived just in time, Miklos.
Have you heard about this morning? It's been chaos, the news spreading everywhere...
Apparently there was a student protest outside the State Radio headquarters...
Another coffee, coming up...
...the AVH showed up, the political police, and arrested the students inside the building.
CLIK CLIK
Then, a crowd cornered the police, and managed to free the students. There have been gunshots, and soldiers showed up...
What's going on, Dad?
No one knows what the hell is happening, including the soldiers who opened fire on the AVH, thinking they were being attacked.
?
Gyula! Get down from there!
Finally, the protestors took the AVH's weapons, with the help of soldiers who have joined the revolt...
And what happened then?
I don't know what happened.
No one knows anything.

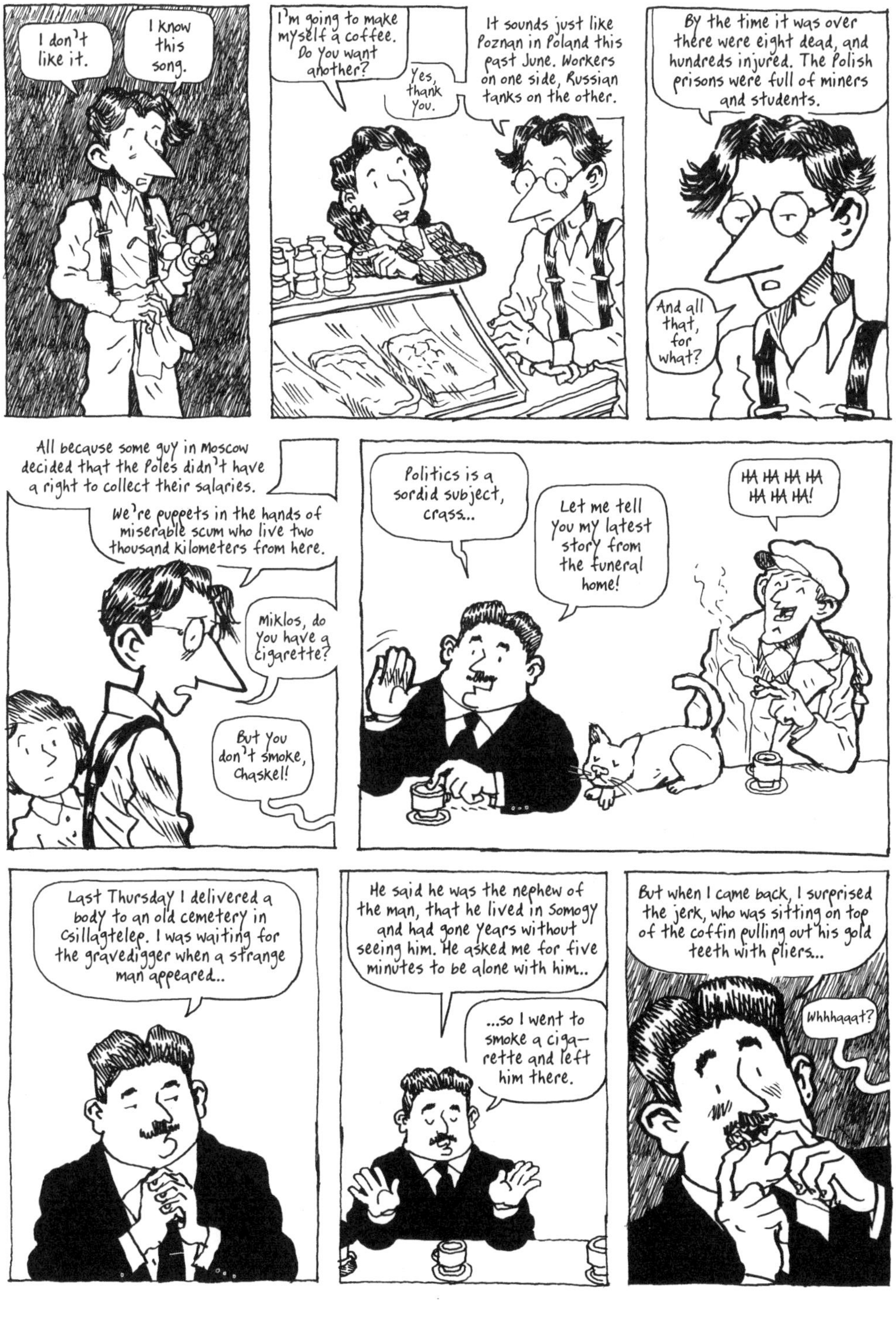
I don't like it.
I know this song.
I'm going to make myself a coffee. Do you want another?
Yes, thank you.
It sounds just like Poznan in Poland this past June. Workers on one side, Russian tanks on the other.
By the time it was over there were eight dead, and hundreds injured. The Polish prisons were full of miners and students.
And all that, for what?
All because some guy in Moscow decided that the Poles didn't have a right to collect their salaries.
We're puppets in the hands of miserable scum who live two thousand kilometers from here.
Miklos, do you have a cigarette?
But you don't smoke, Chaskel!
Politics is a sordid subject, crass...
Let me tell you my latest story from the funeral home!
HA HA HA HA HA HA HA!
Last Thursday I delivered a body to an old cemetery in Csillagtelep. I was waiting for the gravedigger when a strange man appeared..
He said he was the nephew of the man, that he lived in Somogy and had gone years without seeing him. He asked me for five minutes to be alone with him..
...so I went to smoke a cigarette and left him there.
But when I came back, I surprised the jerk, who was sitting on top of the coffin pulling out his gold teeth with pliers...
Whhhaaat?

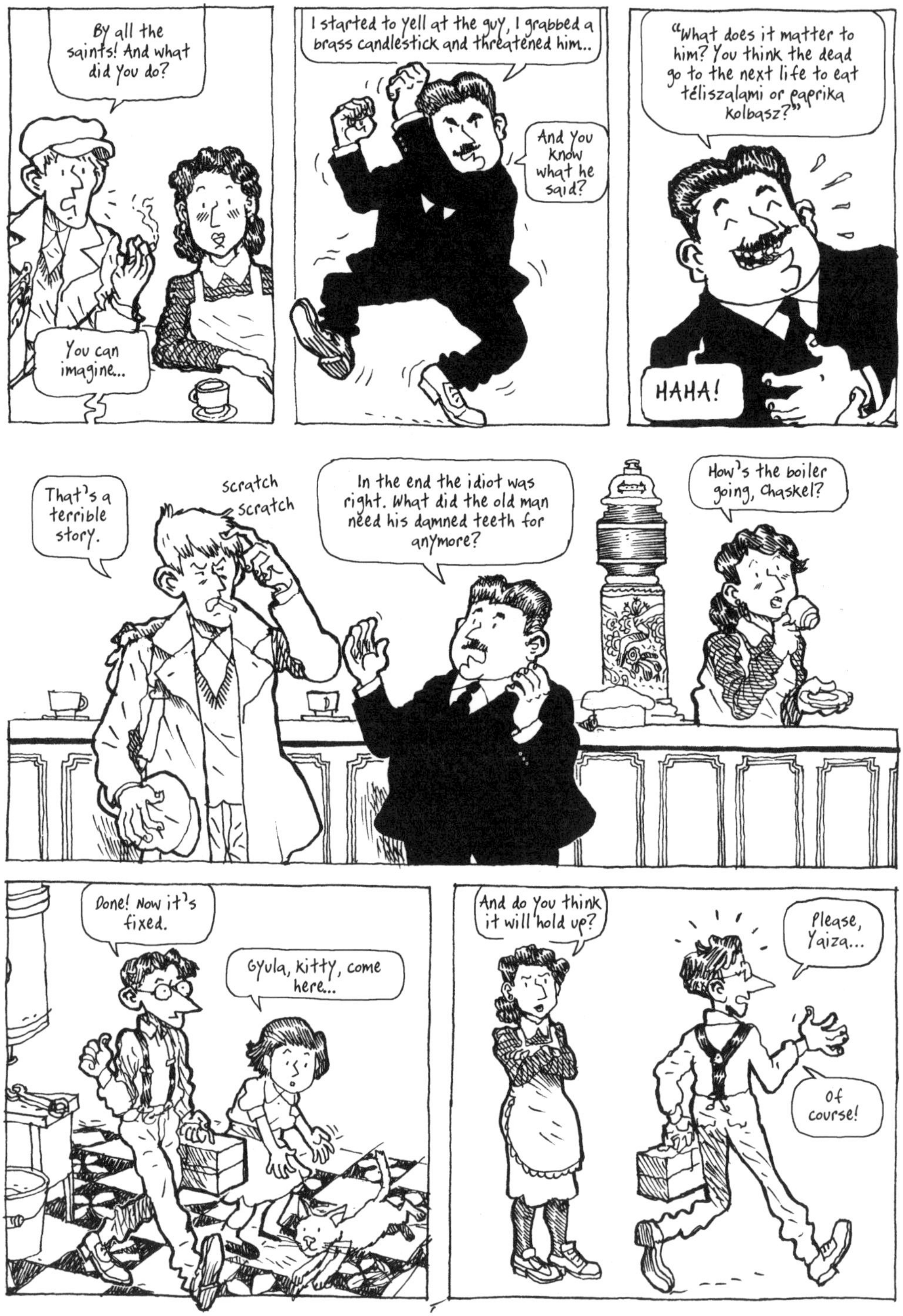
By all the saints! And what did you do?
You can imagine...
I started to yell at the guy, I grabbed a brass candlestick and threatened him..
And you know what he said?
"What does it matter to him? You think the dead go to the next life to eat téliszalami or paprika kolbász?"
HAHA!
That's a terrible story.
scratch scratch
In the end the idiot was right. What did the old man need his damned teeth for anymore?
How's the boiler going, Chaskel?
Done! Now it's fixed.
Gyula, kitty, come here...
And do you think it will hold up?
Please, Yaiza...
Of course!

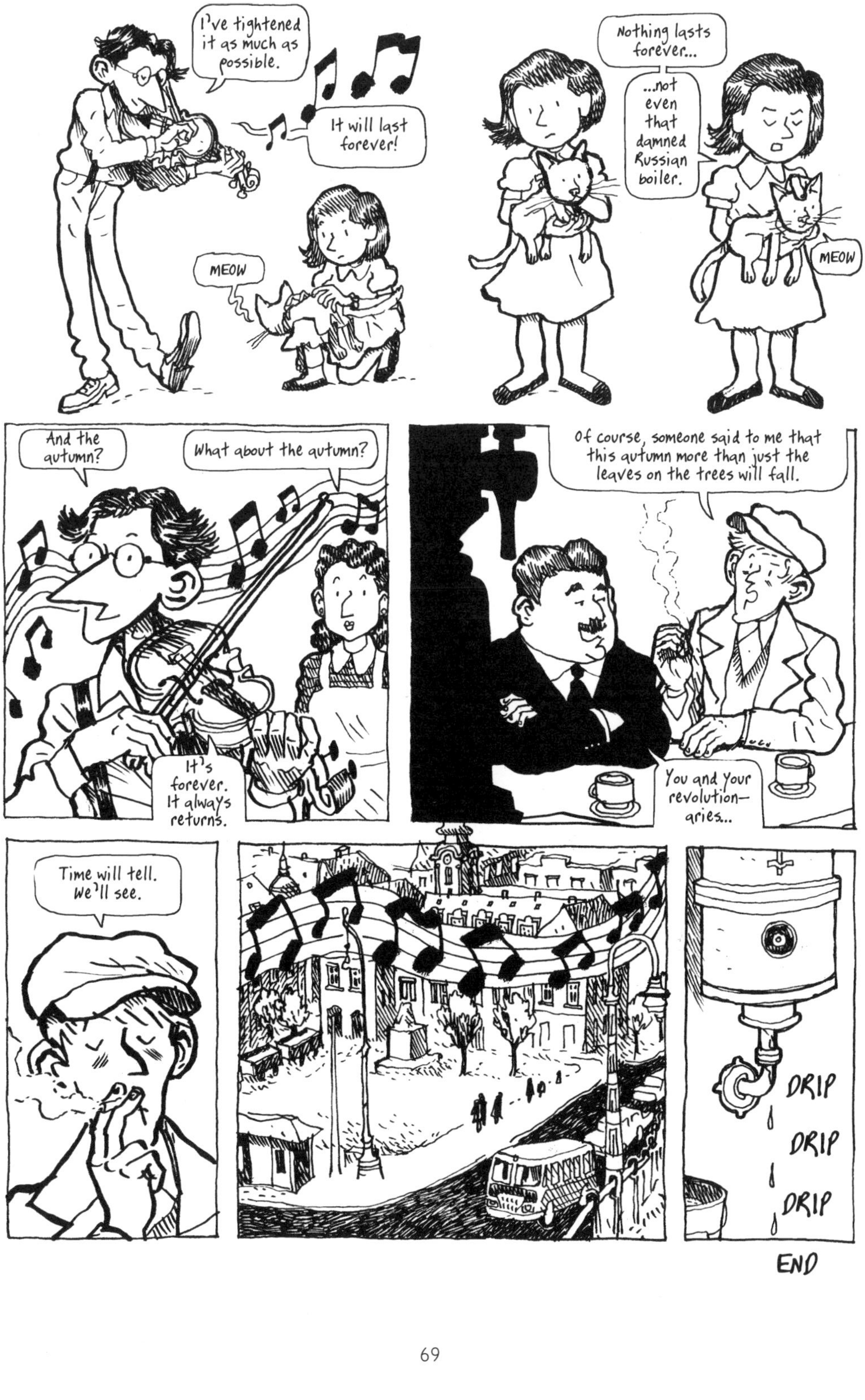
I've tightened it as much as possible.
It will last forever!
MEOW
Nothing lasts forever...
...not even that damned Russian boiler.
MEOW
And the autumn?
What about the autumn?
It's forever. It always returns.
Of course, someone said to me that this autumn more than just the leaves on the trees will fall.
You and your revolution-aries...
Time will tell. We'll see.
DRIP
DRIP
DRIP
END

JUACO VIZUETE
CURIOSITIES, SCIENCE, AND FICTION

Juaco Vizuete was born in Alicante in 1972. An illustrator and animator, he is best known as a cartoonist; he broke out with his series *El resentido* [*The Resentful*] (1996–1998). Afterward, he collaborated with Hernán Migoya on *Julito, el cantante cojito* [*Julito the the Singer Señorito*] (2007), some of which was published in *Mome* (Fantagraphics) in the United States. In recent years, he's published two graphic novels that he both wrote and drew: *El experimento* [*The Experiment*] (2009) and *Lo primero que me viene a la mente* [*The First Thing That Comes To Mind*] (2014). *Yuna*, which has a script by Santiago García, was published in 2015.

CURIOSITIES, SCIENCE, AND FICTION

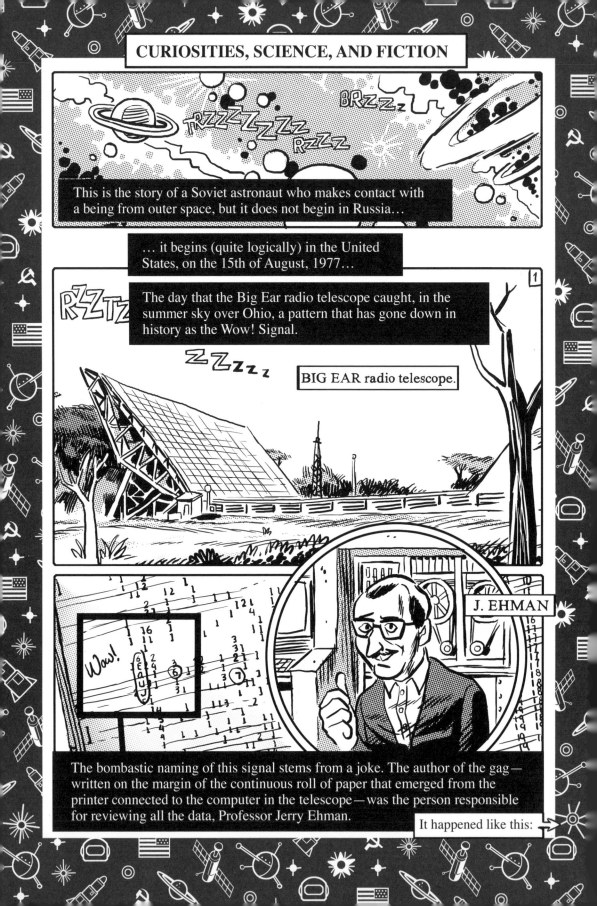

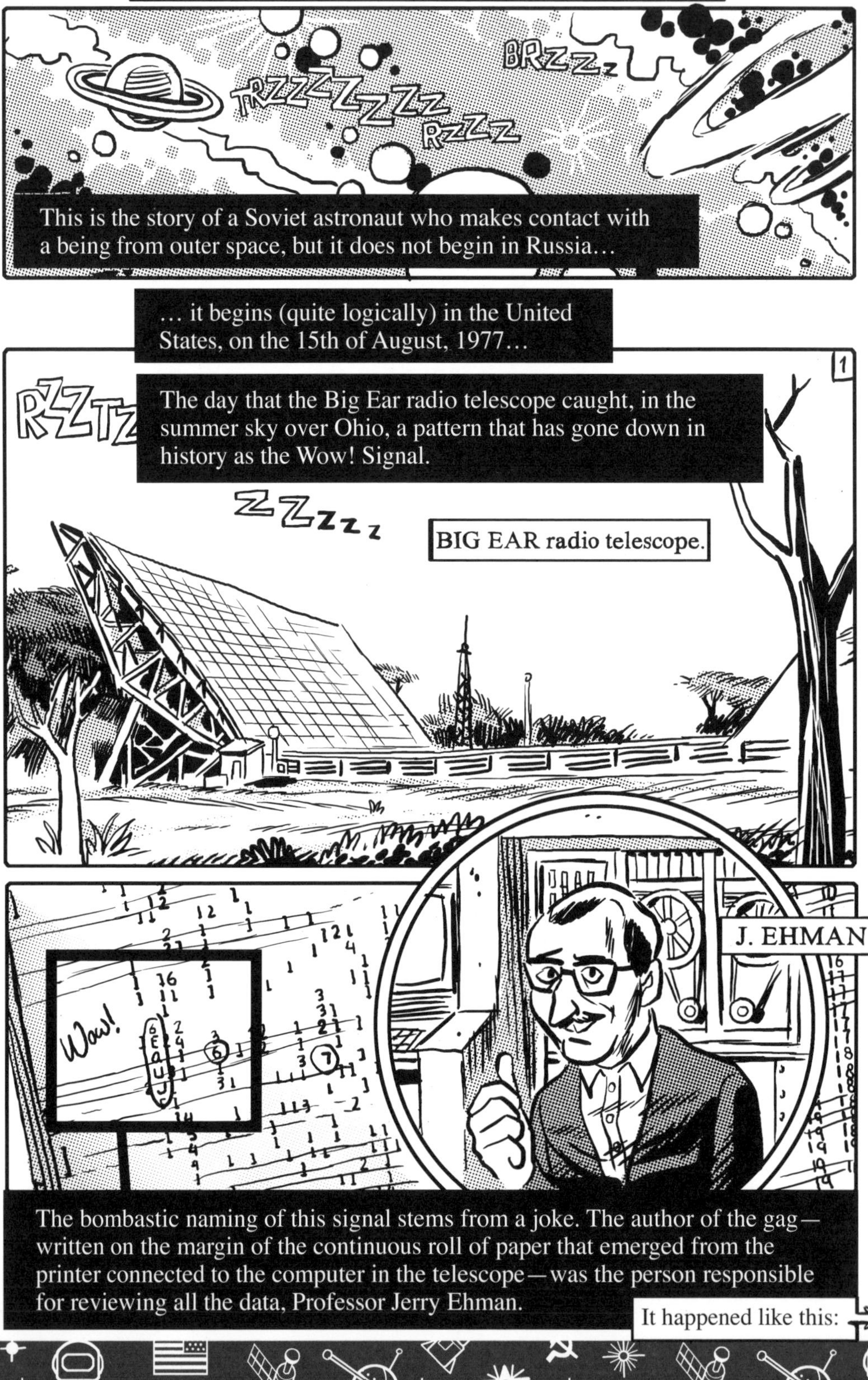
BRZZZz
This is the story of a Soviet astronaut who makes contact with a being from outer space, but it does not begin in Russia…
… it begins (quite logically) in the United States, on the 15th of August, 1977…
1
The day that the Big Ear radio telescope caught, in the summer sky over Ohio, a pattern that has gone down in history as the Wow! Signal.
BIG EAR radio telescope.
Wow!
J. EHMAN
The bombastic naming of this signal stems from a joke. The author of the gag—written on the margin of the continuous roll of paper that emerged from the printer connected to the computer in the telescope—was the person responsible for reviewing all the data, Professor Jerry Ehman.
It happened like this:

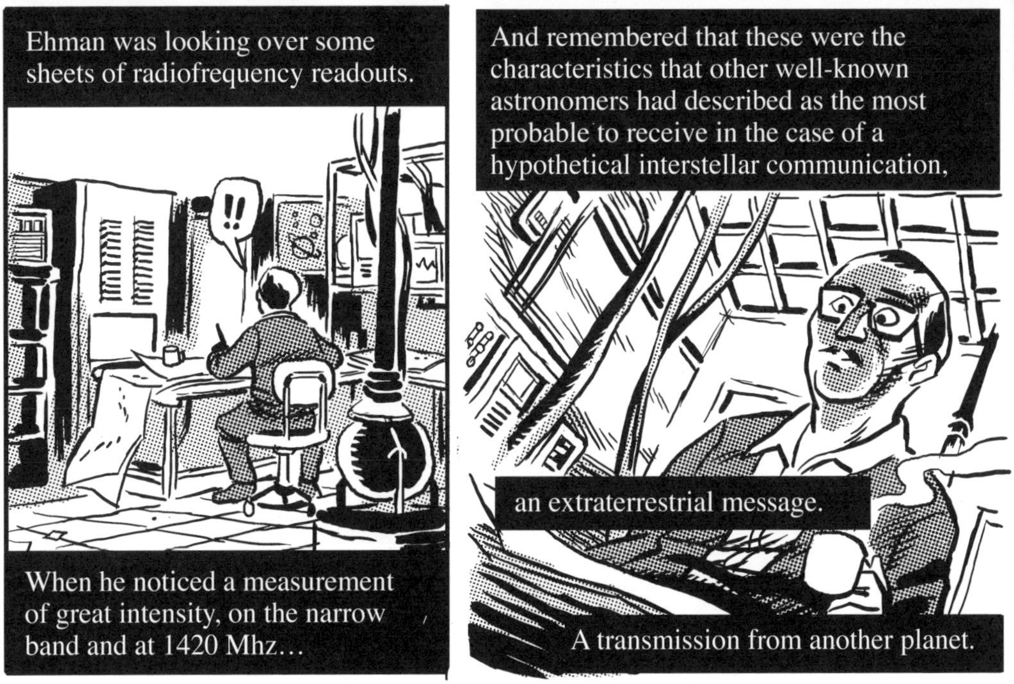
Ehman was looking over some sheets of radiofrequency readouts.
!!
When he noticed a measurement of great intensity, on the narrow band and at 1420 Mhz…
And remembered that these were the characteristics that other well-known astronomers had described as the most probable to receive in the case of a hypothetical interstellar communication,
an extraterrestrial message.
A transmission from another planet.

A number of highly technical reasons, including that nothing in the natural phenomena of the universe emits signals at the narrow bandwidth like this, reinforced the theory.

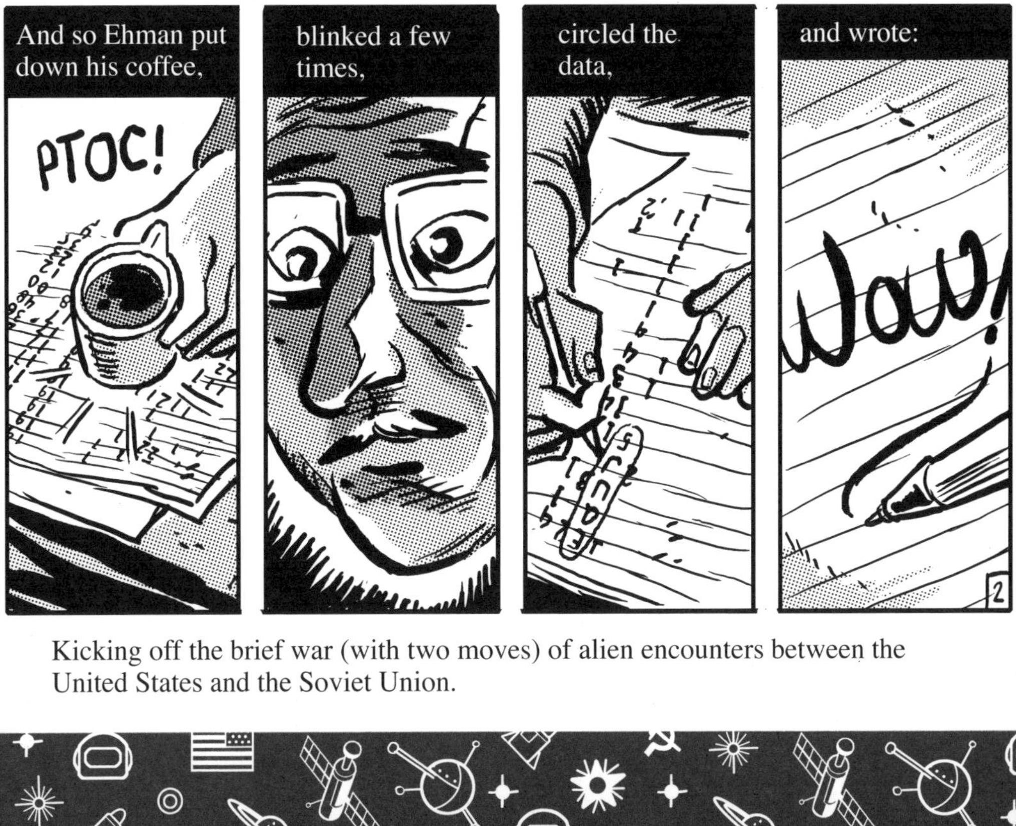
And so Ehman put down his coffee,
PTOC!
blinked a few times,
circled the data,
and wrote:
Wow!

Kicking off the brief war (with two moves) of alien encounters between the United States and the Soviet Union.

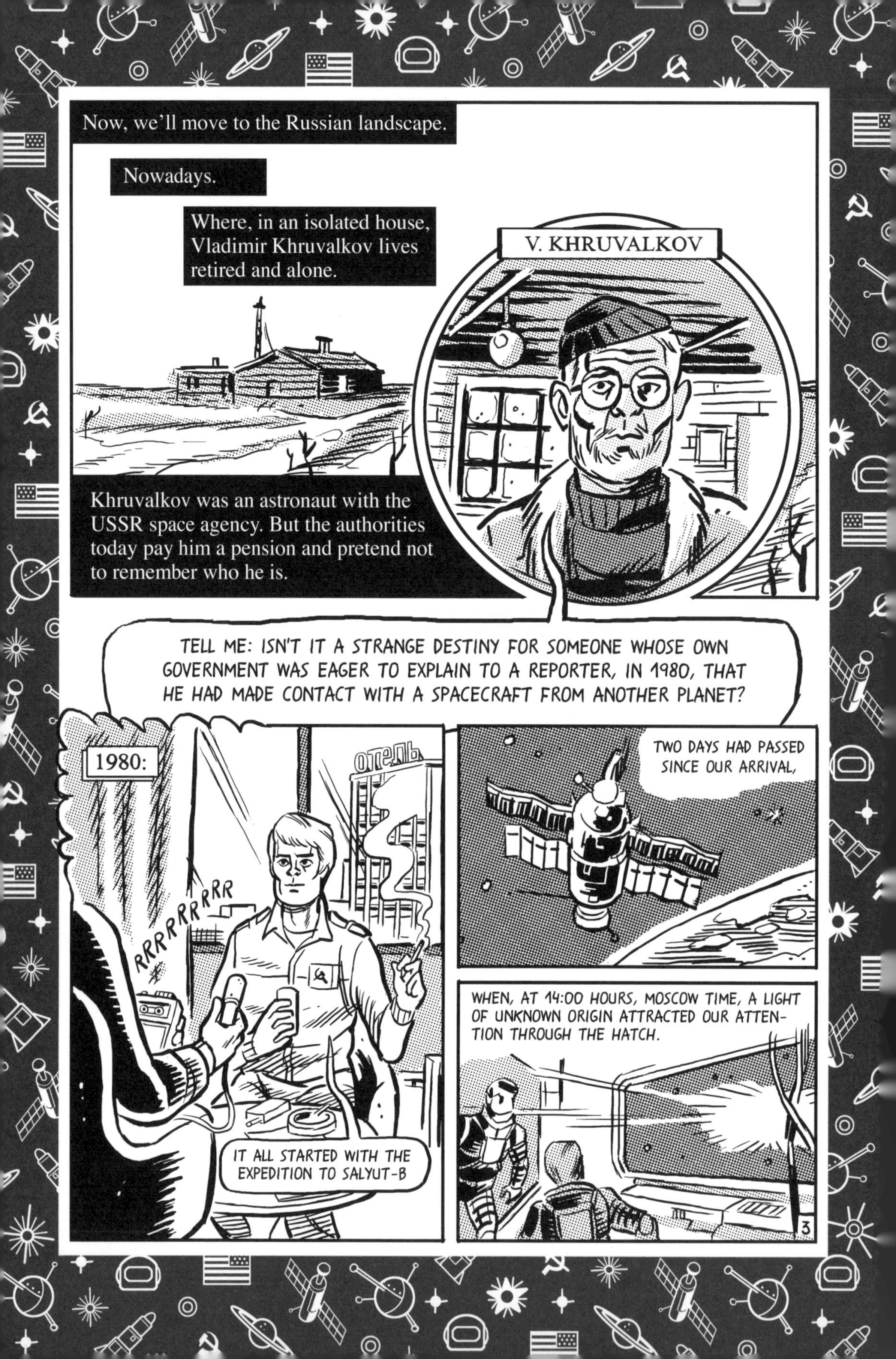
Now, we'll move to the Russian landscape.
Nowadays.
Where, in an isolated house, Vladimir Khruvalkov lives retired and alone.
V. KHRUVALKOV
Khruvalkov was an astronaut with the USSR space agency. But the authorities today pay him a pension and pretend not to remember who he is.
TELL ME: ISN'T IT A STRANGE DESTINY FOR SOMEONE WHOSE OWN GOVERNMENT WAS EAGER TO EXPLAIN TO A REPORTER, IN 1980, THAT HE HAD MADE CONTACT WITH A SPACECRAFT FROM ANOTHER PLANET?
1980:
ОТЕЛЬ
RRRRRRRRRR
IT ALL STARTED WITH THE EXPEDITION TO SALYUT-B
TWO DAYS HAD PASSED SINCE OUR ARRIVAL,
WHEN, AT 14:00 HOURS, MOSCOW TIME, A LIGHT OF UNKNOWN ORIGIN ATTRACTED OUR ATTENTION THROUGH THE HATCH.
3

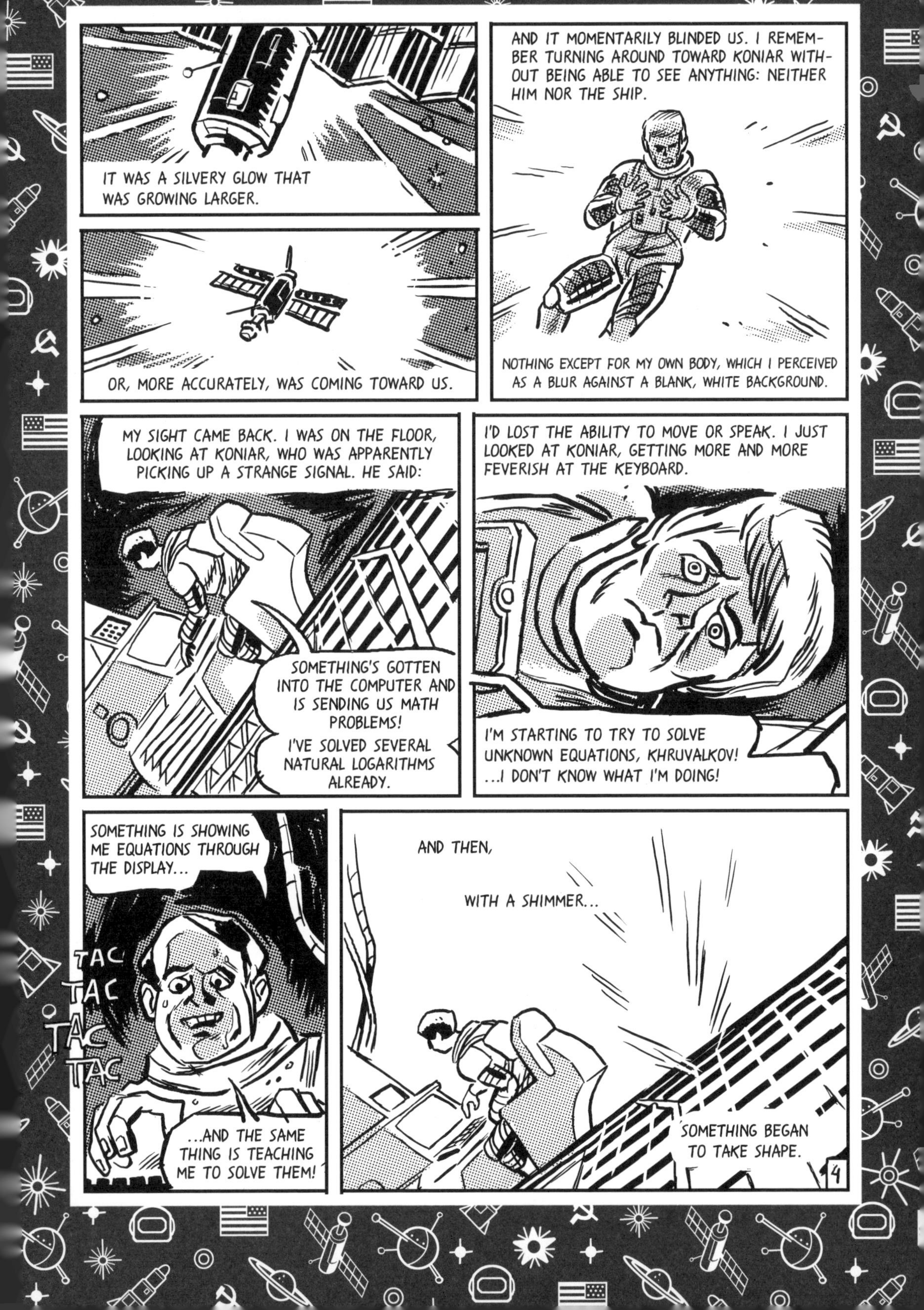
IT WAS A SILVERY GLOW THAT WAS GROWING LARGER.
OR, MORE ACCURATELY, WAS COMING TOWARD US.
AND IT MOMENTARILY BLINDED US. I REMEMBER TURNING AROUND TOWARD KONIAR WITHOUT BEING ABLE TO SEE ANYTHING: NEITHER HIM NOR THE SHIP.
NOTHING EXCEPT FOR MY OWN BODY, WHICH I PERCEIVED AS A BLUR AGAINST A BLANK, WHITE BACKGROUND.
MY SIGHT CAME BACK. I WAS ON THE FLOOR, LOOKING AT KONIAR, WHO WAS APPARENTLY PICKING UP A STRANGE SIGNAL. HE SAID:
SOMETHING'S GOTTEN INTO THE COMPUTER AND IS SENDING US MATH PROBLEMS!
I'VE SOLVED SEVERAL NATURAL LOGARITHMS ALREADY.
I'D LOST THE ABILITY TO MOVE OR SPEAK. I JUST LOOKED AT KONIAR, GETTING MORE AND MORE FEVERISH AT THE KEYBOARD.
I'M STARTING TO TRY TO SOLVE UNKNOWN EQUATIONS, KHRUVALKOV! ...I DON'T KNOW WHAT I'M DOING!
SOMETHING IS SHOWING ME EQUATIONS THROUGH THE DISPLAY...
TAC TAC TAC TAC
...AND THE SAME THING IS TEACHING ME TO SOLVE THEM!
AND THEN,
WITH A SHIMMER...
SOMETHING BEGAN TO TAKE SHAPE.
4

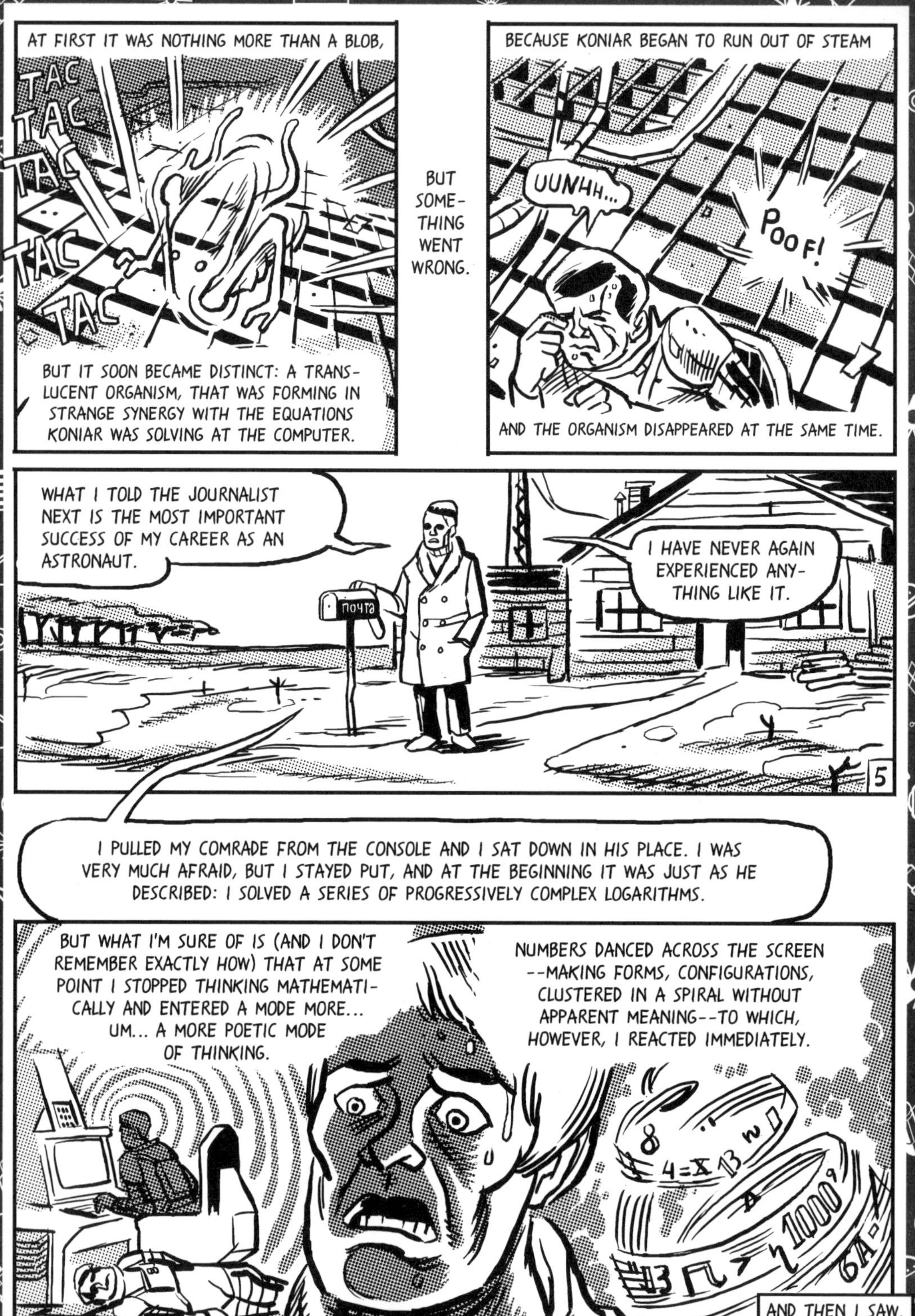
AT FIRST IT WAS NOTHING MORE THAN A BLOB,
TAC TAC TAC TAC TAC
BUT IT SOON BECAME DISTINCT: A TRANSLUCENT ORGANISM, THAT WAS FORMING IN STRANGE SYNERGY WITH THE EQUATIONS KONIAR WAS SOLVING AT THE COMPUTER.
BUT SOMETHING WENT WRONG.
BECAUSE KONIAR BEGAN TO RUN OUT OF STEAM
UUNHH...
POOF!
AND THE ORGANISM DISAPPEARED AT THE SAME TIME.
WHAT I TOLD THE JOURNALIST NEXT IS THE MOST IMPORTANT SUCCESS OF MY CAREER AS AN ASTRONAUT.
ПОЧТА
I HAVE NEVER AGAIN EXPERIENCED ANYTHING LIKE IT.
5
I PULLED MY COMRADE FROM THE CONSOLE AND I SAT DOWN IN HIS PLACE. I WAS VERY MUCH AFRAID, BUT I STAYED PUT, AND AT THE BEGINNING IT WAS JUST AS HE DESCRIBED: I SOLVED A SERIES OF PROGRESSIVELY COMPLEX LOGARITHMS.
BUT WHAT I'M SURE OF IS (AND I DON'T REMEMBER EXACTLY HOW) THAT AT SOME POINT I STOPPED THINKING MATHEMATICALLY AND ENTERED A MODE MORE... UM... A MORE POETIC MODE OF THINKING.
NUMBERS DANCED ACROSS THE SCREEN --MAKING FORMS, CONFIGURATIONS, CLUSTERED IN A SPIRAL WITHOUT APPARENT MEANING--TO WHICH, HOWEVER, I REACTED IMMEDIATELY.
AND THEN I SAW.

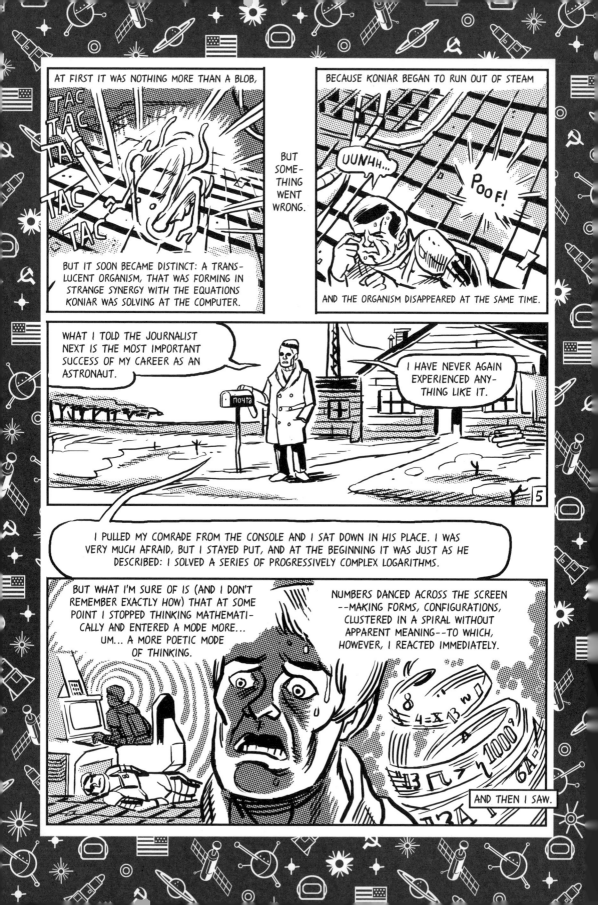

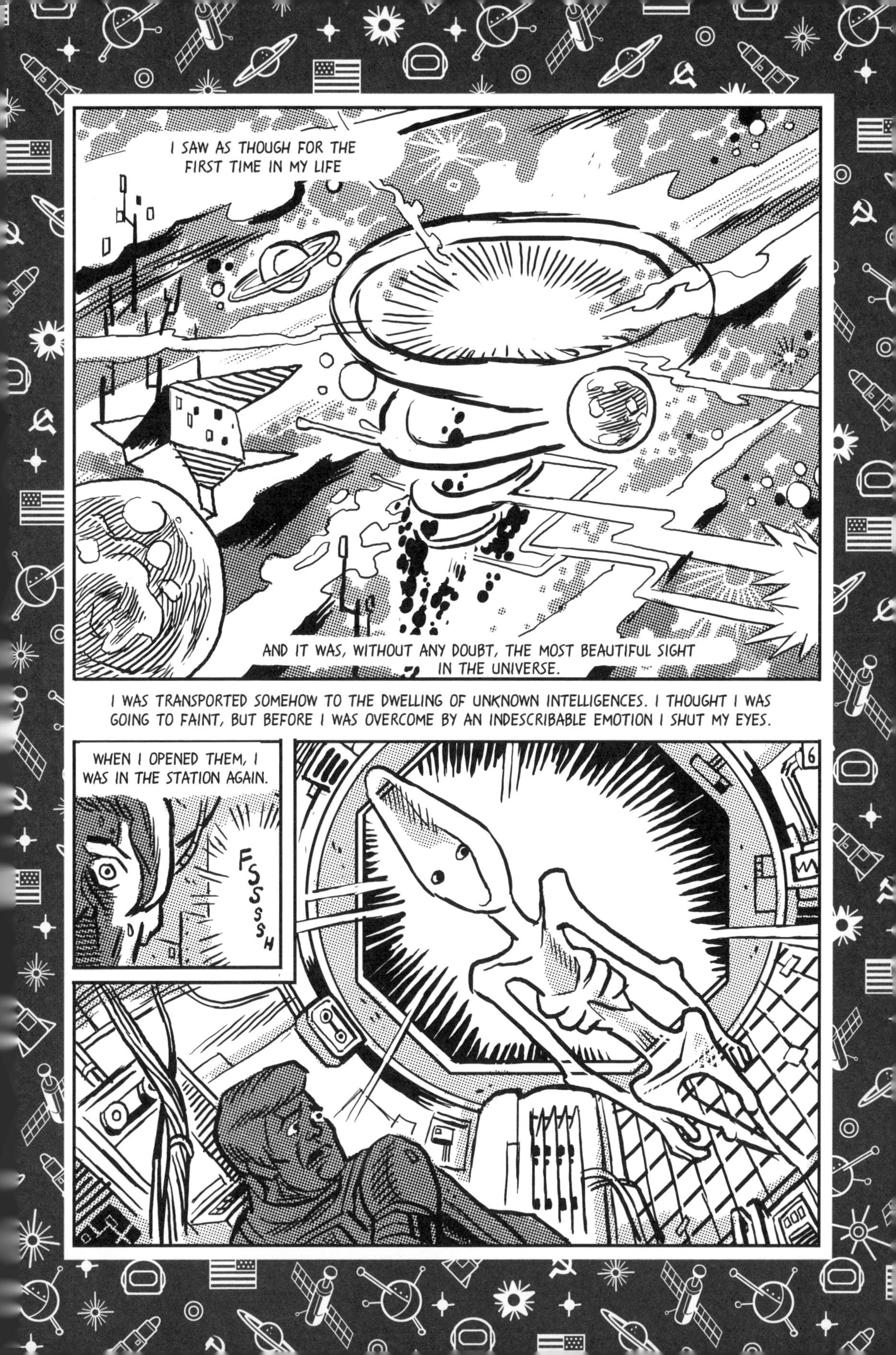
I SAW AS THOUGH FOR THE FIRST TIME IN MY LIFE
AND IT WAS, WITHOUT ANY DOUBT, THE MOST BEAUTIFUL SIGHT IN THE UNIVERSE.
I WAS TRANSPORTED SOMEHOW TO THE DWELLING OF UNKNOWN INTELLIGENCES. I THOUGHT I WAS GOING TO FAINT, BUT BEFORE I WAS OVERCOME BY AN INDESCRIBABLE EMOTION I SHUT MY EYES.
WHEN I OPENED THEM, I WAS IN THE STATION AGAIN.
FSSSSSH

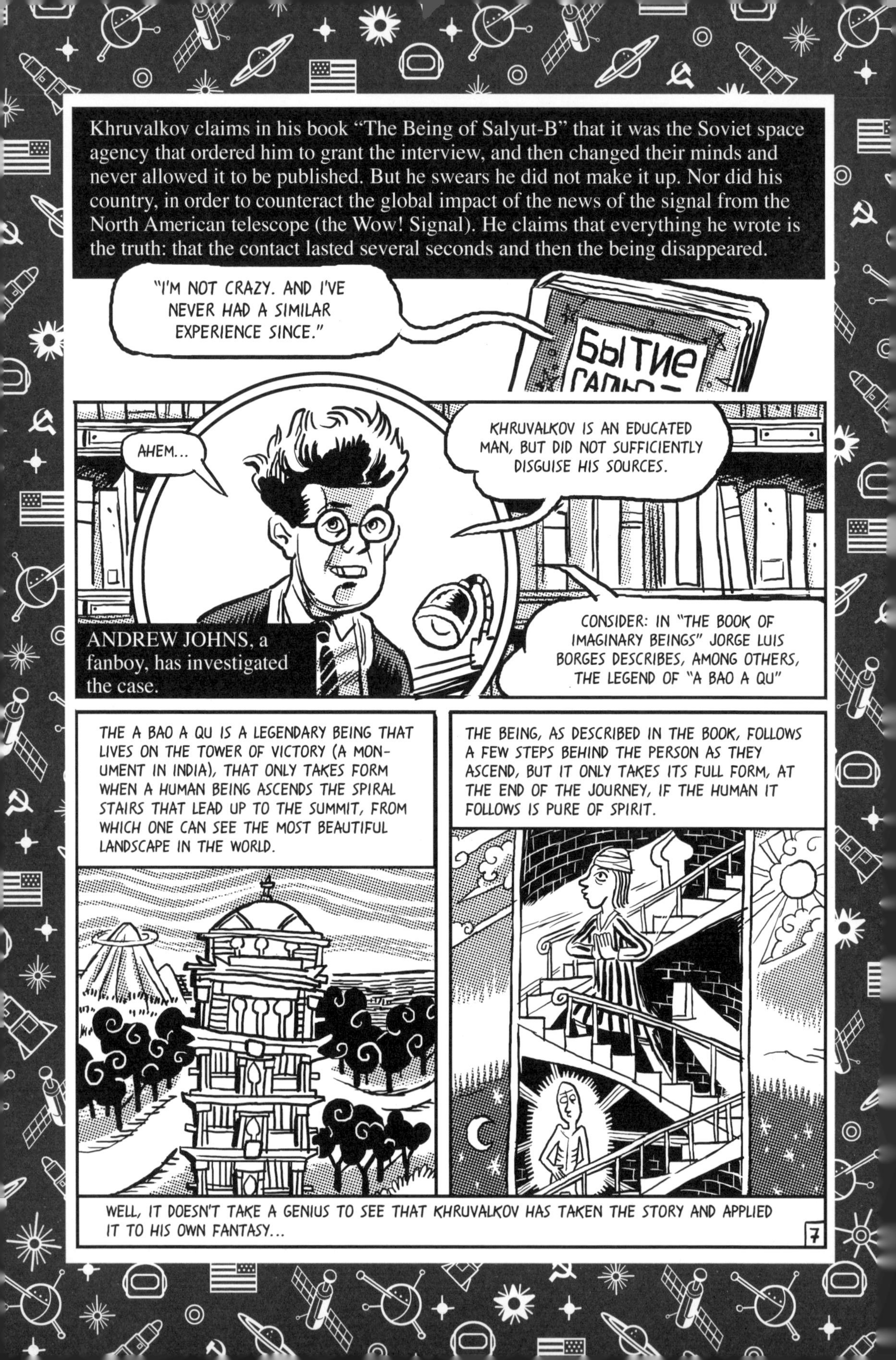
Khruvalkov claims in his book “The Being of Salyut-B” that it was the Soviet space agency that ordered him to grant the interview, and then changed their minds and never allowed it to be published. But he swears he did not make it up. Nor did his country, in order to counteract the global impact of the news of the signal from the North American telescope (the Wow! Signal). He claims that everything he wrote is the truth: that the contact lasted several seconds and then the being disappeared.
"I'M NOT CRAZY. AND I'VE NEVER HAD A SIMILAR EXPERIENCE SINCE."
БЫТИЕ
AHEM...
KHRUVALKOV IS AN EDUCATED MAN, BUT DID NOT SUFFICIENTLY DISGUISE HIS SOURCES.
ANDREW JOHNS, a fanboy, has investigated the case.
CONSIDER: IN "THE BOOK OF IMAGINARY BEINGS" JORGE LUIS BORGES DESCRIBES, AMONG OTHERS, THE LEGEND OF "A BAO A QU"
THE A BAO A QU IS A LEGENDARY BEING THAT LIVES ON THE TOWER OF VICTORY (A MONUMENT IN INDIA), THAT ONLY TAKES FORM WHEN A HUMAN BEING ASCENDS THE SPIRAL STAIRS THAT LEAD UP TO THE SUMMIT, FROM WHICH ONE CAN SEE THE MOST BEAUTIFUL LANDSCAPE IN THE WORLD.
THE BEING, AS DESCRIBED IN THE BOOK, FOLLOWS A FEW STEPS BEHIND THE PERSON AS THEY ASCEND, BUT IT ONLY TAKES ITS FULL FORM, AT THE END OF THE JOURNEY, IF THE HUMAN IT FOLLOWS IS PURE OF SPIRIT.
WELL, IT DOESN'T TAKE A GENIUS TO SEE THAT KHRUVALKOV HAS TAKEN THE STORY AND APPLIED IT TO HIS OWN FANTASY...
7

THE ASCENT UP THE TOWER IS, FOR HIM, A SUCCESSION OF CALCULATIONS "IN A SPIRAL"...

THE LANDSCAPE OF THE STORY, HE TRANSLATED INTO A MAGNIFICENT VISION OF THE COSMOS...

JUST AS, AT THE END, THE ALIEN IS THE A BAO A QU, WHICH FORMS BEHIND HIM AFTER HE "ASCENDS" TO THE PEAK.

I KNOW THAT THERE ARE A NUMBER OF "BELIEVERS" WHO JUSTIFY THIS SIMILARITY BY ARGUING THAT THE STORY "A BAO A QU" COLLECTED BY BORGES IS ALSO THE DESCRIPTION OF AN ENCOUNTER, IN ANTIQUITY, OF A MAN WITH THE SAME RACE OF EXTRATERRESTRIALS.

BUT, ULTIMATELY, I SUGGEST THAT ANYONE WHO BELIEVES THIS SIMPLY WANTS TO BELIEVE.

Can an ancient legend coincide by chance with that of an astronaut? Or is it a literary parody perpetrated by him, or by the space agency of his country? How to resolve what seems to be the latest episode in the "space race"? How shall the myth of the A BAO A QU in outer space end?

THIS MORNING, KHRUVALKOV PICKS UP HIS MAIL.

Mr. Khruvalkov:

We're writing to advise you of the risk run by your book "The Being of Salyut-B," about which an accusation of plagiarism has been made. We're not happy to tell you that you are going to need lawyers, but we're pleased to give you some good news. We at Burner & Staples are your best option!

...immediately to our office... we're offering you every... experience that only...

FSSSSSSSSHHH

MARCOS PRIOR
THE NEW YORK EXPERIMENT

Marcos Prior was born in L'Hospitalet de Llobregat (Barcelona) in 1975. He has worked as an illustrator and storyboard artist for advertising companies such as Ogilvy Bassat, Vinizius Young & Rubicam, and McCann. As a cartoonist he began with *Oropel* (1996) and *Cool Tokio* [*Cool Tokyo*] (1997), together with Marcos Morán, Nacho Antolín, Jordi Borrás, and Artur Laperla, with whom, over the following years, he's collaborated on other projects. In 2008 he published his solo graphic novel *Fallos de raccord,* which was followed by *Fagocitosis* [*Phagocytosis*] *(2012),* with illustrations by Danide; *El año de los 4 emperadores* [*The Year of the 4 Emperors*] (2012), on his own; and *Potlach* (2013), also with Danide. *Necrópolis* came out in 2015, and his collaboration with David Rubín, *Gran Hotel Abismo* [*Grand Hotel Abyss*] will be released in 2016.

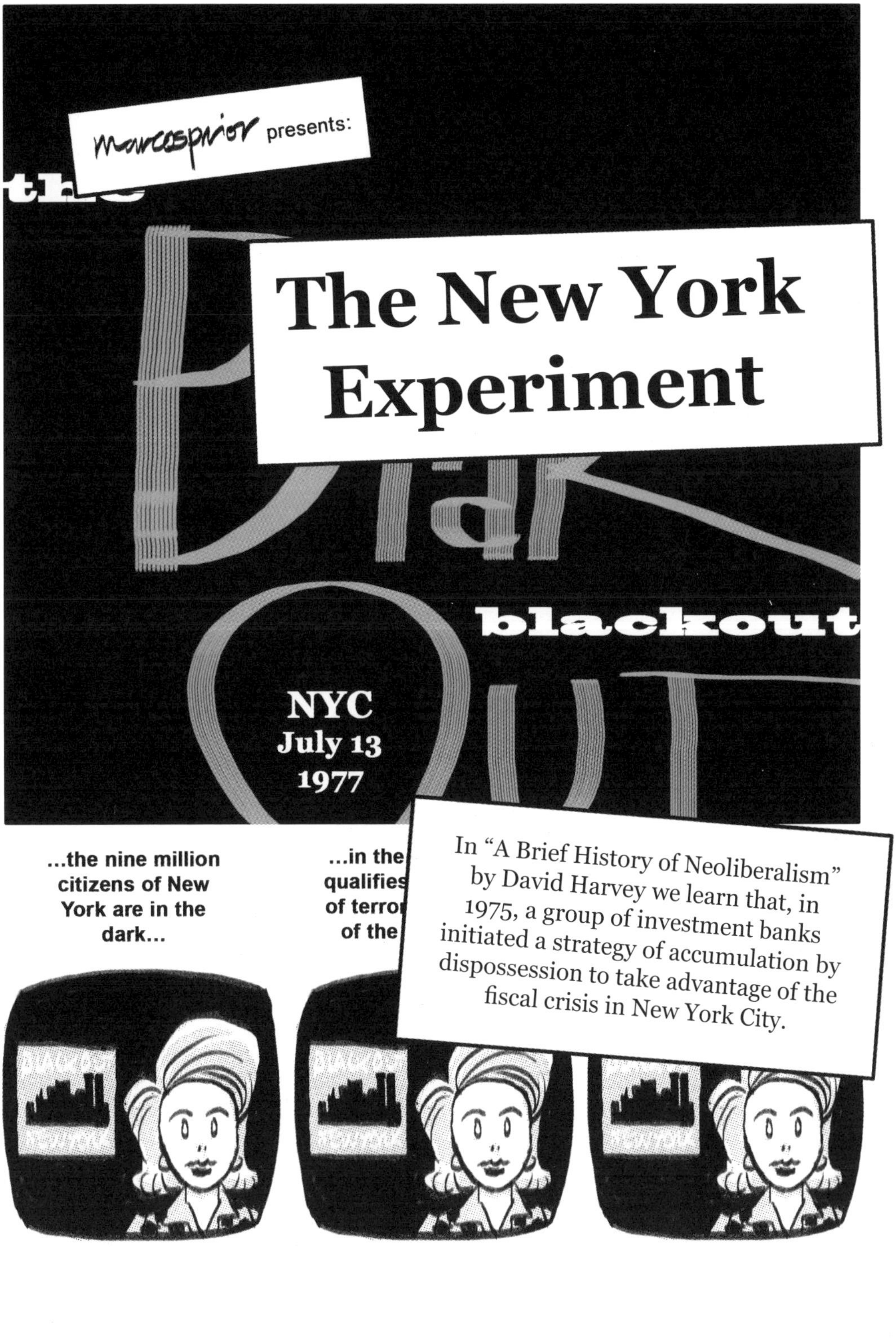
marcospiror presents:
the blackout
The New York Experiment
NYC July 13 1977
...the nine million citizens of New York are in the dark...
...in the qualifies of terro of the
In "A Brief History of Neoliberalism" by David Harvey we learn that, in 1975, a group of investment banks initiated a strategy of accumulation by dispossession to take advantage of the fiscal crisis in New York City.

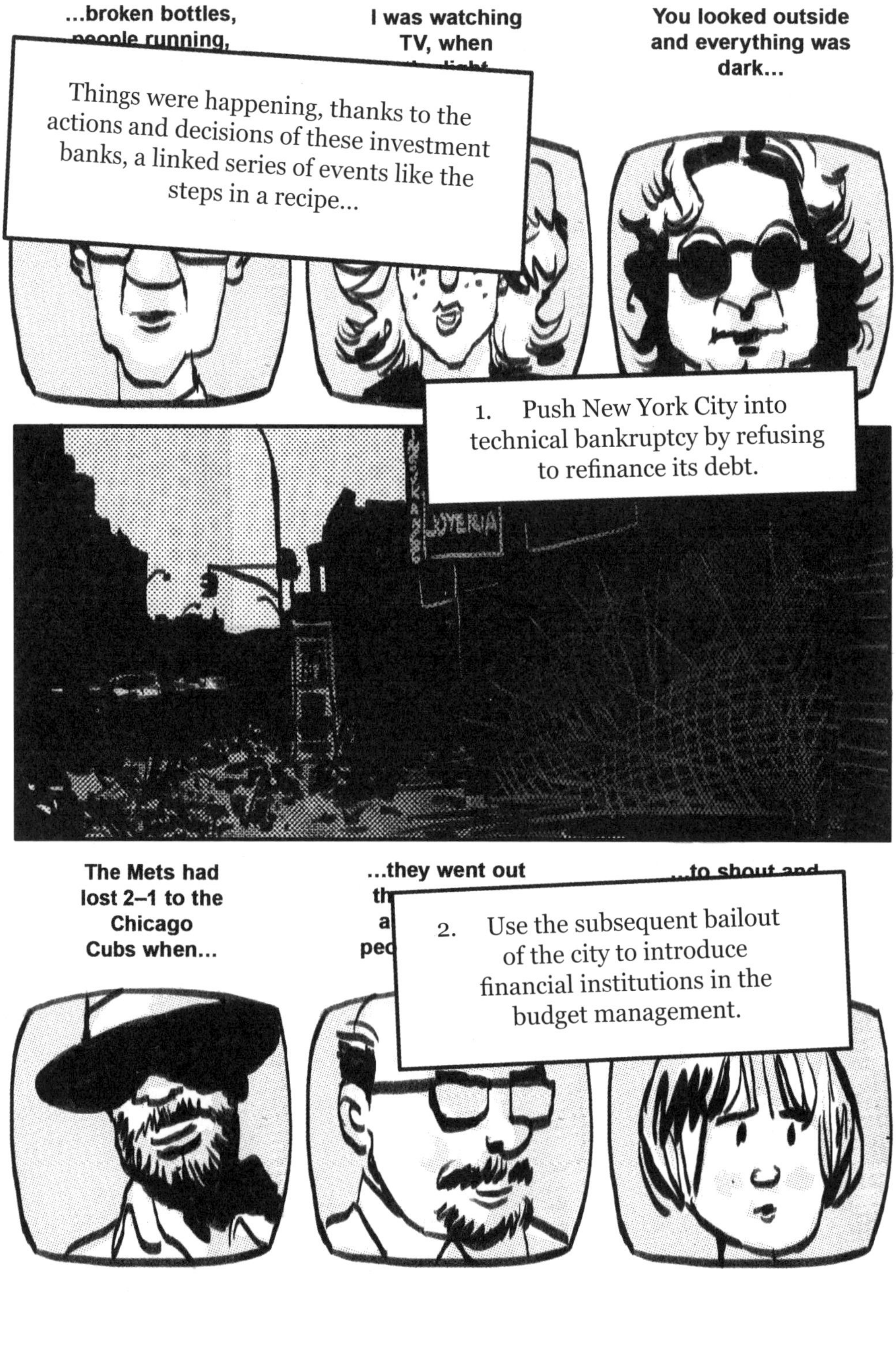
...broken bottles,
people running,
Things were happening, thanks to the actions and decisions of these investment banks, a linked series of events like the steps in a recipe...
I was watching TV, when
You looked outside and everything was dark...
1. Push New York City into technical bankruptcy by refusing to refinance its debt.
JOYERIA
The Mets had lost 2–1 to the Chicago Cubs when...
...they went out
2. Use the subsequent bailout of the city to introduce financial institutions in the budget management.

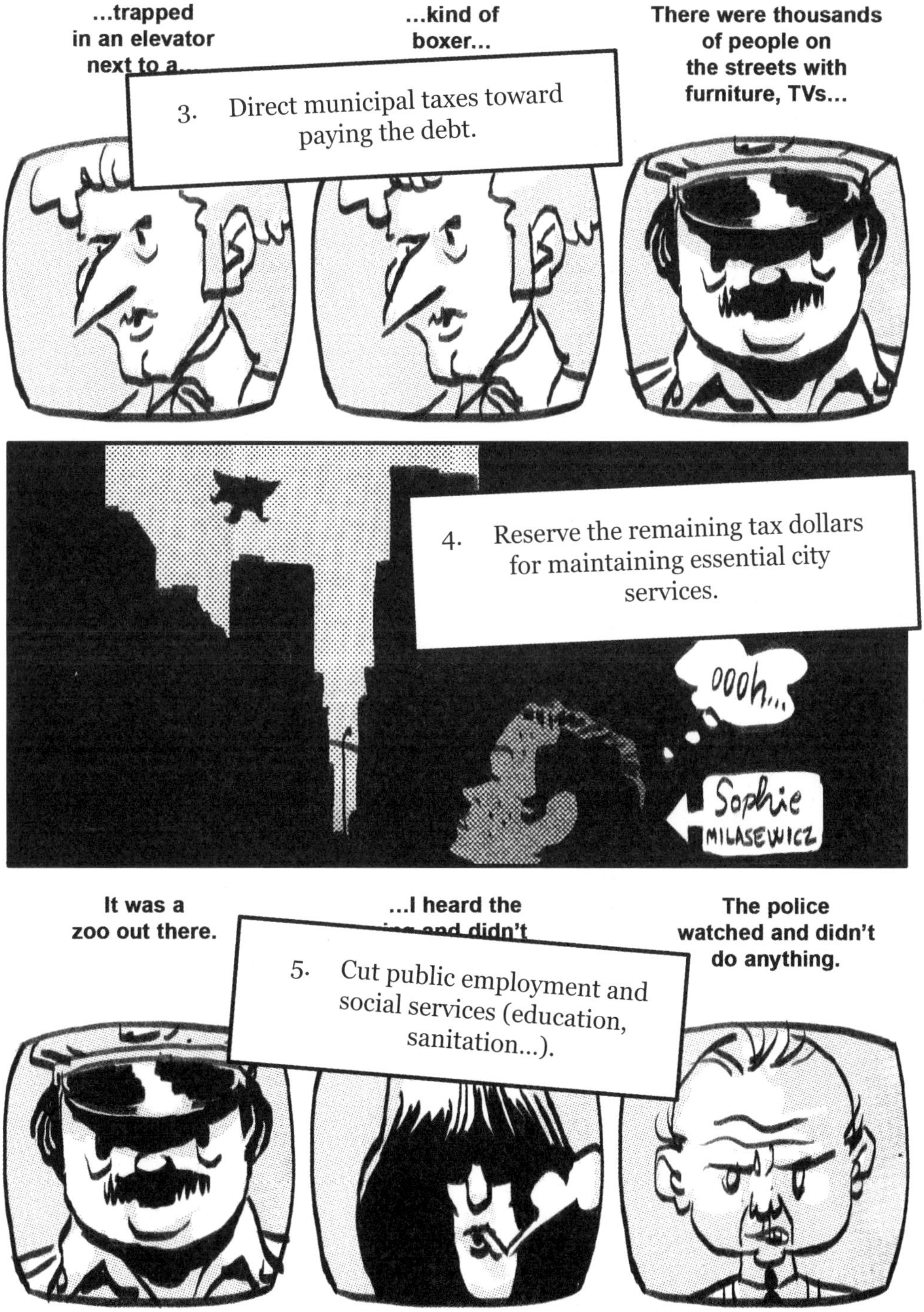
...trapped
in an elevator
next to a...
3. Direct municipal taxes toward paying the debt.
...kind of
boxer...
There were thousands
of people on
the streets with
furniture, TVs...
4. Reserve the remaining tax dollars for maintaining essential city services.
oooh...
Sophie
MILASEWICZ
It was a
zoo out there.
...I heard the
5. Cut public employment and social services (education, sanitation...).
The police
watched and didn't
do anything.

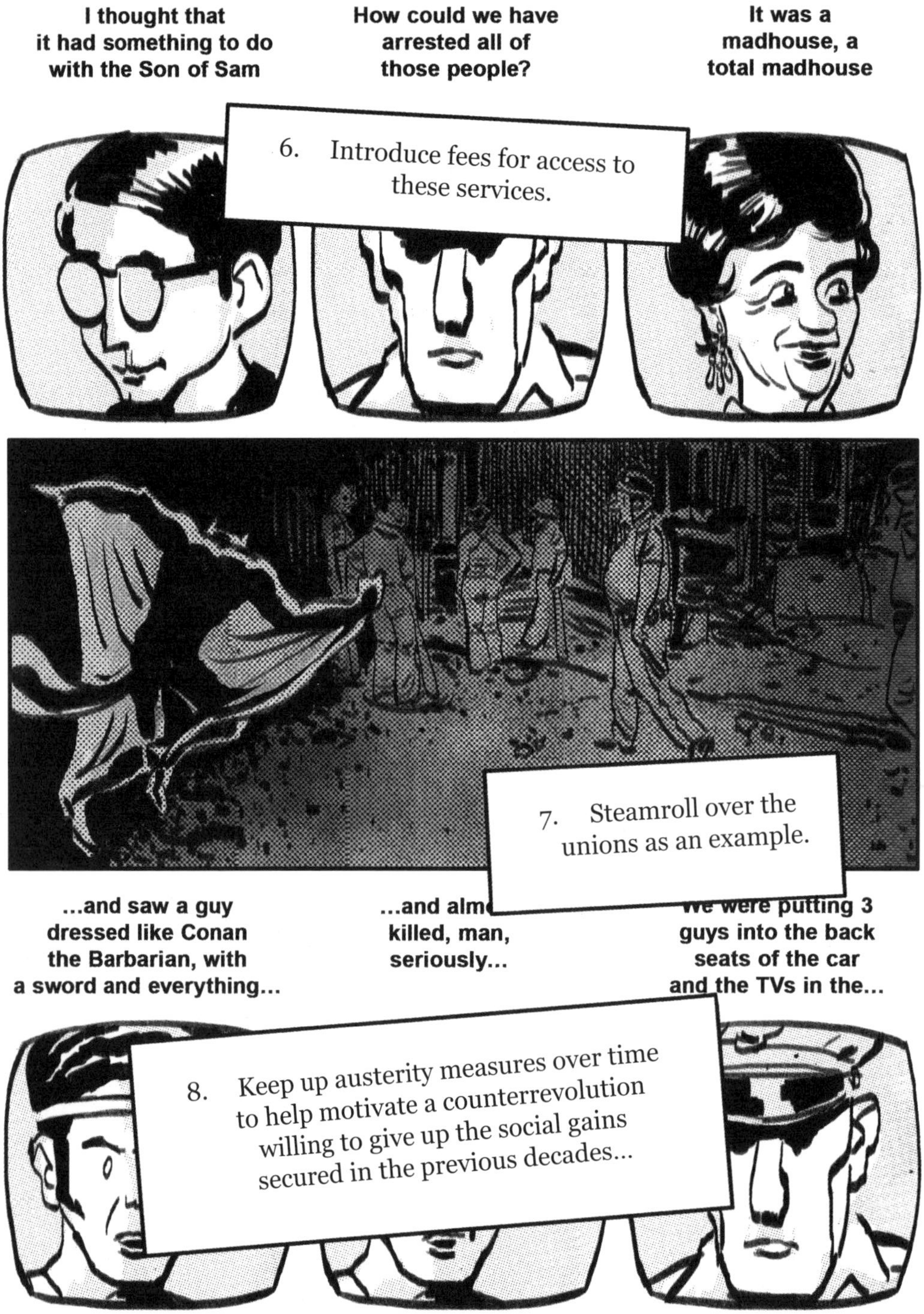
I thought that it had something to do with the Son of Sam
How could we have arrested all of those people?
It was a madhouse, a total madhouse
6. Introduce fees for access to these services.
7. Steamroll over the unions as an example.
...and saw a guy dressed like Conan the Barbarian, with a sword and everything...
...and alm
killed, man, seriously...
We were putting 3 guys into the back seats of the car and the TVs in the...
8. Keep up austerity measures over time to help motivate a counterrevolution willing to give up the social gains secured in the previous decades...

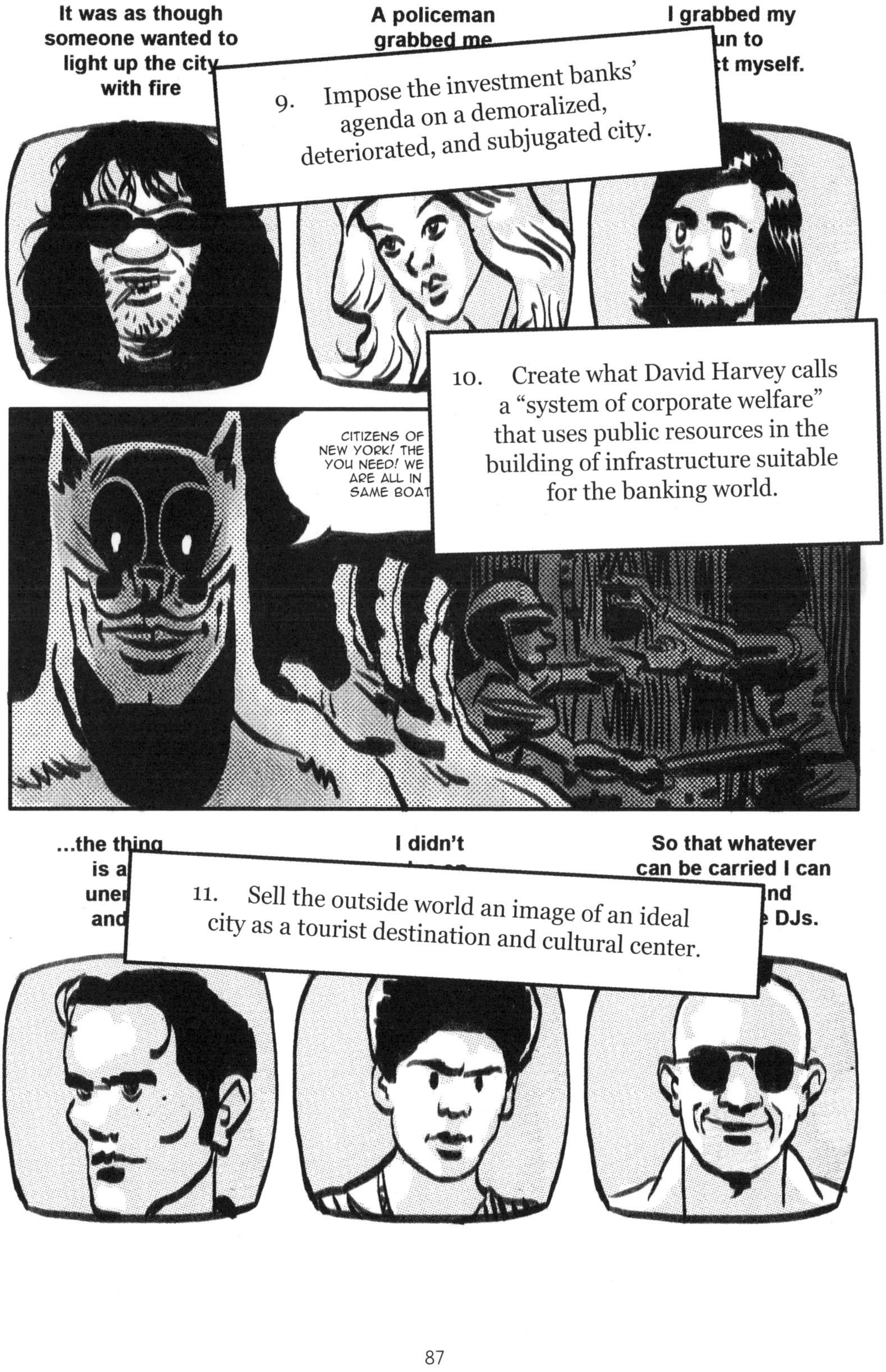
It was as though someone wanted to light up the city with fire
A policeman grabbed me
I grabbed my
un to
t myself.
9. Impose the investment banks' agenda on a demoralized, deteriorated, and subjugated city.
CITIZENS OF NEW YORK! THE YOU NEED! WE ARE ALL IN SAME BOAT
10. Create what David Harvey calls a "system of corporate welfare" that uses public resources in the building of infrastructure suitable for the banking world.
...the thing is a uner and
I didn't
So that whatever can be carried I can
nd
DJs.
11. Sell the outside world an image of an ideal city as a tourist destination and cultural center.

...while the Edison Company speaks of an "act of God"...

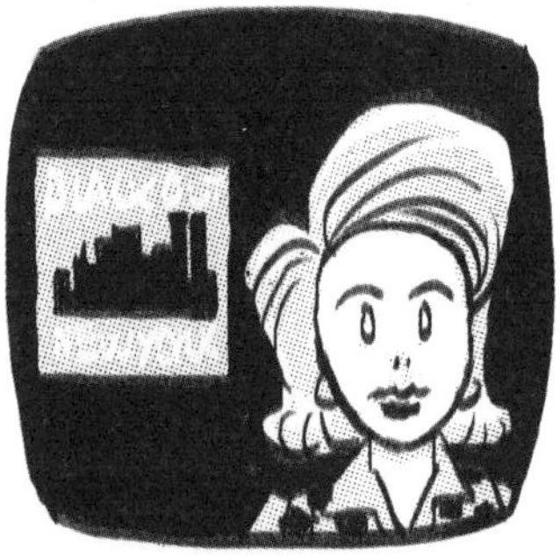

An explanation that does not seem to agree with...

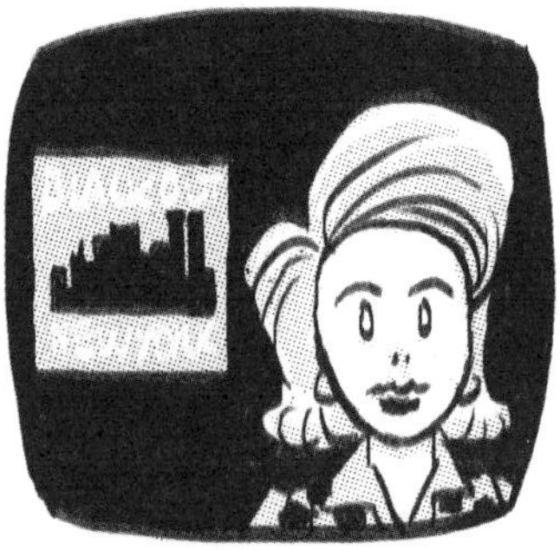

Mayor Abraham Beame, who sees it as a danger to...

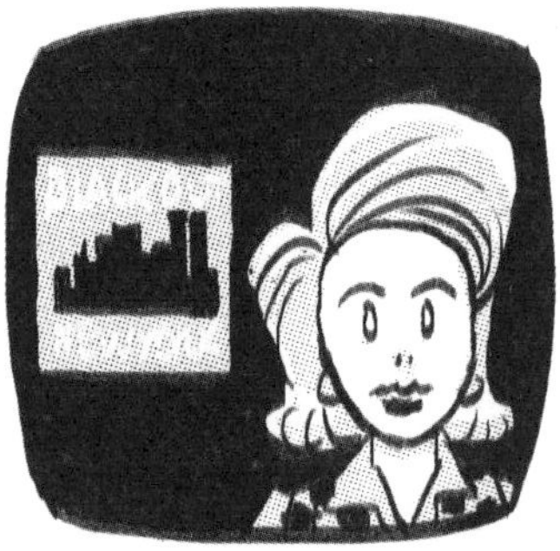

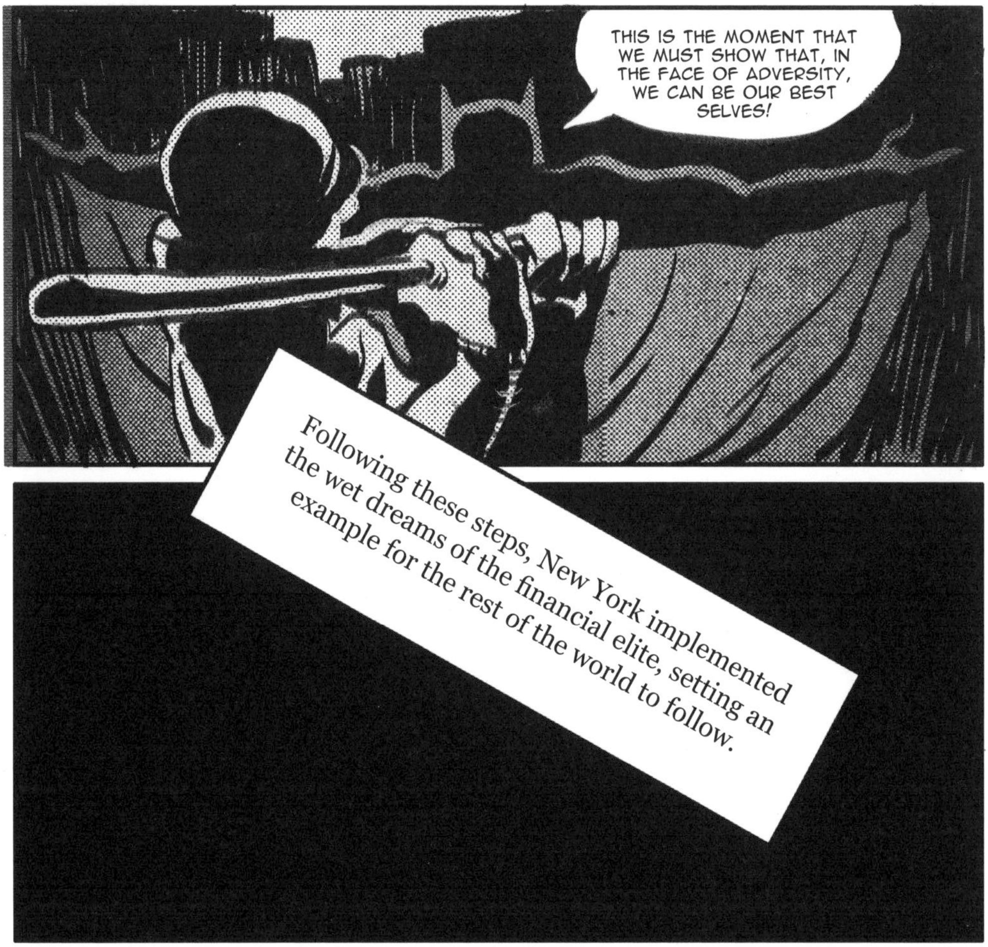
THIS IS THE MOMENT THAT WE MUST SHOW THAT, IN THE FACE OF ADVERSITY, WE CAN BE OUR BEST SELVES!
Following these steps, New York implemented the wet dreams of the financial elite, setting an example for the rest of the world to follow.

MIGUEL ÁNGEL MARTÍN

GUNSLINGER

Miguel Ángel Martín was born in Leon in 1960. His cartooning career
began in the comics magazines that were published during the '80s:
Totem, Makoki, Zona 84, El Víbora. He has been published in the United
States and several European countries, most especially in Italy, where he
won the Yellow Kid prize in 1999 and the Attilio Micheluzzi Award in 2003.
He's created characters such as Brian the Brain and Keibol Black, and has
published the provocatively titled works *Anal Core* (1999), *Snuff 2000*
(1998), *Psychopathia Sexualis* (1992), *Rubber Flesh* (1999–2000), and
Bitch (2008). His latest original graphic novels are *Playlove* (2008) and
Out of My Brain (2014), which concludes the saga of Brian the Brain.

GUNSLINGER

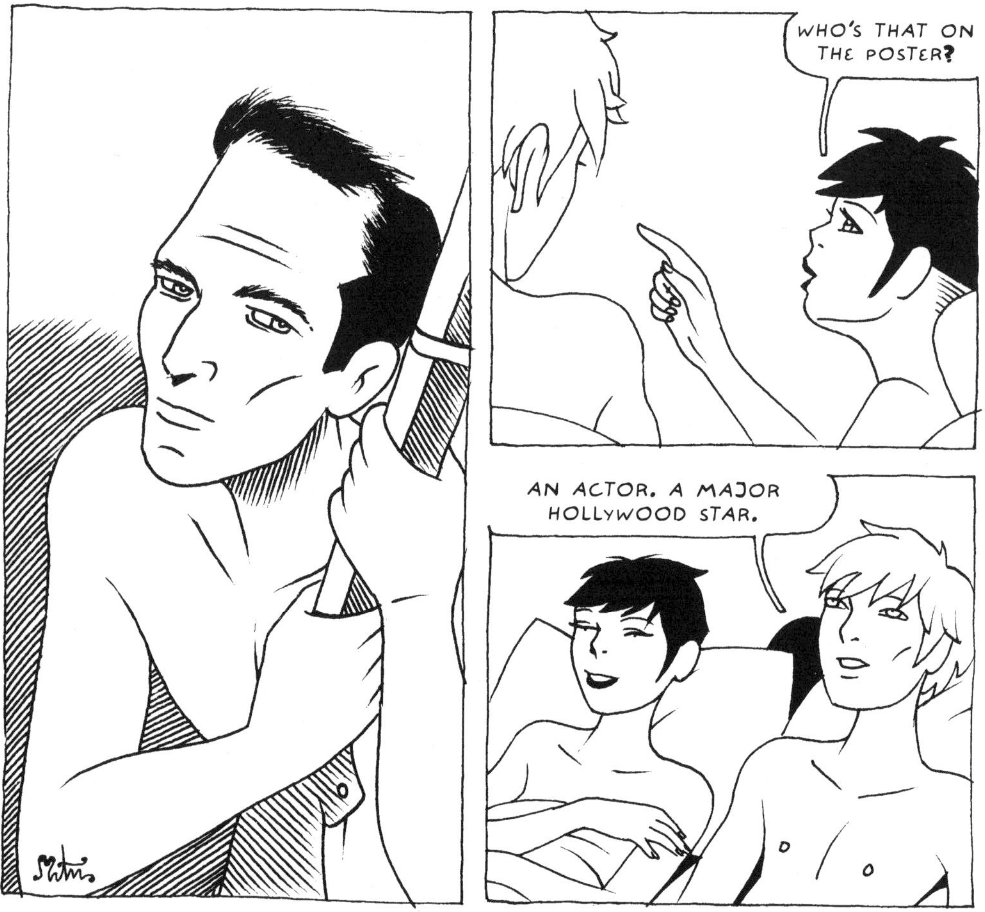
WHO'S THAT ON THE POSTER?
AN ACTOR. A MAJOR HOLLYWOOD STAR.

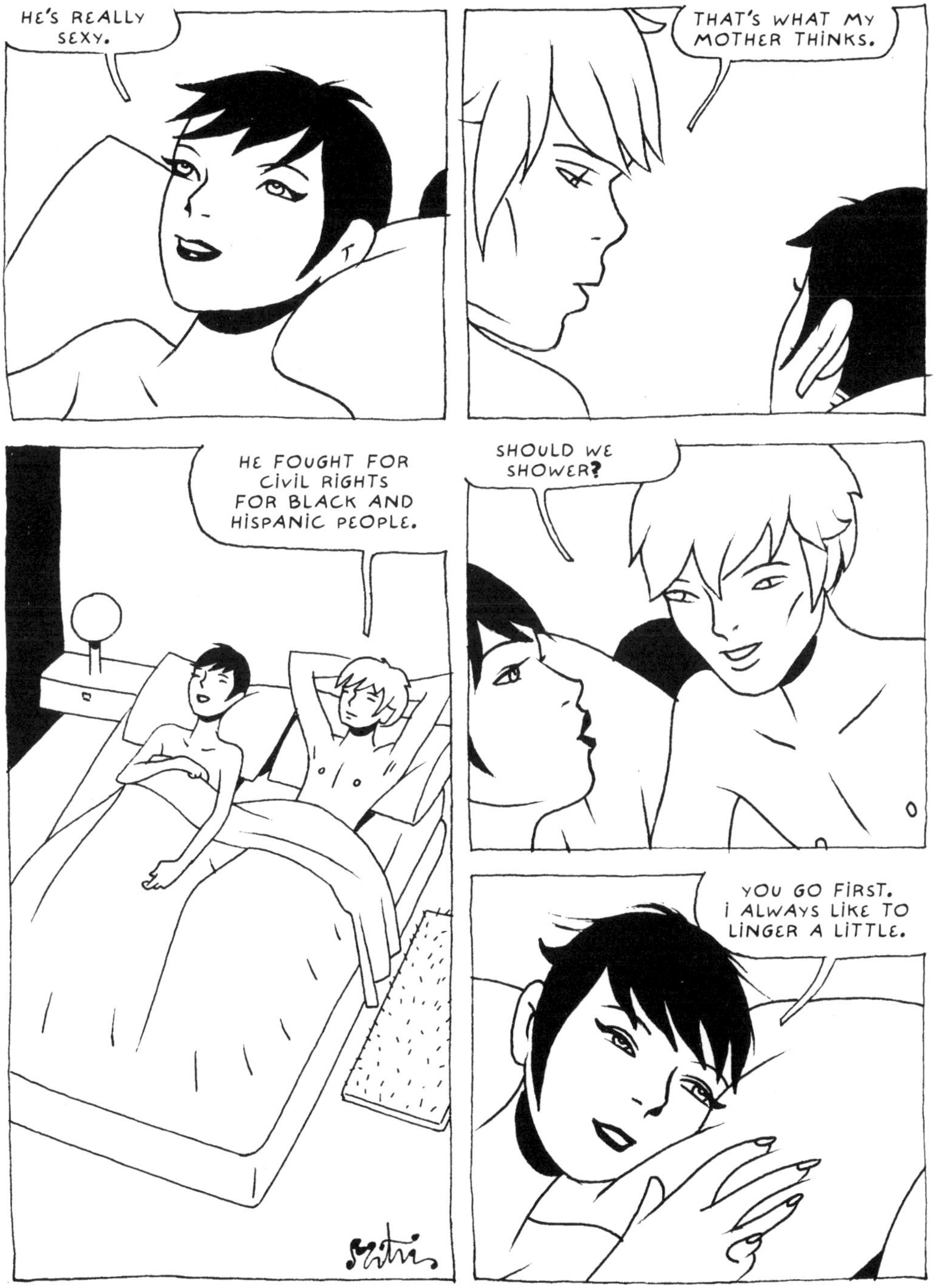
HE'S REALLY SEXY.
THAT'S WHAT MY MOTHER THINKS.
HE FOUGHT FOR CIVIL RIGHTS FOR BLACK AND HISPANIC PEOPLE.
SHOULD WE SHOWER?
YOU GO FIRST. I ALWAYS LIKE TO LINGER A LITTLE.

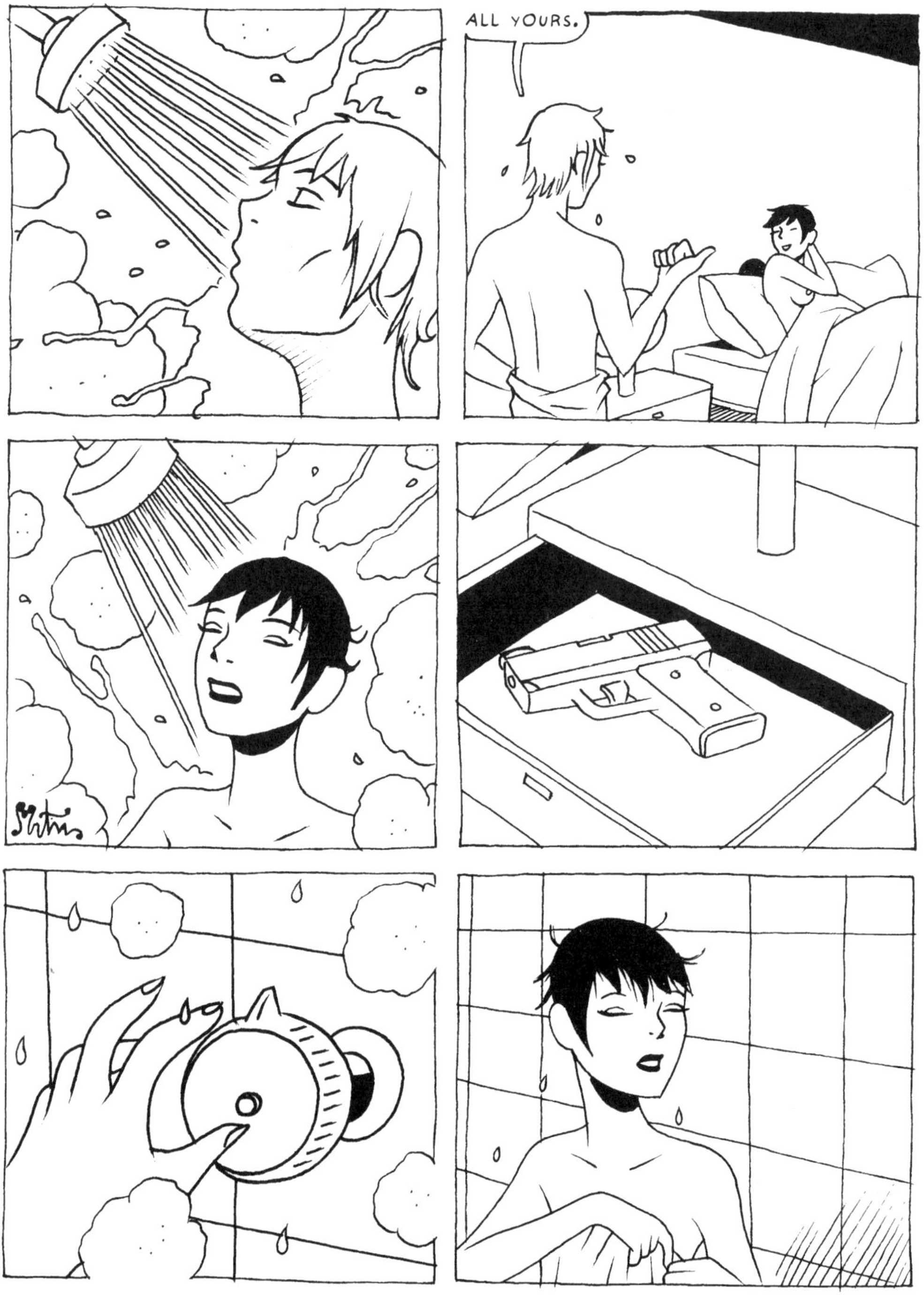
ALL YOURS.

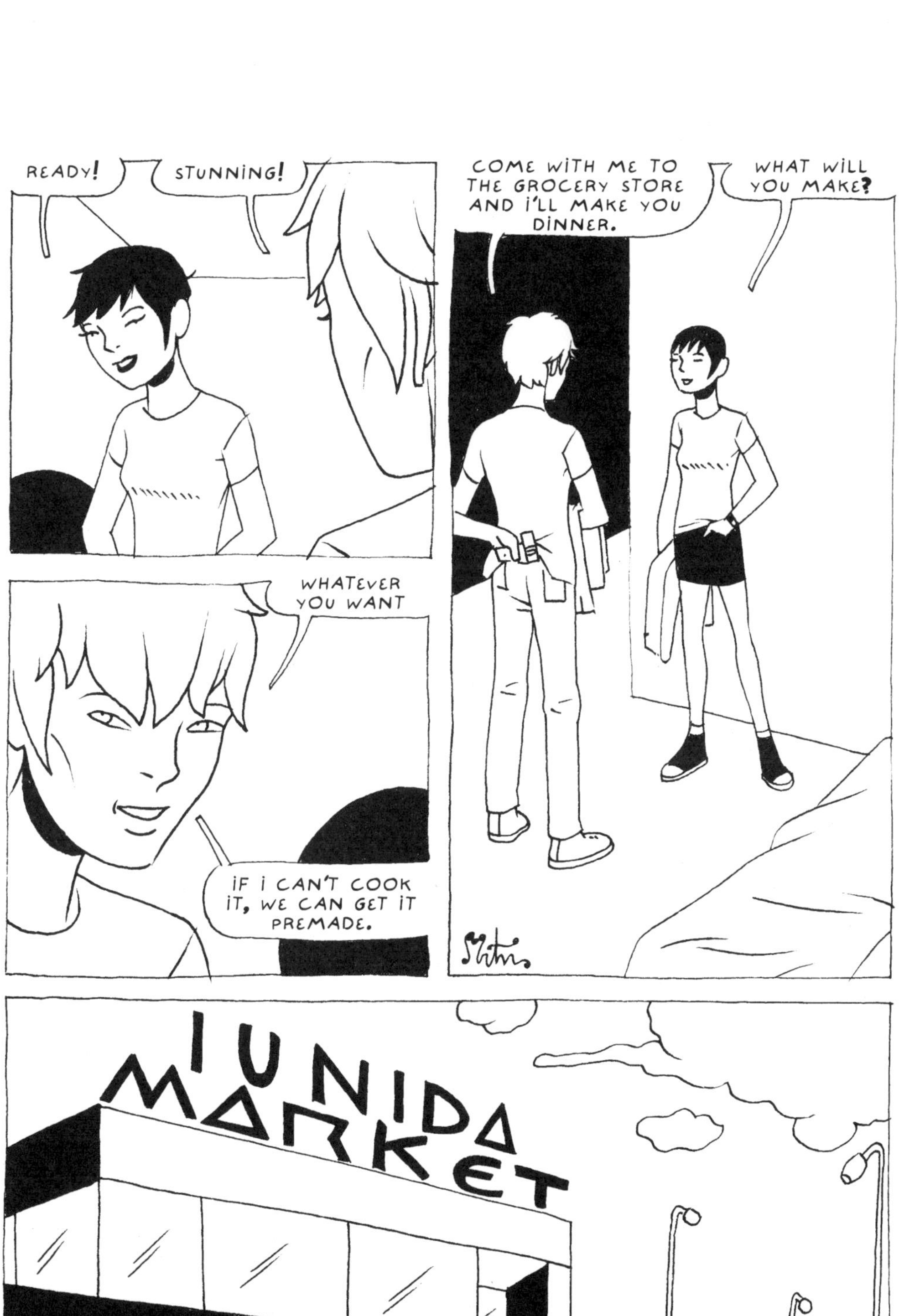
READY!
STUNNING!
COME WITH ME TO THE GROCERY STORE AND I'LL MAKE YOU DINNER.
WHAT WILL YOU MAKE?
WHATEVER YOU WANT
IF I CAN'T COOK IT, WE CAN GET IT PREMADE.
IUNIDA MARKET

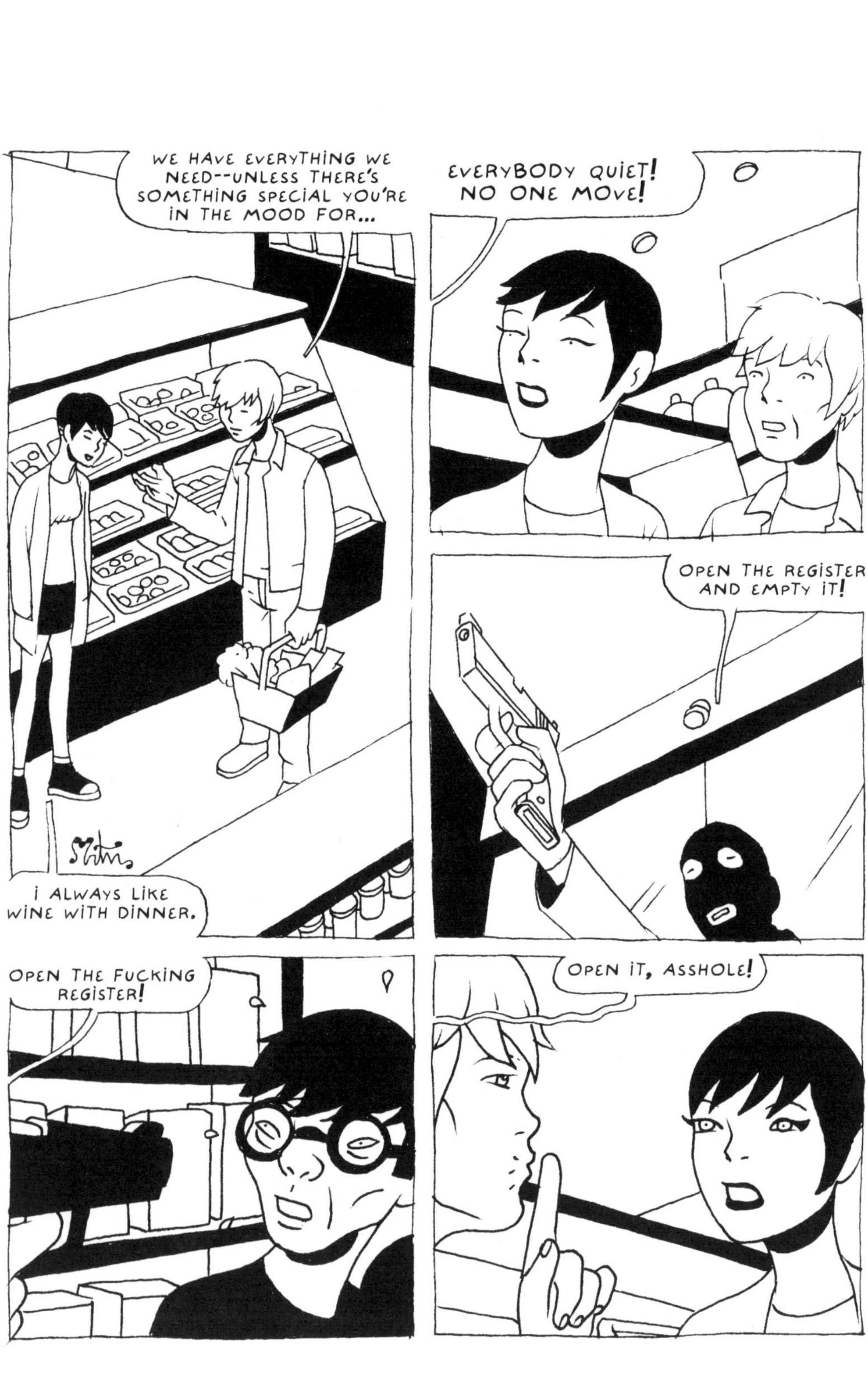
WE HAVE EVERYTHING WE NEED--UNLESS THERE'S SOMETHING SPECIAL YOU'RE IN THE MOOD FOR...
I ALWAYS LIKE WINE WITH DINNER.
EVERYBODY QUIET! NO ONE MOVE!
OPEN THE REGISTER AND EMPTY IT!
OPEN THE FUCKING REGISTER!
OPEN IT, ASSHOLE!

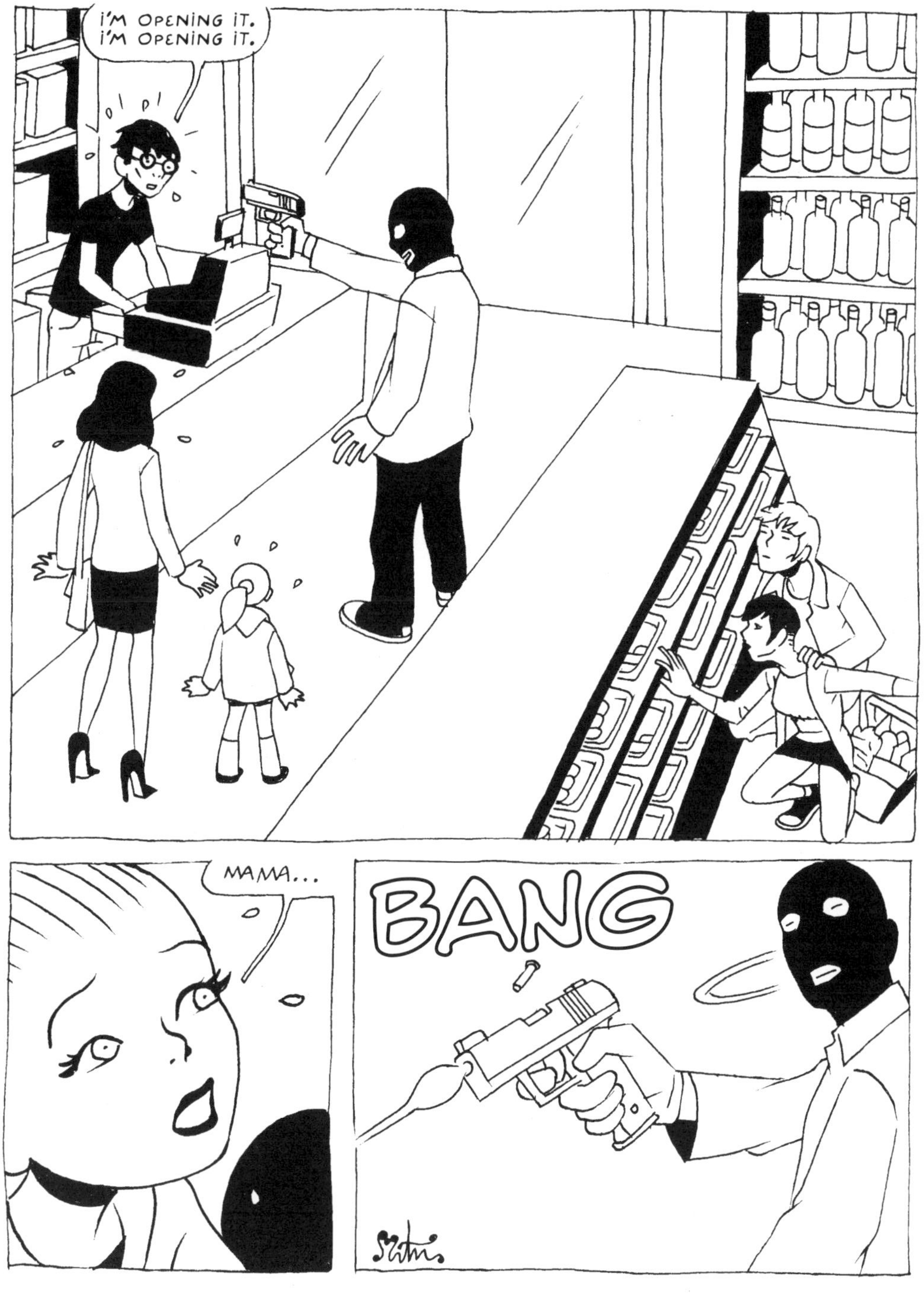
I'M OPENING IT.
I'M OPENING IT.
MAMA...
BANG

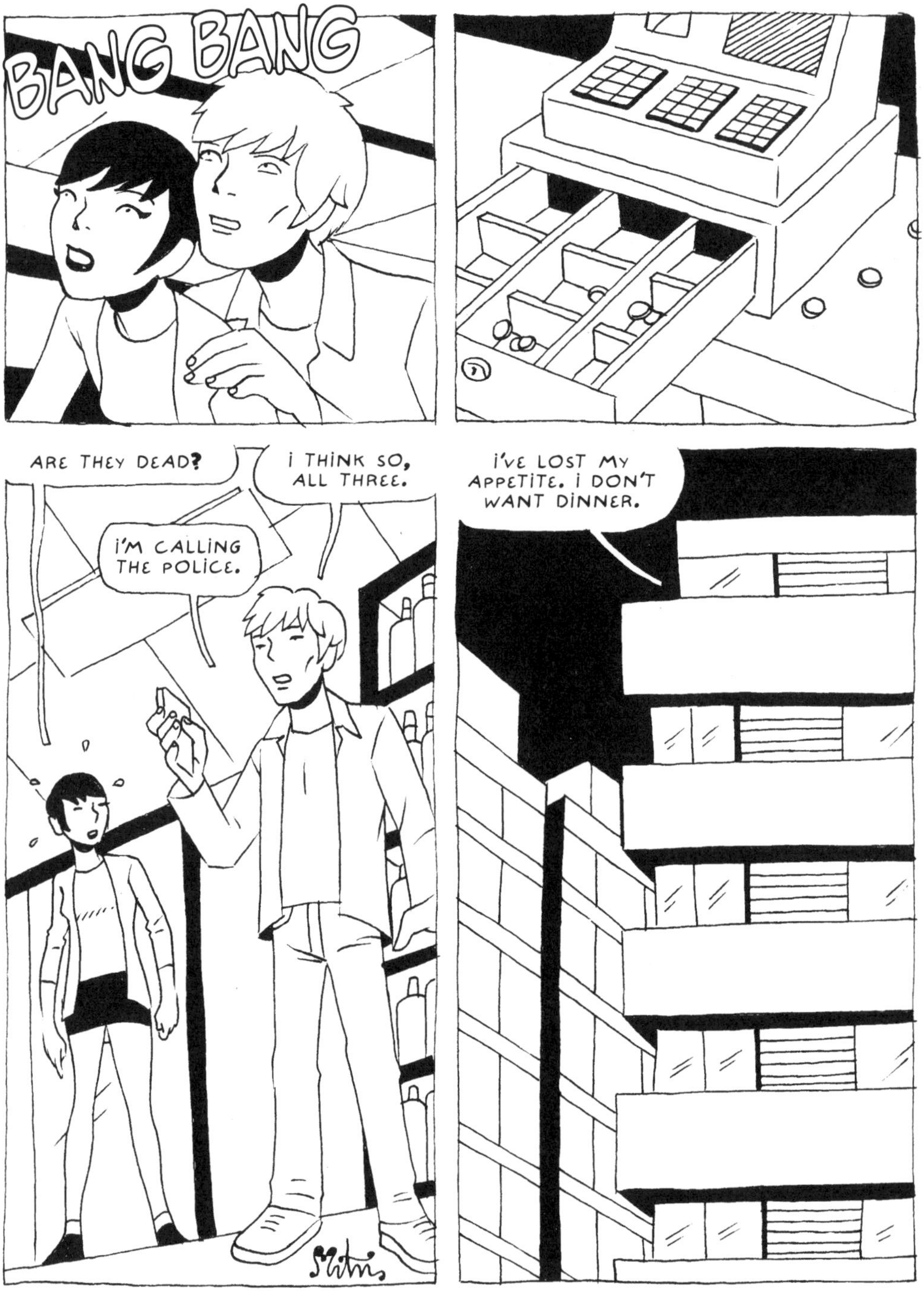
BANG BANG
ARE THEY DEAD?
I THINK SO, ALL THREE.
I'M CALLING THE POLICE.
I'VE LOST MY APPETITE. I DON'T WANT DINNER.

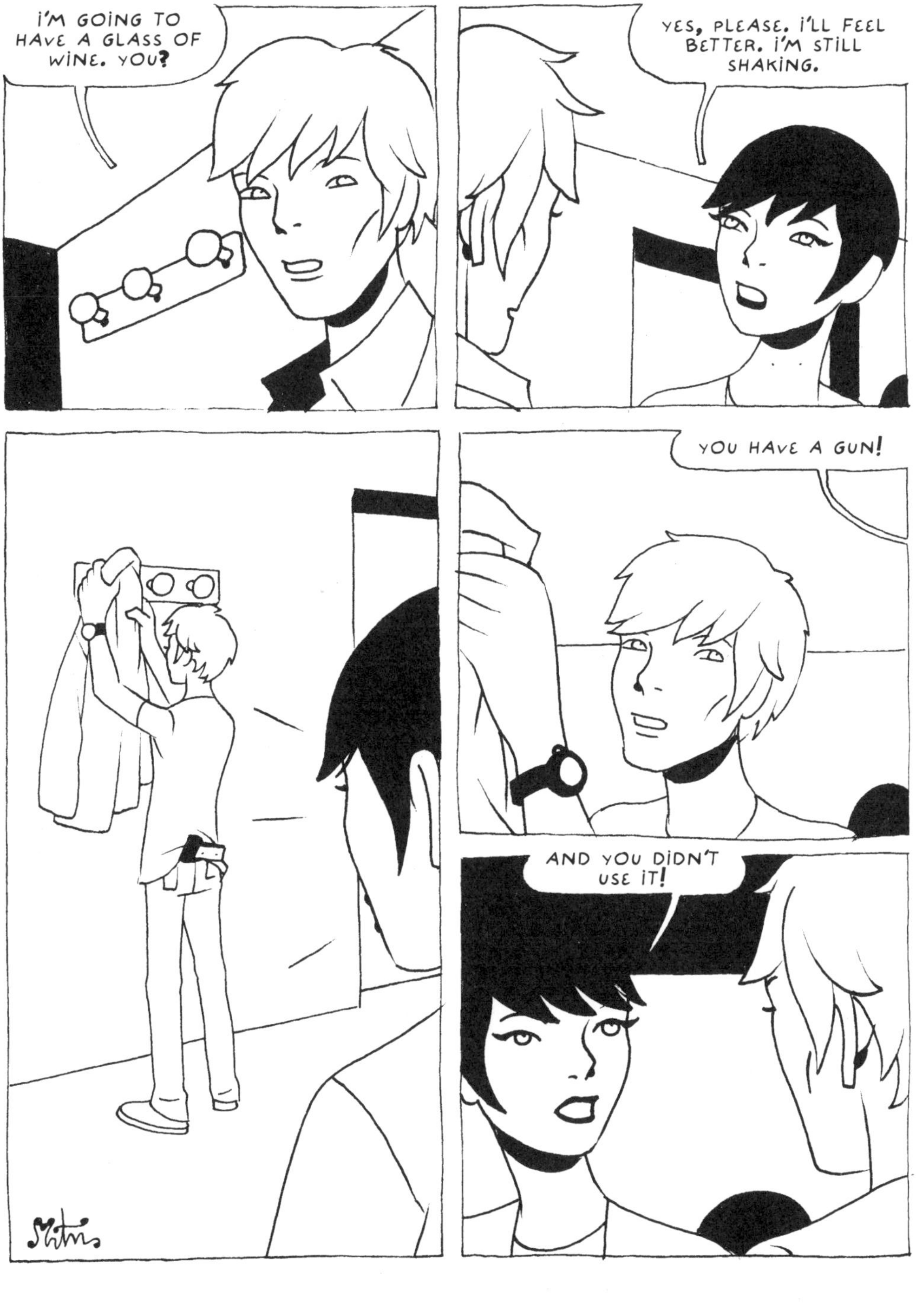
I'M GOING TO HAVE A GLASS OF WINE. YOU?
YES, PLEASE. I'LL FEEL BETTER. I'M STILL SHAKING.
YOU HAVE A GUN!
AND YOU DIDN'T USE IT!

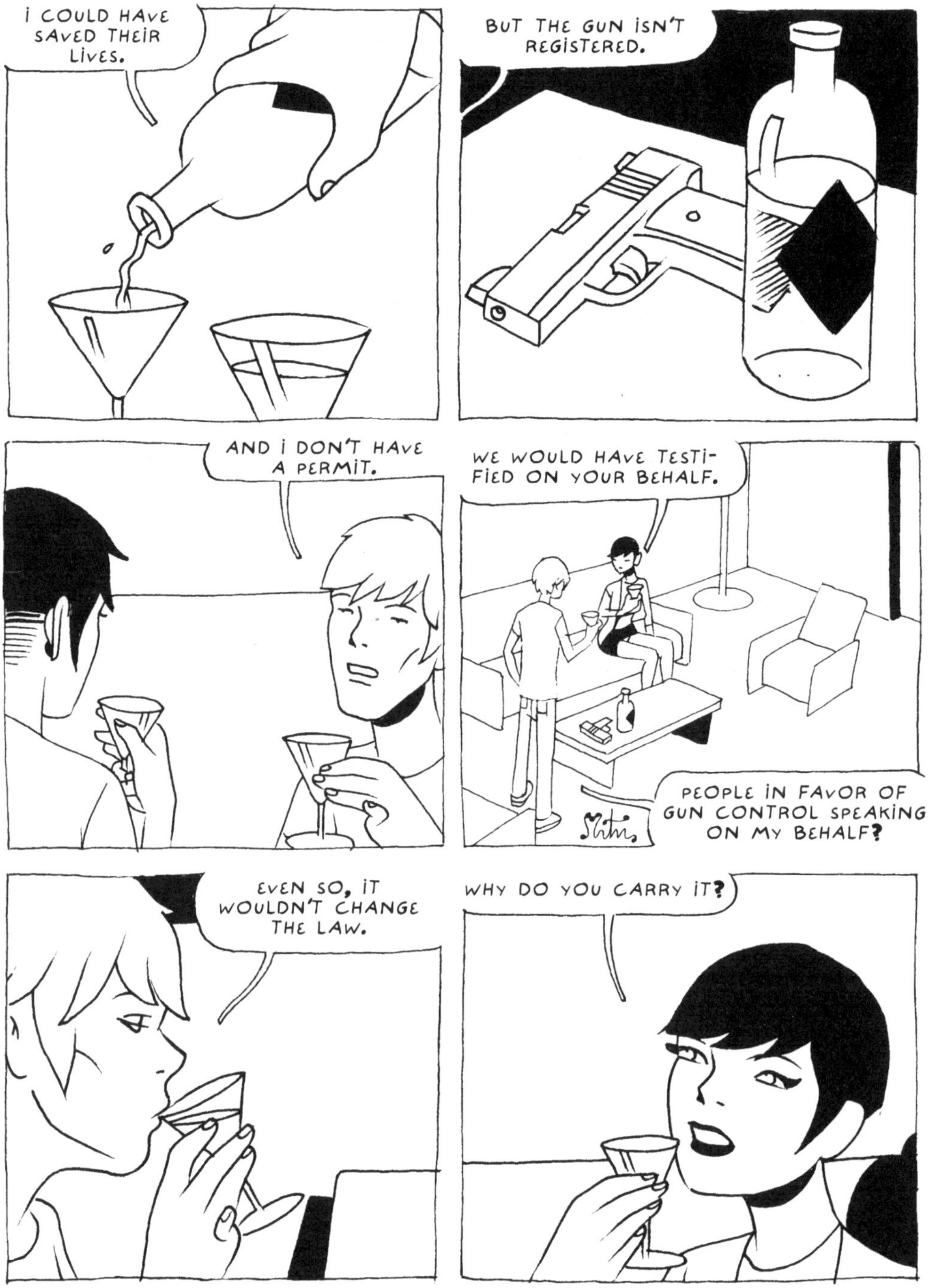
I COULD HAVE SAVED THEIR LIVES.
BUT THE GUN ISN'T REGISTERED.
AND I DON'T HAVE A PERMIT.
WE WOULD HAVE TESTI-FIED ON YOUR BEHALF.
PEOPLE IN FAVOR OF GUN CONTROL SPEAKING ON MY BEHALF?
EVEN SO, IT WOULDN'T CHANGE THE LAW.
WHY DO YOU CARRY IT?

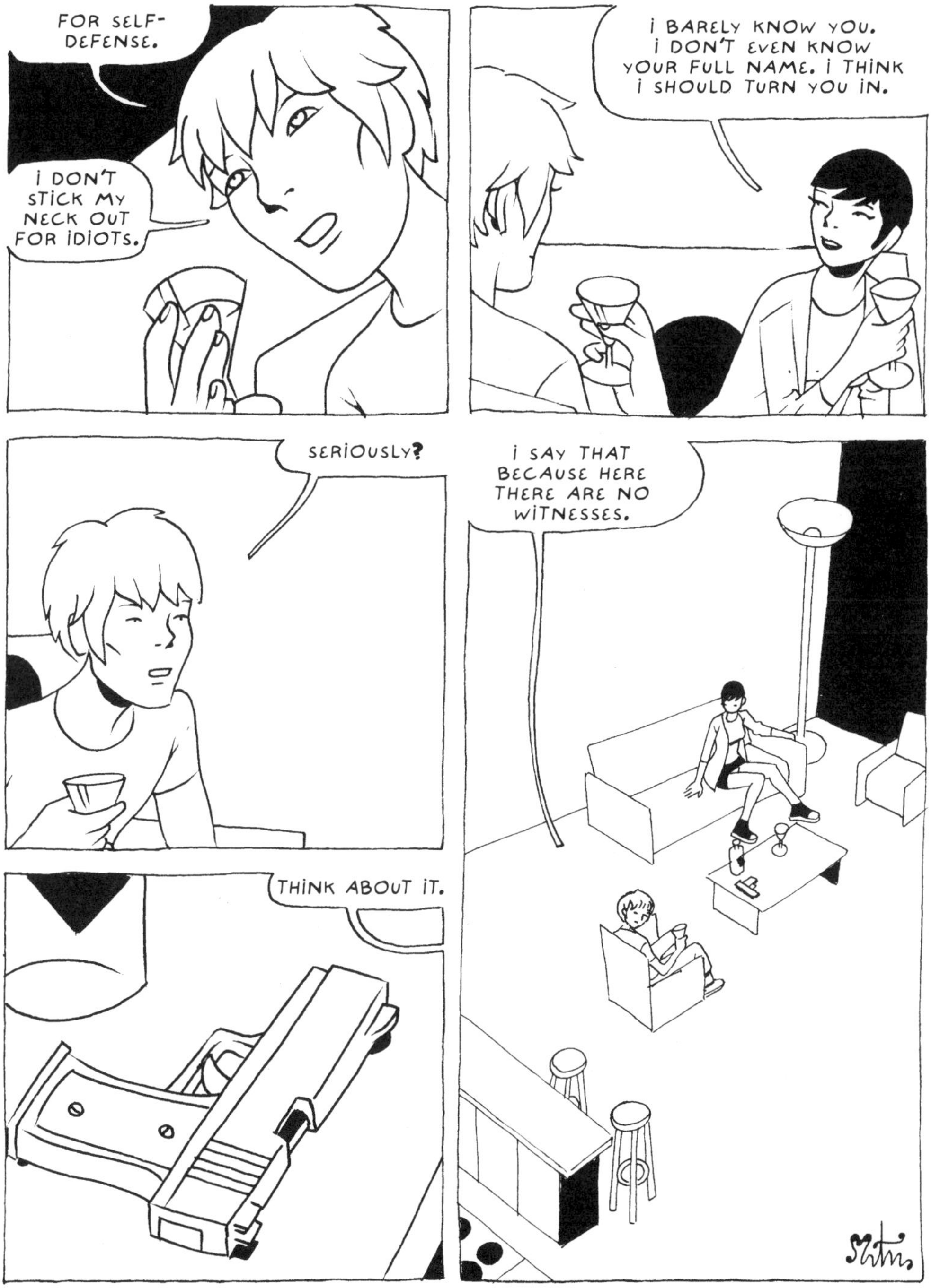
FOR SELF-DEFENSE.
I DON'T STICK MY NECK OUT FOR IDIOTS.
I BARELY KNOW YOU. I DON'T EVEN KNOW YOUR FULL NAME. I THINK I SHOULD TURN YOU IN.
SERIOUSLY?
I SAY THAT BECAUSE HERE THERE ARE NO WITNESSES.
THINK ABOUT IT.

GAME OVER

RAMÓN BOLDÚ
WRITERS NEVER SCORE

Ramón Boldú was born in Tarroja de la Segarra (Lérida) in 1951. A comedian and television writer, in 1976, in the magazine *Interviú,* he began what would be a long career as a cartoonist, graphic artist, and editor of many magazines—during Spain's transition to democracy and the following years—most notably the popular erotic magazine *Lib.* During the '80s he published autobiographical comics in *El Víbora.* Recently, he continued the story of his life in vignettes in a series of graphic novels: *El arte de criar malvas* [*The Art of Growing Mallow*] (2008), *Bohemio pero abstemio, memorias de un hombre de segunda mano* [*Bohemian But Abstinent: Memoirs of a Second-Hand Man*] (2009), and *Sexo, amor y pistachos* [*Sex, Love, and Pistachios*] (2010). He collaborated with Ramón Pereira on *La voz que no cesa, biografía del poeta Miguel Hernández* [*The Voice That Doesn't End: Biography of the Poet Miguel Hernández*] (2014), and his latest project at the moment is *La vida es un tango y te piso bailando* [*Life Is A Tango and I Step on Your Feet While Dancing*] (2015).

Writers Never Score

R. Boldú

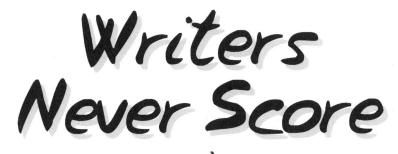

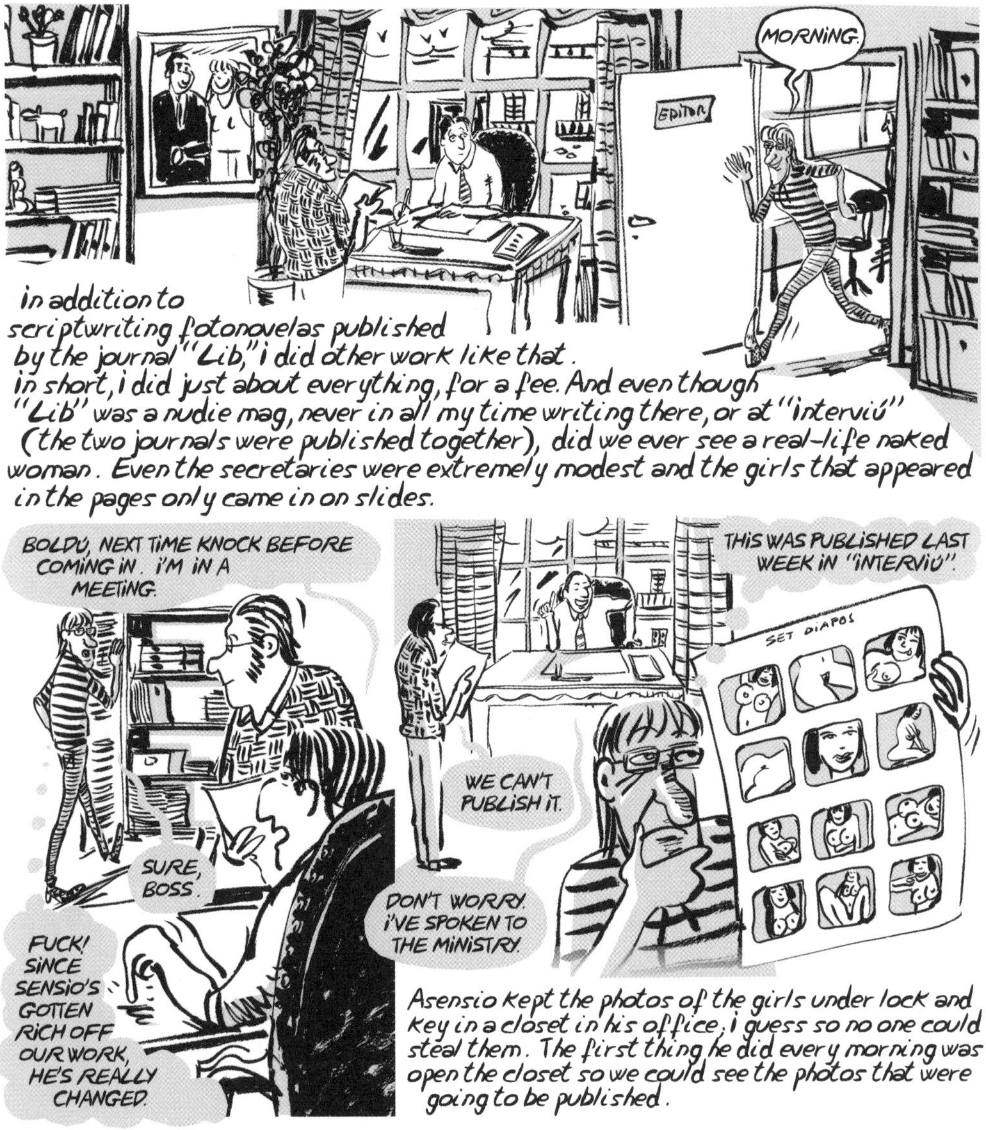
MORNING.
EDITOR
in addition to scriptwriting fotonovelas published by the journal "Lib," i did other work like that. in short, i did just about everything, for a fee. And even though "Lib" was a nudie mag, never in all my time writing there, or at "interviú" (the two journals were published together), did we ever see a real-life naked woman. Even the secretaries were extremely modest and the girls that appeared in the pages only came in on slides.
BOLDÚ, NEXT TIME KNOCK BEFORE COMING IN. I'M IN A MEETING.
SURE, BOSS.
FUCK! SINCE SENSIO'S GOTTEN RICH OFF OUR WORK, HE'S REALLY CHANGED.
THIS WAS PUBLISHED LAST WEEK IN "INTERVIÚ".
SET DIAPOS
WE CAN'T PUBLISH IT.
DON'T WORRY. I'VE SPOKEN TO THE MINISTRY.
Asensio kept the photos of the girls under lock and key in a closet in his office, i guess so no one could steal them. The first thing he did every morning was open the closet so we could see the photos that were going to be published.

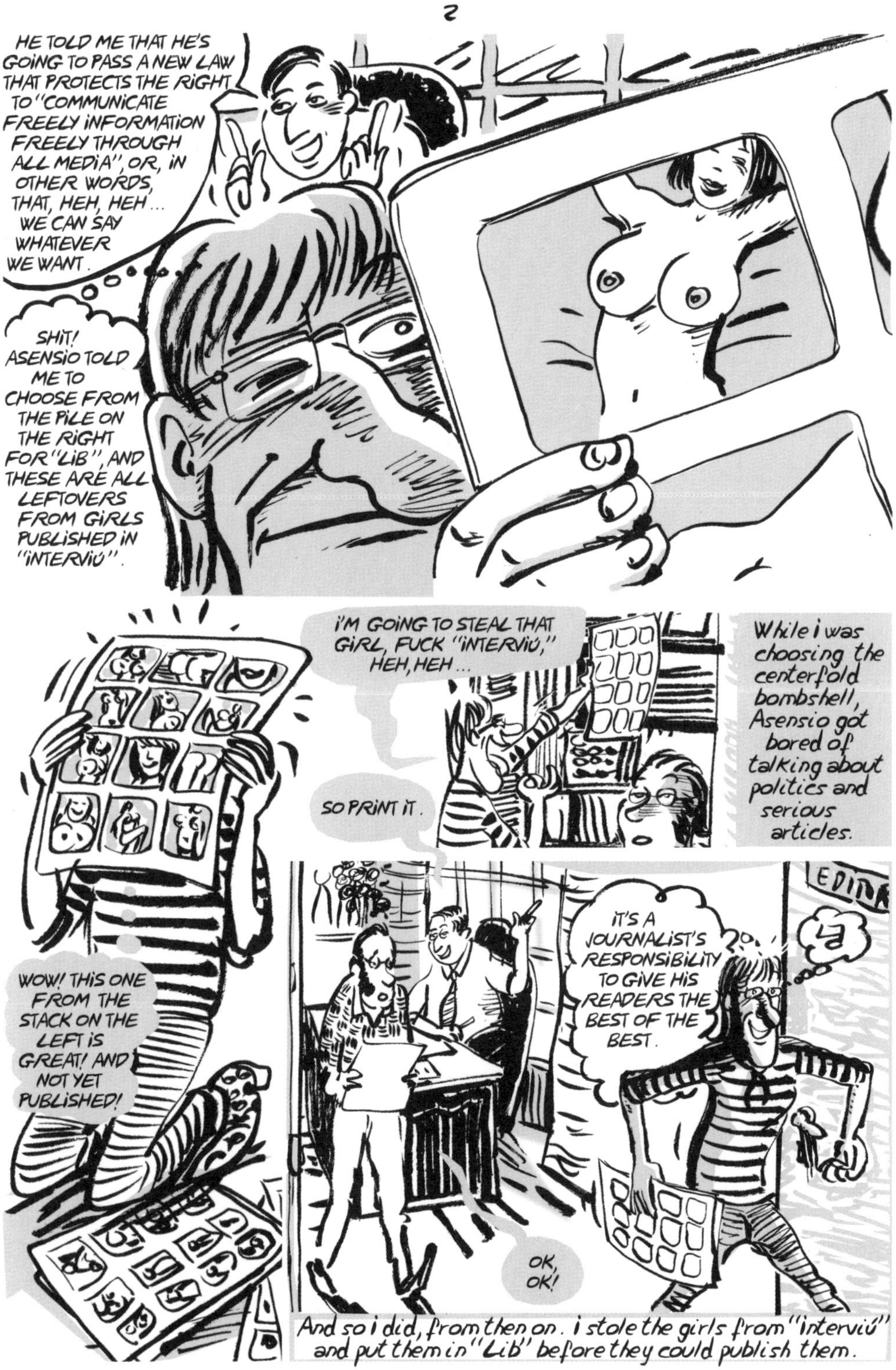
2
HE TOLD ME THAT HE'S GOING TO PASS A NEW LAW THAT PROTECTS THE RIGHT TO "COMMUNICATE FREELY INFORMATION FREELY THROUGH ALL MEDIA", OR, IN OTHER WORDS, THAT, HEH, HEH... WE CAN SAY WHATEVER WE WANT.
SHIT! ASENSIO TOLD ME TO CHOOSE FROM THE PILE ON THE RIGHT FOR "LIB", AND THESE ARE ALL LEFTOVERS FROM GIRLS PUBLISHED IN "INTERVIÚ".
WOW! THIS ONE FROM THE STACK ON THE LEFT IS GREAT! AND NOT YET PUBLISHED!
I'M GOING TO STEAL THAT GIRL, FUCK "INTERVIÚ," HEH, HEH...
SO PRINT IT.
While i was choosing the centerfold bombshell, Asensio got bored of talking about politics and serious articles.
IT'S A JOURNALIST'S RESPONSIBILITY TO GIVE HIS READERS THE BEST OF THE BEST.
OK, OK!
And so i did, from then on. i stole the girls from "interviú" and put them in "Lib" before they could publish them.

3

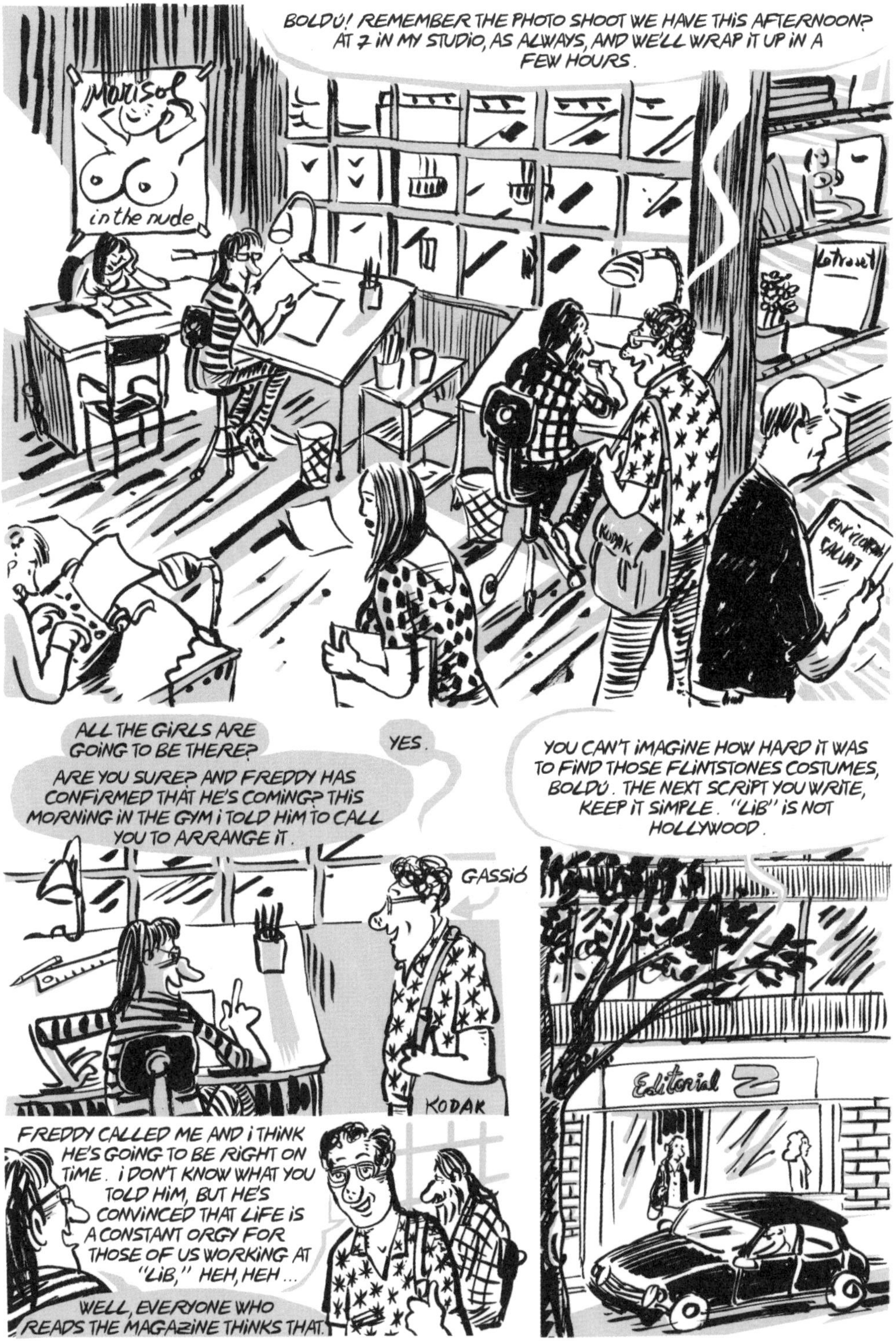
BOLDÚ! REMEMBER THE PHOTO SHOOT WE HAVE THIS AFTERNOON? AT 7 IN MY STUDIO, AS ALWAYS, AND WE'LL WRAP IT UP IN A FEW HOURS.
Marisol
in the nude
KODAK
ALL THE GIRLS ARE GOING TO BE THERE?
ARE YOU SURE? AND FREDDY HAS CONFIRMED THAT HE'S COMING? THIS MORNING IN THE GYM I TOLD HIM TO CALL YOU TO ARRANGE IT.
YES.
GASSIÓ
KODAK
FREDDY CALLED ME AND I THINK HE'S GOING TO BE RIGHT ON TIME. I DON'T KNOW WHAT YOU TOLD HIM, BUT HE'S CONVINCED THAT LIFE IS A CONSTANT ORGY FOR THOSE OF US WORKING AT "LIB," HEH, HEH...
WELL, EVERYONE WHO READS THE MAGAZINE THINKS THAT.
YOU CAN'T IMAGINE HOW HARD IT WAS TO FIND THOSE FLINTSTONES COSTUMES, BOLDÚ. THE NEXT SCRIPT YOU WRITE, KEEP IT SIMPLE. "LIB" IS NOT HOLLYWOOD.
Editorial Z

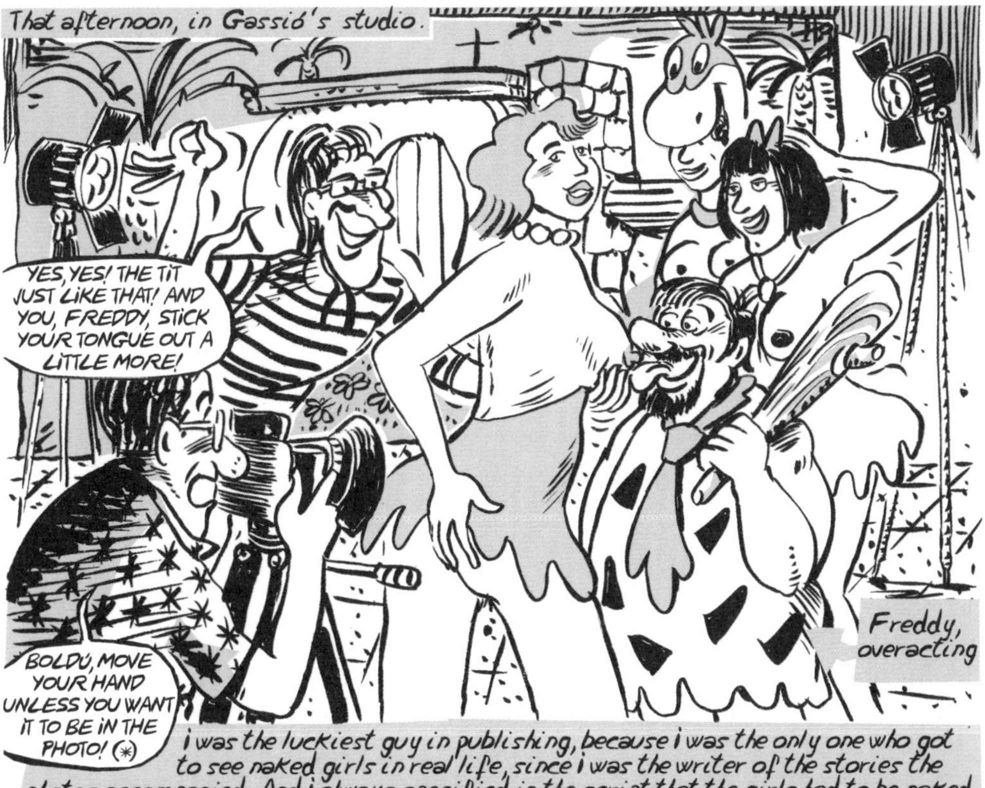
That afternoon, in Gassió's studio.
YES, YES! THE TIT JUST LIKE THAT! AND YOU, FREDDY, STICK YOUR TONGUE OUT A LITTLE MORE!
BOLDÚ, MOVE YOUR HAND UNLESS YOU WANT IT TO BE IN THE PHOTO! (*)
Freddy, overacting
i was the luckiest guy in publishing, because i was the only one who got to see naked girls in real life, since i was the writer of the stories the photos accompanied. And i always specified in the script that the girls had to be naked.

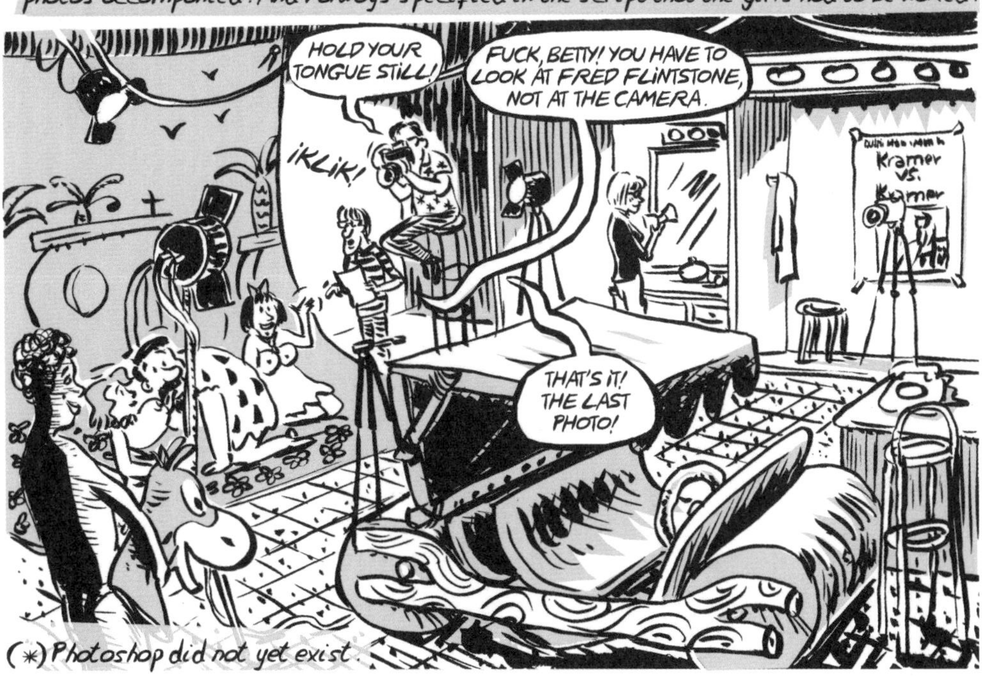
HOLD YOUR TONGUE STILL!
FUCK, BETTY! YOU HAVE TO LOOK AT FRED FLINTSTONE, NOT AT THE CAMERA.
¡KLIK!
Kramer vs. Kramer
THAT'S IT! THE LAST PHOTO!
(*) Photoshop did not yet exist.

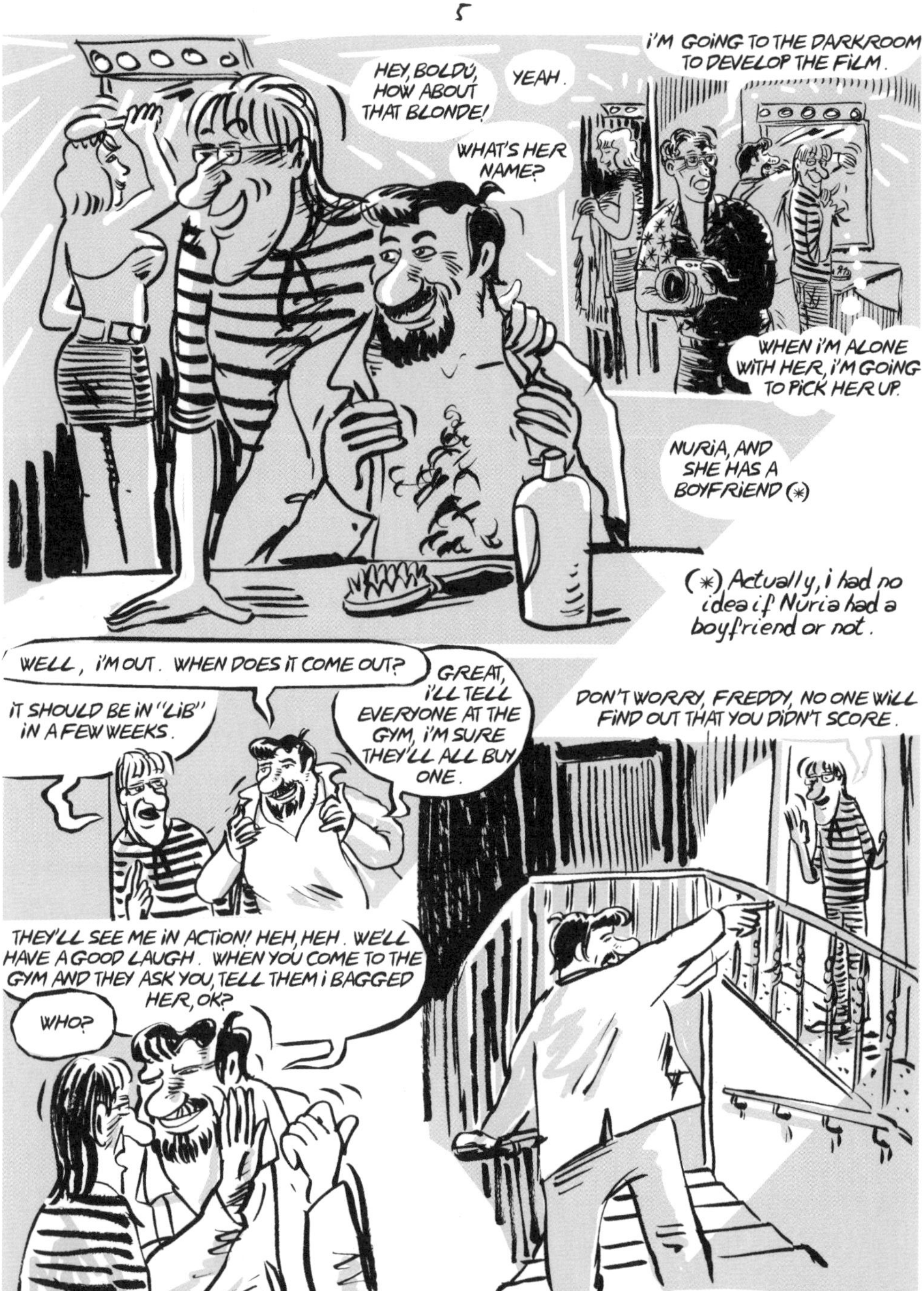
5
HEY, BOLDÚ, HOW ABOUT THAT BLONDE!
YEAH.
WHAT'S HER NAME?
I'M GOING TO THE DARKROOM TO DEVELOP THE FILM.
WHEN I'M ALONE WITH HER, I'M GOING TO PICK HER UP.
NURIA, AND SHE HAS A BOYFRIEND (*)
(*) Actually, i had no idea if Nuria had a boyfriend or not.
WELL, I'M OUT. WHEN DOES IT COME OUT?
IT SHOULD BE IN "LIB" IN A FEW WEEKS.
GREAT, I'LL TELL EVERYONE AT THE GYM, I'M SURE THEY'LL ALL BUY ONE.
THEY'LL SEE ME IN ACTION! HEH, HEH. WE'LL HAVE A GOOD LAUGH. WHEN YOU COME TO THE GYM AND THEY ASK YOU, TELL THEM I BAGGED HER, OK?
WHO?
THE ONE WITH THE HUGE TITS, NURIA.
DON'T WORRY, FREDDY, NO ONE WILL FIND OUT THAT YOU DIDN'T SCORE.
YEAH, I DON'T WANT THEM TO THINK I'M AN ASSHOLE. THEY THINK THIS IS AN ORGY. BUT FUCK, IT'S LIKE A NUNNERY: NAKED, BUT PIOUS.
YEAH.

6

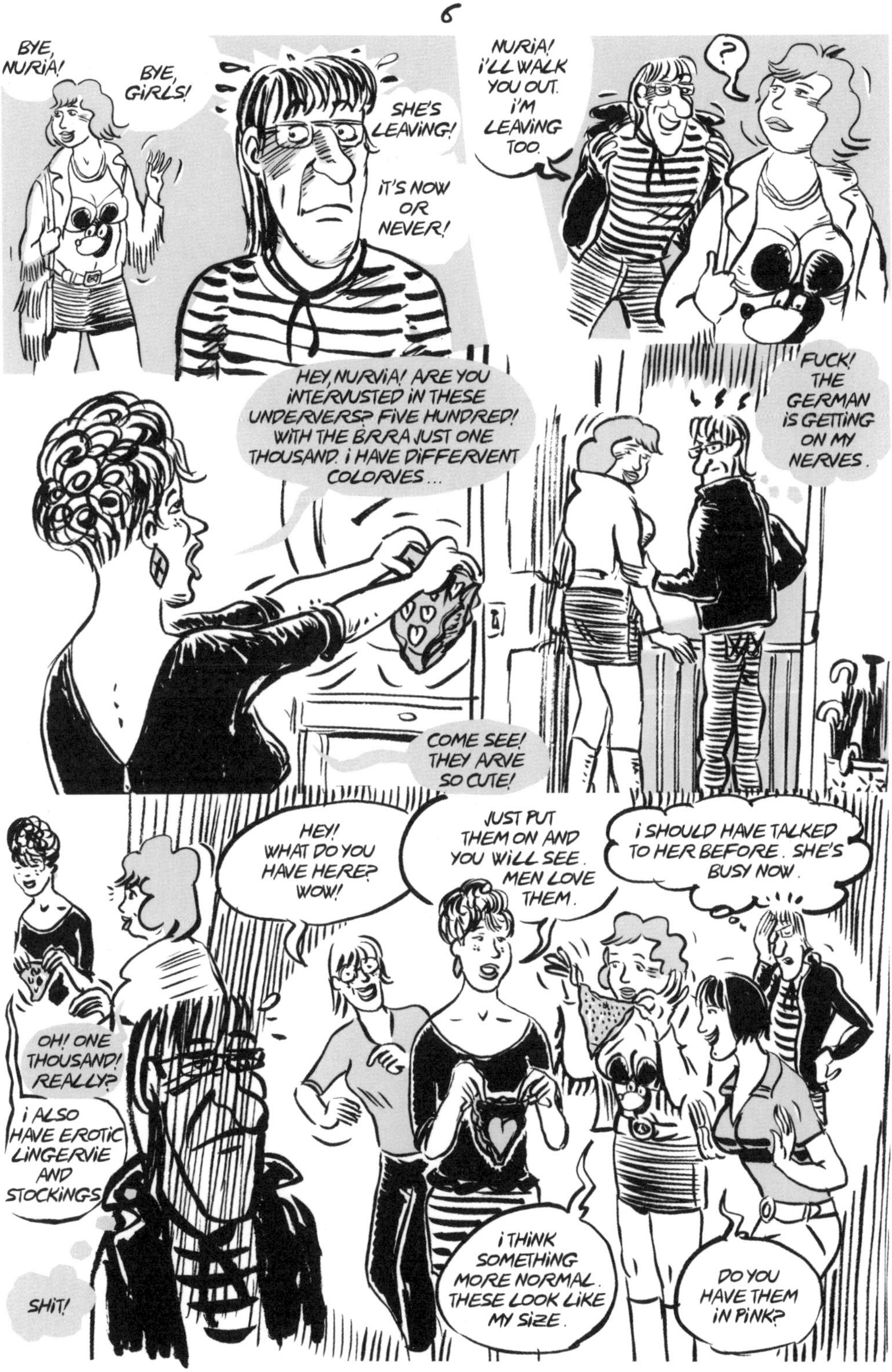

BYE, NURIA!
BYE, GIRLS!
SHE'S LEAVING!
IT'S NOW OR NEVER!
NURIA! I'LL WALK YOU OUT. I'M LEAVING TOO.
?
HEY, NURVIA! ARE YOU INTERVUSTED IN THESE UNDERVERS? FIVE HUNDRED! WITH THE BRRA JUST ONE THOUSAND. I HAVE DIFFERVENT COLORVES...
COME SEE! THEY ARVE SO CUTE!
FUCK! THE GERMAN IS GETTING ON MY NERVES.
OH! ONE THOUSAND! REALLY?
I ALSO HAVE EROTIC LINGERVIE AND STOCKINGS
SHIT!
HEY! WHAT DO YOU HAVE HERE? WOW!
JUST PUT THEM ON AND YOU WILL SEE. MEN LOVE THEM.
I THINK SOMETHING MORE NORMAL. THESE LOOK LIKE MY SIZE.
I SHOULD HAVE TALKED TO HER BEFORE. SHE'S BUSY NOW.
DO YOU HAVE THEM IN PINK?

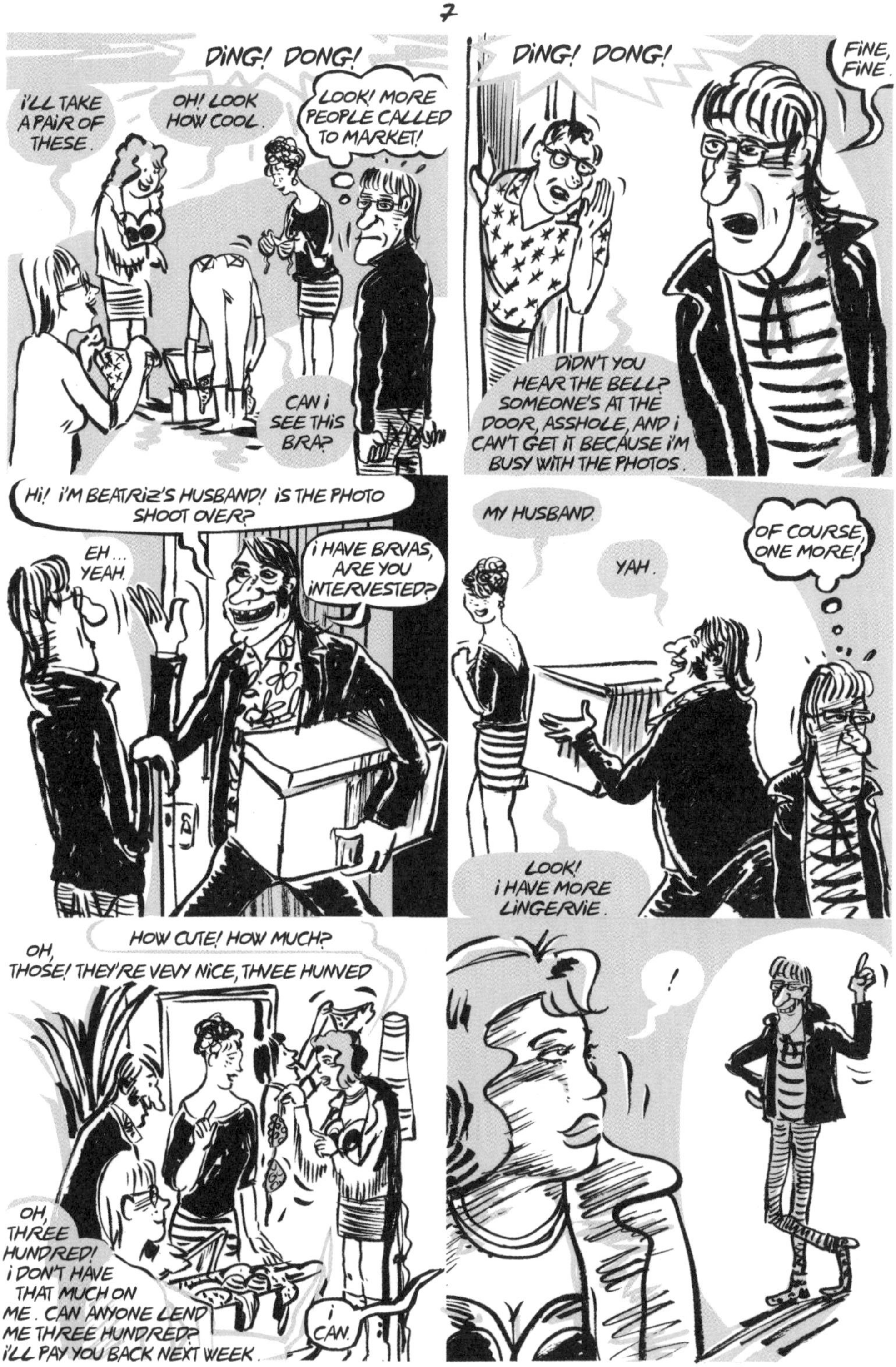
7
DING! DONG!
I'LL TAKE A PAIR OF THESE.
OH! LOOK HOW COOL.
LOOK! MORE PEOPLE CALLED TO MARKET!
CAN I SEE THIS BRA?
DING! DONG!
FINE, FINE.
DIDN'T YOU HEAR THE BELL? SOMEONE'S AT THE DOOR, ASSHOLE, AND I CAN'T GET IT BECAUSE I'M BUSY WITH THE PHOTOS.
HI! I'M BEATRIZ'S HUSBAND! IS THE PHOTO SHOOT OVER?
EH ... YEAH.
I HAVE BRVAS, ARE YOU INTERVESTED?
MY HUSBAND.
YAH.
OF COURSE, ONE MORE!
LOOK! I HAVE MORE LINGERVIE.
HOW CUTE! HOW MUCH?
OH, THOSE! THEY'RE VEVY NICE, THVEE HUNVED
OH, THREE HUNDRED! I DON'T HAVE THAT MUCH ON ME. CAN ANYONE LEND ME THREE HUNDRED? I'LL PAY YOU BACK NEXT WEEK.
I CAN.
!

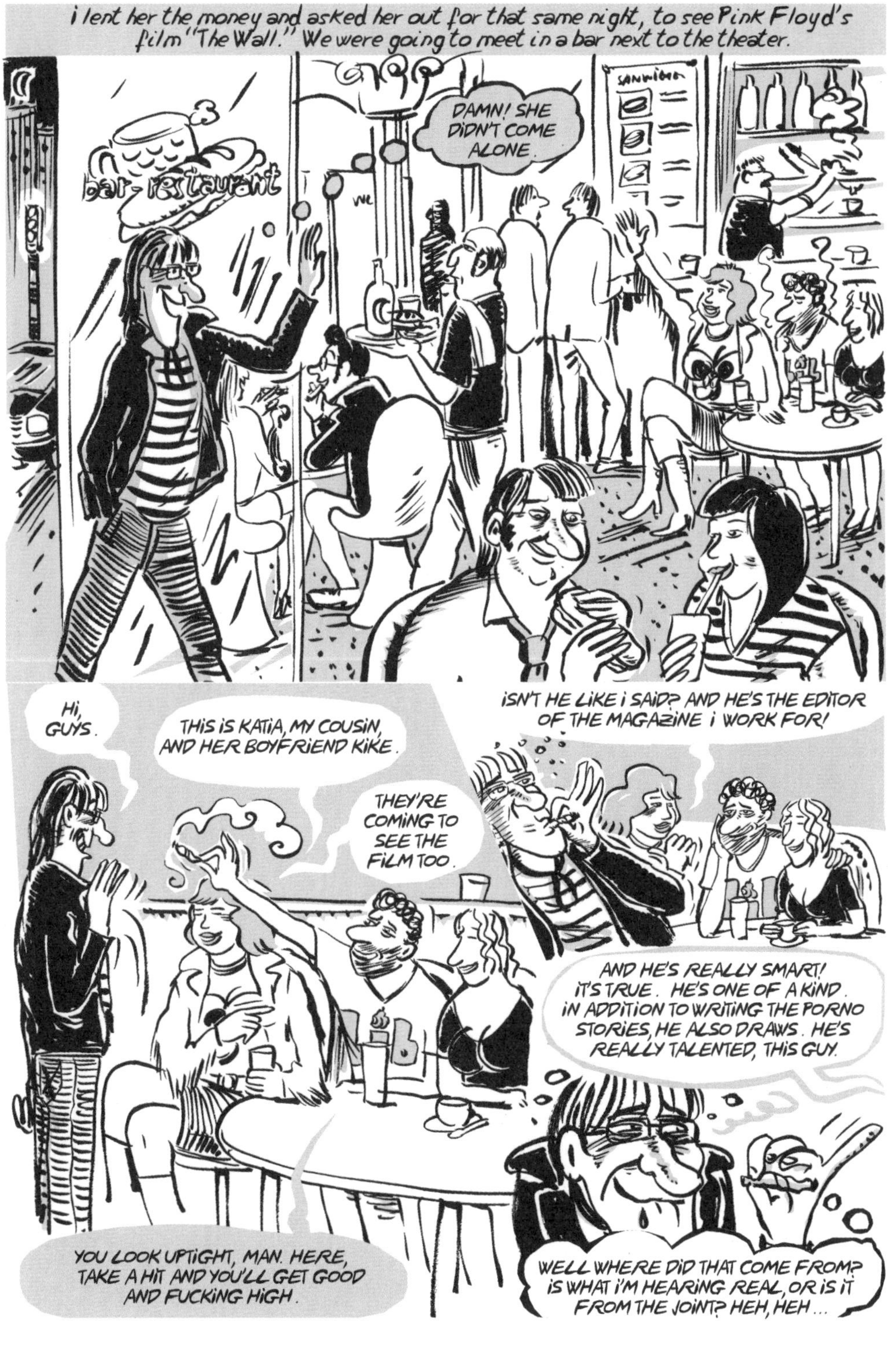
i lent her the money and asked her out for that same night, to see Pink Floyd's film "The Wall." We were going to meet in a bar next to the theater.
bar-restaurant
DAMN! SHE DIDN'T COME ALONE.
HI, GUYS.
THIS IS KATIA, MY COUSIN, AND HER BOYFRIEND KIKE.
THEY'RE COMING TO SEE THE FILM TOO.
YOU LOOK UPTIGHT, MAN. HERE, TAKE A HIT AND YOU'LL GET GOOD AND FUCKING HIGH.
ISN'T HE LIKE I SAID? AND HE'S THE EDITOR OF THE MAGAZINE I WORK FOR!
AND HE'S REALLY SMART! IT'S TRUE. HE'S ONE OF A KIND. IN ADDITION TO WRITING THE PORNO STORIES, HE ALSO DRAWS. HE'S REALLY TALENTED, THIS GUY.
WELL WHERE DID THAT COME FROM? IS WHAT I'M HEARING REAL, OR IS IT FROM THE JOINT? HEH, HEH...

9

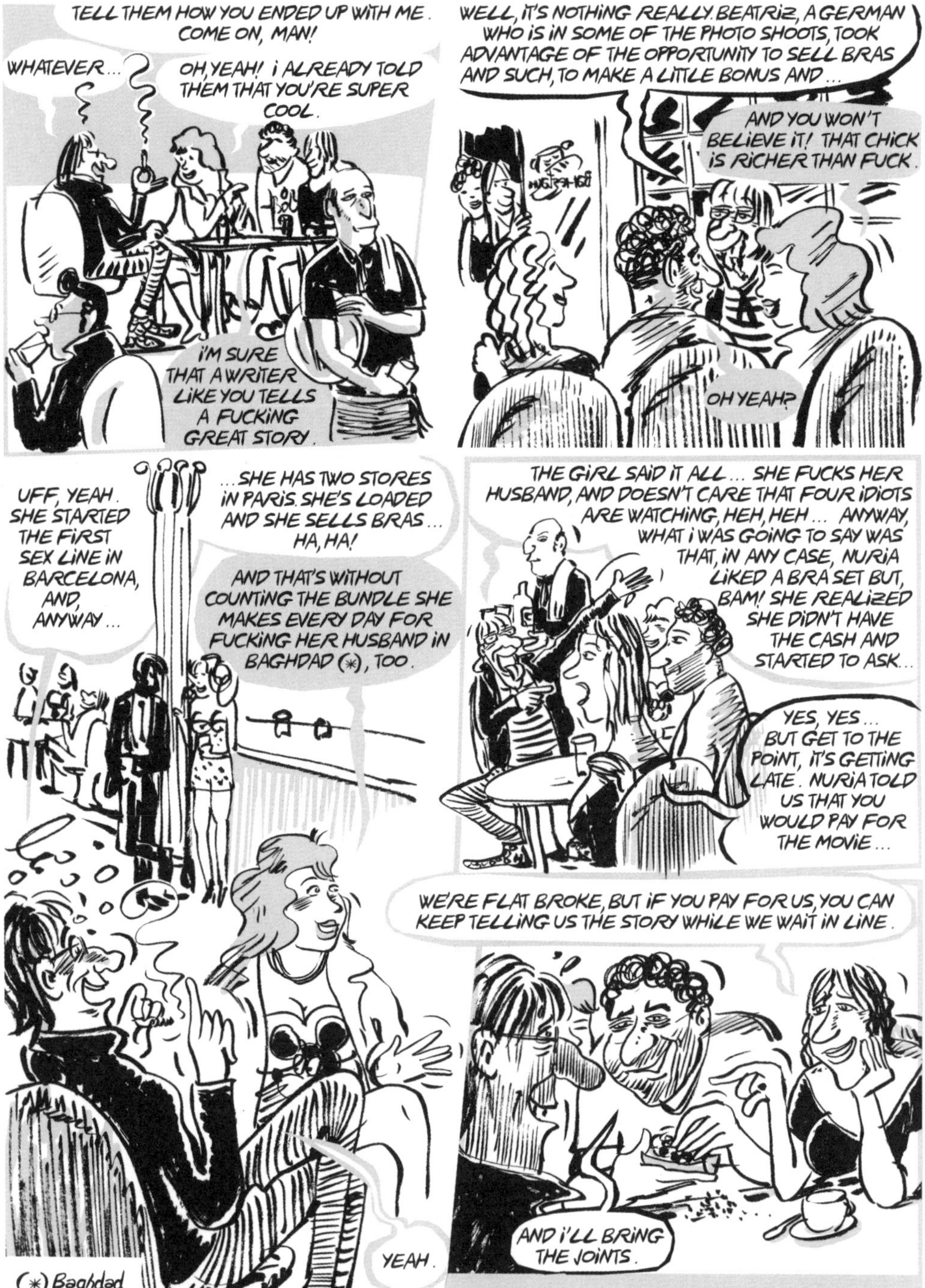
TELL THEM HOW YOU ENDED UP WITH ME. COME ON, MAN!
WHATEVER...
OH, YEAH! I ALREADY TOLD THEM THAT YOU'RE SUPER COOL.
I'M SURE THAT A WRITER LIKE YOU TELLS A FUCKING GREAT STORY.
WELL, IT'S NOTHING REALLY. BEATRIZ, A GERMAN WHO IS IN SOME OF THE PHOTO SHOOTS, TOOK ADVANTAGE OF THE OPPORTUNITY TO SELL BRAS AND SUCH, TO MAKE A LITTLE BONUS AND...
AND YOU WON'T BELIEVE IT! THAT CHICK IS RICHER THAN FUCK.
OH YEAH?
UFF, YEAH. SHE STARTED THE FIRST SEX LINE IN BARCELONA, AND, ANYWAY...
...SHE HAS TWO STORES IN PARIS. SHE'S LOADED AND SHE SELLS BRAS... HA, HA!
AND THAT'S WITHOUT COUNTING THE BUNDLE SHE MAKES EVERY DAY FOR FUCKING HER HUSBAND IN BAGHDAD (*), TOO.
YEAH.
(*) Baghdad was a club famous for having live sex shows.
THE GIRL SAID IT ALL... SHE FUCKS HER HUSBAND, AND DOESN'T CARE THAT FOUR IDIOTS ARE WATCHING, HEH, HEH... ANYWAY, WHAT I WAS GOING TO SAY WAS THAT, IN ANY CASE, NURIA LIKED A BRA SET BUT, BAM! SHE REALIZED SHE DIDN'T HAVE THE CASH AND STARTED TO ASK...
YES, YES... BUT GET TO THE POINT, IT'S GETTING LATE. NURIA TOLD US THAT YOU WOULD PAY FOR THE MOVIE...
WE'RE FLAT BROKE, BUT IF YOU PAY FOR US, YOU CAN KEEP TELLING US THE STORY WHILE WE WAIT IN LINE.
AND I'LL BRING THE JOINTS.
Nuria told me that she'd pay me back for the tickets, and the bras, once the publisher had paid her for the photo shoots.

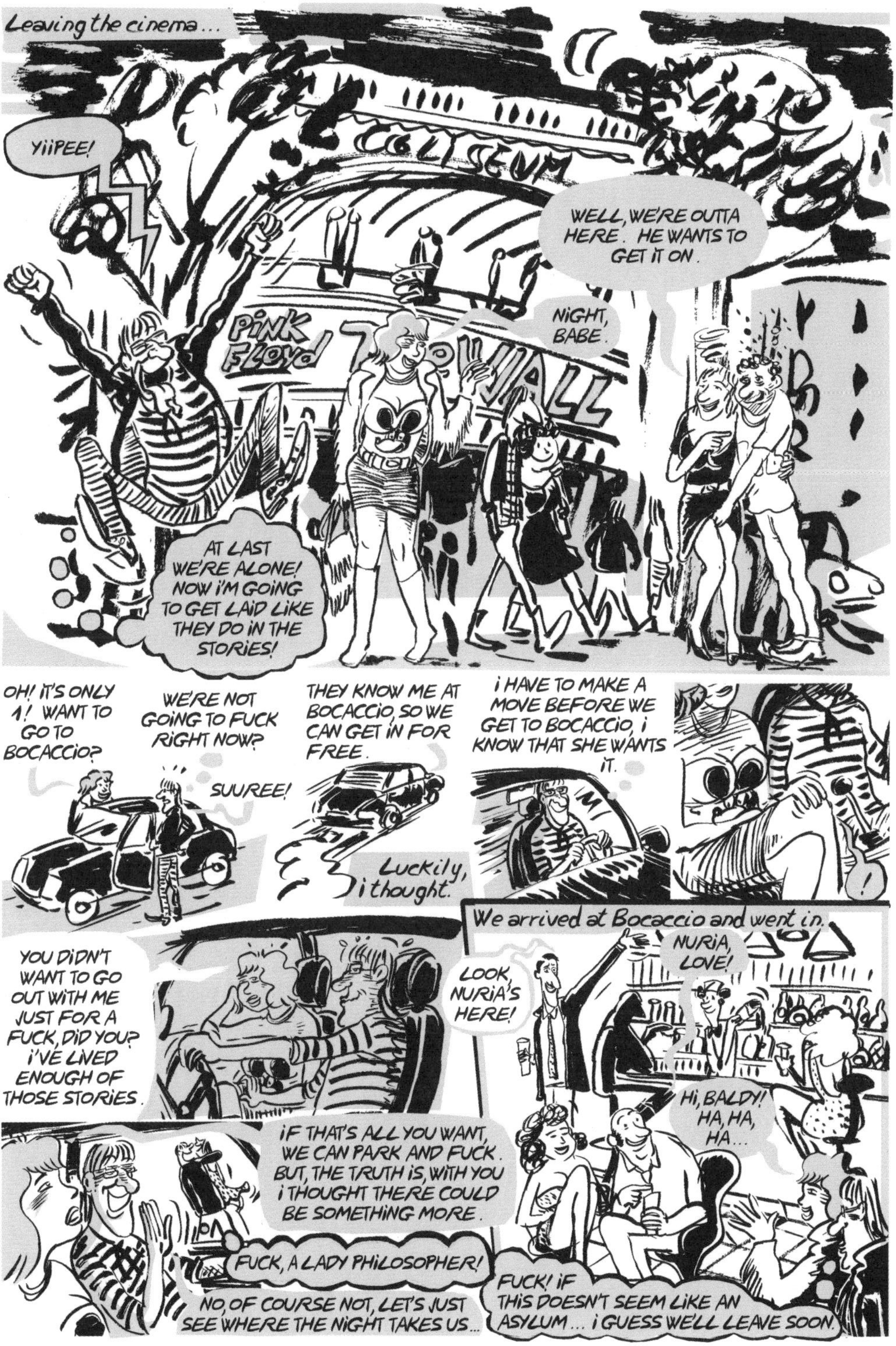
Leaving the cinema...
COLISEUM
YIIPEE!
WELL, WE'RE OUTTA HERE. HE WANTS TO GET IT ON.
NIGHT, BABE.
PINK Floyd
AT LAST WE'RE ALONE! NOW I'M GOING TO GET LAID LIKE THEY DO IN THE STORIES!
OH! IT'S ONLY 1! WANT TO GO TO BOCACCIO?
WE'RE NOT GOING TO FUCK RIGHT NOW?
SUUREE!
THEY KNOW ME AT BOCACCIO, SO WE CAN GET IN FOR FREE.
Luckily, I thought.
I HAVE TO MAKE A MOVE BEFORE WE GET TO BOCACCIO, I KNOW THAT SHE WANTS IT.
!
YOU DIDN'T WANT TO GO OUT WITH ME JUST FOR A FUCK, DID YOU? I'VE LIVED ENOUGH OF THOSE STORIES.
IF THAT'S ALL YOU WANT, WE CAN PARK AND FUCK. BUT, THE TRUTH IS, WITH YOU I THOUGHT THERE COULD BE SOMETHING MORE.
FUCK, A LADY PHILOSOPHER!
NO, OF COURSE NOT, LET'S JUST SEE WHERE THE NIGHT TAKES US...
We arrived at Bocaccio and went in.
LOOK, NURIA'S HERE!
NURIA, LOVE!
HI, BALDY! HA, HA, HA...
FUCK! IF THIS DOESN'T SEEM LIKE AN ASYLUM... I GUESS WE'LL LEAVE SOON.

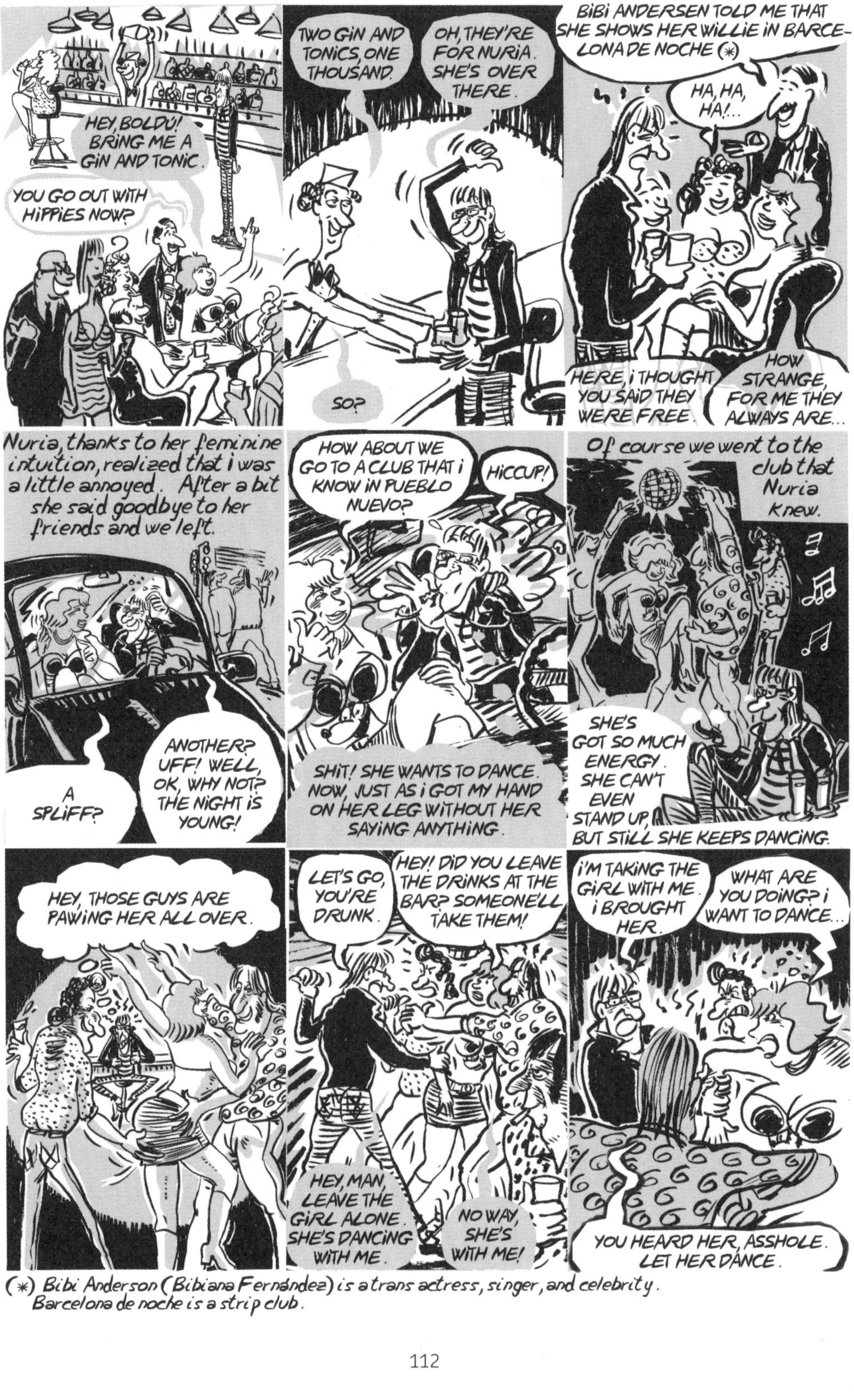
HEY, BOLDÚ! BRING ME A GIN AND TONIC.
YOU GO OUT WITH HIPPIES NOW?
TWO GIN AND TONICS, ONE THOUSAND.
OH, THEY'RE FOR NURIA. SHE'S OVER THERE.
SO?
BIBI ANDERSEN TOLD ME THAT SHE SHOWS HER WILLIE IN BARCELONA DE NOCHE (*)
HA, HA, HA!...
HERE, I THOUGHT YOU SAID THEY WERE FREE.
HOW STRANGE, FOR ME THEY ALWAYS ARE...
Nuria, thanks to her feminine intuition, realized that I was a little annoyed. After a bit she said goodbye to her friends and we left.
A SPLIFF?
ANOTHER? UFF! WELL, OK, WHY NOT? THE NIGHT IS YOUNG!
HOW ABOUT WE GO TO A CLUB THAT I KNOW IN PUEBLO NUEVO?
HICCUP!
SHIT! SHE WANTS TO DANCE. NOW, JUST AS I GOT MY HAND ON HER LEG WITHOUT HER SAYING ANYTHING.
Of course we went to the club that Nuria knew.
SHE'S GOT SO MUCH ENERGY. SHE CAN'T EVEN STAND UP, BUT STILL SHE KEEPS DANCING.
HEY, THOSE GUYS ARE PAWING HER ALL OVER.
LET'S GO, YOU'RE DRUNK.
HEY! DID YOU LEAVE THE DRINKS AT THE BAR? SOMEONE'LL TAKE THEM!
HEY, MAN, LEAVE THE GIRL ALONE. SHE'S DANCING WITH ME.
NO WAY, SHE'S WITH ME!
I'M TAKING THE GIRL WITH ME. I BROUGHT HER.
WHAT ARE YOU DOING? I WANT TO DANCE...
YOU HEARD HER, ASSHOLE. LET HER DANCE.

(*) Bibi Anderson (Bibiana Fernández) is a trans actress, singer, and celebrity. Barcelona de noche is a strip club.

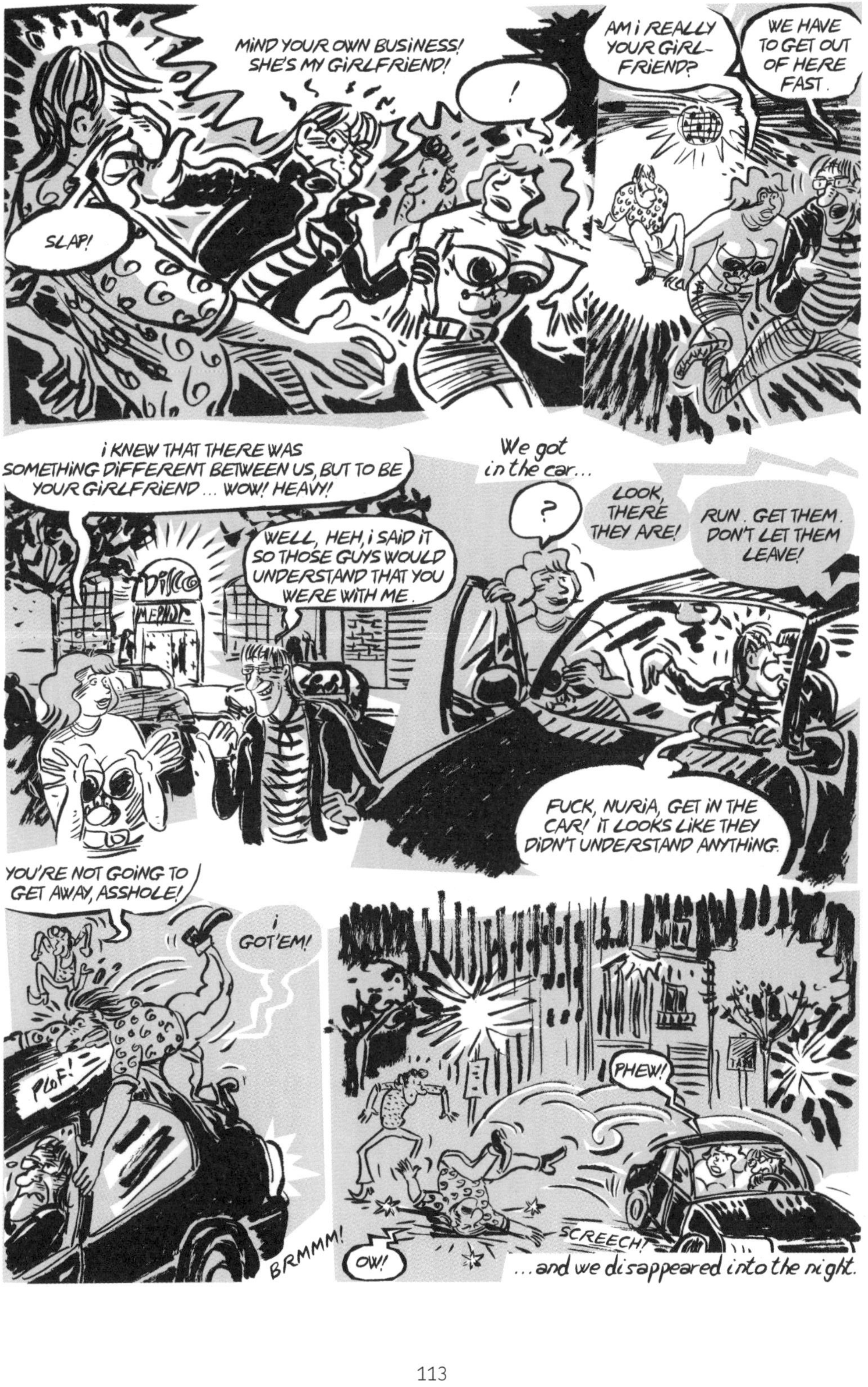
MIND YOUR OWN BUSINESS! SHE'S MY GIRLFRIEND!
SLAP!
!
AM i REALLY YOUR GIRL-FRIEND?
WE HAVE TO GET OUT OF HERE FAST.
i KNEW THAT THERE WAS SOMETHING DIFFERENT BETWEEN US, BUT TO BE YOUR GIRLFRIEND... WOW! HEAVY!
WELL, HEH, i SAID IT SO THOSE GUYS WOULD UNDERSTAND THAT YOU WERE WITH ME.
DISCO
We got in the car...
?
LOOK, THERE THEY ARE!
RUN. GET THEM. DON'T LET THEM LEAVE!
FUCK, NURIA, GET IN THE CAR! IT LOOKS LIKE THEY DIDN'T UNDERSTAND ANYTHING.
YOU'RE NOT GOING TO GET AWAY, ASSHOLE!
i GOT'EM!
PLOF!
BRMMM!
PHEW!
OW!
SCREECH!
...and we disappeared into the night.

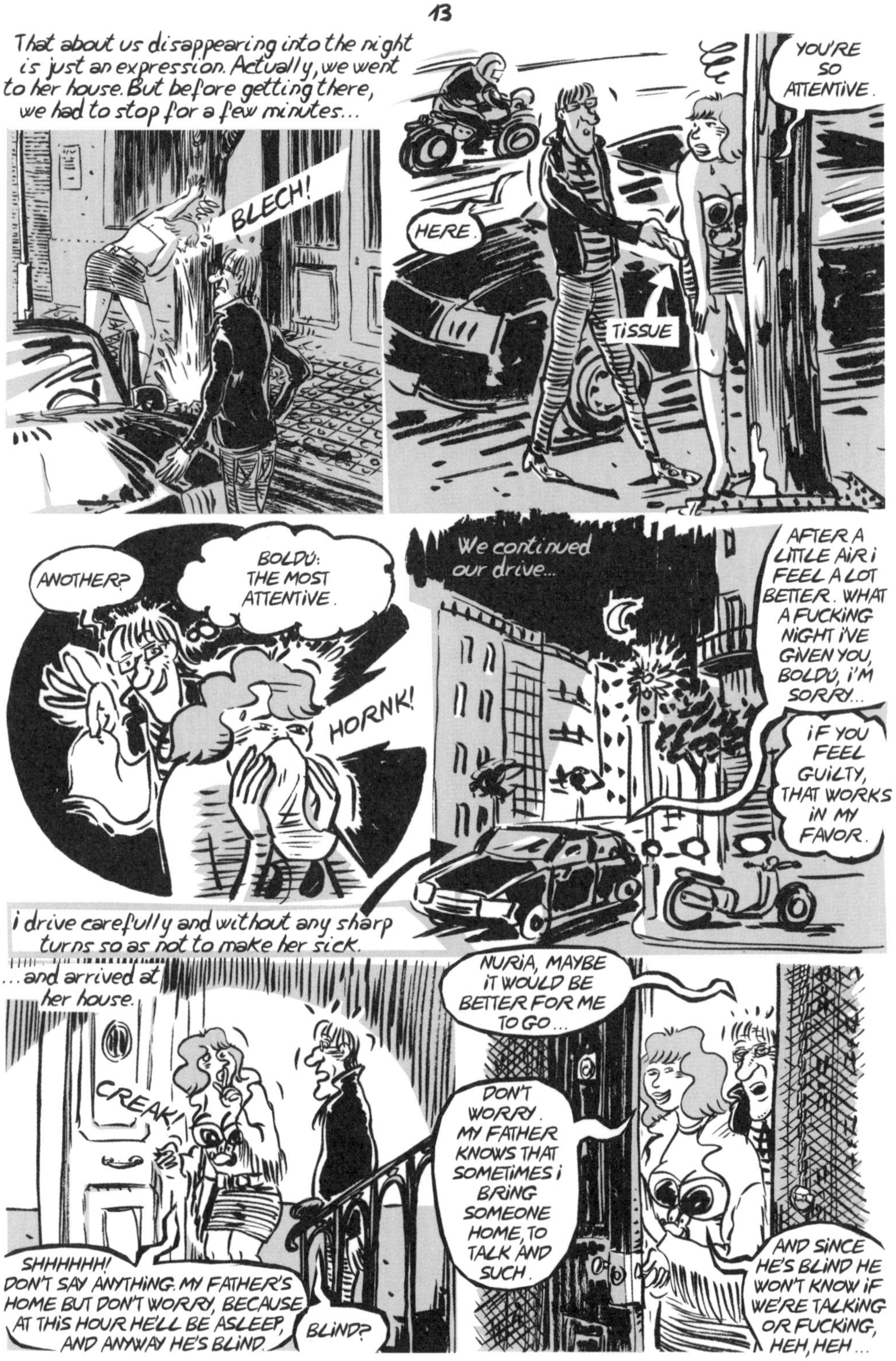
13
That about us disappearing into the night is just an expression. Actually, we went to her house. But before getting there, we had to stop for a few minutes...
BLECH!
YOU'RE SO ATTENTIVE.
HERE.
TISSUE
ANOTHER?
BOLDÚ: THE MOST ATTENTIVE.
HORNK!
We continued our drive...
AFTER A LITTLE AIR I FEEL A LOT BETTER. WHAT A FUCKING NIGHT I'VE GIVEN YOU, BOLDÚ, I'M SORRY...
IF YOU FEEL GUILTY, THAT WORKS IN MY FAVOR.
I drive carefully and without any sharp turns so as not to make her sick.
...and arrived at her house.
CREAK!
SHHHHHH! DON'T SAY ANYTHING. MY FATHER'S HOME BUT DON'T WORRY, BECAUSE AT THIS HOUR HE'LL BE ASLEEP, AND ANYWAY HE'S BLIND.
BLIND?
NURIA, MAYBE IT WOULD BE BETTER FOR ME TO GO...
DON'T WORRY. MY FATHER KNOWS THAT SOMETIMES I BRING SOMEONE HOME, TO TALK AND SUCH.
AND SINCE HE'S BLIND HE WON'T KNOW IF WE'RE TALKING OR FUCKING, HEH, HEH...

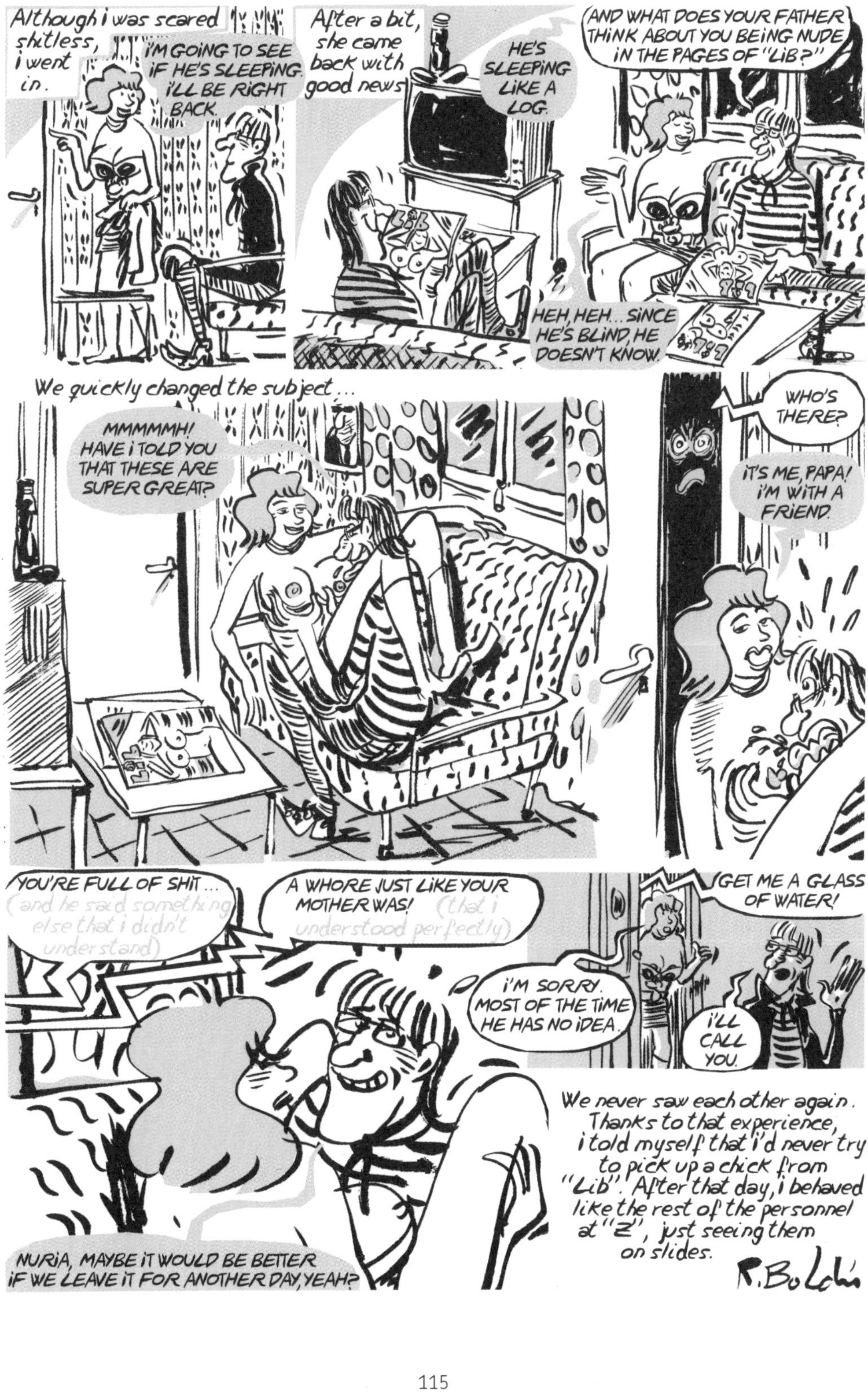
Although i was scared shitless, i went in.
I'M GOING TO SEE IF HE'S SLEEPING. I'LL BE RIGHT BACK.
After a bit, she came back with good news
HE'S SLEEPING LIKE A LOG.
AND WHAT DOES YOUR FATHER THINK ABOUT YOU BEING NUDE IN THE PAGES OF "LIB?"
HEH, HEH... SINCE HE'S BLIND, HE DOESN'T KNOW.
We quickly changed the subject...
MMMMMH! HAVE I TOLD YOU THAT THESE ARE SUPER GREAT?
WHO'S THERE?
IT'S ME, PAPA! I'M WITH A FRIEND.
YOU'RE FULL OF SHIT... (and he said something else that i didn't understand)
A WHORE JUST LIKE YOUR MOTHER WAS! (that i understood perfectly)
NURIA, MAYBE IT WOULD BE BETTER IF WE LEAVE IT FOR ANOTHER DAY, YEAH?
GET ME A GLASS OF WATER!
I'M SORRY. MOST OF THE TIME HE HAS NO IDEA.
I'LL CALL YOU.
We never saw each other again. Thanks to that experience, i told myself that i'd never try to pick up a chick from "Lib". After that day, i behaved like the rest of the personnel at "Z", just seeing them on slides.
R. Bolaño

GABI BELTRÁN
BARTOLOMÉ SEGUÍ
MATHEMATICS

Gabi Beltrán was born in Palma de Mallorca in 1966. An author, scriptwriter, and illustrator, he has contributed to newspapers like *El País* and *Público* and has published comics in the magazine *NSLM*.

Bartolomé Seguí was born in Palma de Mallorca in 1962. He became an illustrator and professional cartoonist starting in the '80s, with his work appearing in magazines like *Metropol*, *El Vibora*, *Cairo*, *El Jueves*, *Madriz*, and NSLM. *A salto de mata* [*Hand to Mouth*] (1989) was the first of many comic books he published. With *Las serpientes ciegas* [*The Blind Serpents*] (2008), together with scriptwriter Felipe Hernández Cava, he won the Premio Nacional de Cómic. His collaboration with Hernández Cava continued in *Hágase el caos* [*Let There be Chaos*] (2011–2012) and *Las oscuras manos del olvido* [*The Dark Hands of Forgetting*] (2014), a history of terrorism.

Beltrán and Seguí have collaborated on *Historias del barrio* [*Neighborhood Stories*] (2011) and *Historias del barrio. Caminos* [*Neighborhood Stories: Streets*] (2014), a series of stories based on the childhood memories of Beltrán, has been translated into French and German. The following story is from the second volume in the series.

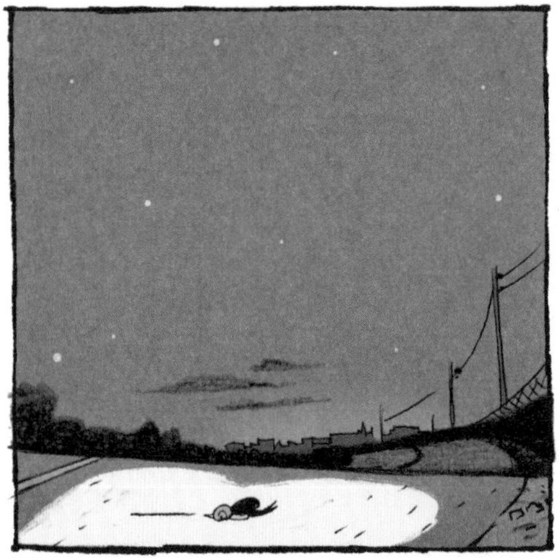

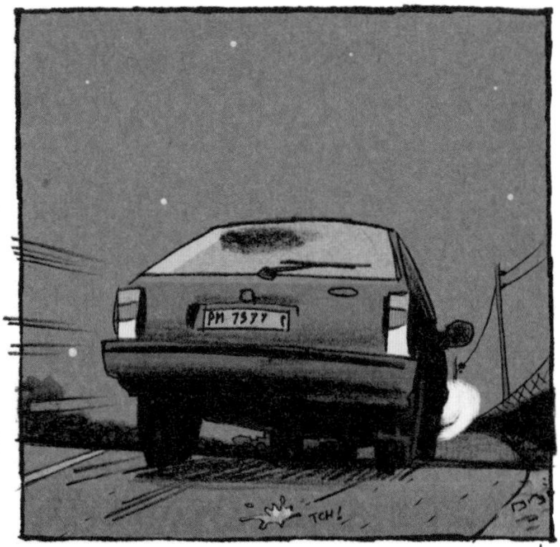
TCH!

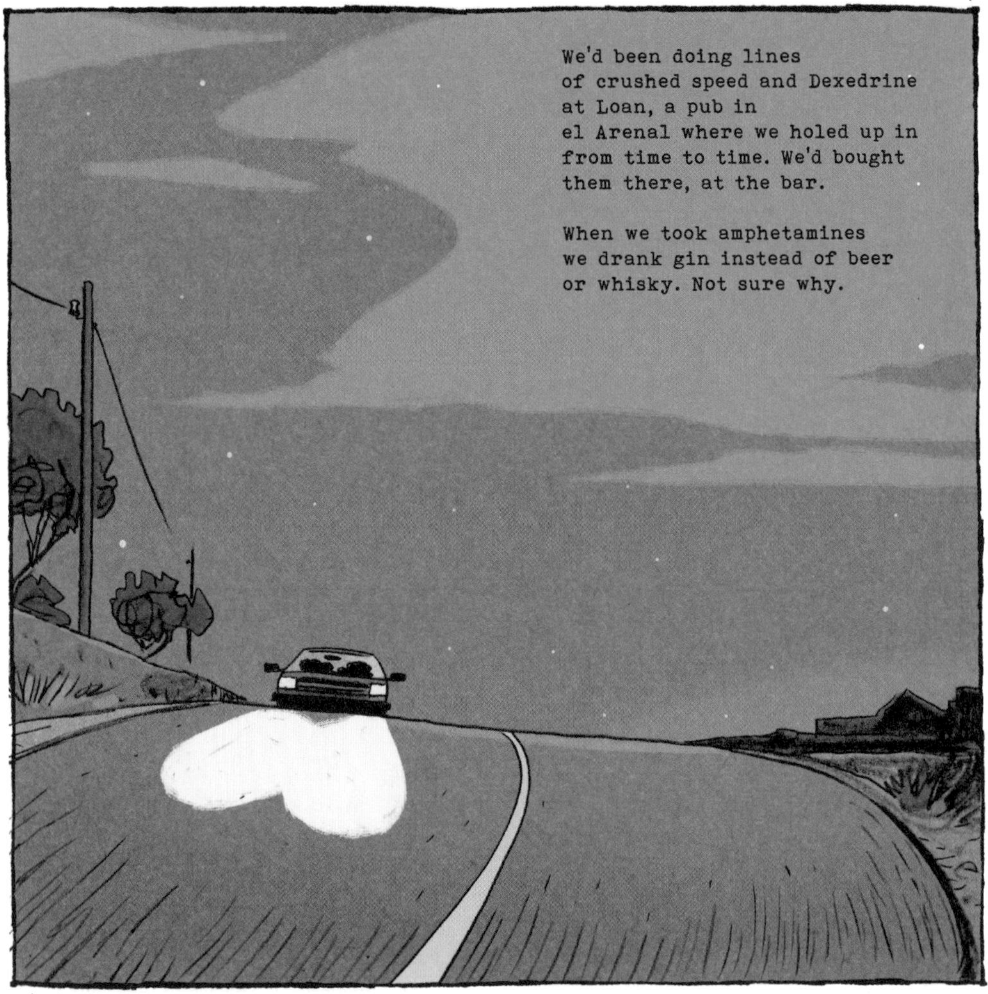
We'd been doing lines
of crushed speed and Dexedrine
at Loan, a pub in
el Arenal where we holed up in
from time to time. We'd bought
them there, at the bar.

When we took amphetamines
we drank gin instead of beer
or whisky. Not sure why.

It was 3 in the morning and we'd stolen a car to get back to Palma.

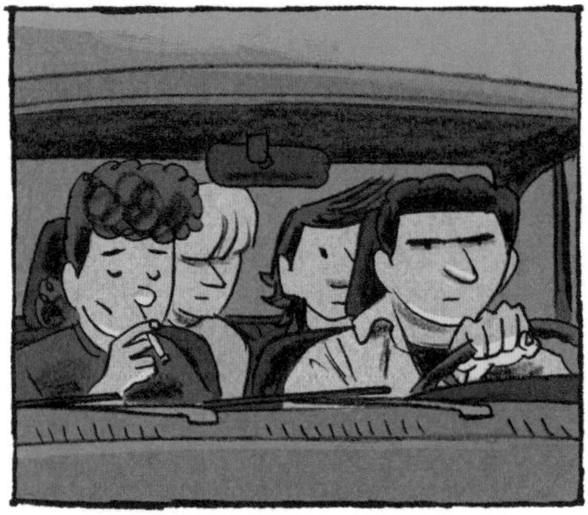

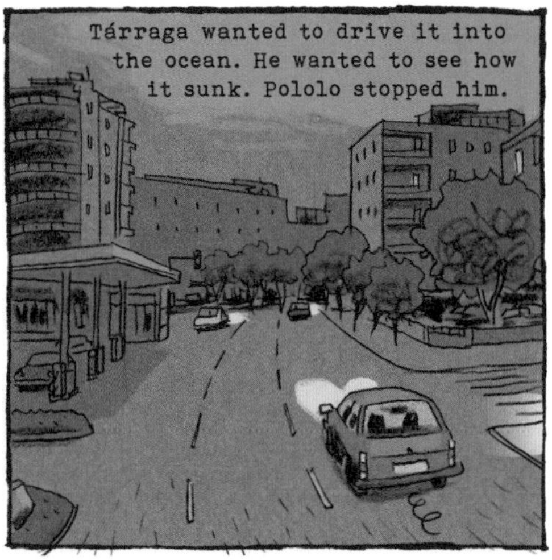
Tárraga wanted to drive it into the ocean. He wanted to see how it sunk. Pololo stopped him.

The other guys had stayed at Loan. Tárraga, Sáez, Pololo, and I went back to Palma and left the car parked in an alley off the main avenue.

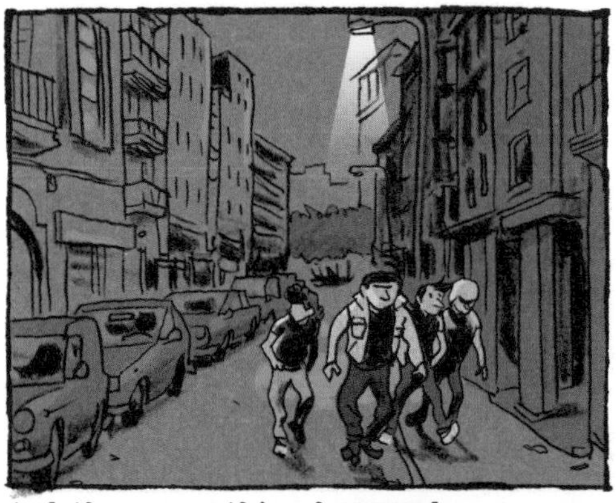

We walked through the Plaza de España on the way home.

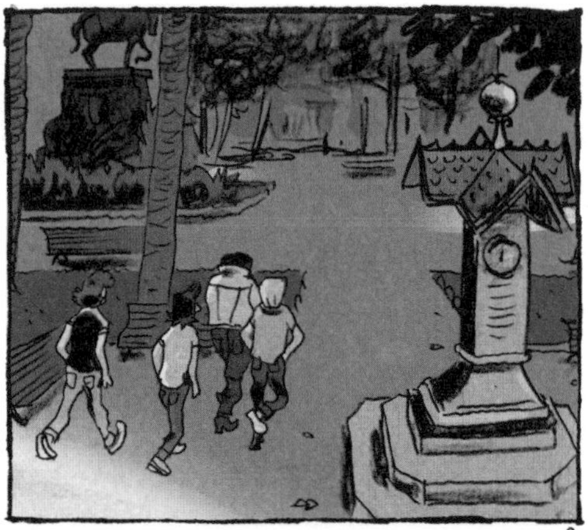

And then everything happened.

2

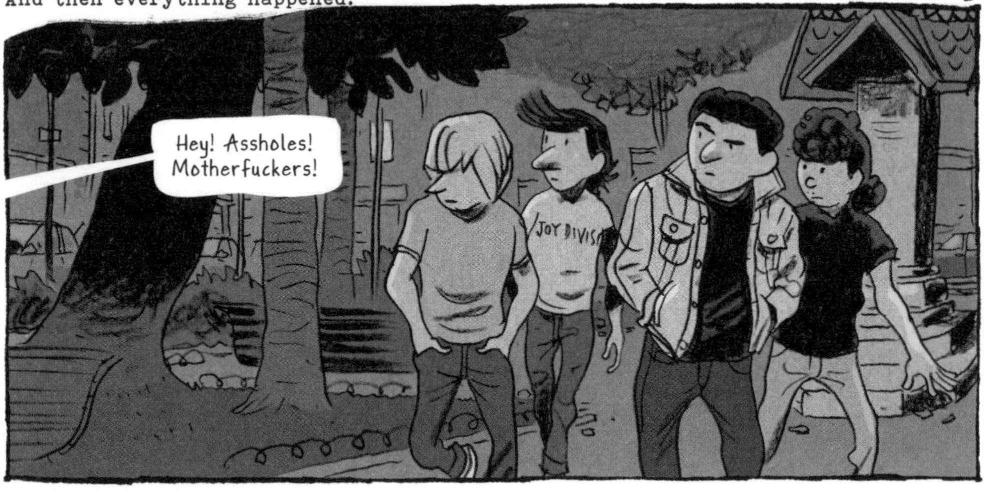
Hey! Assholes! Motherfuckers!
JOY DIVIS

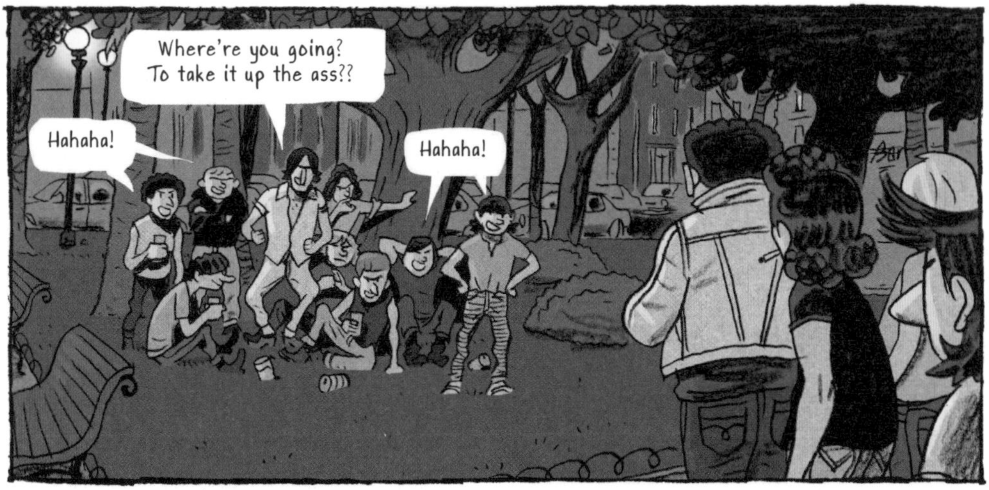
Hahaha!
Where're you going? To take it up the ass??
Hahaha!

I didn't know who they were. I'd never seen them before. But I knew who Sáez and Tárraga were.

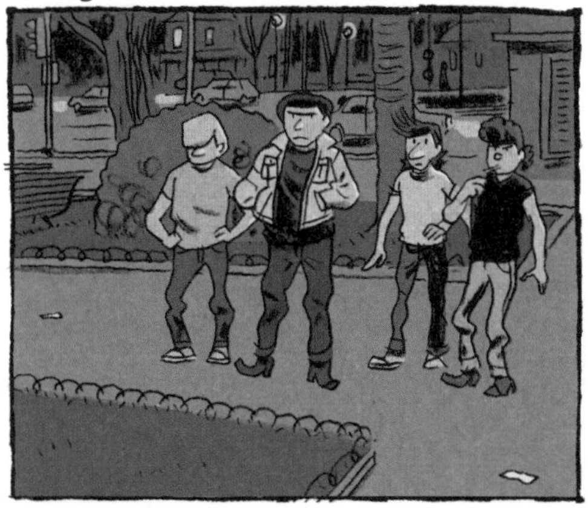

And I also knew this wouldn't end well.

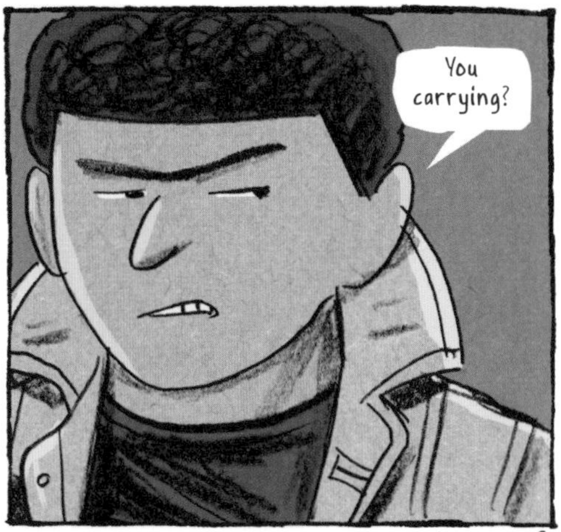
You carrying?

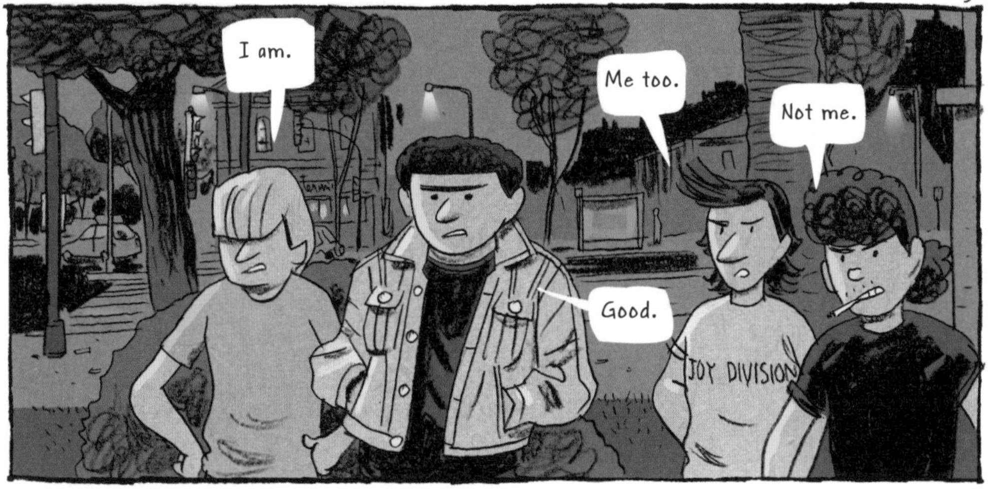
I am.
Good.
Me too.
Not me.
JOY DIVISION

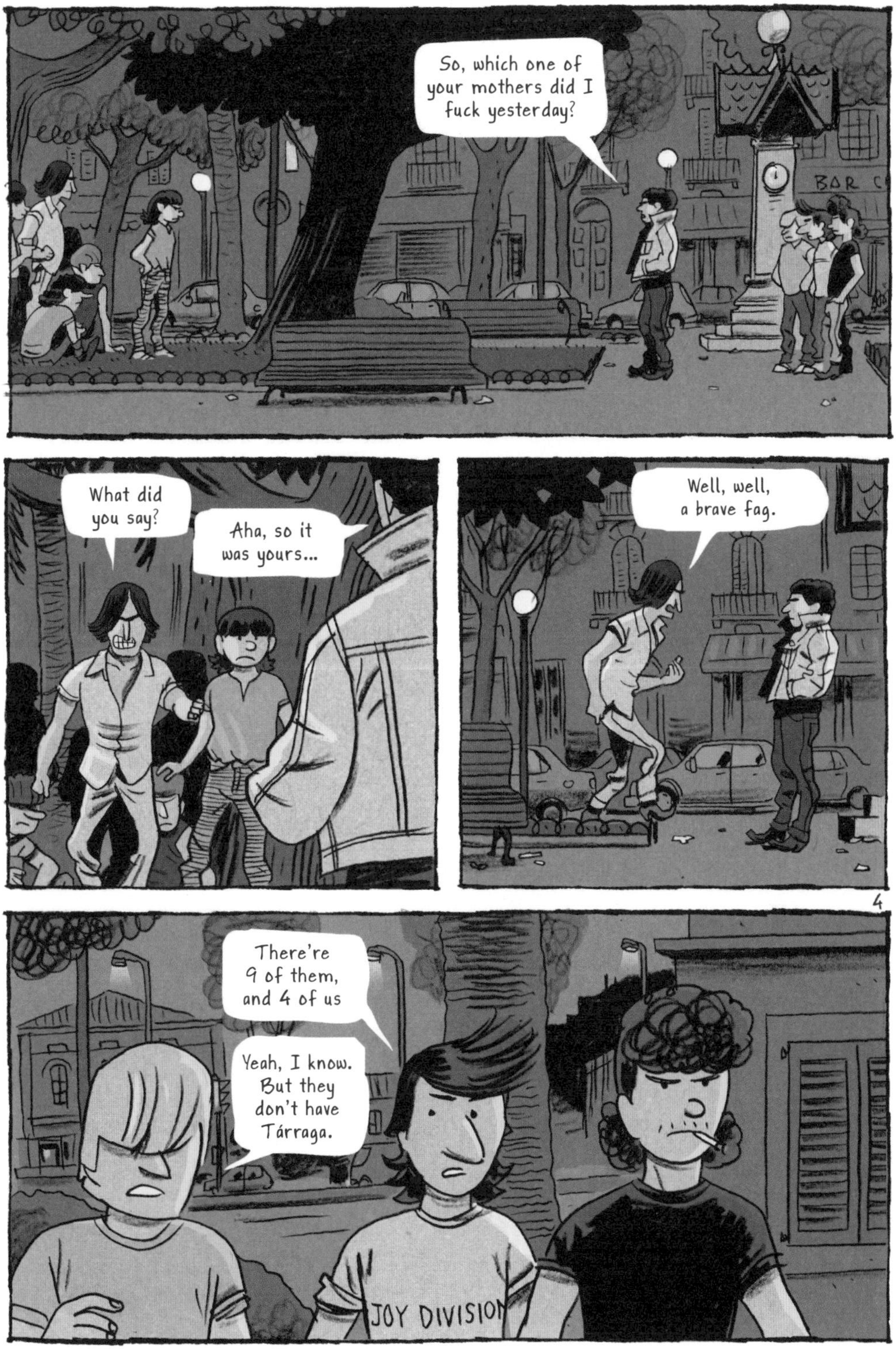
So, which one of your mothers did I fuck yesterday?
BAR
What did you say?
Aha, so it was yours...
Well, well, a brave fag.
4
There're 9 of them, and 4 of us
Yeah, I know. But they don't have Tárraga.
JOY DIVISIO

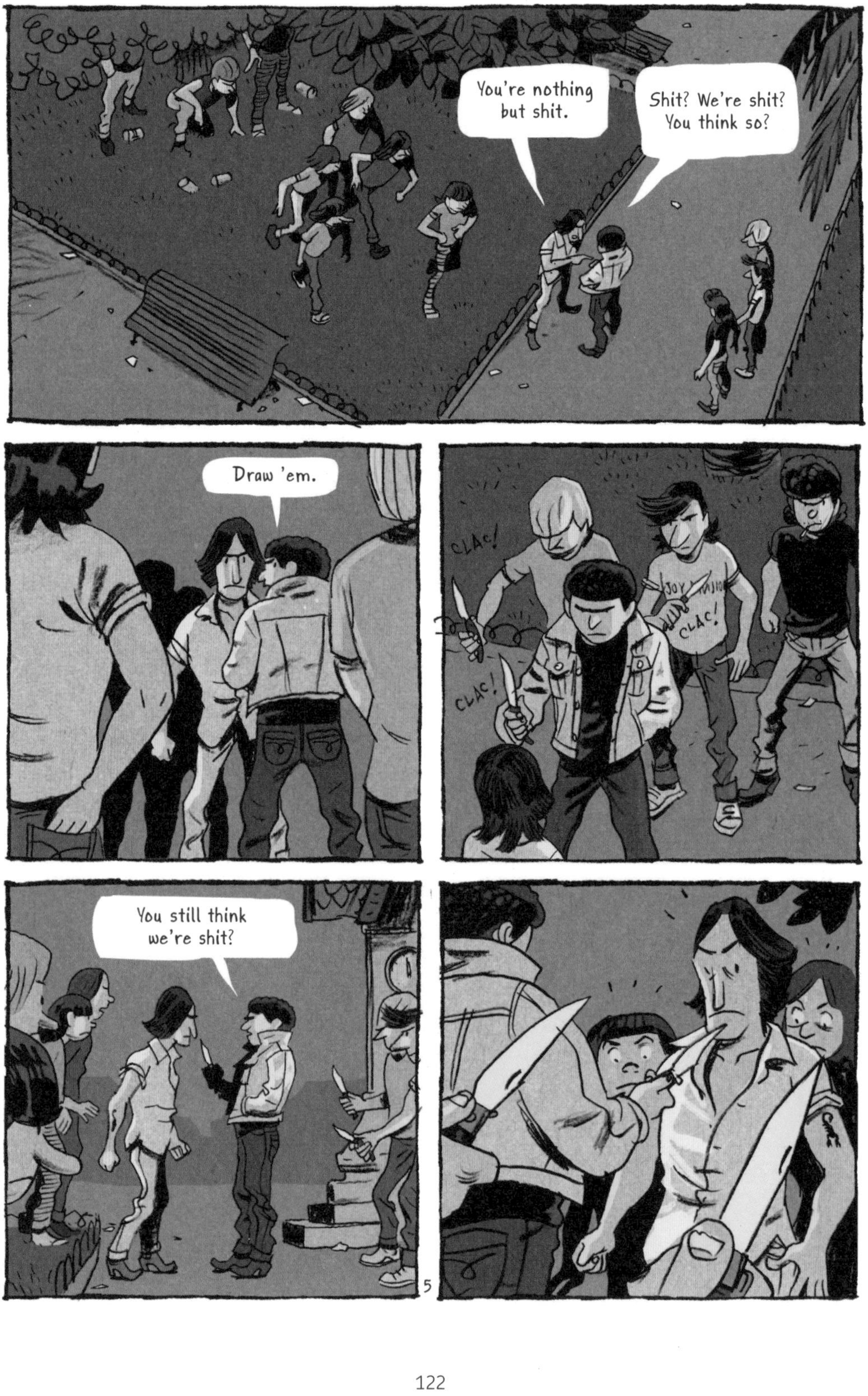
You're nothing but shit.
Shit? We're shit? You think so?
Draw 'em.
CLAC!
CLAC!
CLAC!
You still think we're shit?

The guy was as tall and strong as Tárraga, and as much of an asshole. But he had a weakness that my friend lacked: he wasn't a psychopath.
How about you and me, one on one, on the grass, unarmed?
And he wasn't very smart.
Fine. You and me.
I could see the fear on their faces. There were only four of us, but we weren't running. And when you're at a disadvantage and you don't run, it's because you're willing to go all the way.

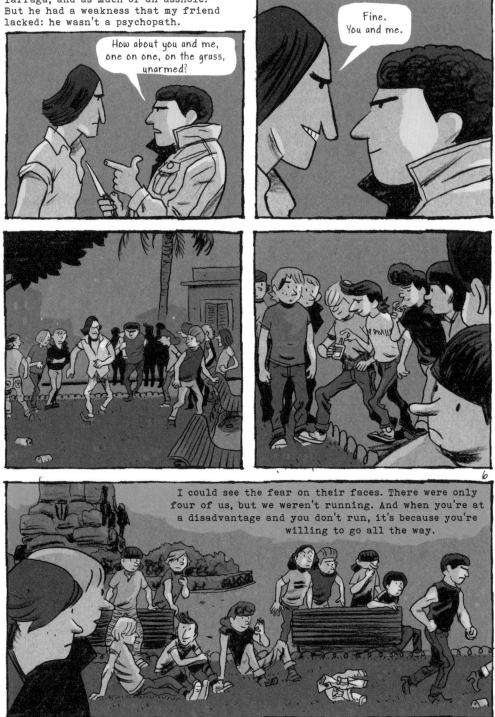

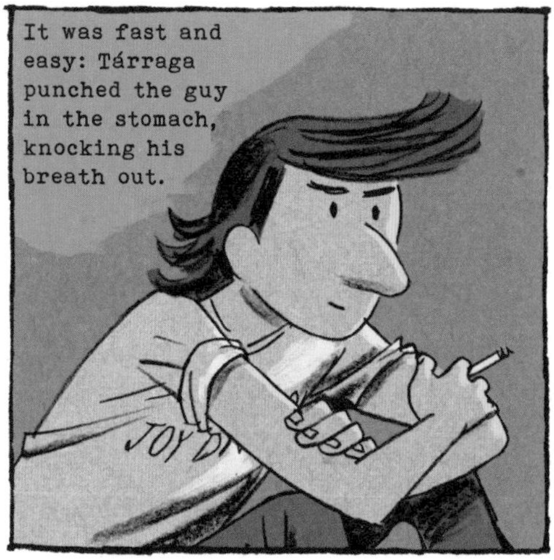
It was fast and easy: Tárraga punched the guy in the stomach, knocking his breath out.

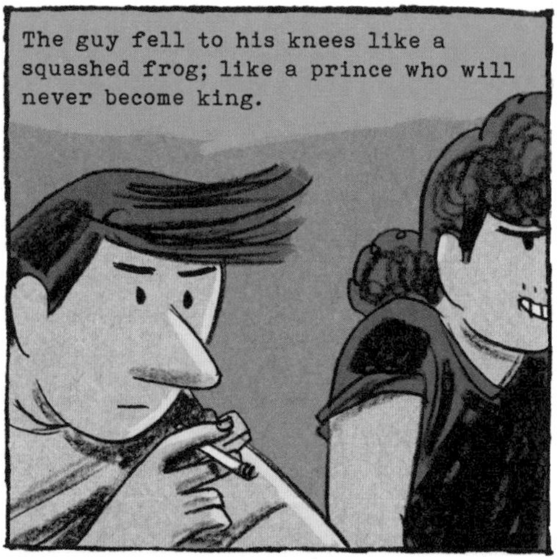
The guy fell to his knees like a squashed frog; like a prince who will never become king.

Tárraga backed away from him a few feet. I watched the guy start drooling and coughing.

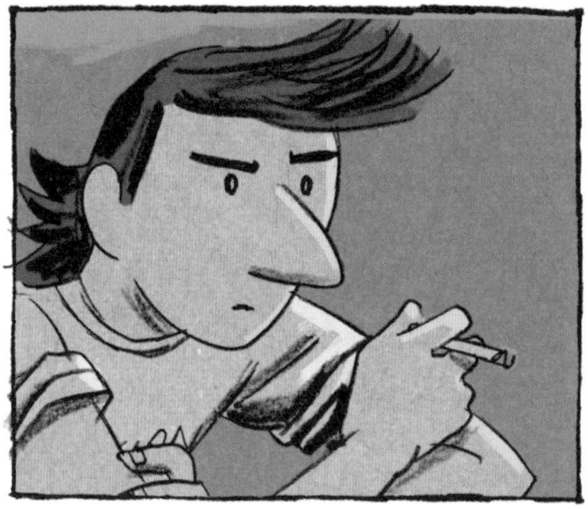

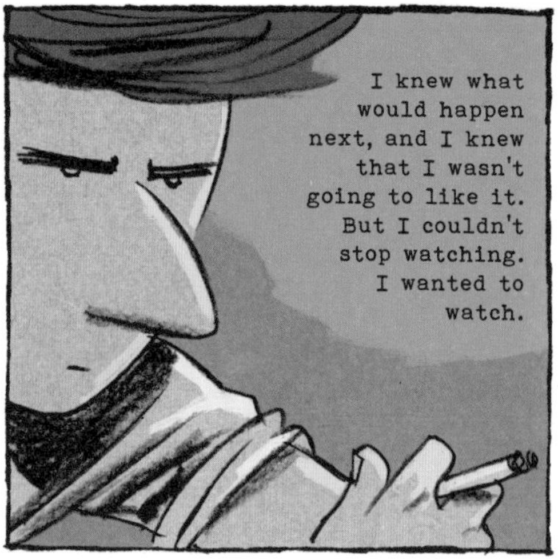
I knew what would happen next, and I knew that I wasn't going to like it. But I couldn't stop watching. I wanted to watch.

I wanted to see that asshole defeated. I wanted to see his stupidity and pride crushed.

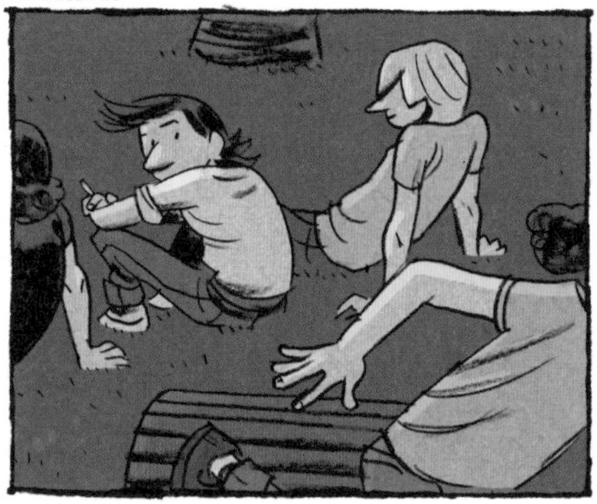

I wanted to see how 4 could beat 9 if you knew how to play your cards.

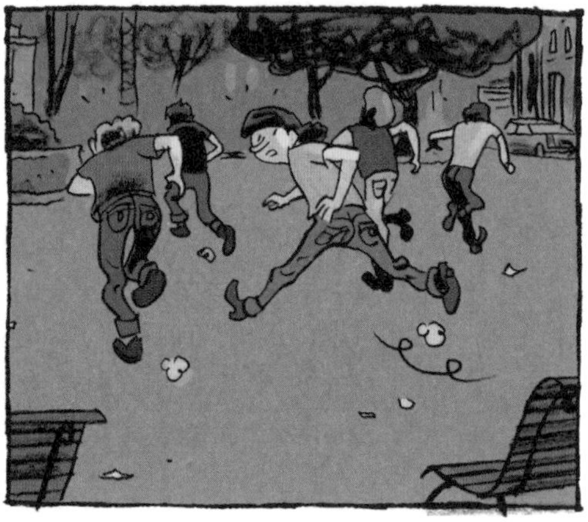

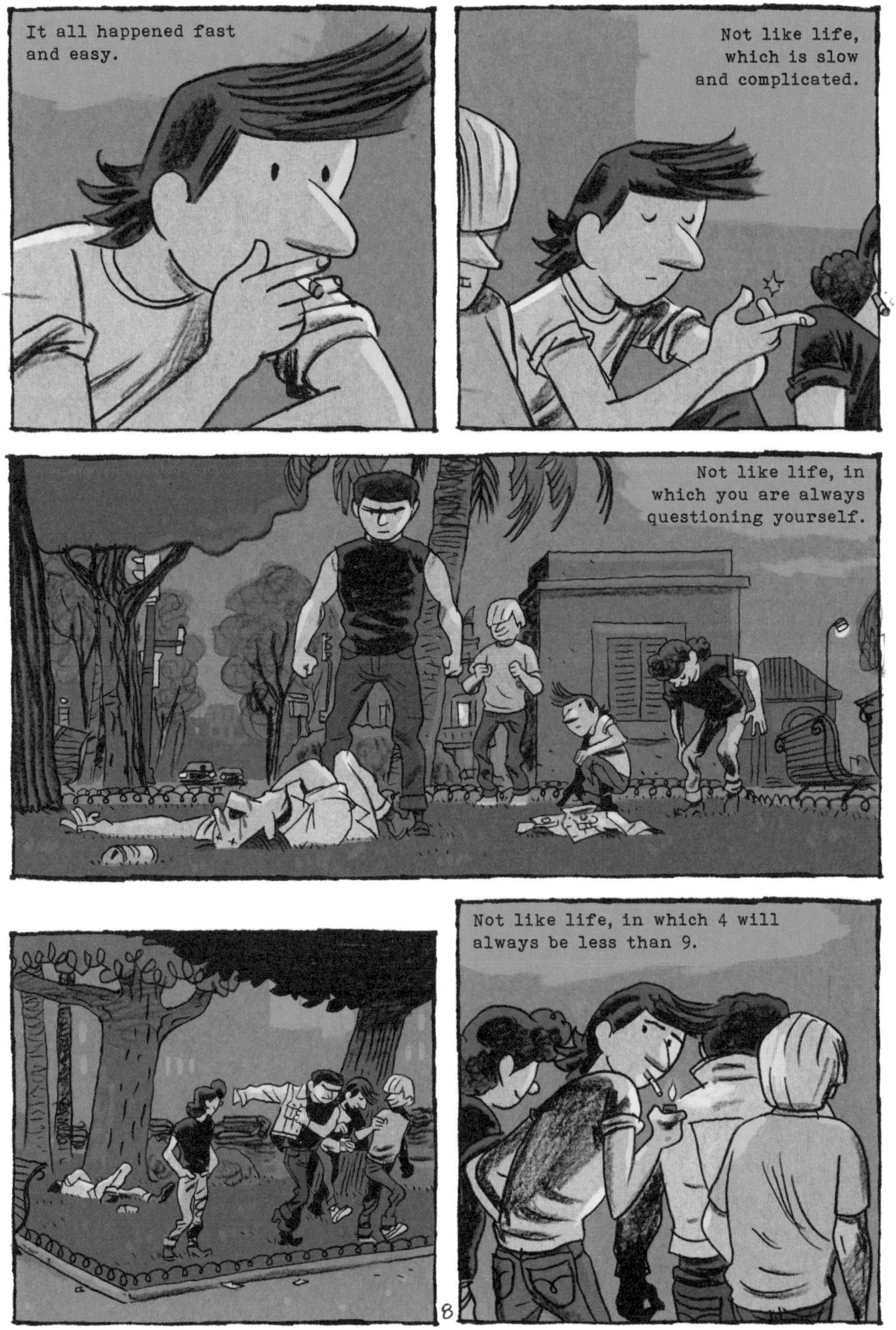
It all happened fast and easy.
Not like life, which is slow and complicated.
Not like life, in which you are always questioning yourself.
Not like life, in which 4 will always be less than 9.

DAVID SÁNCHEZ

MENTAL

David Sánchez was born in Madrid in 1977. He's an illustrator and designer who has worked with publications like *Rolling Stone*, *EP3*, and *Man*. He designs the covers for the publication *Errata Naturae*. He's responsible for the illustrations of the popular shirt line Mong. His first graphic novel, *Tú me has matado* [*You've Killed Me*] (2010), was followed by *No cambies nunca* [*Never Change*] (2013), *La muerte en los ojos* [*Death In The Eyes*] (2012) and *Videojuegos* [*Video games*] (2013). In 2014 he illustrated *Con dos huevos* [*With Two Eggs*], written by Héloïse Guerrier. In 2015, he also illustrated the book *Paul está muerto y otras leyendas urbanas del rock* [*Paul is Dead and other Rock Urban Legends*] written by Héctor Sánchez.

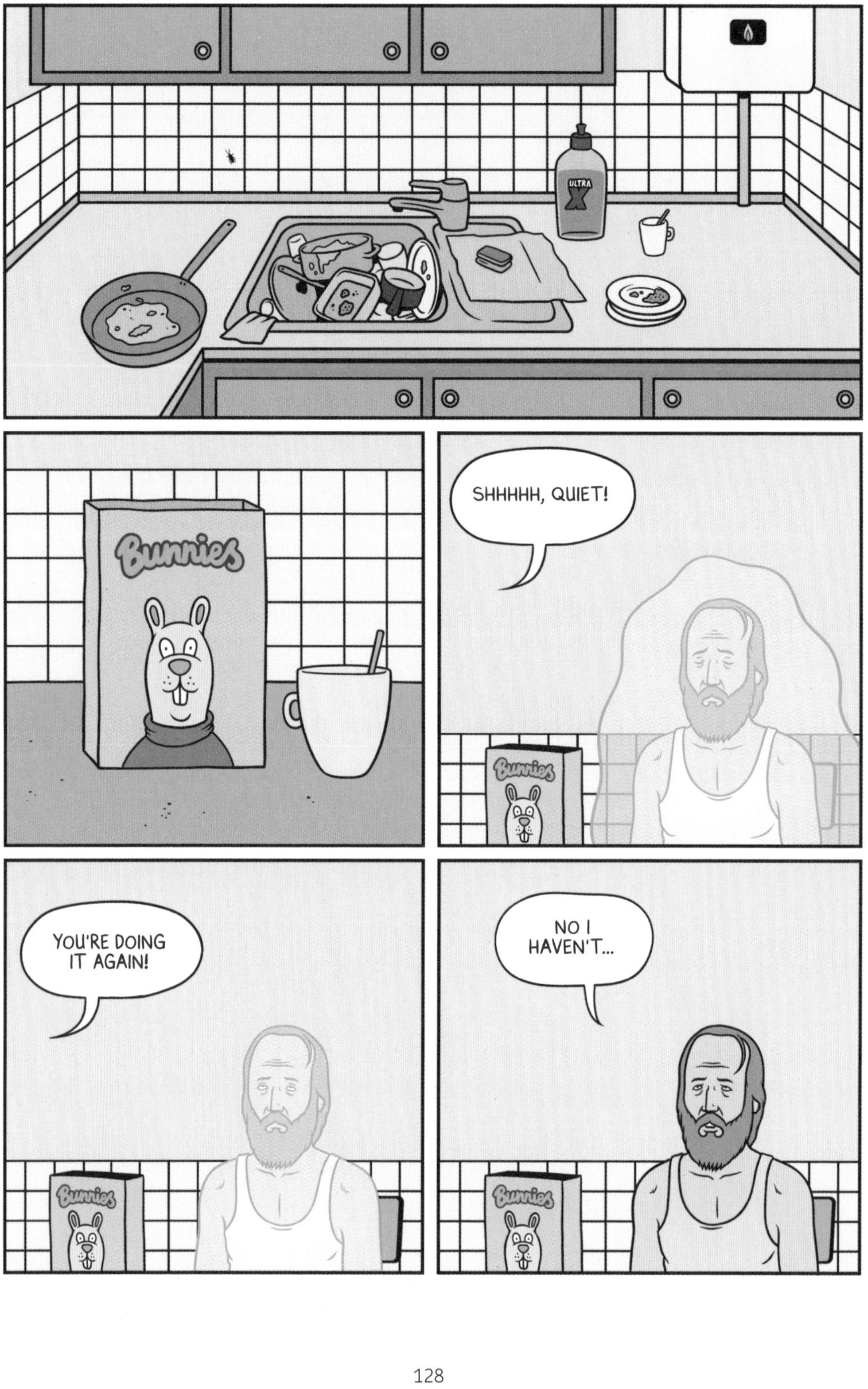
ULTRA X
Bunnies
SHHHHH, QUIET!
YOU'RE DOING IT AGAIN!
NO I HAVEN'T...

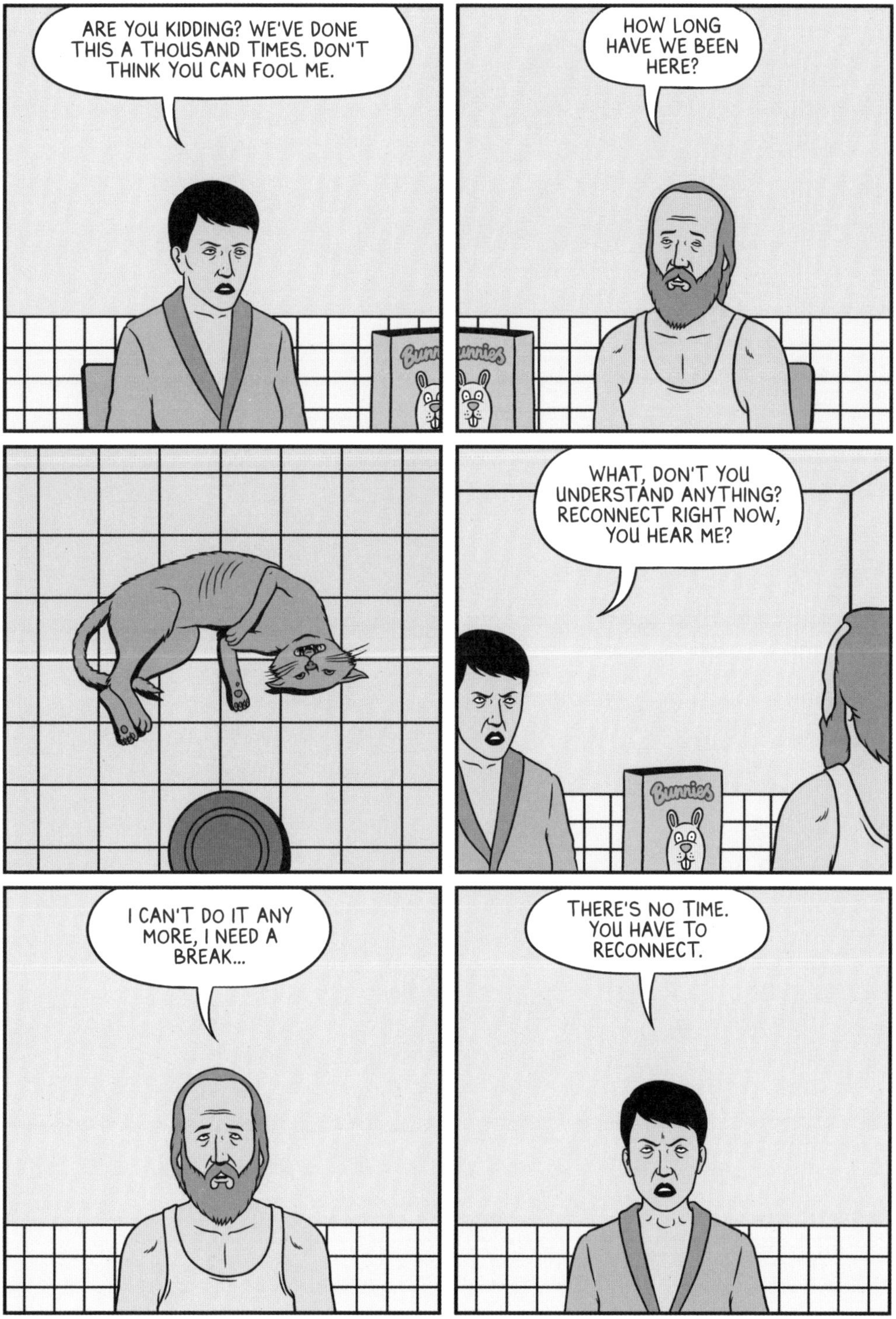
ARE YOU KIDDING? WE'VE DONE THIS A THOUSAND TIMES. DON'T THINK YOU CAN FOOL ME.
HOW LONG HAVE WE BEEN HERE?
Bunnies
Bunnies
WHAT, DON'T YOU UNDERSTAND ANYTHING? RECONNECT RIGHT NOW, YOU HEAR ME?
Bunnies
I CAN'T DO IT ANY MORE, I NEED A BREAK...
THERE'S NO TIME. YOU HAVE TO RECONNECT.

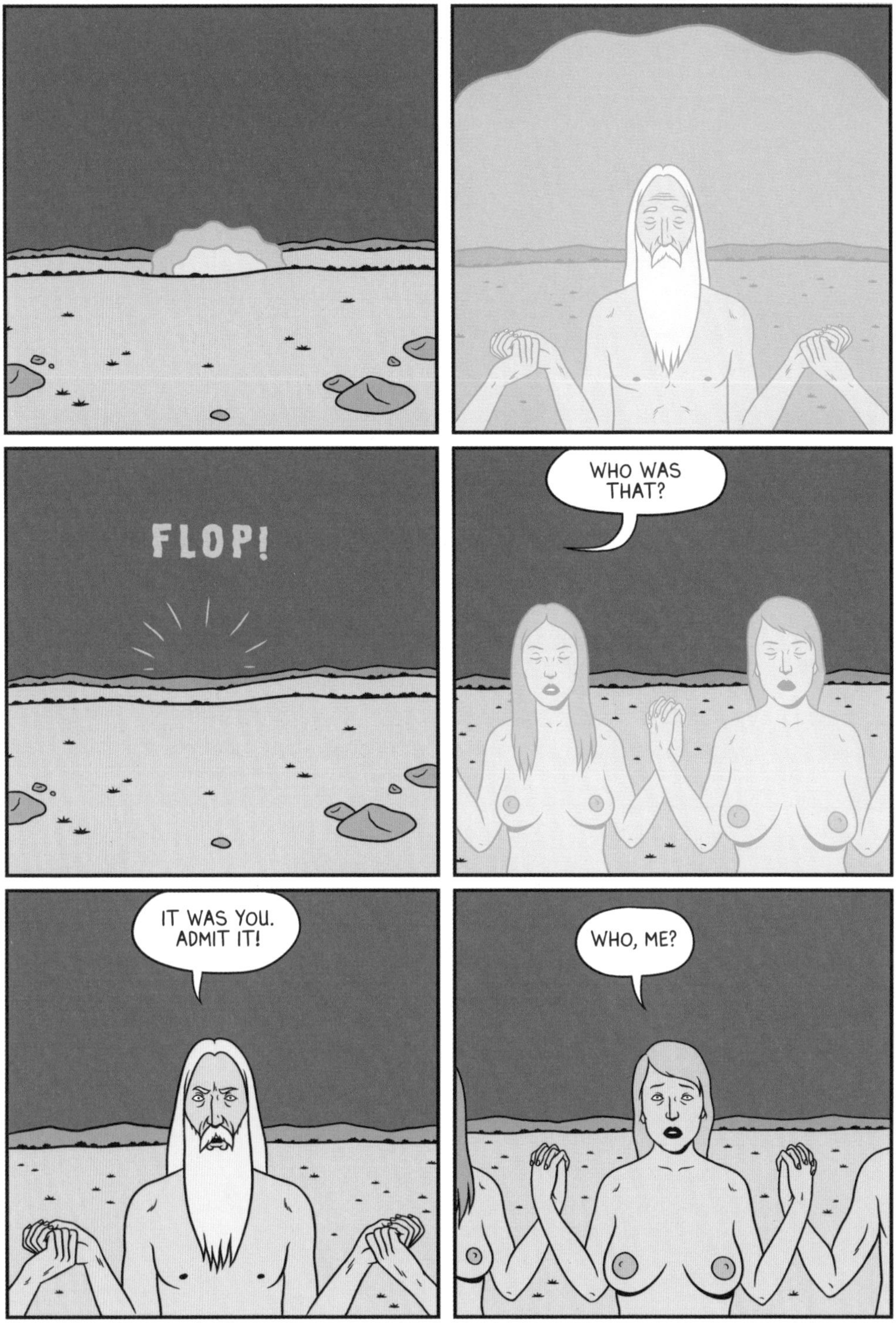
FLOP!
WHO WAS THAT?
IT WAS YOU. ADMIT IT!
WHO, ME?

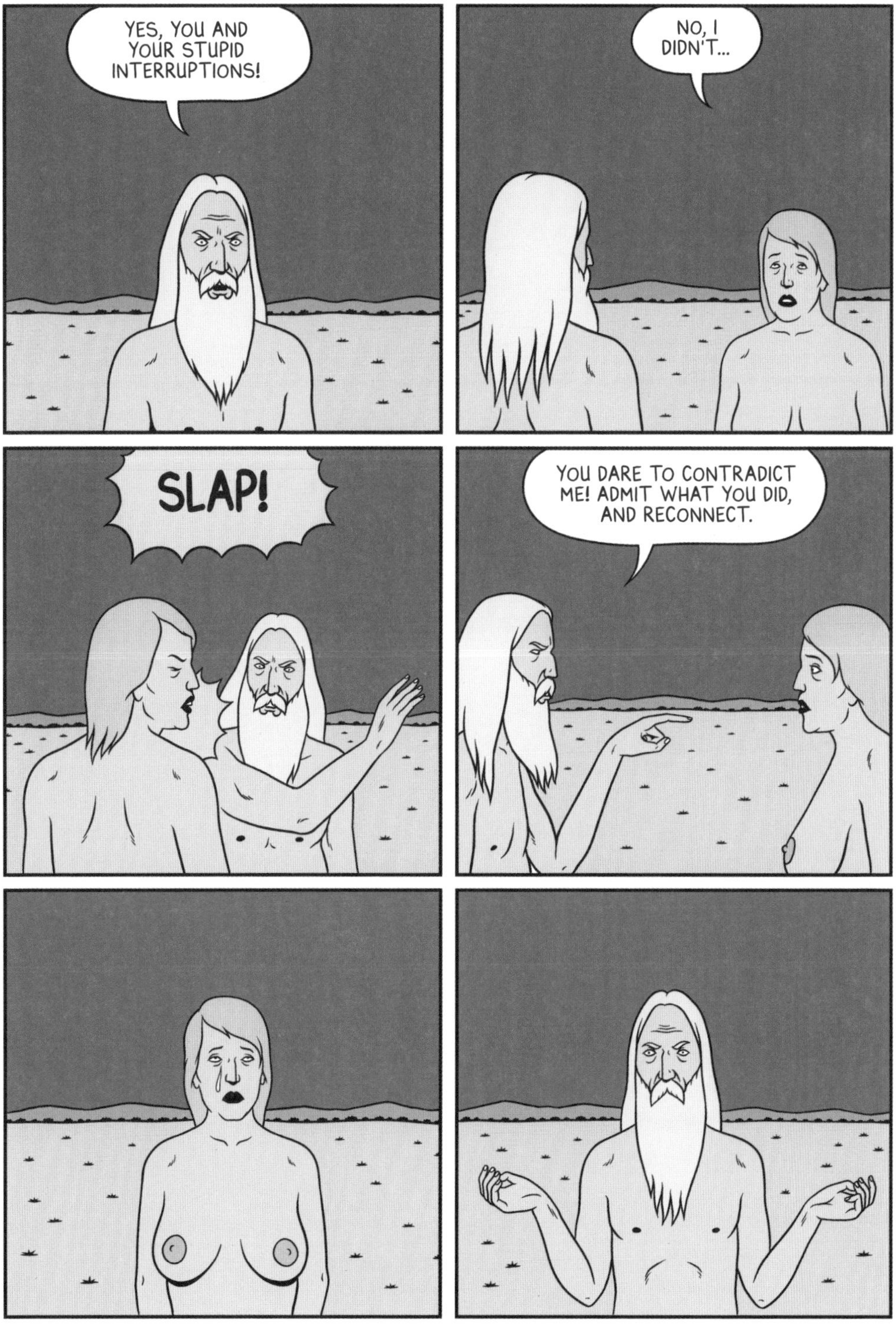
YES, YOU AND YOUR STUPID INTERRUPTIONS!
NO, I DIDN'T...
SLAP!
YOU DARE TO CONTRADICT ME! ADMIT WHAT YOU DID, AND RECONNECT.

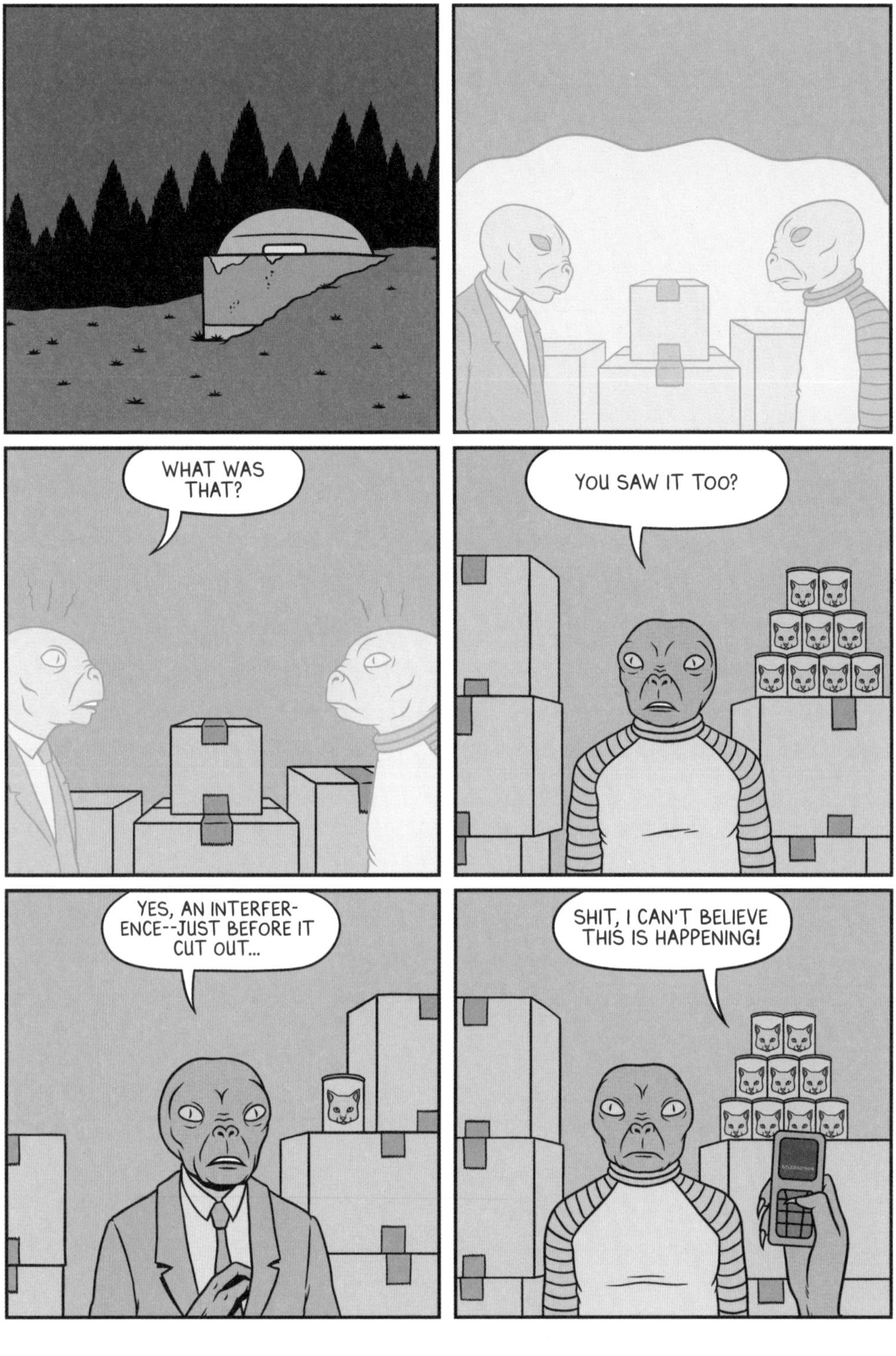
WHAT WAS THAT?
YOU SAW IT TOO?
YES, AN INTERFERENCE--JUST BEFORE IT CUT OUT...
SHIT, I CAN'T BELIEVE THIS IS HAPPENING!

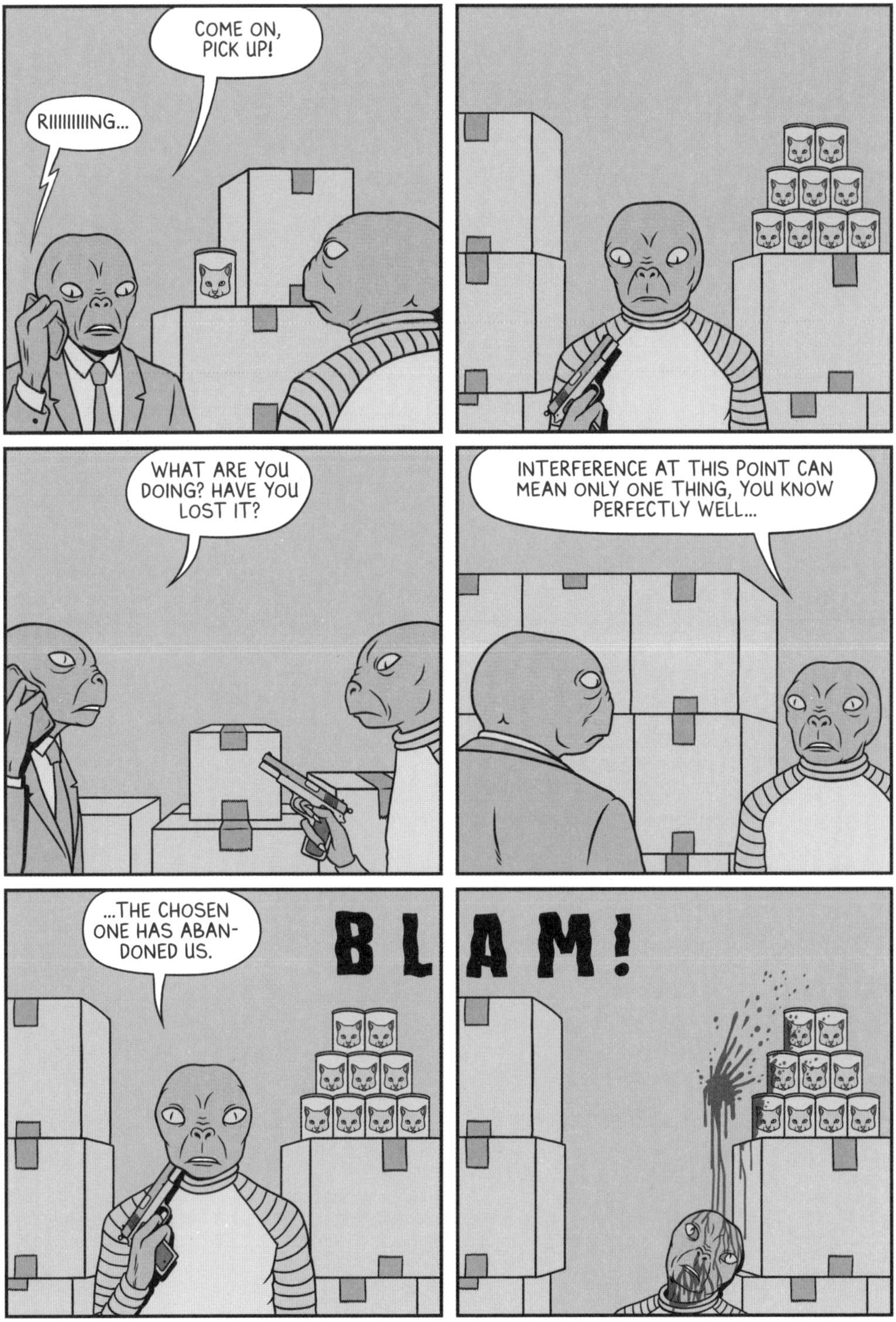
RIIIIIIIIING...
COME ON, PICK UP!
WHAT ARE YOU DOING? HAVE YOU LOST IT?
INTERFERENCE AT THIS POINT CAN MEAN ONLY ONE THING, YOU KNOW PERFECTLY WELL...
...THE CHOSEN ONE HAS ABANDONED US.
BLAM!

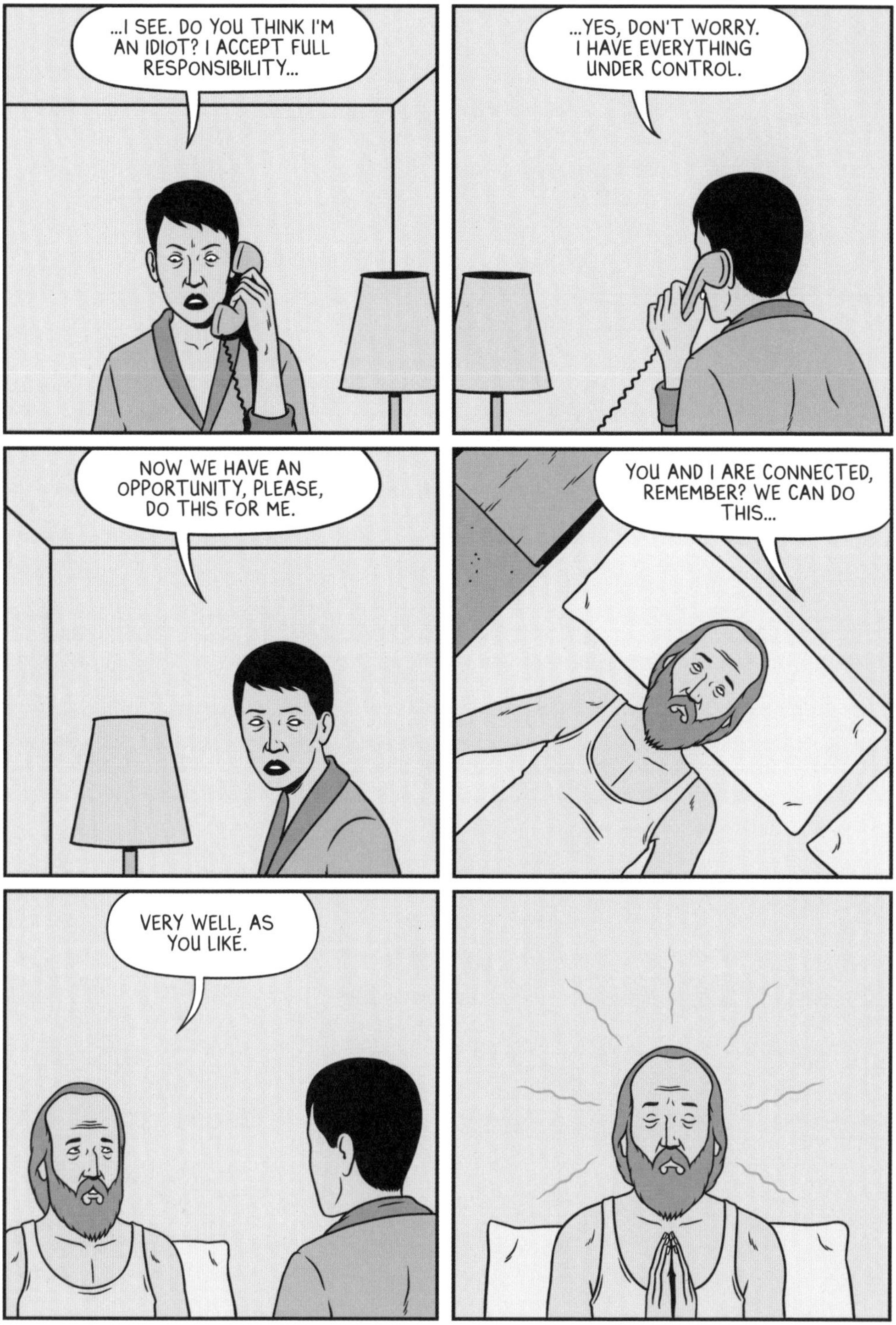
...I SEE. DO YOU THINK I'M AN IDIOT? I ACCEPT FULL RESPONSIBILITY...
...YES, DON'T WORRY. I HAVE EVERYTHING UNDER CONTROL.
NOW WE HAVE AN OPPORTUNITY, PLEASE, DO THIS FOR ME.
YOU AND I ARE CONNECTED, REMEMBER? WE CAN DO THIS...
VERY WELL, AS YOU LIKE.

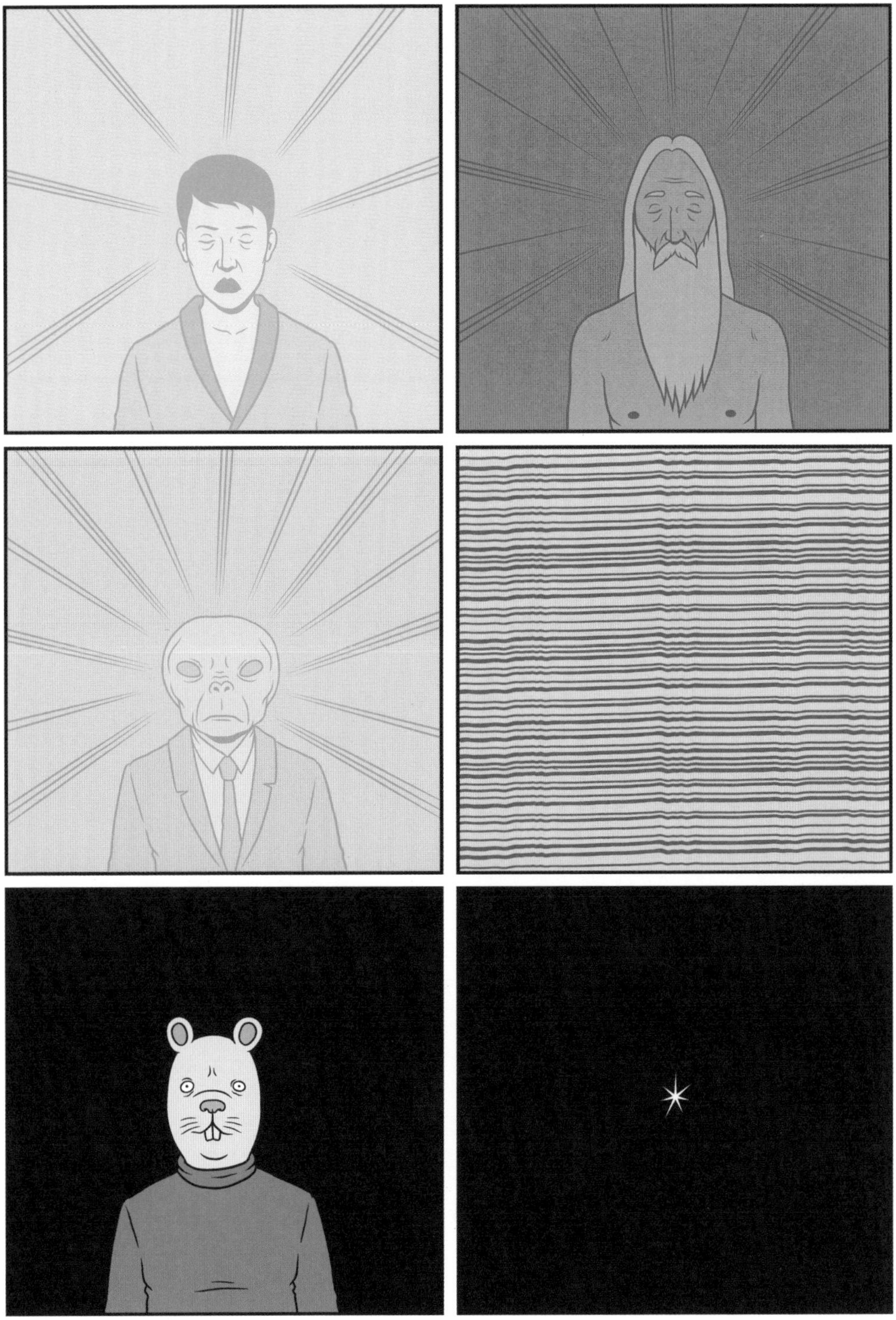

PERE JOAN
ARIZONA STRATOCASTER

Pere Joan was born in Palma de Mallorca in 1956. He is an illustrator and cartoonist who began his career in the tradition of what is called the "nueva línea clara" [new clear line] of the '80s. With Max, he co-edited the acclaimed magazine *NSLM*. He won the Salón del Cómic de Barcelona award for *Mi cabeza bajo el mar* [*My Head Underwater*] (1991). More recently he adapted the "afterpop" novel *Nocilla Experience* [*Nutella Experience*] (2011), by Agustín Fernández Mallo into a comic. The comic featured in this anthology is a new collaboration with Fernández Mallo. His latest works are the experimental *100 pictogramas para un siglo* [*100 Pictograms For A Century*] (forthcoming), his adaptation of Cristóbal Serra's novel *Viaje a Cotiledonia*, and *Agujero* [*Hole*] (with Dani Cardona).

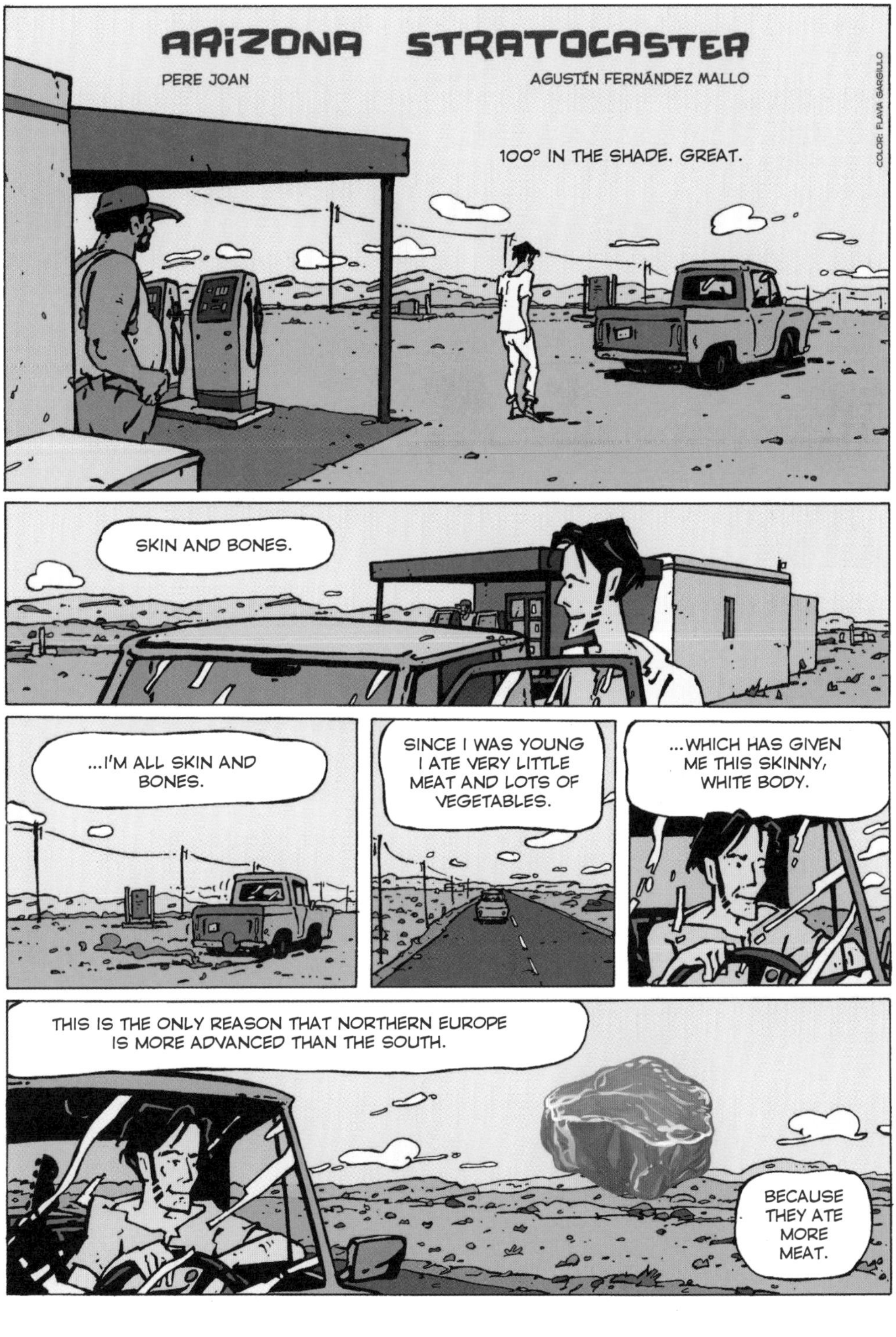
ARIZONA STRATOCASTER
PERE JOAN
AGUSTÍN FERNÁNDEZ MALLO
COLOR: FLAVIA GARGIULO
100° IN THE SHADE. GREAT.
SKIN AND BONES.
...I'M ALL SKIN AND BONES.
SINCE I WAS YOUNG I ATE VERY LITTLE MEAT AND LOTS OF VEGETABLES.
...WHICH HAS GIVEN ME THIS SKINNY, WHITE BODY.
THIS IS THE ONLY REASON THAT NORTHERN EUROPE IS MORE ADVANCED THAN THE SOUTH.
BECAUSE THEY ATE MORE MEAT.

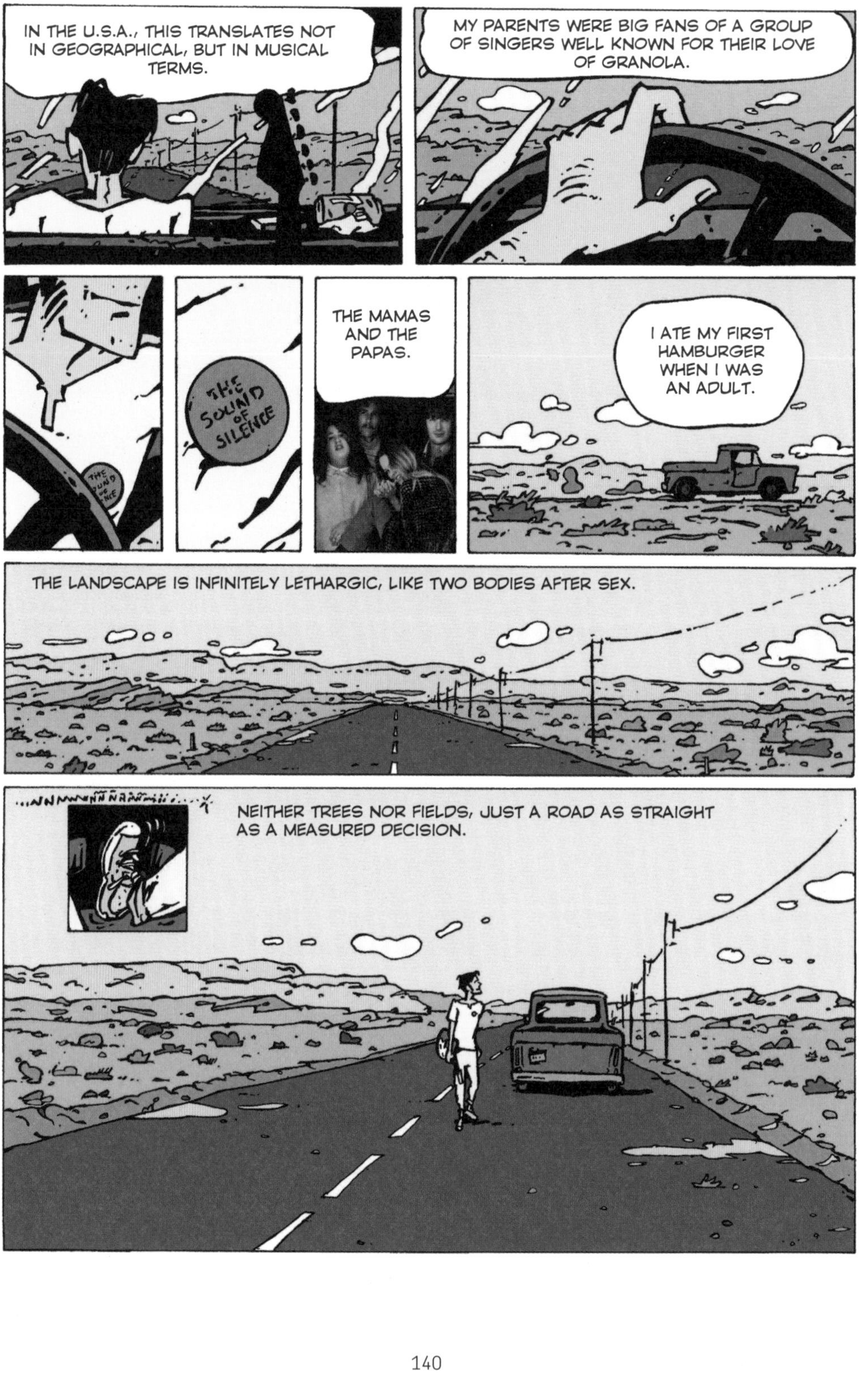
IN THE U.S.A., THIS TRANSLATES NOT IN GEOGRAPHICAL, BUT IN MUSICAL TERMS.
MY PARENTS WERE BIG FANS OF A GROUP OF SINGERS WELL KNOWN FOR THEIR LOVE OF GRANOLA.
THE SOUND OF SILENCE
THE MAMAS AND THE PAPAS.
I ATE MY FIRST HAMBURGER WHEN I WAS AN ADULT.
THE LANDSCAPE IS INFINITELY LETHARGIC, LIKE TWO BODIES AFTER SEX.
NEITHER TREES NOR FIELDS, JUST A ROAD AS STRAIGHT AS A MEASURED DECISION.

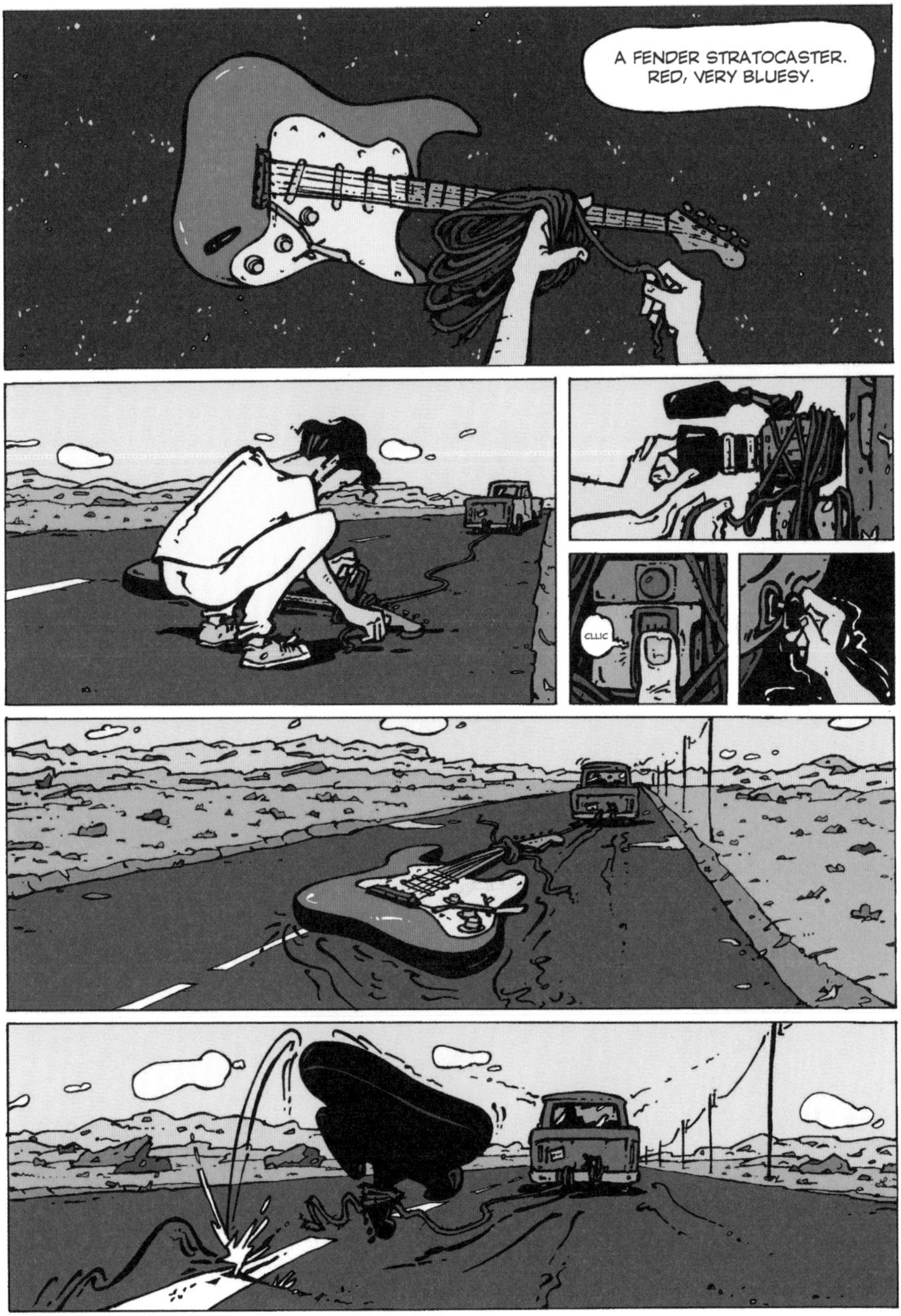
A FENDER STRATOCASTER. RED, VERY BLUESY.
CLLIC

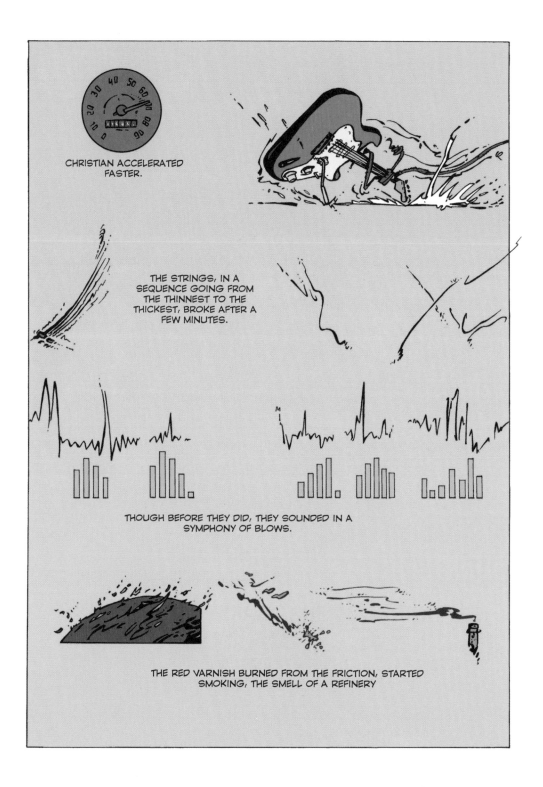

CHRISTIAN ACCELERATED
FASTER.

THE STRINGS, IN A
SEQUENCE GOING FROM
THE THINNEST TO THE
THICKEST, BROKE AFTER A
FEW MINUTES.

THOUGH BEFORE THEY DID, THEY SOUNDED IN A
SYMPHONY OF BLOWS.

THE RED VARNISH BURNED FROM THE FRICTION, STARTED
SMOKING, THE SMELL OF A REFINERY

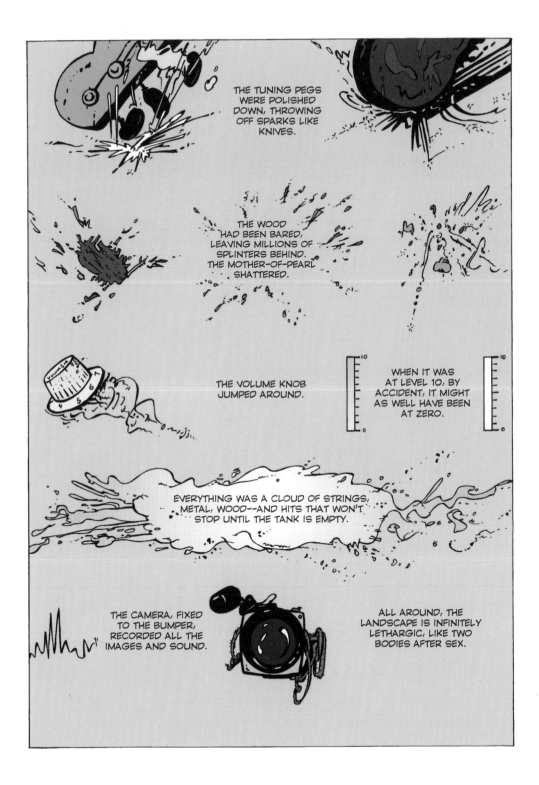

THE TUNING PEGS WERE POLISHED DOWN, THROWING OFF SPARKS LIKE KNIVES.

THE WOOD HAD BEEN BARED, LEAVING MILLIONS OF SPLINTERS BEHIND. THE MOTHER-OF-PEARL SHATTERED.

THE VOLUME KNOB JUMPED AROUND.

WHEN IT WAS AT LEVEL 10, BY ACCIDENT, IT MIGHT AS WELL HAVE BEEN AT ZERO.

EVERYTHING WAS A CLOUD OF STRINGS, METAL, WOOD--AND HITS THAT WON'T STOP UNTIL THE TANK IS EMPTY.

THE CAMERA, FIXED TO THE BUMPER, RECORDED ALL THE IMAGES AND SOUND.

ALL AROUND, THE LANDSCAPE IS INFINITELY LETHARGIC, LIKE TWO BODIES AFTER SEX.

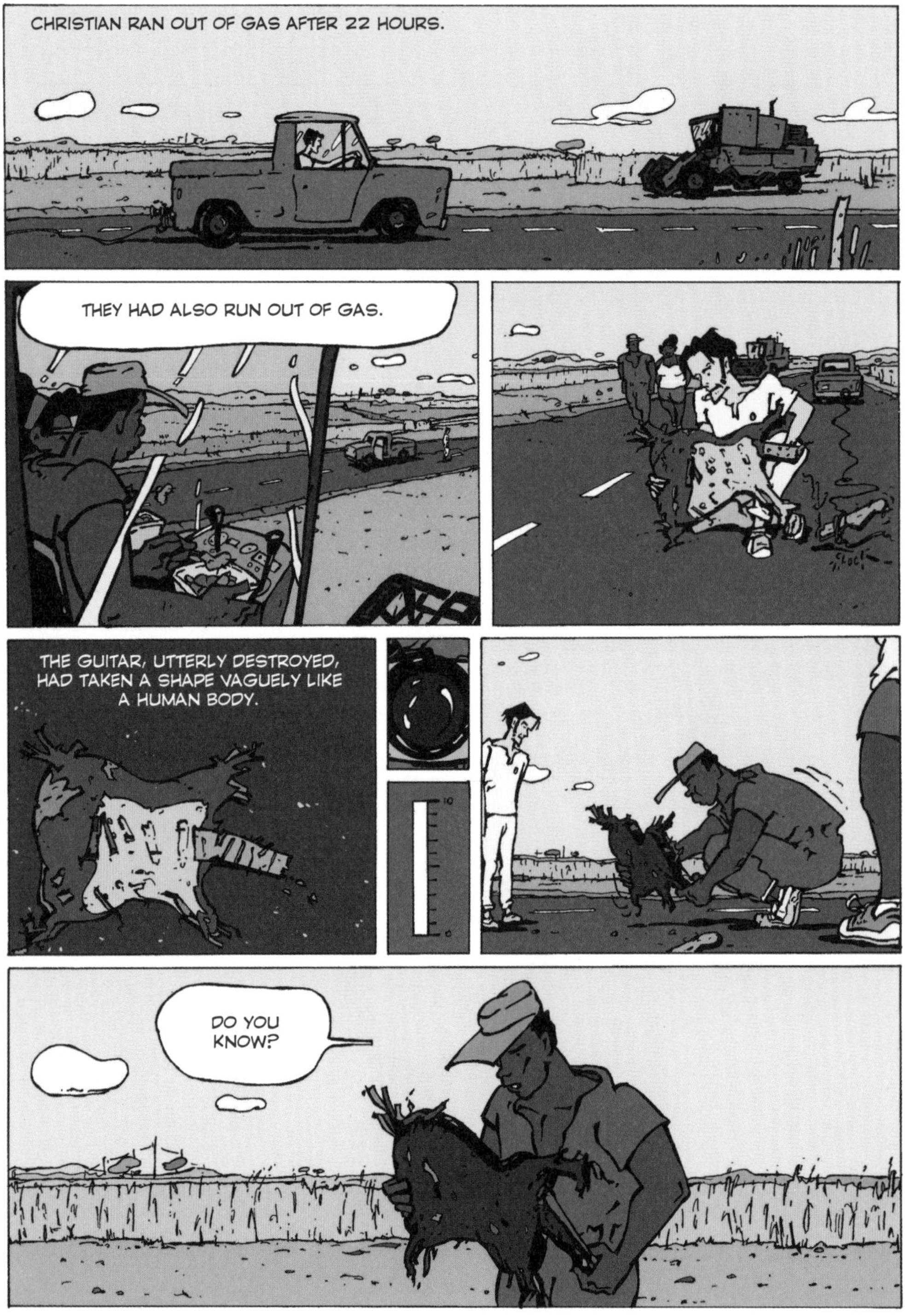
CHRISTIAN RAN OUT OF GAS AFTER 22 HOURS.
THEY HAD ALSO RUN OUT OF GAS.
CLOC!
THE GUITAR, UTTERLY DESTROYED, HAD TAKEN A SHAPE VAGUELY LIKE A HUMAN BODY.
DO YOU KNOW?

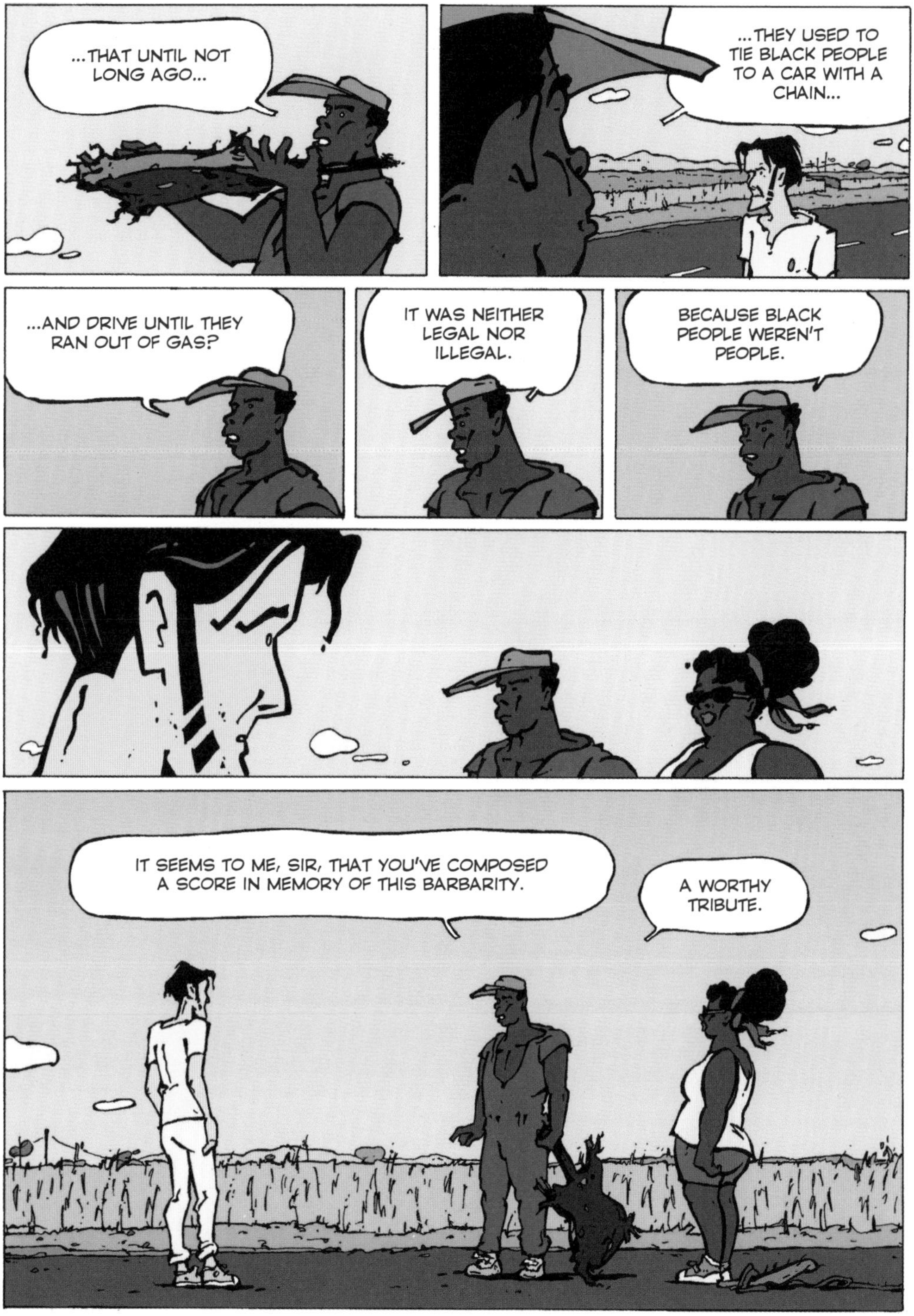
...THAT UNTIL NOT LONG AGO...
...THEY USED TO TIE BLACK PEOPLE TO A CAR WITH A CHAIN...
...AND DRIVE UNTIL THEY RAN OUT OF GAS?
IT WAS NEITHER LEGAL NOR ILLEGAL.
BECAUSE BLACK PEOPLE WEREN'T PEOPLE.
IT SEEMS TO ME, SIR, THAT YOU'VE COMPOSED A SCORE IN MEMORY OF THIS BARBARITY.
A WORTHY TRIBUTE.

MIREIA PÉREZ

THE VISIT

Mireia Pérez was born in Valencia in 1984, and studied fine art in Valencia, Angoulême, and Madrid. She drew comic strips for websites like *El Estafador* [*The Swindler*], and is a member of the collective Ultrarradio. With *La muchacha salvaje* [*The Wild Girl*], she won the Novela Gráfica Fnac Sins Entido Prize in 2010 and was a candidate for Best National Comic at the Barcelona Comic Festival in 2012. Her cartoons have appeared in the newspaper *El País,* the satirical magazine *El Jueves*, the *Caniculadas* webcomic, and the online community *Tik Tok Comics*. In 2013, she did a story for the anthology *Supercómic*, edited by Santiago García and published by Errata Naturae. She belongs to ACDCómic (The Comics Critics Association of Spain) and writes criticism for the bookstore La Central's newspaper, and for magazines like *CuCo. Cuadernos de cómic* [*CuCo. Notebooks on Comics*]*, El Buen Salvaje* [*The Good Wildman*], and *Rockdelux.* Nowadays, she draws and publishes her own fanzine, *Chicos* [*Boys*], and is an active player in the Spanish comics scene. She works for a bookstore and organizes the small press and art comics festival GRAF in Madrid and Barcelona.

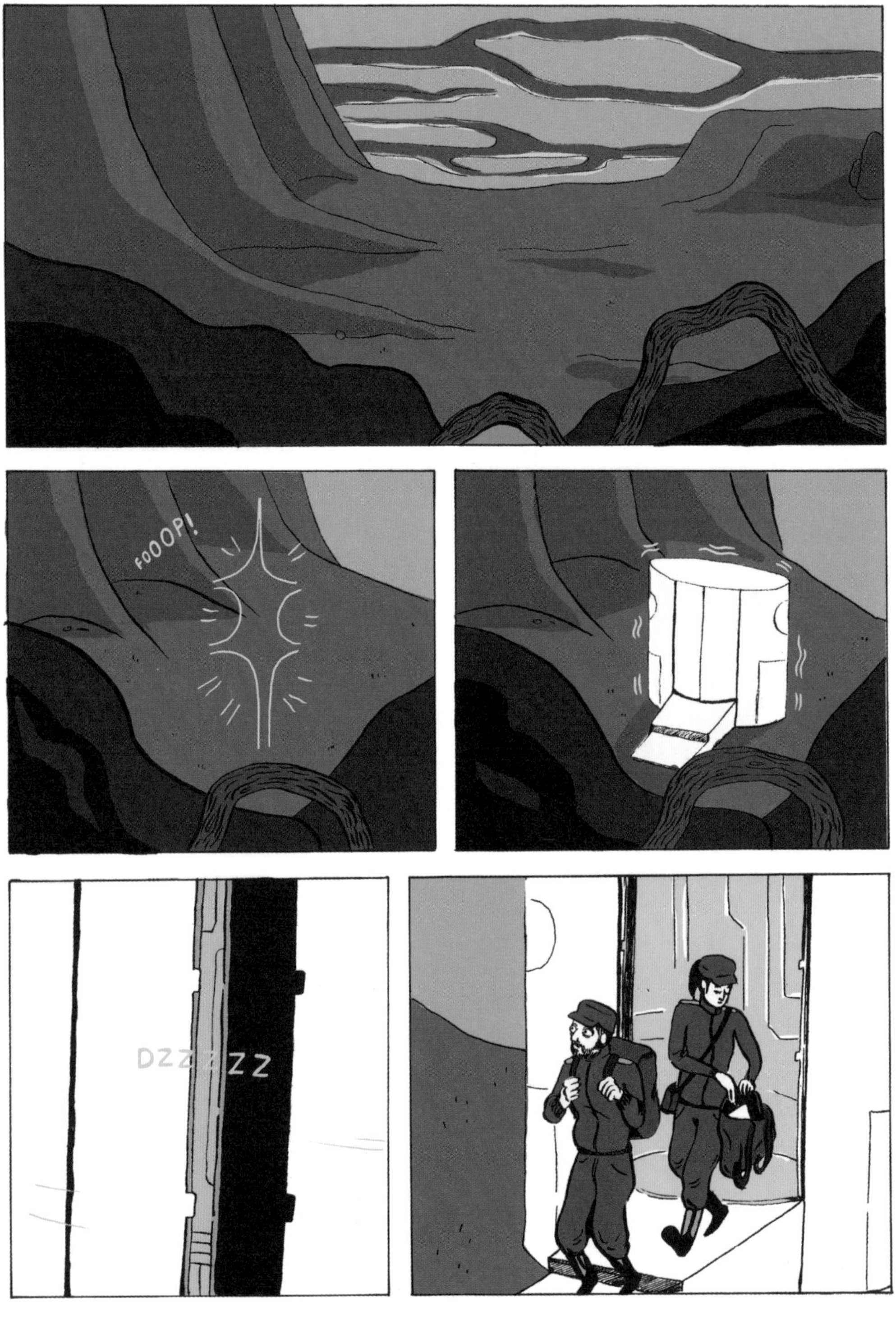
FOOOP!
DZZZZZ

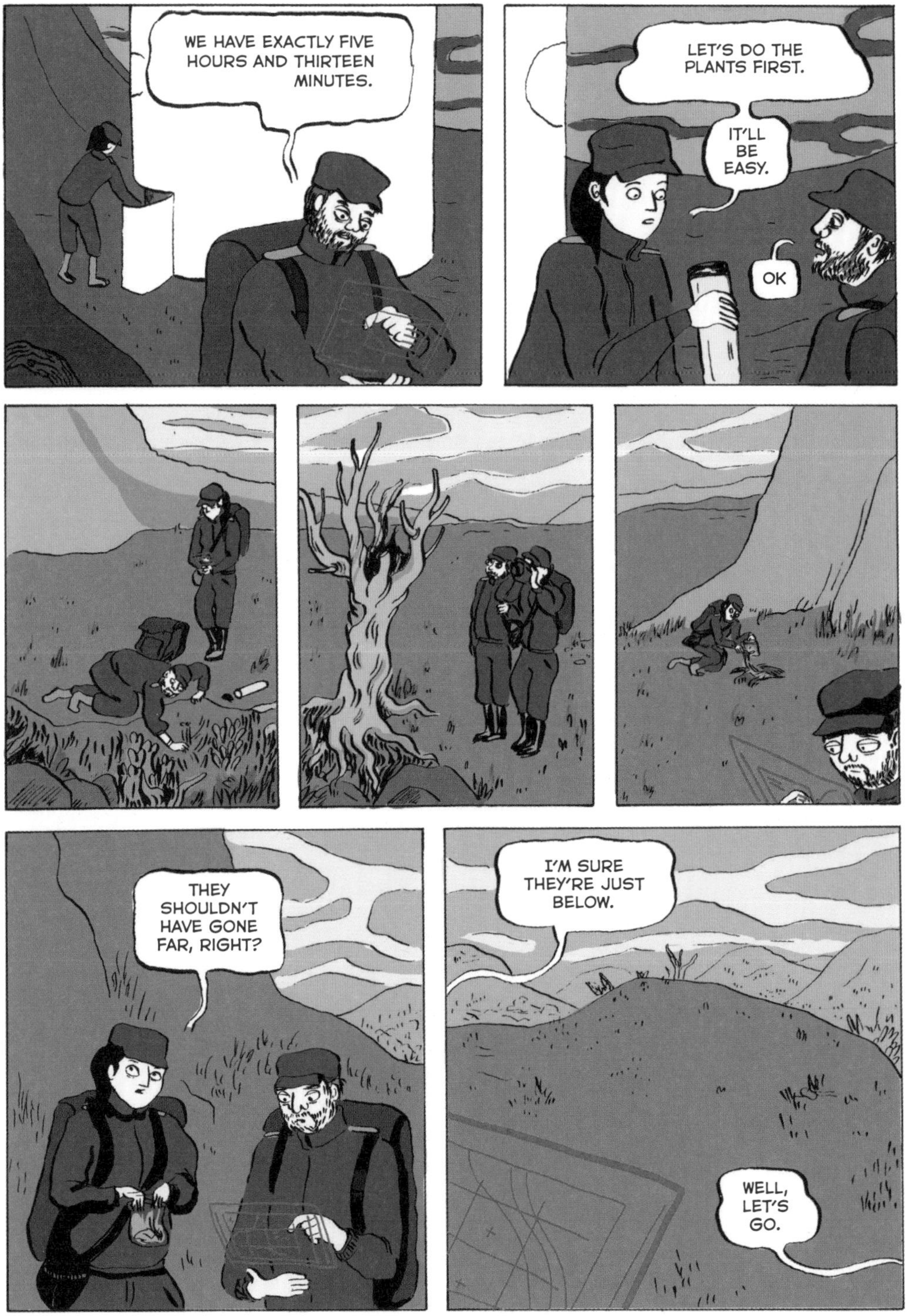
WE HAVE EXACTLY FIVE HOURS AND THIRTEEN MINUTES.
LET'S DO THE PLANTS FIRST.
IT'LL BE EASY.
OK
THEY SHOULDN'T HAVE GONE FAR, RIGHT?
I'M SURE THEY'RE JUST BELOW.
WELL, LET'S GO.

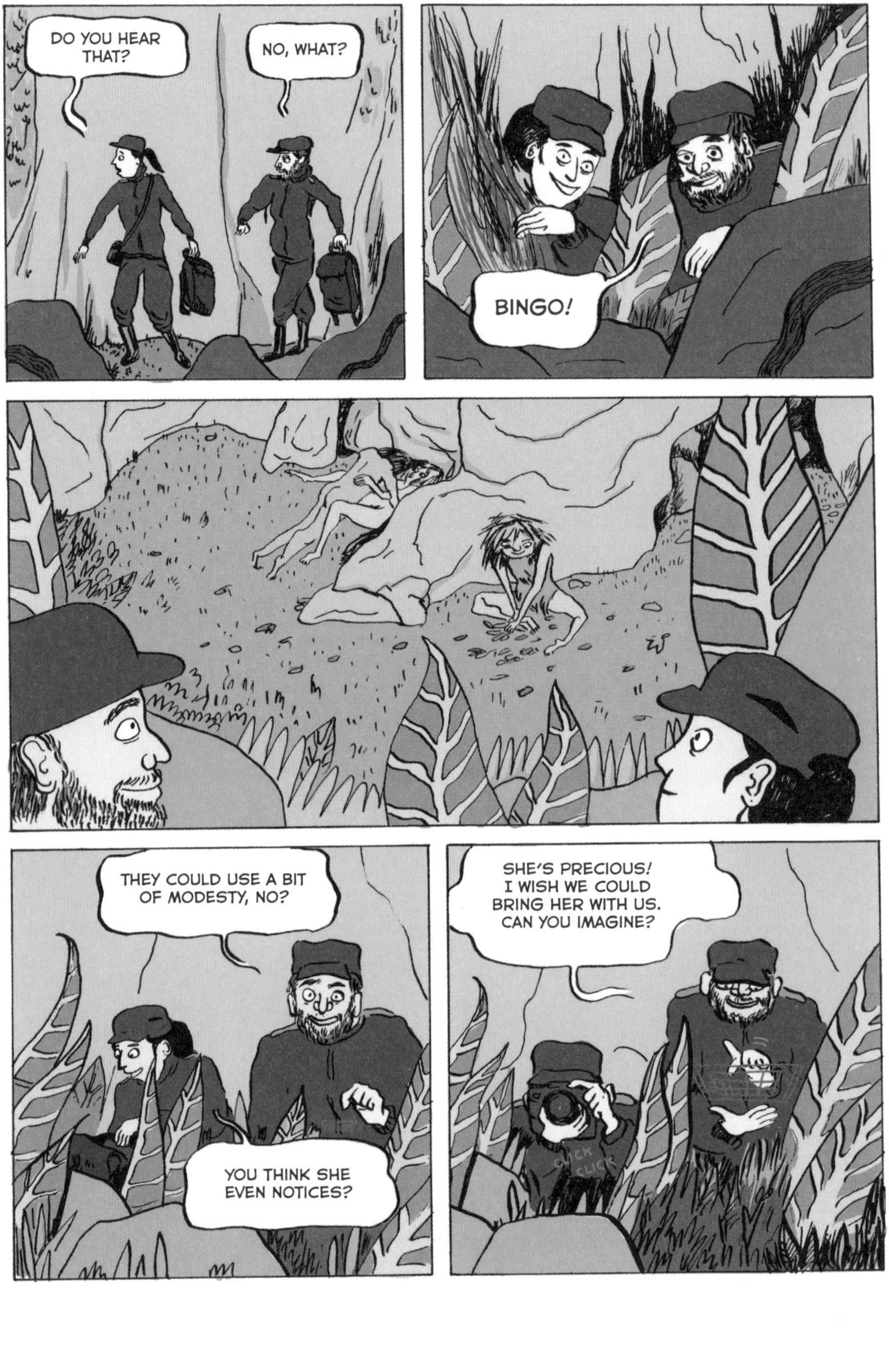
DO YOU HEAR THAT?
NO, WHAT?
BINGO!
THEY COULD USE A BIT OF MODESTY, NO?
YOU THINK SHE EVEN NOTICES?
SHE'S PRECIOUS! I WISH WE COULD BRING HER WITH US. CAN YOU IMAGINE?
CLICK CLICK

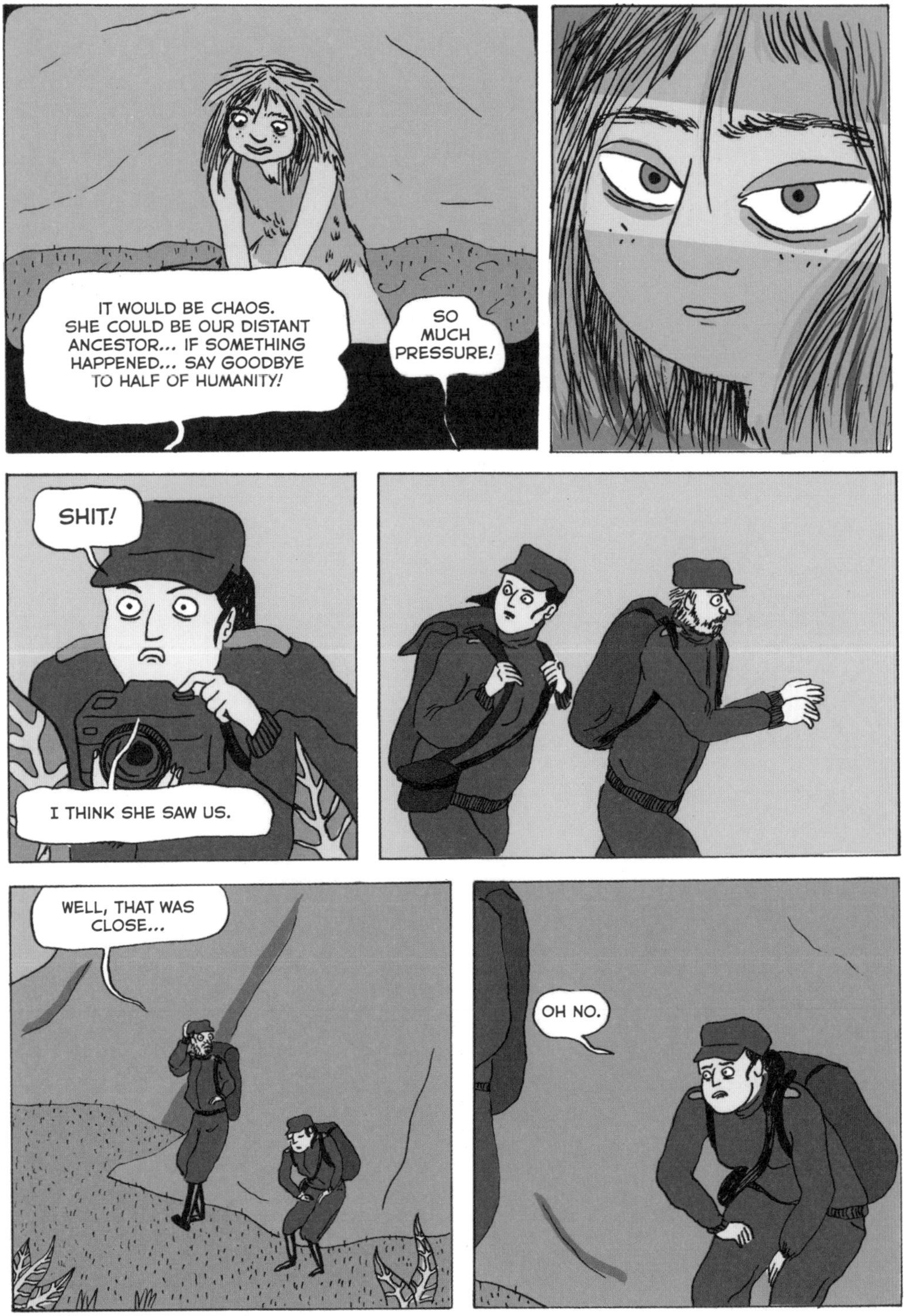
IT WOULD BE CHAOS. SHE COULD BE OUR DISTANT ANCESTOR... IF SOMETHING HAPPENED... SAY GOODBYE TO HALF OF HUMANITY!
SO MUCH PRESSURE!
SHIT!
I THINK SHE SAW US.
WELL, THAT WAS CLOSE...
OH NO.

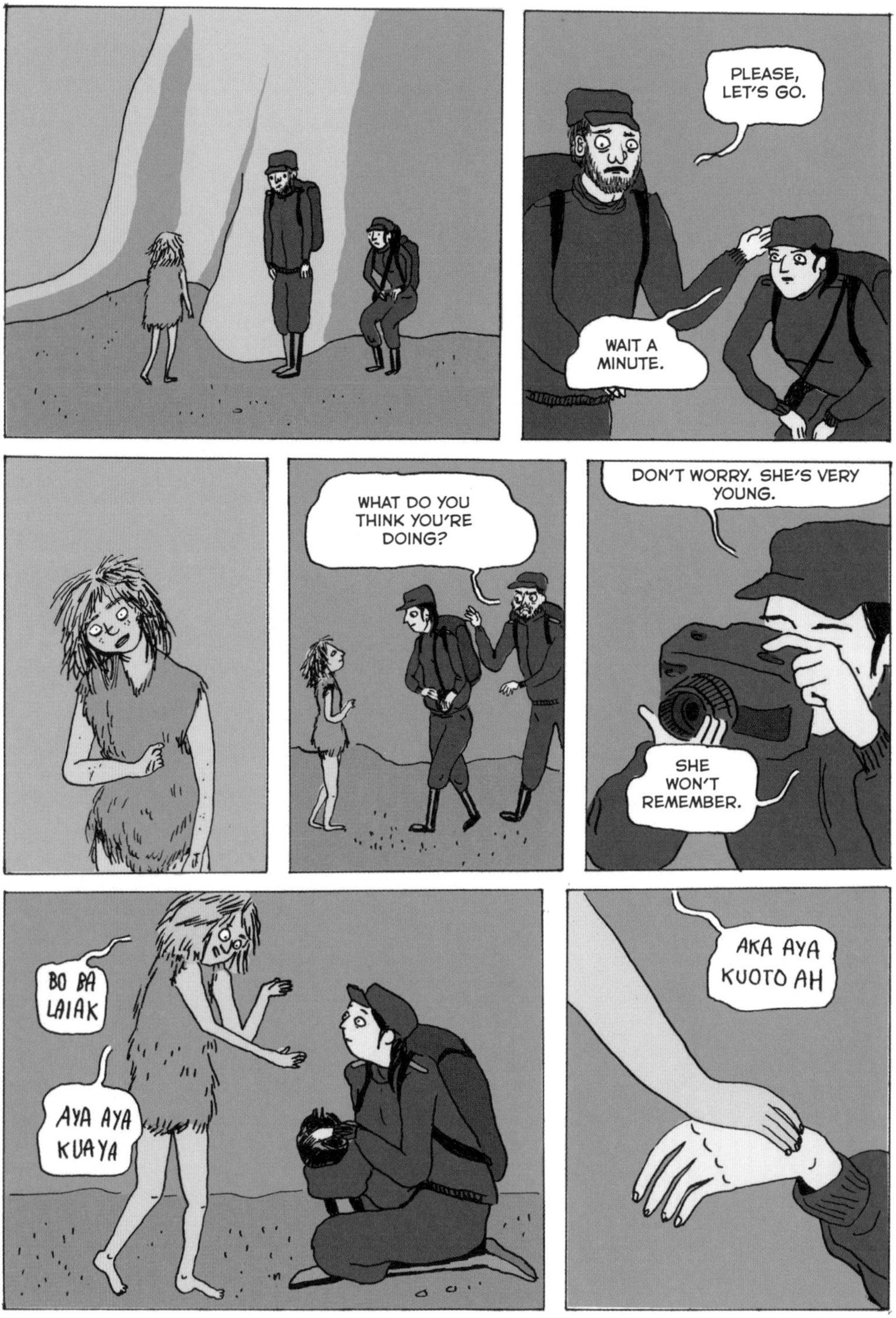
PLEASE, LET'S GO.
WAIT A MINUTE.
WHAT DO YOU THINK YOU'RE DOING?
DON'T WORRY. SHE'S VERY YOUNG.
SHE WON'T REMEMBER.
BO BA LAIAK
AYA AYA KUAYA
AKA AYA KUOTO AH

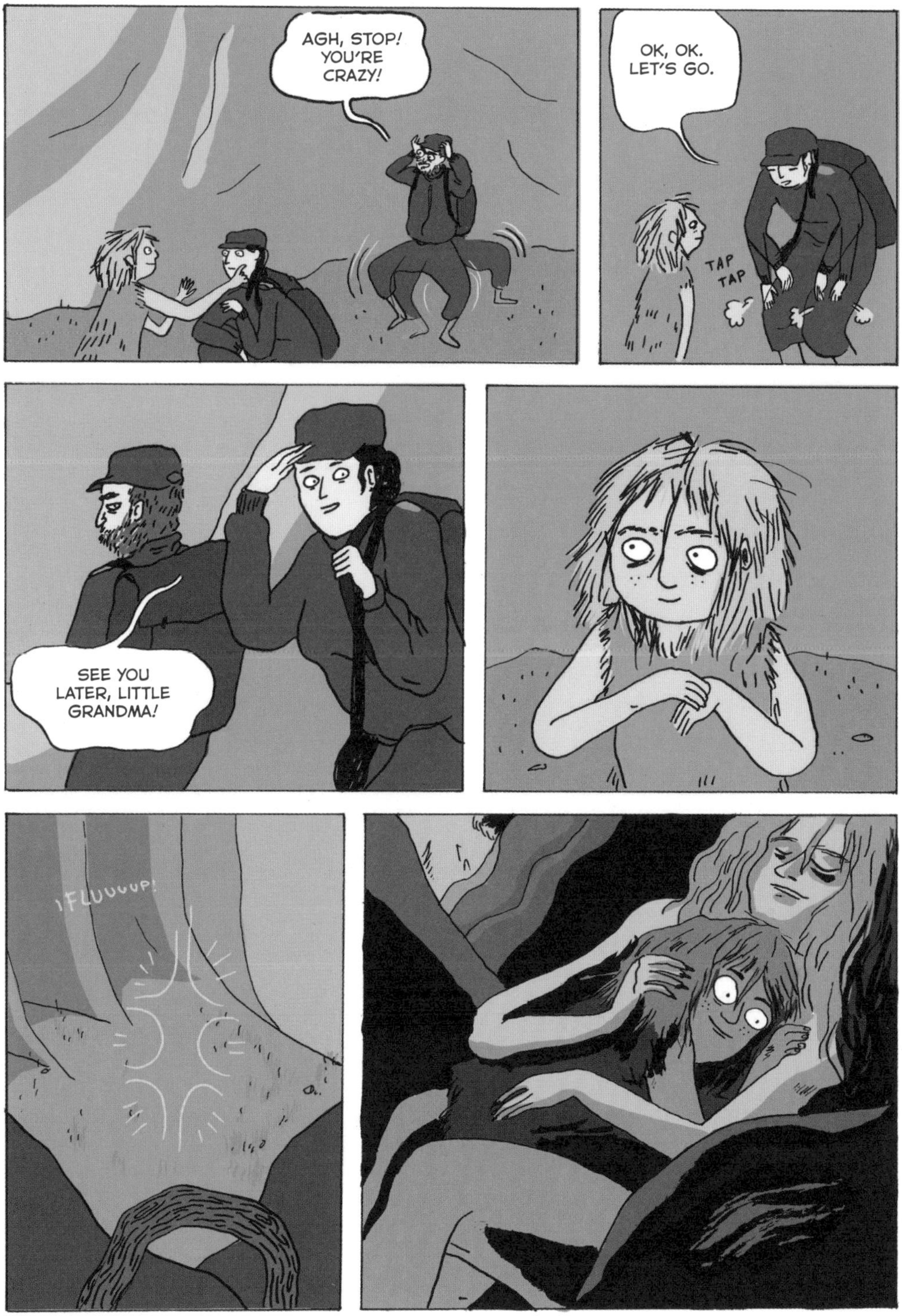
AGH, STOP! YOU'RE CRAZY!
OK, OK. LET'S GO.
TAP TAP
SEE YOU LATER, LITTLE GRANDMA!
¡FLUUUUP!

CLARA-TANIT ARQUÉ

LET'S MOVE TO THE COUNTRY! YOU SAID TO ME

Clara-Tanit Arqué was born in Gerona in 1981. Her comics have appeared in fanzines like *Colibrí*, *Lunettes*, and *Fanzine Enfermo*. She won the AlhóndigaKomik prize in 2008. She's published the graphic novels *Wassalon* (2007), and *¿Quién ama a las fresas?* [*Who Loves Strawberries?*] (2010).

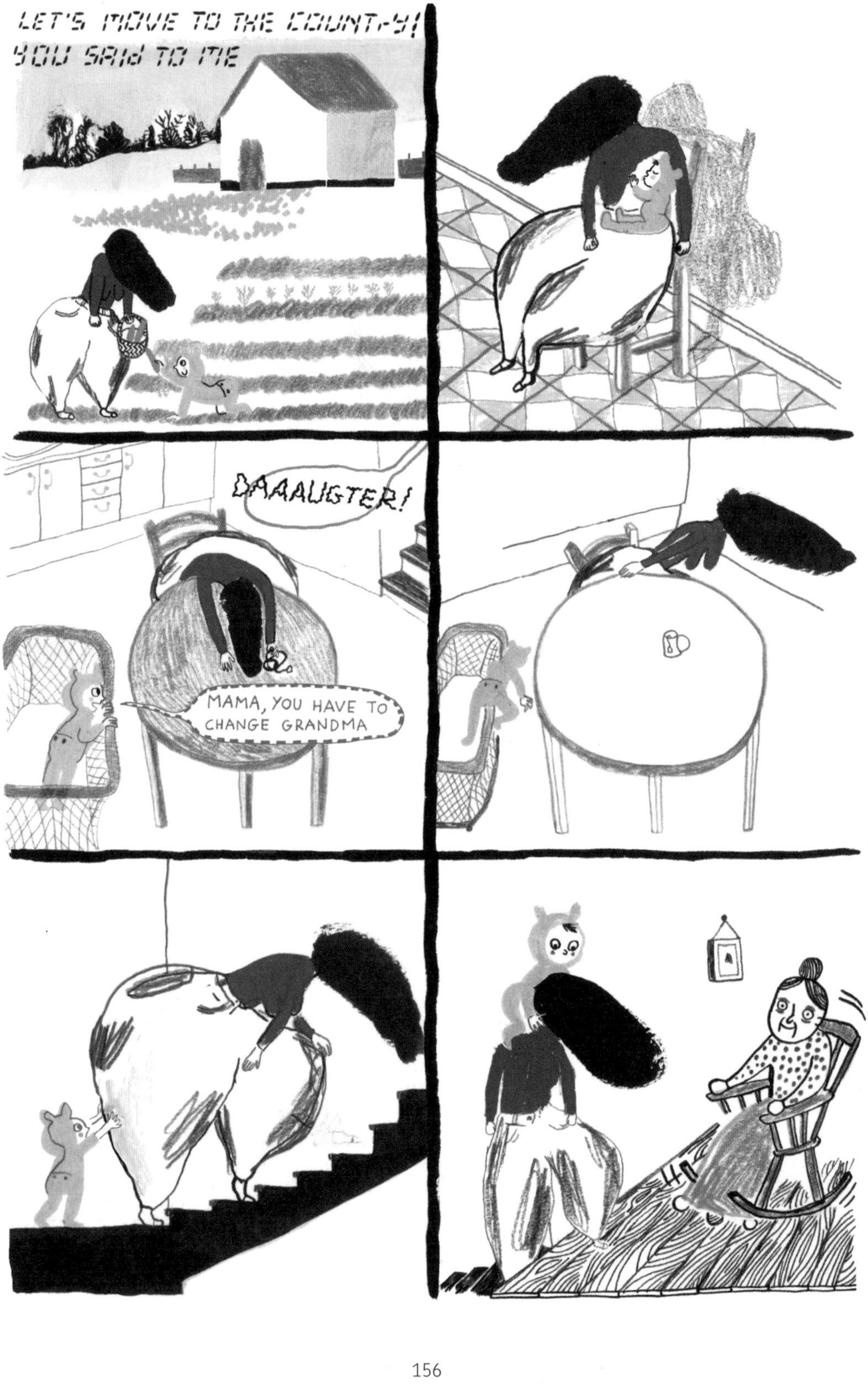
LET'S MOVE TO THE COUNTRY!
YOU SAID TO ME
DAAAUGTER!
MAMA, YOU HAVE TO CHANGE GRANDMA

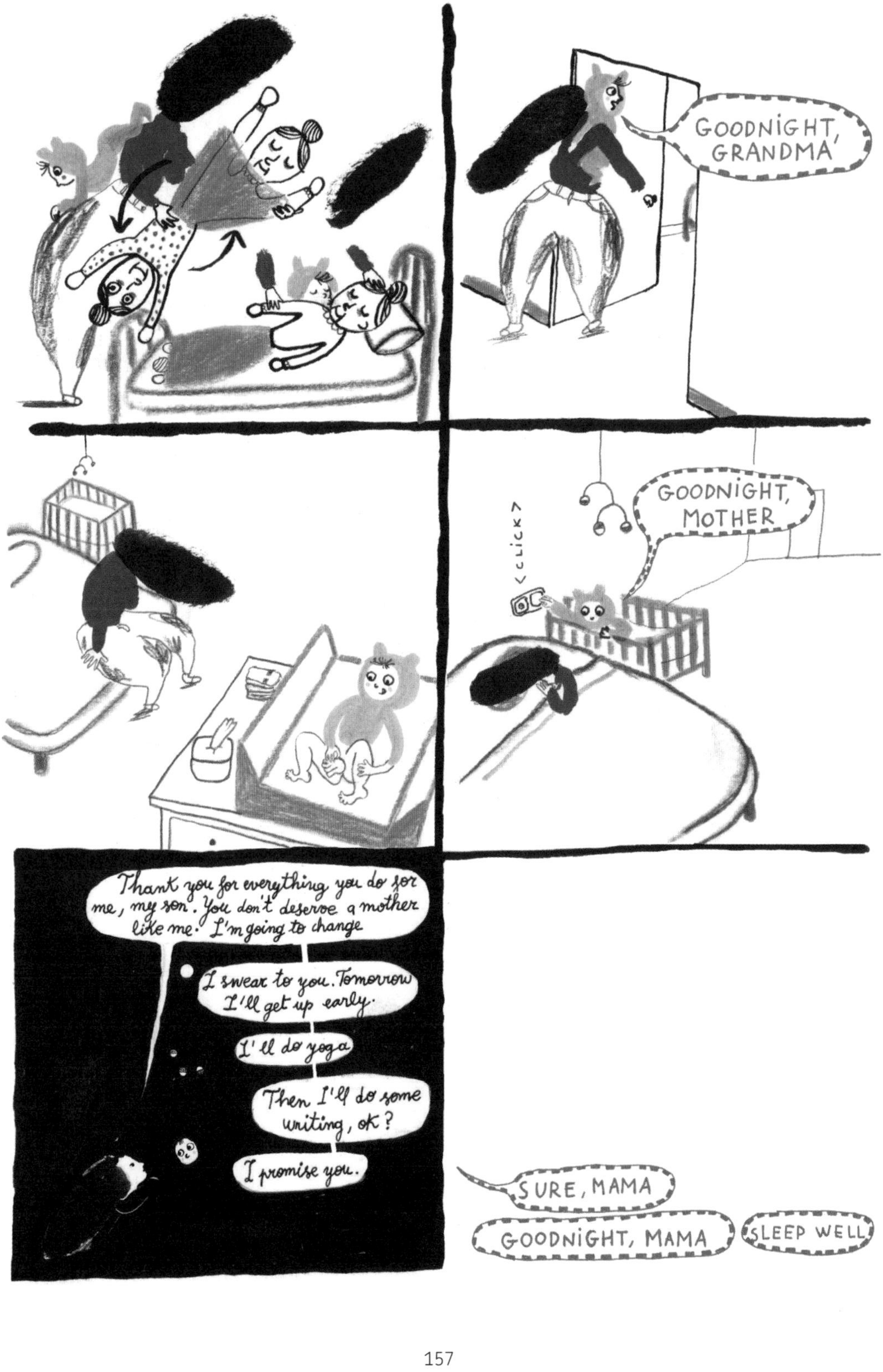
GOODNIGHT, GRANDMA
<CLICK>
GOODNIGHT, MOTHER
Thank you for everything you do for me, my son. You don't deserve a mother like me. I'm going to change
I swear to you. Tomorrow I'll get up early.
I'll do yoga
Then I'll do some writing, ok?
I promise you.
SURE, MAMA
GOODNIGHT, MAMA
SLEEP WELL

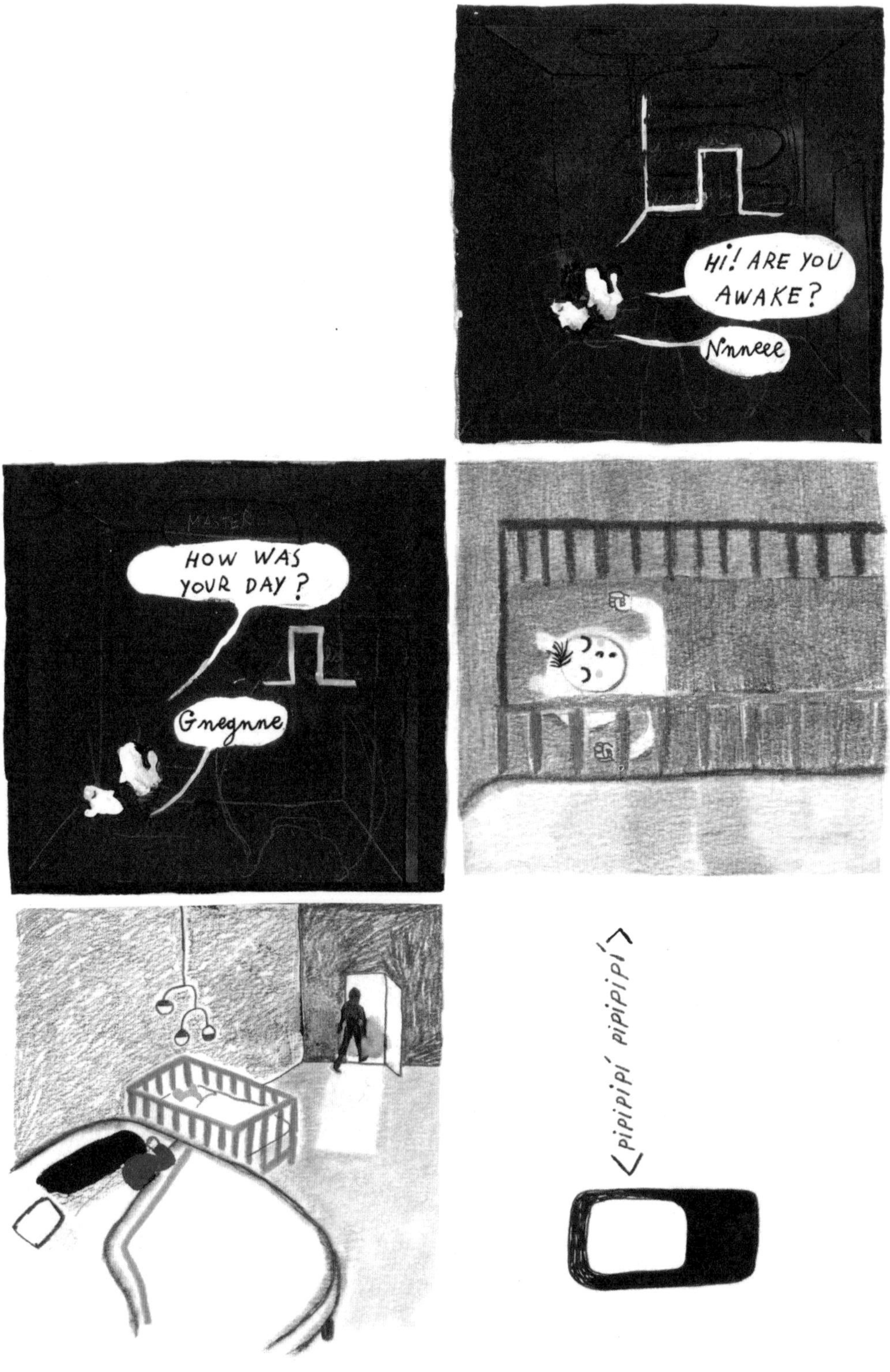
HI! ARE YOU AWAKE?
Nnneee
HOW WAS YOUR DAY?
Gnegnne
pipipipi pipipipi

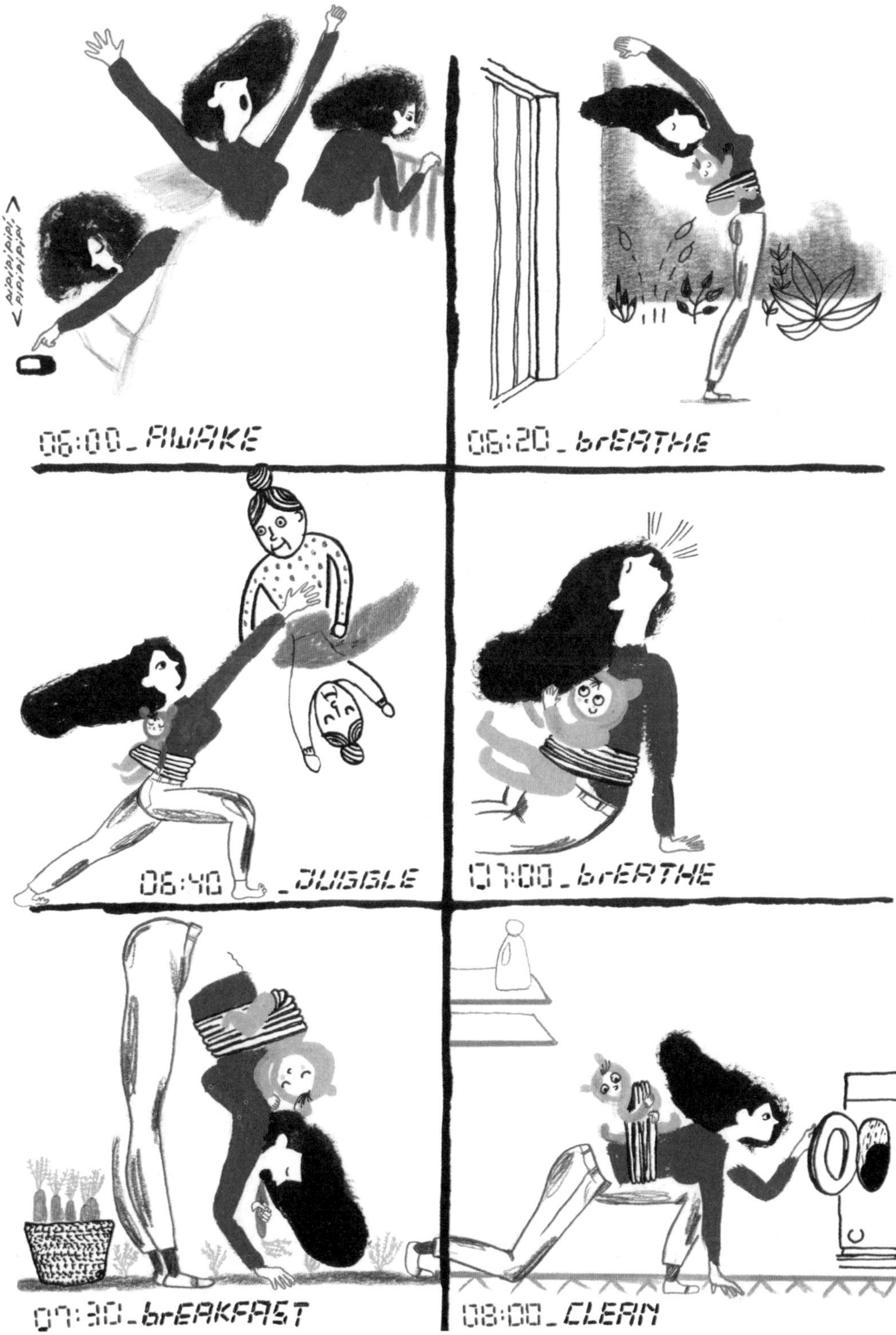
<pipipipipi, pipipipipi>
06:00_AWAKE
06:20_brEATHE
06:40 _JUGGLE
07:00_brEATHE
07:30_brEAKFAST
08:00_CLEAN

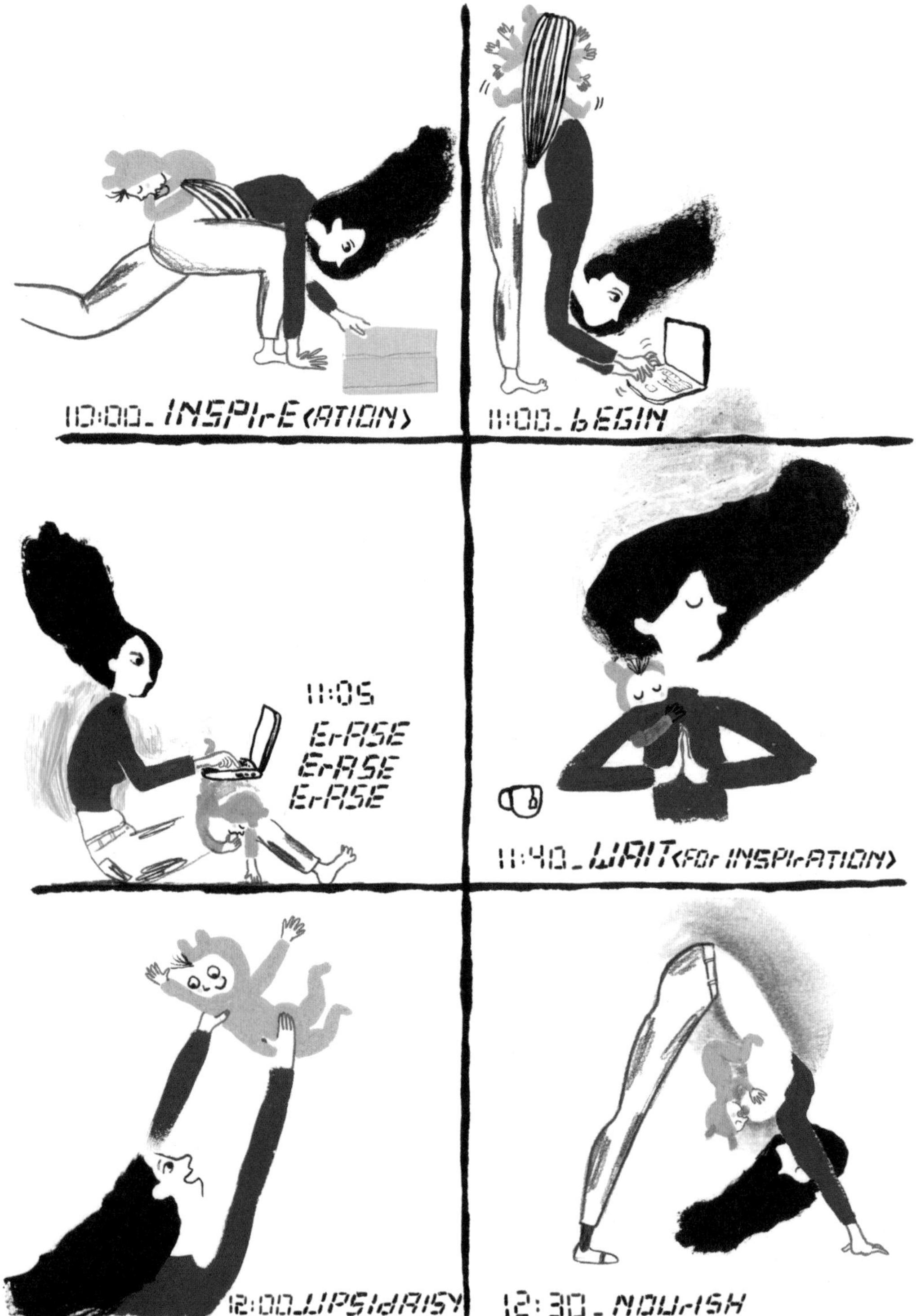
10:00_ INSPIrE(ATION)
11:00_ bEGIN
11:05
ErASE
ErASE
ErASE
11:40_ WAIT(For INSPIrATION)
12:00_UPSIdAISY
12:30_ NOUrISH

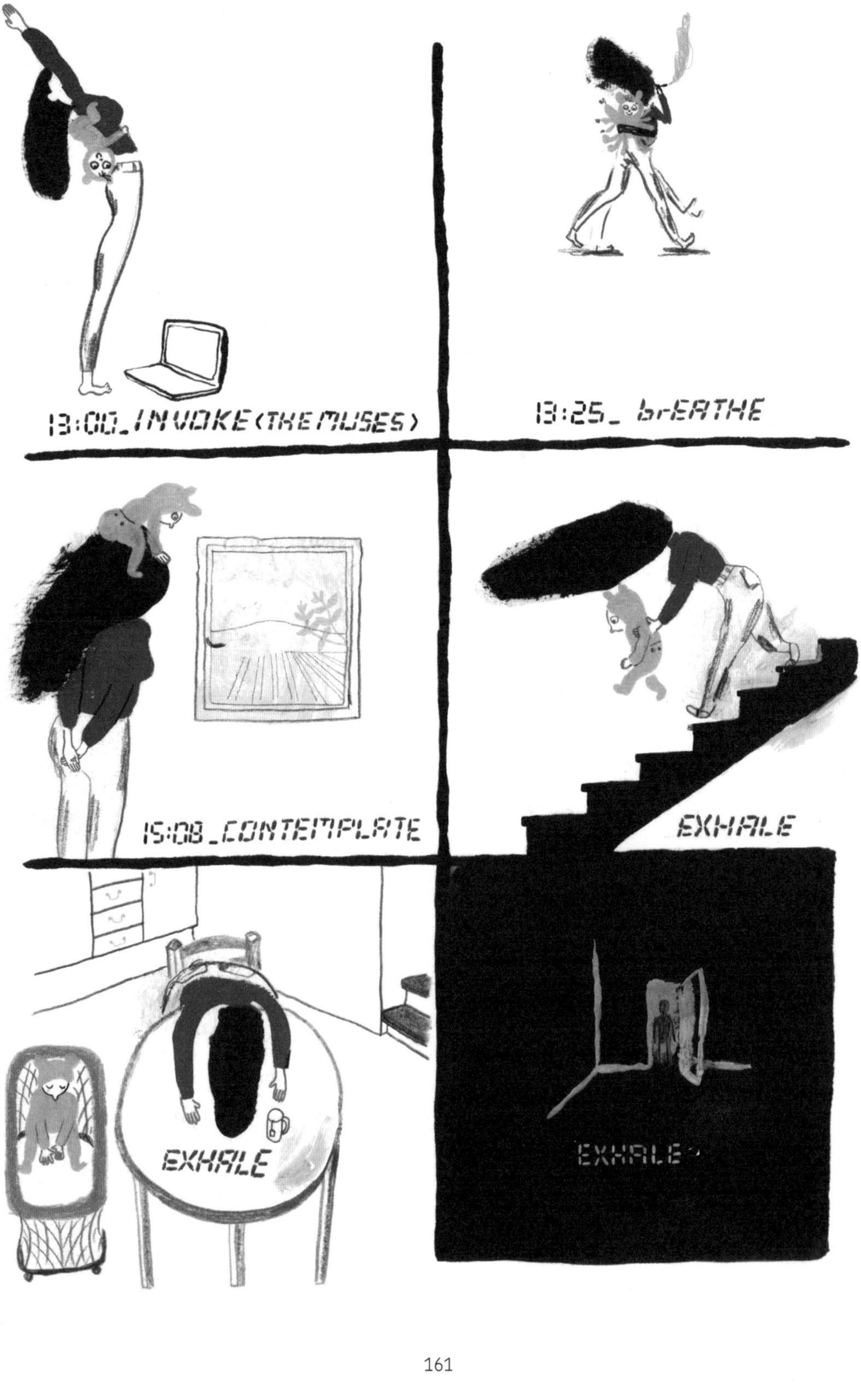
13:00_INVOKE (THE MUSES)
13:25_ brEATHE
15:08_CONTEMPLATE
EXHALE
EXHALE
EXHALE?

MIGUEL GALLARDO
A CHRISTMAS AT HOME

Miguel Gallardo was born in Lérida in 1955. He studied at the Escola Massana in Barcelona. During the '80s he became known as one of the most prominent members of the Barcelona underground, creating the legendary character Makoki. As an illustrator, he's been published in *La Vanguardia*, *El País*, the *New York Times*, and the *New Yorker*. The graphic novel *María y yo* [*Maria and I*] (2007), the story of his relationship with his autistic daughter, won the Premio Nacional del Cómic de Cataluña. The work gave rise to a documentary of the same title. He recently reissued *Un largo silencio* [*A Long Silence*] (2012), which explores the memory of his father, who fought with the Republicans during the Spanish Civil War, and has just published *María cumple 20 años* [*Maria Turns 20*] (2015), a continuation of *María y yo*. *Turista accidental* [*Accidental Tourist*] was released in 2016.

A CHRISTMAS AT HOME

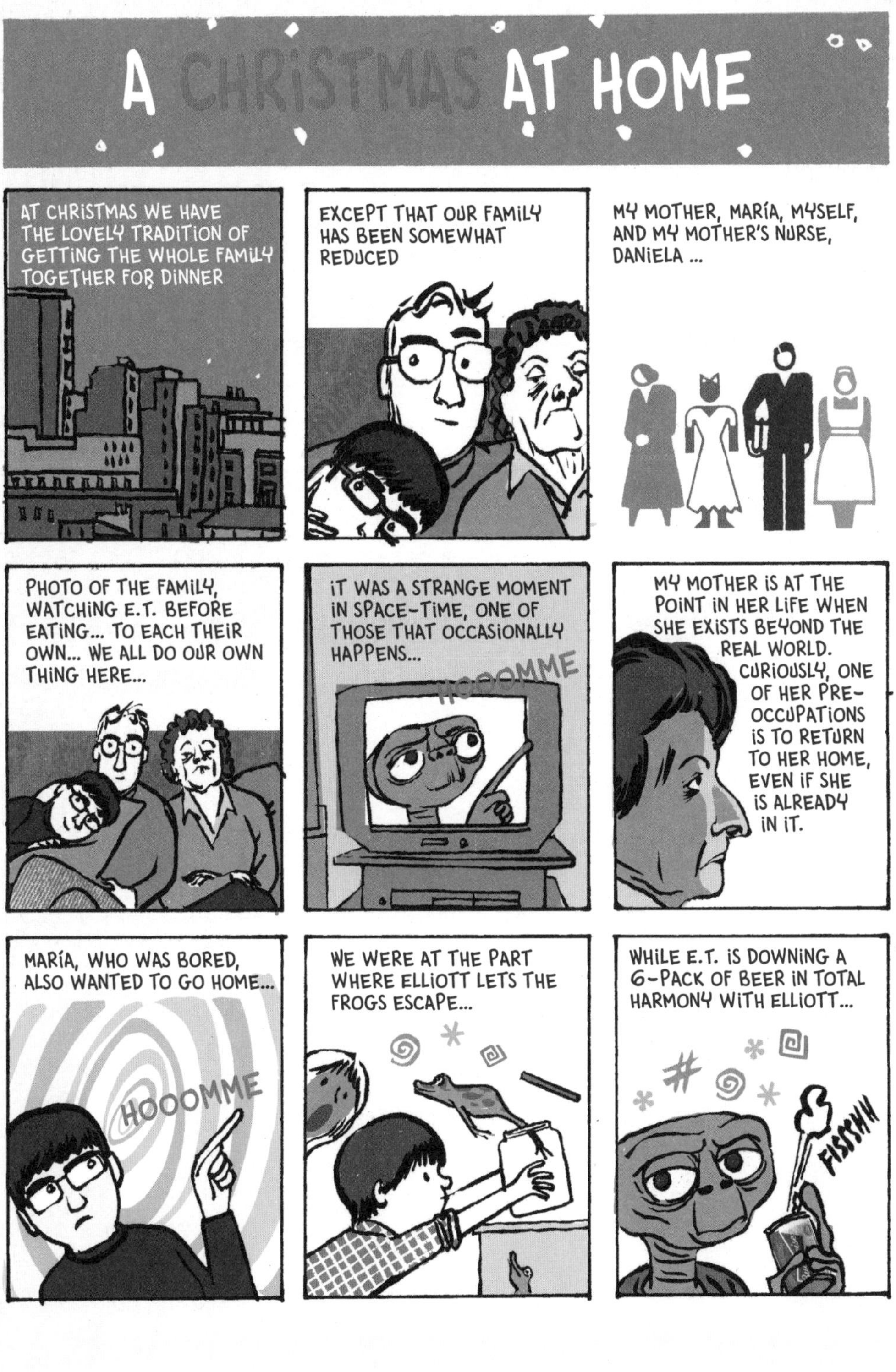
AT CHRISTMAS WE HAVE THE LOVELY TRADITION OF GETTING THE WHOLE FAMILY TOGETHER FOR DINNER
EXCEPT THAT OUR FAMILY HAS BEEN SOMEWHAT REDUCED
MY MOTHER, MARÍA, MYSELF, AND MY MOTHER'S NURSE, DANIELA ...
PHOTO OF THE FAMILY, WATCHING E.T. BEFORE EATING... TO EACH THEIR OWN... WE ALL DO OUR OWN THING HERE...
IT WAS A STRANGE MOMENT IN SPACE-TIME, ONE OF THOSE THAT OCCASIONALLY HAPPENS...
HOOOMME
MY MOTHER IS AT THE POINT IN HER LIFE WHEN SHE EXISTS BEYOND THE REAL WORLD.
CURIOUSLY, ONE OF HER PRE-OCCUPATIONS IS TO RETURN TO HER HOME, EVEN IF SHE IS ALREADY IN IT.
MARÍA, WHO WAS BORED, ALSO WANTED TO GO HOME...
HOOOMME
WE WERE AT THE PART WHERE ELLIOTT LETS THE FROGS ESCAPE...
WHILE E.T. IS DOWNING A 6-PACK OF BEER IN TOTAL HARMONY WITH ELLIOTT...
FISSSHH

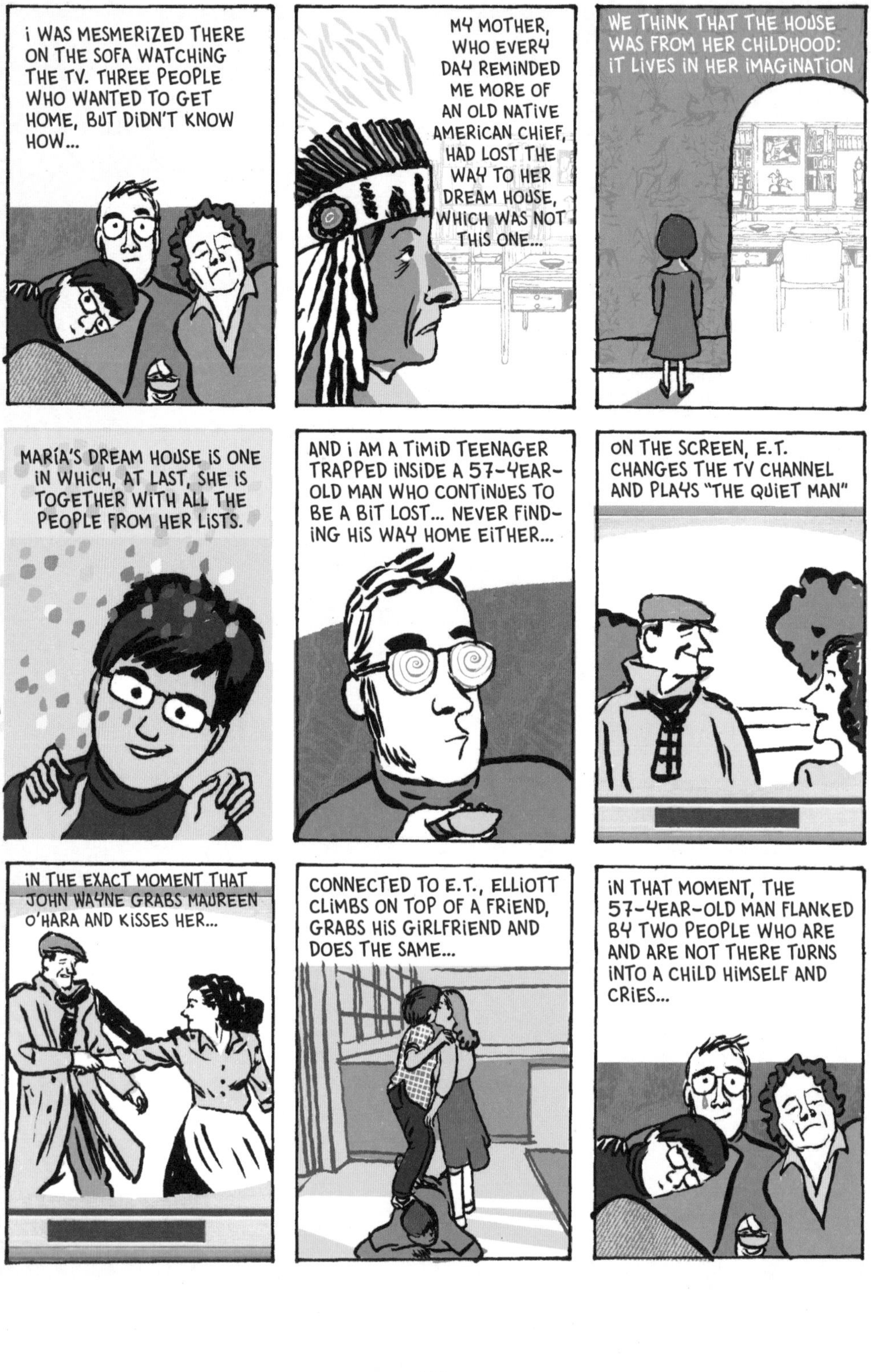

i WAS MESMERIZED THERE ON THE SOFA WATCHiNG THE TV. THREE PEOPLE WHO WANTED TO GET HOME, BUT DIDN'T KNOW HOW...
MY MOTHER, WHO EVERY DAY REMINDED ME MORE OF AN OLD NATiVE AMERiCAN CHiEF, HAD LOST THE WAY TO HER DREAM HOUSE, WHiCH WAS NOT THiS ONE...
WE THiNK THAT THE HOUSE WAS FROM HER CHiLDHOOD: iT LiVES iN HER iMAGiNATiON
MARÍA'S DREAM HOUSE iS ONE iN WHiCH, AT LAST, SHE iS TOGETHER WiTH ALL THE PEOPLE FROM HER LiSTS.
AND i AM A TiMiD TEENAGER TRAPPED iNSiDE A 57-YEAR-OLD MAN WHO CONTiNUES TO BE A BiT LOST... NEVER FiND-iNG HiS WAY HOME EiTHER...
ON THE SCREEN, E.T. CHANGES THE TV CHANNEL AND PLAYS "THE QUiET MAN"
iN THE EXACT MOMENT THAT JOHN WAYNE GRABS MAUREEN O'HARA AND KiSSES HER...
CONNECTED TO E.T., ELLiOTT CLiMBS ON TOP OF A FRiEND, GRABS HiS GiRLFRiEND AND DOES THE SAME...
iN THAT MOMENT, THE 57-YEAR-OLD MAN FLANKED BY TWO PEOPLE WHO ARE AND ARE NOT THERE TURNS iNTO A CHiLD HiMSELF AND CRiES...

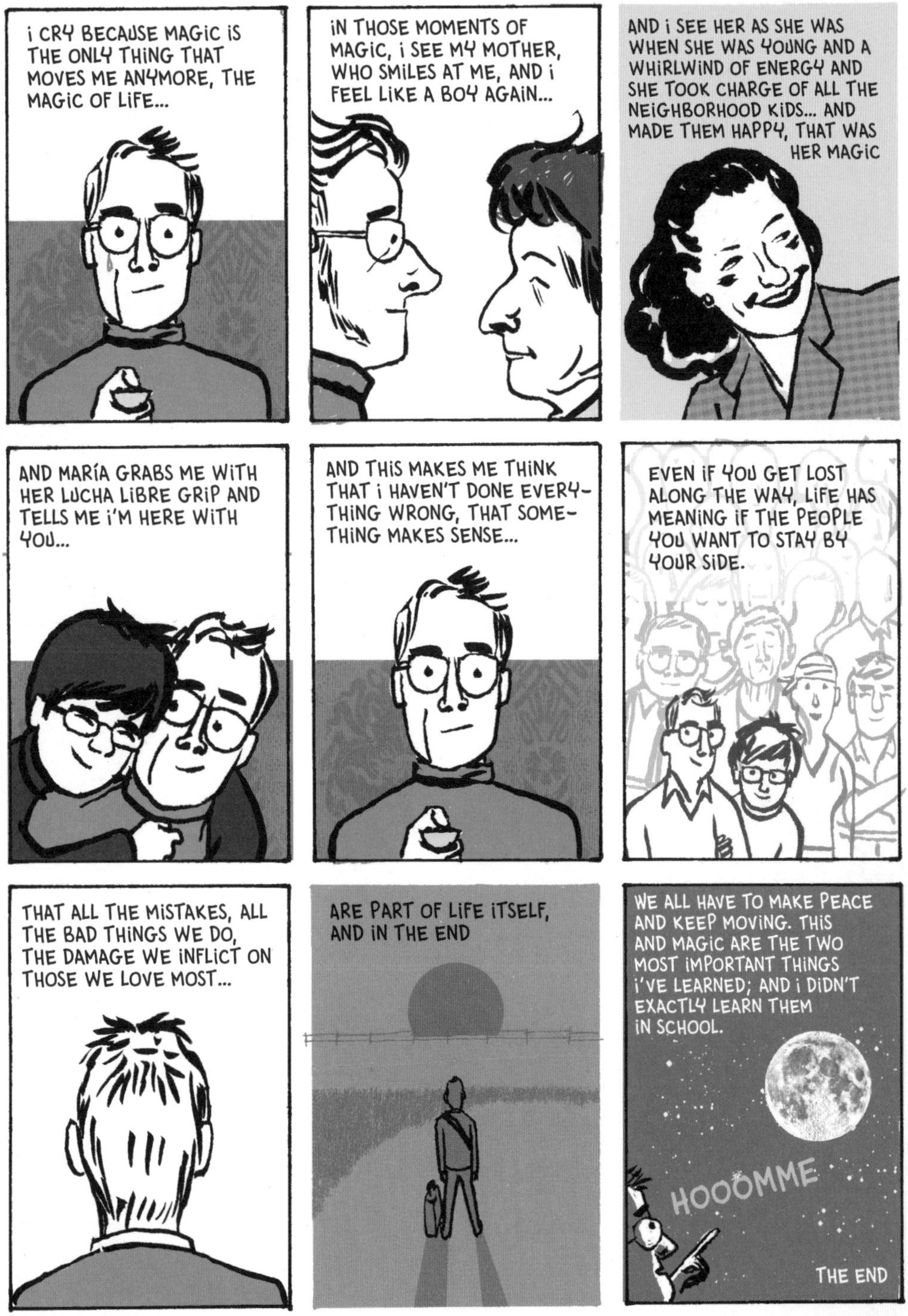
i CRY BECAUSE MAGiC iS THE ONLY THiNG THAT MOVES ME ANYMORE, THE MAGiC OF LiFE...
iN THOSE MOMENTS OF MAGiC, i SEE MY MOTHER, WHO SMiLES AT ME, AND i FEEL LiKE A BOY AGAiN...
AND i SEE HER AS SHE WAS WHEN SHE WAS YOUNG AND A WHiRLWiND OF ENERGY AND SHE TOOK CHARGE OF ALL THE NEiGHBORHOOD KiDS... AND MADE THEM HAPPY, THAT WAS HER MAGiC
AND MARíA GRABS ME WiTH HER LUCHA LiBRE GRiP AND TELLS ME i'M HERE WiTH YOU...
AND THiS MAKES ME THiNK THAT i HAVEN'T DONE EVERY-THiNG WRONG, THAT SOME-THiNG MAKES SENSE...
EVEN iF YOU GET LOST ALONG THE WAY, LiFE HAS MEANiNG iF THE PEOPLE YOU WANT TO STAY BY YOUR SiDE.
THAT ALL THE MiSTAKES, ALL THE BAD THiNGS WE DO, THE DAMAGE WE iNFLiCT ON THOSE WE LOVE MOST...
ARE PART OF LiFE iTSELF, AND iN THE END
WE ALL HAVE TO MAKE PEACE AND KEEP MOVING. THiS AND MAGiC ARE THE TWO MOST iMPORTANT THiNGS i'VE LEARNED; AND i DiDN'T EXACTLY LEARN THEM iN SCHOOL.
HOOOMME
THE END

GALLARDO

MAX

AN ENIGMATIC DREAM

Max was born in Barcelona in 1956. An illustrator for the press, literature and philosophy books, and a prolific and celebrated cartoonist, Max has won the Premio Nacional del Cómic (2007, for *Bardín el Superrealista* [*Bardín the Superrealist*]), the Gran Premio del Salón del Cómic de Barcelona in 2000 and the North American Ignatz (1999). As a cartoonist, he became known in the pages of *El Víbora* in the '80s, where he created popular characters such as Gustavo and Peter Pank. He co-edited the international avant-garde magazine *NSLM*. His graphic novel *Vapor* (2012), was published in the United States by Fantagraphics. Currently he's contributing to *Babelia*, the cultural supplement of *El País*. He worked on the design for the newspaper stand at the ARCO International Art Fair 2013. This experience resulted in the book *Paseo astral* [*Astral Trip*] (2013). Most recently, he published *Conversación de sombras* [*Conversation of Shadows*] (2013) and *¡Oh diabólica ficción!* [*Oh Diabolic Fiction!*] (2015). He is currently working on a comic about the painter Bosch, in collaboration with the Prado Museum.

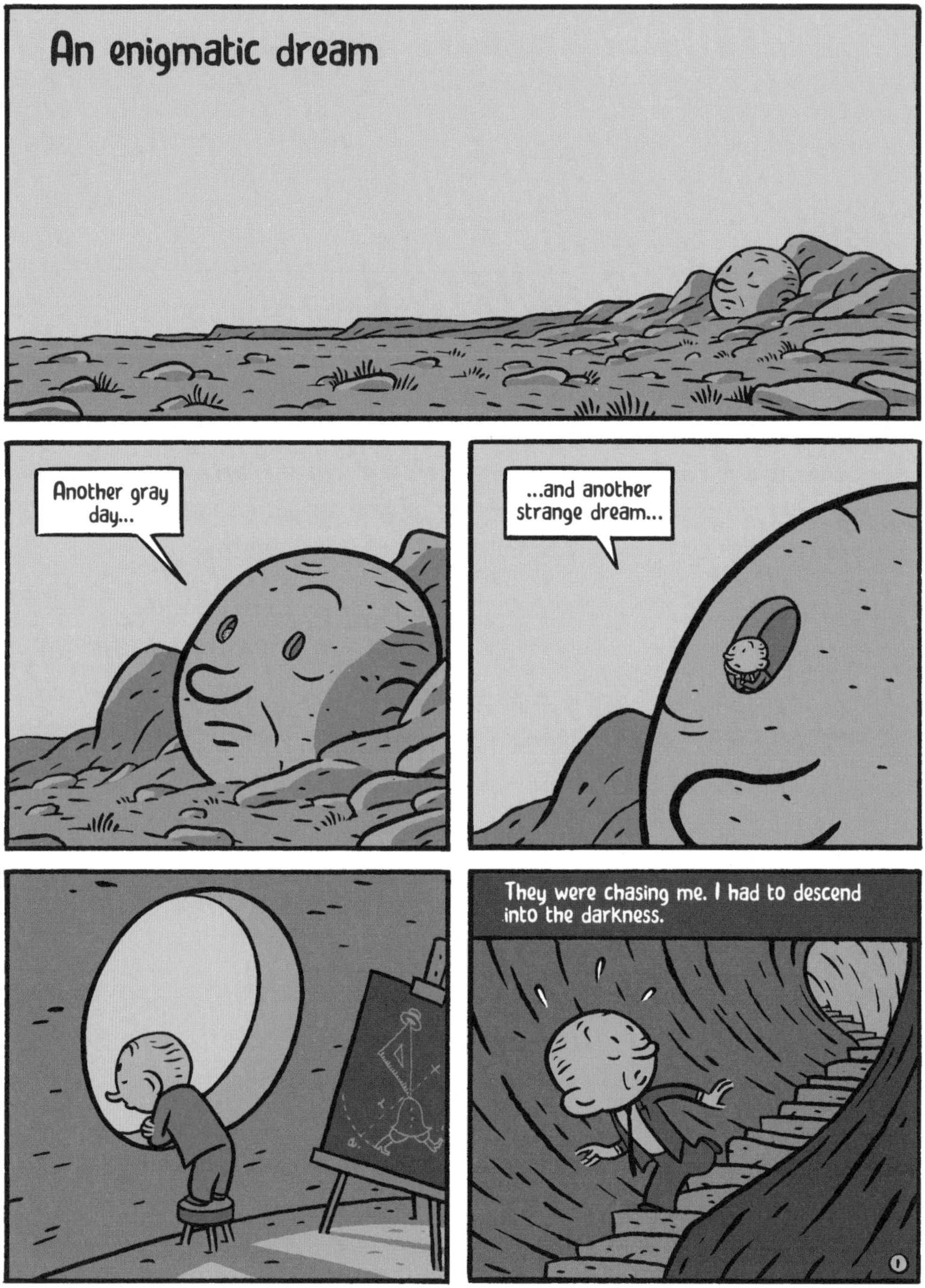
An enigmatic dream
Another gray day...
...and another strange dream...
They were chasing me. I had to descend into the darkness.

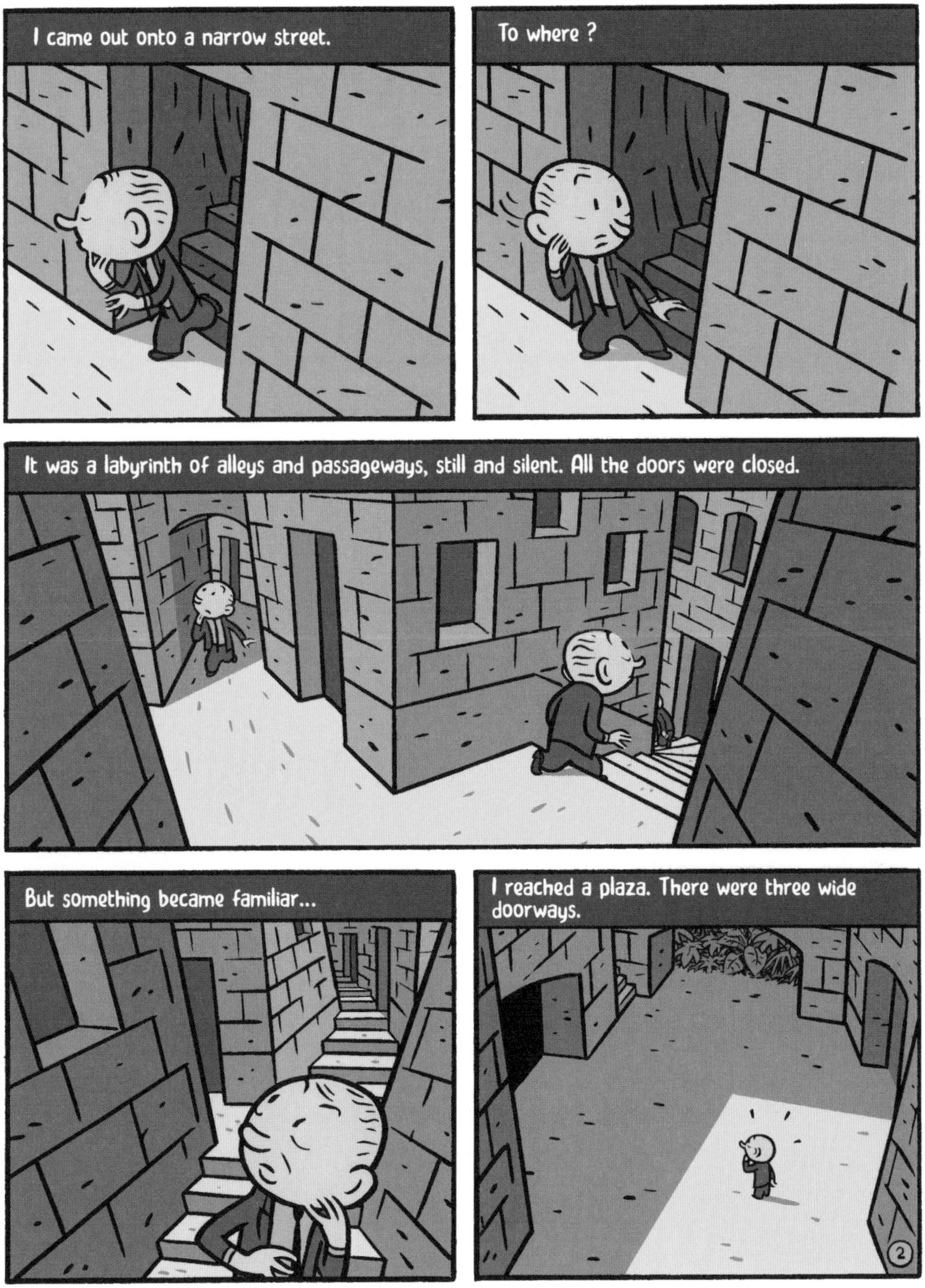
I came out onto a narrow street.
To where ?
It was a labyrinth of alleys and passageways, still and silent. All the doors were closed.
But something became familiar...
I reached a plaza. There were three wide doorways.

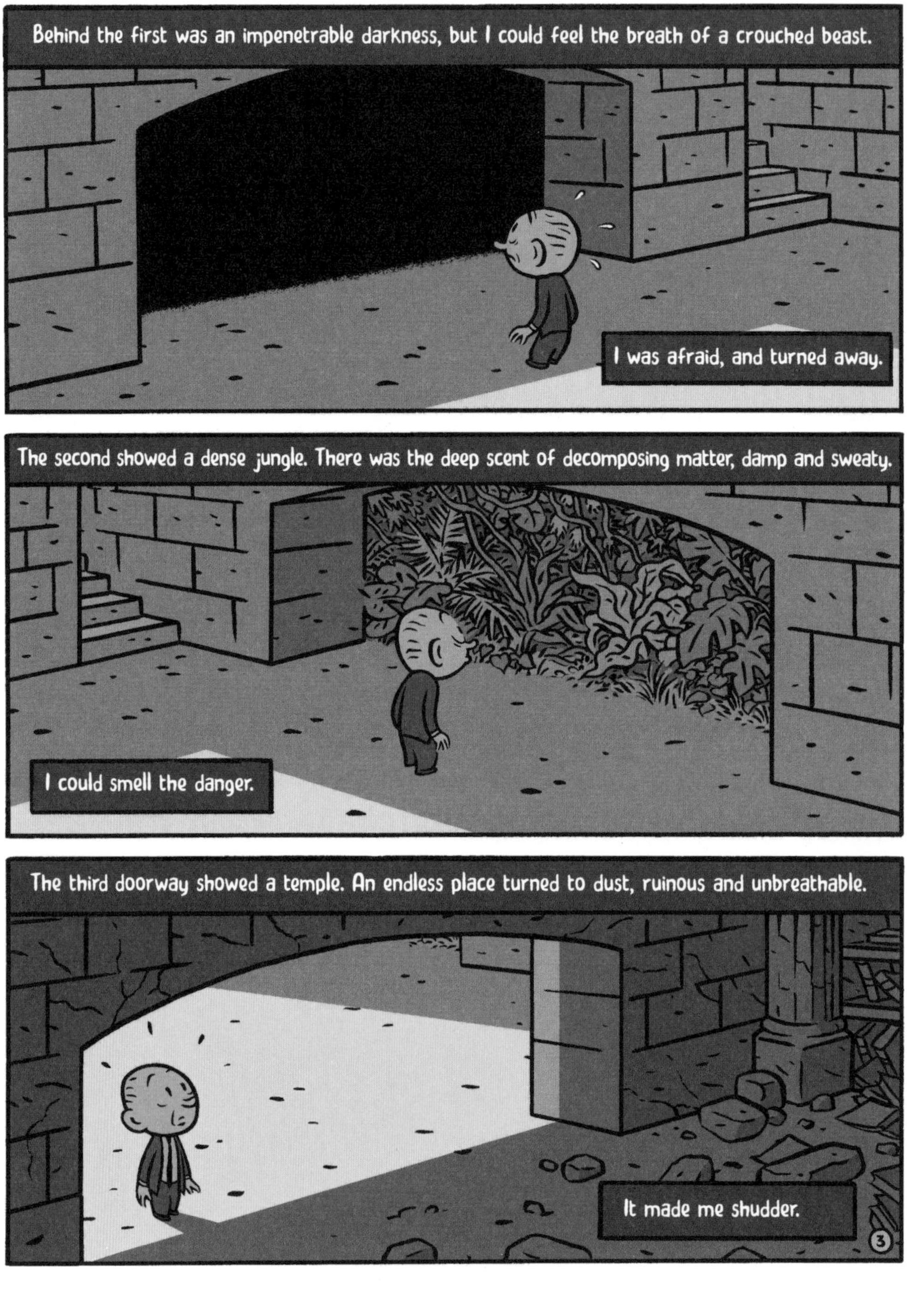
Behind the first was an impenetrable darkness, but I could feel the breath of a crouched beast.
I was afraid, and turned away.
The second showed a dense jungle. There was the deep scent of decomposing matter, damp and sweaty.
I could smell the danger.
The third doorway showed a temple. An endless place turned to dust, ruinous and unbreathable.
It made me shudder.
3

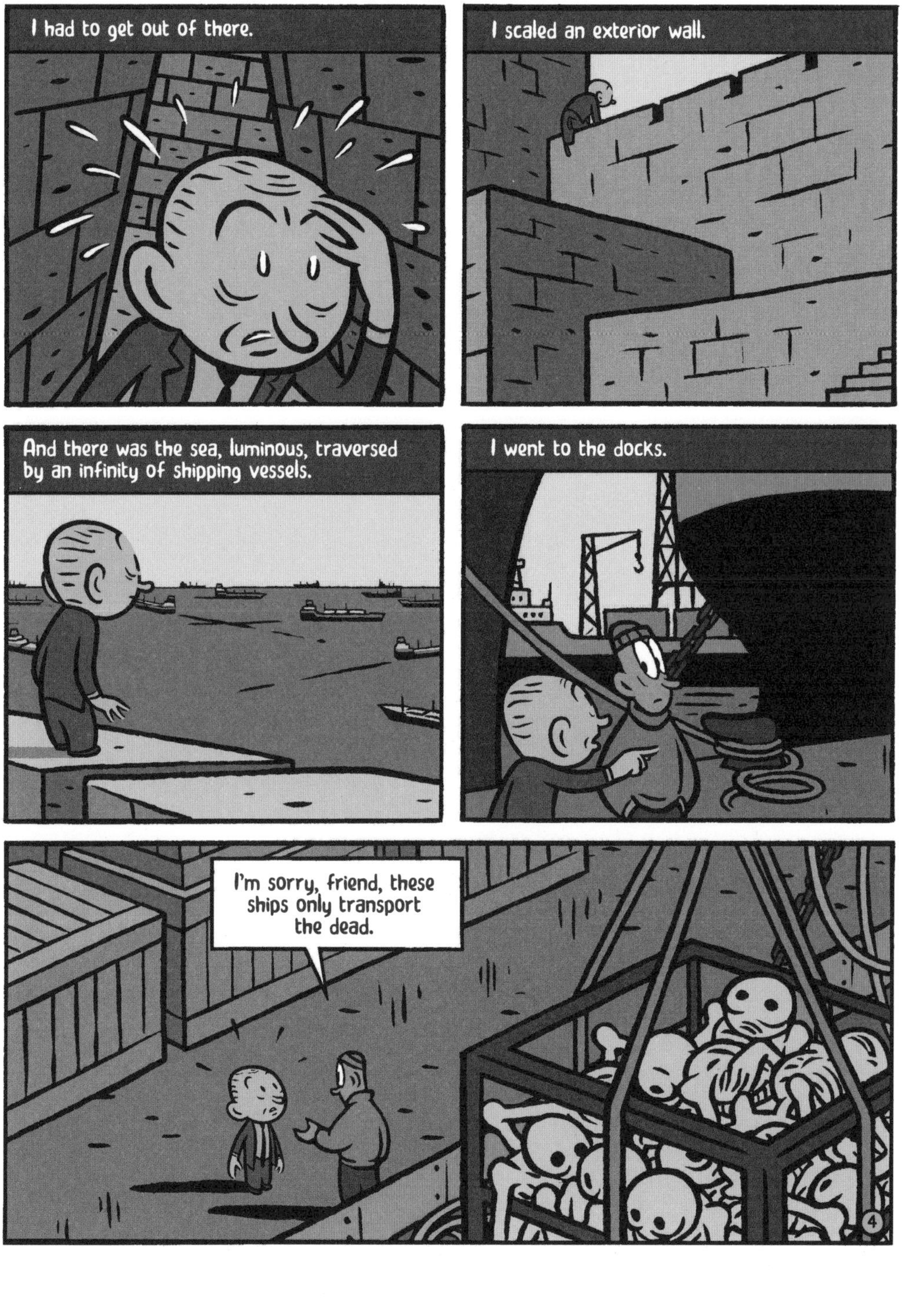
I had to get out of there.
I scaled an exterior wall.
And there was the sea, luminous, traversed by an infinity of shipping vessels.
I went to the docks.
I'm sorry, friend, these ships only transport the dead.
4

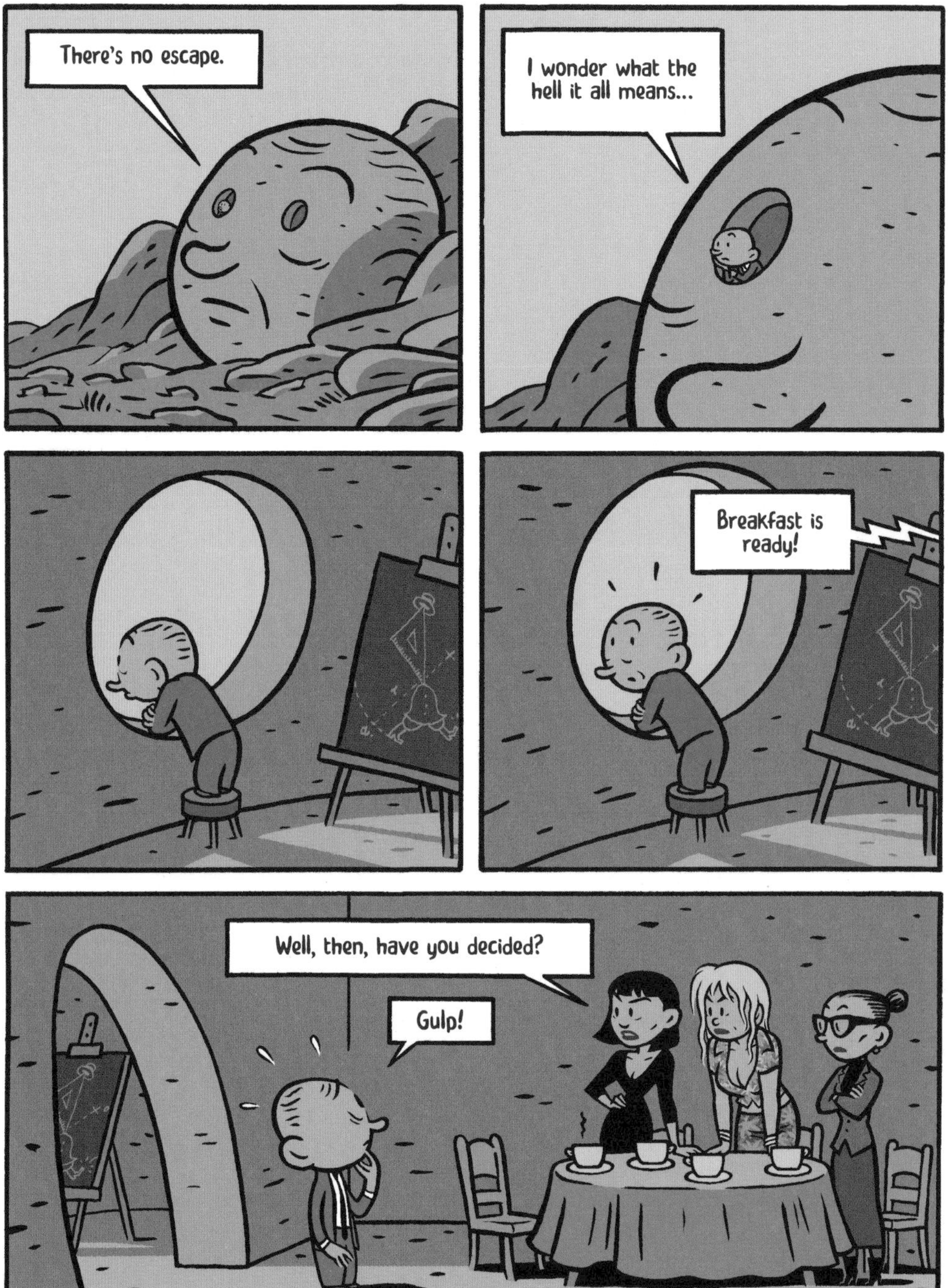
There's no escape.
I wonder what the hell it all means...
Breakfast is ready!
Well, then, have you decided?
Gulp!

MICHARMUT

TIME IN TIME OUT

Micharmut was born in El Cabañal (Valencia) in 1953. He is one of the most prominent cartoonists of the "nueva línea clara" [new clear line] 1980s Valencia movement. Micharmut's career has resulted in a handful of scattered comics and a number of albums, always on the cutting edge of graphic art with an intensely personal vision. The standouts among them are *Dogón* (1983), *Futurama: la mascara de goma* [*Futurama: The Rubber Mask*] (1984), *Raya* [*Ray*] (2009), *Marisco* [*Seafood*] (1990), *Venticuatro horas* [*Twenty-Four Hours*] (2995), *Pip* (2004), and *Arf!* (2005). His latest work is *Sólo para moscas* [*Only For Flies*] (2012).

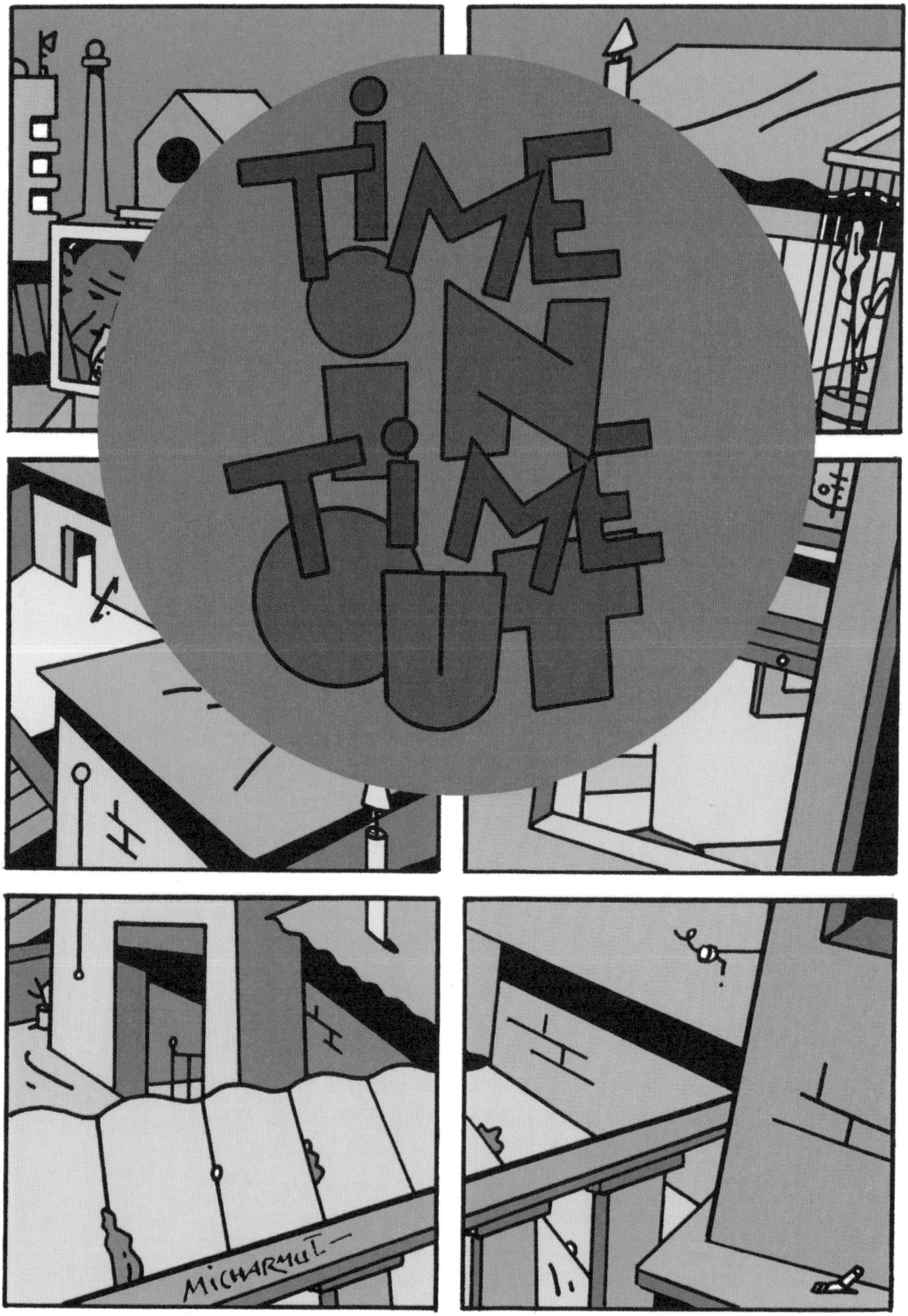
TIME IN TIME OUT
MICHARMUT

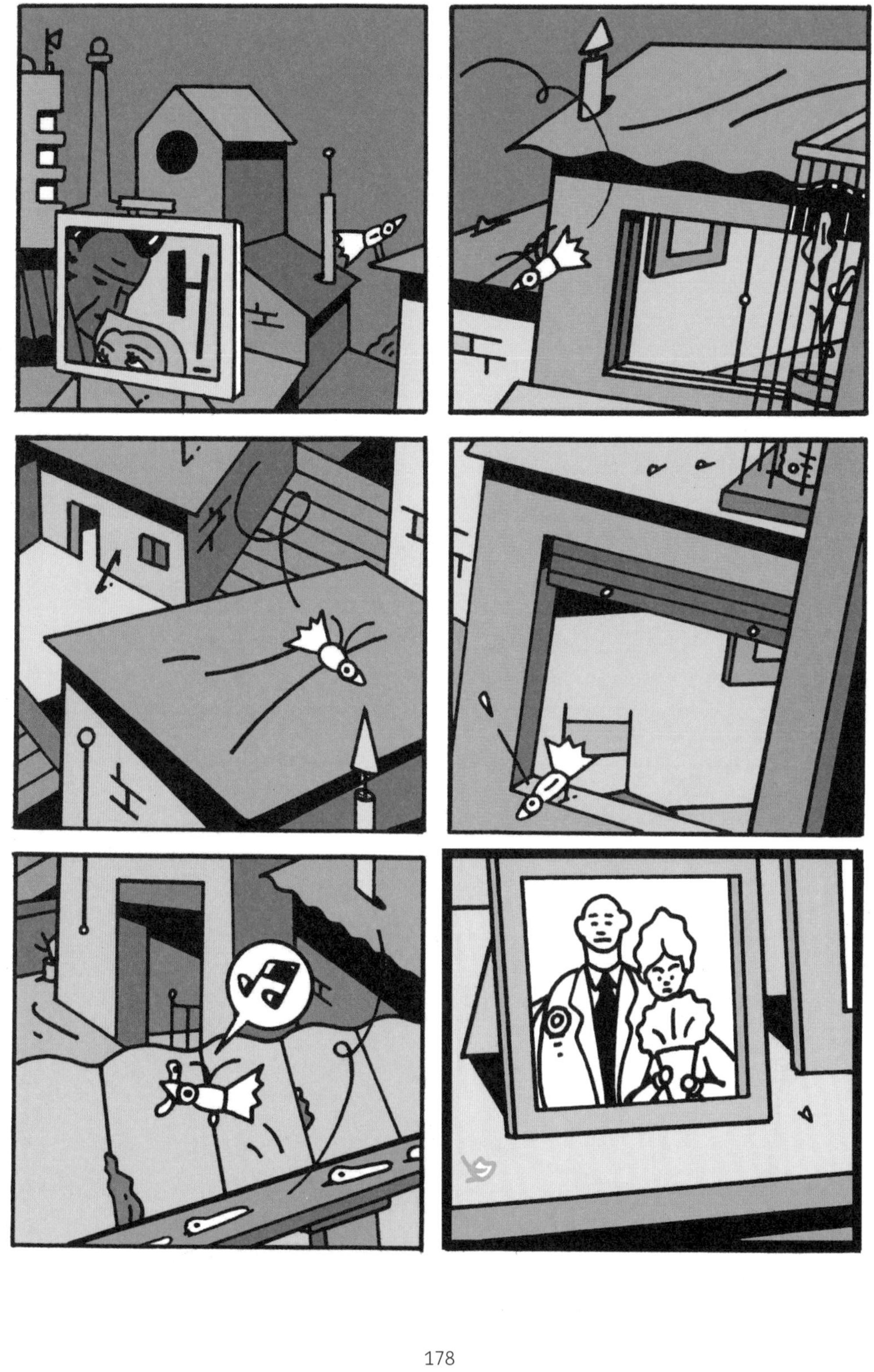

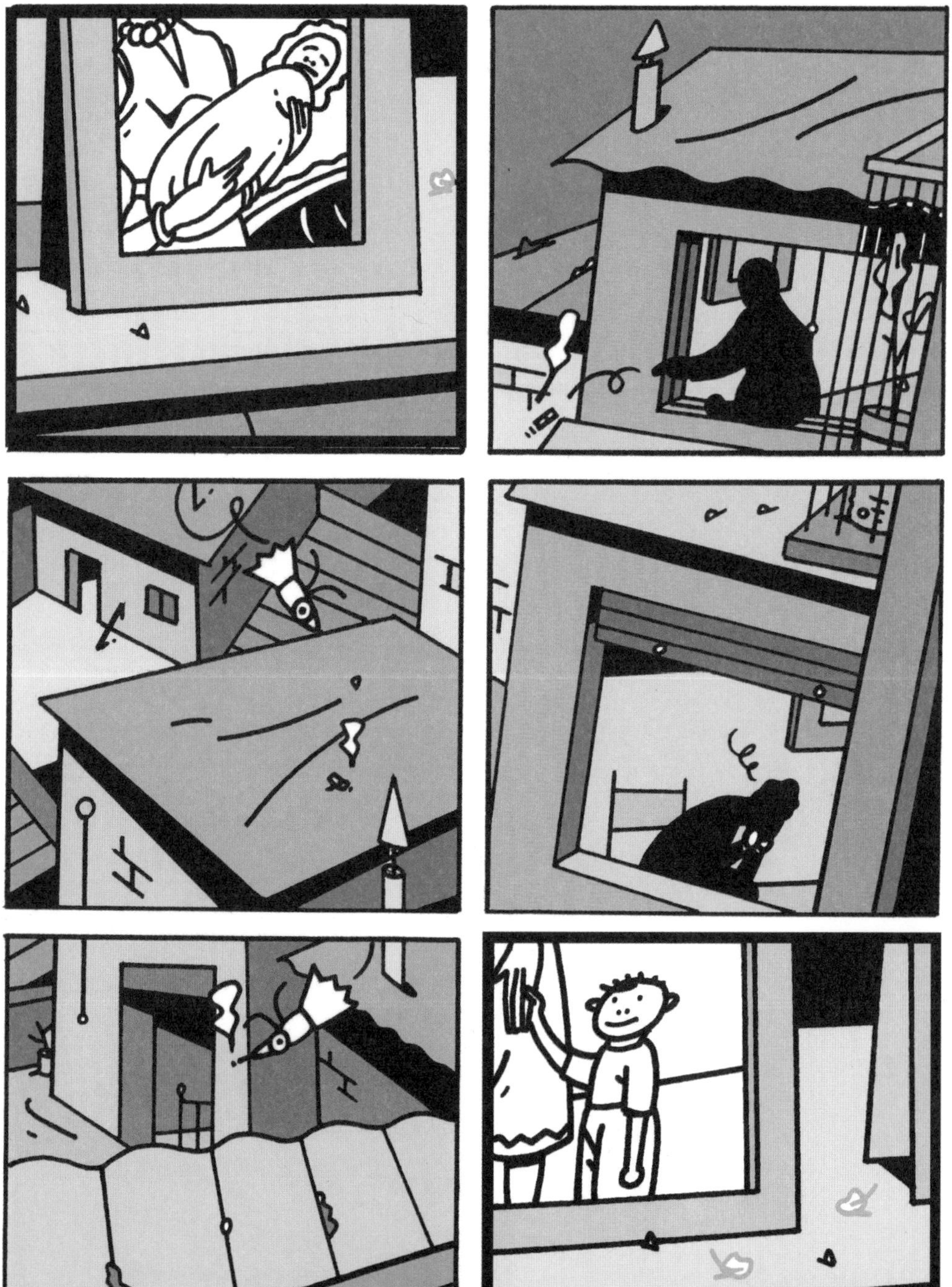

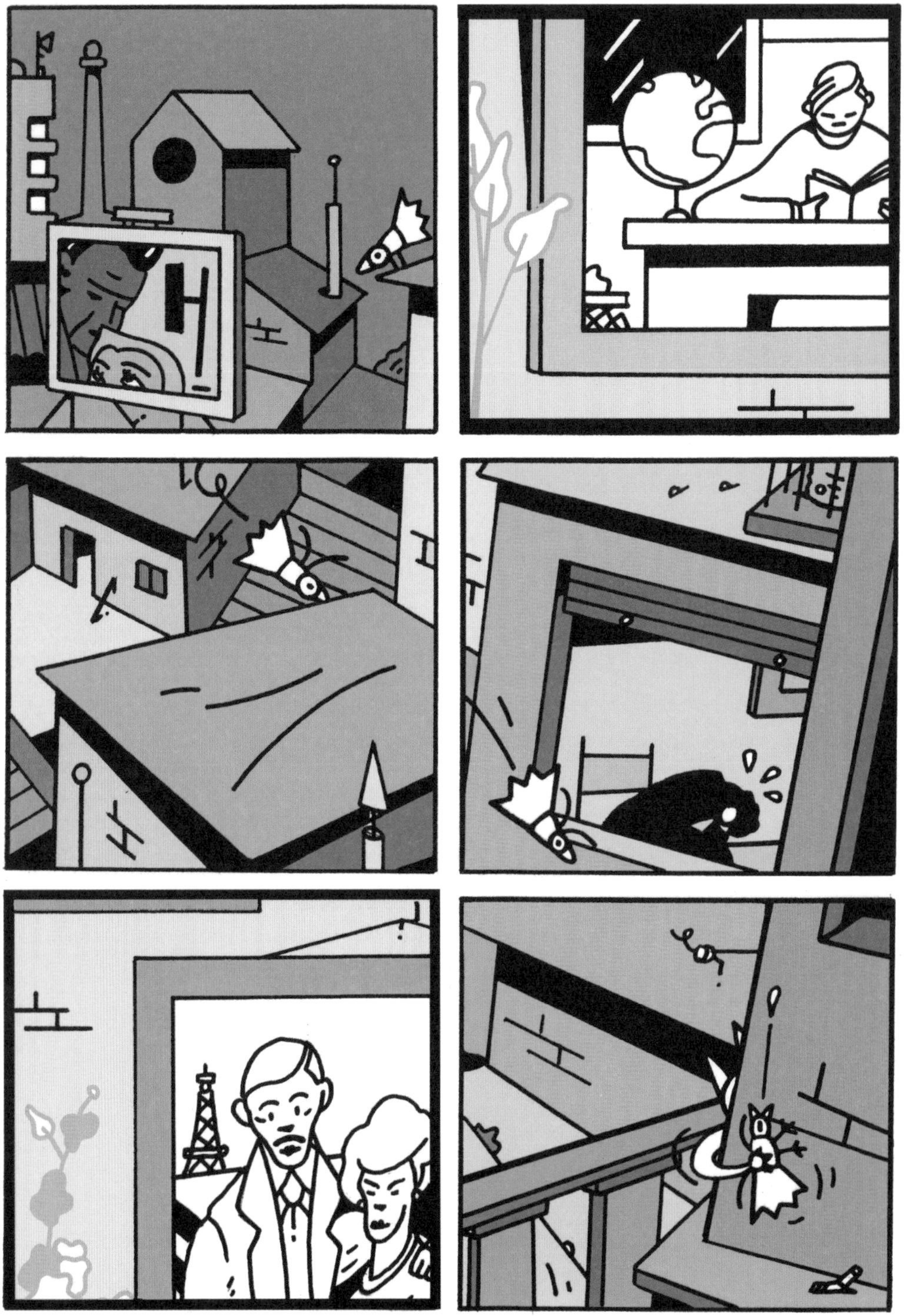

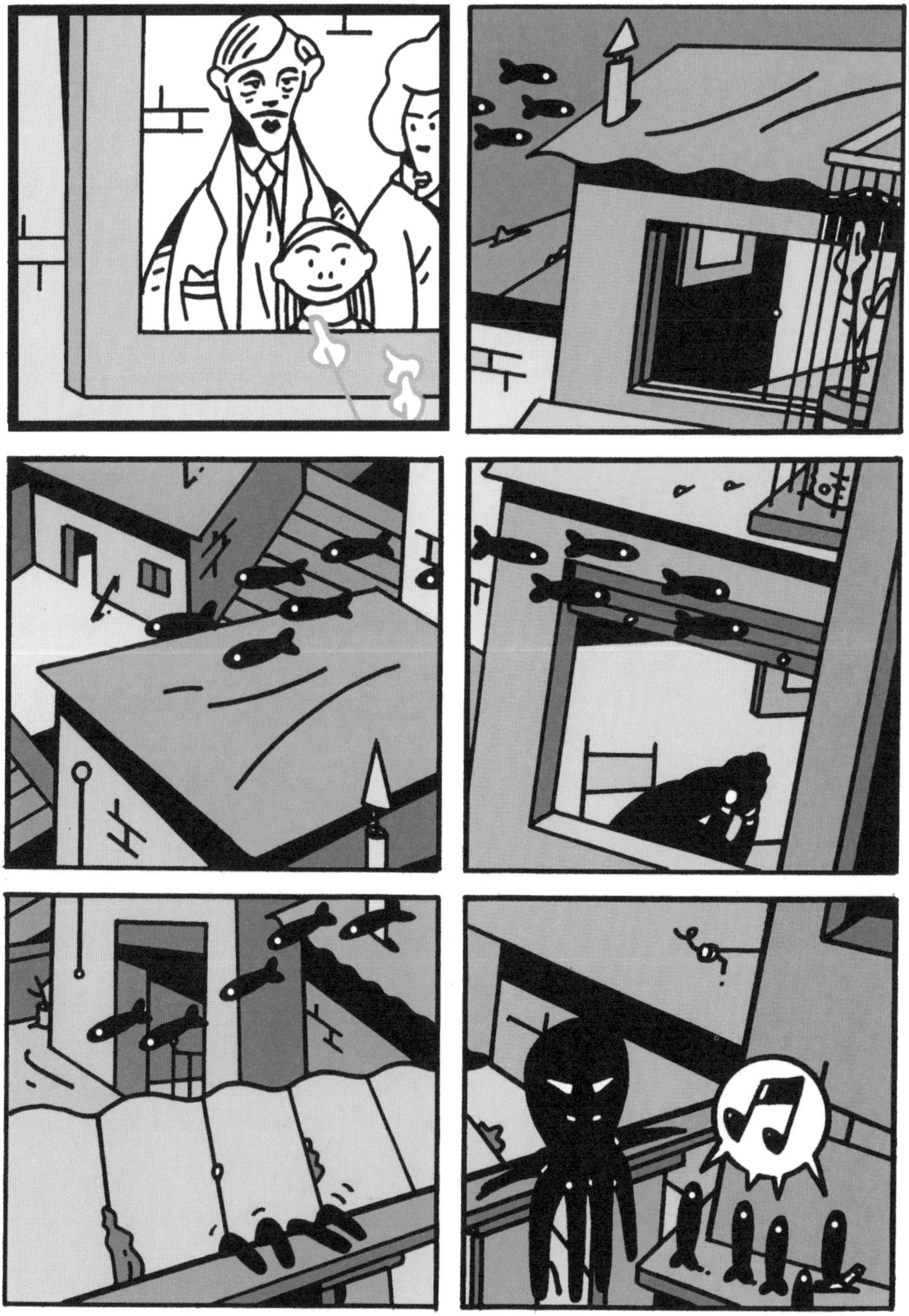

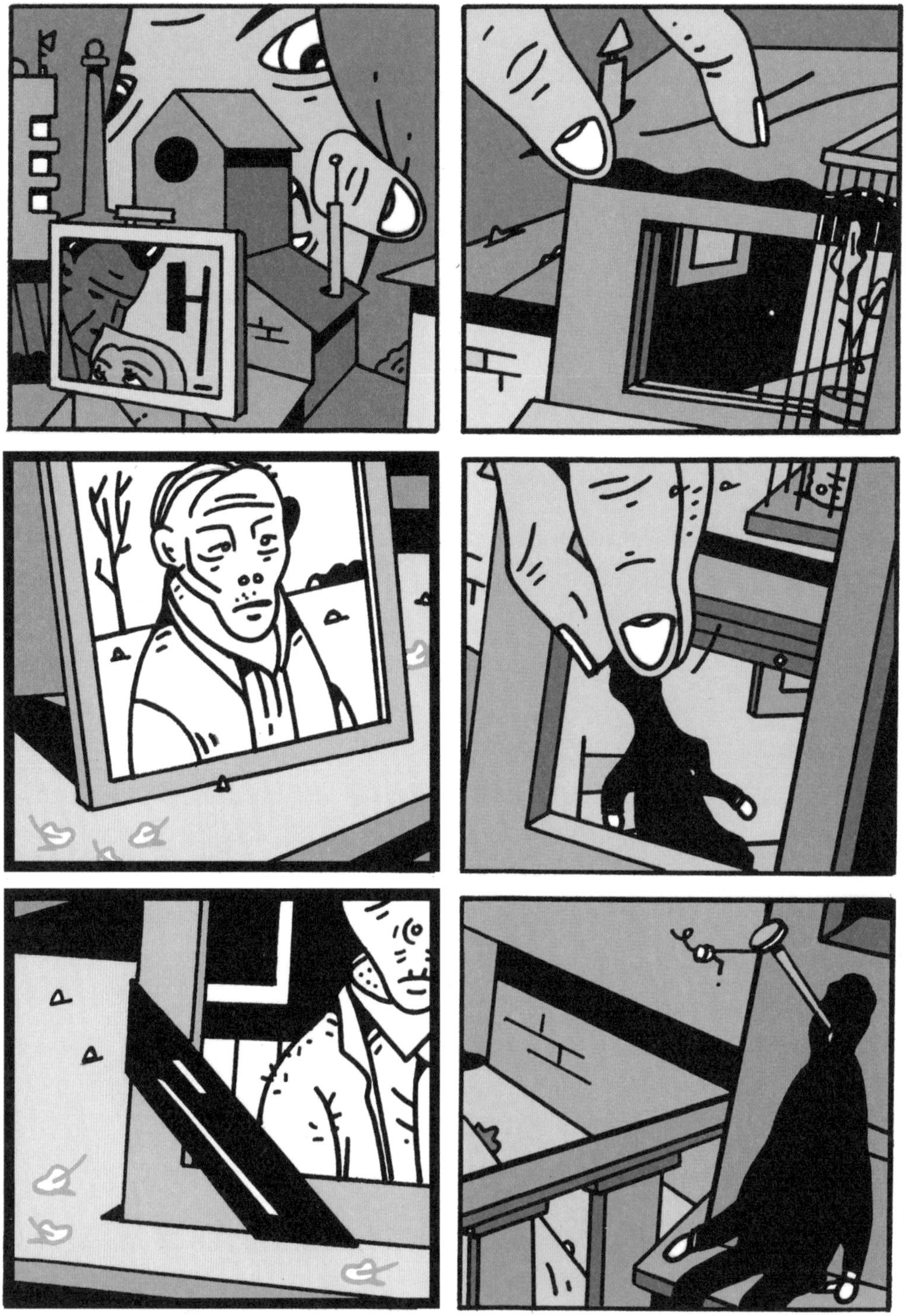

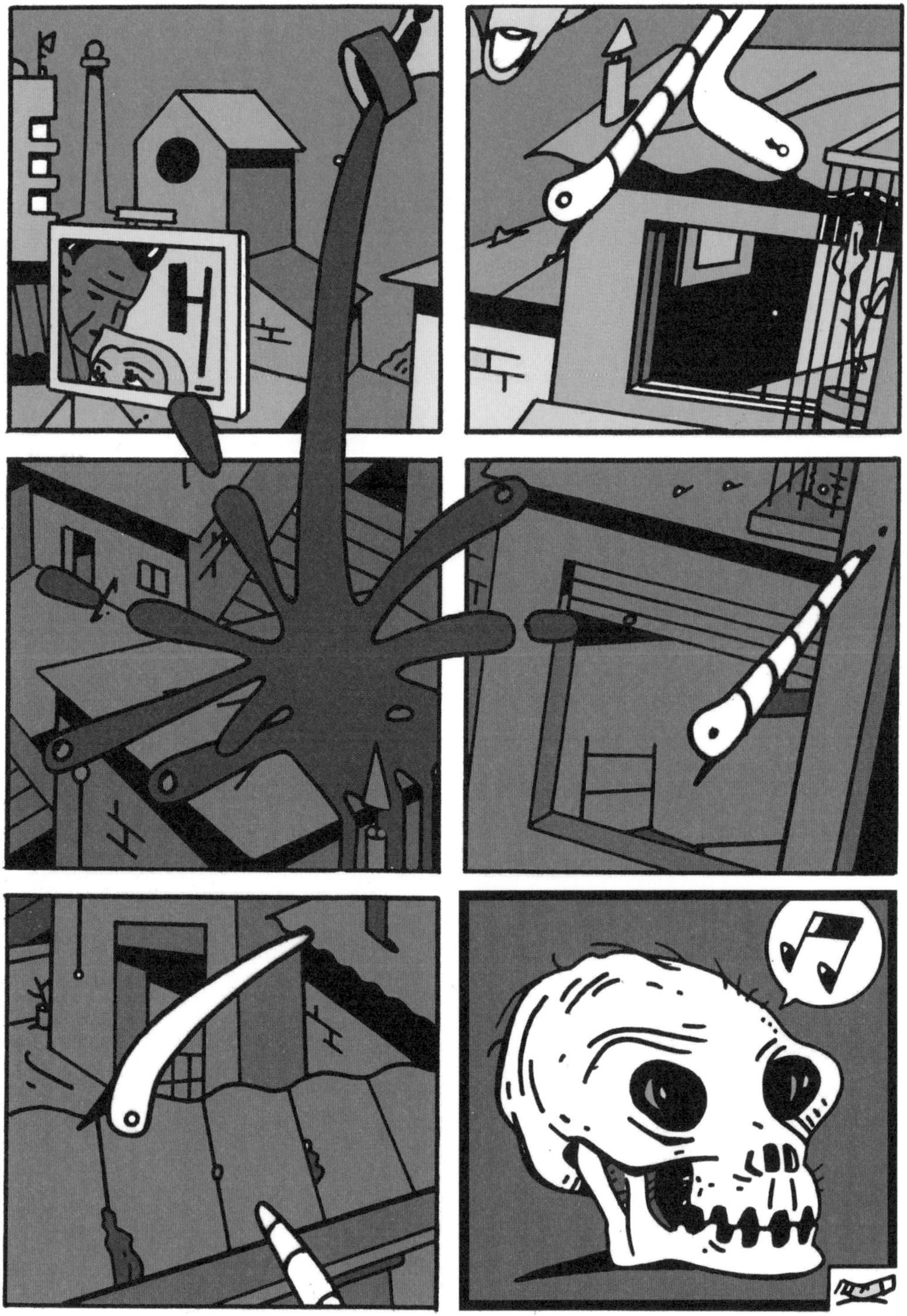

ANA GALVAÑ

HORSE MEAT

Ana Galvañ was born in Murcia in 1975. After her time in the faculty of Fine Arts in Valencia, Ana Galvañ moved to Madrid, where she specialized in creative and art direction. Later she left advertising to pursue comics and illustration full time. Her work has appeared in publications such as *Mortland*, *Nobrow*, *Off Life*, *Clift*, *Ferocious Quarterly*, *Autsaider* comics, *Skunk Art Mag*, and *Tik Tok*. She was also a participant in *Vertigo Quarterly: CMYK no. 4: Black.* Recently, she published the comic book *Trabajo de clase* [*Classwork*] (2014). Additionally, she runs the website www.tiktokcomics.com, on which she has published various short comics.

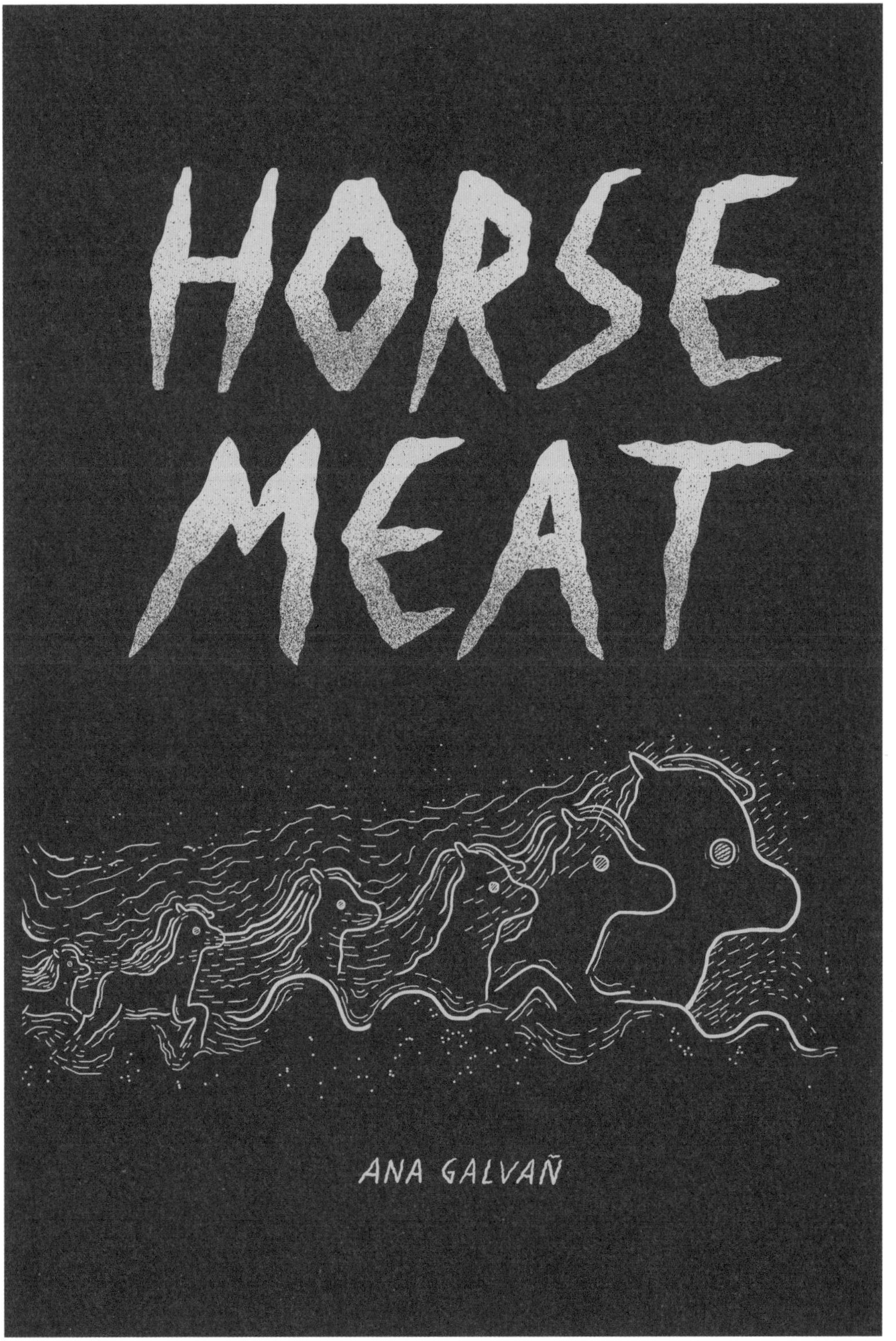
HORSE
MEAT
ANA GALVAÑ

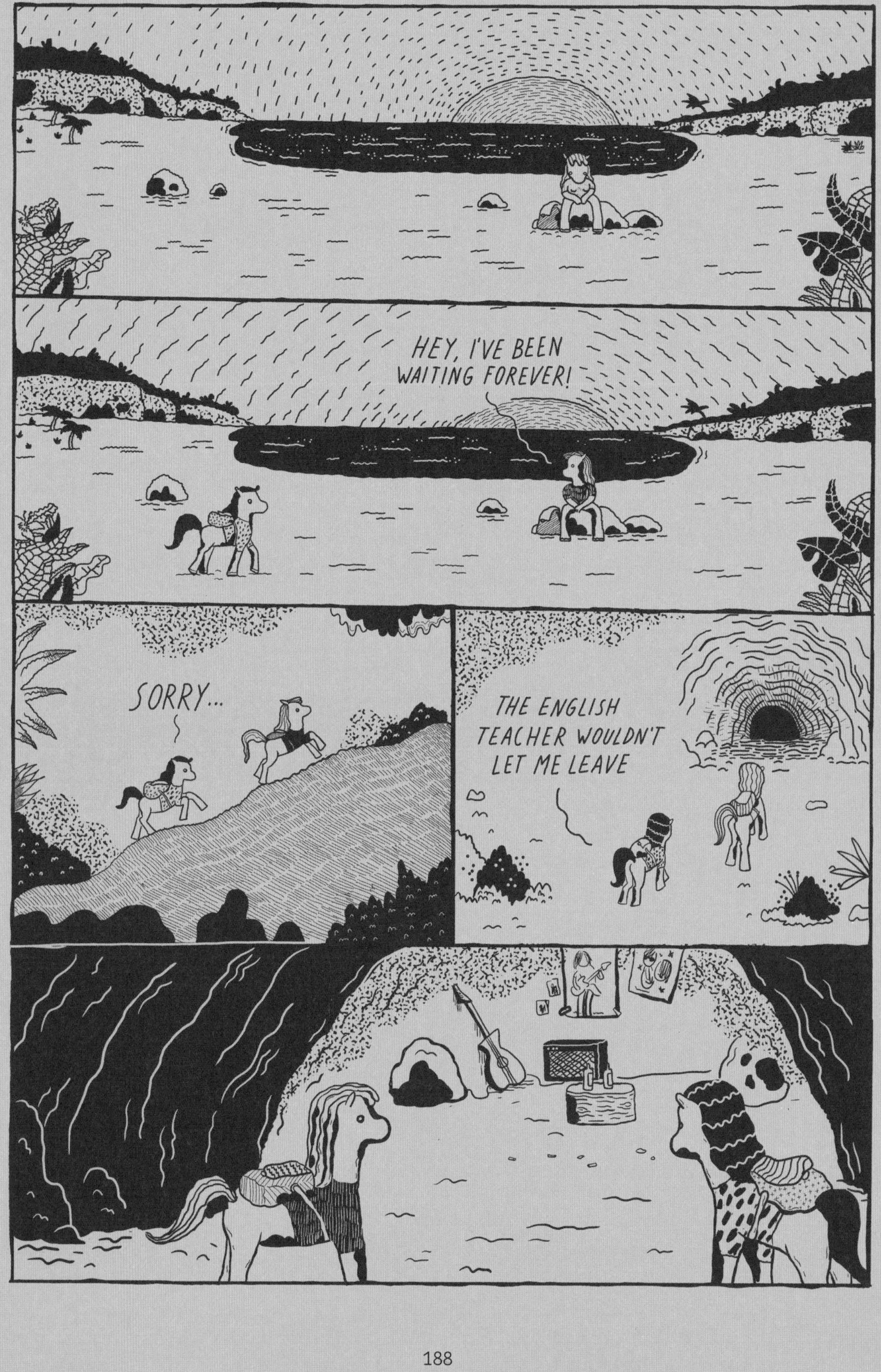
HEY, I'VE BEEN WAITING FOREVER!
SORRY...
THE ENGLISH TEACHER WOULDN'T LET ME LEAVE

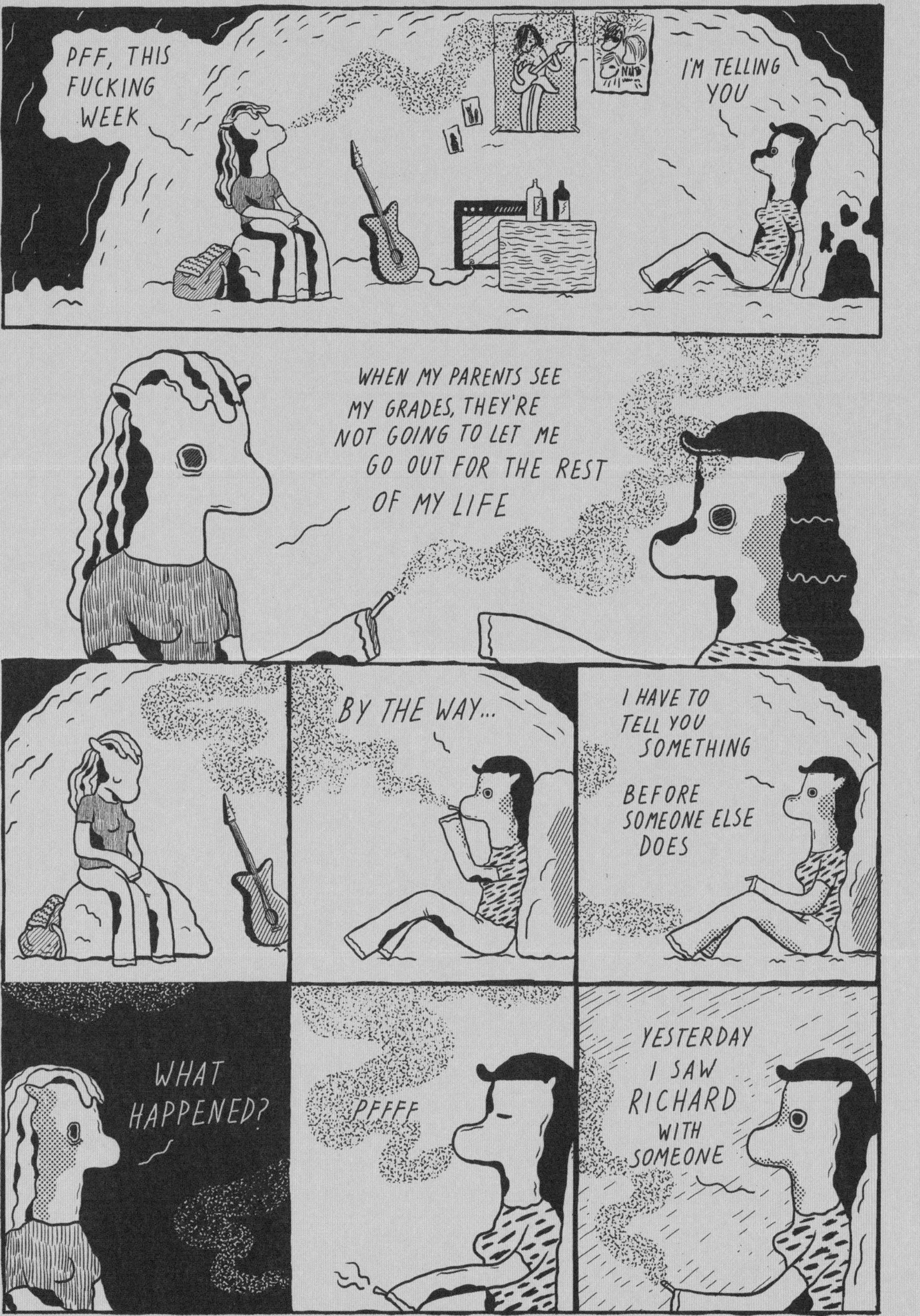
PFF, THIS FUCKING WEEK
I'M TELLING YOU
WHEN MY PARENTS SEE MY GRADES, THEY'RE NOT GOING TO LET ME GO OUT FOR THE REST OF MY LIFE
BY THE WAY...
I HAVE TO TELL YOU SOMETHING
BEFORE SOMEONE ELSE DOES
WHAT HAPPENED?
PFFFF
YESTERDAY I SAW RICHARD WITH SOMEONE

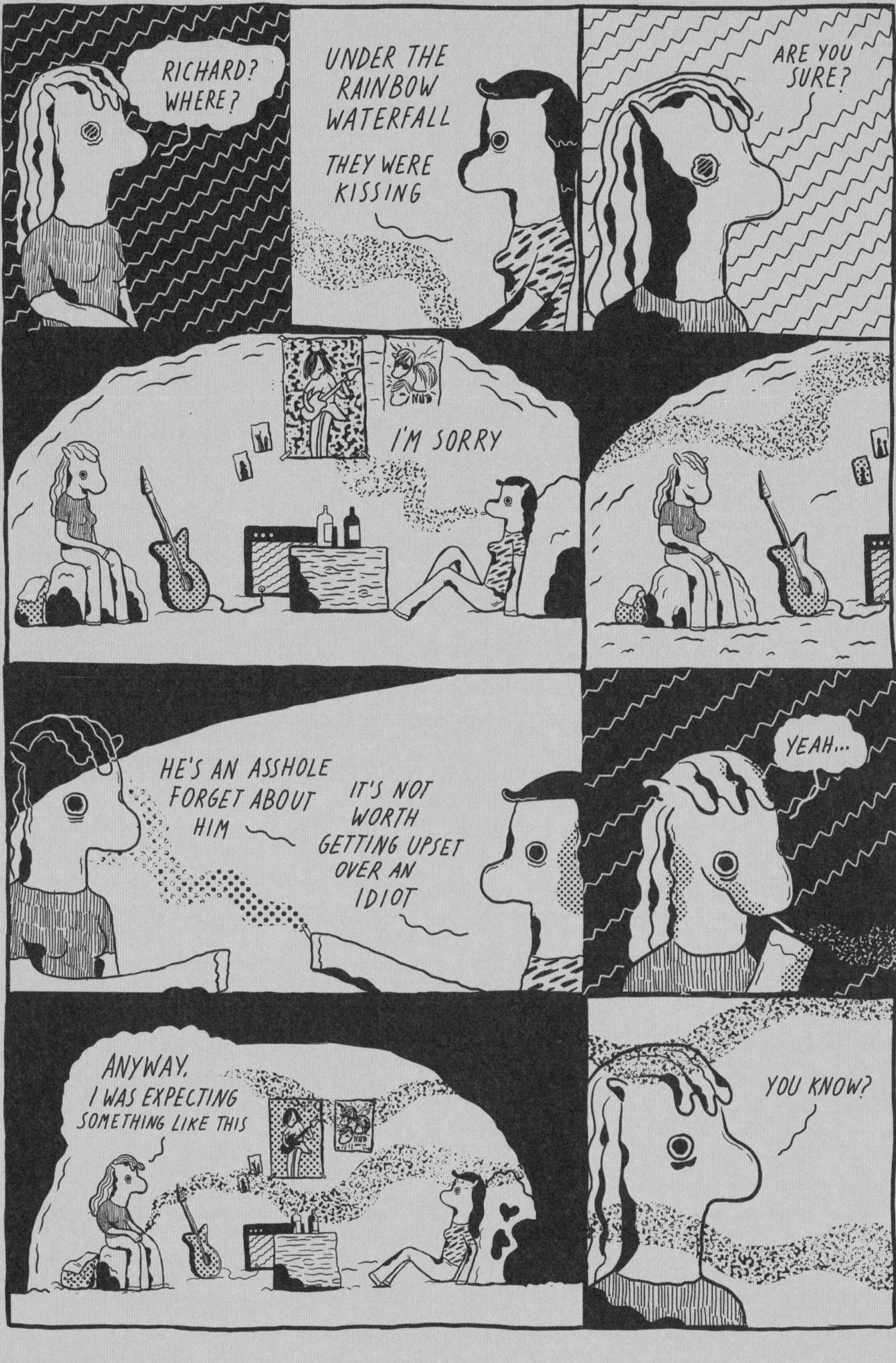
RICHARD? WHERE?
UNDER THE RAINBOW WATERFALL
THEY WERE KISSING
ARE YOU SURE?
I'M SORRY
HE'S AN ASSHOLE
FORGET ABOUT HIM
IT'S NOT WORTH GETTING UPSET OVER AN IDIOT
YEAH...
ANYWAY, I WAS EXPECTING SOMETHING LIKE THIS
YOU KNOW?

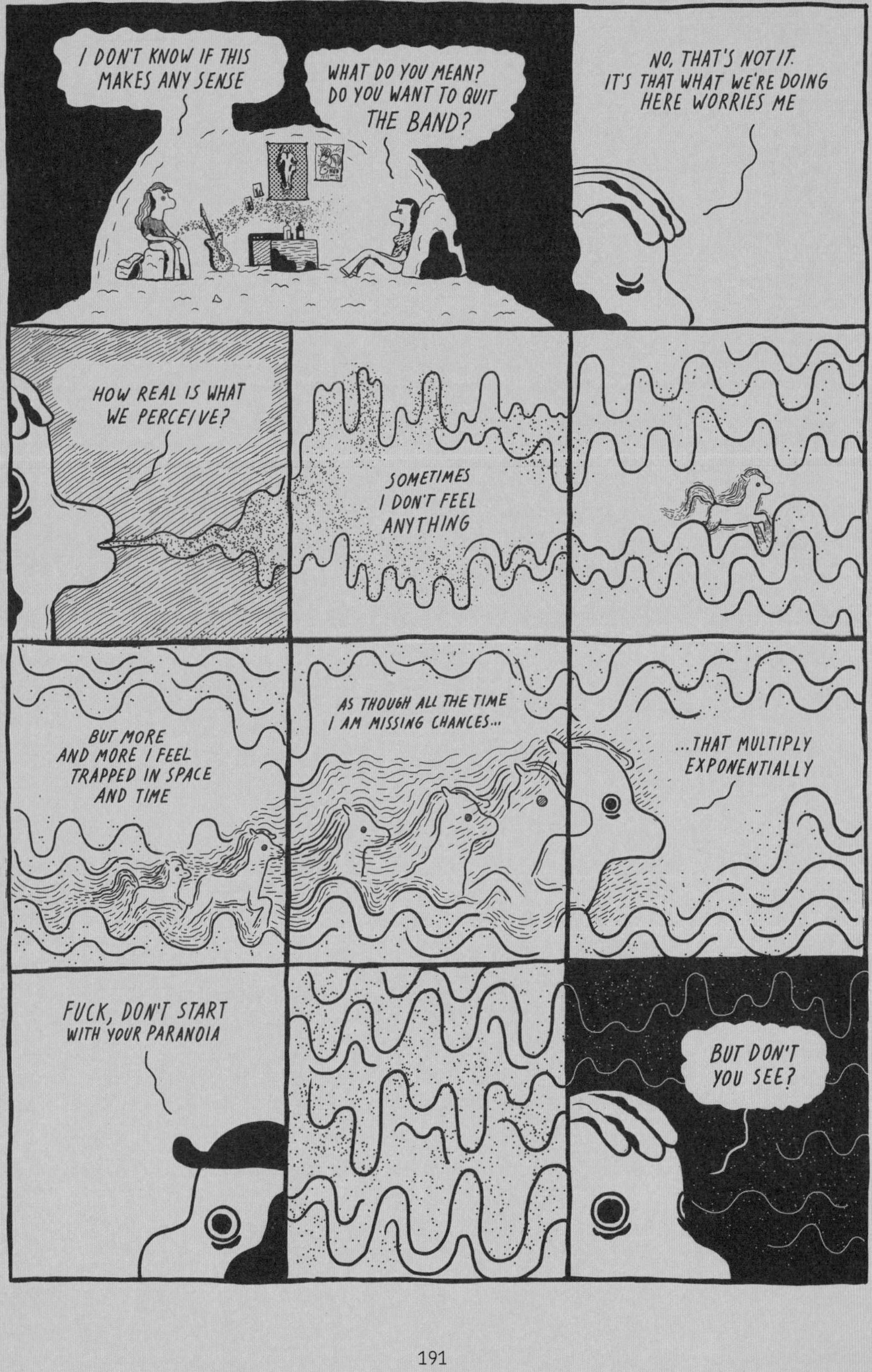
I DON'T KNOW IF THIS MAKES ANY SENSE
WHAT DO YOU MEAN? DO YOU WANT TO QUIT THE BAND?
NO, THAT'S NOT IT. IT'S THAT WHAT WE'RE DOING HERE WORRIES ME
HOW REAL IS WHAT WE PERCEIVE?
SOMETIMES I DON'T FEEL ANYTHING
BUT MORE AND MORE I FEEL TRAPPED IN SPACE AND TIME
AS THOUGH ALL THE TIME I AM MISSING CHANCES...
...THAT MULTIPLY EXPONENTIALLY
FUCK, DON'T START WITH YOUR PARANOIA
BUT DON'T YOU SEE?

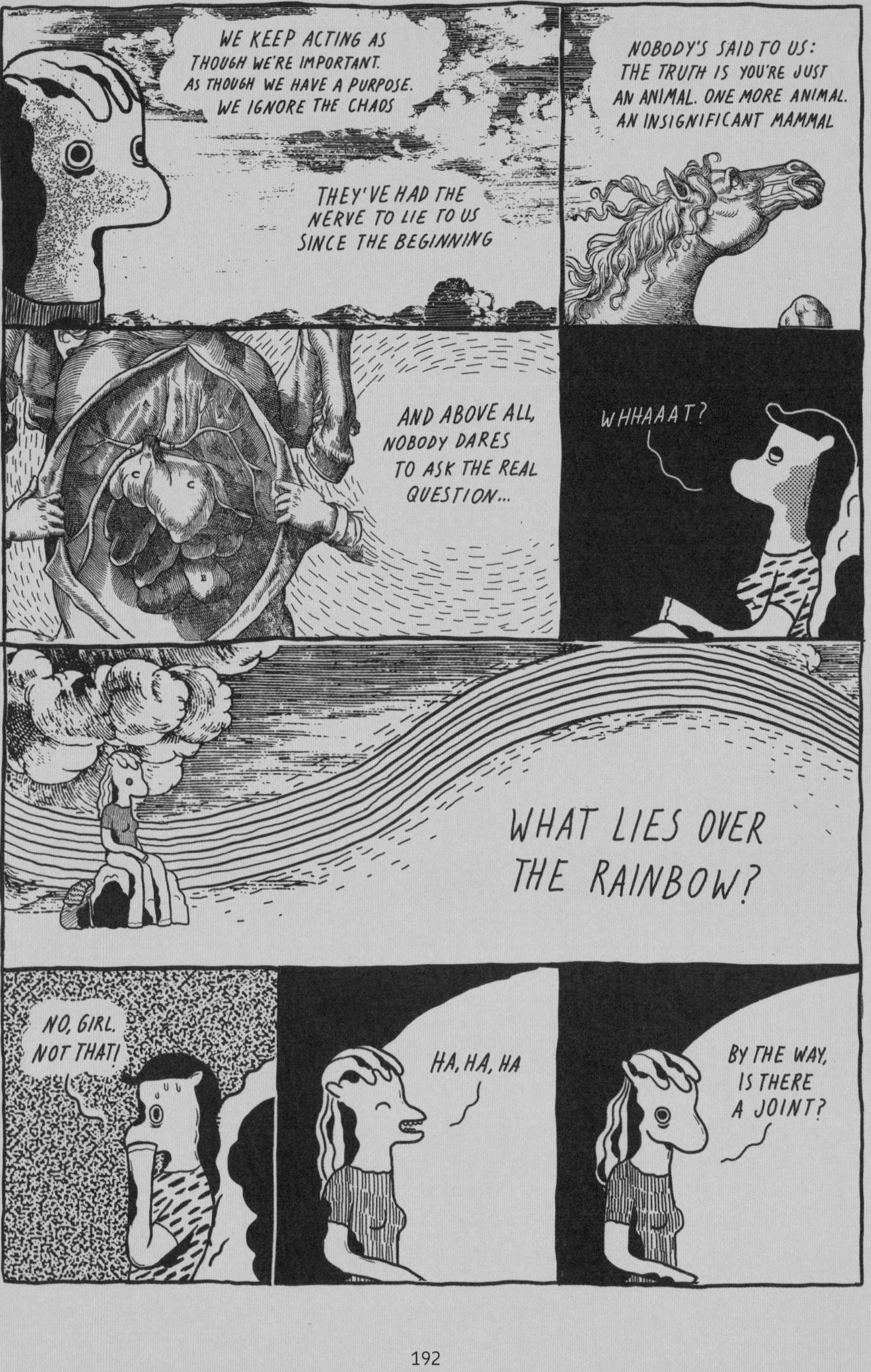
WE KEEP ACTING AS THOUGH WE'RE IMPORTANT. AS THOUGH WE HAVE A PURPOSE. WE IGNORE THE CHAOS
THEY'VE HAD THE NERVE TO LIE TO US SINCE THE BEGINNING
NOBODY'S SAID TO US: THE TRUTH IS YOU'RE JUST AN ANIMAL. ONE MORE ANIMAL. AN INSIGNIFICANT MAMMAL
AND ABOVE ALL, NOBODY DARES TO ASK THE REAL QUESTION...
WHHAAAT?
WHAT LIES OVER THE RAINBOW?
NO, GIRL. NOT THAT!
HA, HA, HA
BY THE WAY, IS THERE A JOINT?

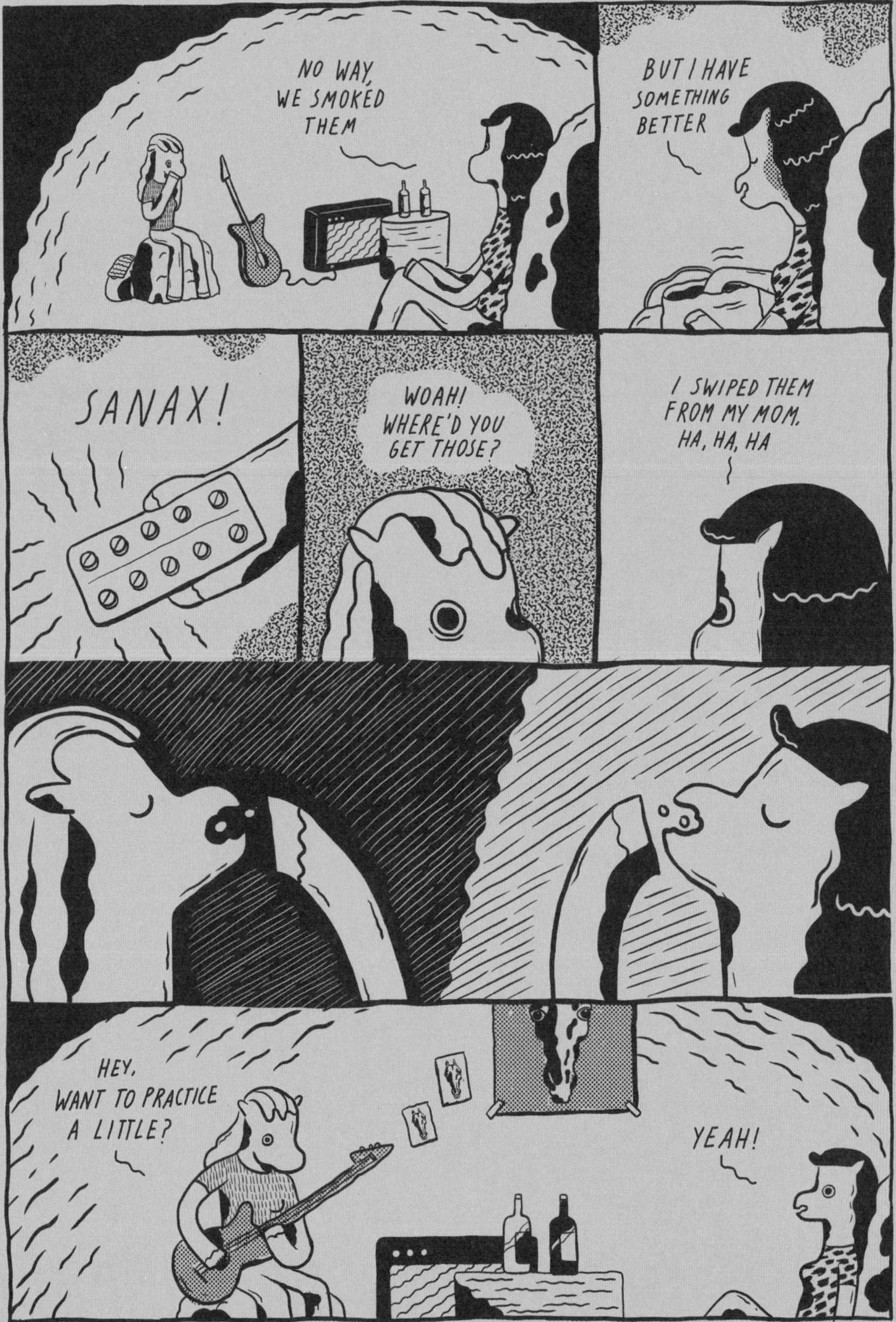
NO WAY, WE SMOKED THEM
BUT I HAVE SOMETHING BETTER
SANAX!
WOAH! WHERE'D YOU GET THOSE?
I SWIPED THEM FROM MY MOM. HA, HA, HA
HEY, WANT TO PRACTICE A LITTLE?
YEAH!

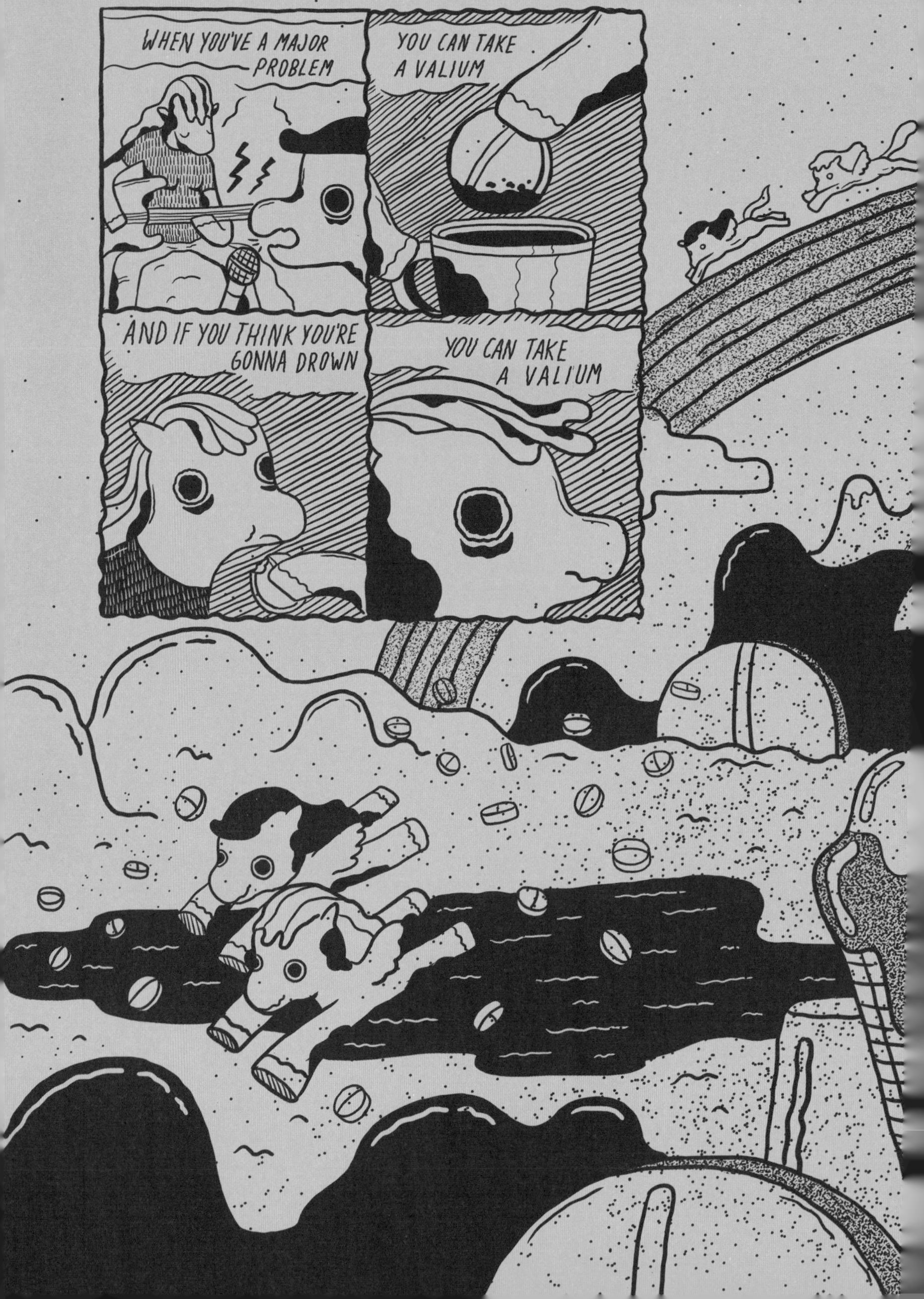
WHEN YOU'VE A MAJOR PROBLEM
YOU CAN TAKE A VALIUM
AND IF YOU THINK YOU'RE GONNA DROWN
YOU CAN TAKE A VALIUM

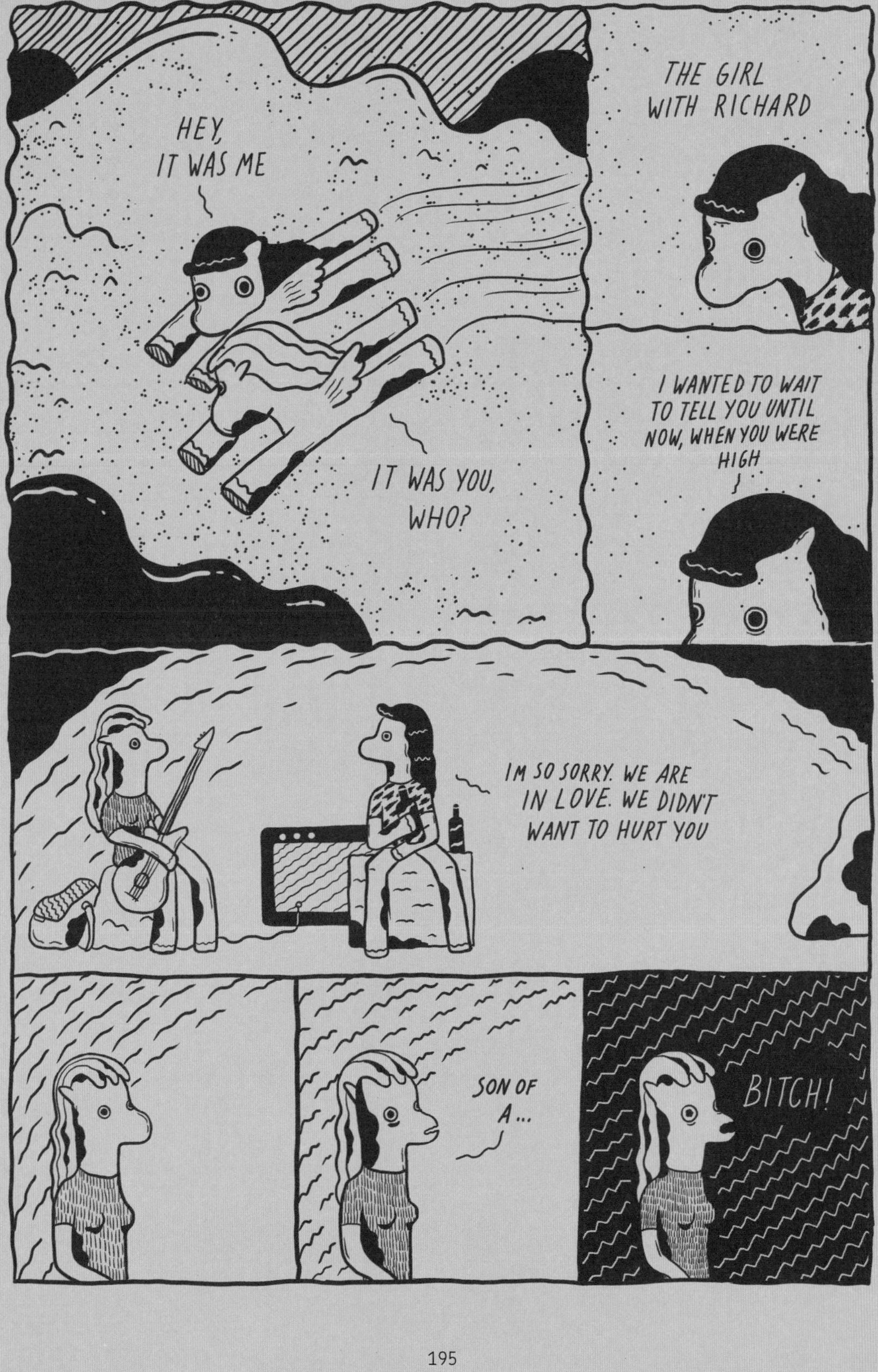
HEY, IT WAS ME
IT WAS YOU, WHO?
THE GIRL WITH RICHARD
I WANTED TO WAIT TO TELL YOU UNTIL NOW, WHEN YOU WERE HIGH
IM SO SORRY. WE ARE IN LOVE. WE DIDN'T WANT TO HURT YOU
SON OF A...
BITCH!

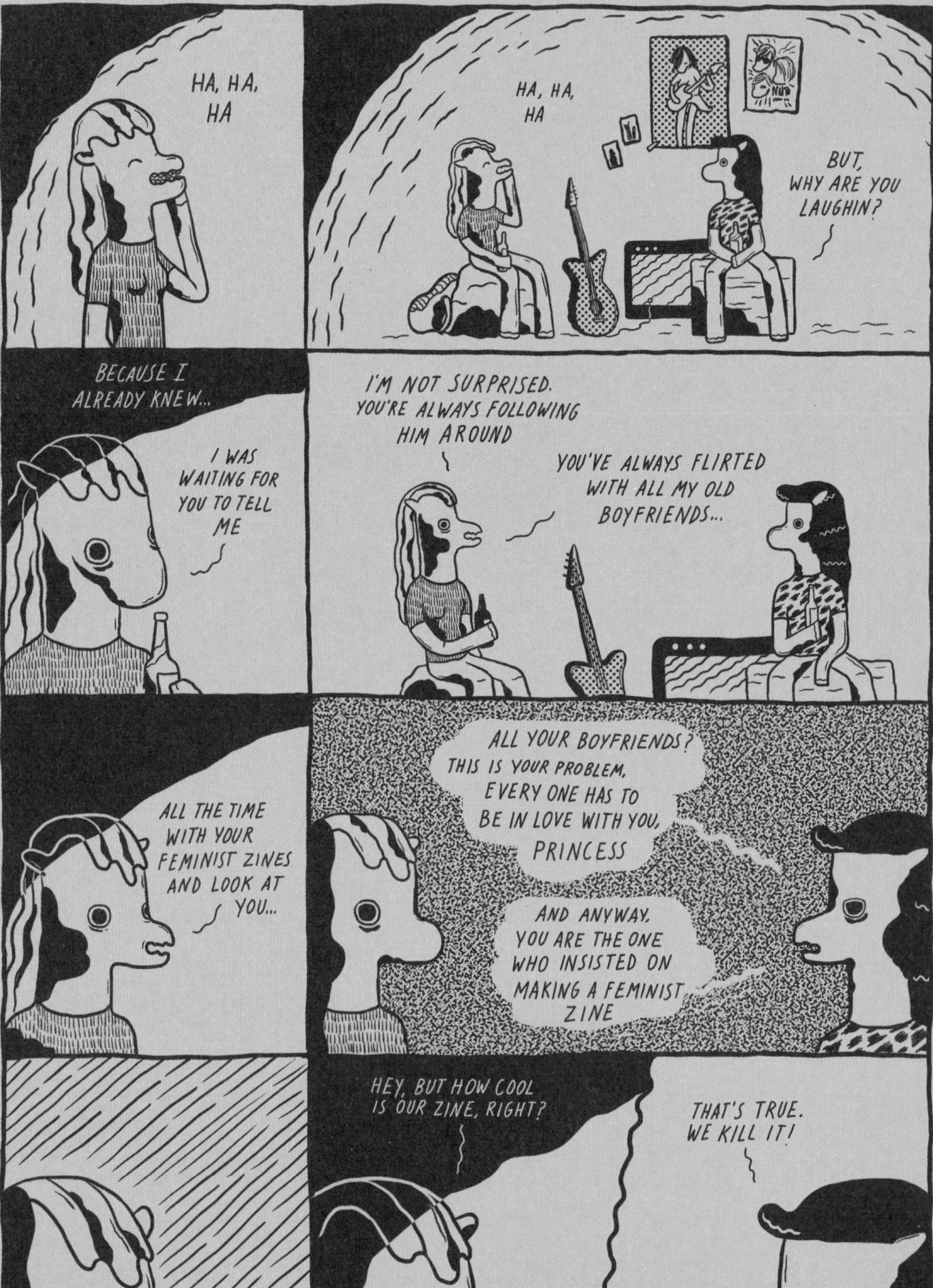
HA, HA, HA
HA, HA, HA
BUT, WHY ARE YOU LAUGHIN?
BECAUSE I ALREADY KNEW...
I WAS WAITING FOR YOU TO TELL ME
I'M NOT SURPRISED. YOU'RE ALWAYS FOLLOWING HIM AROUND
YOU'VE ALWAYS FLIRTED WITH ALL MY OLD BOYFRIENDS...
ALL THE TIME WITH YOUR FEMINIST ZINES AND LOOK AT YOU...
ALL YOUR BOYFRIENDS? THIS IS YOUR PROBLEM, EVERY ONE HAS TO BE IN LOVE WITH YOU, PRINCESS
AND ANYWAY, YOU ARE THE ONE WHO INSISTED ON MAKING A FEMINIST ZINE
HEY, BUT HOW COOL IS OUR ZINE, RIGHT?
THAT'S TRUE. WE KILL IT!

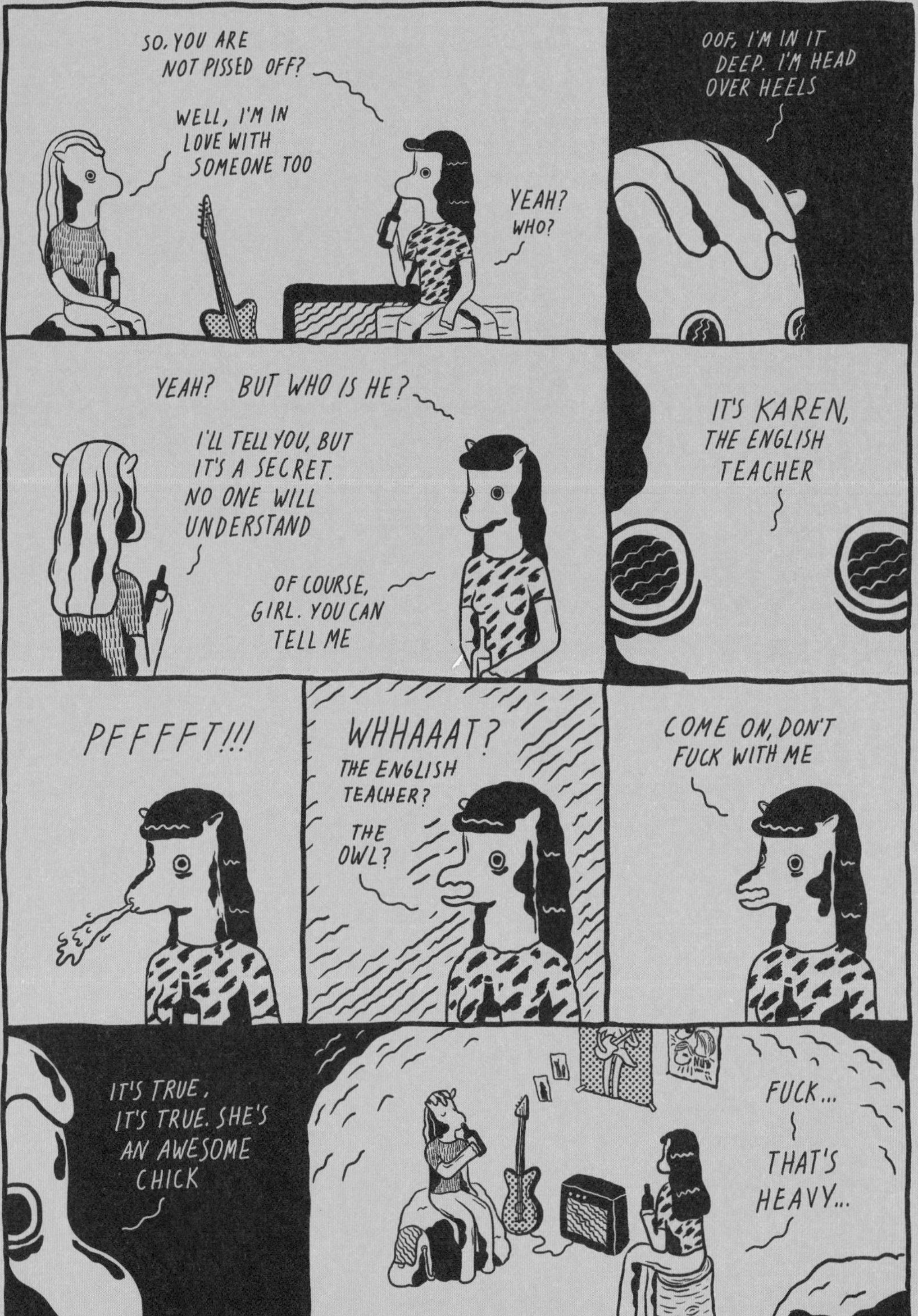
SO, YOU ARE NOT PISSED OFF?
WELL, I'M IN LOVE WITH SOMEONE TOO
YEAH? WHO?
OOF, I'M IN IT DEEP. I'M HEAD OVER HEELS
YEAH? BUT WHO IS HE?
I'LL TELL YOU, BUT IT'S A SECRET. NO ONE WILL UNDERSTAND
OF COURSE, GIRL. YOU CAN TELL ME
IT'S KAREN, THE ENGLISH TEACHER
PFFFFT!!!
WHHAAAT?
THE ENGLISH TEACHER?
THE OWL?
COME ON, DON'T FUCK WITH ME
IT'S TRUE, IT'S TRUE. SHE'S AN AWESOME CHICK
FUCK...
THAT'S HEAVY...

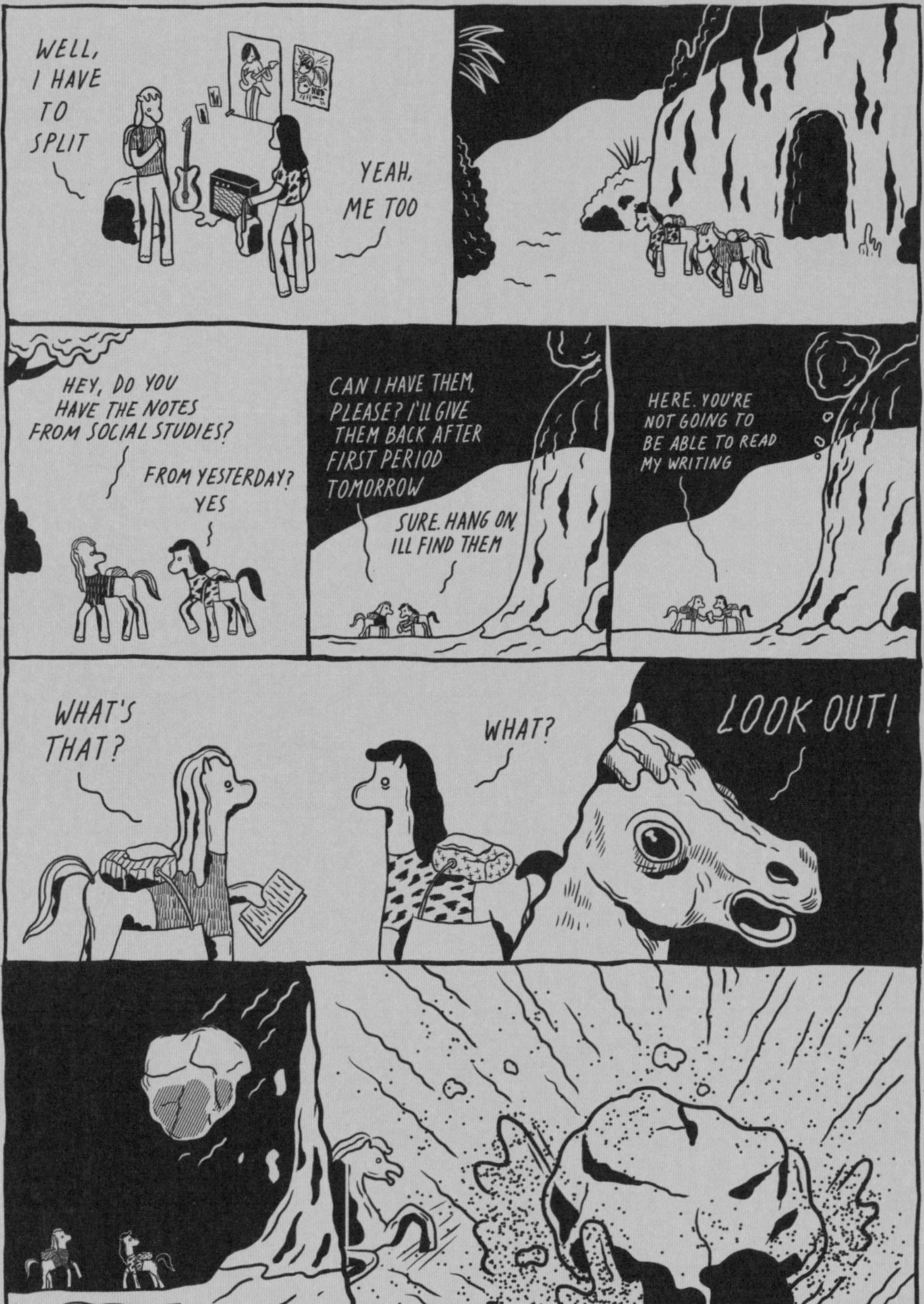
WELL, I HAVE TO SPLIT
YEAH, ME TOO
HEY, DO YOU HAVE THE NOTES FROM SOCIAL STUDIES?
FROM YESTERDAY? YES
CAN I HAVE THEM, PLEASE? I'LL GIVE THEM BACK AFTER FIRST PERIOD TOMORROW
SURE. HANG ON, ILL FIND THEM
HERE. YOU'RE NOT GOING TO BE ABLE TO READ MY WRITING
WHAT'S THAT?
WHAT?
LOOK OUT!

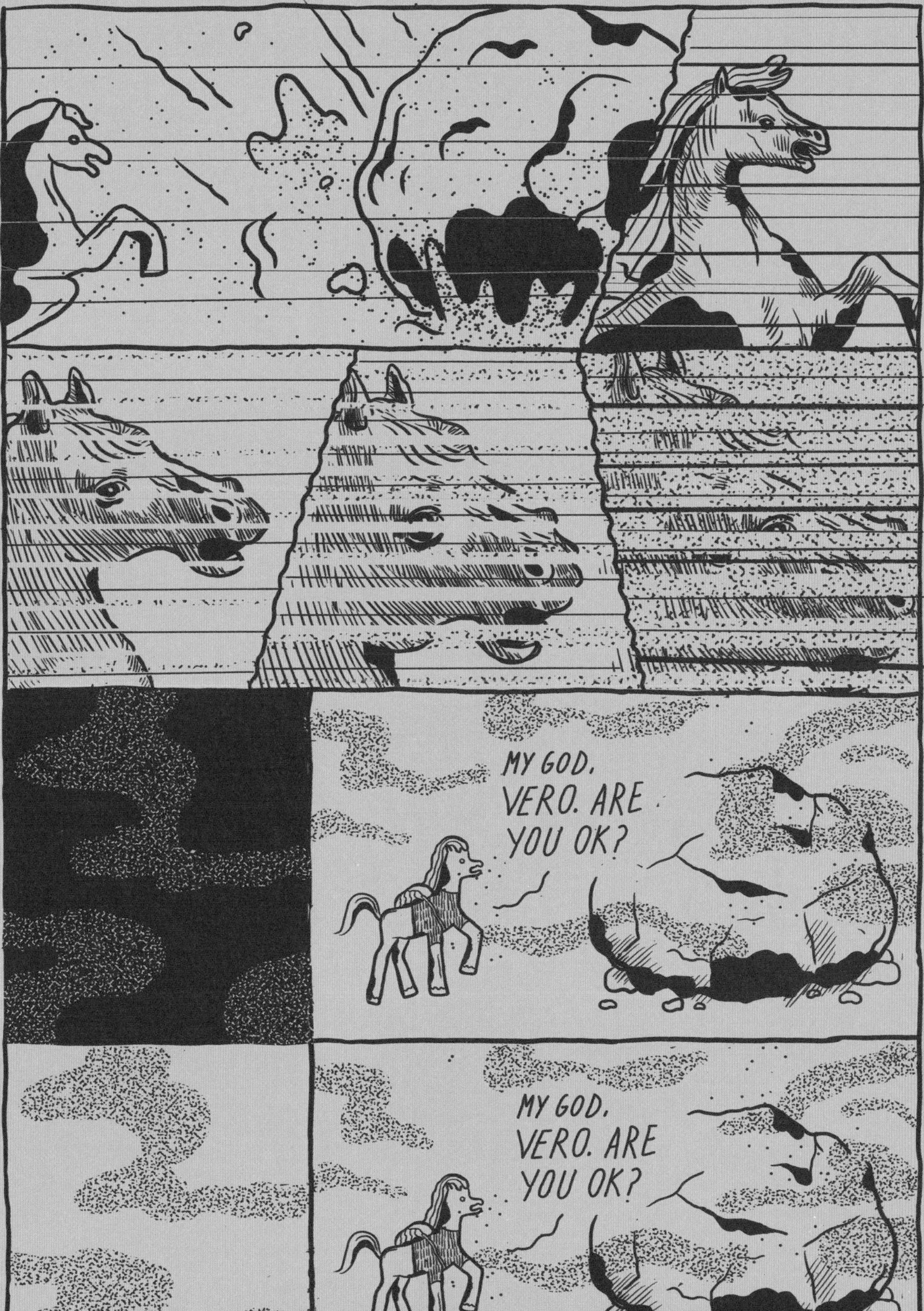
MY GOD. VERO. ARE YOU OK?
MY GOD. VERO. ARE YOU OK?

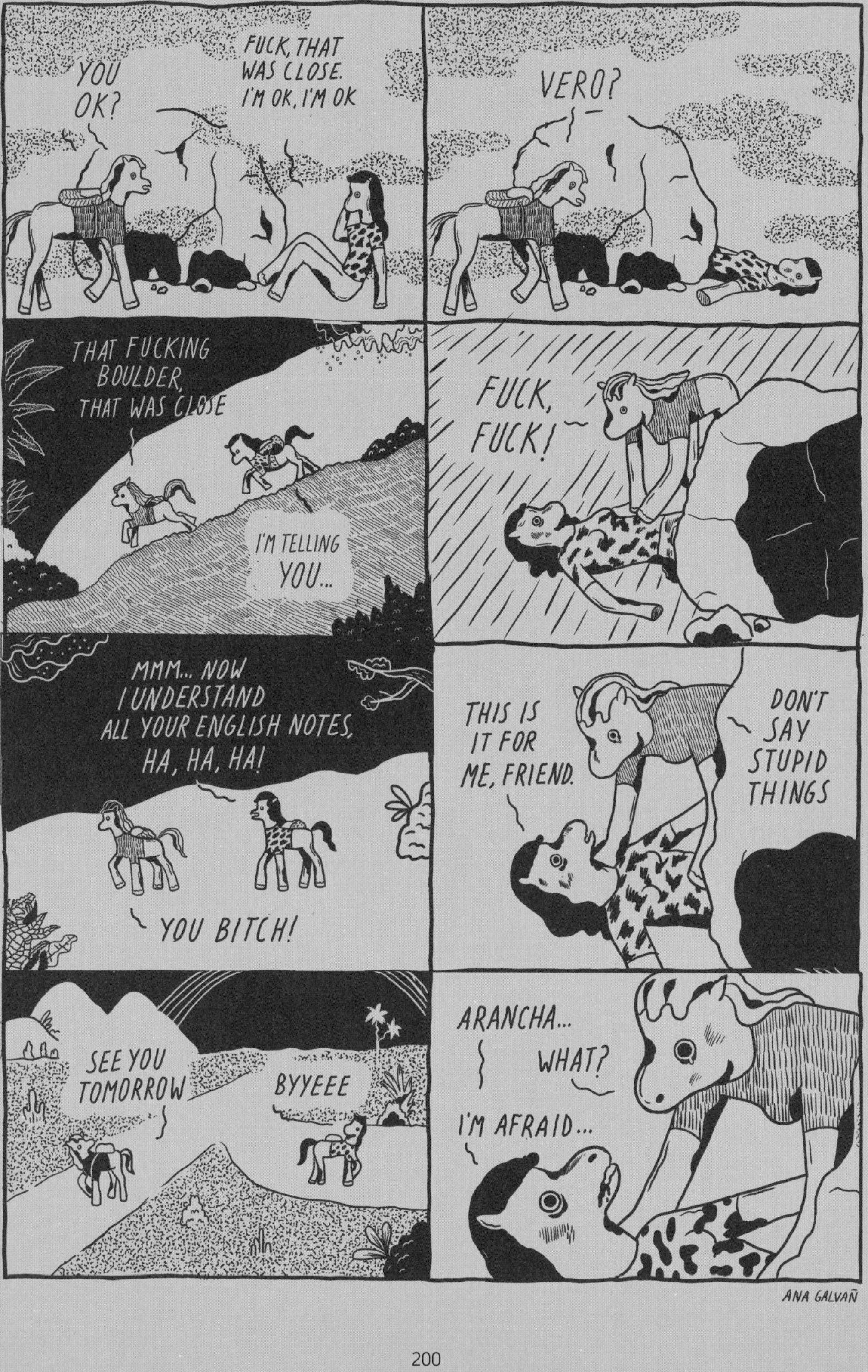
YOU OK?
FUCK, THAT WAS CLOSE. I'M OK, I'M OK
VERO?
THAT FUCKING BOULDER, THAT WAS CLOSE
I'M TELLING YOU...
FUCK, FUCK!
MMM... NOW I UNDERSTAND ALL YOUR ENGLISH NOTES, HA, HA, HA!
YOU BITCH!
THIS IS IT FOR ME, FRIEND.
DON'T SAY STUPID THINGS
SEE YOU TOMORROW
BYYEEE
ARANCHA...
WHAT?
I'M AFRAID...

ANA GALVAÑ

SANTIAGO VALENZUELA
CALL IT X

Santiago Valenzuela was born in San Sebastián in 1971. He has had an extensive career as a cartoonist: his titles include *Sociedad limitadísima* [*Limited Company*] (2005), *El gabinete del doctor Salgari* [*The Cabinet of Dr. Salgari*] (2007), and *Nietos del rock 'n' roll* [*Rock 'n' Roll Grandkids*] (2010), drawn by David Ortega. The work he's best known for is his massive series about Capitán Torrezno, which, to date, has spanned nine volumes: *Horizontes lejanos* [*Distant Horizons*] (2001), *Escala real* [*True Scale*] (2003), *Limbo sin fin* [*Endless Limbo*] (2003), *Extramuros* [*Outside the Walls*] (2004), *Capital de provincias del dolor* [*Capital of the Provinces of Sorrow*] (2005), *Los años oscuros* [*The Dark Years*] (2006), *Plaza Elíptica* [*Elliptical Plaza*] (2010), which won the Premio Nacional del Cómic, *La estrella de la mañana* [*The Morning Star*] (2012), and *Babel* (2015).

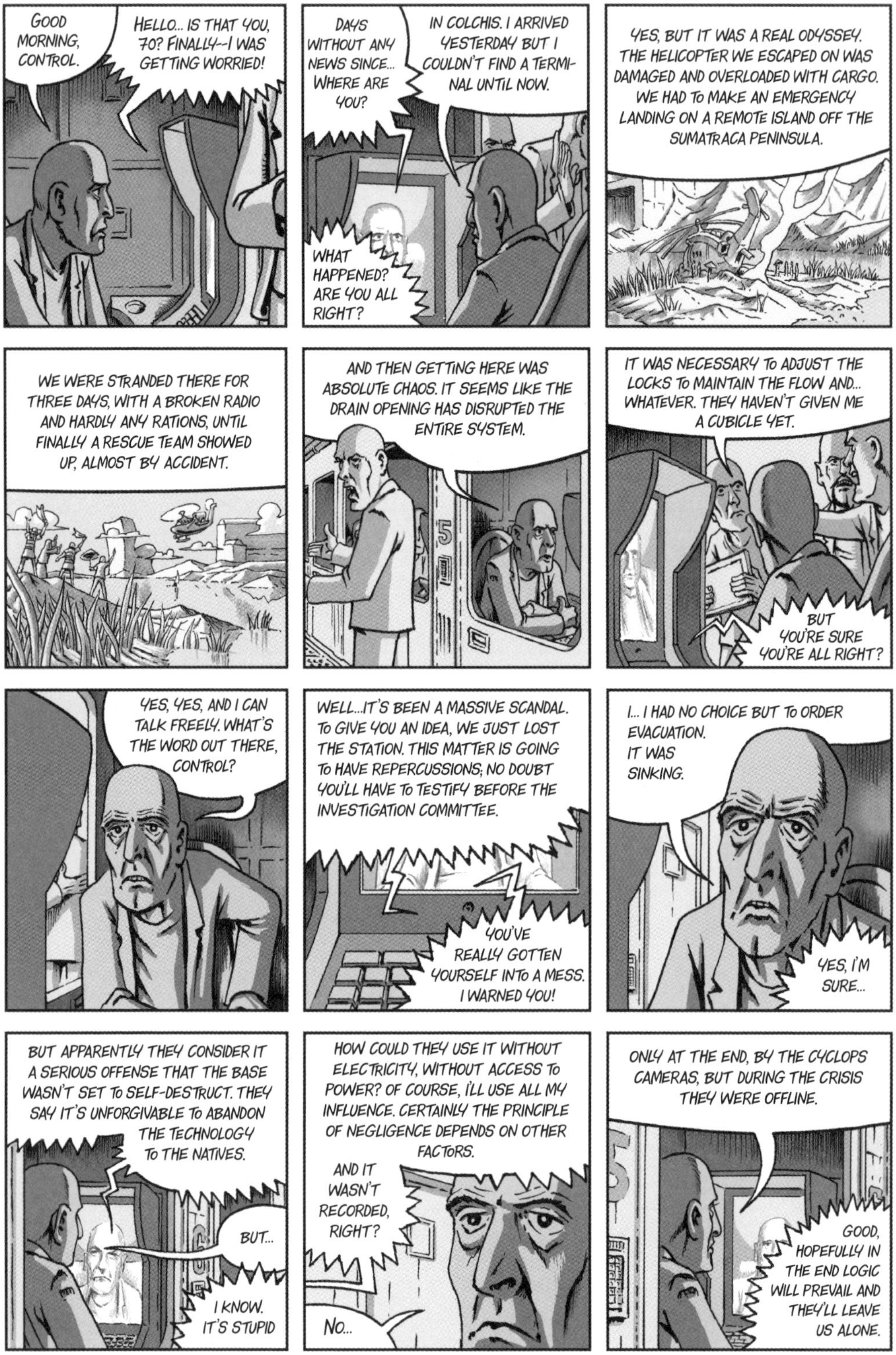
GOOD MORNING, CONTROL.
HELLO... IS THAT YOU, 70? FINALLY--I WAS GETTING WORRIED!
DAYS WITHOUT ANY NEWS SINCE... WHERE ARE YOU?
IN COLCHIS. I ARRIVED YESTERDAY BUT I COULDN'T FIND A TERMINAL UNTIL NOW.
WHAT HAPPENED? ARE YOU ALL RIGHT?
YES, BUT IT WAS A REAL ODYSSEY. THE HELICOPTER WE ESCAPED ON WAS DAMAGED AND OVERLOADED WITH CARGO. WE HAD TO MAKE AN EMERGENCY LANDING ON A REMOTE ISLAND OFF THE SUMATRACA PENINSULA.
WE WERE STRANDED THERE FOR THREE DAYS, WITH A BROKEN RADIO AND HARDLY ANY RATIONS, UNTIL FINALLY A RESCUE TEAM SHOWED UP, ALMOST BY ACCIDENT.
AND THEN GETTING HERE WAS ABSOLUTE CHAOS. IT SEEMS LIKE THE DRAIN OPENING HAS DISRUPTED THE ENTIRE SYSTEM.
IT WAS NECESSARY TO ADJUST THE LOCKS TO MAINTAIN THE FLOW AND... WHATEVER. THEY HAVEN'T GIVEN ME A CUBICLE YET.
BUT YOU'RE SURE YOU'RE ALL RIGHT?
YES, YES, AND I CAN TALK FREELY. WHAT'S THE WORD OUT THERE, CONTROL?
WELL...IT'S BEEN A MASSIVE SCANDAL. TO GIVE YOU AN IDEA, WE JUST LOST THE STATION. THIS MATTER IS GOING TO HAVE REPERCUSSIONS; NO DOUBT YOU'LL HAVE TO TESTIFY BEFORE THE INVESTIGATION COMMITTEE.
YOU'VE REALLY GOTTEN YOURSELF INTO A MESS. I WARNED YOU!
I... I HAD NO CHOICE BUT TO ORDER EVACUATION. IT WAS SINKING.
YES, I'M SURE...
BUT APPARENTLY THEY CONSIDER IT A SERIOUS OFFENSE THAT THE BASE WASN'T SET TO SELF-DESTRUCT. THEY SAY IT'S UNFORGIVABLE TO ABANDON THE TECHNOLOGY TO THE NATIVES.
BUT...
I KNOW. IT'S STUPID
HOW COULD THEY USE IT WITHOUT ELECTRICITY, WITHOUT ACCESS TO POWER? OF COURSE, I'LL USE ALL MY INFLUENCE. CERTAINLY THE PRINCIPLE OF NEGLIGENCE DEPENDS ON OTHER FACTORS.
AND IT WASN'T RECORDED, RIGHT?
NO...
ONLY AT THE END, BY THE CYCLOPS CAMERAS, BUT DURING THE CRISIS THEY WERE OFFLINE.
GOOD, HOPEFULLY IN THE END LOGIC WILL PREVAIL AND THEY'LL LEAVE US ALONE.

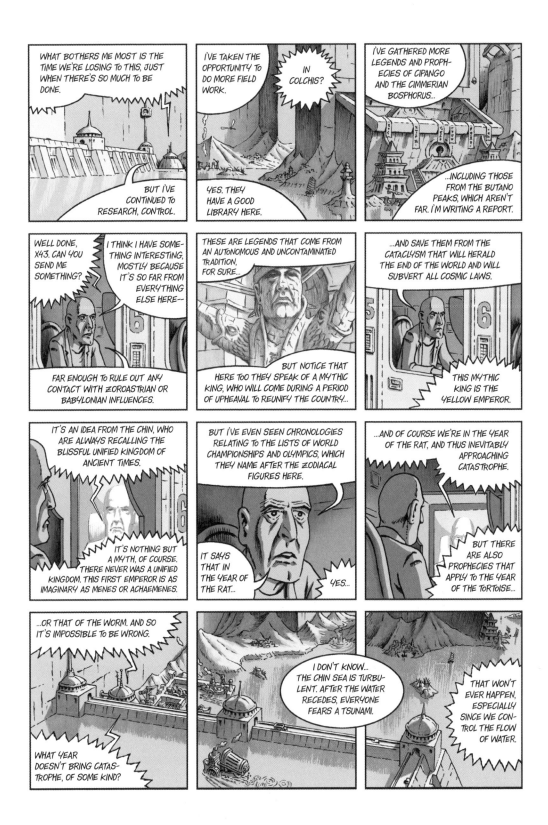

WHAT BOTHERS ME MOST IS THE TIME WE'RE LOSING TO THIS, JUST WHEN THERE'S SO MUCH TO BE DONE.

BUT I'VE CONTINUED TO RESEARCH, CONTROL.

I'VE TAKEN THE OPPORTUNITY TO DO MORE FIELD WORK.

IN COLCHIS?

YES. THEY HAVE A GOOD LIBRARY HERE.

I'VE GATHERED MORE LEGENDS AND PROPH-ECIES OF CIPANGO AND THE CIMMERIAN BOSPHORUS...

...INCLUDING THOSE FROM THE BUTANO PEAKS, WHICH AREN'T FAR. I'M WRITING A REPORT.

WELL DONE, X43. CAN YOU SEND ME SOMETHING?

I THINK I HAVE SOME-THING INTERESTING, MOSTLY BECAUSE IT'S SO FAR FROM EVERYTHING ELSE HERE--

FAR ENOUGH TO RULE OUT ANY CONTACT WITH ZOROASTRIAN OR BABYLONIAN INFLUENCES.

THESE ARE LEGENDS THAT COME FROM AN AUTONOMOUS AND UNCONTAMINATED TRADITION, FOR SURE...

BUT NOTICE THAT HERE TOO THEY SPEAK OF A MYTHIC KING, WHO WILL COME DURING A PERIOD OF UPHEAVAL TO REUNIFY THE COUNTRY...

...AND SAVE THEM FROM THE CATACLYSM THAT WILL HERALD THE END OF THE WORLD AND WILL SUBVERT ALL COSMIC LAWS.

THIS MYTHIC KING IS THE YELLOW EMPEROR.

IT'S AN IDEA FROM THE CHIN, WHO ARE ALWAYS RECALLING THE BLISSFUL UNIFIED KINGDOM OF ANCIENT TIMES.

IT'S NOTHING BUT A MYTH, OF COURSE. THERE NEVER WAS A UNIFIED KINGDOM. THIS FIRST EMPEROR IS AS IMAGINARY AS MENES OR ACHAEMENES.

BUT I'VE EVEN SEEN CHRONOLOGIES RELATING TO THE LISTS OF WORLD CHAMPIONSHIPS AND OLYMPICS, WHICH THEY NAME AFTER THE ZODIACAL FIGURES HERE.

IT SAYS THAT IN THE YEAR OF THE RAT...

YES...

...AND OF COURSE WE'RE IN THE YEAR OF THE RAT, AND THUS INEVITABLY APPROACHING CATASTROPHE.

BUT THERE ARE ALSO PROPHECIES THAT APPLY TO THE YEAR OF THE TORTOISE...

...OR THAT OF THE WORM. AND SO IT'S IMPOSSIBLE TO BE WRONG.

WHAT YEAR DOESN'T BRING CATAS-TROPHE, OF SOME KIND?

I DON'T KNOW... THE CHIN SEA IS TURBU-LENT. AFTER THE WATER RECEDES, EVERYONE FEARS A TSUNAMI.

THAT WON'T EVER HAPPEN, ESPECIALLY SINCE WE CON-TROL THE FLOW OF WATER.

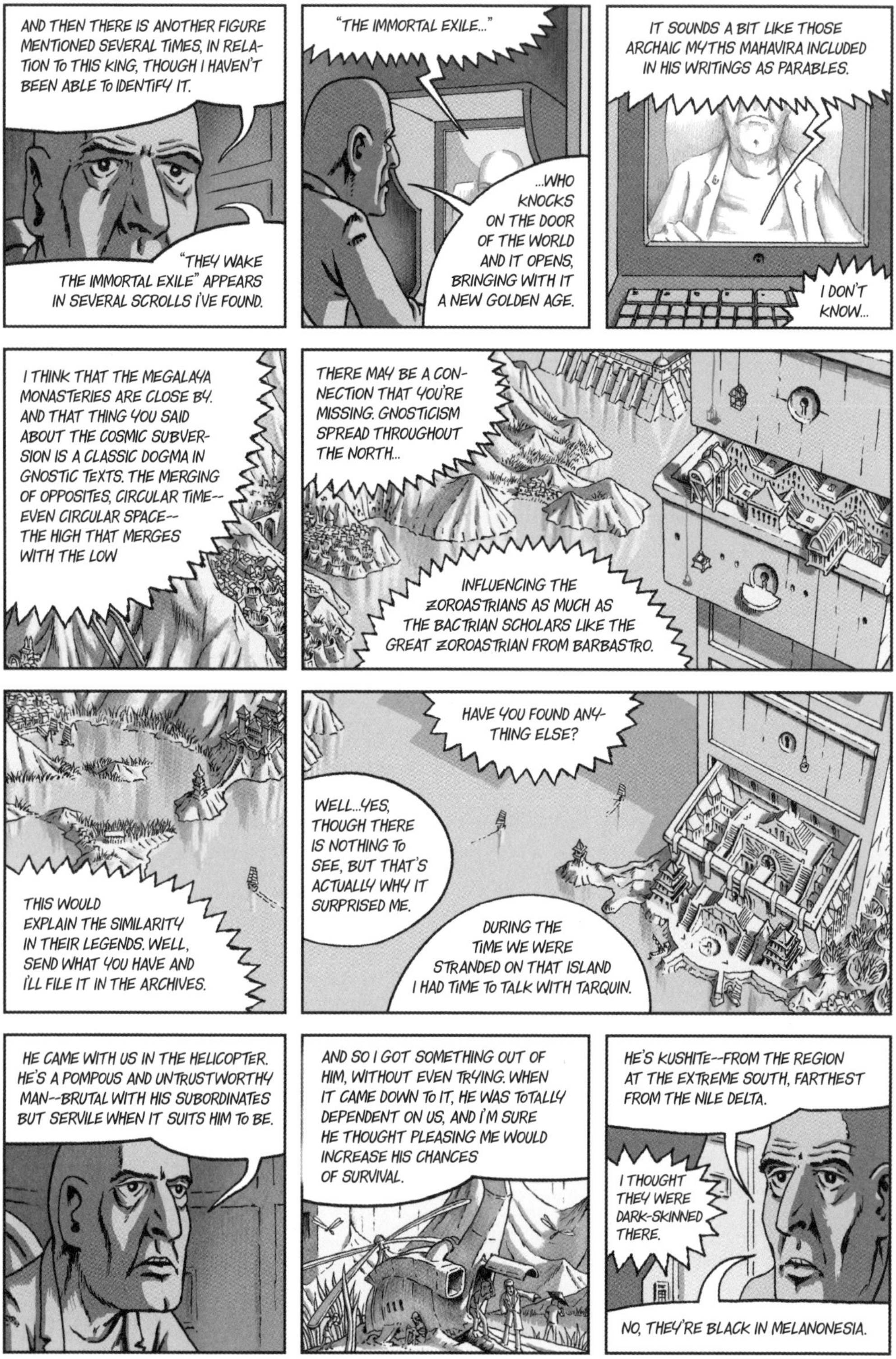
AND THEN THERE IS ANOTHER FIGURE MENTIONED SEVERAL TIMES, IN RELATION TO THIS KING, THOUGH I HAVEN'T BEEN ABLE TO IDENTIFY IT.
"THEY WAKE THE IMMORTAL EXILE" APPEARS IN SEVERAL SCROLLS I'VE FOUND.
"THE IMMORTAL EXILE..."
...WHO KNOCKS ON THE DOOR OF THE WORLD AND IT OPENS, BRINGING WITH IT A NEW GOLDEN AGE.
IT SOUNDS A BIT LIKE THOSE ARCHAIC MYTHS MAHAVIRA INCLUDED IN HIS WRITINGS AS PARABLES.
I DON'T KNOW...
I THINK THAT THE MEGALAYA MONASTERIES ARE CLOSE BY. AND THAT THING YOU SAID ABOUT THE COSMIC SUBVERSION IS A CLASSIC DOGMA IN GNOSTIC TEXTS. THE MERGING OF OPPOSITES, CIRCULAR TIME-- EVEN CIRCULAR SPACE-- THE HIGH THAT MERGES WITH THE LOW
THERE MAY BE A CONNECTION THAT YOU'RE MISSING. GNOSTICISM SPREAD THROUGHOUT THE NORTH...
INFLUENCING THE ZOROASTRIANS AS MUCH AS THE BACTRIAN SCHOLARS LIKE THE GREAT ZOROASTRIAN FROM BARBASTRO.
THIS WOULD EXPLAIN THE SIMILARITY IN THEIR LEGENDS. WELL, SEND WHAT YOU HAVE AND I'LL FILE IT IN THE ARCHIVES.
HAVE YOU FOUND ANYTHING ELSE?
WELL...YES, THOUGH THERE IS NOTHING TO SEE, BUT THAT'S ACTUALLY WHY IT SURPRISED ME.
DURING THE TIME WE WERE STRANDED ON THAT ISLAND I HAD TIME TO TALK WITH TARQUIN.
HE CAME WITH US IN THE HELICOPTER. HE'S A POMPOUS AND UNTRUSTWORTHY MAN--BRUTAL WITH HIS SUBORDINATES BUT SERVILE WHEN IT SUITS HIM TO BE.
AND SO I GOT SOMETHING OUT OF HIM, WITHOUT EVEN TRYING. WHEN IT CAME DOWN TO IT, HE WAS TOTALLY DEPENDENT ON US, AND I'M SURE HE THOUGHT PLEASING ME WOULD INCREASE HIS CHANCES OF SURVIVAL.
HE'S KUSHITE--FROM THE REGION AT THE EXTREME SOUTH, FARTHEST FROM THE NILE DELTA.
I THOUGHT THEY WERE DARK-SKINNED THERE.
NO, THEY'RE BLACK IN MELANONESIA.

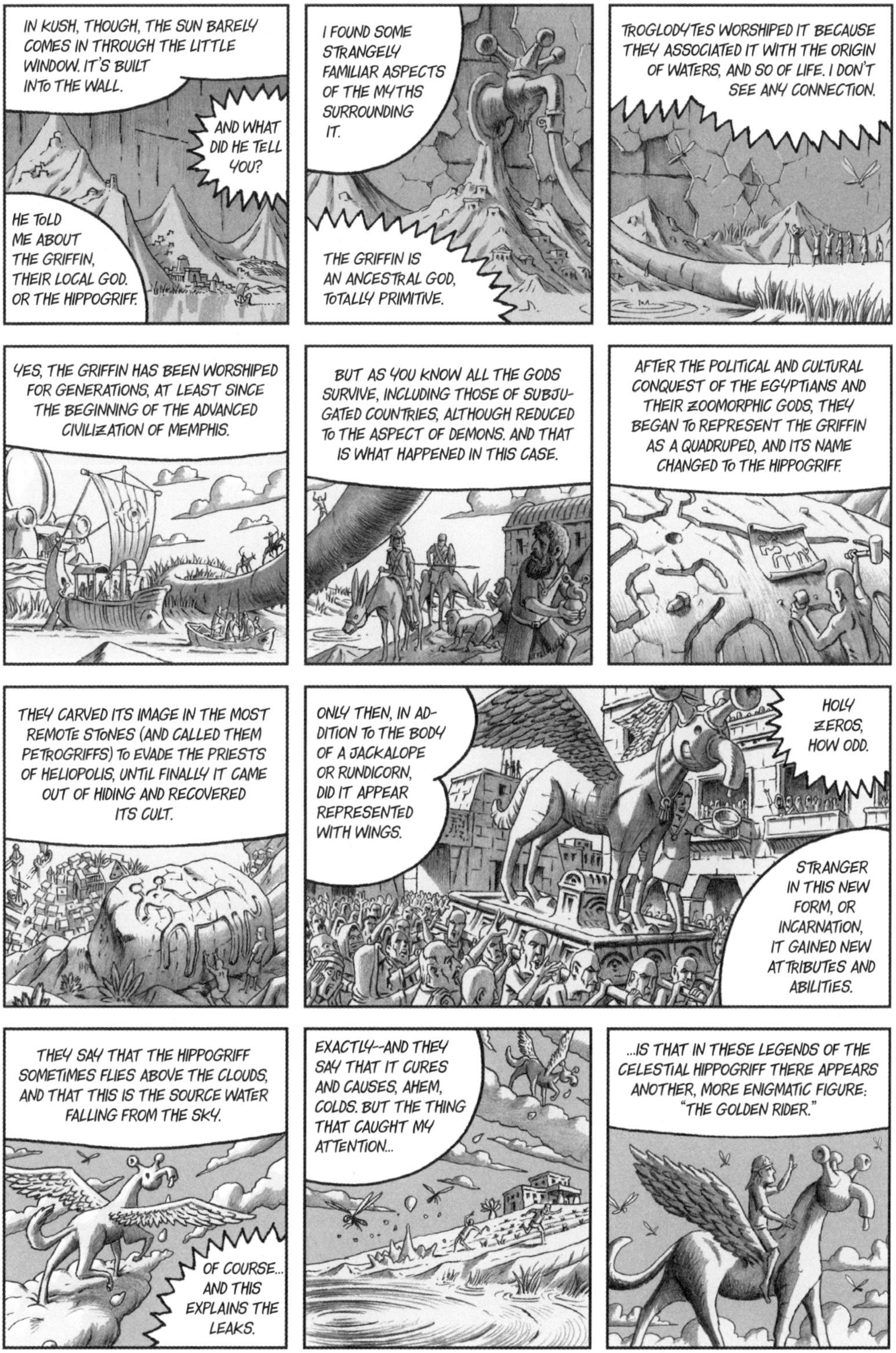
IN KUSH, THOUGH, THE SUN BARELY COMES IN THROUGH THE LITTLE WINDOW. IT'S BUILT INTO THE WALL.
AND WHAT DID HE TELL YOU?
HE TOLD ME ABOUT THE GRIFFIN, THEIR LOCAL GOD. OR THE HIPPOGRIFF.
I FOUND SOME STRANGELY FAMILIAR ASPECTS OF THE MYTHS SURROUNDING IT.
THE GRIFFIN IS AN ANCESTRAL GOD, TOTALLY PRIMITIVE.
TROGLODYTES WORSHIPED IT BECAUSE THEY ASSOCIATED IT WITH THE ORIGIN OF WATERS, AND SO OF LIFE. I DON'T SEE ANY CONNECTION.
YES, THE GRIFFIN HAS BEEN WORSHIPED FOR GENERATIONS, AT LEAST SINCE THE BEGINNING OF THE ADVANCED CIVILIZATION OF MEMPHIS.
BUT AS YOU KNOW ALL THE GODS SURVIVE, INCLUDING THOSE OF SUBJUGATED COUNTRIES, ALTHOUGH REDUCED TO THE ASPECT OF DEMONS. AND THAT IS WHAT HAPPENED IN THIS CASE.
AFTER THE POLITICAL AND CULTURAL CONQUEST OF THE EGYPTIANS AND THEIR ZOOMORPHIC GODS, THEY BEGAN TO REPRESENT THE GRIFFIN AS A QUADRUPED, AND ITS NAME CHANGED TO THE HIPPOGRIFF.
THEY CARVED ITS IMAGE IN THE MOST REMOTE STONES (AND CALLED THEM PETROGRIFFS) TO EVADE THE PRIESTS OF HELIOPOLIS, UNTIL FINALLY IT CAME OUT OF HIDING AND RECOVERED ITS CULT.
ONLY THEN, IN ADDITION TO THE BODY OF A JACKALOPE OR RUNDICORN, DID IT APPEAR REPRESENTED WITH WINGS.
HOLY ZEROS, HOW ODD.
STRANGER IN THIS NEW FORM, OR INCARNATION, IT GAINED NEW ATTRIBUTES AND ABILITIES.
THEY SAY THAT THE HIPPOGRIFF SOMETIMES FLIES ABOVE THE CLOUDS, AND THAT THIS IS THE SOURCE WATER FALLING FROM THE SKY.
OF COURSE... AND THIS EXPLAINS THE LEAKS.
EXACTLY--AND THEY SAY THAT IT CURES AND CAUSES, AHEM, COLDS. BUT THE THING THAT CAUGHT MY ATTENTION...
...IS THAT IN THESE LEGENDS OF THE CELESTIAL HIPPOGRIFF THERE APPEARS ANOTHER, MORE ENIGMATIC FIGURE: "THE GOLDEN RIDER."

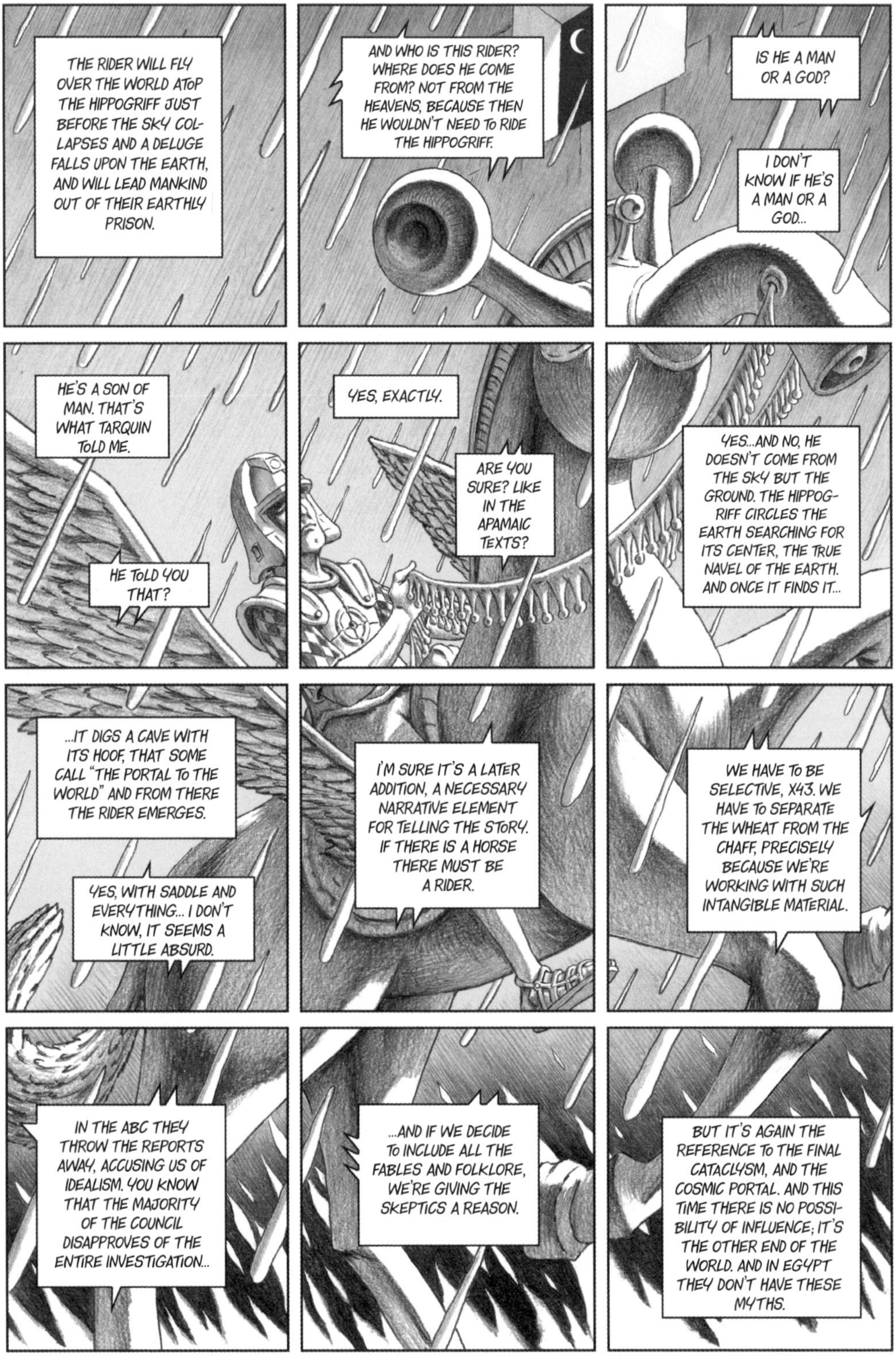
THE RIDER WILL FLY OVER THE WORLD ATOP THE HIPPOGRIFF JUST BEFORE THE SKY COL-LAPSES AND A DELUGE FALLS UPON THE EARTH, AND WILL LEAD MANKIND OUT OF THEIR EARTHLY PRISON.
AND WHO IS THIS RIDER? WHERE DOES HE COME FROM? NOT FROM THE HEAVENS, BECAUSE THEN HE WOULDN'T NEED TO RIDE THE HIPPOGRIFF.
IS HE A MAN OR A GOD?
I DON'T KNOW IF HE'S A MAN OR A GOD...
HE'S A SON OF MAN. THAT'S WHAT TARQUIN TOLD ME.
HE TOLD YOU THAT?
YES, EXACTLY.
ARE YOU SURE? LIKE IN THE APAMAIC TEXTS?
YES...AND NO, HE DOESN'T COME FROM THE SKY BUT THE GROUND. THE HIPPOG-RIFF CIRCLES THE EARTH SEARCHING FOR ITS CENTER, THE TRUE NAVEL OF THE EARTH. AND ONCE IT FINDS IT...
...IT DIGS A CAVE WITH ITS HOOF, THAT SOME CALL "THE PORTAL TO THE WORLD" AND FROM THERE THE RIDER EMERGES.
YES, WITH SADDLE AND EVERYTHING... I DON'T KNOW, IT SEEMS A LITTLE ABSURD.
I'M SURE IT'S A LATER ADDITION, A NECESSARY NARRATIVE ELEMENT FOR TELLING THE STORY. IF THERE IS A HORSE THERE MUST BE A RIDER.
WE HAVE TO BE SELECTIVE, X43. WE HAVE TO SEPARATE THE WHEAT FROM THE CHAFF, PRECISELY BECAUSE WE'RE WORKING WITH SUCH INTANGIBLE MATERIAL.
IN THE ABC THEY THROW THE REPORTS AWAY, ACCUSING US OF IDEALISM. YOU KNOW THAT THE MAJORITY OF THE COUNCIL DISAPPROVES OF THE ENTIRE INVESTIGATION...
...AND IF WE DECIDE TO INCLUDE ALL THE FABLES AND FOLKLORE, WE'RE GIVING THE SKEPTICS A REASON.
BUT IT'S AGAIN THE REFERENCE TO THE FINAL CATACLYSM, AND THE COSMIC PORTAL. AND THIS TIME THERE IS NO POSSI-BILITY OF INFLUENCE; IT'S THE OTHER END OF THE WORLD. AND IN EGYPT THEY DON'T HAVE THESE MYTHS.

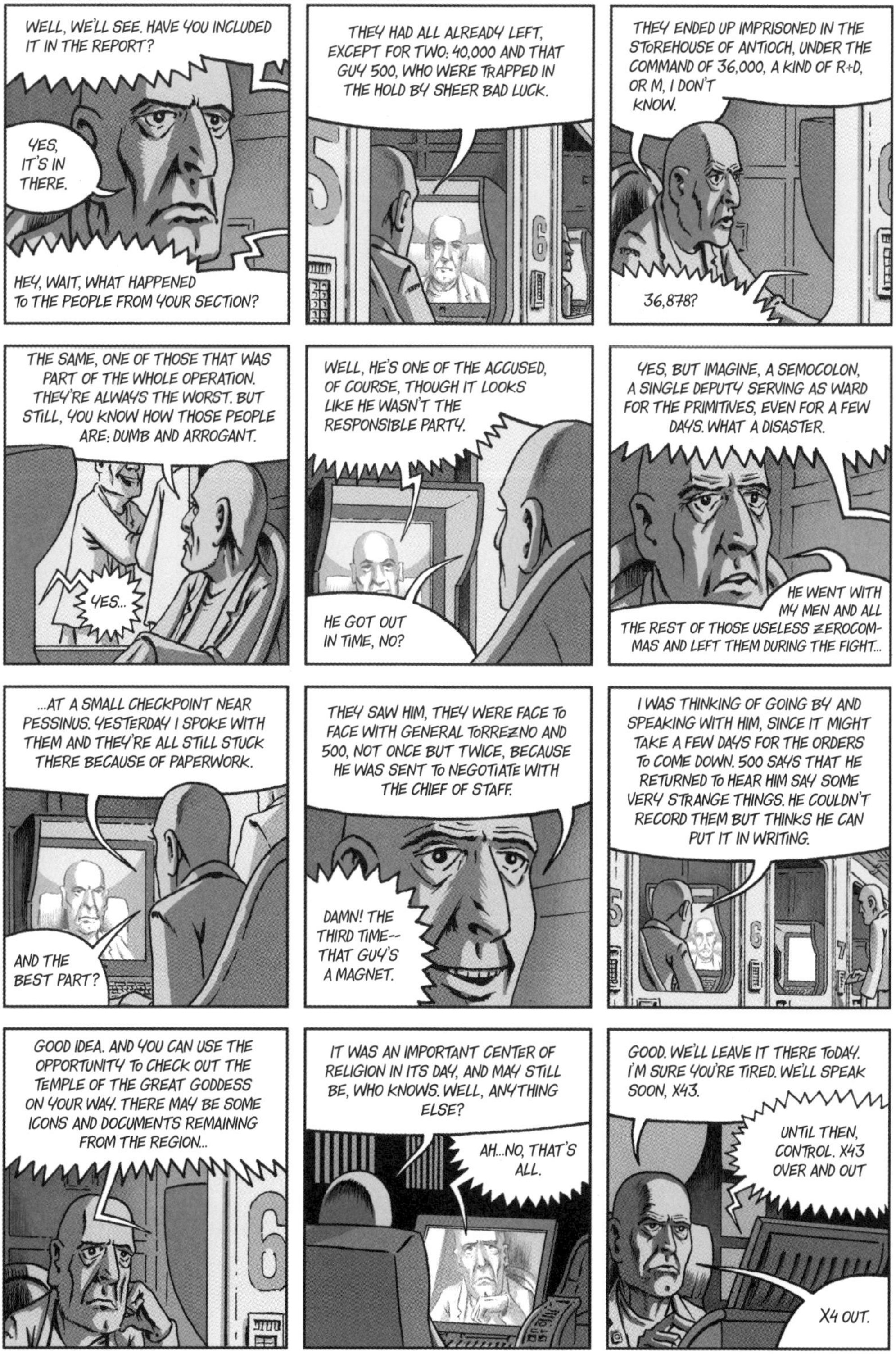
WELL, WE'LL SEE. HAVE YOU INCLUDED IT IN THE REPORT?
YES, IT'S IN THERE.
HEY, WAIT, WHAT HAPPENED TO THE PEOPLE FROM YOUR SECTION?
THEY HAD ALL ALREADY LEFT, EXCEPT FOR TWO: 40,000 AND THAT GUY 500, WHO WERE TRAPPED IN THE HOLD BY SHEER BAD LUCK.
THEY ENDED UP IMPRISONED IN THE STOREHOUSE OF ANTIOCH, UNDER THE COMMAND OF 36,000, A KIND OF R+D, OR M, I DON'T KNOW.
36,878?
THE SAME, ONE OF THOSE THAT WAS PART OF THE WHOLE OPERATION. THEY'RE ALWAYS THE WORST. BUT STILL, YOU KNOW HOW THOSE PEOPLE ARE: DUMB AND ARROGANT.
YES...
WELL, HE'S ONE OF THE ACCUSED, OF COURSE, THOUGH IT LOOKS LIKE HE WASN'T THE RESPONSIBLE PARTY.
HE GOT OUT IN TIME, NO?
YES, BUT IMAGINE, A SEMOCOLON, A SINGLE DEPUTY SERVING AS WARD FOR THE PRIMITIVES, EVEN FOR A FEW DAYS. WHAT A DISASTER.
HE WENT WITH MY MEN AND ALL THE REST OF THOSE USELESS ZEROCOMMAS AND LEFT THEM DURING THE FIGHT...
...AT A SMALL CHECKPOINT NEAR PESSINUS. YESTERDAY I SPOKE WITH THEM AND THEY'RE ALL STILL STUCK THERE BECAUSE OF PAPERWORK.
AND THE BEST PART?
THEY SAW HIM, THEY WERE FACE TO FACE WITH GENERAL TORREZNO AND 500, NOT ONCE BUT TWICE, BECAUSE HE WAS SENT TO NEGOTIATE WITH THE CHIEF OF STAFF.
DAMN! THE THIRD TIME-- THAT GUY'S A MAGNET.
I WAS THINKING OF GOING BY AND SPEAKING WITH HIM, SINCE IT MIGHT TAKE A FEW DAYS FOR THE ORDERS TO COME DOWN. 500 SAYS THAT HE RETURNED TO HEAR HIM SAY SOME VERY STRANGE THINGS. HE COULDN'T RECORD THEM BUT THINKS HE CAN PUT IT IN WRITING.
GOOD IDEA. AND YOU CAN USE THE OPPORTUNITY TO CHECK OUT THE TEMPLE OF THE GREAT GODDESS ON YOUR WAY. THERE MAY BE SOME ICONS AND DOCUMENTS REMAINING FROM THE REGION...
IT WAS AN IMPORTANT CENTER OF RELIGION IN ITS DAY, AND MAY STILL BE, WHO KNOWS. WELL, ANYTHING ELSE?
AH...NO, THAT'S ALL.
GOOD. WE'LL LEAVE IT THERE TODAY. I'M SURE YOU'RE TIRED. WE'LL SPEAK SOON, X43.
UNTIL THEN, CONTROL. X43 OVER AND OUT
X4 OUT.

JOSÉ DOMINGO

NUMBER 2 HAS BEEN MURDERED

José Domingo was born in Zaragoza in 1982. An illustrator, cartoonist, and animator, Domingo is part of the Polaqia Collective. His first long comic was *Cuimhne*: *El fuego distante* [*Cuimhne: The Distant Fire*] (2008), with a script by Kike Benlloch. With *Aventuras de un oficinista japonés* [*Adventures of a Japanese Businessman*] (2011) he won the Salón del Cómic de Barcelona prize. This work has been published in the UK and the US. His latest works are *Conspiraciones* (2013), and *Pablo and Jane and the Hot Air Contraption* (2015).

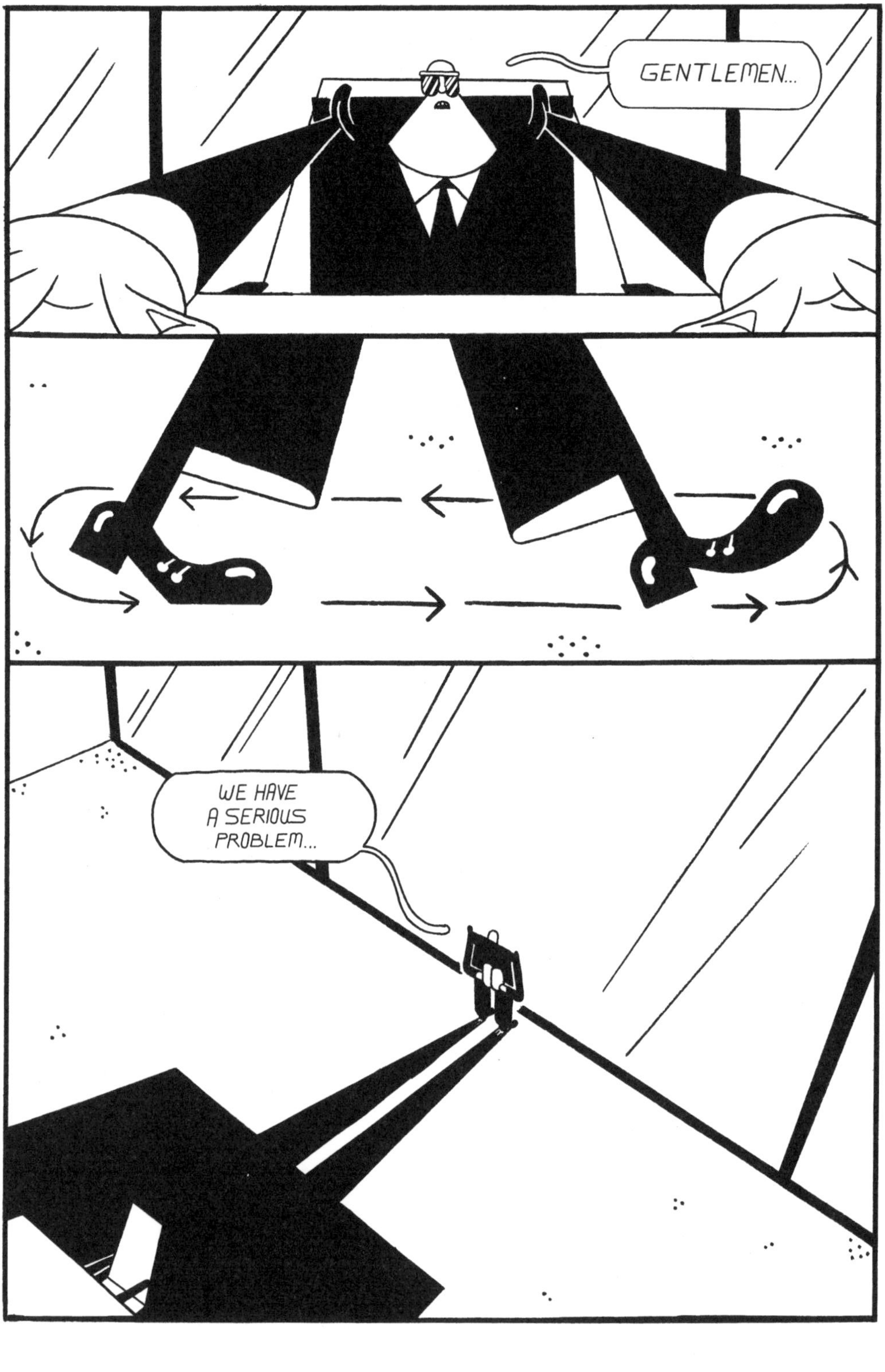
GENTLEMEN...
WE HAVE A SERIOUS PROBLEM...

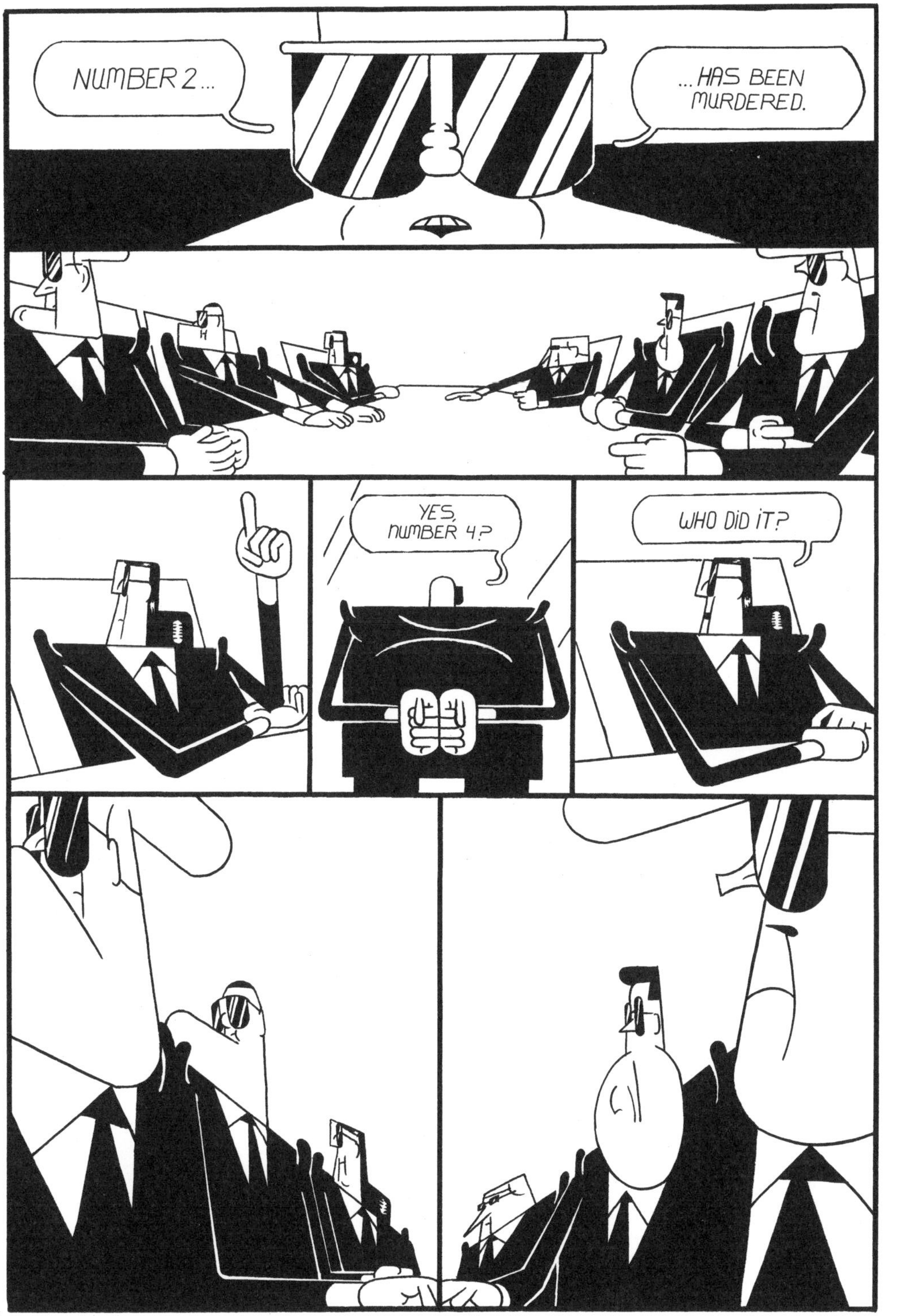
NUMBER 2...
...HAS BEEN MURDERED.
YES, NUMBER 4?
WHO DID IT?

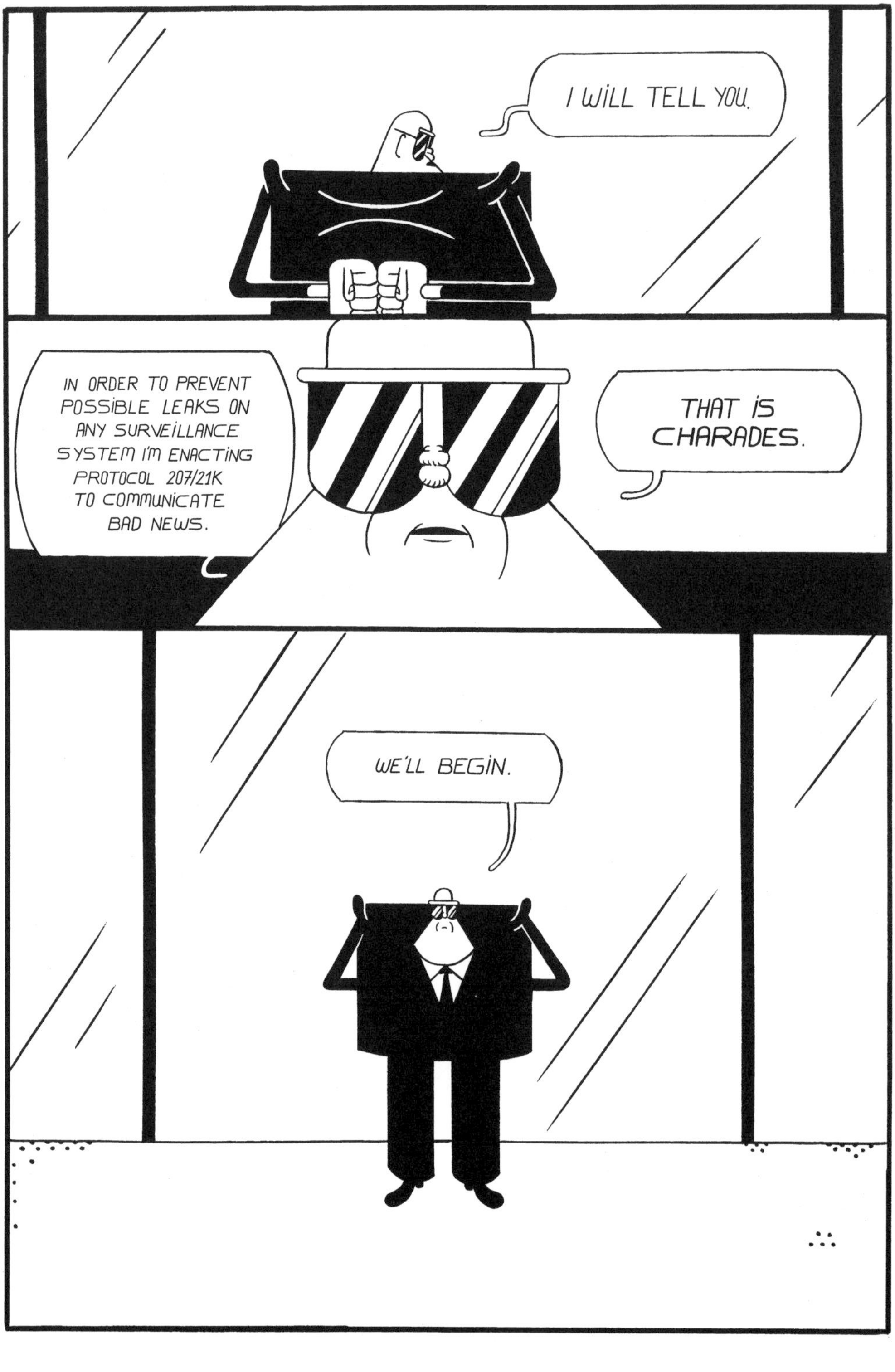
I WILL TELL YOU.
IN ORDER TO PREVENT POSSIBLE LEAKS ON ANY SURVEILLANCE SYSTEM I'M ENACTING PROTOCOL 207/21K TO COMMUNICATE BAD NEWS.
THAT IS CHARADES.
WE'LL BEGIN.

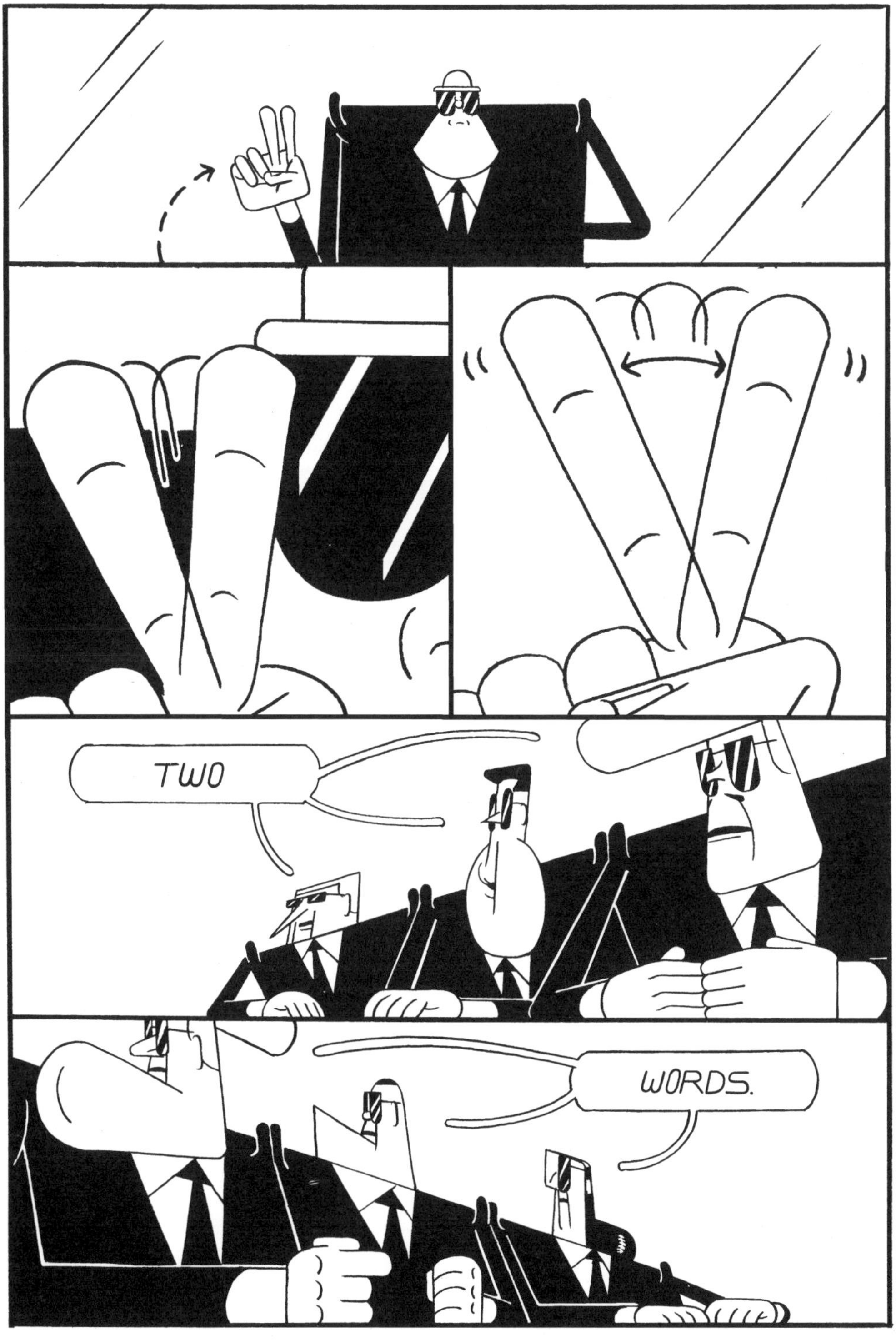
TWO
WORDS.

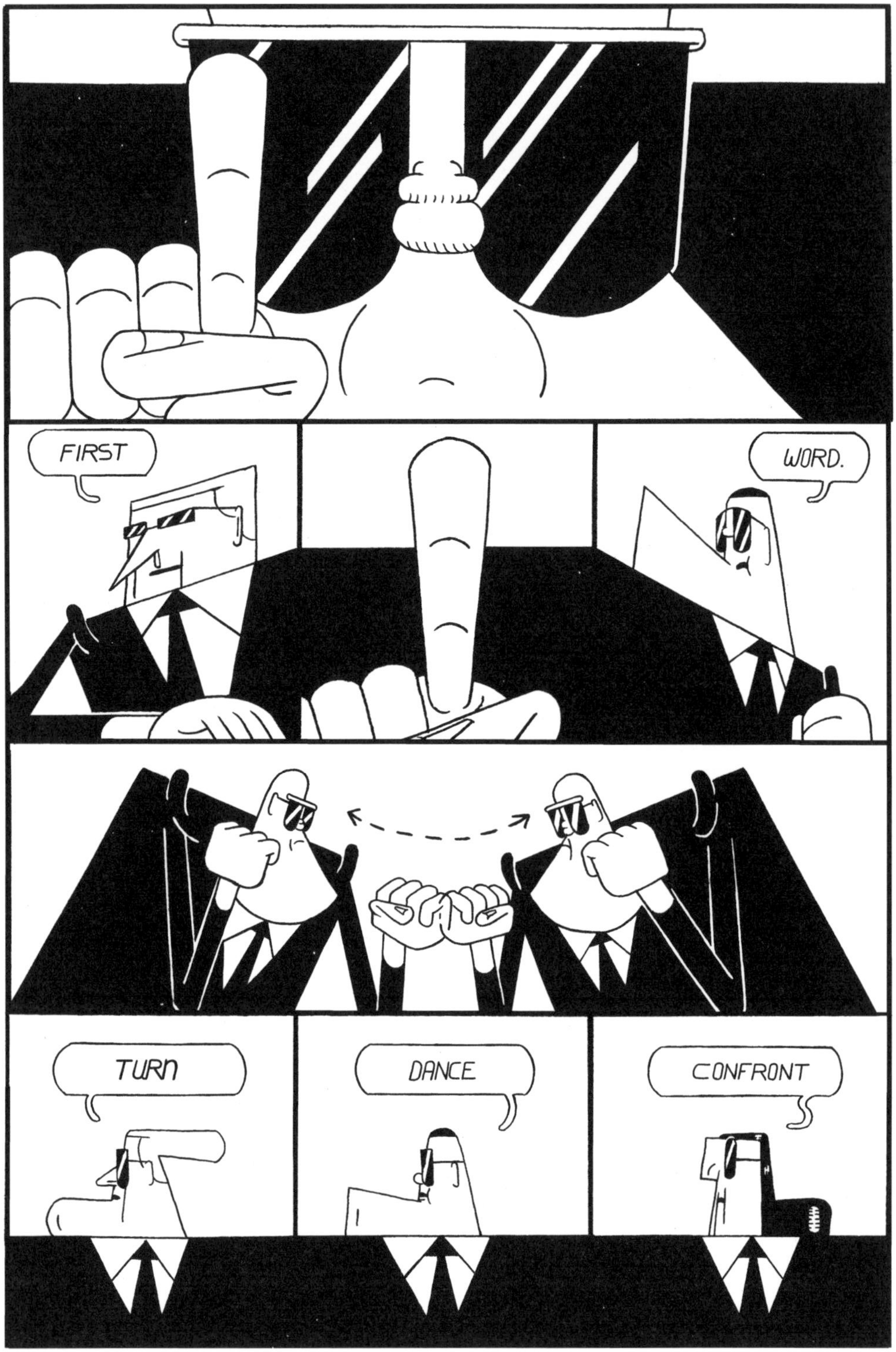
FIRST
WORD.
TURN
DANCE
CONFRONT

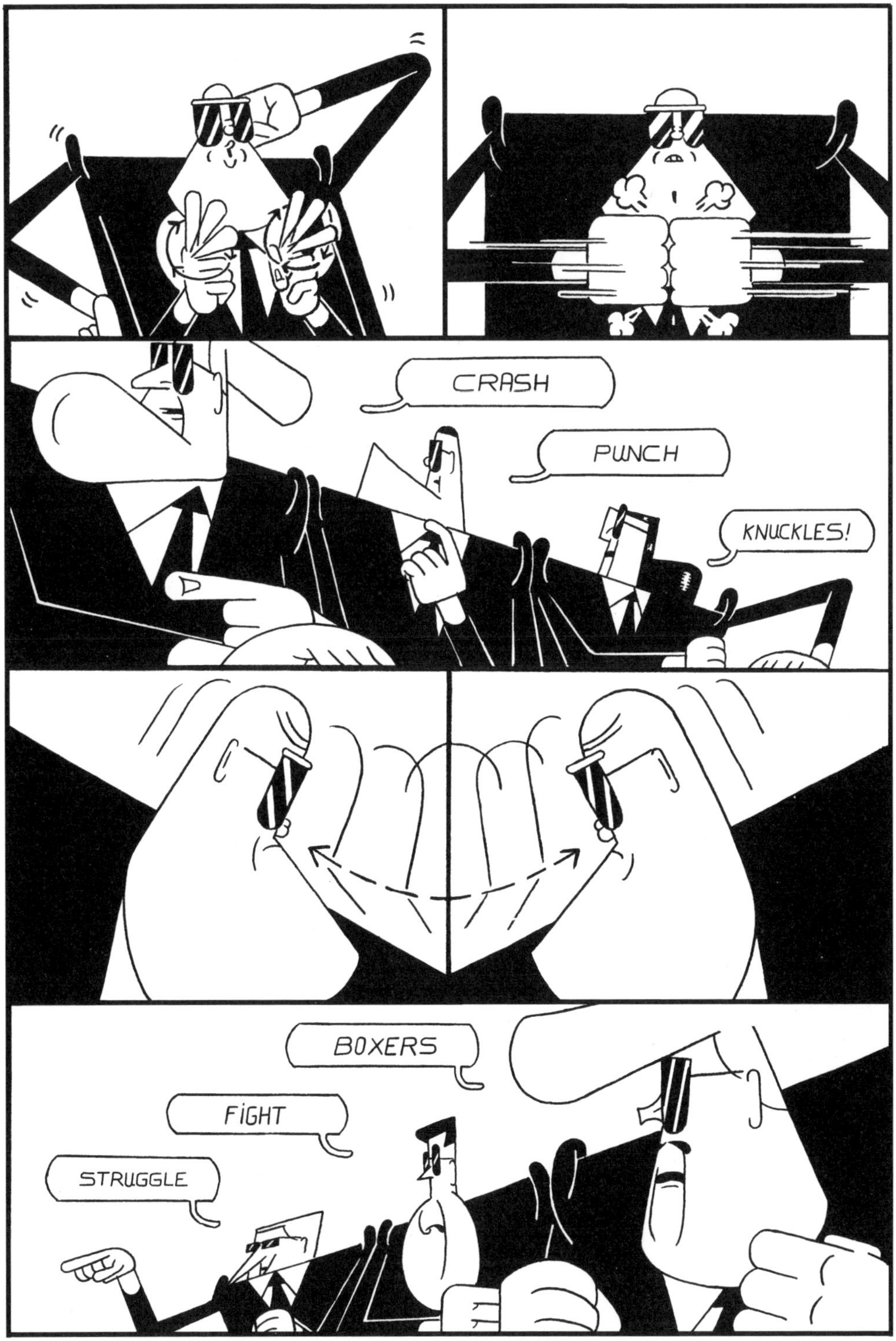
CRASH
PUNCH
KNUCKLES!
STRUGGLE
FIGHT
BOXERS

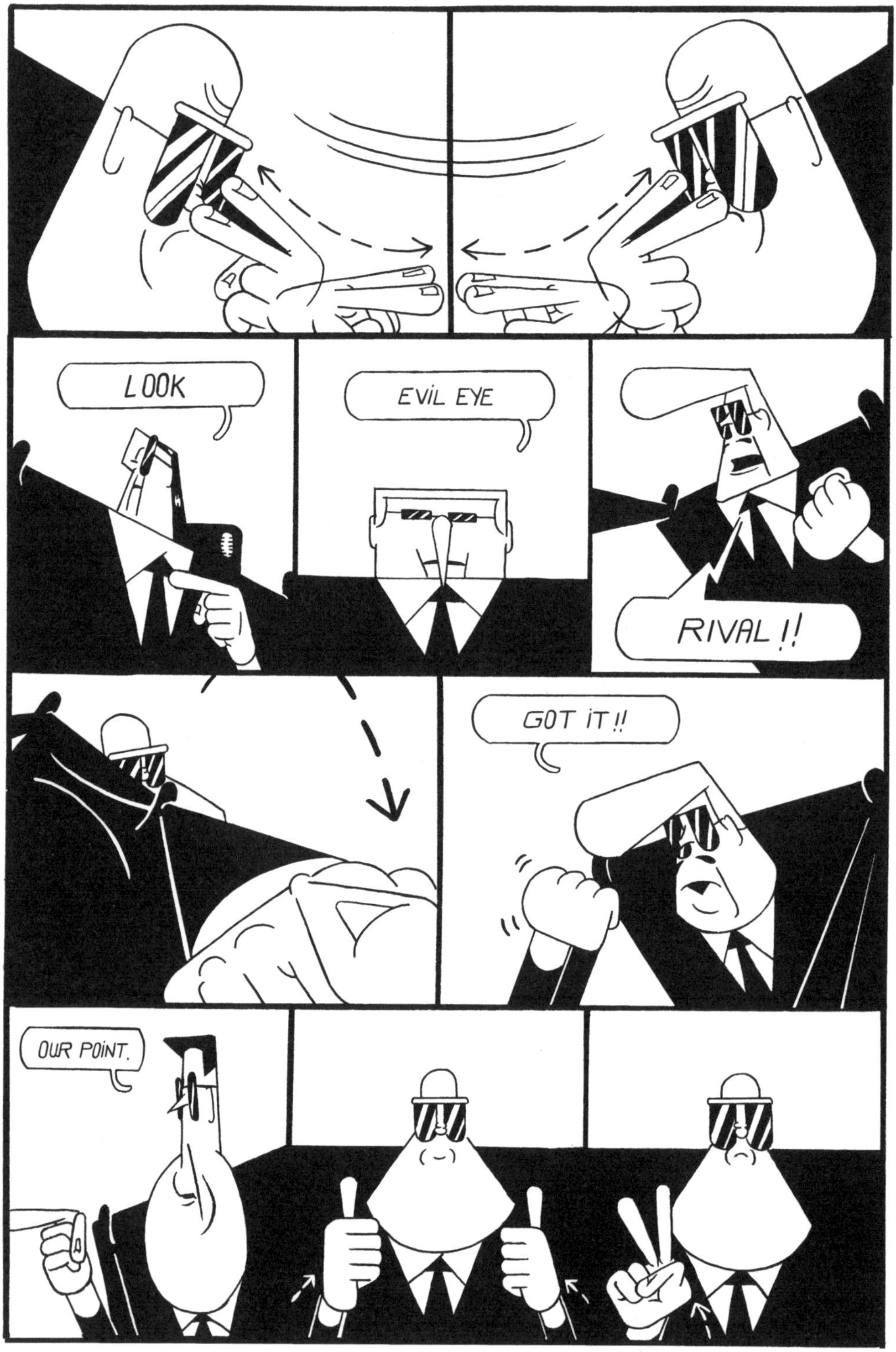
LOOK
EVIL EYE
RIVAL !!
GOT IT !!
OUR POINT.

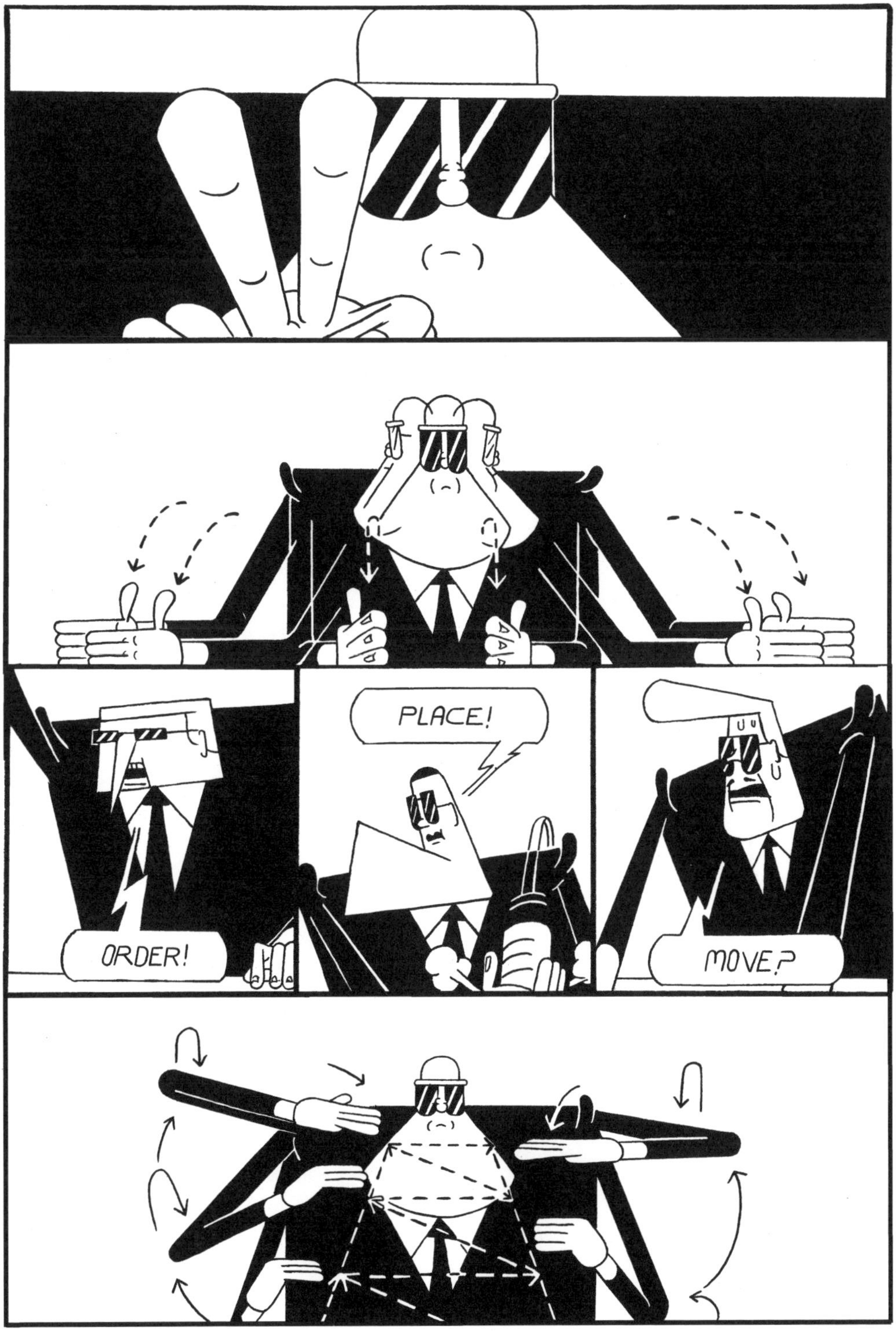
ORDER!
PLACE!
MOVE?

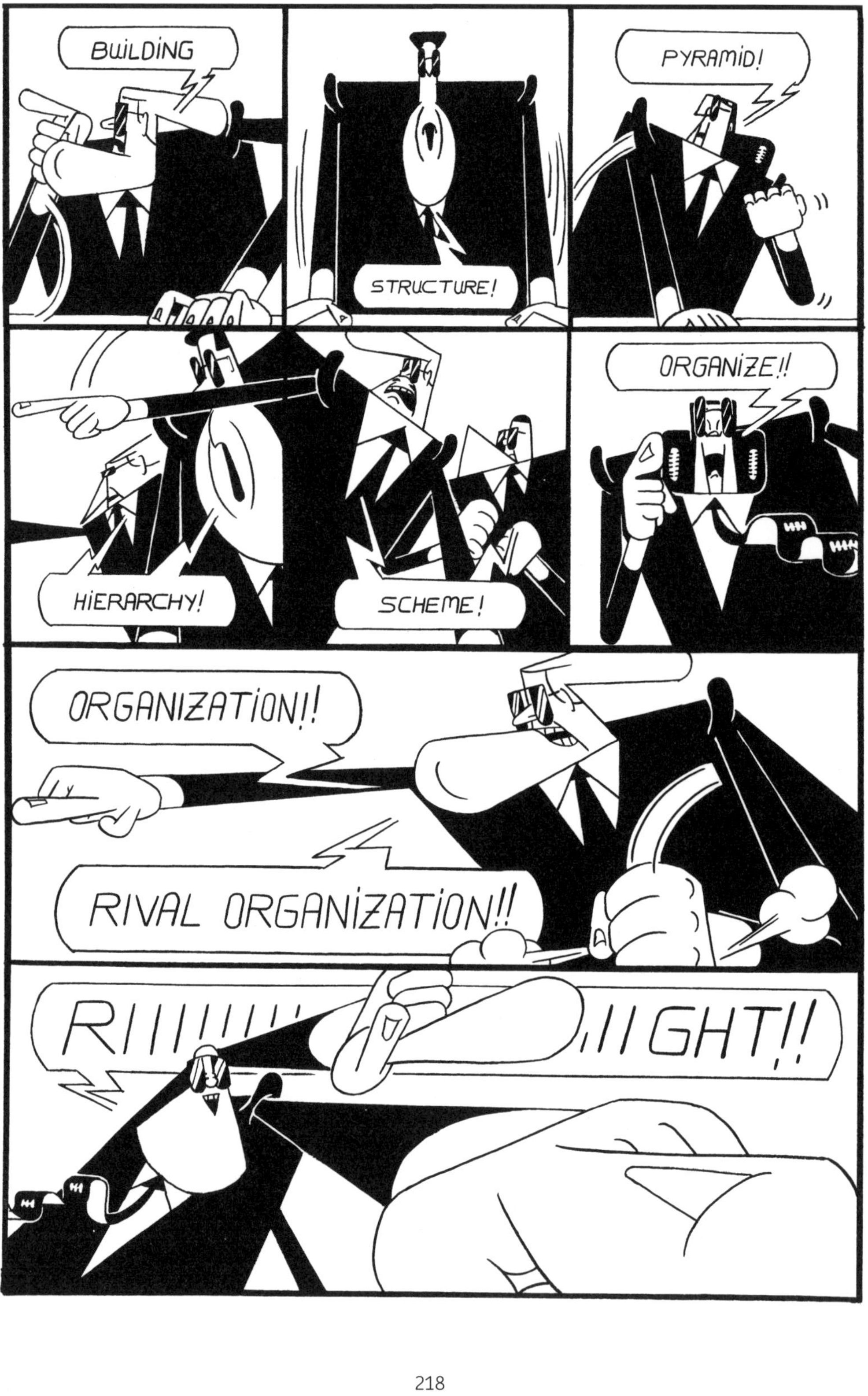
BUILDING
STRUCTURE!
PYRAMID!
HIERARCHY!
SCHEME!
ORGANIZE!!
ORGANIZATION!!
RIVAL ORGANIZATION!!
RIIIIIIIIIIGHT!!

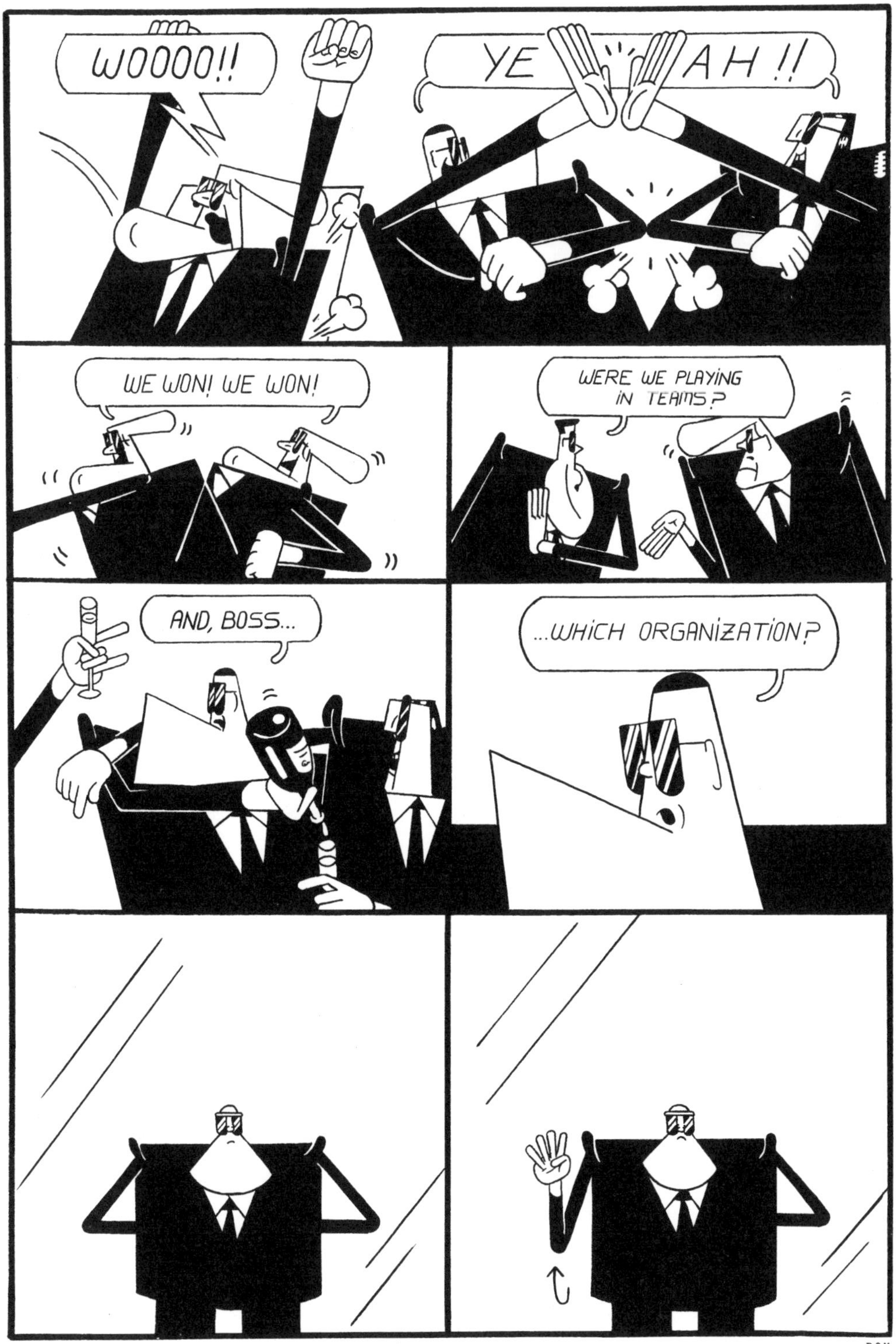
WOOOO!!
YE
AH!!
WE WON! WE WON!
WERE WE PLAYING IN TEAMS?
AND, BOSS...
...WHICH ORGANIZATION?
DOM

SERGI PUYOL

ARRABIATA

Sergi Puyol was born in Barcelona in 1980. A graphic designer, Puyol is a cartoonist by vocation, which has led him to contribute to numerous zines—especially *Colibrí*, which he coedited with Toni Mascaró. He's published the comic *Una caja, una silla* [*One Box, One Chair*] (2008), *Cárcel de amor* [*Prison of Love*] (2011), *Francisco* (2013) and *Una blanda oscuridad* [*A Soft Darkness*] (2014).

ARRABIATA

BY SERGI PUYOL

I... I JUST WANT ALL OF
THIS TO STOP FOR ONCE...
MMHHH?
IS SOMEONE THERE?
IS THAT YOU, MARTÍN?
CLAC!

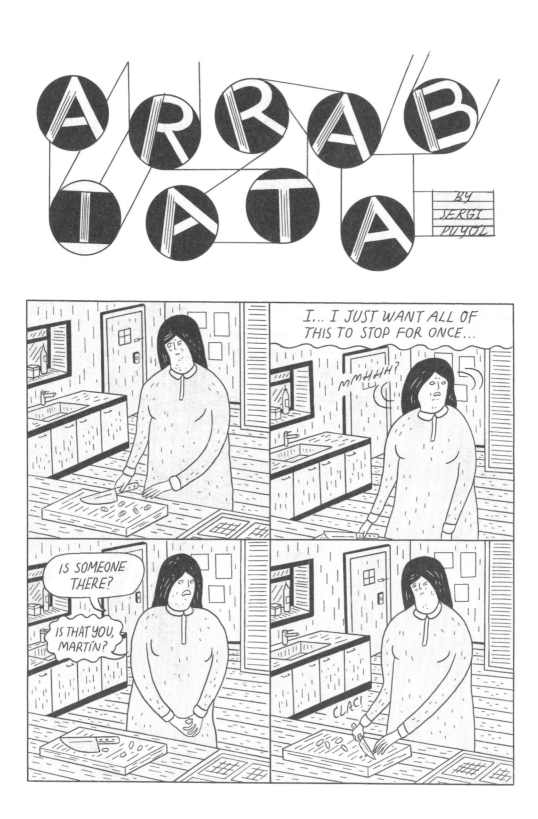

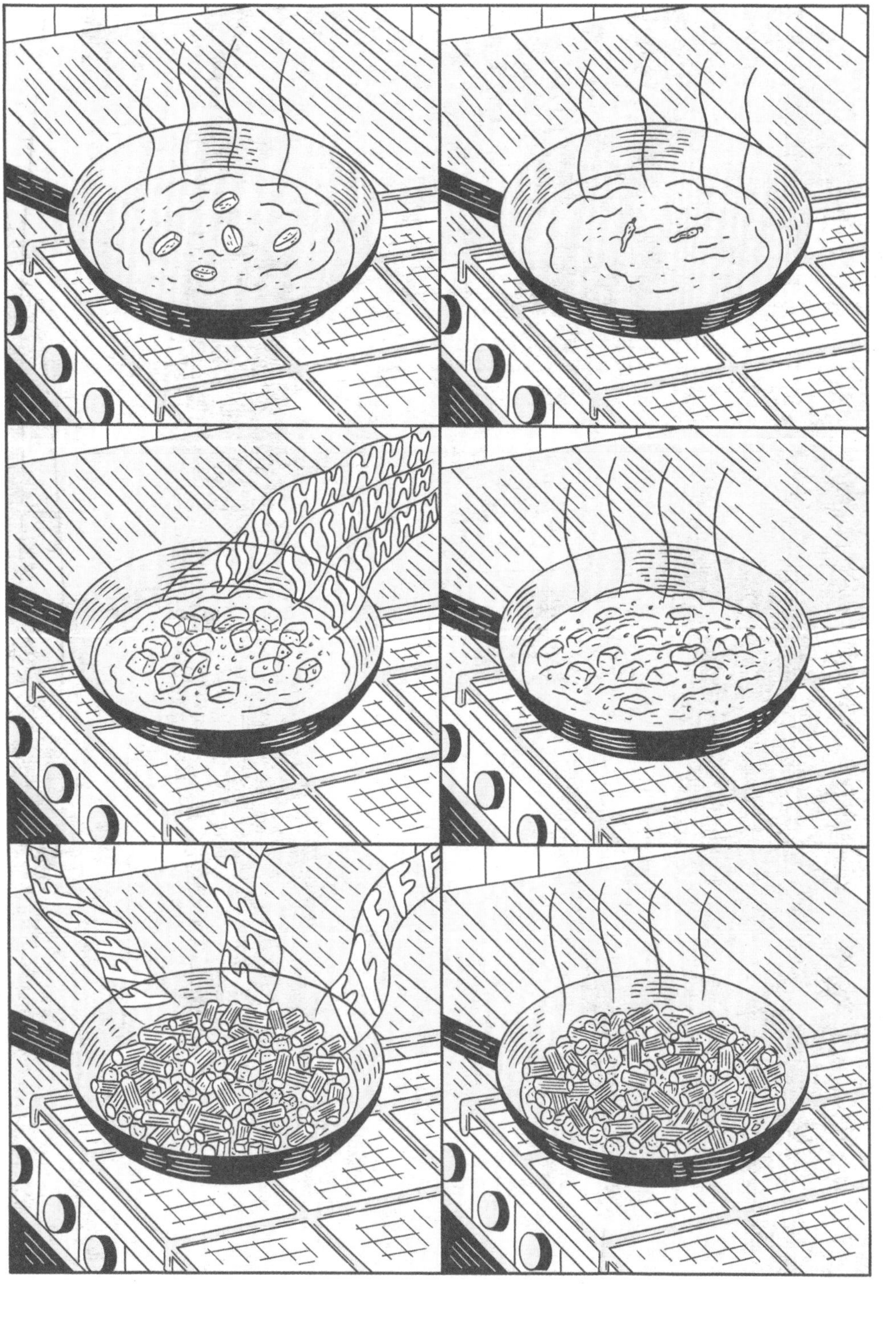
SSSHHHHHH
SSSHHHHH
SSSHHHHH
FFFF
FFFF
FFFF

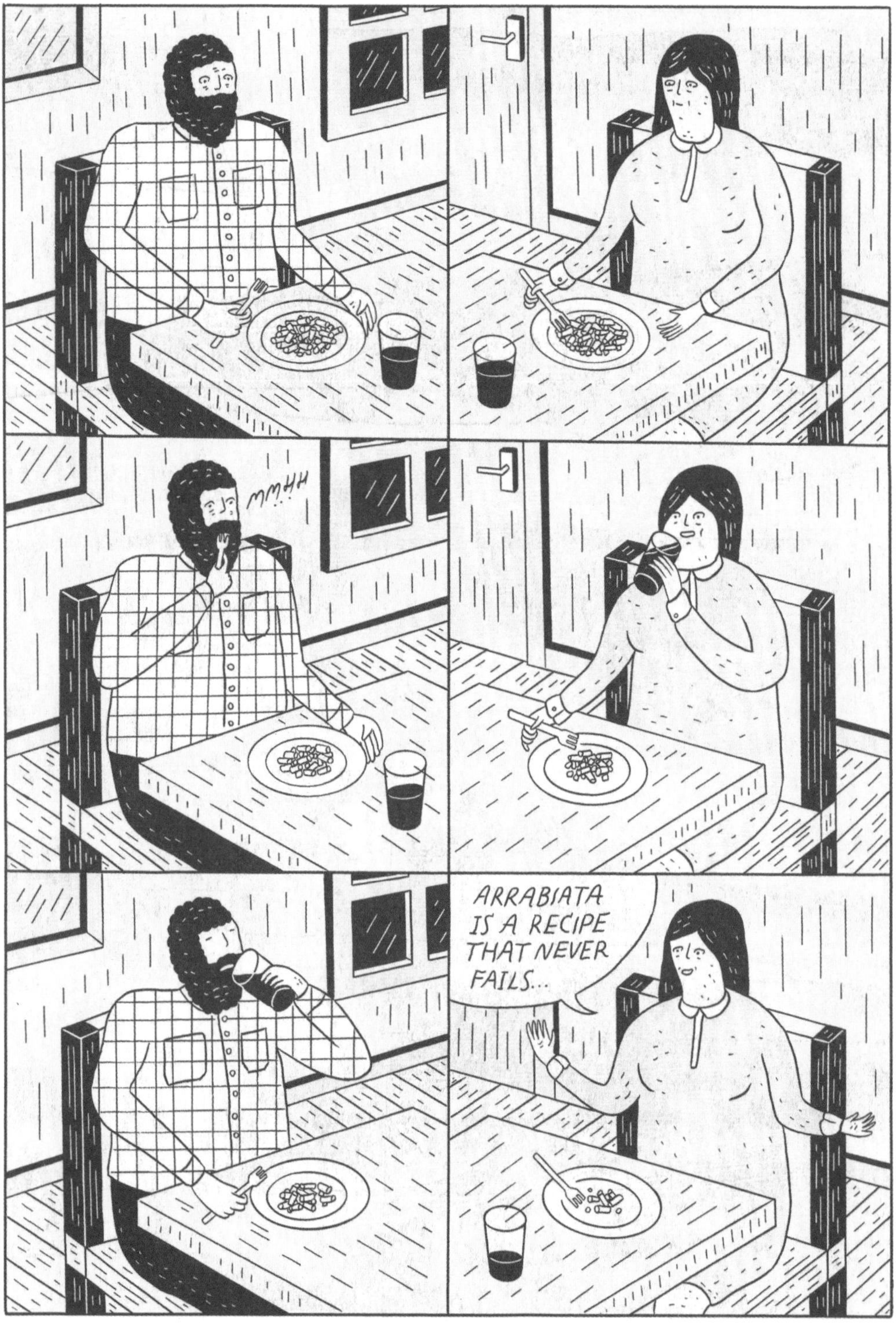
MMHH
ARRABIATA IS A RECIPE THAT NEVER FAILS...

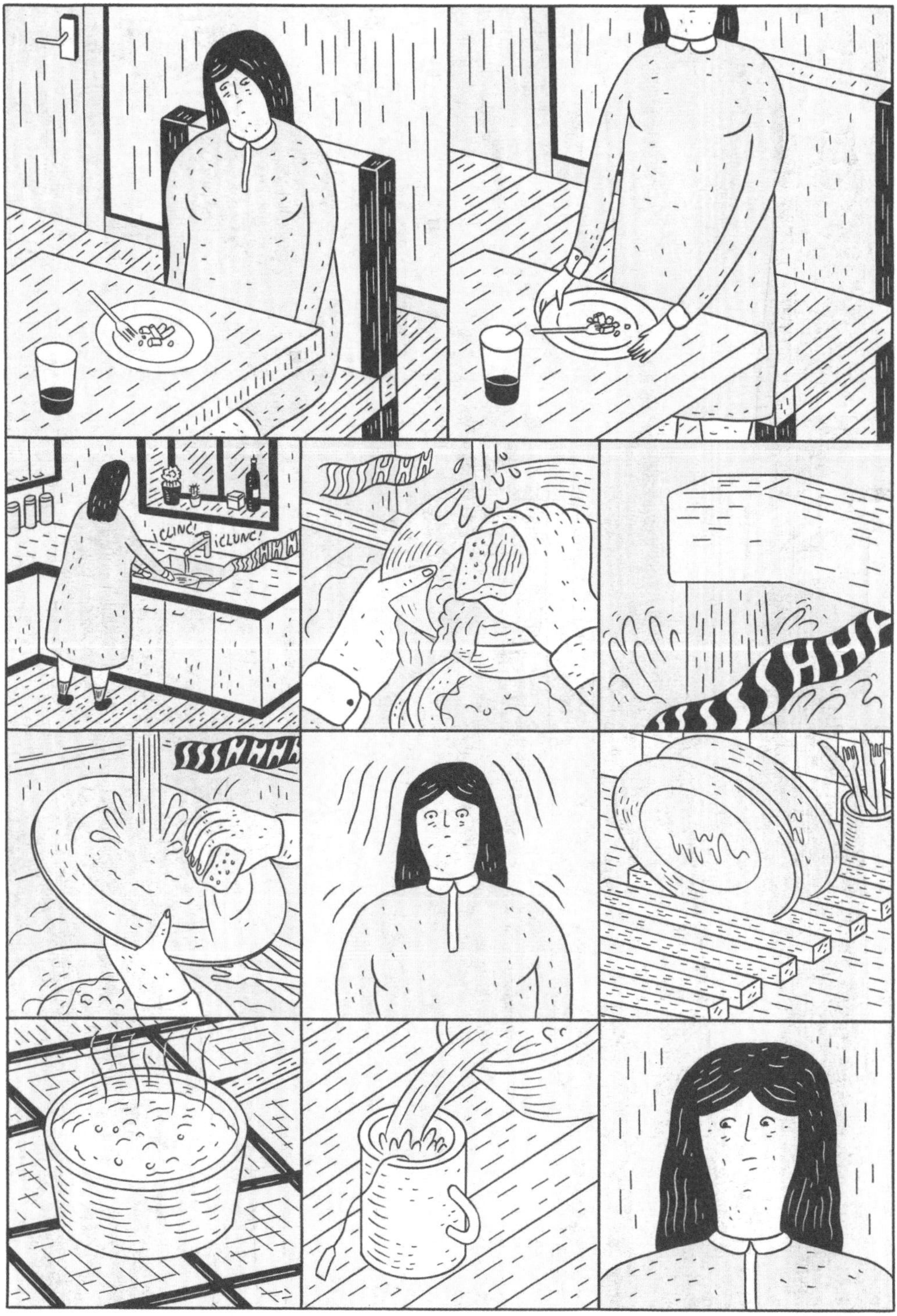
¡CLINC!
¡CLUNC!

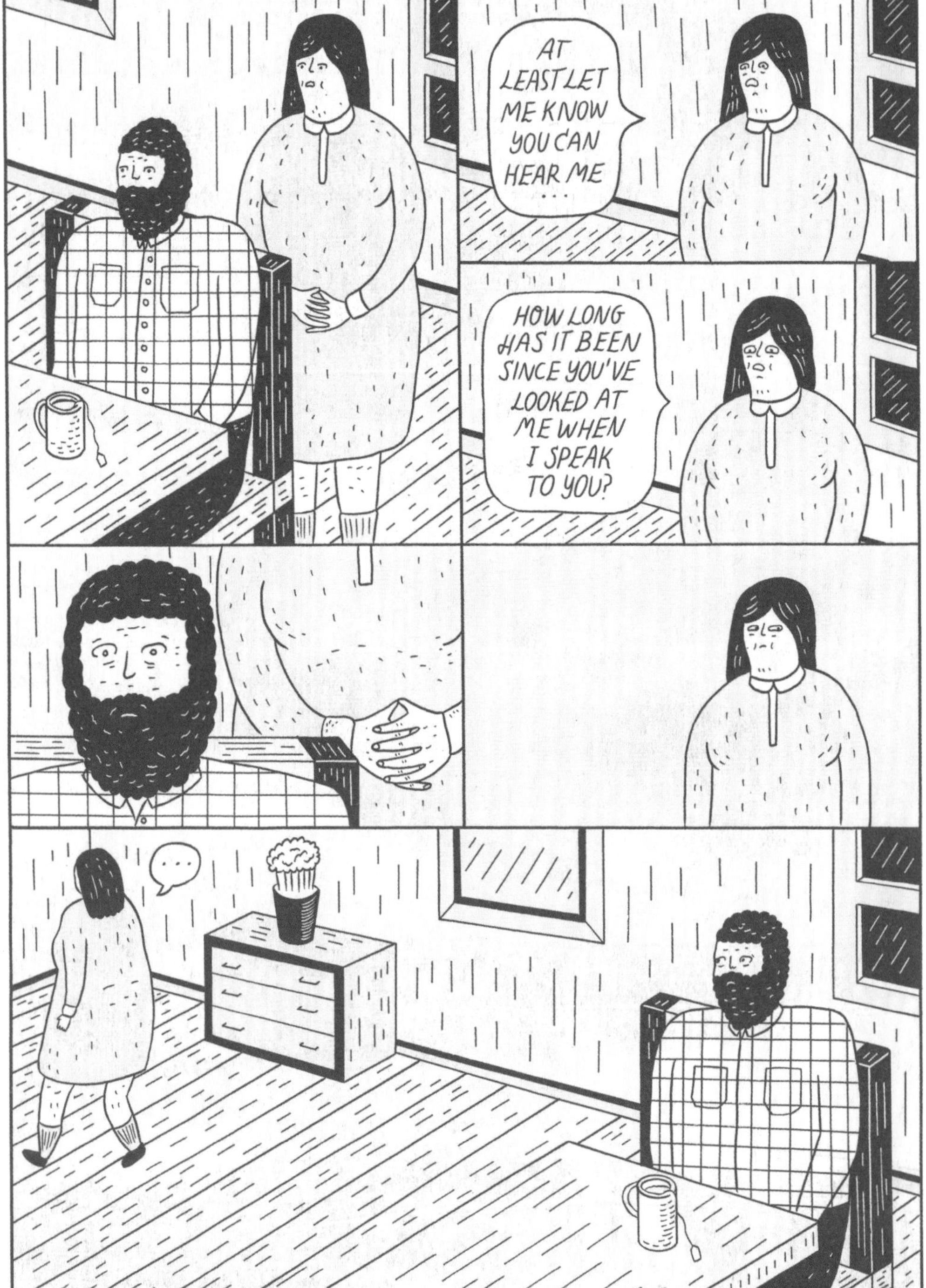
AT LEAST LET ME KNOW YOU CAN HEAR ME
...
HOW LONG HAS IT BEEN SINCE YOU'VE LOOKED AT ME WHEN I SPEAK TO YOU?
...

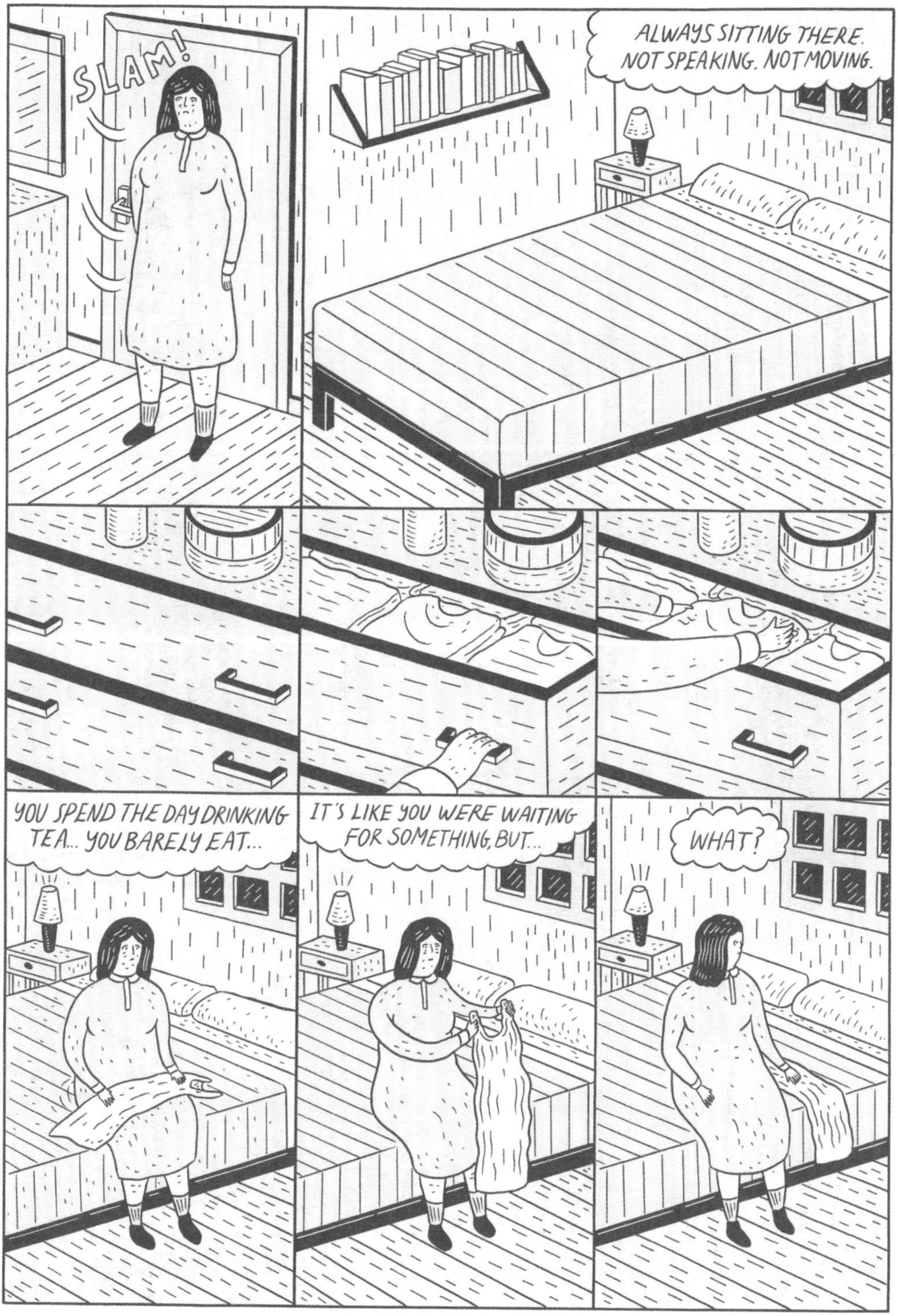
SLAM!
ALWAYS SITTING THERE. NOT SPEAKING. NOT MOVING.
YOU SPEND THE DAY DRINKING TEA... YOU BARELY EAT...
IT'S LIKE YOU WERE WAITING FOR SOMETHING, BUT...
WHAT?

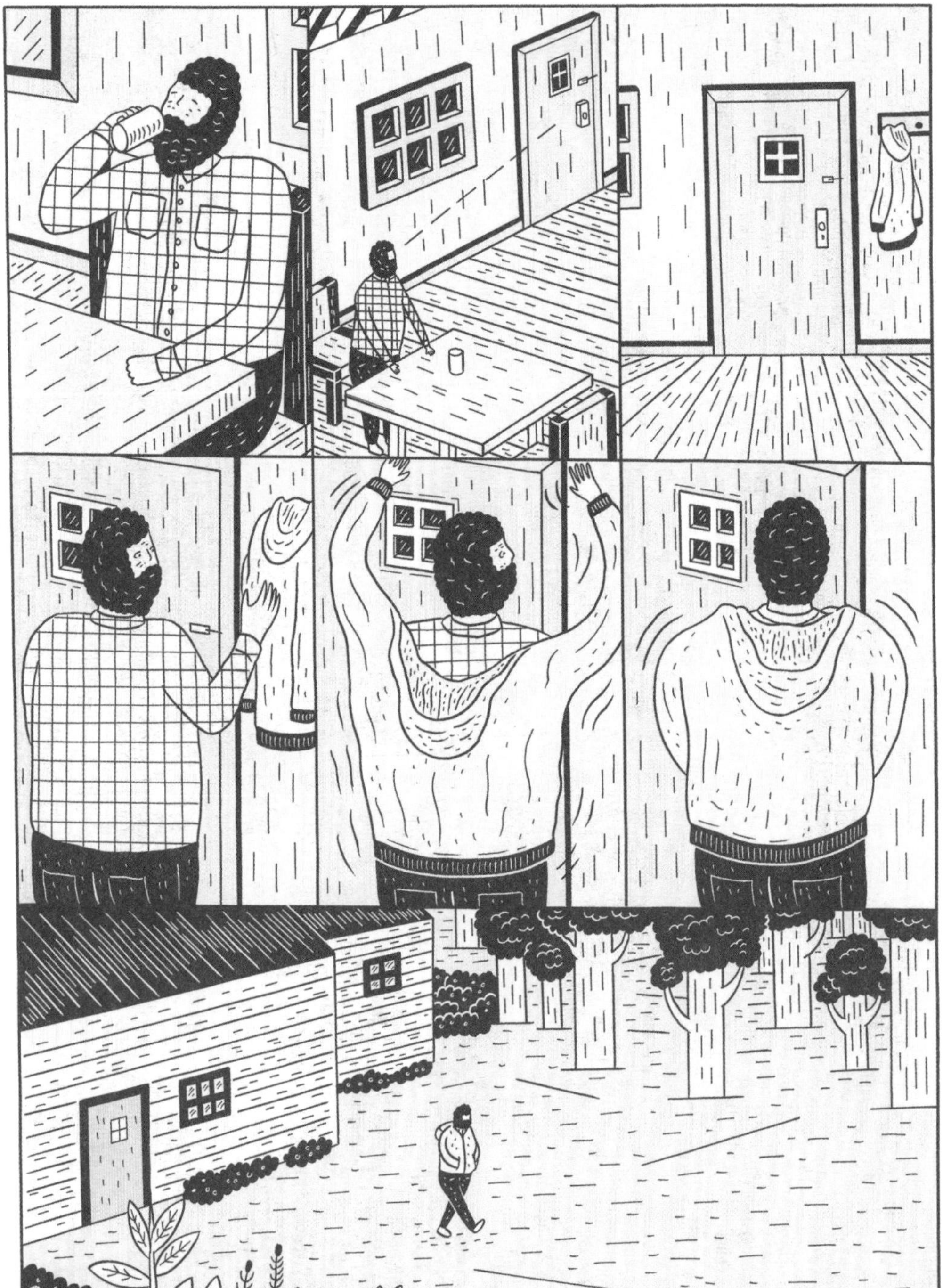

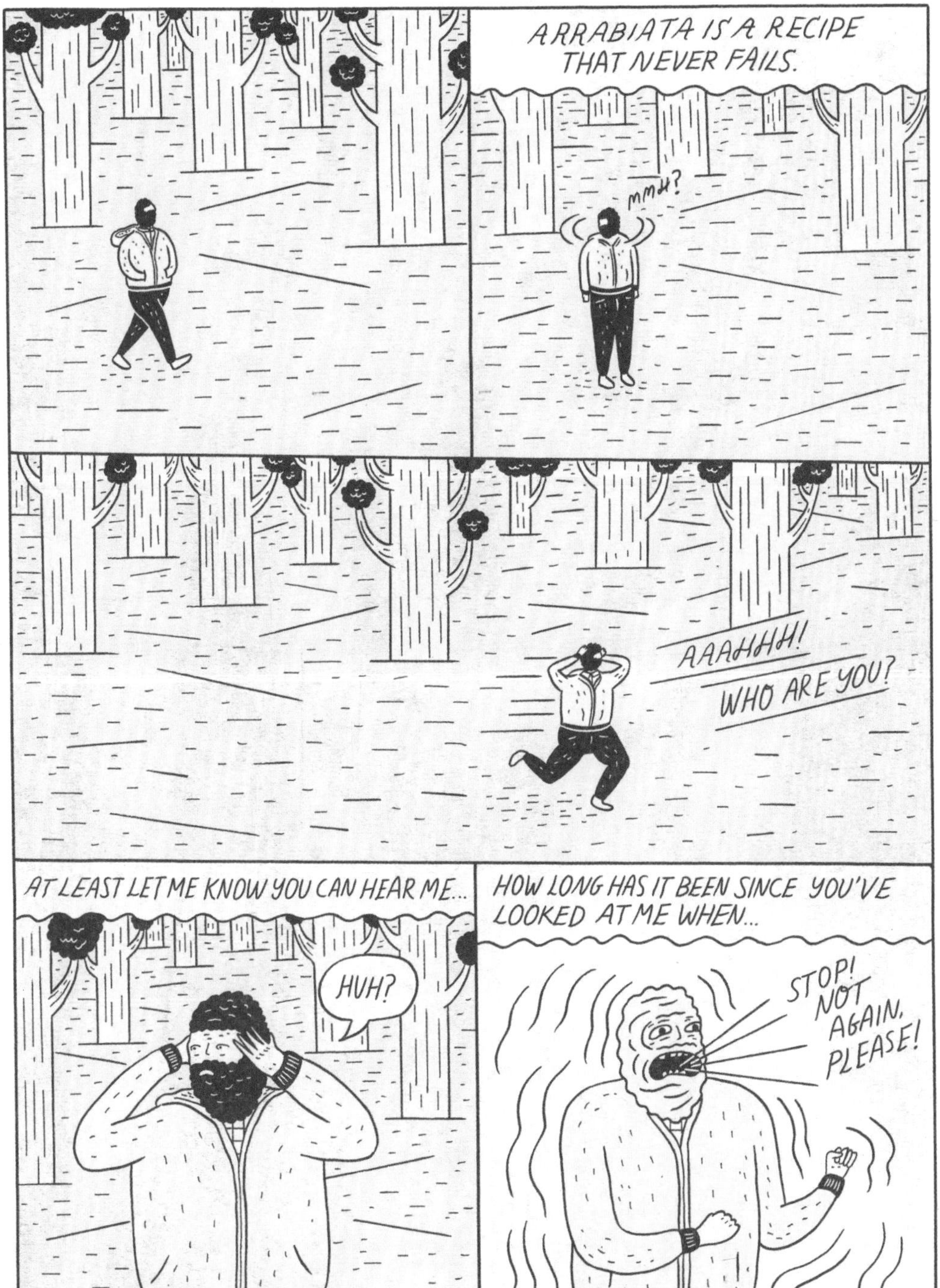
ARRABIATA IS A RECIPE THAT NEVER FAILS.
MMH?
AAAHHH!
WHO ARE YOU?
AT LEAST LET ME KNOW YOU CAN HEAR ME...
HUH?
HOW LONG HAS IT BEEN SINCE YOU'VE LOOKED AT ME WHEN...
STOP! NOT AGAIN, PLEASE!

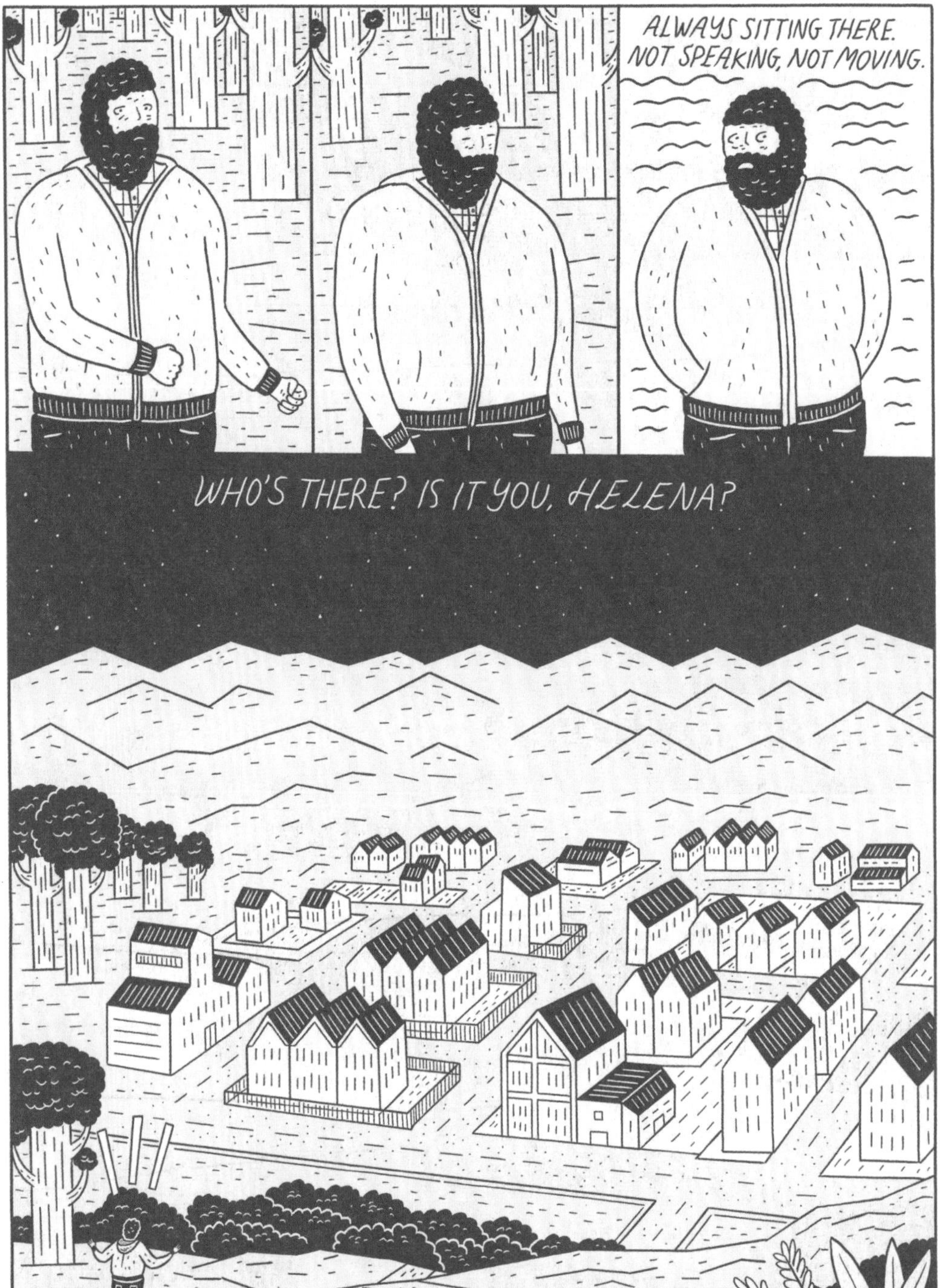
ALWAYS SITTING THERE.
NOT SPEAKING, NOT MOVING.
WHO'S THERE? IS IT YOU, HELENA?

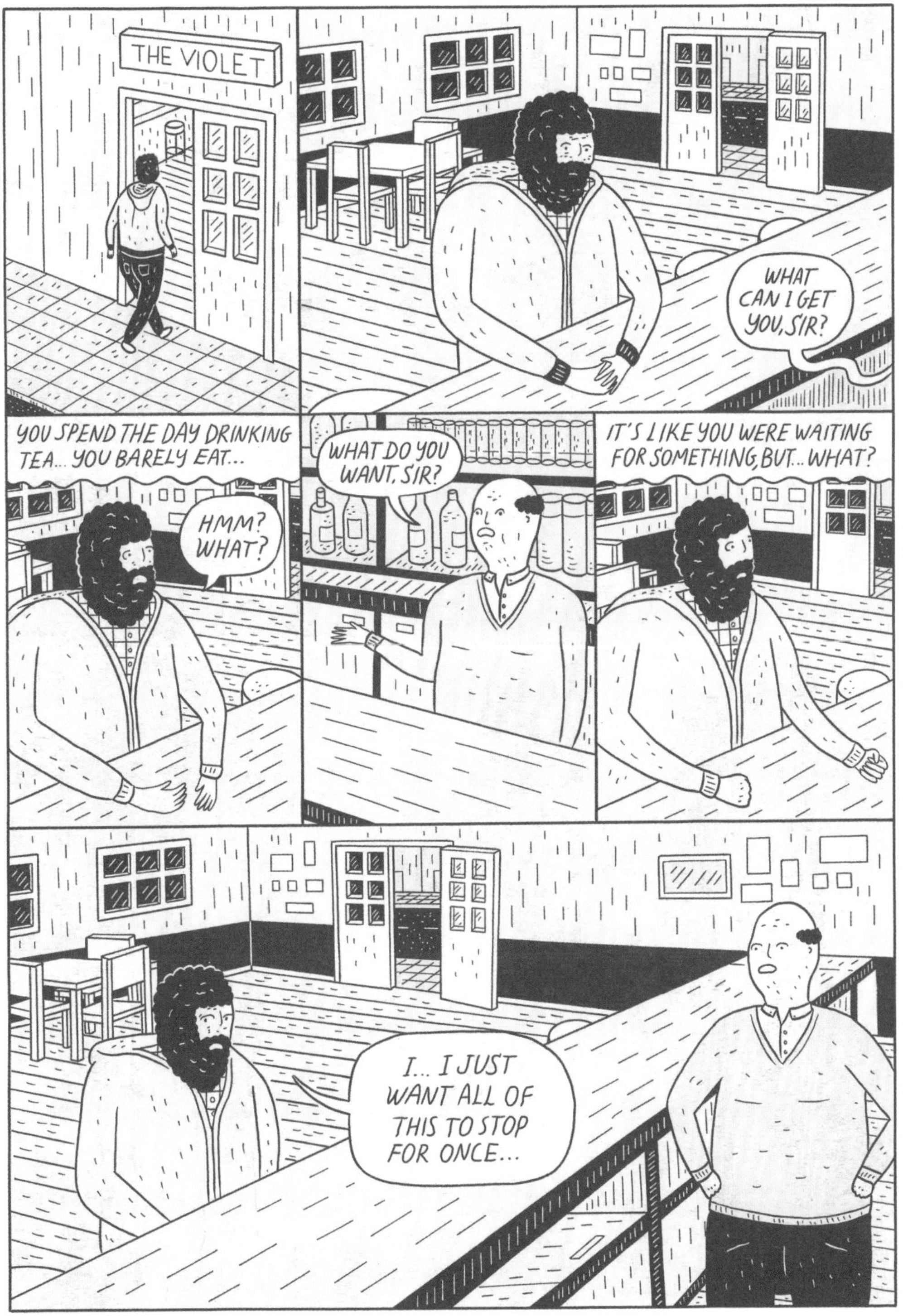
THE VIOLET
WHAT CAN I GET YOU, SIR?
YOU SPEND THE DAY DRINKING TEA... YOU BARELY EAT...
HMM? WHAT?
WHAT DO YOU WANT, SIR?
IT'S LIKE YOU WERE WAITING FOR SOMETHING, BUT... WHAT?
I... I JUST WANT ALL OF THIS TO STOP FOR ONCE...

JAVIER OLIVARES

FINLAND

Javier Olivares was born in Madrid in 1964. An illustrator and cartoonist, he started the journal *Madriz* in the '80s, and since then has contributed work to numerous magazines like *El País Semanal* and newspapers like *El Mundo*, as well as illustrating books both for children and adults. Among his best known comic books are *Cuentos de la estrella legumbre* [*Stories from the Legume Star*] (2005), *La caja negra* [*The Black Box*] (2001), *Las crónicas de Ono y Hop* [*The Chronicles of Ono and Hop*] (2007) and *El extraño caso del doctor Jekyll y mister Hyde* [*The Strange Case of Dr. Jekyll and Mr. Hyde*] (2009), this last one with a script by Santiago García, as well as his most recent graphic novel *Las meninas* (2014), which has been translated into French. It also won the National Comic Award. The comic "Finland," which is included here, was adapted from an original story by Argentine author Hernán Casciari.

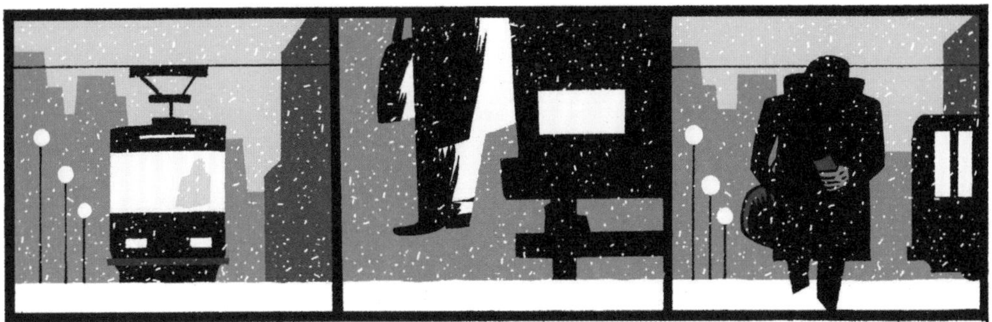

On November 14, 1995, I accidentally killed my sister's oldest daughter, backing up the car. Between the sharp impact, the panicked screams of my family, and the discovery that I had actually hit a log, passed the ten most intense seconds of my life.

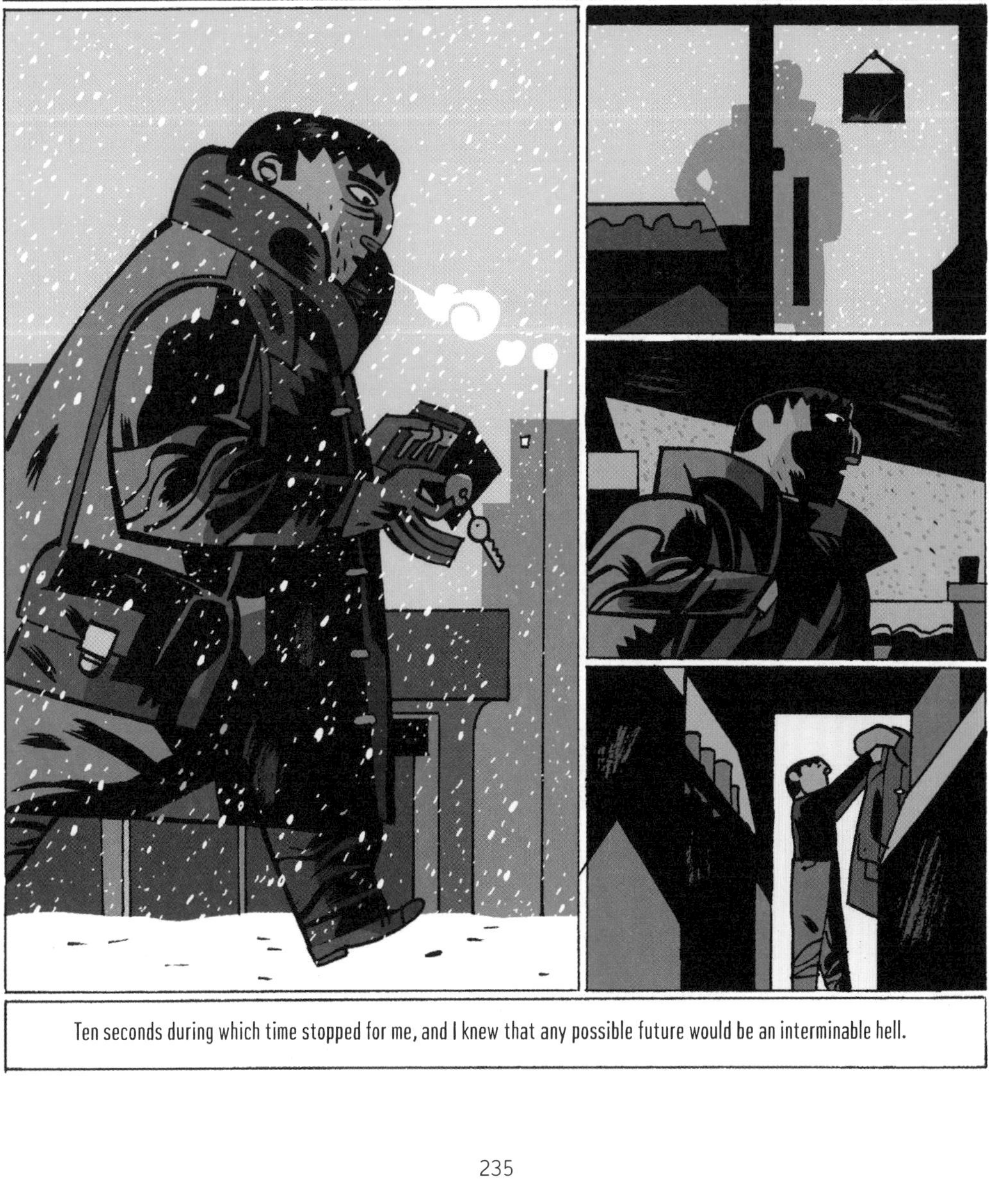

Ten seconds during which time stopped for me, and I knew that any possible future would be an interminable hell.

I was living in Buenos Aires and had traveled to Mercedes to celebrate my father's mother's 80th birthday. We celebrated my grandmother's birthday with a barbecue in the country; we were already onto the familiar after-dinner conversation. At three in the afternoon I asked to borrow Roberto's car to go to the paper and turn in an article.

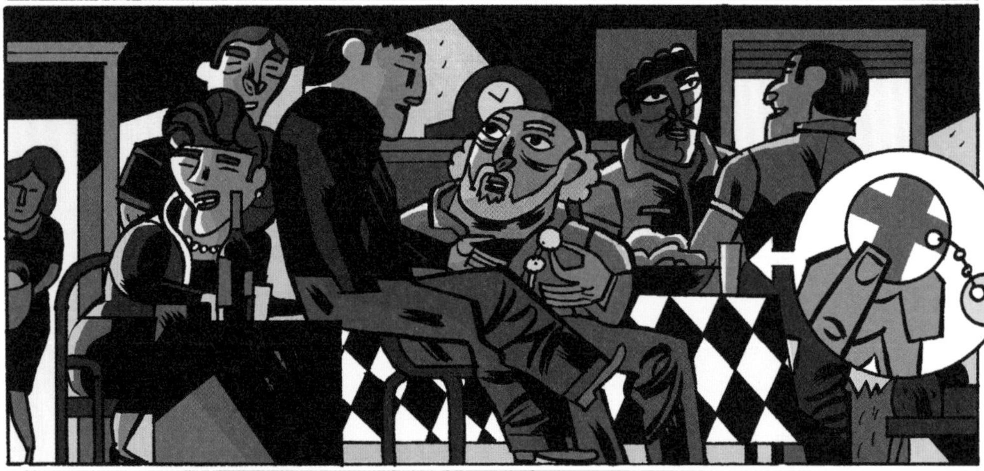

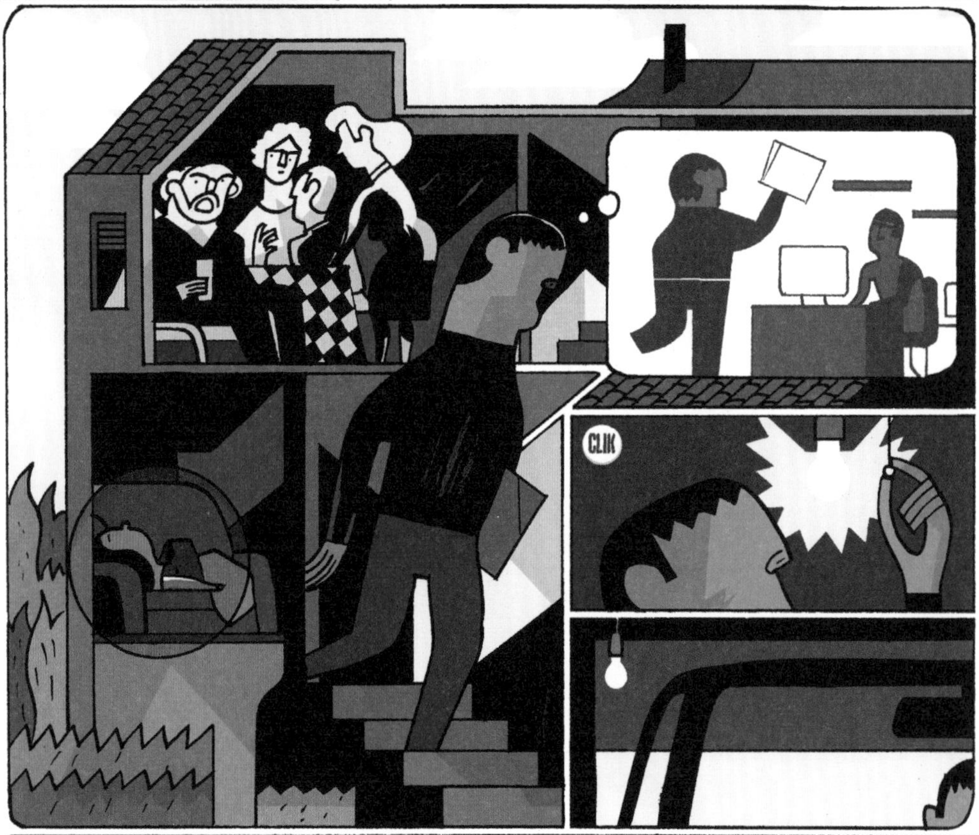
CLIK

I got in the car, checked the rearview mirror to make sure there were no children around, and put it in reverse to back out of the gate and into the street.

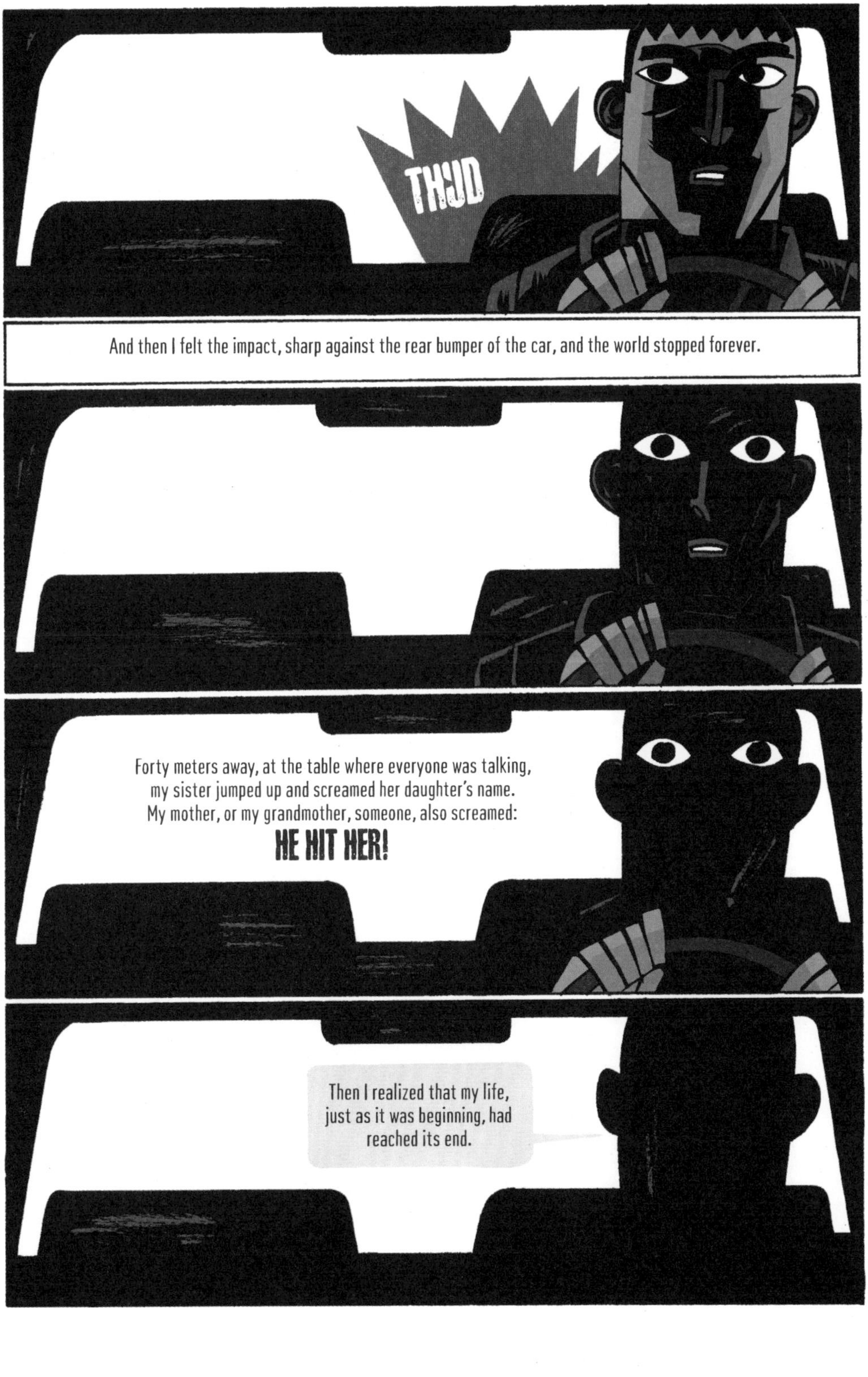
THUD
And then I felt the impact, sharp against the rear bumper of the car, and the world stopped forever.
Forty meters away, at the table where everyone was talking, my sister jumped up and screamed her daughter's name. My mother, or my grandmother, someone, also screamed:
HE HIT HER!
Then I realized that my life, just as it was beginning, had reached its end.

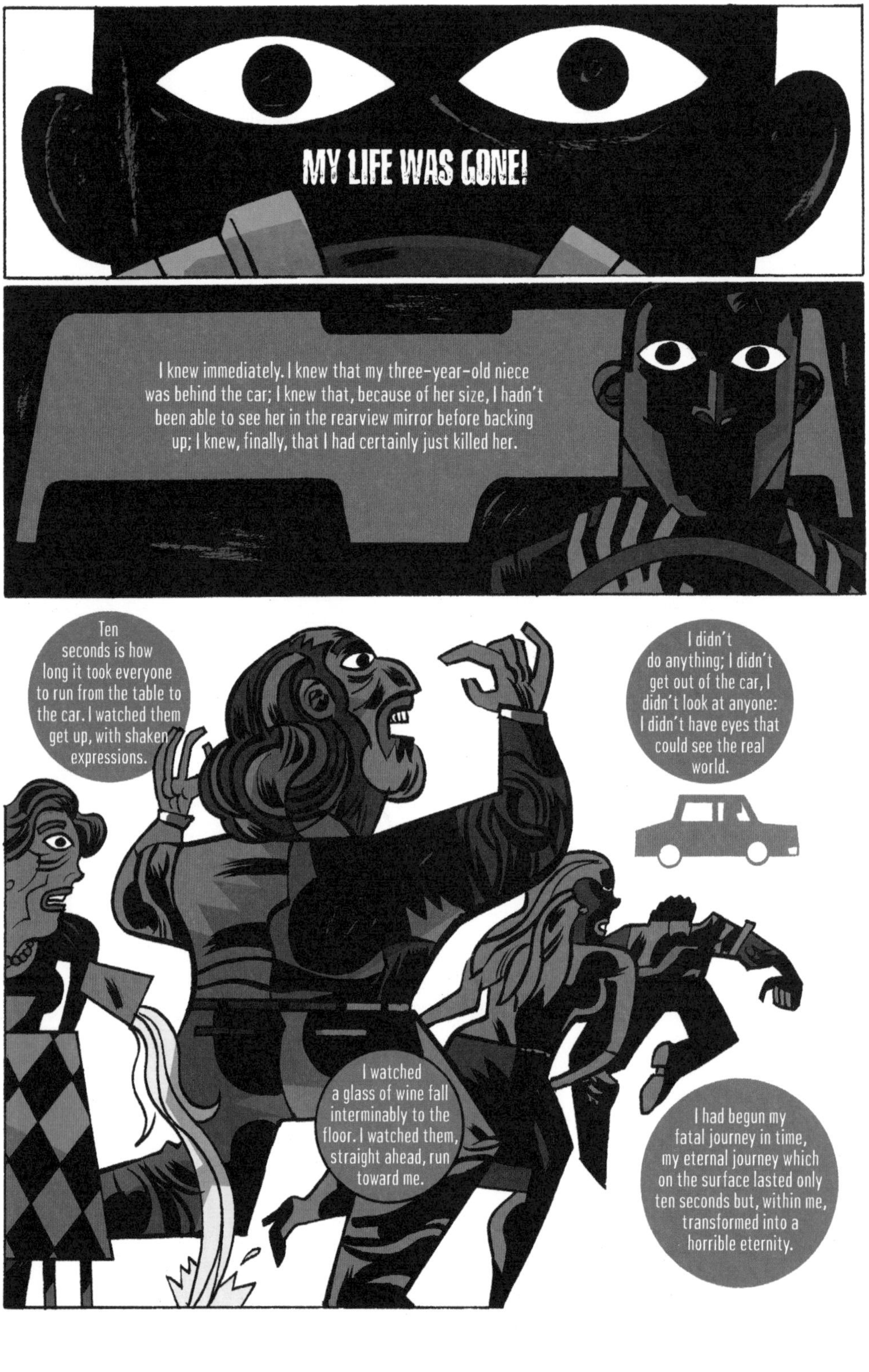
MY LIFE WAS GONE!
I knew immediately. I knew that my three-year-old niece was behind the car; I knew that, because of her size, I hadn't been able to see her in the rearview mirror before backing up; I knew, finally, that I had certainly just killed her.
Ten seconds is how long it took everyone to run from the table to the car. I watched them get up, with shaken expressions.
I didn't do anything; I didn't get out of the car, I didn't look at anyone: I didn't have eyes that could see the real world.
I watched a glass of wine fall interminably to the floor. I watched them, straight ahead, run toward me.
I had begun my fatal journey in time, my eternal journey which on the surface lasted only ten seconds but, within me, transformed into a horrible eternity.

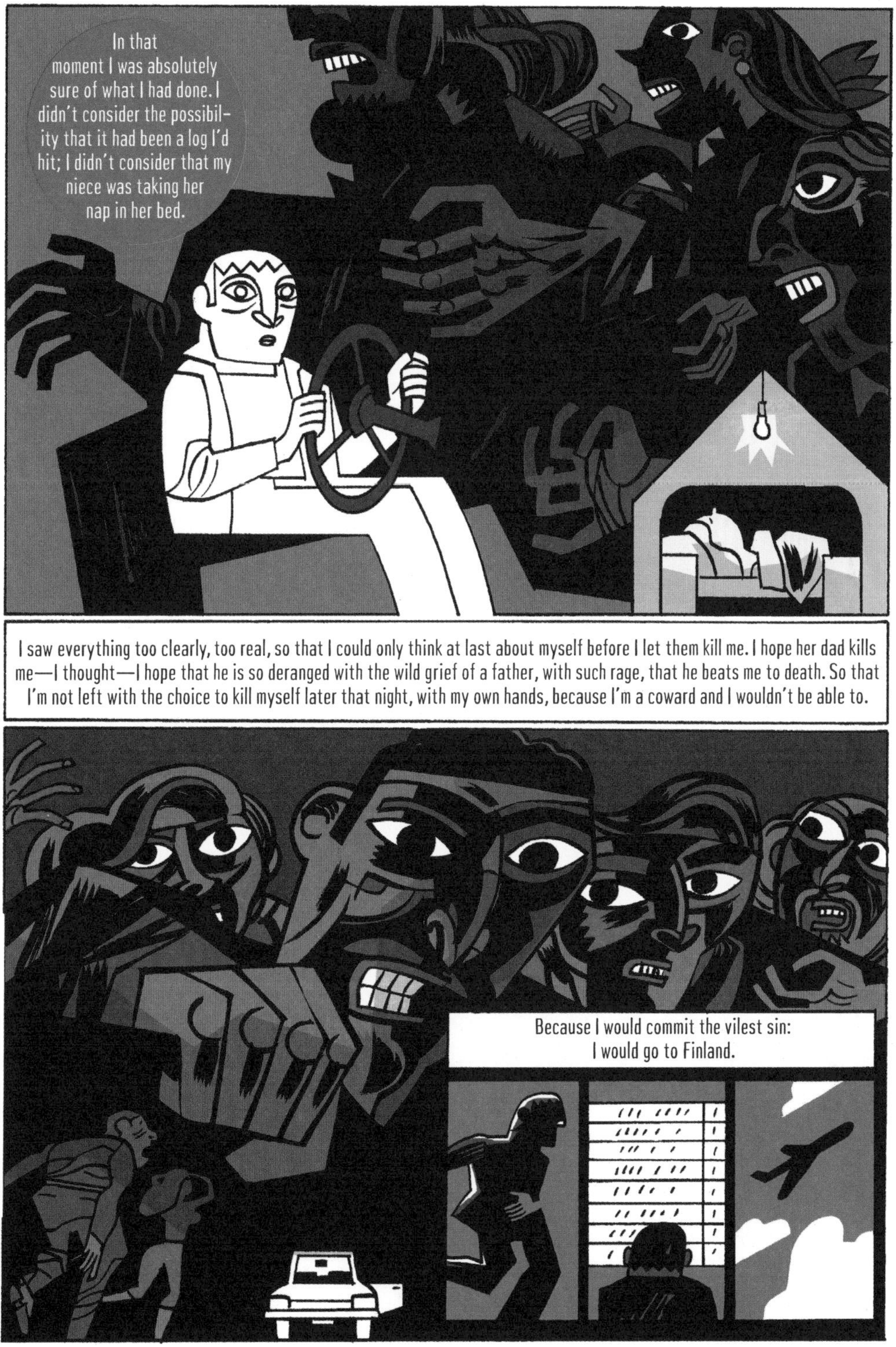
In that moment I was absolutely sure of what I had done. I didn't consider the possibility that it had been a log I'd hit; I didn't consider that my niece was taking her nap in her bed.
I saw everything too clearly, too real, so that I could only think at last about myself before I let them kill me. I hope her dad kills me—I thought—I hope that he is so deranged with the wild grief of a father, with such rage, that he beats me to death. So that I'm not left with the choice to kill myself later that night, with my own hands, because I'm a coward and I wouldn't be able to.
Because I would commit the vilest sin:
I would go to Finland.

I was almost twenty-five years old. I was writing a long and pleasant novel. I lived in a lovely house in Villa Urquiza—with a pingpong table on the patio and my whole life ahead of me—working for a newspaper that paid me well, with a full social life; I was happy.

And then I killed my three-year-old goddaughter and all the lights in all the rooms of all the houses in which I could ever be happy again went out.

I think in this way, dispassionate, because I no longer have a body to tremble in.

TCHAK

?!

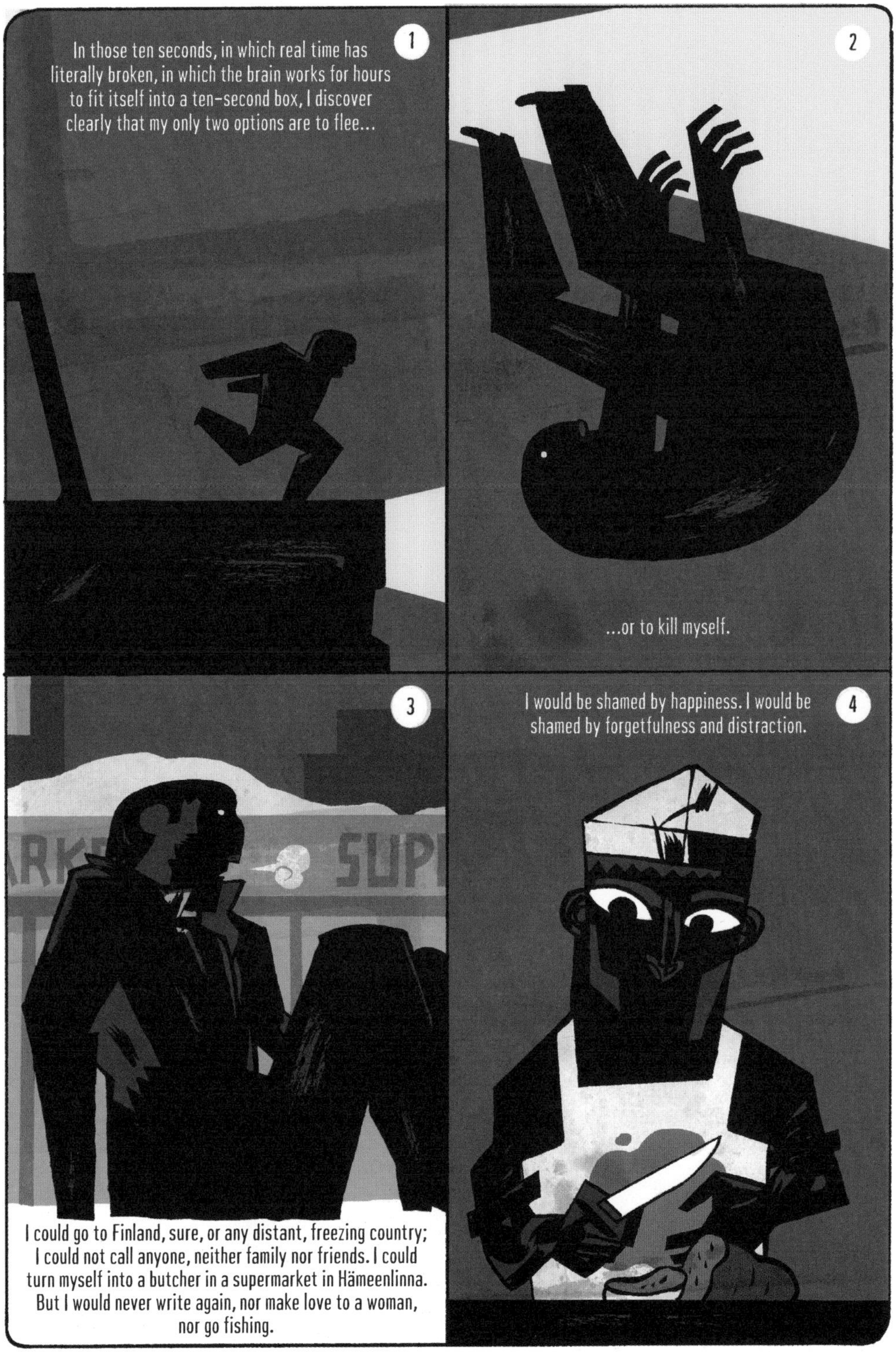
In those ten seconds, in which real time has literally broken, in which the brain works for hours to fit itself into a ten-second box, I discover clearly that my only two options are to flee...
...or to kill myself.
I could go to Finland, sure, or any distant, freezing country; I could not call anyone, neither family nor friends. I could turn myself into a butcher in a supermarket in Hämeenlinna. But I would never write again, nor make love to a woman, nor go fishing.
I would be shamed by happiness. I would be shamed by forgetfulness and distraction.

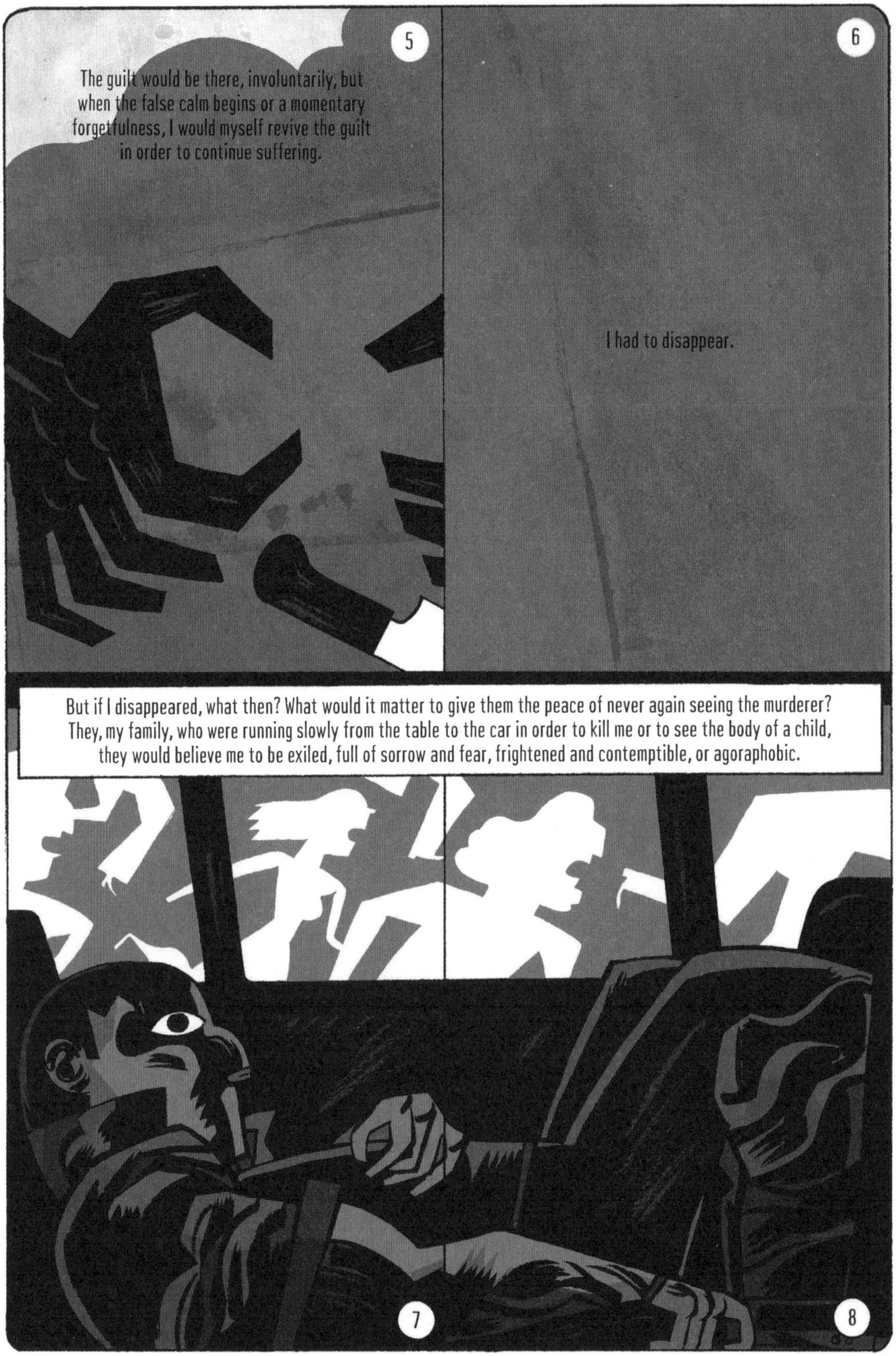
5
The guilt would be there, involuntarily, but when the false calm begins or a momentary forgetfulness, I would myself revive the guilt in order to continue suffering.
6
I had to disappear.
But if I disappeared, what then? What would it matter to give them the peace of never again seeing the murderer? They, my family, who were running slowly from the table to the car in order to kill me or to see the body of a child, they would believe me to be exiled, full of sorrow and fear, frightened and contemptible, or agoraphobic.
7
8

They would kill anyone who would blaspheme my memory, anyone who said he had seen me laugh in a Finnish city, anyone who said he had seen me drinking in a bar with whores, writing a story, earning money, seducing a woman, or petting a cat. They would not believe that anyone would be capable of such weakness, such pitiful forgetfulness, to kill and not weep, to flee and not continue thinking in the summer afternoon about a girl of your own blood dead beneath the wheels of a car.

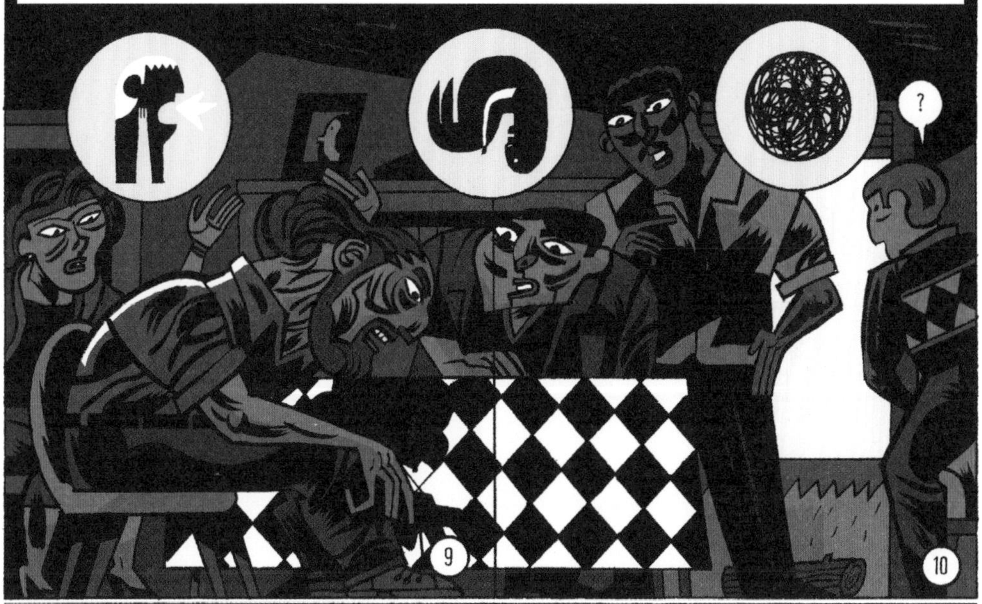
?
9
10

Ten endless seconds until someone saw the log and everyone forgot what happened.

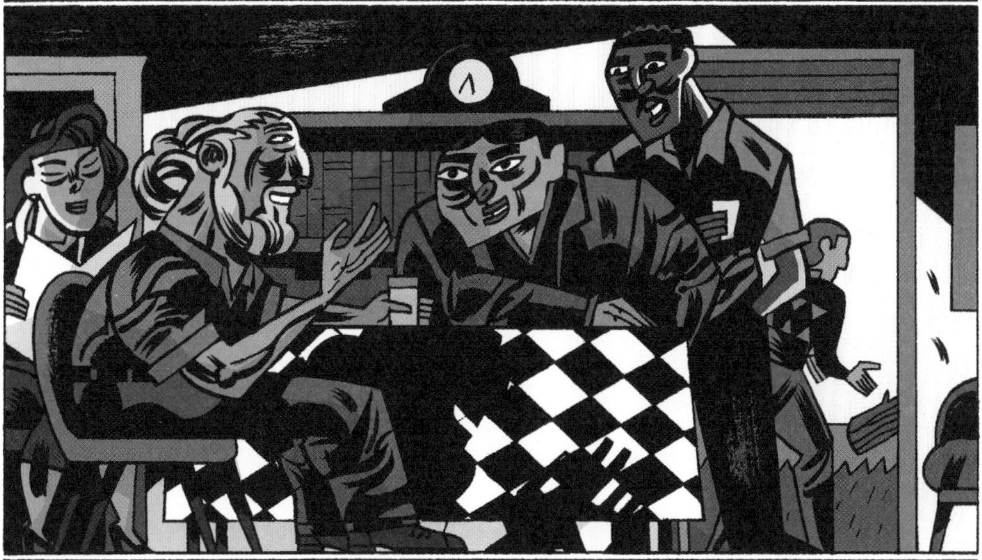

No one, none of the people who were at lunch that afternoon ten years ago in Mercedes, remember this episode. No one has nightmares with these images: I alone have woken covered in sweat for years, when those 10 seconds return for the night, without the final grace of the log. For them, it was nothing more than a dent in the bumper at the end of spring.

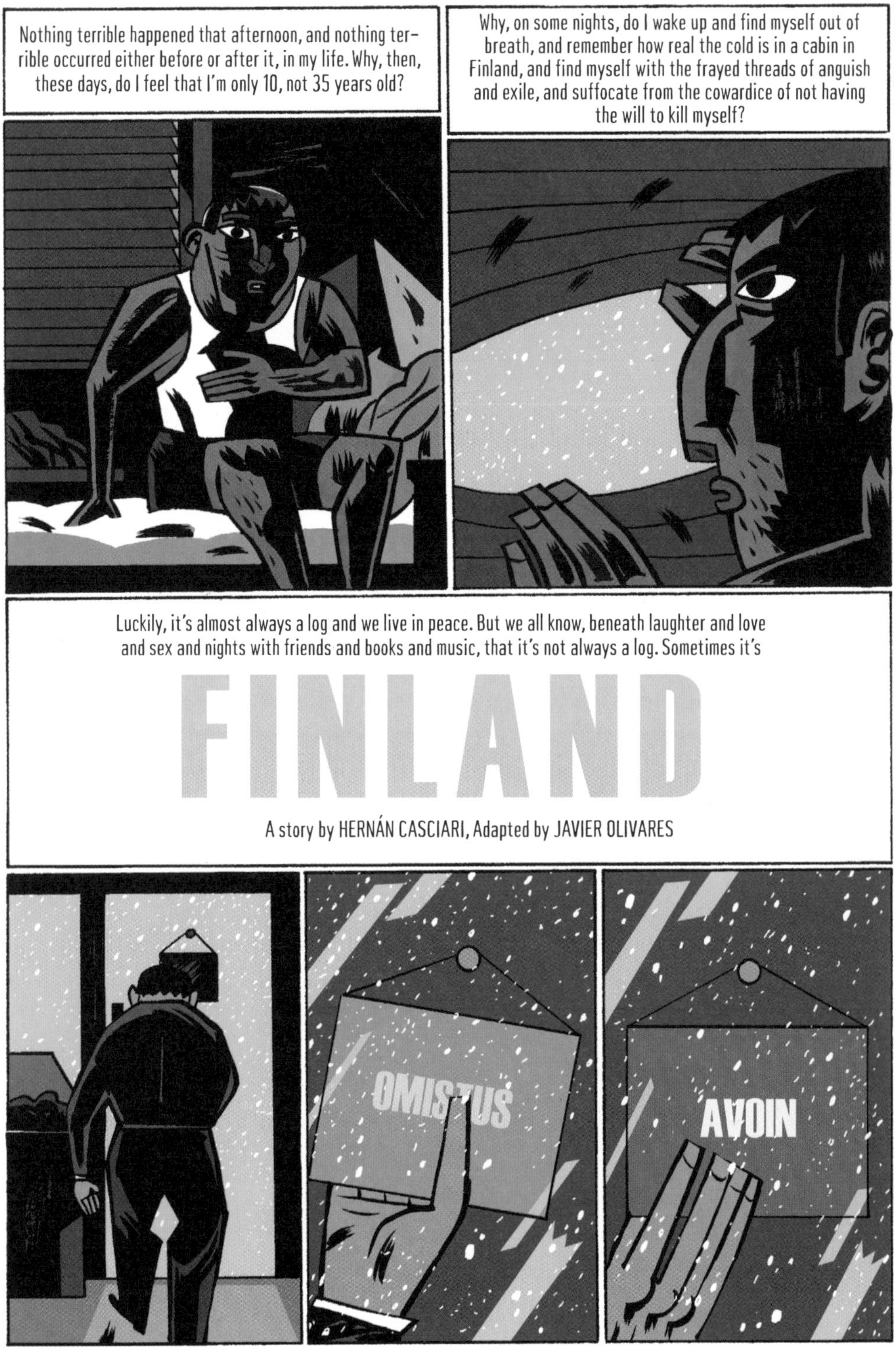
Nothing terrible happened that afternoon, and nothing terrible occurred either before or after it, in my life. Why, then, these days, do I feel that I'm only 10, not 35 years old?
Why, on some nights, do I wake up and find myself out of breath, and remember how real the cold is in a cabin in Finland, and find myself with the frayed threads of anguish and exile, and suffocate from the cowardice of not having the will to kill myself?
Luckily, it's almost always a log and we live in peace. But we all know, beneath laughter and love and sex and nights with friends and books and music, that it's not always a log. Sometimes it's
FINLAND
A story by HERNÁN CASCIARI, Adapted by JAVIER OLIVARES
OMISTUS
AVOIN

CARLOS DE DIEGO

TICKET TO MALTA

Carlos de Diego was born in Barcelona in 1975. He is a physical science student in Barcelona. He's part of the group Los Pioneros del siglo XXI [The Pioneers of the 21st Century] and he writes for television and film, including the feature film *Mi loco Erasmus* [*My Crazy Erasmus*] (2012). He's published comics in *El Víbora, El Manglar, NSLM,* and *El Estafador.* His first book of comics is *Grandes verdades de la humanidad* [*Great Truths of Humanity*] (2013).

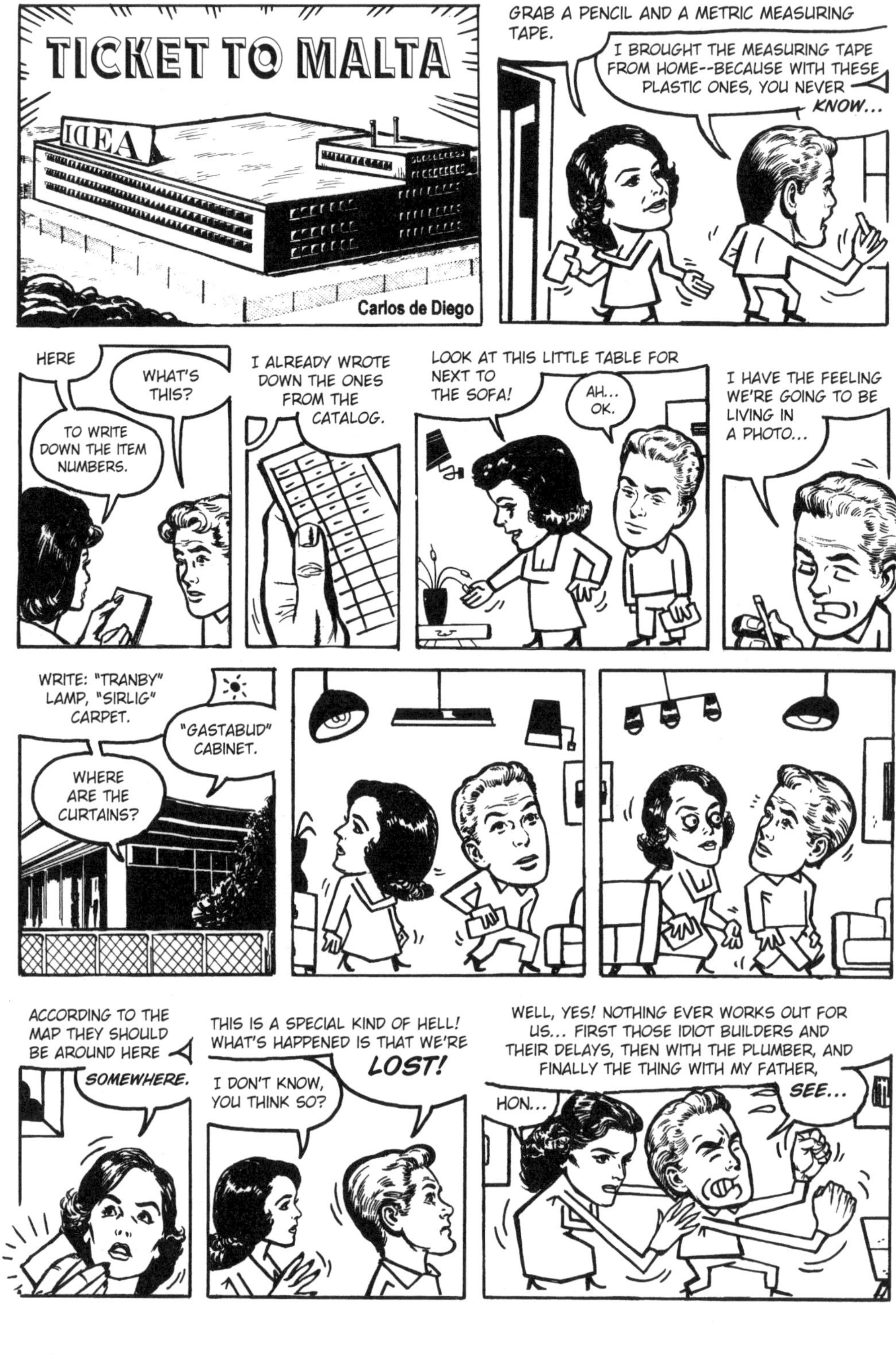
TICKET TO MALTA
IDEA
Carlos de Diego
GRAB A PENCIL AND A METRIC MEASURING TAPE.
I BROUGHT THE MEASURING TAPE FROM HOME--BECAUSE WITH THESE PLASTIC ONES, YOU NEVER *KNOW...*
HERE
TO WRITE DOWN THE ITEM NUMBERS.
WHAT'S THIS?
I ALREADY WROTE DOWN THE ONES FROM THE CATALOG.
LOOK AT THIS LITTLE TABLE FOR NEXT TO THE SOFA!
AH... OK.
I HAVE THE FEELING WE'RE GOING TO BE LIVING IN A PHOTO...
WRITE: "TRANBY" LAMP, "SIRLIG" CARPET.
WHERE ARE THE CURTAINS?
"GASTABUD" CABINET.
ACCORDING TO THE MAP THEY SHOULD BE AROUND HERE *SOMEWHERE.*
THIS IS A SPECIAL KIND OF HELL! WHAT'S HAPPENED IS THAT WE'RE *LOST!*
I DON'T KNOW, YOU THINK SO?
WELL, YES! NOTHING EVER WORKS OUT FOR US... FIRST THOSE IDIOT BUILDERS AND THEIR DELAYS, THEN WITH THE PLUMBER, AND FINALLY THE THING WITH MY FATHER, *SEE...*
HON...

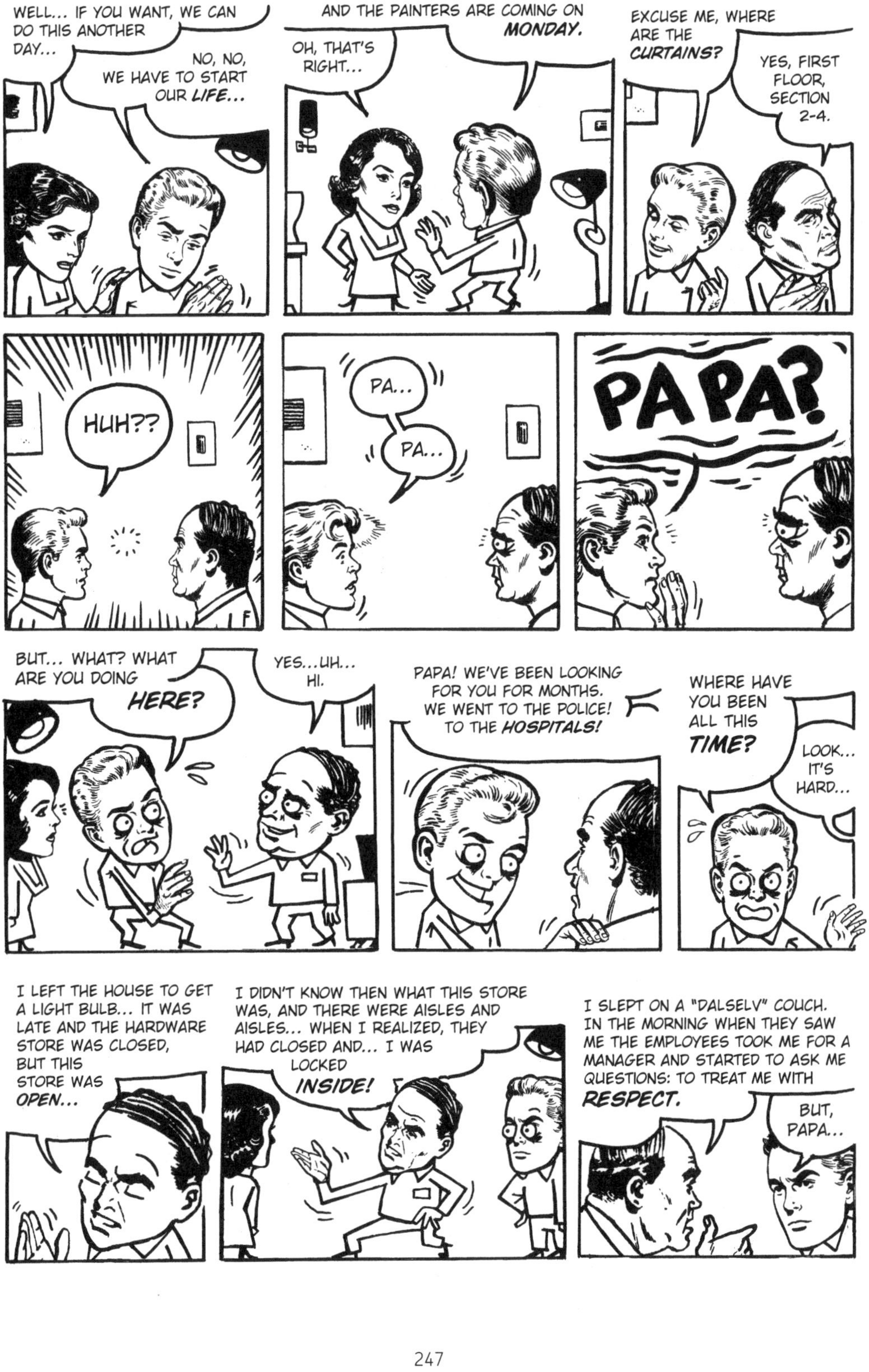
WELL... IF YOU WANT, WE CAN DO THIS ANOTHER DAY...
NO, NO, WE HAVE TO START OUR LIFE...
AND THE PAINTERS ARE COMING ON MONDAY.
OH, THAT'S RIGHT...
EXCUSE ME, WHERE ARE THE CURTAINS?
YES, FIRST FLOOR, SECTION 2-4.
HUH??
PA...
PA...
PAPA?
BUT... WHAT? WHAT ARE YOU DOING HERE?
YES...UH... HI.
PAPA! WE'VE BEEN LOOKING FOR YOU FOR MONTHS. WE WENT TO THE POLICE! TO THE HOSPITALS!
WHERE HAVE YOU BEEN ALL THIS TIME?
LOOK... IT'S HARD...
I LEFT THE HOUSE TO GET A LIGHT BULB... IT WAS LATE AND THE HARDWARE STORE WAS CLOSED, BUT THIS STORE WAS OPEN...
I DIDN'T KNOW THEN WHAT THIS STORE WAS, AND THERE WERE AISLES AND AISLES... WHEN I REALIZED, THEY HAD CLOSED AND... I WAS LOCKED INSIDE!
I SLEPT ON A "DALSELV" COUCH. IN THE MORNING WHEN THEY SAW ME THE EMPLOYEES TOOK ME FOR A MANAGER AND STARTED TO ASK ME QUESTIONS: TO TREAT ME WITH RESPECT.
BUT, PAPA...

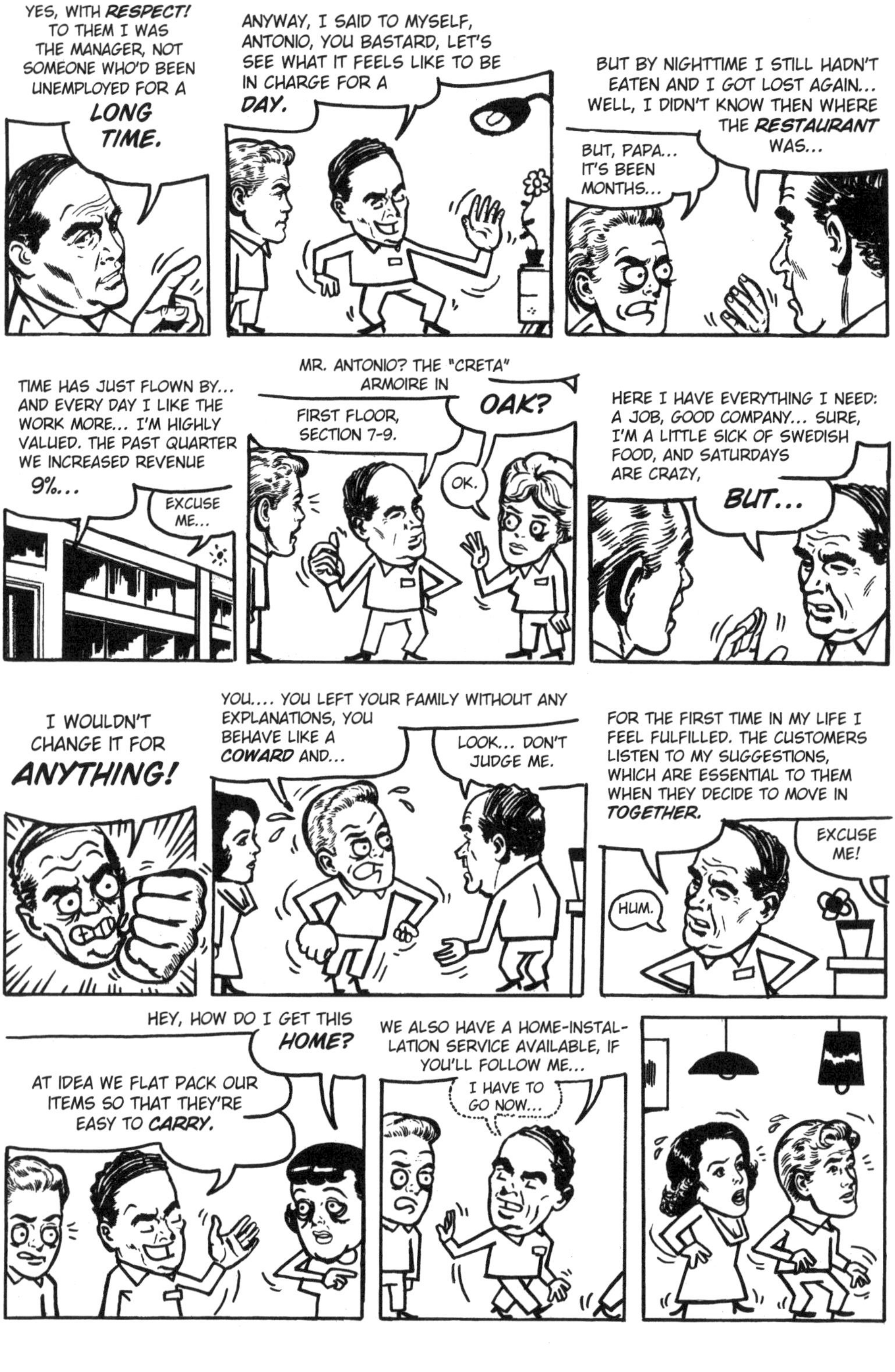

YES, WITH RESPECT! TO THEM I WAS THE MANAGER, NOT SOMEONE WHO'D BEEN UNEMPLOYED FOR A LONG TIME.
ANYWAY, I SAID TO MYSELF, ANTONIO, YOU BASTARD, LET'S SEE WHAT IT FEELS LIKE TO BE IN CHARGE FOR A DAY.
BUT BY NIGHTTIME I STILL HADN'T EATEN AND I GOT LOST AGAIN... WELL, I DIDN'T KNOW THEN WHERE THE RESTAURANT WAS...
BUT, PAPA... IT'S BEEN MONTHS...
TIME HAS JUST FLOWN BY... AND EVERY DAY I LIKE THE WORK MORE... I'M HIGHLY VALUED. THE PAST QUARTER WE INCREASED REVENUE 9%...
EXCUSE ME...
MR. ANTONIO? THE "CRETA" ARMOIRE IN OAK?
FIRST FLOOR, SECTION 7-9.
OK.
HERE I HAVE EVERYTHING I NEED: A JOB, GOOD COMPANY... SURE, I'M A LITTLE SICK OF SWEDISH FOOD, AND SATURDAYS ARE CRAZY, BUT...
I WOULDN'T CHANGE IT FOR ANYTHING!
YOU.... YOU LEFT YOUR FAMILY WITHOUT ANY EXPLANATIONS, YOU BEHAVE LIKE A COWARD AND...
LOOK... DON'T JUDGE ME.
FOR THE FIRST TIME IN MY LIFE I FEEL FULFILLED. THE CUSTOMERS LISTEN TO MY SUGGESTIONS, WHICH ARE ESSENTIAL TO THEM WHEN THEY DECIDE TO MOVE IN TOGETHER.
EXCUSE ME!
HUM.
HEY, HOW DO I GET THIS HOME?
AT IDEA WE FLAT PACK OUR ITEMS SO THAT THEY'RE EASY TO CARRY.
WE ALSO HAVE A HOME-INSTALLATION SERVICE AVAILABLE, IF YOU'LL FOLLOW ME...
I HAVE TO GO NOW...

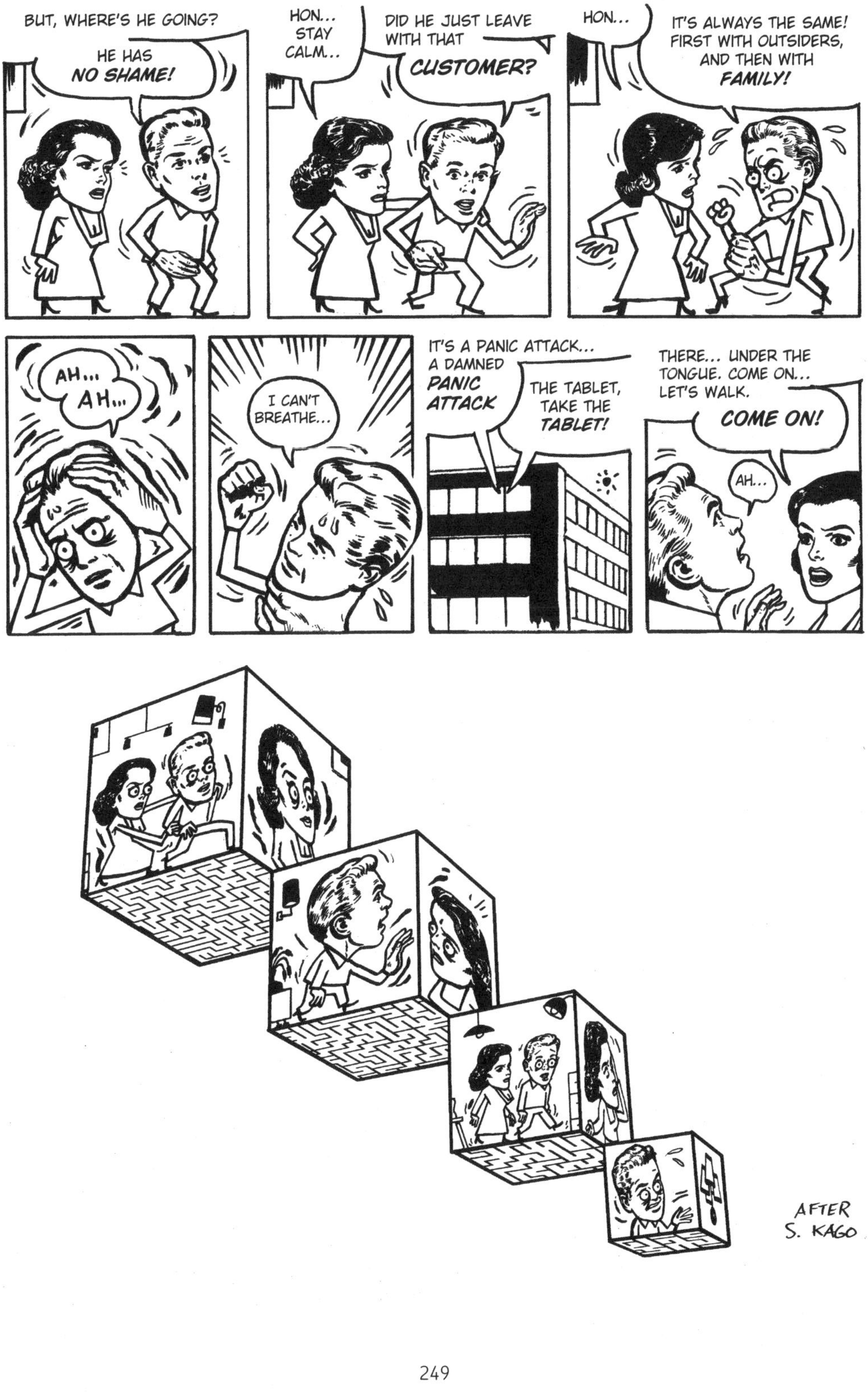
BUT, WHERE'S HE GOING?
HE HAS NO SHAME!
HON... STAY CALM...
DID HE JUST LEAVE WITH THAT CUSTOMER?
HON...
IT'S ALWAYS THE SAME! FIRST WITH OUTSIDERS, AND THEN WITH FAMILY!
AH... AH...
I CAN'T BREATHE...
IT'S A PANIC ATTACK... A DAMNED PANIC ATTACK
THE TABLET, TAKE THE TABLET!
THERE... UNDER THE TONGUE. COME ON... LET'S WALK.
COME ON!
AH...
AFTER S. KAGO

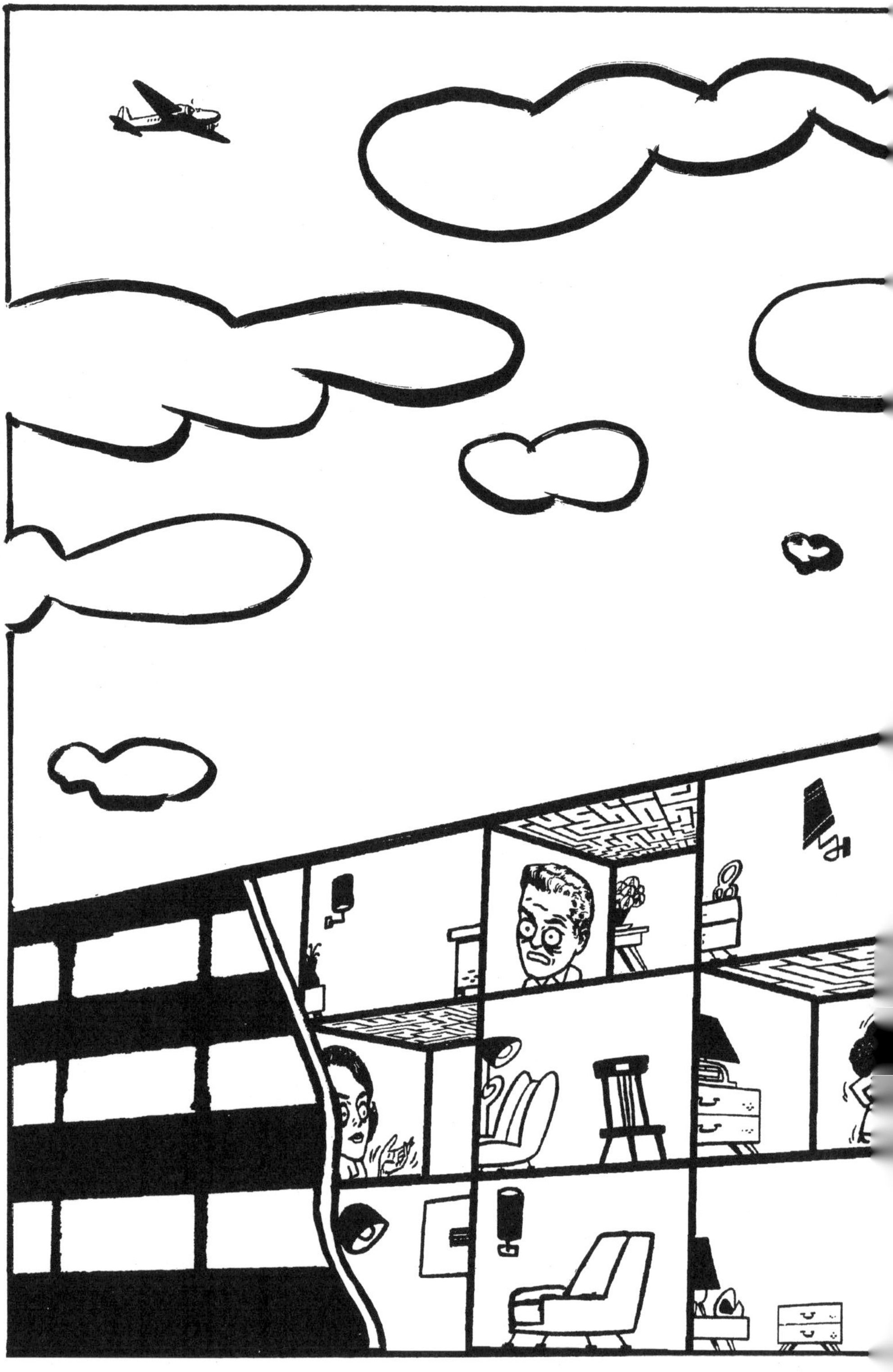

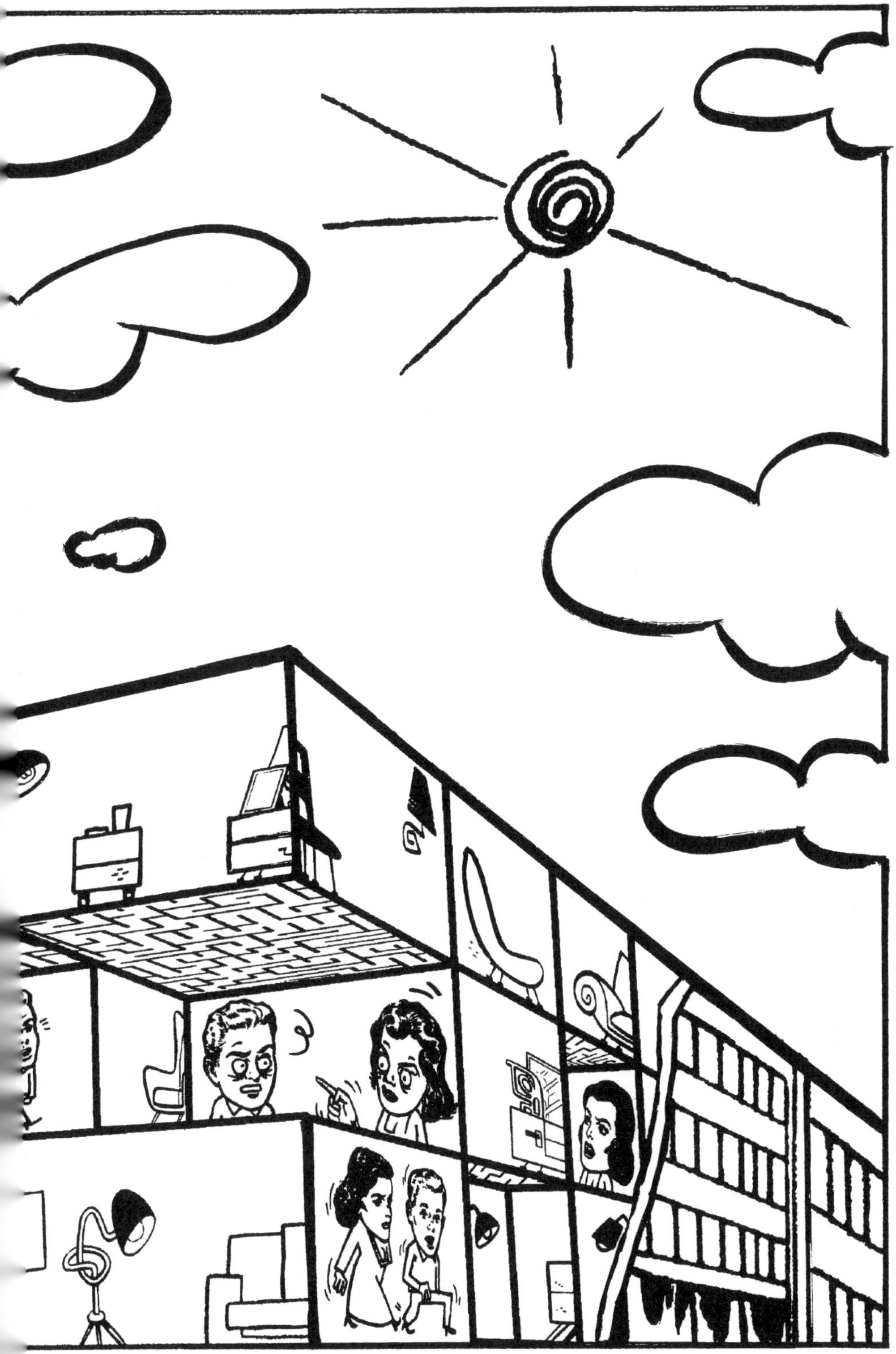

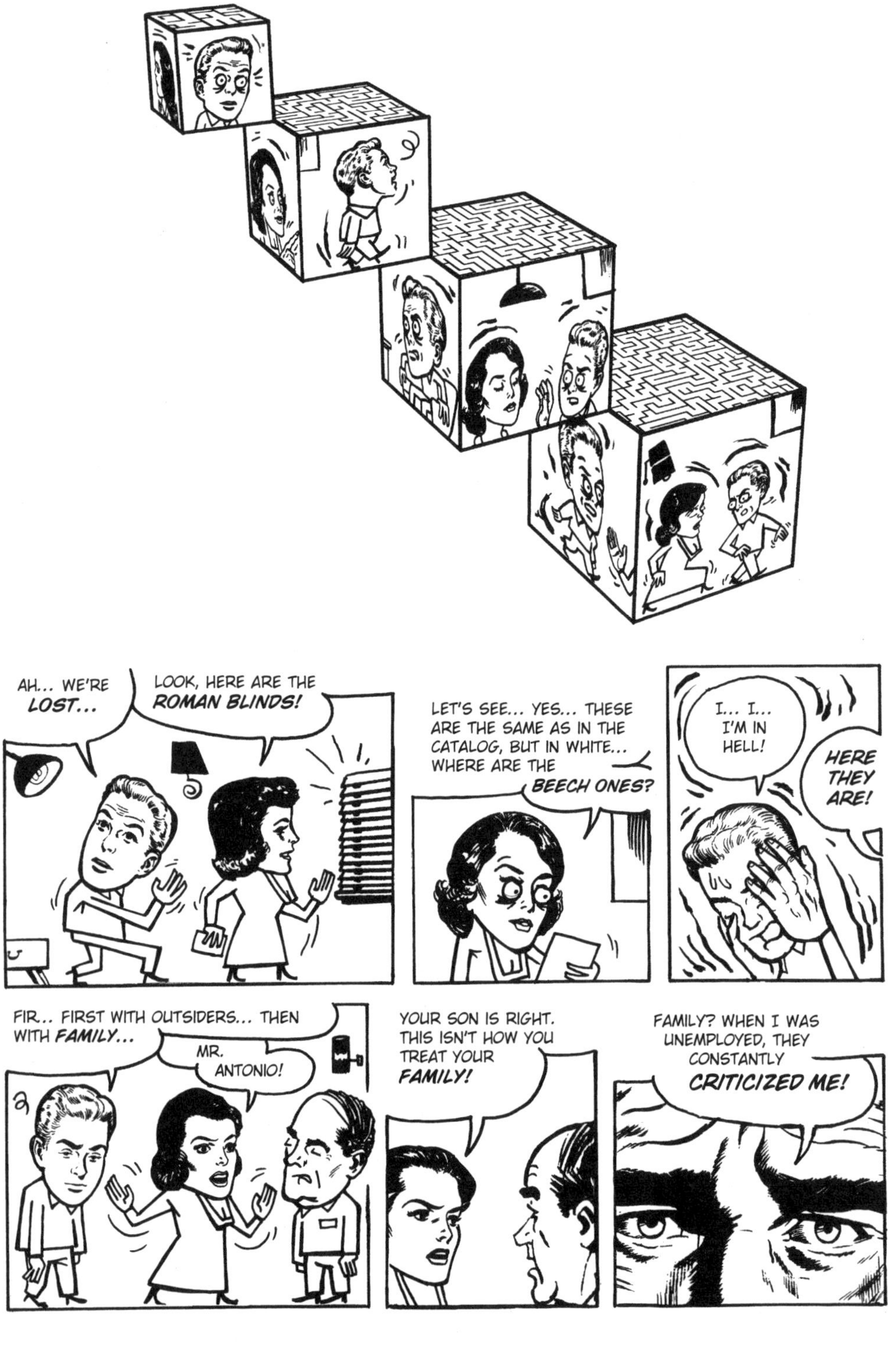
AH... WE'RE LOST...
LOOK, HERE ARE THE ROMAN BLINDS!
LET'S SEE... YES... THESE ARE THE SAME AS IN THE CATALOG, BUT IN WHITE... WHERE ARE THE BEECH ONES?
I... I... I'M IN HELL!
HERE THEY ARE!
FIR... FIRST WITH OUTSIDERS... THEN WITH FAMILY...
MR. ANTONIO!
YOUR SON IS RIGHT. THIS ISN'T HOW YOU TREAT YOUR FAMILY!
FAMILY? WHEN I WAS UNEMPLOYED, THEY CONSTANTLY CRITICIZED ME!

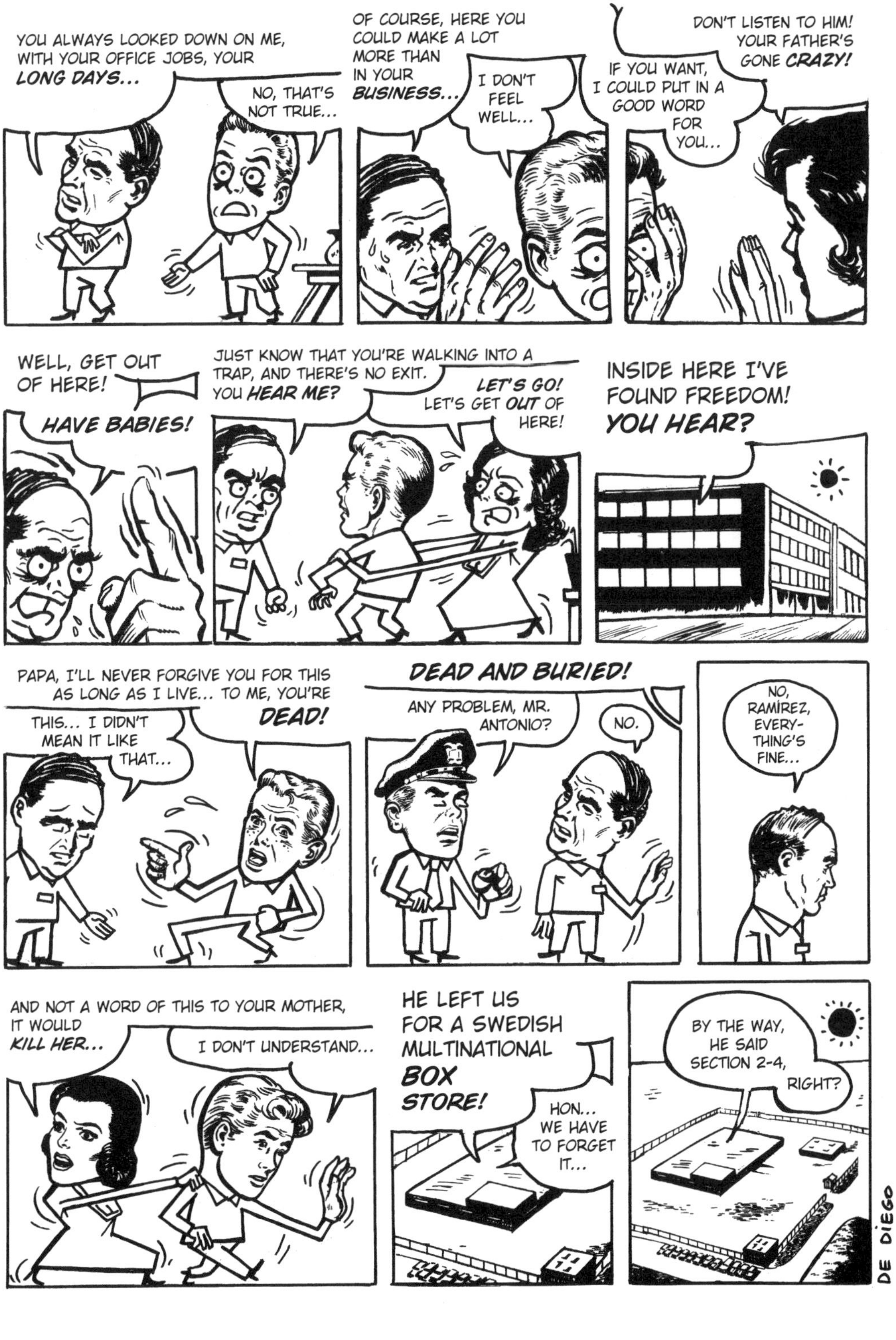
YOU ALWAYS LOOKED DOWN ON ME, WITH YOUR OFFICE JOBS, YOUR **LONG DAYS...**
NO, THAT'S NOT TRUE...
OF COURSE, HERE YOU COULD MAKE A LOT MORE THAN IN YOUR **BUSINESS...**
I DON'T FEEL WELL...
IF YOU WANT, I COULD PUT IN A GOOD WORD FOR YOU...
DON'T LISTEN TO HIM! YOUR FATHER'S GONE **CRAZY!**
WELL, GET OUT OF HERE!
HAVE BABIES!
JUST KNOW THAT YOU'RE WALKING INTO A TRAP, AND THERE'S NO EXIT. YOU **HEAR ME?**
LET'S GO! LET'S GET **OUT** OF HERE!
INSIDE HERE I'VE FOUND FREEDOM! **YOU HEAR?**
PAPA, I'LL NEVER FORGIVE YOU FOR THIS AS LONG AS I LIVE... TO ME, YOU'RE **DEAD!**
THIS... I DIDN'T MEAN IT LIKE THAT...
DEAD AND BURIED!
ANY PROBLEM, MR. ANTONIO?
NO.
NO, RAMÍREZ, EVERY-THING'S FINE...
AND NOT A WORD OF THIS TO YOUR MOTHER, IT WOULD **KILL HER...**
I DON'T UNDERSTAND...
HE LEFT US FOR A SWEDISH MULTINATIONAL **BOX STORE!**
HON... WE HAVE TO FORGET IT...
BY THE WAY, HE SAID SECTION 2-4, RIGHT?
DE DIEGO

PACO ALCÁZAR
BAGGAGE

Paco Alcázar was born in Cádiz in 1970. He got his start as a cartoonist in the fanzines of the '90s. His work as an illustrator and comic artist appears in *El Víbora, Recto, NLSM, El País Semanal, 40, Rolling Stone, MAN, Cinemanía*, and *Rockdelux*. He's a member of the band Humbert Humbert, and produces music that is digitally distributed under the label Mal Amigo. In 2005 he began the series *Silvio José, el buen parásito* [*Silvio José, the Good Parasite*] in the satirical weekly *El Jueves*, which lasted until the summer of 2014 when he left the magazine to begin a new digital project, *Orgullo y Satisfacción* [*Pride and Satisfaction*]. His books are *El manual de mi mente* [*Manual to my Mind*] (2008), *Silvio José, Emperador* [*Silvio José, Emperor*] (2009), *Daño gratuito* [*Damage Free*] (2010), *La industria de los sueños* [*The Dream Industry*] (2012), *Silvio José, Faraón* [*Silvio José, Pharaoh*] (2012), *Huracán de sensatez* [*Hurricane of Sense*] (2013), *Silvio José, Destronado* [*Silvio José, Dethroned*] (2013), *Silvio José, Enamorado* [*Silvio José, in Love*] (2014), and *Silvio José, Rescatado* [*Silvio José, Rescued*] (2015).

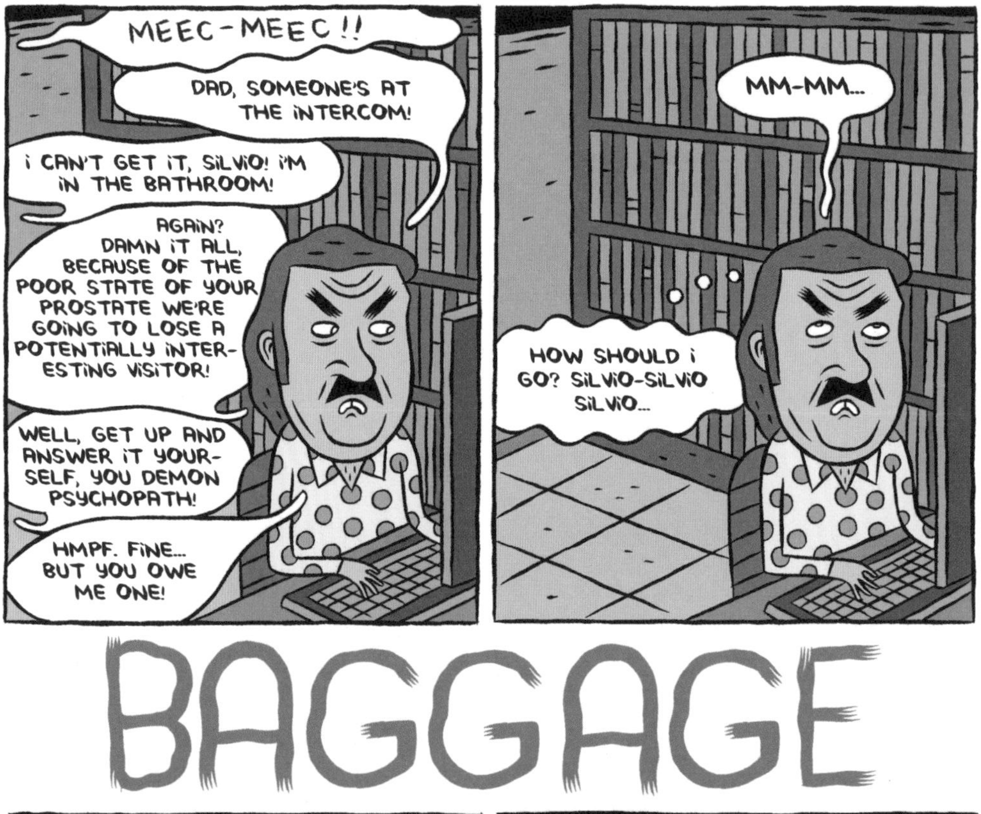
MEEC-MEEC!!
DAD, SOMEONE'S AT THE INTERCOM!
I CAN'T GET IT, SILVIO! I'M IN THE BATHROOM!
AGAIN? DAMN IT ALL, BECAUSE OF THE POOR STATE OF YOUR PROSTATE WE'RE GOING TO LOSE A POTENTIALLY INTERESTING VISITOR!
WELL, GET UP AND ANSWER IT YOURSELF, YOU DEMON PSYCHOPATH!
HMPF. FINE... BUT YOU OWE ME ONE!
MM-MM...
HOW SHOULD I GO? SILVIO-SILVIO SILVIO...

BAGGAGE

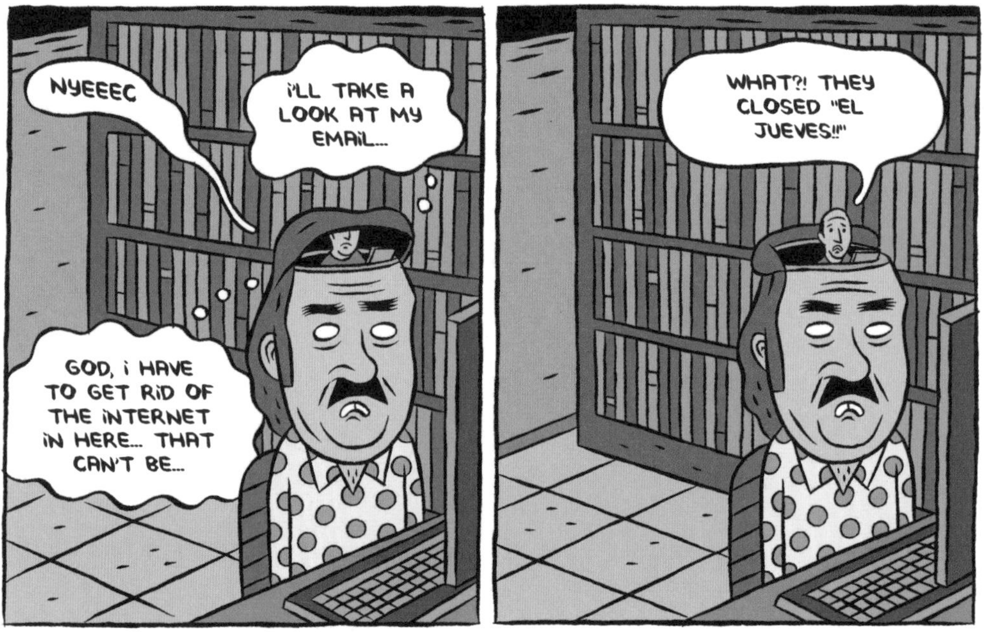
NYEEEC
I'LL TAKE A LOOK AT MY EMAIL...
GOD, I HAVE TO GET RID OF THE INTERNET IN HERE... THAT CAN'T BE...
WHAT?! THEY CLOSED "EL JUEVES!!"

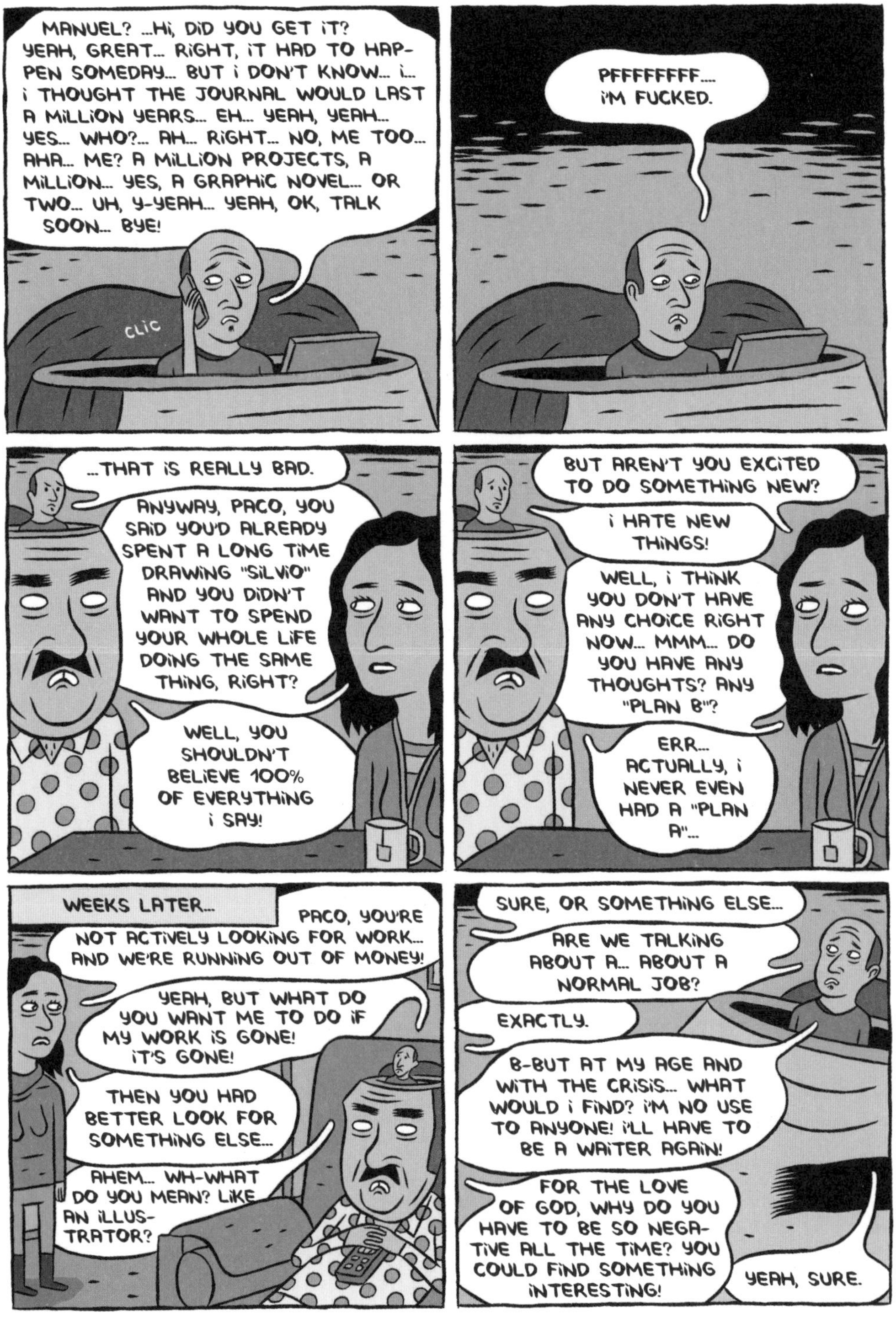
MANUEL? ...Hi, DiD YOU GET iT? YEAH, GREAT... RiGHT, iT HAD TO HAPPEN SOMEDAY... BUT i DON'T KNOW... i... i THOUGHT THE JOURNAL WOULD LAST A MiLLiON YEARS... EH... YEAH, YEAH... YES... WHO?... AH... RiGHT... NO, ME TOO... AHA... ME? A MiLLiON PROJECTS, A MiLLiON... YES, A GRAPHiC NOVEL... OR TWO... UH, Y-YEAH... YEAH, OK, TALK SOON... BYE!
CLiC
PFFFFFFFF.... i'M FUCKED.
...THAT iS REALLY BAD.
ANYWAY, PACO, YOU SAiD YOU'D ALREADY SPENT A LONG TiME DRAWiNG "SiLViO" AND YOU DiDN'T WANT TO SPEND YOUR WHOLE LiFE DOiNG THE SAME THiNG, RiGHT?
WELL, YOU SHOULDN'T BELiEVE 100% OF EVERYTHiNG i SAY!
BUT AREN'T YOU EXCiTED TO DO SOMETHiNG NEW?
i HATE NEW THiNGS!
WELL, i THiNK YOU DON'T HAVE ANY CHOiCE RiGHT NOW... MMM... DO YOU HAVE ANY THOUGHTS? ANY "PLAN B"?
ERR... ACTUALLY, i NEVER EVEN HAD A "PLAN A"...
WEEKS LATER...
PACO, YOU'RE NOT ACTiVELY LOOKiNG FOR WORK... AND WE'RE RUNNiNG OUT OF MONEY!
YEAH, BUT WHAT DO YOU WANT ME TO DO iF MY WORK iS GONE! iT'S GONE!
THEN YOU HAD BETTER LOOK FOR SOMETHiNG ELSE...
AHEM... WH-WHAT DO YOU MEAN? LiKE AN iLLUSTRATOR?
SURE, OR SOMETHiNG ELSE...
ARE WE TALKiNG ABOUT A... ABOUT A NORMAL JOB?
EXACTLY.
B-BUT AT MY AGE AND WiTH THE CRiSiS... WHAT WOULD i FiND? i'M NO USE TO ANYONE! i'LL HAVE TO BE A WAiTER AGAiN!
FOR THE LOVE OF GOD, WHY DO YOU HAVE TO BE SO NEGATiVE ALL THE TiME? YOU COULD FiND SOMETHiNG iNTERESTiNG!
YEAH, SURE.

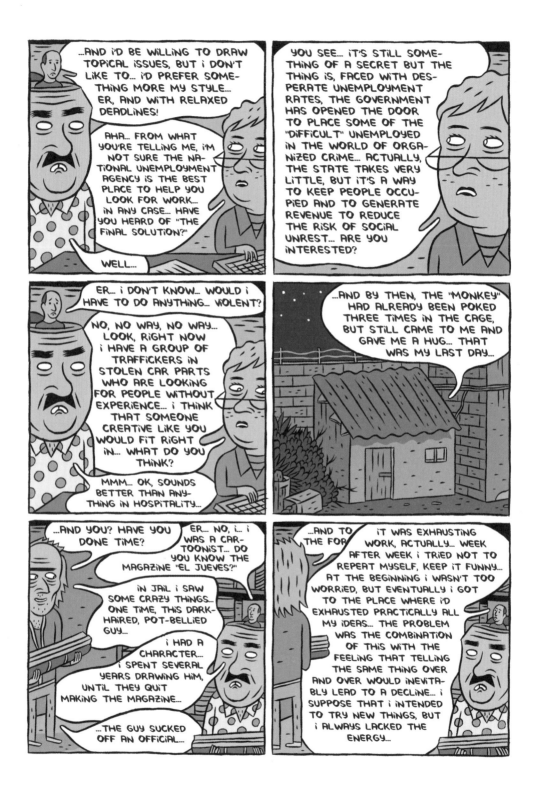

...AND i'D BE WILLING TO DRAW TOPICAL ISSUES, BUT i DON'T LIKE TO... i'D PREFER SOMETHING MORE MY STYLE... ER, AND WITH RELAXED DEADLINES!

AHA... FROM WHAT YOU'RE TELLING ME, i'M NOT SURE THE NATIONAL UNEMPLOYMENT AGENCY IS THE BEST PLACE TO HELP YOU LOOK FOR WORK... IN ANY CASE... HAVE YOU HEARD OF "THE FINAL SOLUTION?"

WELL...

YOU SEE... IT'S STILL SOMETHING OF A SECRET BUT THE THING IS, FACED WITH DESPERATE UNEMPLOYMENT RATES, THE GOVERNMENT HAS OPENED THE DOOR TO PLACE SOME OF THE "DIFFICULT" UNEMPLOYED IN THE WORLD OF ORGANIZED CRIME... ACTUALLY, THE STATE TAKES VERY LITTLE, BUT IT'S A WAY TO KEEP PEOPLE OCCUPIED AND TO GENERATE REVENUE TO REDUCE THE RISK OF SOCIAL UNREST... ARE YOU INTERESTED?

ER... i DON'T KNOW... WOULD i HAVE TO DO ANYTHING... VIOLENT?

NO, NO WAY, NO WAY... LOOK, RIGHT NOW i HAVE A GROUP OF TRAFFICKERS IN STOLEN CAR PARTS WHO ARE LOOKING FOR PEOPLE WITHOUT EXPERIENCE... i THINK THAT SOMEONE CREATIVE LIKE YOU WOULD FIT RIGHT IN... WHAT DO YOU THINK?

MMM... OK, SOUNDS BETTER THAN ANYTHING IN HOSPITALITY...

...AND BY THEN, THE "MONKEY" HAD ALREADY BEEN POKED THREE TIMES IN THE CAGE, BUT STILL CAME TO ME AND GAVE ME A HUG... THAT WAS MY LAST DAY...

...AND YOU? HAVE YOU DONE TIME?

ER... NO, i.. i WAS A CARTOONIST... DO YOU KNOW THE MAGAZINE "EL JUEVES?"

IN JAIL i SAW SOME CRAZY THINGS... ONE TIME, THIS DARK-HAIRED, POT-BELLIED GUY...

i HAD A CHARACTER... i SPENT SEVERAL YEARS DRAWING HIM, UNTIL THEY QUIT MAKING THE MAGAZINE...

...THE GUY SUCKED OFF AN OFFICIAL...

...AND TO THE FOR...

IT WAS EXHAUSTING WORK, ACTUALLY... WEEK AFTER WEEK i TRIED NOT TO REPEAT MYSELF, KEEP IT FUNNY... AT THE BEGINNING i WASN'T TOO WORRIED, BUT EVENTUALLY i GOT TO THE PLACE WHERE i'D EXHAUSTED PRACTICALLY ALL MY IDEAS... THE PROBLEM WAS THE COMBINATION OF THIS WITH THE FEELING THAT TELLING THE SAME THING OVER AND OVER WOULD INEVITABLY LEAD TO A DECLINE... i SUPPOSE THAT i INTENDED TO TRY NEW THINGS, BUT i ALWAYS LACKED THE ENERGY...

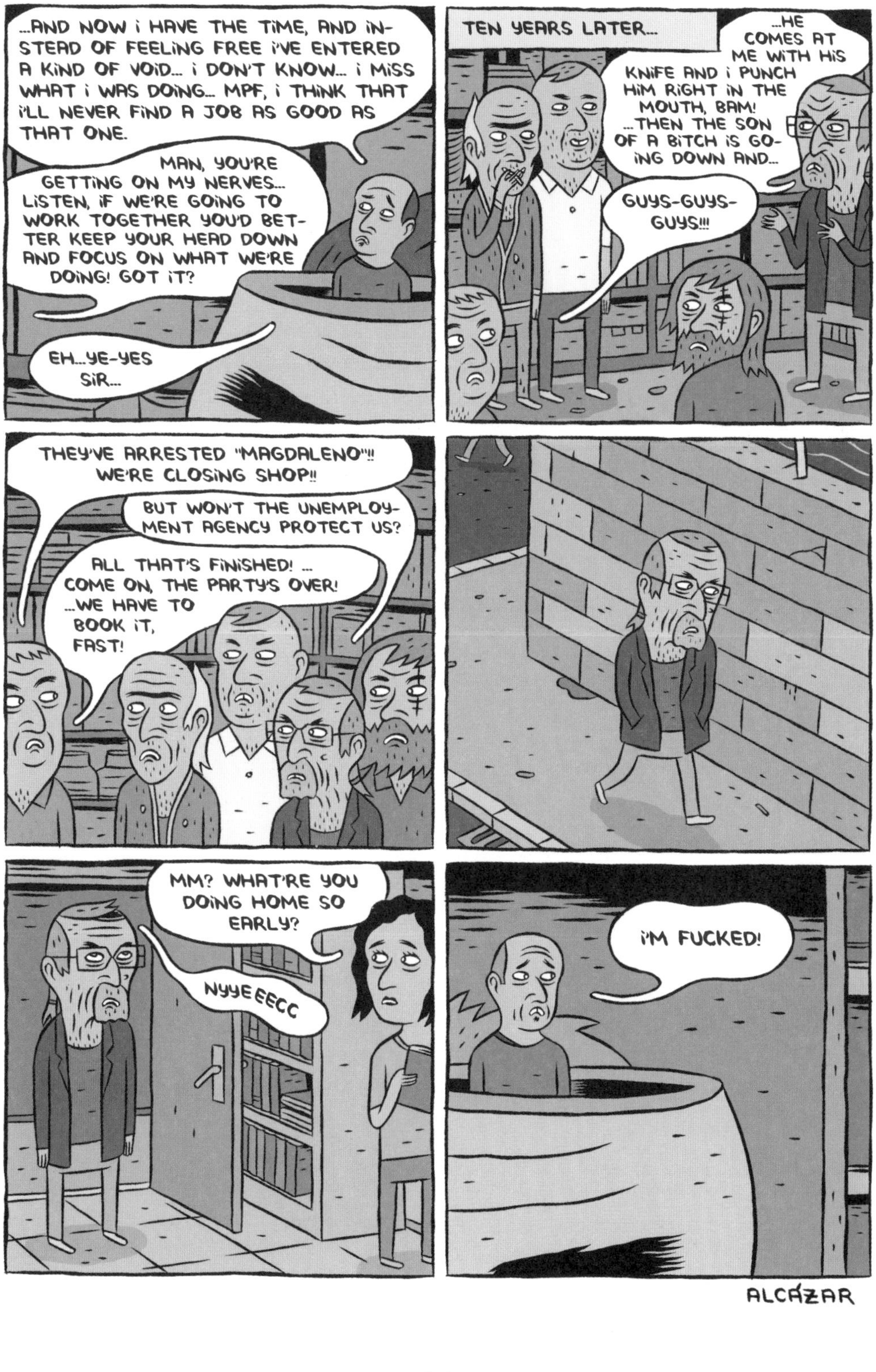
...AND NOW i HAVE THE TiME, AND iNSTEAD OF FEELiNG FREE i'VE ENTERED A KiND OF VOiD... i DON'T KNOW... i MiSS WHAT i WAS DOiNG... MPF, i THiNK THAT i'LL NEVER FiND A JOB AS GOOD AS THAT ONE.
MAN, YOU'RE GETTiNG ON MY NERVES... LiSTEN, iF WE'RE GOiNG TO WORK TOGETHER YOU'D BETTER KEEP YOUR HEAD DOWN AND FOCUS ON WHAT WE'RE DOiNG! GOT iT?
EH...YE-YES SiR...
TEN YEARS LATER...
...HE COMES AT ME WiTH HiS KNiFE AND i PUNCH HiM RiGHT iN THE MOUTH, BAM! ...THEN THE SON OF A BiTCH iS GOiNG DOWN AND...
GUYS-GUYS-GUYS!!!
THEY'VE ARRESTED "MAGDALENO"!! WE'RE CLOSiNG SHOP!!
BUT WON'T THE UNEMPLOYMENT AGENCY PROTECT US?
ALL THAT'S FiNiSHED! ...COME ON, THE PARTY'S OVER! ...WE HAVE TO BOOK iT, FAST!
MM? WHAT'RE YOU DOiNG HOME SO EARLY?
NYYEEECC
i'M FUCKED!
ALCÁZAR

JUAN BERRIO
DREAMS

Juan Berrio was born in Valladolid in 1964. Though he is from Valladolid, he is a Madrileño by choice. He has had a long career as an illustrator and cartoonist. He's been published in magazines like *Marie Claire*, *Elle*, *GQ*, and *Cinemanía*, and in newspapers like *El País*, *ABC*, and *El Periódico de Catalunya*. Coeditor of the comics magazine *Usted está aquí*, his books include *A Saltos* [*Jumps*] (2003), *Siempre la misma historia* [*Always the Same Story*] (2004), *Calles contadas* [*Recounting Streets*] (2008), and *Dentro de nada* [*In No Time*] (2010). He won the Premio de Novela Gráfica Fnac/Sins Entido for *Miércoles* [*Wednesday*] (2012. His latest book is *Kiosco* [*Kiosk*] (2014). In 2012 an English translation of *Calles contatas* was published in the United States as *Recounting Streets*.

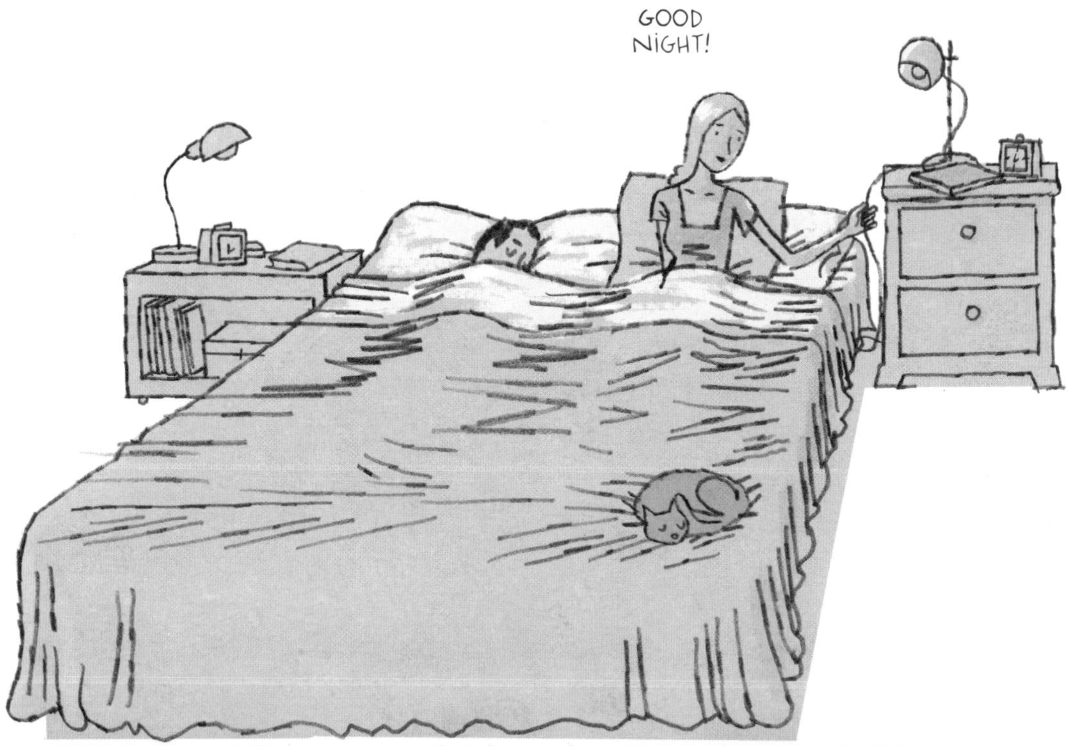
GOOD NIGHT!

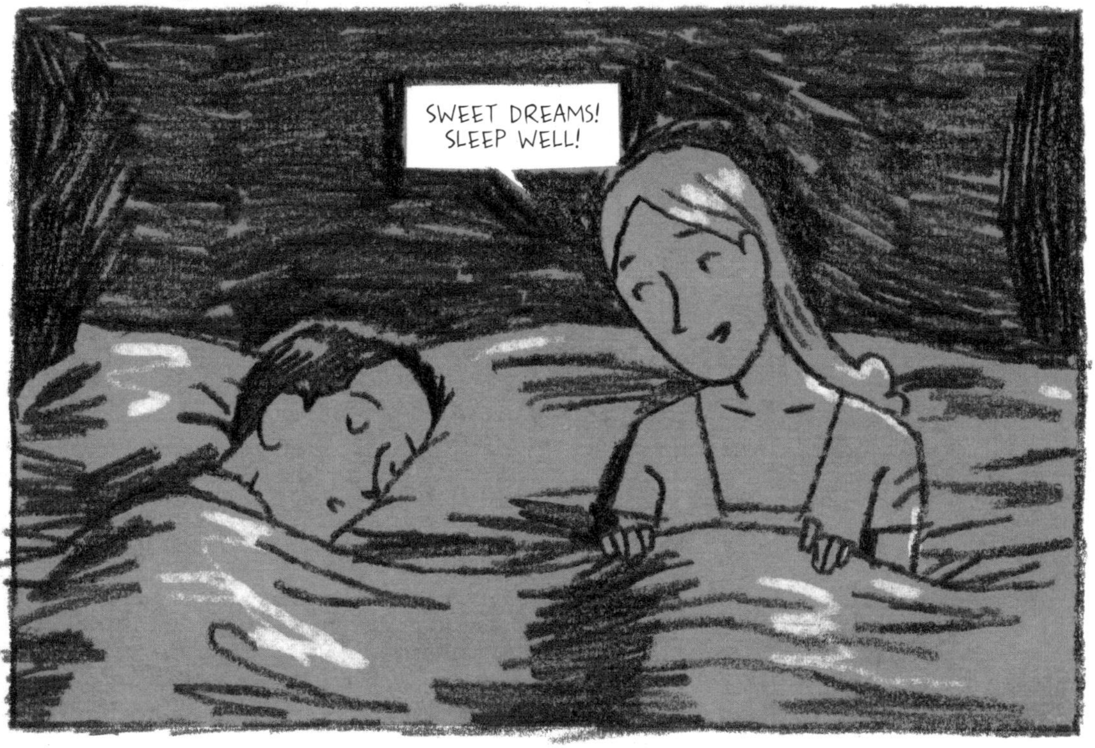
SWEET DREAMS! SLEEP WELL!

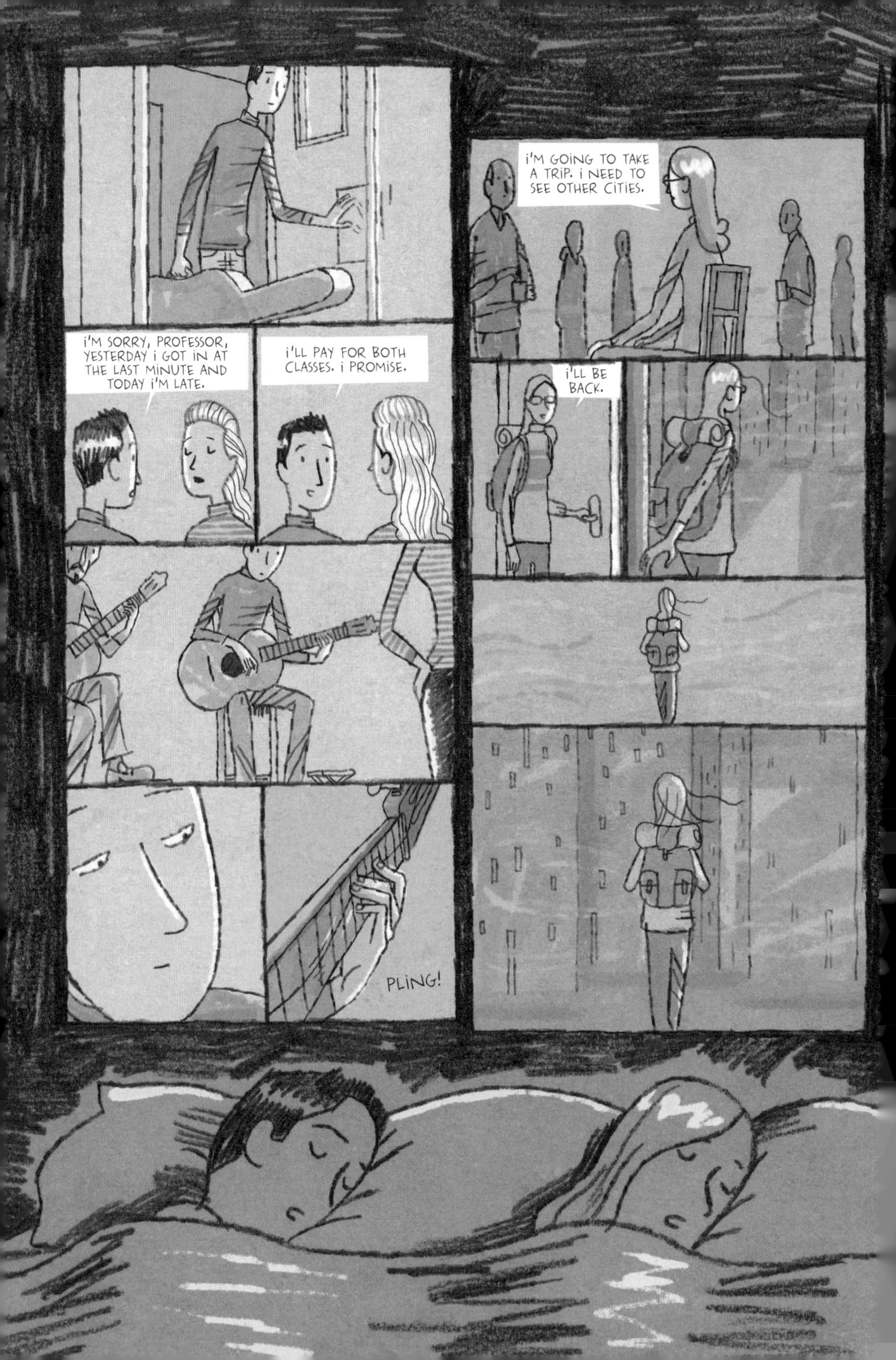
I'M SORRY, PROFESSOR, YESTERDAY I GOT IN AT THE LAST MINUTE AND TODAY I'M LATE.
I'LL PAY FOR BOTH CLASSES. I PROMISE.
PLING!
I'M GOING TO TAKE A TRIP. I NEED TO SEE OTHER CITIES.
I'LL BE BACK.

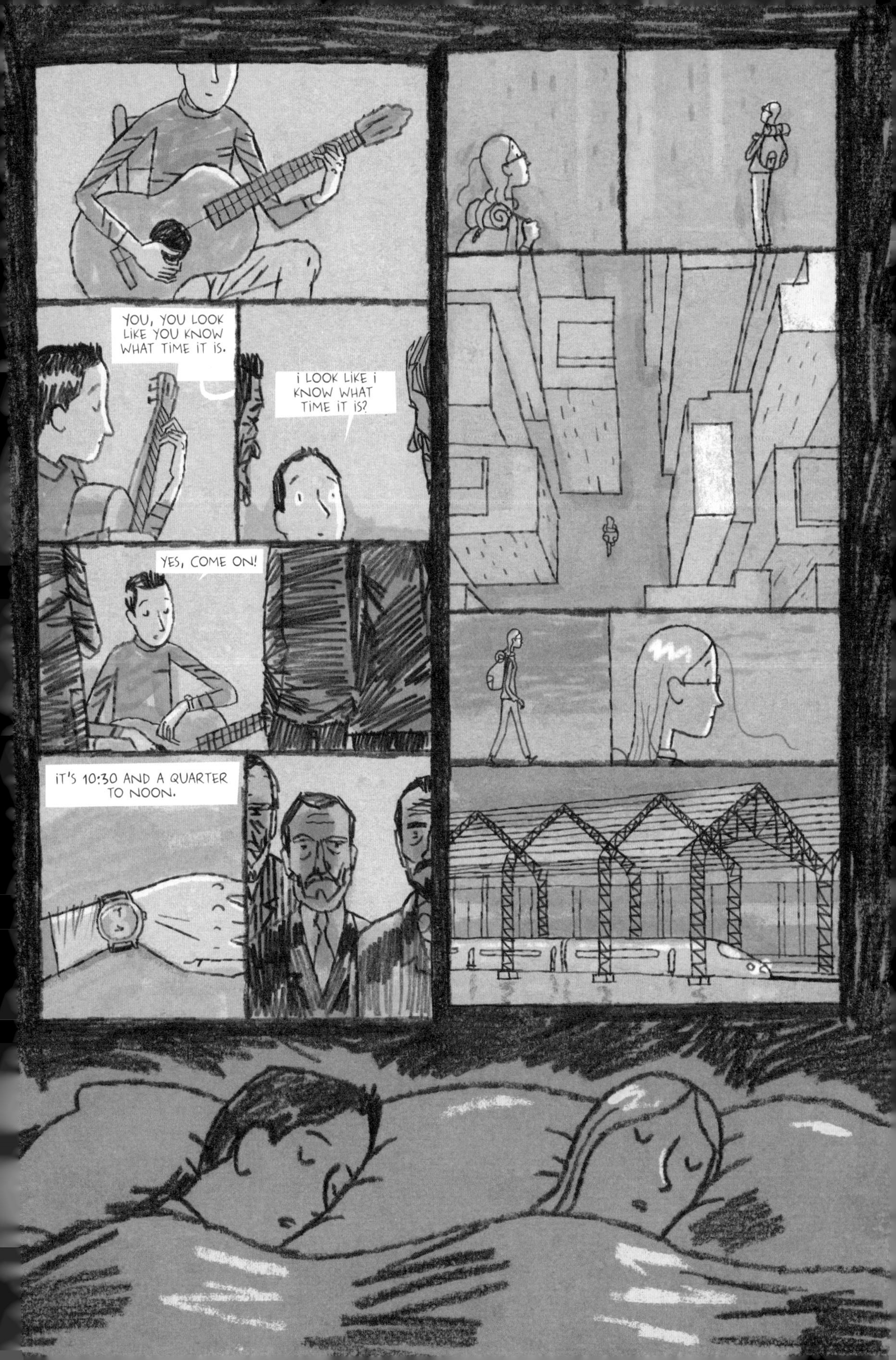
YOU, YOU LOOK LIKE YOU KNOW WHAT TIME IT IS.
I LOOK LIKE I KNOW WHAT TIME IT IS?
YES, COME ON!
IT'S 10:30 AND A QUARTER TO NOON.

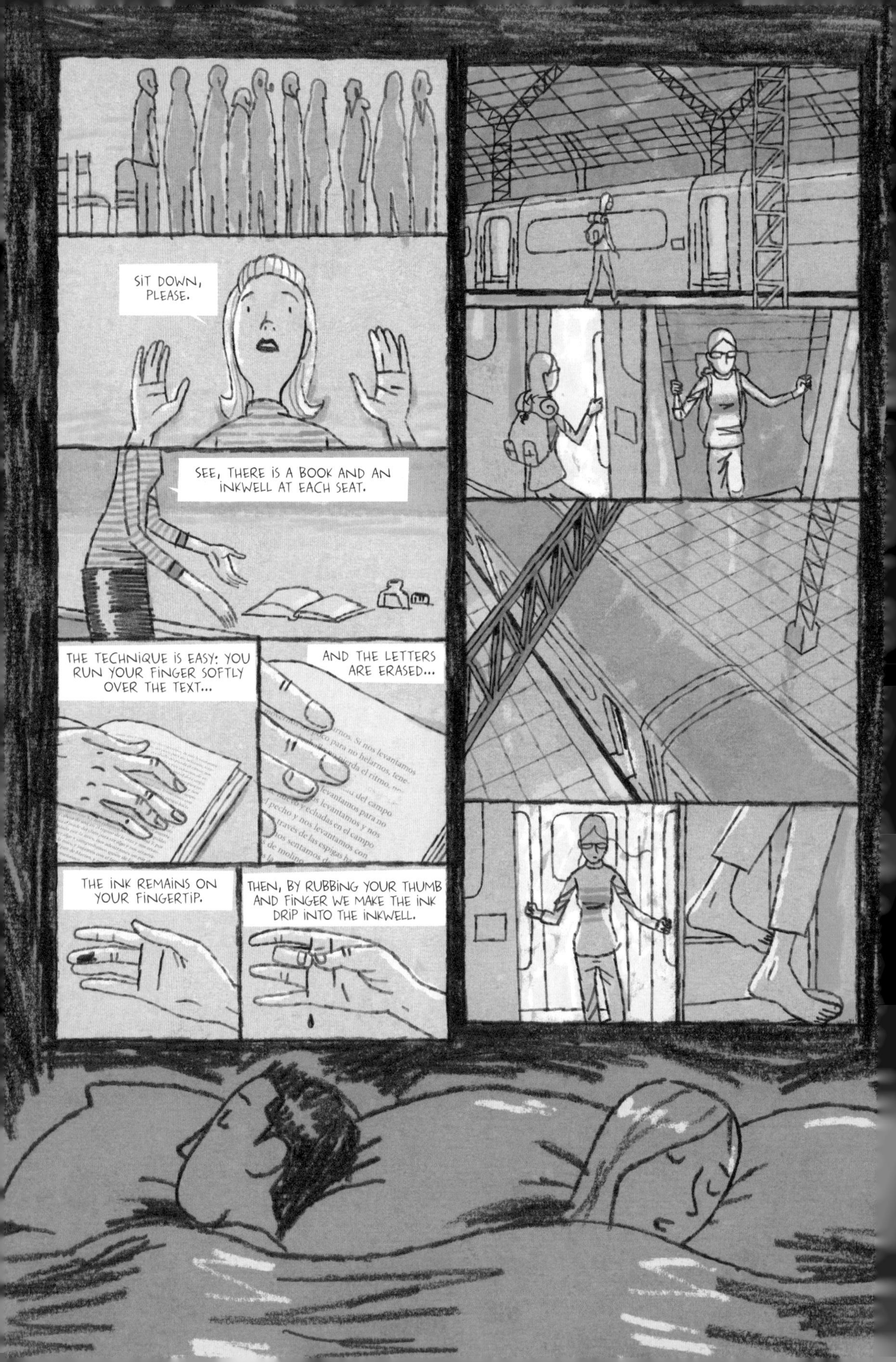
SIT DOWN, PLEASE.
SEE, THERE IS A BOOK AND AN INKWELL AT EACH SEAT.
THE TECHNIQUE IS EASY: YOU RUN YOUR FINGER SOFTLY OVER THE TEXT...
AND THE LETTERS ARE ERASED...
THE INK REMAINS ON YOUR FINGERTIP.
THEN, BY RUBBING YOUR THUMB AND FINGER WE MAKE THE INK DRIP INTO THE INKWELL.

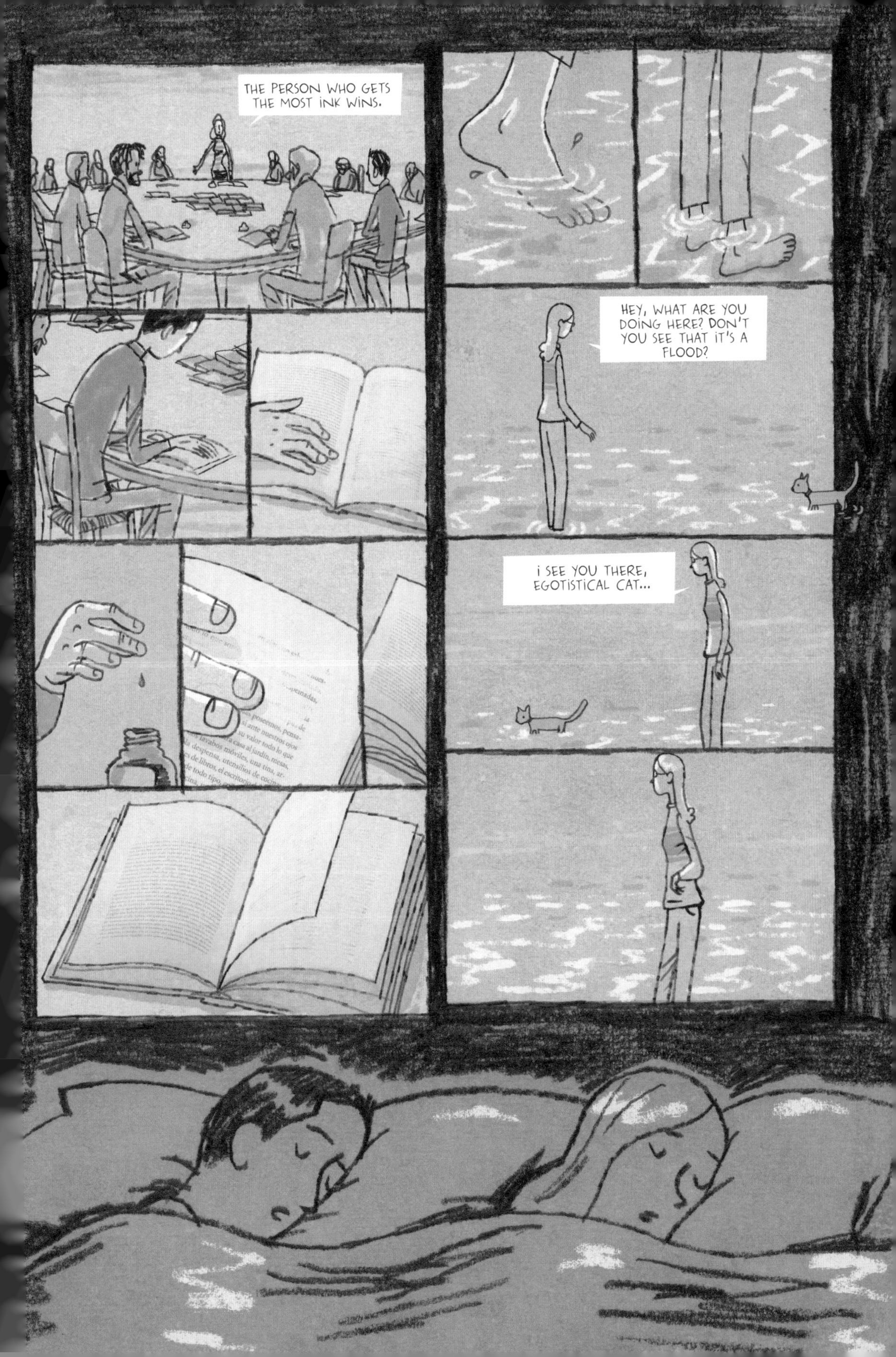
THE PERSON WHO GETS THE MOST INK WINS.
HEY, WHAT ARE YOU DOING HERE? DON'T YOU SEE THAT IT'S A FLOOD?
I SEE YOU THERE, EGOTISTICAL CAT...

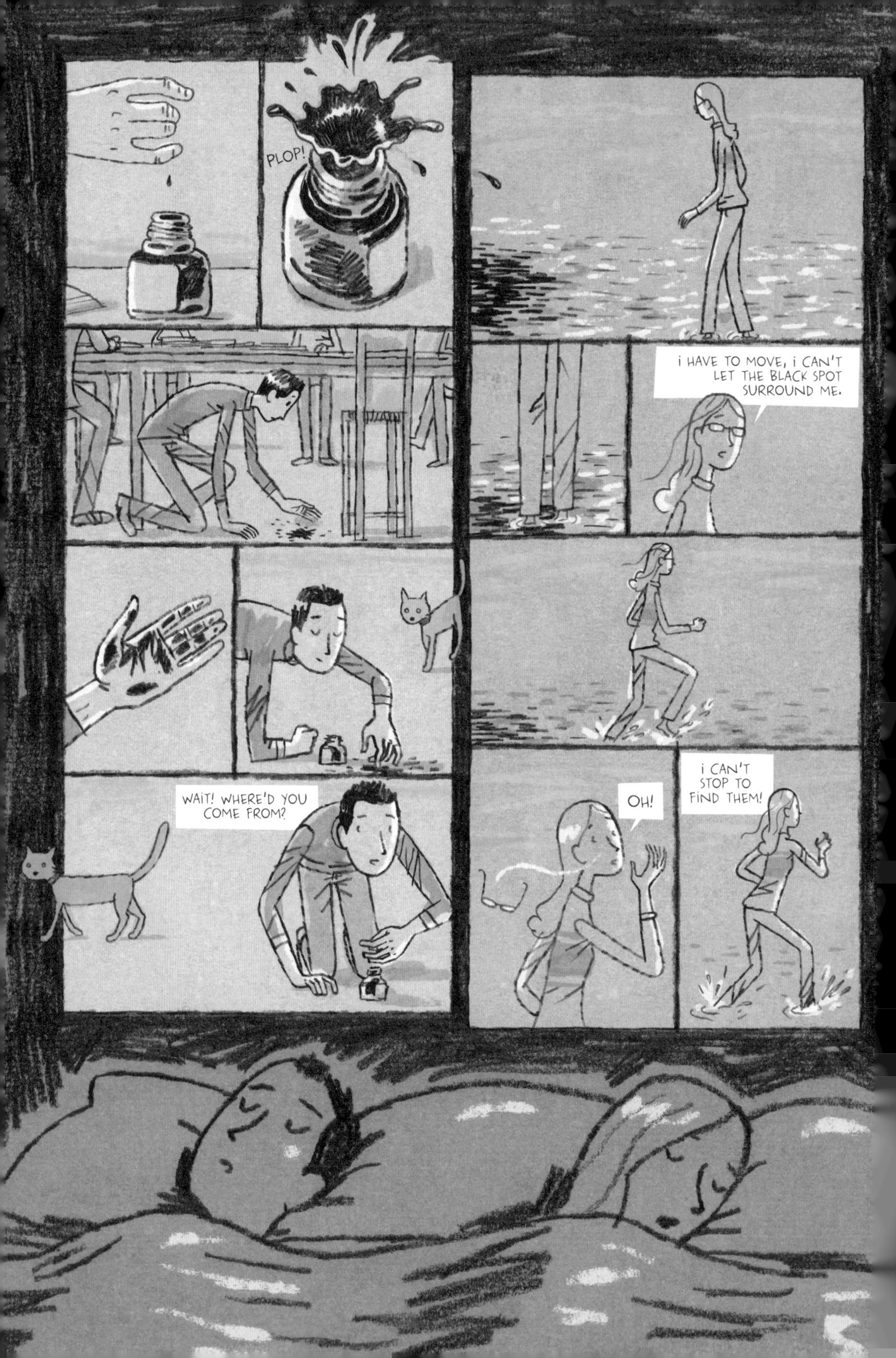
PLOP!
WAIT! WHERE'D YOU COME FROM?
i HAVE TO MOVE, i CAN'T LET THE BLACK SPOT SURROUND ME.
OH!
i CAN'T STOP TO FiND THEM!

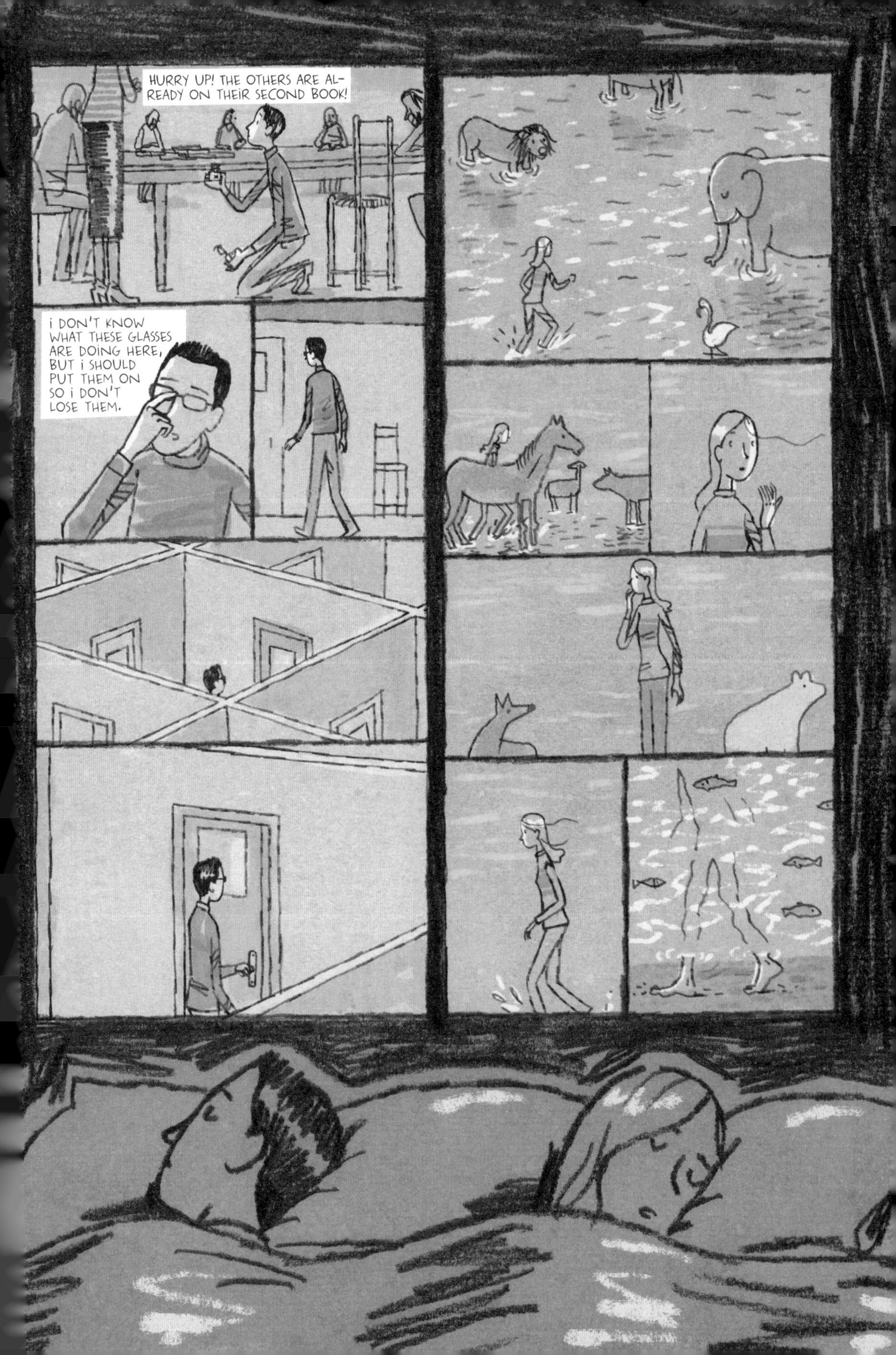
HURRY UP! THE OTHERS ARE AL-
READY ON THEIR SECOND BOOK!
i DON'T KNOW WHAT THESE GLASSES ARE DOiNG HERE, BUT i SHOULD PUT THEM ON SO i DON'T LOSE THEM.

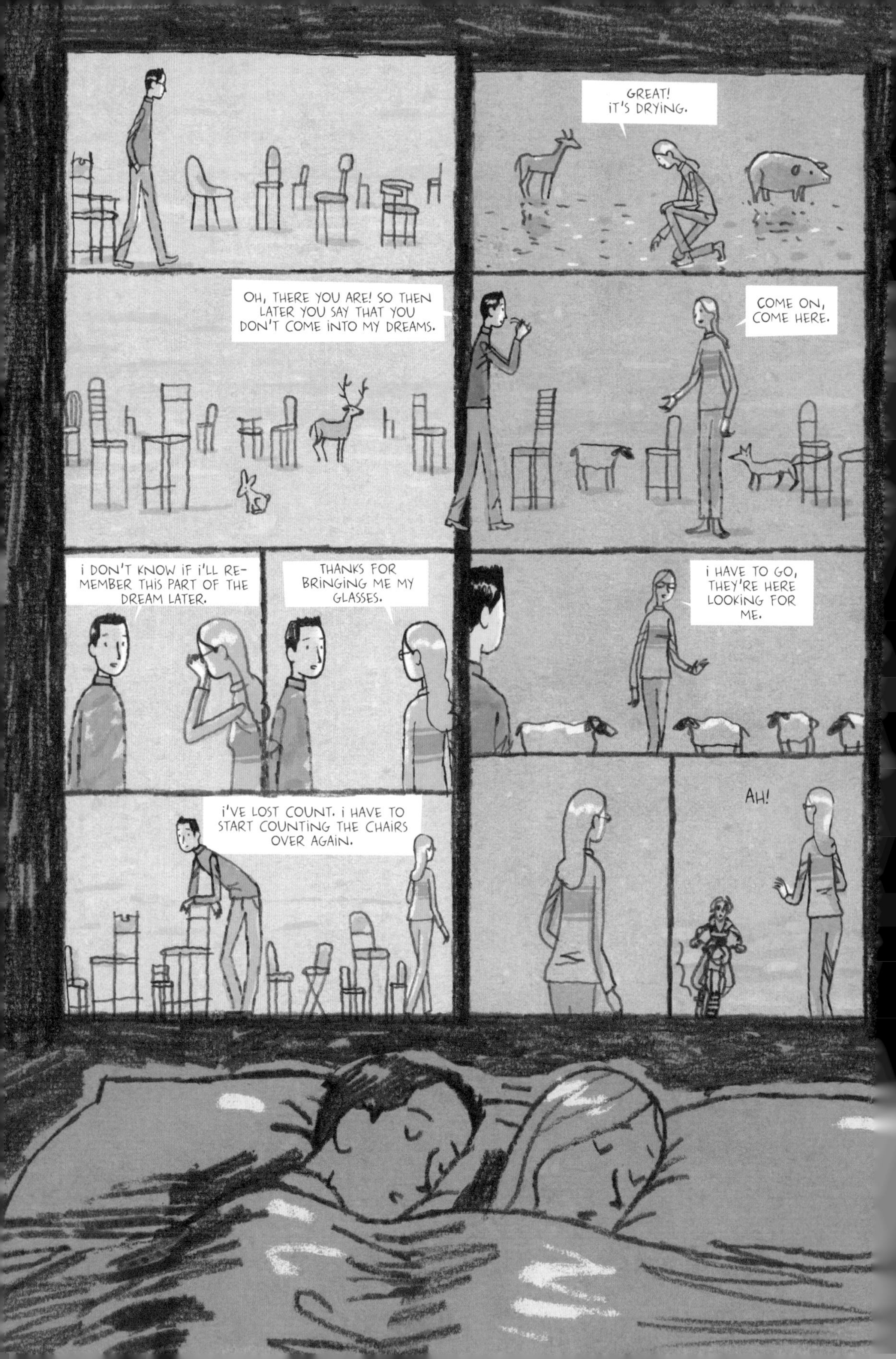
GREAT!
iT'S DRYiNG.
OH, THERE YOU ARE! SO THEN LATER YOU SAY THAT YOU DON'T COME iNTO MY DREAMS.
COME ON, COME HERE.
i DON'T KNOW iF i'LL RE-MEMBER THIS PART OF THE DREAM LATER.
THANKS FOR BRiNGiNG ME MY GLASSES.
i HAVE TO GO, THEY'RE HERE LOOKiNG FOR ME.
i'VE LOST COUNT. i HAVE TO START COUNTiNG THE CHAiRS OVER AGAiN.
AH!

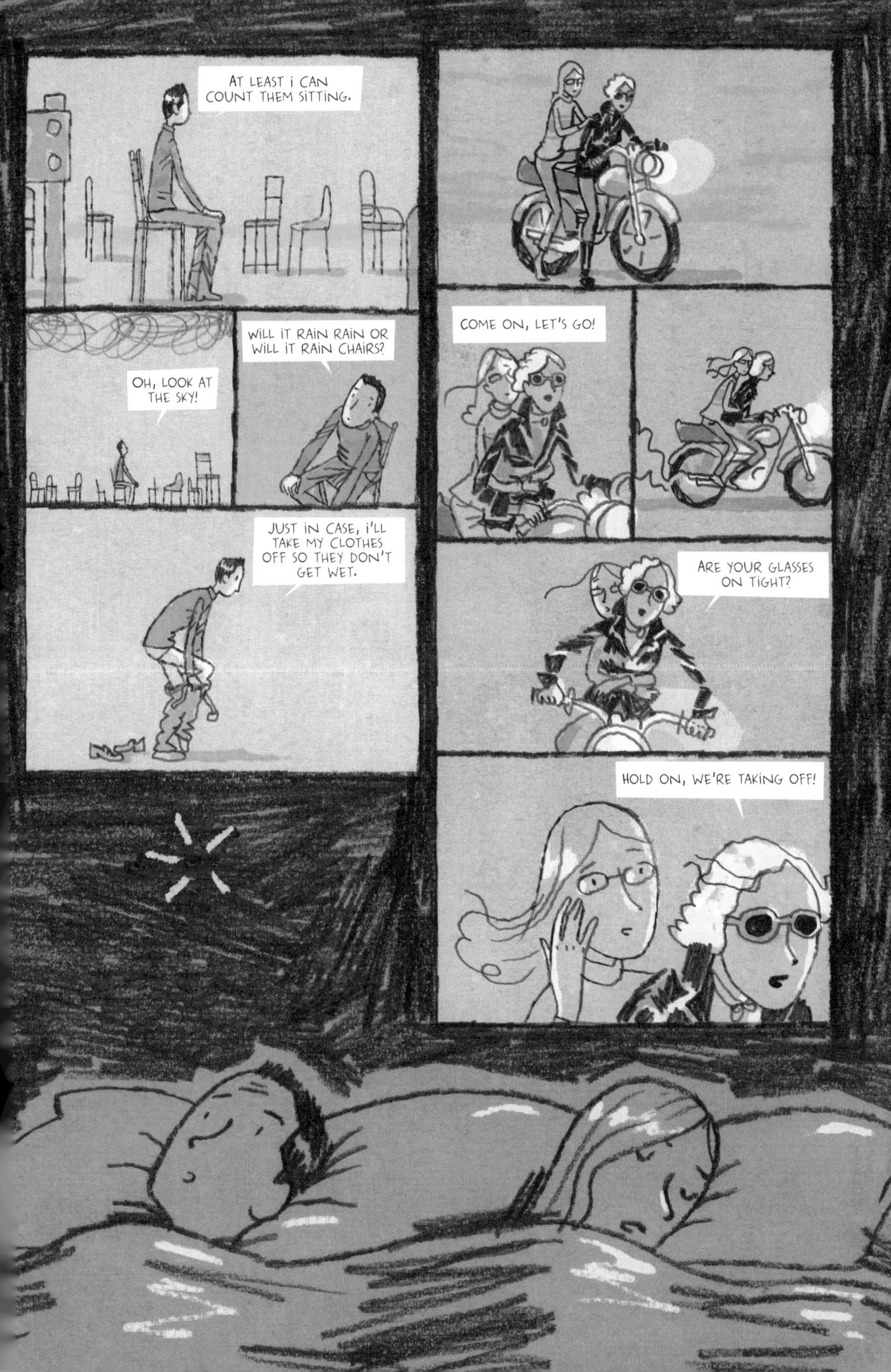
AT LEAST i CAN COUNT THEM SITTING.
OH, LOOK AT THE SKY!
WiLL iT RAiN RAiN OR WiLL iT RAiN CHAiRS?
JUST iN CASE, i'LL TAKE MY CLOTHES OFF SO THEY DON'T GET WET.
COME ON, LET'S GO!
ARE YOUR GLASSES ON TiGHT?
HOLD ON, WE'RE TAKiNG OFF!

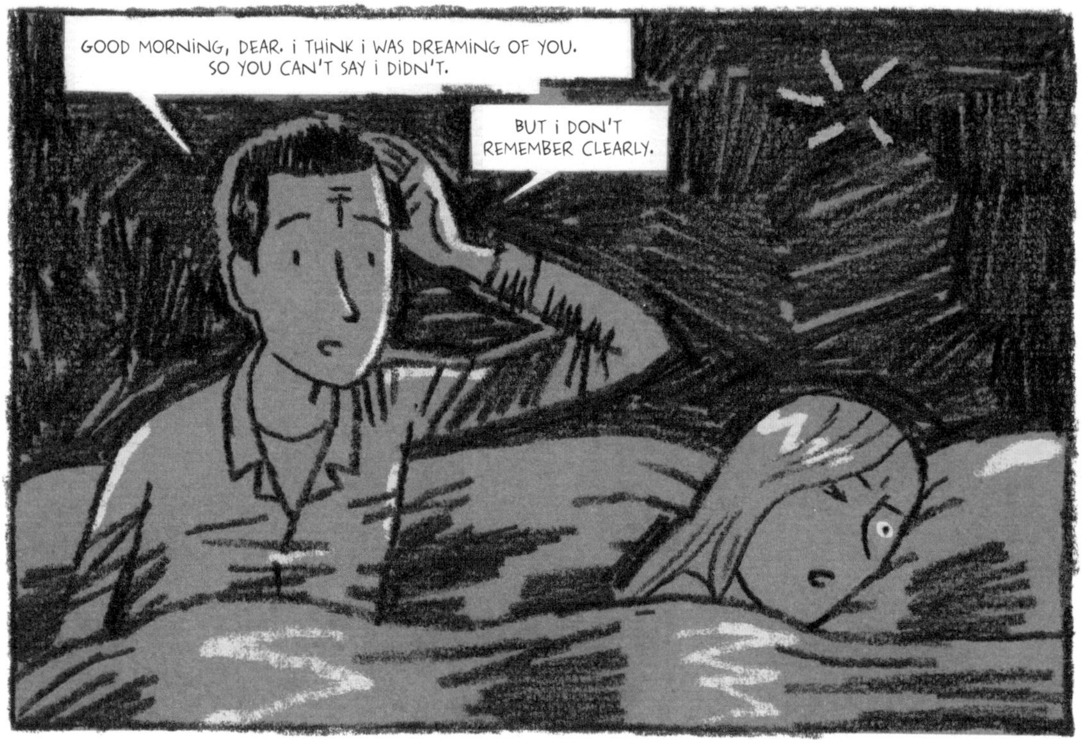
GOOD MORNING, DEAR. i THINK i WAS DREAMING OF YOU. SO YOU CAN'T SAY i DIDN'T.
BUT i DON'T REMEMBER CLEARLY.

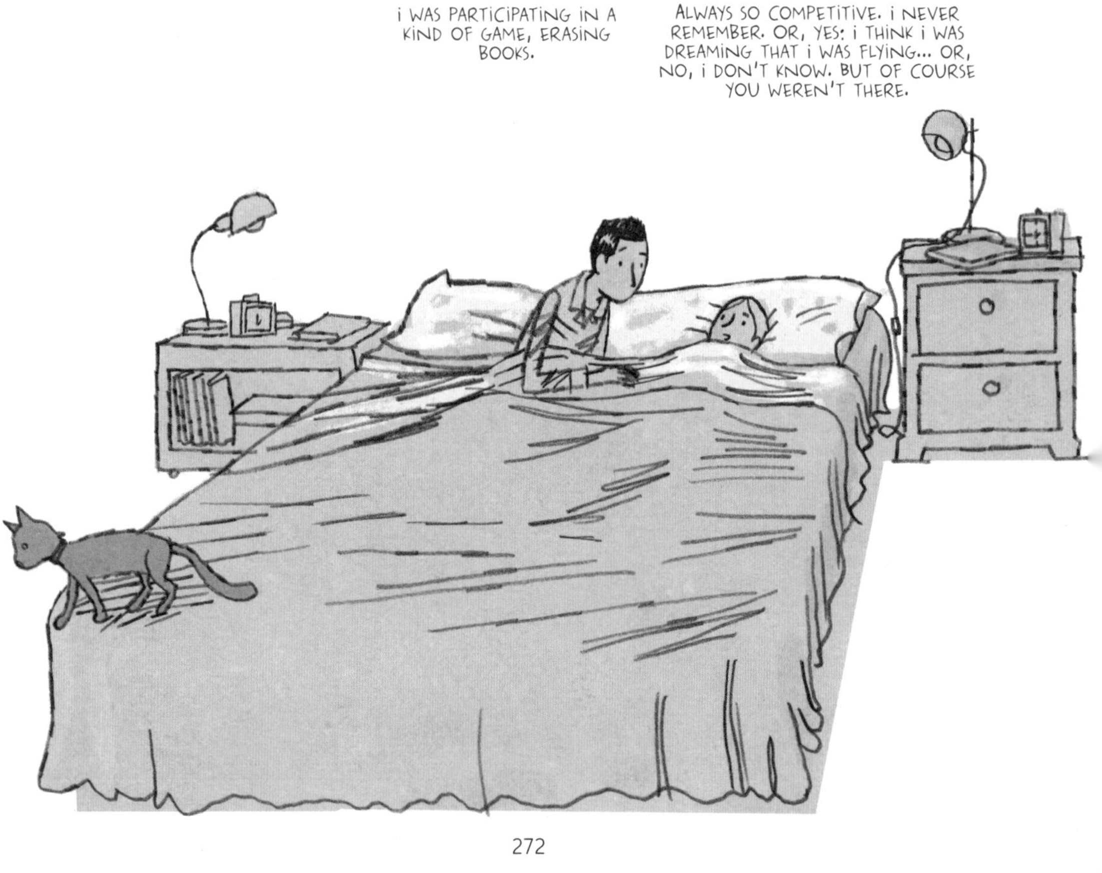
i WAS PARTICIPATING IN A KIND OF GAME, ERASING BOOKS.
ALWAYS SO COMPETITIVE. i NEVER REMEMBER. OR, YES: i THINK i WAS DREAMING THAT i WAS FLYING... OR, NO, i DON'T KNOW. BUT OF COURSE YOU WEREN'T THERE.

DAVID RUBÍN
DEMOLITION

David Rubín was born in Orense in 1977. He is a comics and animation illustrator, who codirected the full-length animated film *El espíritu del bosque* [*The Spirit of the Forest*] (2008). He's a founding member of the Polaqia Collective and has contributed to many journals and fanzines. His first graphic novel is *El circo de desaliento* [*The Circus of Discouragement*] (2005), after which followed *La tetería del oso malayo* [*The Tea Room of the Sun Bear*] (2006) and *Cuaderno de tormentas* [*Notebook of Storms*] (2008). He subsequently published the ambitious *El Héroe* [*The Hero*] (2011–2012), a graphic novel in two parts that retells the myth of Hercules from the perspective of superheroes, which was translated into English in 2015 and published by Dark Horse. Following that he adapted *Beowulf* with a script by Santiago García, also forthcoming in the United States. Currently, he's working with scriptwriter Marcos Prior on the graphic novel *Gran Hotel Abismo* [*Great Chasm Hotel*], slated to be published at the end of 2015. His works have been published in Italy and France, but in the last few years he's begun working directly in the United States, where he's completed two volumes of *The Rise of Aurora West* with scripts by Paul Pope and J. T. Petty, and *The Fiction* (2015) written by Curt Pires.

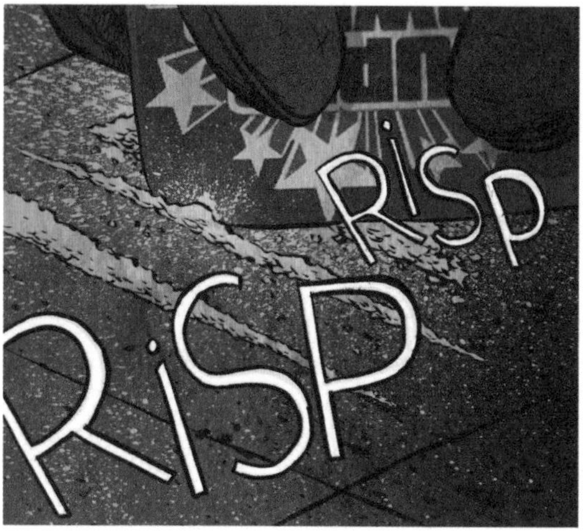
RISP
RISP

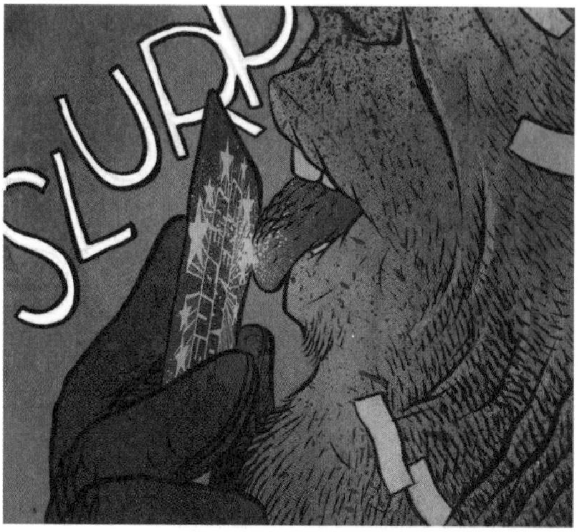
SLUR

DON'T YOU THINK YOU'RE TOO OLD FOR THESE THINGS?

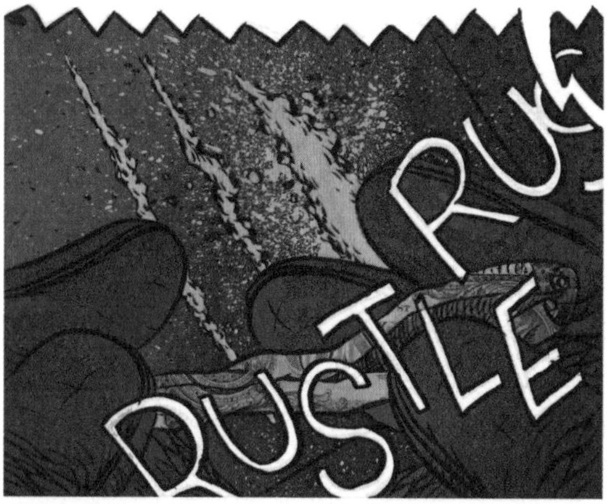
RUSTLE

MY TIME PASSED A WHILE AGO, BUT... YOU KNOW WHAT? ...I DON'T CARE.

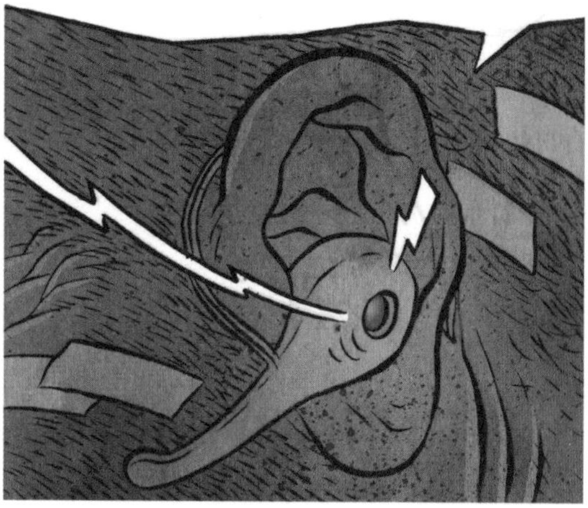

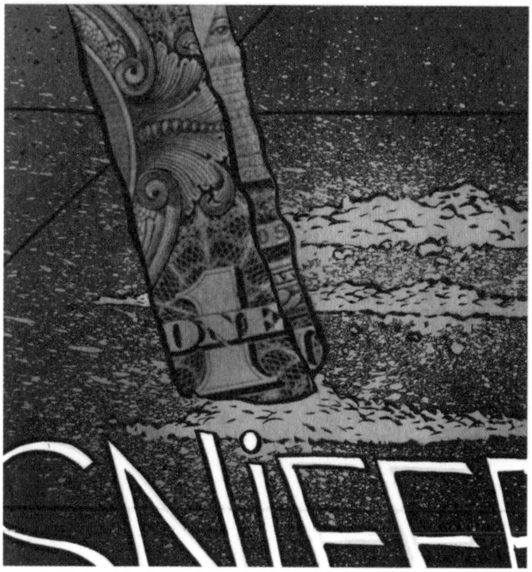
SNIFF

I'M NOT THAT AGILE, STRONG 30-SOMETHING ANYMORE, BUT I STILL HOLD MY OWN.

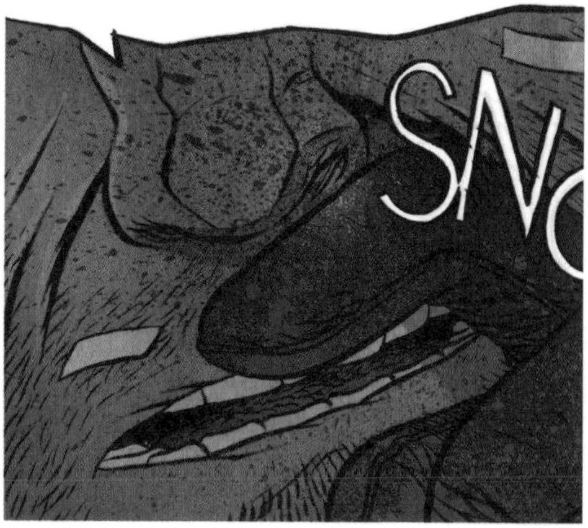

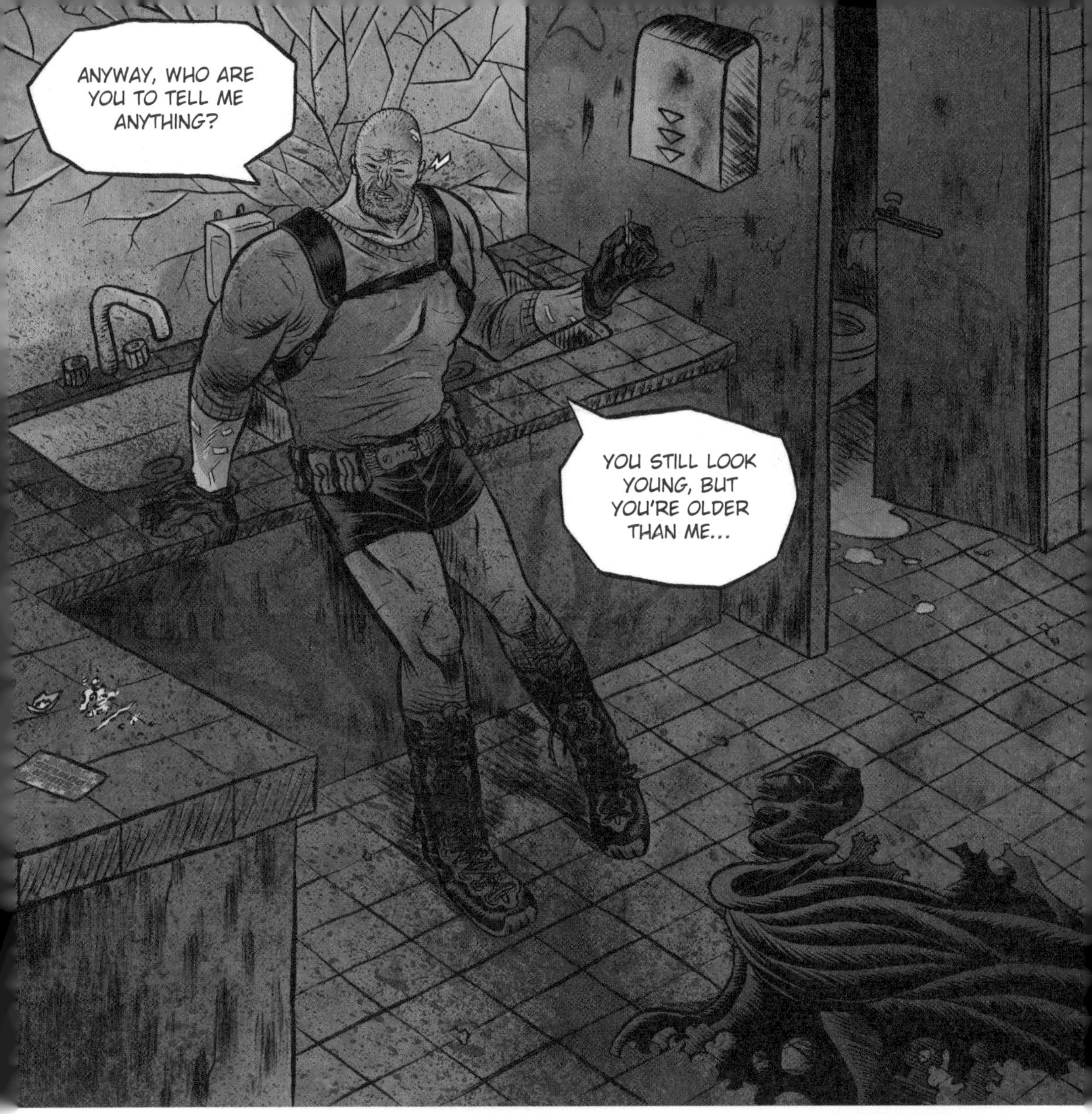
ANYWAY, WHO ARE YOU TO TELL ME ANYTHING?
YOU STILL LOOK YOUNG, BUT YOU'RE OLDER THAN ME...

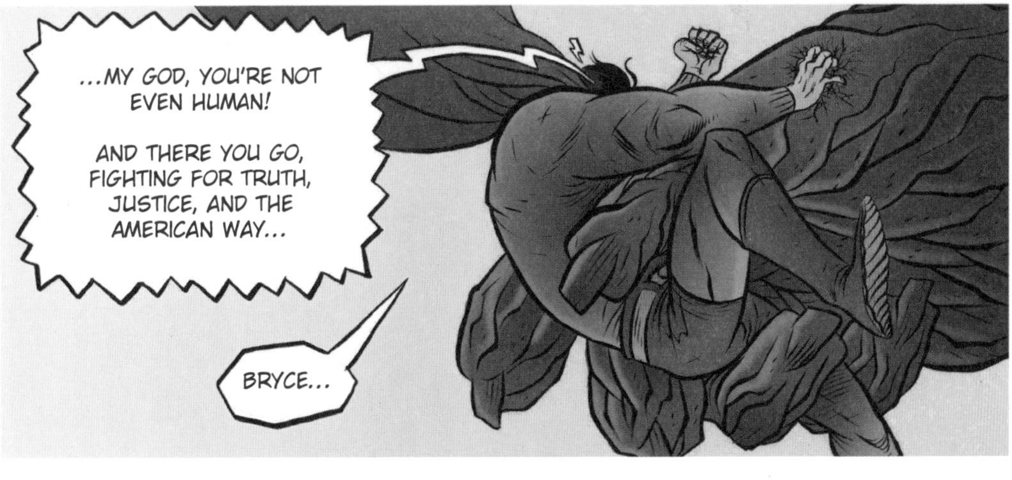
...MY GOD, YOU'RE NOT EVEN HUMAN!
AND THERE YOU GO, FIGHTING FOR TRUTH, JUSTICE, AND THE AMERICAN WAY...
BRYCE...

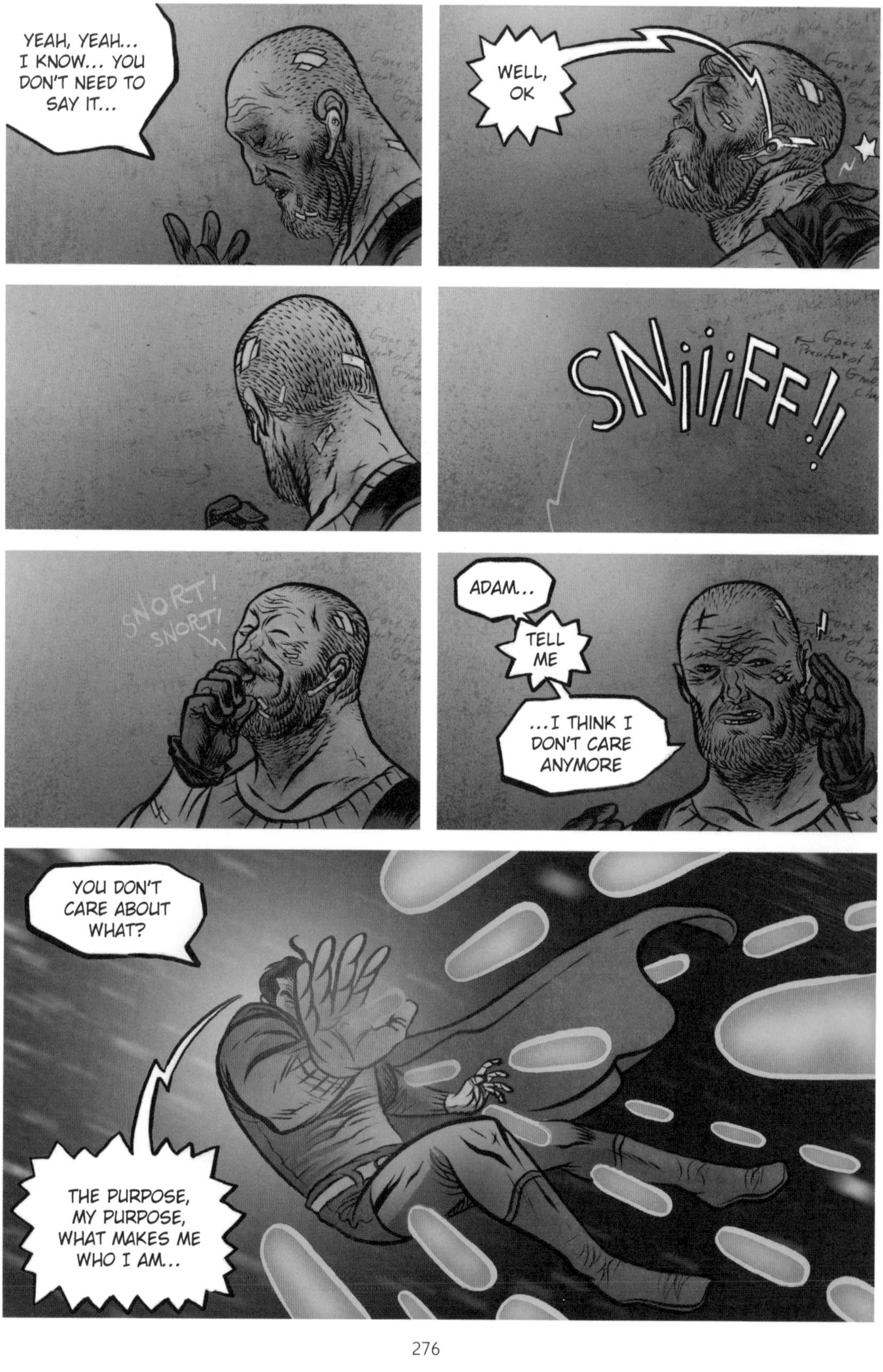
YEAH, YEAH... I KNOW... YOU DON'T NEED TO SAY IT...
WELL, OK
SNiiiFF!!
SNORT! SNORT!
ADAM...
TELL ME
...I THINK I DON'T CARE ANYMORE
YOU DON'T CARE ABOUT WHAT?
THE PURPOSE, MY PURPOSE, WHAT MAKES ME WHO I AM...

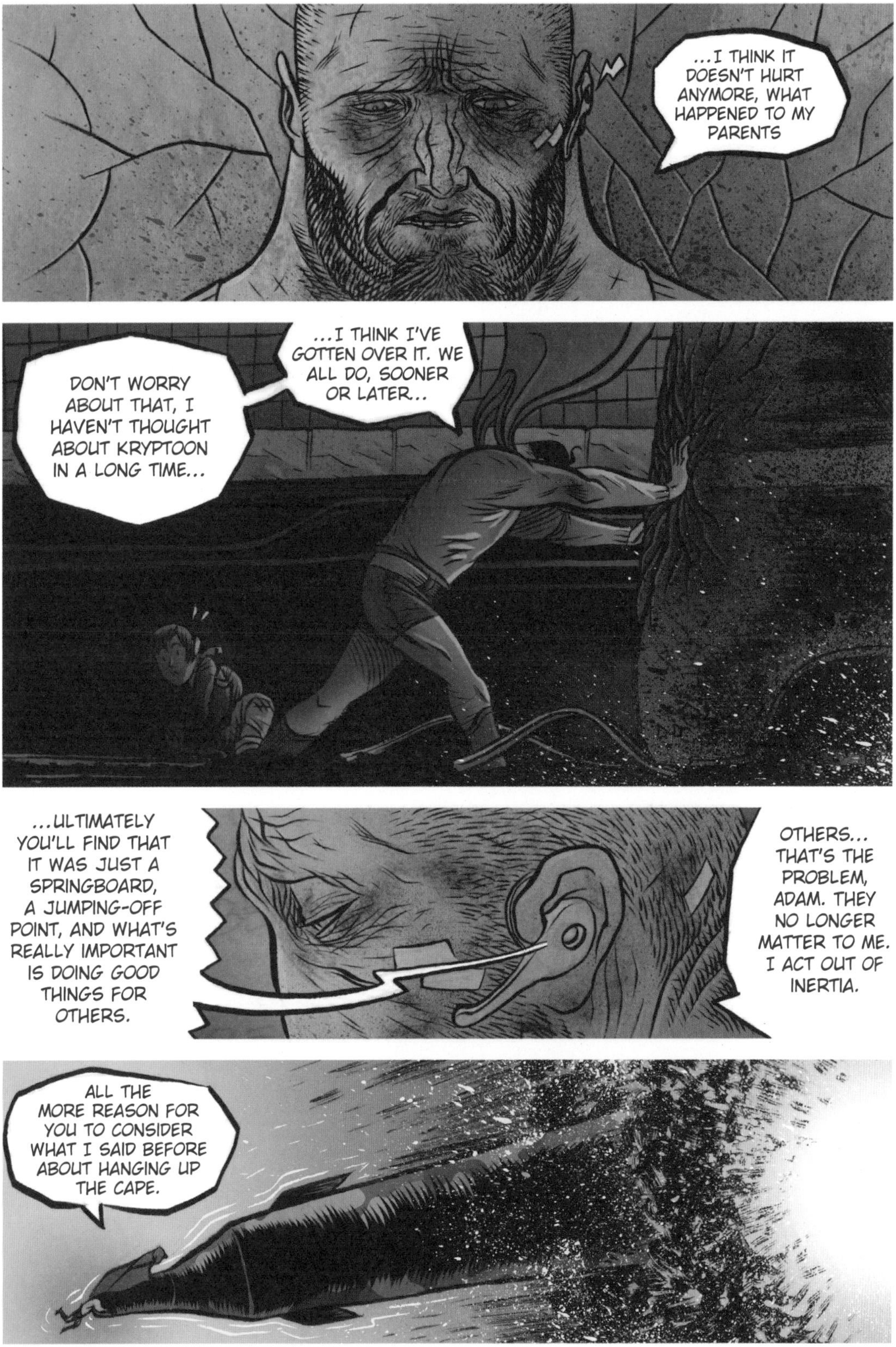
...I THINK IT DOESN'T HURT ANYMORE, WHAT HAPPENED TO MY PARENTS
DON'T WORRY ABOUT THAT, I HAVEN'T THOUGHT ABOUT KRYPTOON IN A LONG TIME...
...I THINK I'VE GOTTEN OVER IT. WE ALL DO, SOONER OR LATER...
...ULTIMATELY YOU'LL FIND THAT IT WAS JUST A SPRINGBOARD, A JUMPING-OFF POINT, AND WHAT'S REALLY IMPORTANT IS DOING GOOD THINGS FOR OTHERS.
OTHERS... THAT'S THE PROBLEM, ADAM. THEY NO LONGER MATTER TO ME. I ACT OUT OF INERTIA.
ALL THE MORE REASON FOR YOU TO CONSIDER WHAT I SAID BEFORE ABOUT HANGING UP THE CAPE.

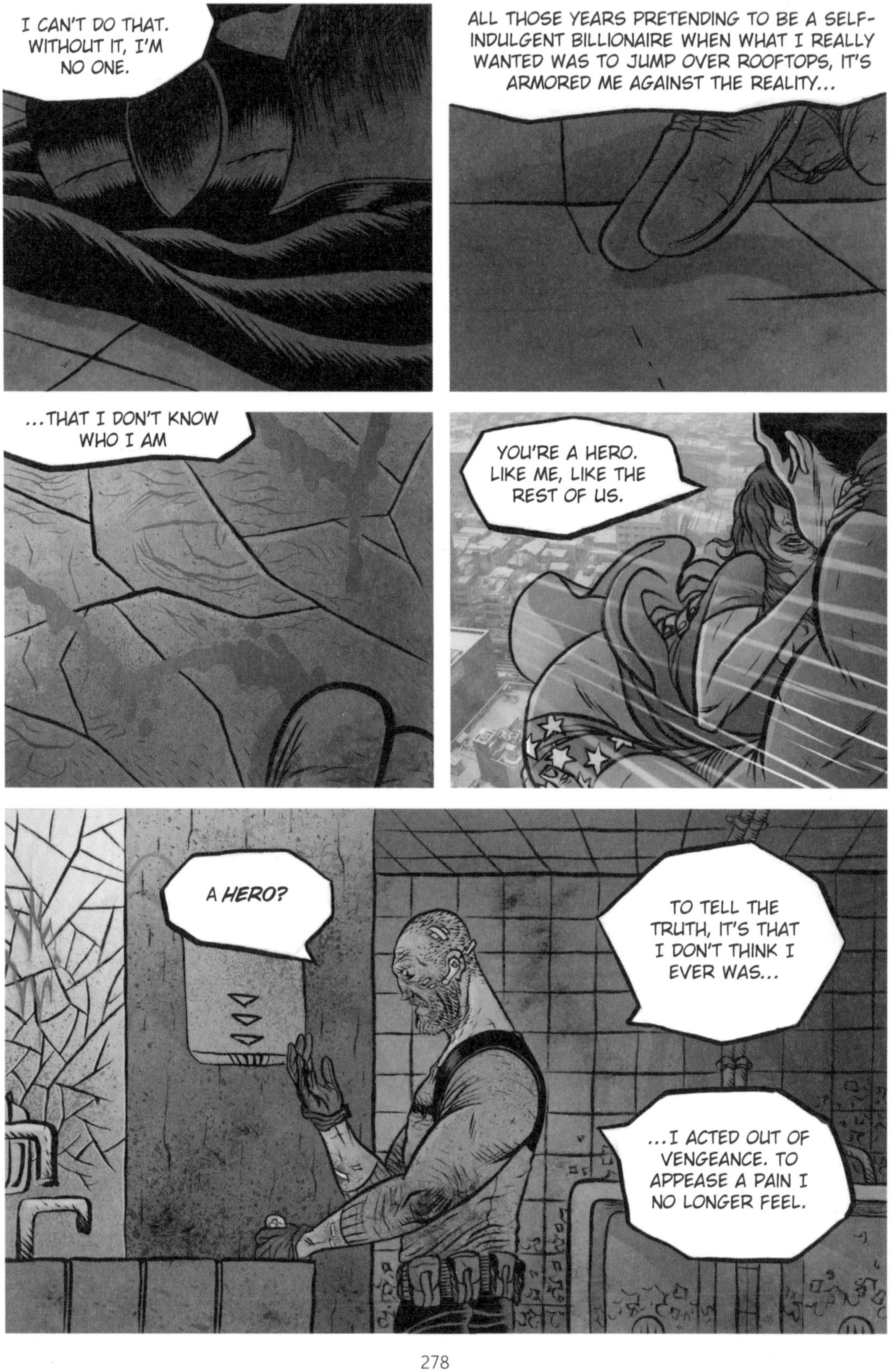
I CAN'T DO THAT. WITHOUT IT, I'M NO ONE.
ALL THOSE YEARS PRETENDING TO BE A SELF-INDULGENT BILLIONAIRE WHEN WHAT I REALLY WANTED WAS TO JUMP OVER ROOFTOPS, IT'S ARMORED ME AGAINST THE REALITY...
...THAT I DON'T KNOW WHO I AM
YOU'RE A HERO. LIKE ME, LIKE THE REST OF US.
A *HERO*?
TO TELL THE TRUTH, IT'S THAT I DON'T THINK I EVER WAS...
...I ACTED OUT OF VENGEANCE. TO APPEASE A PAIN I NO LONGER FEEL.

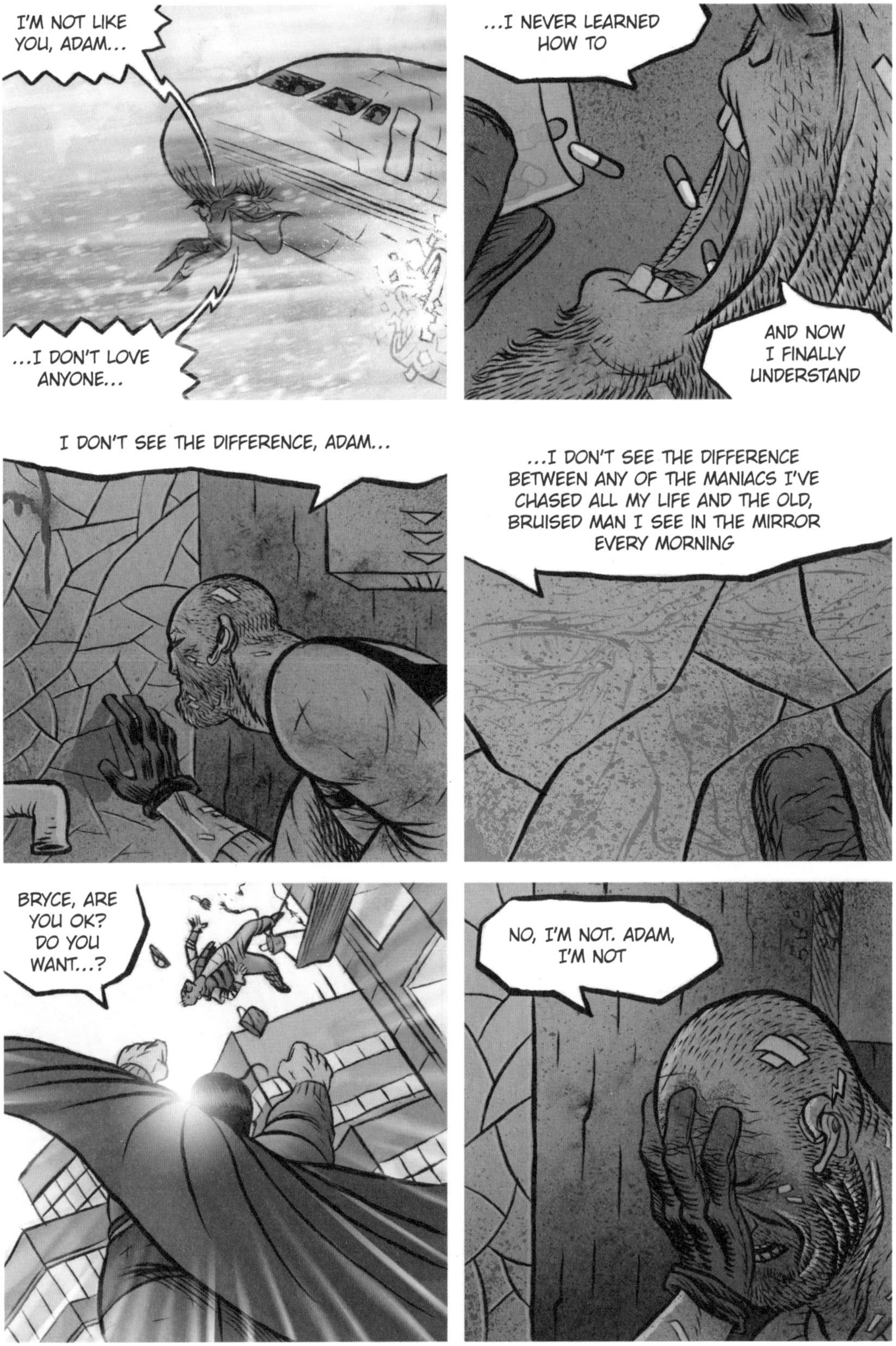
I'M NOT LIKE YOU, ADAM...
...I DON'T LOVE ANYONE...
...I NEVER LEARNED HOW TO
AND NOW I FINALLY UNDERSTAND
I DON'T SEE THE DIFFERENCE, ADAM...
...I DON'T SEE THE DIFFERENCE BETWEEN ANY OF THE MANIACS I'VE CHASED ALL MY LIFE AND THE OLD, BRUISED MAN I SEE IN THE MIRROR EVERY MORNING
BRYCE, ARE YOU OK? DO YOU WANT...?
NO, I'M NOT. ADAM, I'M NOT

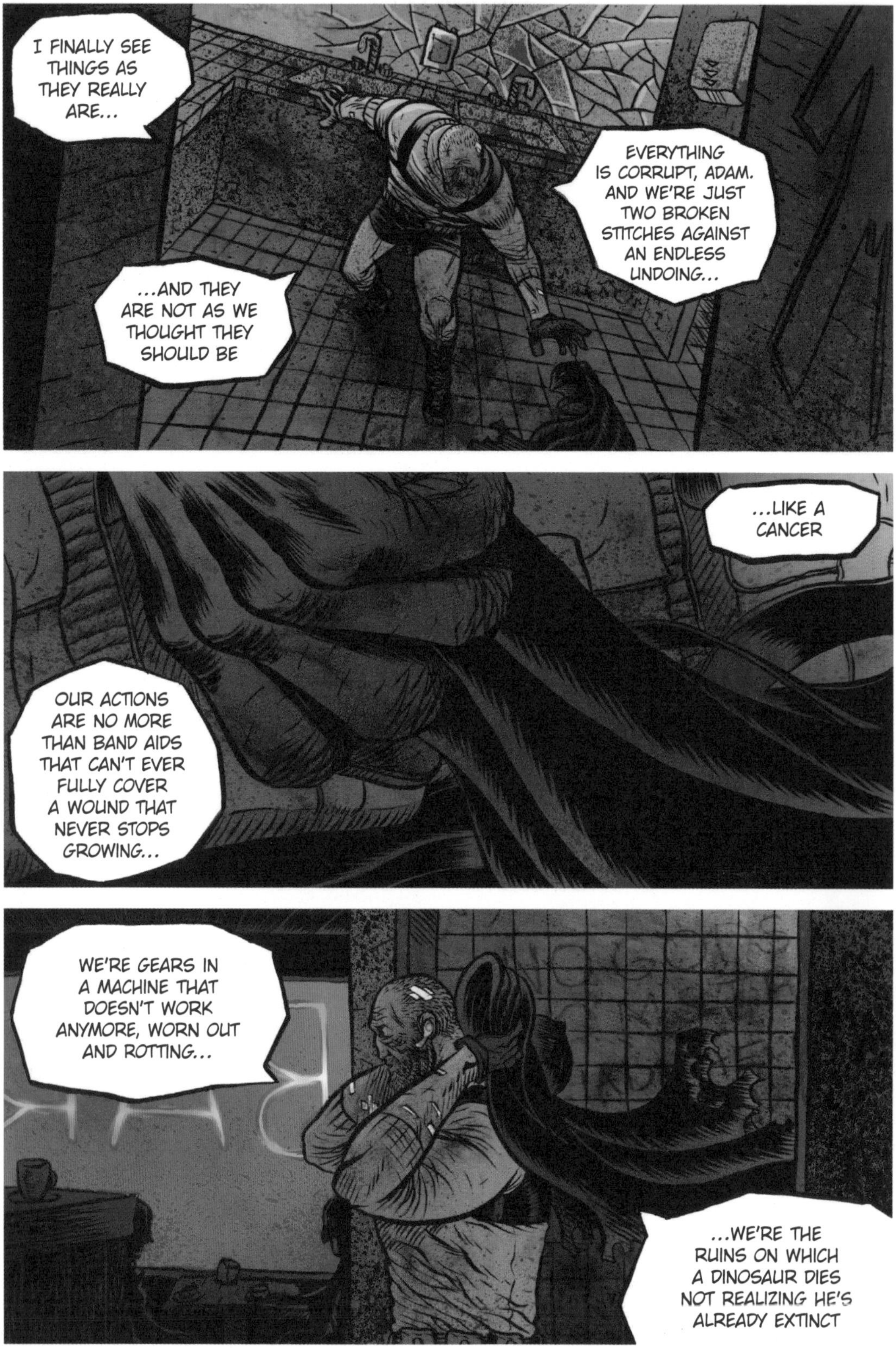
I FINALLY SEE THINGS AS THEY REALLY ARE...
EVERYTHING IS CORRUPT, ADAM. AND WE'RE JUST TWO BROKEN STITCHES AGAINST AN ENDLESS UNDOING...
...AND THEY ARE NOT AS WE THOUGHT THEY SHOULD BE
...LIKE A CANCER
OUR ACTIONS ARE NO MORE THAN BAND AIDS THAT CAN'T EVER FULLY COVER A WOUND THAT NEVER STOPS GROWING...
WE'RE GEARS IN A MACHINE THAT DOESN'T WORK ANYMORE, WORN OUT AND ROTTING...
...WE'RE THE RUINS ON WHICH A DINOSAUR DIES NOT REALIZING HE'S ALREADY EXTINCT

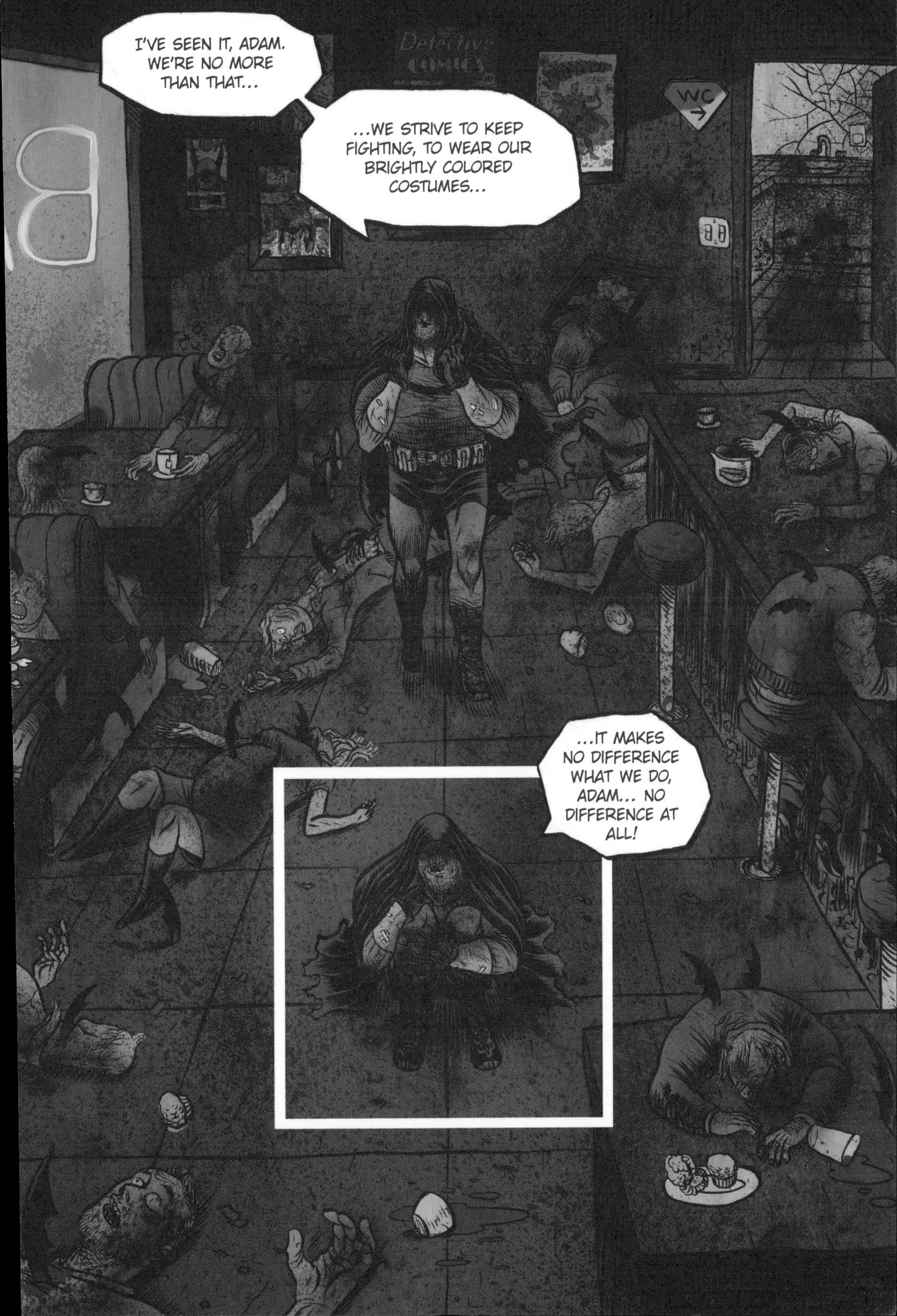
I'VE SEEN IT, ADAM. WE'RE NO MORE THAN THAT...
...WE STRIVE TO KEEP FIGHTING, TO WEAR OUR BRIGHTLY COLORED COSTUMES...
...IT MAKES NO DIFFERENCE WHAT WE DO, ADAM... NO DIFFERENCE AT ALL!
Detective Comics
WC

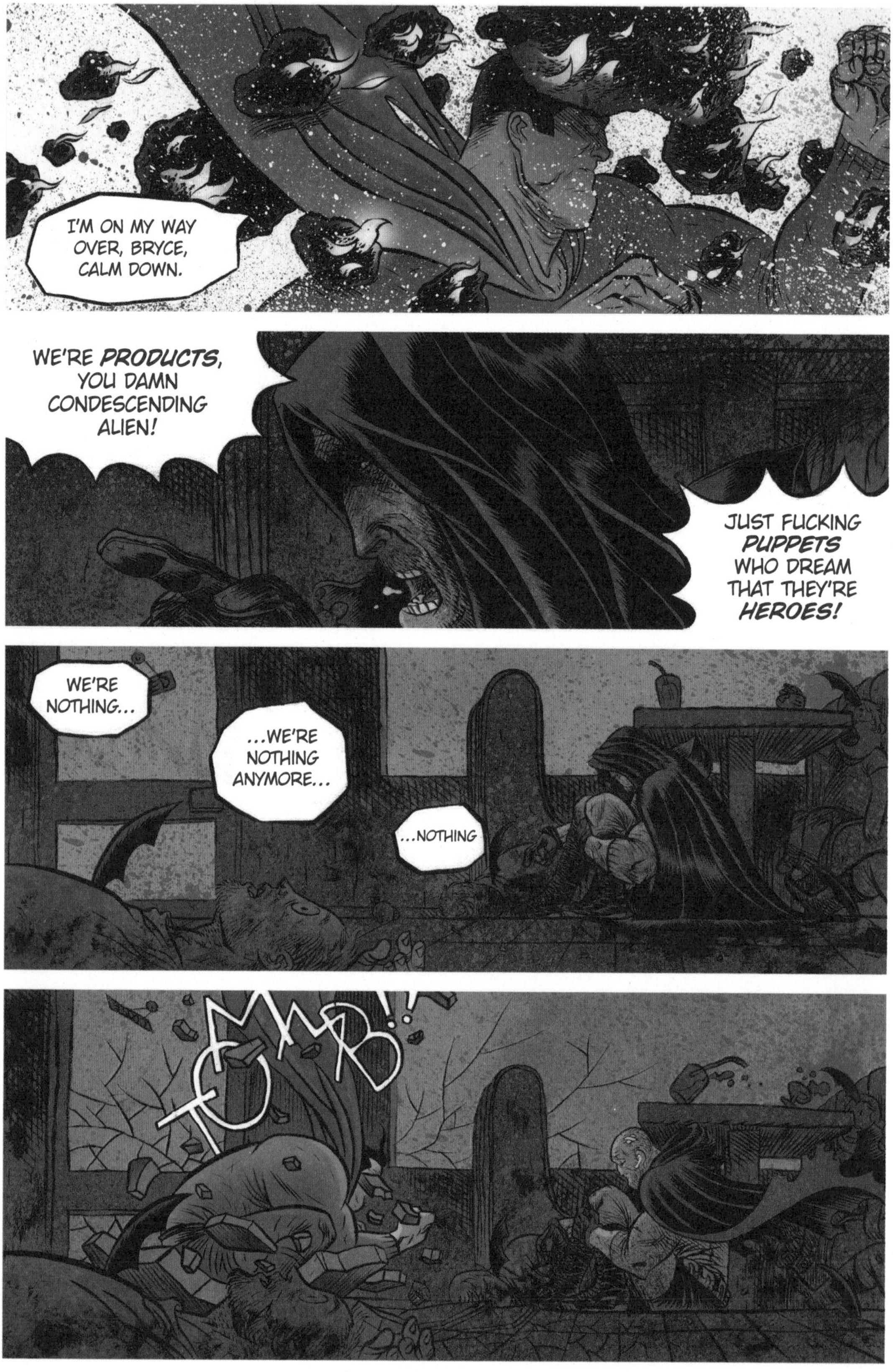
I'M ON MY WAY OVER, BRYCE, CALM DOWN.
WE'RE *PRODUCTS*, YOU DAMN CONDESCENDING ALIEN!
JUST FUCKING *PUPPETS* WHO DREAM THAT THEY'RE *HEROES!*
WE'RE NOTHING...
...WE'RE NOTHING ANYMORE...
...NOTHING
TOMMB!!

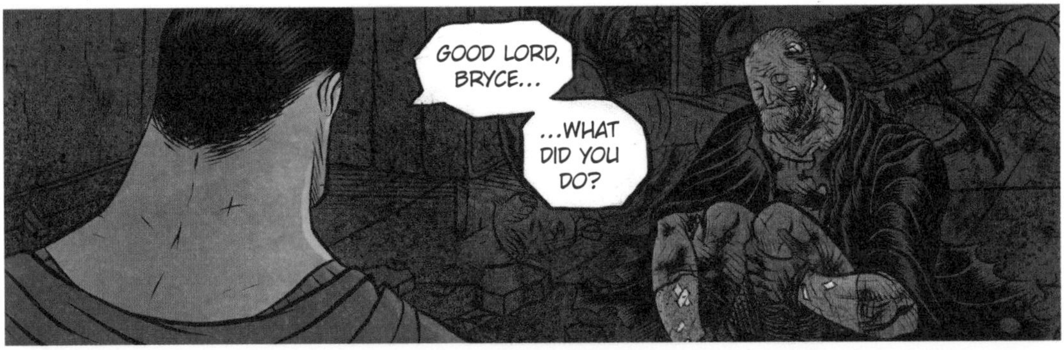
GOOD LORD, BRYCE...
...WHAT DID YOU DO?

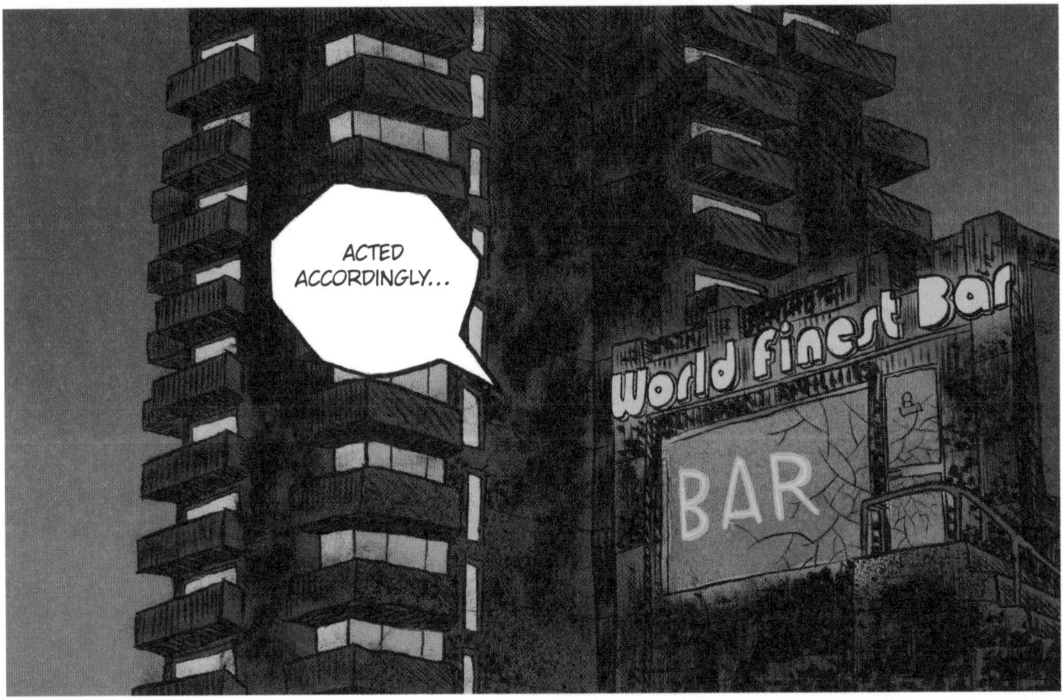
ACTED ACCORDINGLY...
World Finest Bar
BAR

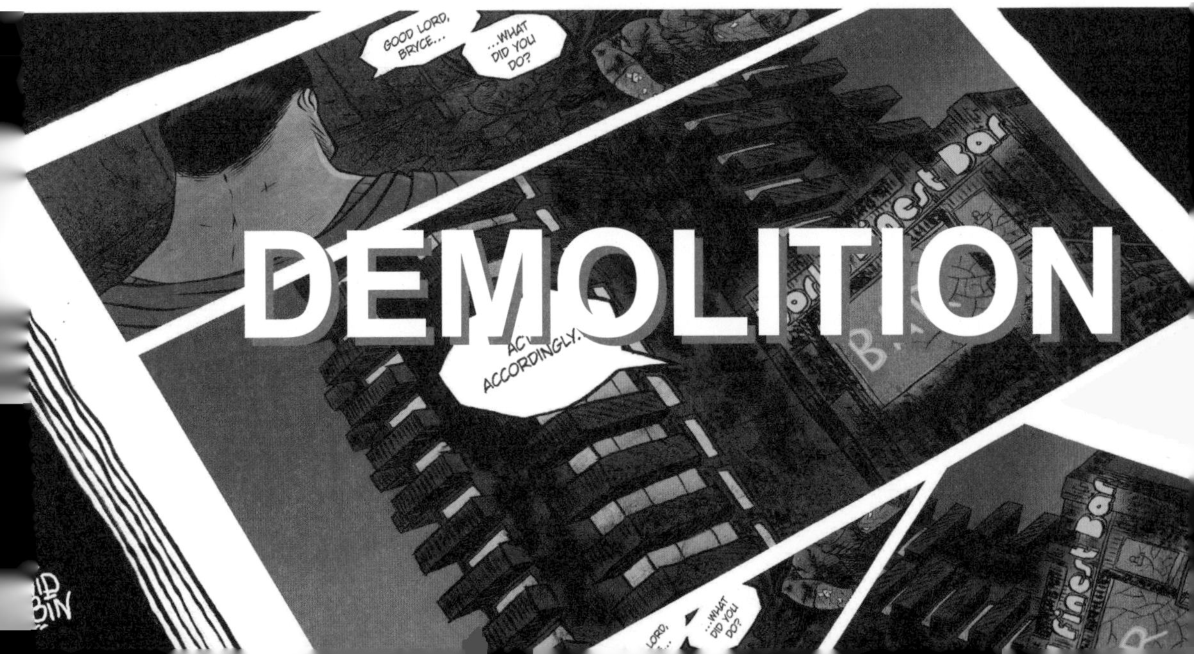
GOOD LORD, BRYCE...
...WHAT DID YOU DO?
DEMOLITION
ACCORDINGLY.
Finest Bar
...WHAT DID YOU DO?

THE EDITOR

Santiago García was born in Madrid in 1968. He has written comics and about comics for more than twenty years. He was a founding member of *U* and *Volumen*, magazines specializing in comic reviews and news, for which he served as editor. He has written about comics for the cultural supplement of *ABC* and is the author of *La novela gráfica* (2010), which has been translated into Portuguese in Brazil and into English for the University Press of Mississippi as *On the Graphic Novel* (2015). In 2011 he received the outreach prize at the Salón del Cómic de Barcelona. As a cartoonist, he has collaborated with artists like Pepo Pérez on *El Vecino* [*The Neighbor*] (2004–2009) and Javier Peinado on *La tempestad* [*The Tempest*] (2008). More recently he published the graphic novels *Beowulf* (2013) with David Rubín, *Fútbol* [*Soccer*] (2014) with Pablo Ríos, and *Las meninas* [*The Maids of Honor*] (2014) with Javier Olivares, which will be published by Fantagraphics in 2017. It won the National Prize in 2015. His newest graphic novels are *Yuna*, with Juaco Vizuete, and *¡García!* (two volumes) with Luis Bustos. He edited the essay anthologies *Supercómic: Mutaciones de la novela gráfica contemporánea* [*Supercomic: Mutations of the Contemporary Graphic Novel*] (2013), and *Cómics sensacionales* [*Sensational Comics*].

THE TRANSLATOR

Erica Mena is a poet, translator, and editor. She holds an MFA in Literary Translation from the University of Iowa, and is an MFA candidate in poetry from Brown. Her original poetry has appeared in *Vanitas*, the *Dos Passos Review*, *Pressed Wafer*, and Arrowsmith Press. Her translations have appeared in *The Eternaut* (Fantagraphics, 2015), *Two Lines*, *Asymptote*, *PEN America*, and *Words Without Borders*, among other venues. She is the founding editor of Anomalous Press.

SPANISH FEVER: STORIES BY THE NEW SPANISH CARTOONISTS © 2016 Fantagraphics Books, Inc. Foreword © 2016 Eddie Campbell. Introduction © 2016 Santiago García. Translation © 2016 Erica Mena. Comics stories © 2016 Juanjo Sáez, Antonio Altarriba and Kim, Álvaro Ortiz, Paco Roca, Rayco Pulido, Fermín Solís, Alfonso Zapico, Juaco Vizuete, Marcos Prior, Miguel Ángel Martín, Ramón Boldú, Gabi Beltrán and Bartolomé Seguí, David Sánchez, Pere Joan, Mireia Pérez, Clara-Tanit Arqué, Miguel Gallardo, Max, Micharmut, Ana Galvañ, Santiago Valenzuela, José Domingo, Sergi Puyol, Javier Olivares, Carlos de Diego, Paco Alcázar, Juan Berrio, and David Rubín.

Published by agreement with Astiberri ediciones.

Special thanks to Astiberri, Héloïse Guerrier, and Cristina Ruiz. This anthology was made possible thanks to the generous support of the Spain-USA Foundation and its SPAIN arts & culture program www.spainculture.us.

SPAIN/USA/
/ Foundation /

Translator: Erica Mena
Cover Design: Jacob Covey
Layout Design: Manuel Bartual and Jacob Covey
Editors: Santiago García, Héloïse Guerrier, Kristy Valenti, Gary Groth
Production: Paul Baresh
Editorial Assistance: Erin Keaton, Emily Hendrickson, Michael McHugh, Emily Silva
Associate Publisher: Eric Reynolds
Publisher: Gary Groth

Printed in Hong Kong
First edition: September 2016
ISBN: 978-1-60699-944-8
LCCN: 2016935476

FANTAGRAPHICS BOOKS